THE BODY GOD GIVES

A BIBLICAL RESPONSE TO
TRANSGENDER THEORY

"This is a remarkably gracious, insightful, and clear book on a highly contested issue in the Western world today. Robert Smith combines the analysis of a scholar and the heart of a pastor and has done us all a terrific service in the process. Very highly recommended."

—Sam Allberry, associate pastor, Immanuel Nashville

"The breadth of this book is stunning! A taxonomy of transgender categories and a discussion of its core thesis and main axioms. A historical presentation of the disconnecting of gender from sex and the dissolving of sex into gender. A robust development of biblical perspectives on male and female and sex and gender, with implications for trans theory and transgenderism. All conclusions are biblically grounded, theologically sound, person affirming, and God honoring. *The Body God Gives* has my highest recommendation!"

—Gregg R. Allison, professor of Christian theology, The Southern Baptist Theological Seminary; secretary, Evangelical Theological Society

"This book tackles complicated issues with analytic rigour. The conclusions are not reached lightly but follow careful biblical reasoning. An important addition to a difficult debate."

—Kirsten Birkett, Church Society, UK

"In the rapidly expanding literature on this topic, no volume of which I am aware combines, as this one does, careful unpacking of the opening chapters of Genesis, thoughtful interaction with the views of other scholars (not least those with whom he disagrees), and good writing that makes this volume a joy to read. Don't bother picking up this book if all you want is a crisp slogan or two. But if you want judicious arguments that reflect years of work grounded in exact and compassionate reading of the evidence, this is the book to read."

—D. A. Carson, emeritus professor of New Testament, Trinity Evangelical Divinity School

"In this fine book, Robert Smith makes an important contribution to a vexed subject. His approach to transgenderism assumes a high view of biblical authority, engages the relevant social sciences adroitly and is judicious in its judgments and tone. An important contribution in this cultural moment."

—Graham A. Cole, emeritus dean and emeritus professor of biblical and systematic theology, Trinity Evangelical Divinity School

"This is an in-depth, fair-minded, and delightfully clear examination of contemporary trans and gender theories. There are no 'straw men' to be found here. That this book also includes a compelling account of biblical theological anthropology makes it a must-read for Christians who desire thoughtful and faithful engagement on these questions."

—Abigail Favale, author of *The Genesis of Gender: A Christian Theory*

"In this judicious work, Dr. Smith tackles a question that tends to generate more heat than light, and leads us more fully into the light. His wide-ranging effort to root the transgender question in the deep structures of creation (and, to some extent, eschatology) reflects a commendable, necessary commitment to think today with the Scriptures rather than beyond them. This alone—alongside many other grounds for praise—suggests this work will prove useful and edifying beyond the demands of our particular moment."

—Mark A. Garcia, president and fellow in Scripture and theology, Greystone Theological Institute; associate professor of systematic theology, Westminster Theological Seminary

"In his important new work, Dr. Rob Smith has given the church an excellent resource examining both the claims made by those who advocate for the validity of transgender identities, as well as how Scripture speaks to sexed embodiment. His breadth of engagement will benefit both those newer to the conversation as well as those who are familiar with the terrain. This volume is required reading for anyone who is serious about understanding how the Bible speaks to contemporary conversations of sex and gender."

—Rachel Gilson, author of *Born Again This Way*

"Questions of sex, gender, and identity are the hot topics of our age and often leave Christians confused. Rob Smith leads us through the wilds of transgender theories and evangelical responses and offers a careful theological discussion grounded in Scripture and shaped by the gospel of Christ—just what we need at present. While not a 'how to' guide for pastoral care or public engagement, *The Body God Gives* sets out a secure basis for both."

—John McClean, lecturer in systematic theology, Christ College

"In this genuinely compassionate and deeply convictional work, Robert Smith offers a serious and thoughtful engagement with modern gender theory and transgender claims. Smith affirms the truth that both Scripture and Christian theology confirm that our Creator reveals our gender in our bodies. Christians will deeply appreciate his scholarship and his courage."

—R. Albert Mohler Jr., president, The Southern Baptist Theological Seminary

"This book provides an excellent biblical and theological assessment of the transgender movement and of the long-term sociocultural influences which have made transgender self-identification not just plausible but attractively fashionable today. It is therefore a valuable resource for those who want to—or find they need to—discuss and debate issues associated with transgender identity. Its clear articulation of the issues makes it a good reference tool for those who are confronted with these issues and need to make a quick but well-informed response to them."

—Patricia Weerakoon, sexologist, academic, and writer

THE BODY GOD GIVES

A BIBLICAL RESPONSE TO TRANSGENDER THEORY

ROBERT S. SMITH

The Body God Gives: A Biblical Response to Transgender Theory

Copyright 2025 Robert S. Smith

Lexham Academic, an imprint of Lexham Press
1313 Commercial St., Bellingham, WA 98225
LexhamPress.com

You may use brief quotations from this resource in presentations, articles, and books. For all other uses, please write Lexham Press for permission. Email us at permissions@lexhampress.com.

Unless otherwise noted, Scripture quotations are from ESV® Bible (*The Holy Bible, English Standard Version®*), copyright © 2001 by Crossway Bibles, a publishing ministry of Good News Publishers. Used by permission. All rights reserved.

Scripture quotations marked (KJV) are from the King James Version. Public domain.

Scripture quotations marked (NIV) are from the Holy Bible, NEW INTERNATIONAL VERSION®. Copyright © 1973, 1978, 1984, 2011 by Biblica, Inc. Used by permission. All rights reserved worldwide.

Scripture quotations marked (GNT) or (GNB) are from the Good News Translation in Today's English Version—Second Edition Copyright © 1992 by American Bible Society. Used by Permission.

Scripture quotations marked (HCSB) are from the Holman Christian Standard Bible®, Copyright © 1999, 2000, 2002, 2003, 2009 by Holman Bible Publishers. Used by permission. Holman Christian Standard Bible®, Holman CSB®, and HCSB® are federally registered trademarks of Holman Bible Publishers.

Scripture quotations marked (CSB) are from the Christian Standard Bible®, Copyright © 2017 by Holman Bible Publishers. Used by permission. Christian Standard Bible® and CSB® are federally registered trademarks of Holman Bible Publishers.

Scripture quotations marked (LSV) are from the Literal Standard Version®, Copyright © 2020, by Covenant Press. Used by Permission.

Print ISBN 9781683598121
Digital ISBN 9781683598138

Lexham Editorial: Todd Hains, Elliot Ritzema, Jessi Strong
Cover Design: Gabriel Eason
Typesetting: Mandi Newell

25 26 27 28 29 30 31 / US / 12 11 10 9 8 7 6 5 4 3 2

To my late father, Rev. Bruce Smith—
for teaching me the truth and showing me the way.

Your hands have made and fashioned me;
give me understanding that I may
learn your commandments.

Psalm 119:73

Almighty God, you see that we have no power of our own to help ourselves: keep us both outwardly in our bodies and inwardly in our souls so that we may be defended from all ills that may befall the body and from all evil thoughts that may assault and hurt the soul, through Jesus Christ our Lord. Amen.

Collect for the Second Sunday in Lent

CONTENTS

LIST OF TABLES

ABBREVIATIONS

ANF	*The Ante-Nicene Fathers*, ed. A. Roberts and J. Donaldson, rev. A. C. Coxe (repr., Grand Rapids: Eerdmans, 1969–1973)
AOTC	Apollos Old Testament Commentary Series
ATR	*Anglican Theology Review*
BBR	*Bulletin for Biblical Research*
BBRS	Bulletin for Biblical Research Supplements
BDD	body dysmorphic disorder
BECNT	Baker Exegetical Commentary on the New Testament
BET	*Bulletin of Ecclesial Theology*
BHS	Biblia Hebraica Stuttgartensia
BIID	body integrity identity disorder
BJRL	*Bulletin of the John Rylands University Library of Manchester*
BLS	Biblical Limits Series
BRev	*Bible Review*
BST	The Bible Speaks Today
BTC	Brazos Theological Commentary
CBMW	Council for Biblical Manhood and Womanhood
CBQ	*Catholic Biblical Quarterly*
CD	Karl Barth, *Church Dogmatics*, trans. Geoffrey W. Bromiley, 14 vols. (Edinburgh: T&T Clark, 1956–1977)
CHT	cross-sex hormone therapy
CSB	Christian Standard Bible
CT	*Christianity Today*
CTJ	*Calvin Theological Journal*
CTQ	*Concordia Theological Quarterly*

DRB	Douay–Rheims Bible
DSD^{1}	disorders of sex development
DSD^{2}	disorders of sex differentiation
DSD^{3}	differences of sex development
DSD^{4}	divergences of sex development
DSM-5	American Psychiatric Association, *Diagnostic and Statistical Manual of Mental Disorders*, 5th ed. (Washington, DC: American Psychiatric Publishing, 2013)
DW	*Deutsche Welle*
EGGNT	Exegetical Guide to the Greek New Testament
EQ	*Evangelical Quarterly*
ER	*Ecclesia Reformanda*
ESV	English Standard Version
FtM	female-to-male transsexual
GCS	gender confirmation surgery
GD	gender dysphoria
GNB	Good News Bible
GRS	gender reassignment surgery
HCSB	Holman Christian Standard Bible
HTR	*Harvard Theological Review*
IBC	Interpretation: A Bible Commentary for Teaching and Preaching
ICC	International Critical Commentary
IJST	*International Journal of Systematic Theology*
IJT	*International Journal of Transgenderism*
Institutes	John Calvin, *Institutes of the Christian Religion*, 2 volumes, ed. John T. McNeill, trans. Ford Lewis Battles (Philadelphia: Westminster Press, 1960)
ISV	International Standard Version
JATS	*Journal of the Adventist Theological Society*
JBL	*Journal of Biblical Literature*
JBMW	*Journal of Biblical Manhood and Womanhood*
JECS	*Journal of Early Christian Studies*
JETS	*Journal of the Evangelical Theological Society*
JFSR	*Journal of Feminist Studies in Religion*
JRE	*The Journal of Religious Ethics*

JRT	*Journal of Reformed Theology*
JSNT	*Journal for the Study of the New Testament*
JSOT	*Journal for the Study of the Old Testament*
JSNTSup	Journal for the Study of the New Testament Supplement Series
JSOTSup	Journal for the Study of the Old Testament Supplement Series
JTI	*Journal of Theological Interpretation*
JTS	*Journal of Theological Studies*
KJV	King James Version
LCL	Loeb Classical Library
LNTS	Library of New Testament Studies
LSV	Literal Standard Version
LW	*Luther's Works*, ed. Jaroslav Pelikan, American edition, 55 vols. (St. Louis: Concordia; Philadelphia: Fortress, 1955–1974)
MFF	*Medieval Feminist Forum*
MSJ	*Master's Seminary Journal*
MtF	male-to-female transsexual
NAC	New American Commentary
NASB	New American Standard Bible
NCBC	New Cambridge Bible Commentary
NET	New English Translation
NICNT	New International Commentary on the New Testament
NICOT	New International Commentary on the Old Testament
NIDOTTE	*New International Dictionary of Old Testament Theology and Exegesis*, ed. W. A. VanGemeren, 5 vols. (Grand Rapids: Eerdmans, 1997)
NIGTC	New International Greek Testament Commentary
NIV	New International Version
NPNF^{1}	*Nicene and Post-Nicene Fathers of the Christian Church*, first series, ed. Philip Schaff (repr., Grand Rapids: Eerdmans, 1978–1979)
NPNF^{2}	*Nicene and Post-Nicene Fathers of the Christian Church*, second series, ed. Philip Schaff (repr., Grand Rapids: Eerdmans, 1979)

NRSA	New Revised Standard Version with Apocrypha
NSBT	New Studies in Biblical Theology
NTS	*New Testament Studies*
PNTC	Pillar New Testament Commentary
ROGD	Rapid Onset Gender Dysphoria
SBJT	*Southern Baptist Journal of Theology*
SBT	Studies in Biblical Theology
SJT	*Scottish Journal of Theology*
SRS	sex reassignment surgery
STR	*Southeastern Theological Review*
TB	*Tyndale Bulletin*
TERF	trans exclusionary radical feminist
TOTC	Tyndale Old Testament Commentaries
TRINJ	*Trinity Journal*
UBC	Understanding the Bible Commentary Series
USQR	*Union Seminary Quarterly Review*
VT	*Vetus Testamentum*
WBC	Word Bible Commentary
WCF	Westminster Confession of Faith
WTJ	*Westminster Theological Journal*
ZAW	*Zeitschrift für die Alttestamentliche Wissenschaft*
ZECNT	Zondervan Exegetical Commentary on the New Testament

ACKNOWLEDGMENTS

If it takes a village to raise a child, then something similar has to be said about the writing of this book, which is a developed (and, I trust, improved) version of my PhD dissertation. While this work (including its inevitable flaws) is my own, it would not have been possible without the prayers and support of many brothers and sisters, particularly those belonging to the various "villages" I have been privileged to inhabit during the period of its writing—Sydney Missionary & Bible College, Christ College, Ministry Training & Development, and St. Andrew's Cathedral, Sydney.

Nor would this book have arrived at its final form without the generosity of many capable friends and colleagues, whose careful reading, insightful criticisms, editorial suggestions, and many corrections have proved invaluable. While I am tempted to elaborate their respective contributions in detail (some truly herculean), I can here only name them alphabetically: Tim Bradford, Rachel Ciano, Dr. Glenn Davies, Dr. Katherine Davis, Dr. Karl Deenick, Dr. Abigail Favale, Dr. Melanie Fung, Rachel Gilson, Dr. Geoffrey Harper, Janet Kirk, Emily Maurits, Dr. Daniel Patterson, Andrew Pole, Dr. Joshua Reeve, Dr. Claire Smith, David Stanley, Dr. Christopher Watkin, Dr. Patricia Weerakoon, and Dr. Sarah Williams.

Most importantly, I want to express my profound thanks to my doctoral supervisor, Dr. John McClean, whose wise counsel and constant encouragement not only guided me through the dissertation process but have been an immense blessing to me personally. I am indebted also to my secondary supervisors, Dr. David Burke and Dr. Cameron Clausing, for their attentive engagement with my work, as I am to my three dissertation examiners, Dr. Marc Cortez, Dr. Graham Cole, and Dr. Mark Garcia, for their astute comments and suggested improvements.

My deepest appreciation, however, goes to my wife, Claire. While her own doctoral work had minimal impact upon my life, the same cannot be said in reverse. I am grateful for her tireless assistance and unfailing wisdom at every point in the writing of my dissertation and now this book. True is the proverb: "House and wealth are inherited from fathers, but a prudent wife is from the LORD" (Prov 19:14).

Finally, I wish to express my heartfelt thanks to Dr. Todd Hains, Elliot Ritzema, and the team at Lexham Press for their enthusiasm to see this book published and for their editorial expertise.

Roseville, Australia
January 21, 2024

A NOTE TO READERS

In my approach to referencing, I have followed the advice of the second edition of the *SBL Handbook of Style* and have not included the issue numbers (or the month and season information) of journal volumes in footnotes, except where a particular volume is not paginated consecutively. However, these details are included in the bibliography.

In order to minimize footnotes, where I have two or more quotes from the same source in the same paragraph, I have usually held off inserting a footnote until the final quote. I have then sought to make clear in the footnote the different page numbers from which the various quotes have come (e.g., Butler, *Gender Trouble*, 9, 34, 76).

In chapters 7–11, I have included a significant number of Hebrew and Greek words and phrases. However, for those not conversant with these languages, and with very few exceptions (and mostly in footnotes), I have given the English translation first (or, occasionally, a transliteration) and then put the Hebrew or Greek in brackets.

Readers will also note that I have alternated between speaking of *transgender theory* and *trans theory*. This is purely for variation—although it reflects the lack of terminological consistency in the broader literature on this subject. The key thing to note is that, in my usage, there is no difference in meaning between the two expressions.

At several points in the body of my argument, I have interacted with web articles or blog posts written by reputable theologians (e.g., Terrance Tiessen). While these publications are not peer-reviewed, the significance of their content made them either suitable for reference or (in Tiessen's case) worthy of sustained engagement.

PART 1

SEX, GENDER, AND TRANSGENDER: SETTING THE SCENE

CHAPTER 1

THE CONTEMPORARY SEX AND GENDER CRISIS

Many people confuse sex with gender. Sex is biological, whereas gender is psychosocial. So if biology does not truly dictate gender or personality, then dichotomies of masculinity and femininity only serve to coerce or restrict the potential variety of ways of being human.[1]

—Holly Boswell

For transgenderism to be coherent, the society in which it occurs needs to place a decisive priority on the psychological over the physical in determining identity.[2]

—Carl R. Trueman

This book is an exercise in theo-anthropology and theo-ethics. Its primary purpose is to evaluate the central ontological claim of transgender theory: that the sexed body *does not* determine the gendered self. In so doing, it will also assess the moral and practical implication of this claim: that biological sex *should not* (or, at least, *need not*) ground gender identity, guide gender roles, and govern gender expression.

---

1. Holly Boswell, "The Transgender Alternative," *Chrysalis Quarterly* 1, no. 22 (1991): 29.

2. Carl R. Trueman, *The Rise and Triumph of the Modern Self: Cultural Amnesia, Expressive Individualism, and the Road to Sexual Revolution* (Wheaton, IL: Crossway, 2020), 351.

This, then, is not a book about the lived experience of those with gender incongruence (and the dysphoria it typically generates), or the pastoral care they typically require. Addressing such matters is vital, and I have written on this elsewhere.[3] But in the pages that follow I seek to do something more foundational. This does not mean that it will be without benefit for those who are personally navigating gender conflicts—far from it! It simply means that, like Helen Joyce's *Trans*, this is not so much "a book about trans people" but "a book about an idea."[4] Unlike Joyce, however, I aim to investigate this idea from an *evangelical perspective*—that is, one that regards the Bible as the written word of the Triune God.[5]

Accordingly, my evaluation of transgender theory will be primarily through a detailed theological exposition of Genesis 1 and 2 (chs. 7–9). I will then seek to show how the remainder of Scripture affirms the creational pattern (despite the disruption of the fall), reclaims it through the covenant of redemption (that culminates in the work of Christ and the Spirit), and indicates its restoration and transformation in the consummation (chs. 10–11). These chapters will comprise part 3 of the book.

In addition to this biblical evaluation, and as an important prelude to it, part 2 of the book (chs. 4–6) will provide a philosophical appraisal of trans theory via a historical analysis of the journey of sex and gender from 1949 to the present. While not definitive, this exercise will unearth the genealogy of trans theory (and, in the process, its relationship to and difference from queer theory) and highlight the main problems with its claims—at least from a critical realist perspective.

Before engaging in either of these assessments, however, part 1 is given over to several preliminary tasks. The first is to outline the controversy currently being generated (both outside and inside the church) by the transgender phenomenon and, in the process, to define trans theory (ch. 1); the

---

3. Robert S. Smith, "Discipleship and the Transgender Convert: Issues and Proposals," *Eikon* 1, no. 2 (Fall 2019): 60–74; Robert S. Smith, *How Should We Think about Gender and Identity?* (Bellingham, WA: Lexham Press, 2022), 65–68; Patricia Weerakoon, with Robert Smith and Kamal Weerakoon, *The Gender Revolution: A Biblical, Biological and Compassionate Response* (Sydney: Matthias Media, 2023).

4. Helen Joyce, *Trans: When Ideology Meets Reality* (London: Oneworld, 2021), 5, 1.

5. In ch. 2, I will discuss the imprecision and elasticity of the term "evangelical" and explain why I have defined an evangelical perspective in this way. In ch. 3, I will outline the kind of evangelical theological method I intend to employ in the second half of the book.

second is to review the history of evangelical attempts to engage transgender questions (ch. 2); and the third is to explicate the evangelical theological method I will use in part 3 of the book (ch. 3).

I begin with a brief unpacking of what many have called "the transgender moment."[6]

UNPACKING THE TRANSGENDER MOMENT

THE ADVENT OF "THE TRANSGENDER TIPPING POINT"

Cultural commentators are generally agreed that sometime toward the end of 2013 a "transgender tipping point" was reached in Western society.[7] Sociologically speaking, a tipping point is a way of referring to the moment when a social or political (or, in this case, sexual) minority is able to change the thinking and/or behavior of the majority—a change that presupposes the weakening, if not the abandoning, of long-held attitudes, convictions, and practices.[8] Such changes are often the result of the work of a small group of "committed agents who consistently proselytize the opposing opinion and are immune to influence."[9]

So it is, in this case. Although impossible apart from other societal changes (e.g., changing attitudes to homosexuality), philosophical developments (e.g., the rise of queer theory),[10] and technological advances (e.g., sex change procedures), it is well recognized that the revolution in cultural attitudes toward transgender experience and expression "has largely been

---

6. E.g., Sonali Kohli, "Pop Culture's Transgender Moment: Why Online TV Is Leading the Way," *The Atlantic* (September 26, 2014), https://www.theatlantic.com/entertainment/archive/2014/09/why-online-streaming-wins-with-transgender-portrayals/380822; Brandon Griggs, "America's Transgender Moment," *CNN* (June 1, 2015), https://www.cnn.com/2015/04/23/living/transgender-moment-jenner-feat/index.html; Rand Richards Cooper, "The Transgender Moment," *Commonweal* (December 16, 2015), https://www.commonwealmagazine.org/transgender-moment.

7. Katy Steinmetz, "The Transgender Tipping Point," *TIME* (May 29, 2014), http://time.com/135480/transgender-tipping-point.

8. See Malcolm Gladwell, *The Tipping Point: How Little Things Can Make a Big Difference* (London: Abacus, 2000).

9. J. Xie, S. Sreenivasan, G. Korniss, W. Zhang, C. Lim, and B. K. Szymanski, "Social Consensus through the Influence of Committed Minorities," *Physical Review E* 84, 011130 (July 22, 2011), https://pdfs.semanticscholar.org/21ce/52e518edef55a4eb05edb19286132c5eb1a6.pdf.

10. See further Noreen Giffney, "Introduction: The 'q' Word," in *Ashgate Research Companion to Queer Theory*, ed. Noreen Giffney and Michael O'Rourke (Burlington, VT: Ashgate, 2009), 19–27.

the result of a targeted campaign by transgender activist organizations."[11] Nor is this simply the opinion of critics. American gender theorist, trans activist, and trans woman Susan Stryker is quite candid about the fact that the "deep but hard-to-define shifts" in how gender is now understood in mainstream Western culture are "the cumulative consequence of decades of activism."[12]

The transgender moment is what lies on the other side of the transgender tipping point. Admittedly, the arrival of this moment was not entirely unforeseen. Early in 2008, an article appeared in *Christianity Today* with precisely this title.[13] The following year, Kevin Vanhoozer mooted the idea that "Transsexuality may soon become the new homosexuality—the latest hot button dispute to send shock waves through society, the courts, and the church." Again, his prediction was not overly prescient. As he was only too aware, ever since the 1980s the transgender cause has been positioning itself as "the next chapter in the civil rights movement."[14]

THE ORIGINS OF "THE TRANSGENDER MOMENT"

Clearly, then, the transgender moment has been in the making for some decades. In fact, some have even traced its origins to the publication of a 1857 article, "The Man Who Thought Himself a Woman."[15] A more obvious starting point, however, is the launch of *Transvestia: The Journal of the American Society for Equality in Dress* in 1952.[16] Even so, it was not until the development of queer theory and performative notions of gender in the late 1980s and early 1990s that a *transgender movement* can really be said to have begun in earnest. Gaining impetus from Judith Butler's groundbreaking work *Gender Trouble* (1990) and finding expression in

11. Ryan T. Anderson, *When Harry Became Sally: Responding to the Transgender Moment* (New York: Encounter Books, 2018), 19.

12. Susan Stryker, *Transgender History: The Roots of Today's Revolution* (New York: Seal, 2017), 195–96.

13. John W. Kennedy, "The Transgender Moment," *Christianity Today* (February 12, 2008), http://www.christianitytoday.com/ct/2008/february/25.54.html.

14. Kevin J. Vanhoozer, "A Drama of Redemption Model: Always Performing?," in *Four Views on Moving Beyond the Bible to Theology*, ed. Gary T. Meadors (Grand Rapids: Zondervan, 2009), 192–93.

15. Christopher Looby, "The Man Who Thought Himself a Woman," *The Knickerbocker* 50 (1857): 599–610.

16. This was also the year George Jorgensen, a former US soldier, made international headlines after undergoing sex-change surgery and changing his name to Christine Jorgensen.

Kate Bornstein's provocative *Gender Outlaw* (1994),[17] this movement "emphasized the instability of gender boundaries, rejected the 'binary' of male and female, and tried in various ways to live outside, or beyond, or across, gender categories."[18]

Whichever version best accounts for the rise of the transgender movement, it is beyond dispute that, since the 2013 tipping point, the transgender phenomenon has moved from the margins to the mainstream of Western cultural awareness and contemporary political concerns. As a consequence, society, the courts, and churches (as well as schools, sports, hospitals, universities, and the military) have felt its impact and have, indeed, all been playing catch-up.[19]

THE CONTROVERSY GENERATED BY "THE TRANSGENDER MOMENT"

Examples of resistance

The transgender moment has not been met with unequivocal enthusiasm or unqualified support, however. The "bathroom wars," particularly in the United States, are one example of resistance.[20] The more recent pushback against trans women in women's sports is another.[21] Mounting evidence that "social and peer contagion" is largely responsible for the escalation of instances of "Rapid Onset Gender Dysphoria" (ROGD) among teenagers is also raising urgent questions about the influence of trans activists and the validity of the view that "the only way to support

17. Judith Butler, *Gender Trouble: Feminism and the Subversion of Identity* (New York: Routledge, 1990); Kate Bornstein, *Gender Outlaw: On Men, Women, and the Rest of Us* (New York: Routledge, 1994).

18. Raewyn Connell and Rebecca Pearse, *Gender: In World Perspective* (Cambridge: Polity, 2015), 108.

19. See the wide range of issues treated in Patrick J. Byrne, with John Whitehall and Lane Anderson, *Transgender: One Shade of Grey: The Legal Consequences for Man & Woman, Schools, Sports, Politics, Democracy* (Melbourne: Wilkinson, 2018).

20. Michael Scherer, "Battle of the Bathroom," TIME (May 19, 2016), https://time.com/4341419/battle-of-the-bathroom; Joyce, *Trans*, 159–68; Brooke Migdon, "Idaho Governor Signs Transgender Bathroom Bill," *The Hill* (March 24, 2023), https://thehill.com/homenews/state-watch/3916944-idaho-governor-signs-transgender-bathroom-bill.

21. Jörg Strohschein, "How Sports Are Handling Transgender Women in Competition," *DW* (October 1, 2023), https://www.dw.com/en/how-sports-are-handling-transgender-women-in-competition/a-66973847.

a transgender identifying teen is to immediately accede to all requested changes, including potential medical intervention."[22] Finally, widespread concerns about the medical appropriateness of the "affirmative model of care" for treating gender dysphoric or gender nonconforming children and youth has not only led to the collapse of the major gender service for children in London,[23] but also to a number of counter initiatives such as the formation of Genspect and the Clinical Advisory Network on Sex and Gender (CAN-SG).[24]

Gender-critical feminist reactions

Moreover, it is not just cultural, political, religious, and medical conservatives who have expressed concerns over the steady march of transgender rights. Opposition has also come from gender-critical feminists and other advocates of women's rights.[25] Behind this opposition lies a long history of feminist critique of transsexuality dating back to 1979 and the publication of Janice Raymond's *The Transsexual Empire*. For Raymond, the issues are straightforward: "Maleness and femaleness are governed by certain chromosomes, and the subsequent history of being a chromosomal male or female." For this reason, transsexual surgeries "violate a dynamic process of be-ing [*sic*] and becoming that includes the integrity of the body, the total person, and the society." Consequently, sex-reassignment surgery (SRS) is, quite simply, the wrong solution to the problem of gender discontentment—a problem created by "a gender-defined society whose

22. This is certainly the finding of Lisa Littman, "Parent Reports of Adolescents and Young Adults Perceived to Show Signs of a Rapid Onset of Gender Dysphoria," *PLoS ONE* 13, no. 8 (August 16, 2018): 1–41: https://doi.org/10.1371/journal.pone.0202330; "Correction: Parent Reports of Adolescents and Young Adults Perceived to Show Signs of a Rapid Onset of Gender Dysphoria," *PLoS ONE* 14 (March 19, 2019), https://doi.org/10.1371/journal.pone.0214157; see also Lisa Marchiano, "Trans Activism's Dangerous Myth of Parental Rejection," *Quillette* (July 20, 2018), https://quillette.com/2018/07/20/trans-activisms-dangerous-myth-of-parental-rejection.

23. See Hannah Barnes, *Time to Think: The Inside Story of the Collapse of the Tavistock's Gender Service for Children* (London: Swift, 2023).

24. Genspect is particularly concerned with "the role that the healthcare, media and educational establishments play in guiding vulnerable youth toward a singular explanation for their distress" (https://genspect.org/about). CAN-SG describes itself as "a group of UK and Ireland based clinicians calling for greater understanding of the effects of sex and gender in healthcare" (https://can-sg.org).

25. Sheila Jeffreys, *Gender Hurts: A Feminist Analysis of the Politics of Transgenderism* (New York: Routledge, 2014); Holly Lawford-Smith, *Gender-Critical Feminism* (Oxford: Oxford University Press, 2022).

norms of masculinity and femininity generate the desire to be transsexed," but one better solved by "morally mandating it out of existence."[26]

Many contemporary feminists agree with Raymond's critique.[27] Political philosopher Rebecca Reilly-Cooper, for example, argues that by conceiving of gender as a spectrum, queer theorists and trans activists have confused gender with personality. In her view, gender is the system of socially prescribed norms that (supposedly) correspond to the two sex classes—male and female—a system that is socially constructed, arbitrarily imposed, and oppressive of females. Reilly-Cooper's solution "is not to reify gender by insisting on ever more gender categories that define the complexity of human personality in rigid and essentialist ways. The solution is to abolish gender altogether."[28]

While other feminists do not go quite so far,[29] and others still advocate for a more trans-inclusive approach,[30] the responses of many trans activists to non-trans (i.e., gender-critical) feminists have often been visceral, personal, and intemperate.[31] Consequently, those who question whether it is right that "someone born and raised male, who is therefore reasonably perceived as male, be included in spaces reserved for women—changing rooms, domestic violence shelters and prison wings"—are often accused of transphobia, cissexism, being a bigot or a "genderist" (akin to a "racist"), and even inciting hatred.[32] As Julian Vigo reports, "when women dare to voice their concerns about transgenderism, they are called a TERF

---

26. Janice G. Raymond, *The Transsexual Empire: The Making of the She-Male* (1979; repr., New York: Teachers College, 1994), 4, 17–18, 16, 178. Instead of making SRS illegal, however, Raymond recommended undermining "the network of sex-role stereotyping that produces the schizoid state of a 'female mind in a male body' " (179).

27. Holly Lawford-Smith, *Sex Matters: Essays in Gender-Critical Philosophy* (Oxford: Oxford University Press, 2023).

28. Rebecca Reilly-Cooper, "Gender Is Not a Spectrum," *Aeon* (June 28, 2016), https://aeon.co/essays/the-idea-that-gender-is-a-spectrum-is-a-new-gender-prison.

29. E.g., Kathleen Stock, *Material Girls: Why Reality Matters for Feminism* (London: Fleet, 2021).

30. E.g., Laura Kacere, "Why the Feminist Movement Must Be Trans-Inclusive," *Everyday Feminism* (February 24, 2014), https://everydayfeminism.com/2014/02/trans-inclusive-feminist-movement.

31. See, e.g., Samantha Bergeson, "J. K. Rowling Doubles Down on Transphobia in International Women's Day Twitter Rant," *IndieWire* (March 8, 2022), https://www.indiewire.com/2022/03/jk-rowling-transphobia-international-womens-day-rant-1234705640.

32. Judith Green, "Transgender Activists and the Real War on Women: A Dispatch from the New Front Line in Free Speech," *The Spectator* (March 10, 2018), https://www.spectator.co.au/2018/03/transgender-activists-and-the-real-war-on-women.

(trans exclusionary radical feminist), and face No Platforming, cyberstalking, death and rape threats, and social scorn."[33] Such reactions have only strengthened the resolve of many to resist giving trans women "unrestricted access to protected spaces originally introduced to shield females from sexual violence from males."[34]

An uncertain future

All of this suggests that the transgender moment is less secure and decisive than advocates might have hoped. Indeed, there is a tense (and increasingly ugly) culture war raging over the whole transgender question. Stryker, then, is right to see the transgender tipping point as being "more like the fulcrum of a teeter-totter, tipping backward as well as forward, than like a summit where, after a long upward climb, progress toward legal and social equality starts rolling effortlessly downhill."[35] Nevertheless, there is no denying a growing awareness of "transgender experience" (i.e., the mismatch that some people feel between their inner sense of self and the sex of their body) and the challenge that such experience poses for a world that, traditionally, has assumed a binary understanding of both sex and gender, and also a stable connection between them.

At a deeper level, the claims of many transgender theorists have raised a series of complex philosophical quandaries—ontological, epistemological, and ethical—that require urgent attention and exploration. For example: "Is the self prior to the institution of gender identity? Is sex the 'hardware' on which the program of gender is run, or is sex itself thoroughly cultural? If the self is irrevocably immersed in cultural gender, how is resistance to gender oppression possible at all?"[36]

These are just some of the more important questions raised by the transgender moment and, as we shall see, answers to them are highly contested.

---

33. Julian Vigo, "Why Women Should Stand Up to the Trans Ideology," *Spiked* (November 29, 2017), http://www.spiked-online.com/newsite/article/why-women-should-stand-up-to-the-trans-ideology.

34. Kathleen Stock, "Changing the Concept of 'Woman' Will Cause Unintended Harms," *The Economist* (July 6, 2018), https://www.economist.com/open-future/2018/07/06/changing-the-concept-of-woman-will-cause-unintended-harms.

35. Stryker, *Transgender History*, 196.

36. Talia Bettcher, "Feminist Perspectives on Trans Issues," *The Stanford Encyclopedia of Philosophy* (Spring 2014 Edition), http://plato.stanford.edu/archives/spr2014/entries/feminism-trans.

MAPPING AND DEFINING "TRANSGENDER"

A COMPLEX AND CONFUSING HISTORY

Part of the difficulty in addressing the issues raised by the trans phenomenon has to do with differing definitions of the term "transgender." To what particular claim or experience does this word refer? How is it best defined?

These are not simple questions to answer. Since the mid-1960s, "transgender" has had a rather complex and confusing history and, as Stryker acknowledges, "has meant many contradictory things at different times."[37] In one stream of contemporary usage, the term refers to those who experience "a disjunction between their physical sex and gender identity."[38] As such, "transgenderism" may be distinguished from both "transvestitism" (i.e., the practice of cross-dressing) and "transsexualism," which "refers more specifically to people who have undertaken surgery or hormone therapy to make their bodies 'fit' their gender identities."[39] However, it is increasingly common for the category of "transgender" to embrace (and so replace) both transvestites and transsexuals.[40]

As a discrete term, "transgender" was coined in 1965 by John Oliven, a Columbia University psychiatrist. He applied it specifically to people who wished to live as the gender opposite to their sex but without surgically altering their bodies.[41] As an alternative, in the December 1969 issue of *Transvestia*, Virginia Prince employed the term "transgenderal" (again, in contrast to transsexual). But this failed to catch on.[42] By the mid-1970s, however, "transgenderist" was regularly functioning as a broad umbrella term, encompassing both transvestites and transsexuals, and also anyone in between.[43]

---

37. Stryker, *Transgender History*, 36.

38. Susannah Cornwall, "Intersex and Transgender People," in *The Oxford Handbook of Theology, Sexuality, and Gender*, ed. Adrian Thatcher (Oxford: Oxford University Press, 2014), 659.

39. Cornwall, "Intersex and Transgender People," 659.

40. Stryker, for example, applies the term "transgender" to "the widest imaginable range of gender-variant practices and identities" (*Transgender History*, 38).

41. John F. Oliven, *Sexual Hygiene and Pathology* (Philadelphia: J. B. Lippincott, 1965), 514.

42. Richard Ekins and Dave King, *The Transgender Phenomenon* (London: SAGE, 2006), 13.

43. Ekins and King, *The Transgender Phenomenon*, 14.

The first major challenge to this more elastic and expansive use of the term came from trans activist Holly Boswell in her 1991 article "The Transgender Alternative." In it, she contends that being transgender should be seen as "a viable option between crossdresser and transsexual," and that it is better to "view each of these three zones within the greater spectrum of gender." She further argues that finding such "middle ground" is not unprecedented, claiming that "transgender" has "a firm foundation in the ancient tradition of androgyny." Indeed, Boswell saw androgyny as "offering the broadest opportunity for psychological integration and evolution."[44]

THE CURRENT CONSENSUS

Whatever the merits of defining transgender more narrowly, at the level of popular discourse it is becoming increasingly common for it to be applied to "the widest range of gender-variant practices and identities."[45] The way here was paved by the lesbian transgender activist and revolutionary communist Leslie Feinberg in her 1996 publication *Transgender Warriors*.[46] While respectful of more restrictive applications of the term, for Feinberg, transgender is best defined as "an umbrella term to include everyone who challenges the boundaries of sex and gender."[47] Trans man Jay Prosser, similarly, sees it as covering "any form of what's been dubbed a 'gender outlaw.' "[48] Some have gone even further. For Anne Finn Enke, the following array of persons all belong under the transgender umbrella: "FTM, MTF, gender queer, trans woman, trans man, butch queen, fem queen, tranny, transy, drag king, bi-gender, pan-gender, femme, butch, stud, two spirit, people with intersex conditions, androgynous, gender fluid, gender euphoric, third gender, *and* man and woman."[49]

---

44. Boswell, "The Transgender Alternative," 29–31.

45. Stryker, *Transgender History*, 38.

46. Leslie Feinberg, *Transgender Warriors: Making History from Joan of Arc to Dennis Rodman* (Boston: Beacon, 1996).

47. Feinberg, *Transgender Warriors*, x.

48. Jay Prosser, "Transgender," in *Lesbian and Gay Studies: A Critical Introduction*, ed. Andy Medhurst and Sally R. Munt (London: Cassell, 1997), 310.

49. Anne Finn Enke "Introduction," in *Transfeminist Perspectives in and Beyond Transgender and Gender Studies*, ed. Anne Finn Enke (Philadelphia: Temple University Press, 2012), 4 (emphasis original).

However, the problem with this degree of expansiveness (and particularly the inclusion of "man and woman") is that the category is stretched beyond meaningfulness.[50] Consequently, most of those currently engaged in transgender studies apply the term in a moderately expansive way; i.e., to those who "do not conform to prevailing expectations about gender."[51] In other words, transgender (or increasingly trans) now refers not only to those who experience and/or exhibit some degree of cross-gender or non-binary identification but also to "transsexuals, drag queens and kings, some butch lesbians, and (heterosexual) male cross dressers."[52] This breadth is often signaled by the addition of an asterisk: trans*. Consistent with this understanding, the American Psychological Association offers the following definition: "Transgender is an umbrella term for persons whose *gender identity*, *gender expression*, or behavior does not conform to that typically associated with the sex to which they were assigned at birth. … 'Trans' is sometimes used as shorthand for 'transgender.' "[53] Despite the dangers inherent in the description of sex as *assigned* (rather than *recognized*) at birth,[54] it is this broader definition that has been adopted in this book.

ROGERS BRUBAKER'S TAXONOMY

As a way of encompassing the various groups covered by this definition, but without blurring the distinctions between them, American sociologist Rogers Brubaker distinguishes between three trans categories: the "trans of migration," the "trans of between," and the "trans of beyond." He explains his taxonomy as follows:

50. It is also vitally important to distinguish intersexuality from transgender experience, even though both can generate experiences of GD.

51. Andrew Heywood, *Political Ideologies: An Introduction* (London: Palgrave, 2017), 241.

52. Bettcher, "Feminist Perspectives."

53. "Answers to Your Questions About Transgender People, Gender Identity, and Gender Expression," *American Psychological Association* (2018), http://www.apa.org/topics/lgbt/transgender.aspx (emphasis original).

54. It is noteworthy that the association's definition speaks not of "biological sex" or "physical sex" (or even "birth sex" or "natal sex"), but of sex as something that is "*assigned* at birth." This language (intentionally) opens up the possibility that a person's true sexed identity is not, finally, determined by their *body* (i.e., their "chromosomes, hormone prevalence, and external and internal anatomy"), but by their *gender identity* (i.e., their "internal sense of being male, female or something else"). Accordingly, a person's sex may later need to be "reassigned" in order to match their gender identity.

> The *trans of migration* involves moving from one established sex/gender category to another, often by surgically and hormonally transforming one's body and formally changing one's legal identity. The *trans of between* involves defining oneself with reference to the two established categories, without belonging entirely or unambiguously to either one, and without moving definitively from one to the other. The *trans of beyond* involves positioning oneself in a space that is not defined with reference to established categories. It is characterised by the claim to transcend existing categories—or to transcend categorization altogether.[55]

Brubaker's categories are helpful for three reasons. First, they helpfully capture the three main identity groups that fall under the transgender umbrella while also signaling "the many, many different ways there are of being trans."[56] Second, they alert us to the complex imbrications of trans ideology and queer theory (a point to which we shall return). Third, they reveal that although the precise boundary between a number of the letters in the LGBTQQIAAP2S acronym is far from clear,[57] this lack of clarity serves to highlight a crucial point of commonality: what those under the "T" umbrella share with those who identify as queer, questioning, androgynous, asexual, and two-spirit (and, we might add, non-binary) is a rejection of the idea that *the sexed body reveals and determines the gendered self and, as a consequence, should ground gender identity, guide gender roles, and govern gender expression.*

---

55. Rogers Brubaker, *Trans: Gender and Race in an Age of Unsettled Identities* (Princeton: Princeton University Press, 2016), 10.

56. Jennifer Finney Boylan, "Throwing Our Voices: An Introduction," in *"Trans Bodies, Trans Selves": A Resource for the Transgender Community*, ed. Laura Erickson-Schroth (Oxford: Oxford University Press, 2014), xvi. Boylan notes at least nine "different ways there are of being trans" (xvii).

57. LGBTQQIAAP2S stands for Lesbian, Gay, Bisexual, Transgender, Queer, Questioning, Intersex, Androgynous, Asexual, Pansexual, and Two-Spirit.

THE CENTRAL CLAIM OF TRANSGENDER THEORY

THE CONTENTION OF THIS BOOK

In this book I contend that at the heart of transgender theory lies the denial that *the sexed body reveals and determines the gendered self*. The accuracy of this contention is confirmed by Stryker, who avers that

> the sex of the body ... does not bear any *necessary* or *predetermined* relationship to the social category in which that body lives or to the identity and subjective sense of self of the person who lives in the world through that body. This assertion, drawn from the observation of human social, psychological, and biological variability, is political precisely because it contradicts the common belief that whether a person is a man or a woman in the social sense is fundamentally determined by bodily sex, which is self-apparent and can be clearly and unambiguously perceived.[58]

Here, in fact, Stryker offers two distinct denials. At the end of the citation, it is denied that bodily sex is "self-apparent." Presumably, this is a reference to the reality of intersex conditions—i.e., medically identifiable developmental disorders in which "genetic sex (chromosomes) and phenotypic sex (genital appearance) do not match, or are somehow different from the 'standard' definition of male or female."[59] The significance of such conditions and the questions they raise will be discussed at various points in this book. At this point, however, it is sufficient to note that for more than 99.98 percent of human beings their sex, as either male or female, is "self-apparent."[60]

The denial at the beginning of the citation, however, is not only entirely independent of the one at the end but is also far more radical. According to Stryker, the sex of a person's body, even when it is unambiguously male or female, "does not bear any *necessary* or *predetermined* relationship" to either their social sex (how they present and perform in the world) or

---

58. Stryker, *Transgender History*, 16 (emphasis original).

59. This description is taken from http://www.intersexinitiative.org.

60. Leonard Sax, "How Common Is Intersex? A Response to Anne Fausto-Sterling," *The Journal of Sex Research* 39, no. 3 (2002): 177.

their psychological sex (how they perceive or believe themselves to be). In brief, the sexed body does not determine the gendered self.

PARSING TRANS THEORY

So, if not sex, then what determines the gendered self? According to trans woman Julia Serano, the answer is one's *subconscious sex*—which can be inferred from a person's "intuition that there is something 'wrong' with the sex they were assigned at birth" or "that they should have been born as or wish they could be the other sex."[61] More commonly, this is referred to as gender identity, which (in a similarly subjective way) the preamble of the Yogyakarta Principles defines as

> each person's deeply felt internal and individual experience of gender, which may or may not correspond with the sex assigned at birth, including the personal sense of the body (which may involve, if freely chosen, modification of bodily appearance or function by medical, surgical or other means) and other expressions of gender, including dress, speech and mannerisms.[62]

Not surprisingly, what I am calling transgender theory (or more often just trans theory) others refer to as gender identity theory or gender-identity ideology, or just gender theory or gender ideology.[63] In each case, however, the theory is essentially the same and, according to Kathleen Stock's analysis, can be broken down into four main axioms: (1) everyone has an inner gender identity; (2) not everyone's gender identity matches their biological sex; (3) gender identity, not sex, is what determines whether you

61. Julia Serano, *Whipping Girl: A Transsexual Woman on Sexism and The Scapegoating of Femininity*, 2nd ed. (Emeryville, CA: Seal, 2016), 27 (emphasis original).

62. The Yogyakarta Principles is a statement that seeks to apply international human rights law to sexual orientation and gender identity. It was produced by a meeting of human rights experts in Yogyakarta, Indonesia, in November 2006. An additional nine principles were added in 2017 to cover "the distinct and intersectional grounds of gender expression and sex characteristics." The definition of gender identity above appears twice in the 2006 statement: once in the introduction (6n2) and again in the preamble (8). See https://yogyakartaprinciples.org/principles-en.

63. For the first, see Stock, *Material Girls*, 12; for the second, see Joyce, *Trans*, 53–70; for the third and fourth, see Sharon James, *Gender Ideology: What Do Christians Need to Know?* (Fearn: Christian Focus Publications, 2019). James alternates between the two labels throughout her book.

are a man or a woman (or neither); and (4) human societies are obliged to recognize and legally protect gender identity, not biological sex.[64]

If, for the sake of argument, we grant the validity of the first two axioms, we still need to ask *what* gender identity is, *where* it comes from, *why* it does not always align with sex, and *why* axioms 3 and 4 should follow. To answer these questions, Stock considers four possible explanatory models: the "stick of rock" model (in which "gender identity is a fundamental part of the self, and determines who you 'really are' "[65]); the medical model (in which a misaligned gender identity—or, at least, the dysphoria it typically generates—is considered to be a psychiatric disorder); the queer theory model (which emphasizes the performative nature of gender and "the impermanence and fluidity of gender identity"); and the identification model (in which a misaligned gender identity is a result of a strong psychological identification with either a particular member of the opposite sex or the sex itself "as a general object or ideal"[66]).

While people who identify as transgender may adopt any (or none, or a combination) of these models, transgender theory is committed to the "stick of rock" (or "real me") model. As the third of the Yogyakarta Principles expresses, "Each person's self-defined ... gender identity is integral to their personality."[67] In short, biology is no longer destiny; gender identity is. As Helen Joyce explains, "It is innate and ineffable: something like a sexed soul."[68] Consequently, a person's "strong yearning to be of a different sex, or disaffection for [their] own sexed body, or attempts to pass as the opposite sex, and so on, are treated as expressions or evidence of [their] innate gender identity."[69] Furthermore, given the experiential reality of axiom 2—that not everyone's gender identity matches their

64. Stock, *Material Girls*, 11.

65. Stock, *Material Girls*, 112. As Stock explains, a "stick of rock" is a type of UK candy that is typically brightly colored on the outside and white on the inside, and has a place name (e.g., Brighton) or some other message printed through its interior in dark-colored sugar.

66. Stock, *Material Girls*, 124, 129.

67. Yogyakarta Principles, 11. Stonewall (UK) similarly defines "gender identity" as a person's "innate sense of their own gender, whether male, female or something else" ("List of LGBTQ+ terms," *Stonewall*, https://www.stonewall.org.uk/help-advice/faqs-and-glossary/list-lgbtq-terms).

68. Joyce, *Trans*, 2.

69. Stock, *Material Girls*, 113.

biological sex—this would seem to provide prima facie evidence that gender identity, whatever its origin, is not infallibly determined by biological sex.

TROUBLING TRANS THEORY

However, none of this suggests that axiom 3—that gender identity, and not biological sex, determines whether one is a man or woman—is true. For even if gender identity was innate and immutable, biological sex can make precisely the same claim.[70] So why should gender identity trump sex, psychology biology, or subjectivity objectivity, particularly when there is strong evidence that trans identities are neither innate nor immutable?[71] Furthermore, as the work of Lisa Littman (and others) has exposed, gender identity (particularly, but not only, in teenage girls) is both highly malleable and easily manipulable, and so is susceptible to a range of social influences.[72] But when it comes to sex and the distinctions between the sexes, these, by their very nature, are "not likely to be at all amenable to social engineering, no matter how much some people want it to be."[73]

There is, then, no reason why gender identity, rather than biological sex, should determine whether a person is a man or woman.[74] Axiom 3 is

---

70. Debra Soh, *The End of Gender: Debunking the Myths about Sex and Identity in Our Society* (New York: Threshold Editions, 2020), 15–38.

71. This is clear from both the desistence rate for childhood GD (70–98 percent of natal males; 50–88 percent of natal females) and the phenomenon of late-onset GD, which also indicates the mutability of gender identity. See American Psychiatric Association, *Diagnostic and Statistical Manual of Mental Disorders*, 5th ed [*DSM-5*] (Washington, DC: American Psychiatric Publishing, 2013), 455; Kenneth J. Zucker, "The Myth of Persistence: Response to 'A Critical Commentary on Follow-Up Studies and "Desistance" Theories about Transgender and Gender Non-Conforming Children' by Temple Newhook et al. (2018)," *IJT* 19, no. 2 (2018): 231–45. Lisa Littman, "Individuals Treated for Gender Dysphoria with Medical and/or Surgical Transition Who Subsequently Detransitioned: A Survey of 100 Detransitioners," *Archives of Sexual Behavior* 50 (2021): 3353–69, https://doi.org/10.1007/s10508-021-02163-w; Soh, *End of Gender*, 139–88.

72. See the research cited in fn. 22 of this chapter; compare Abigail Shrier, *Irreversible Damage: The Transgender Craze Seducing Our Daughters* (Washington, DC: Regnery, 2020).

73. Joyce, *Trans*, 4.

74. It is not my intention to engage at any length with the "body-brain mismatch hypothesis"—the idea that "there are significant natural in-born sex differences found [in] the brains of those called transsexual people" (Milton Diamond, "Transsexualism as an Intersex Condition," in *Transsexuality in Theology and Neuroscience: Findings, Controversies, and Perspectives*, ed. Gerhard Schreiber [Boston: de Gruyter, 2016], 43). Although I will offer a further comment in ch. 6, may it here suffice to say that many who have examined the relevant brain-research studies have concluded that "the supposed sex differences in the brain are overplayed at best and fabricated at worst" (Sprinkle, *Embodied*, 133).

simply an assertion that rests on the assumption that "the body is not of primary relevance to gender identity" and then, on this basis, "excludes bodily considerations from the definition of what it means to be a man or a woman." The problem, however, as Carl Trueman espies, is that this is "a circular argument. Its conclusion is already contained in its premise."[75] Moreover, this is far from the only problem to trouble trans theory, as we shall see. And yet, despite such obstacles, the idea that *trans women are women* (by virtue of their self-declaration) is fast embedding itself in the social imagination of Western society.[76]

TWO VERSIONS OF TRANS THEORY

The increasing prevalence of the notion of gender self-identification—that is, that a person's legal sex is determined by their declared gender identity without any medical diagnosis or intervention—has created two distinct versions of trans theory, both of which can be distinguished from feminist *non-trans theory* and *queer theory*.

TABLE 1: NON-TRANS, TRANS, & QUEER THEORIES CONTRASTED

Type of Theory	*Sex is*	*Gender is*
Non-Trans Theory	Determined by biology	Socially constructed upon sex
Soft Trans Theory	Determined by biology	Determined by gender identity
Hard Trans Theory	Determined by gender identity	Determined by gender identity
Queer Theory	Determined by gender	Performatively constituted

The common conviction that unites both forms of trans theory is that *gender is determined by gender identity* (not by biological sex). But for soft trans theory, sex remains biologically determined. This is what gives rise to the experience of gender incongruence, and usually to a diagnosis of gender dysphoria (GD), and often creates the desire to alter the body to bring it into line with the mind.

In short, there is no evidence that a person can have the brain of one sex and the body of the other. "Indeed, the brain is part of the body" (Weerakoon, et al., *Gender Revolution*, 58).

75. Carl R. Trueman, *Strange New World: How Thinkers and Activists Redefined Identity and Sparked the Sexual Revolution* (Wheaton, IL: Crossway, 2022), 138.

76. Heather Brunskell-Evans, *Transgender: Body Politics* (North Geelong: Spinifex, 2020), 157 (emphasis original).

According to hard trans theory, however, the sex of a person's body is determined by their gender identity. The body requires no reshaping, therefore, only reclassifying. This means that if a person's gender identity is female, then their whole body is female. This is why the trans-inclusive feminist philosopher Katharine Jenkins can insist that "some women do have penises,"[77] and others that "some men menstruate."[78] It is also why principle 3 of the Yogyakarta Principles states, "No one shall be forced to undergo medical procedures, including sex reassignment surgery, sterilisation or hormonal therapy, as a requirement for legal recognition of their gender identity."[79]

In sum, hard trans theory claims that gender incongruence is not necessary to be trans; self-identification is all that is required. Consequently, many non-dysphoric people now identify as trans "for a variety of political to social to emotional reasons."[80]

A QUESTION IN NEED OF URGENT RESOLUTION

THE PURPOSE AND IMPETUS OF THIS BOOK

As significant as the distinction between soft and hard trans theory is for society, it is important to note that both versions of the theory contain a common core: a denial of the view that the sexed body determines the gendered self and so should ground gender identity, guide gender roles, and govern gender expression.

The purpose of this book is to evaluate both the indicative (that the sexed body does not determine the gendered self) and the imperative (that it ought not, or at least need not, ground gender identity, guide gender roles, and govern gender expression) inherent in this denial, and to do so from an evangelical theological perspective.

---

77. Katharine Jenkins, "Can a Woman Have a Penis? How to Understand Disagreements about Gender Recognition," *The Conversation* (August 28, 2018), https://theconversation.com/can-a-woman-have-a-penis-how-to-understand-disagreements-about-gender-recognition-101991.

78. Kabir Trivedi, "Some Men Menstruate Too. Can We Talk About It Now?," *Feminism in India* (July 13, 2018), https://feminisminindia.com/2018/07/13/men-menstruate-talk-about-it.

79. Yogyakarta Principles, 11–12.

80. Jessie Earl, "Do You Need Gender Dysphoria to Be Trans?," *Advocate* (January 18, 2019), www.advocate.com/commentary/2019/1/18/do-you-need-gender-dysphoria-be-trans.

The impetus for this book stems not only from the fact that this negative claim—that sex neither signifies nor determines gender—has generated a major social, political, and medical crisis in many Western societies, but also because it has provoked intense discussion, considerable confusion, and, often, deep division in many Christian churches, dioceses, and denominations. Perhaps not surprisingly, this is also the case among those who claim the label "evangelical."[81]

THE PROBLEM OF EVANGELICAL DIVISION

The depth and seriousness of intra-evangelical division was highlighted by the wide range of responses to the release of the 2017 "Nashville Statement: A Coalition for Biblical Sexuality."[82] In the course of fulfilling its aim to bring biblical clarity to a broad range of issues concerning human sexuality, the statement offered the following five affirmations concerning transgender claims: first, "that divinely ordained differences between male and female reflect God's original creation design and are meant for human good and human flourishing" (Art. 4); second, "that the differences between male and female reproductive structures are integral to God's design for self-conception as male or female" (Art. 5); third, "that self-conception as male or female should be defined by God's holy purposes in creation and redemption as revealed in Scripture" (Art. 7); fourth, "that it is sinful to approve of ... transgenderism and that such approval constitutes an essential departure from Christian faithfulness and witness" (Art. 10); and fifth, "that the grace of God in Christ enables sinners to forsake transgender self-conceptions and by divine forbearance to accept the God-ordained link between one's biological sex and one's self-conception as male or female" (Art. 13).

The statement also contains the following five denials that likewise bear on transgender questions: first, it denies that differences between male and female "are a result of the Fall or are a tragedy to be overcome" (Art. 4); second, it denies "that physical anomalies or psychological conditions

---

81. "The Evangelical Divide," editorial, *The Economist* (October 14, 2017), https://www.economist.com/united-states/2017/10/14/the-evangelical-divide.

82. The "Nashville Statement" is an evangelical statement of faith, produced by the Council on Biblical Manhood and Womanhood (CBMW). It can be viewed here: https://cbmw.org/wp-content/uploads/2017/08/The-Nashville-Statement.pdf.

nullify the God-appointed link between biological sex and self-conception as male or female" (Art. 5); third, it denies that adopting a "transgender self-conception is consistent with God's holy purposes in creation and redemption" (Art. 7); fourth, it denies that the approval of transgender ideology "is a matter of moral indifference about which otherwise faithful Christians should agree to disagree" (Art. 10); and fifth, it denies that "that the grace of God in Christ sanctions self-conceptions that are at odds with God's revealed will" (Art. 13).

As my evaluation of trans theory will in due course reveal, I stand in firm agreement with the Nashville Statement. My purpose here, however, is not to defend it but to note the broad spectrum of evangelical responses to it. At one end were those who praised it for its mix of clarity and compassion,[83] while at the other were those who denounced it as "tone-deaf" and claimed it would result in further "suffering, rejection, shame, and despair" for LGBTQ people.[84] And then there were those who positioned themselves somewhere in the middle and sought to be more even handed.[85]

THE REALITY OF EVANGELICAL CONFUSION

One of the main reasons for this lack of evangelical unanimity is that the term "evangelical" is becoming increasingly elastic.[86] Consequently, professed evangelicals often have widely differing conceptions of biblical inspiration, different convictions about biblical authority, different approaches to biblical hermeneutics, and different views regarding how the Bible addresses contemporary ethical questions.[87]

---

83. Alistair Begg (@Alistair Begg), "This is a clear, courageous, compassionate statement on human sexuality. https://cbmw.org/nashville-statement... #NashvilleStatement," *Twitter.com* (August 29, 2017, 1:17pm), https://twitter.com/AlistairBegg/status/902626348484755456.

84. Jen Hatmaker (@JenHatmaker), "The fruit of the 'Nashville Statement' is suffering, rejection, shame, and despair. The timing is callous beyond words," *Twitter.com* (August 29, 2017, 10:55am), https://twitter.com/JenHatmaker/status/902590545578643456.

85. Preston Sprinkle, "My Nashville Statement," *Preston Sprinkle* (September 3, 2017), https://www.prestonsprinkle.com/blog/2017/9/3/my-nashville-statement.

86. Jonathan Merritt, "Defining 'Evangelical': Its Meaning Has Shifted throughout Christianity's Long History and Changes Depending on Who You Ask. Why?," *The Atlantic* (December 7, 2015), https://www.theatlantic.com/politics/archive/2015/12/evangelical-christian/418236.

87. On the first two points, see James R. A. Merrick and Stephen M. Garrett, eds., *Five Views on Biblical Inerrancy* (Grand Rapids: Zondervan, 2013). On the last two, see Meadors, ed., *Four Views on Moving Beyond the Bible to Theology*.

Furthermore, for the last quarter-century or more, many evangelicals have tended to be less culturally conservative and more world affirming.[88] In a reversal of the old aphorism "as goes the church, so goes society," the reality now tends to be *as goes society, so goes the church*. Consequently, the fact that Western nations are "increasingly influenced by the promise that human flourishing can come by what is styled as sexual liberation and the overthrowing of historic Christianity's witness to God's purpose in making us as sexual beings—even making us as male and female"[89]—is unsettling the convictions of many evangelicals.

CONCLUDING REFLECTIONS

The net effect of the developments described in this chapter is that many churches have found themselves unready for, confused by, and (in some cases) deeply divided over "the transgender moment." This is not helped by the fact that evangelical scholars, for the most part, are still in the early stages of grappling with the theological, ethical, and pastoral issues raised by transgender experience and, in particular, trans theory. Indeed, as we shall see in the next chapter, there is still only a relatively small number of in-depth, exegetical, and theological evaluations of trans theory from an evangelical perspective.[90]

This does not mean that no significant steps have been taken in this direction. In fact, the evangelical literature addressing transgender questions, which dates from the early 1980s, is laden with valuable insights and, in the main, provides a firm foundation on which to build. The task of the next chapter, then, is to present a brief survey and summary of the more notable contributions to this body of literature.

---

88. Mark A. Shibley, "Contemporary Evangelicals: Born-Again and World Affirming," *The Annals of the American Academy of Political and Social Science* 558 (1998): 67–87; Thomas S. Kidd, *Who Is an Evangelical? The History of a Movement in Crisis* (New Haven: Yale University Press, 2019).

89. R. Albert Mohler Jr., "I Signed the Nashville Statement. It's an Expression of Love for Same-Sex Attracted People," *The Washington Post* (September 3, 2017), https://www.washingtonpost.com/news/acts-of-faith/wp/2017/09/03/i-signed-the-nashville-statement-its-an-expression-of-love-for-same-sex-attracted-people.

90. For example, there is currently no treatment of transgender questions comparable to Robert A. J. Gagnon's *The Bible and Homosexual Practice: Texts and Hermeneutics* (Nashville: Abingdon, 2002).

CHAPTER 2

EVANGELICALS AND TRANSGENDER QUESTIONS

Only with the corrective lens of Scripture can we discern what is normative in the tangled mass of psychological and sociological data on sexual mores in different cultures.[1]

—Albert M. Wolters

The Bible begins by drawing certain global distinctions, including those between the Creator and the creation, the heavens and the earth, humans and all other creatures, male and female. We must do more than restate propositions ... to learn the wisdom implied in these distinctions. We must rather adopt a habit of judging that respects these distinctions in whatever language, conceptuality, and culture we happen to be speaking, thinking, and living.[2]

—Kevin J. Vanhoozer

The purpose of this chapter is to present a brief survey and summary of the more notable attempts by evangelicals to address transgender questions. Before we get underway, however, two additional comments are necessary.

1. Albert M. Wolters, *Creation Regained: Biblical Basics for a Reformational Worldview* (Grand Rapids: Eerdmans, 2005), 109.

2. Kevin J. Vanhoozer, "Love's Wisdom: The Authority of Scripture's Form and Content for Faith's Understanding and Theological Judgment," *JRT* 5 (2011): 266–67.

First, the scope of the literature reviewed in this chapter is deliberately narrow. I will not be surveying works that address transgender questions from a non-evangelical perspective (many of these will be engaged with in chs. 7–11). Neither will I refer to the vast body of secular writing on the subject (much of this literature will be explored in chs. 4–6). My purpose, rather, is to register the main evangelical attempts to engage with transgender questions and, in the process, gain a clear appreciation of the current state of play in the world of evangelical thought.

Second, to give the (admittedly elastic) term "evangelical" a simple and stable point of reference, I will use it in line with the theological affirmations contained in the "Doctrinal Basis" of the Evangelical Theological Society (as stated in article III of the society's constitution), to which all members must subscribe annually. The affirmations are two: (1) "The Bible alone, and the Bible in its entirety, is the Word of God written and is therefore inerrant in the autographs"; and (2) "God is a Trinity, Father, Son, and Holy Spirit, each an uncreated person, one in essence, equal in power and glory."[3]

OLIVER O'DONOVAN, *TRANSSEXUALISM AND CHRISTIAN MARRIAGE*

The story of evangelical attempts to engage transgender questions begins in 1982, when the British ethicist Oliver O'Donovan produced a small booklet titled *Transsexualism and Christian Marriage*.[4] This carefully argued account of the implications of sex change for marriage defends the thesis that a person who is "unambiguously a member of one biological sex cannot then become a member of the other." This leads to the conclusion that the marriage of a man and a trans woman (or vice versa), from a Christian perspective, would "not be the union of a man and a woman" but a same-sex union, and for that reason would "not be a marriage at all."[5]

3. "ETS Constitution," The Evangelical Theological Society (originally adopted in 1949 and last amended in 2008), https://www.etsjets.org/about/constitution#A4.

4. Oliver O'Donovan, *Transsexualism and Christian Marriage* (Bramcote: Grove Books, 1982). In 1983, the booklet was slightly expanded and published as "Transsexualism and Christian Marriage," *JRE* 11 (1983): 135–62. While the original booklet was reprinted by Grove in 2007, the following page numbers refer to the *JRE* publication.

5. O'Donovan, "Transsexualism," 135, 155–56.

O'Donovan considers two cases against this conclusion. The *psychological case* argues that, since biological sex cannot be considered on its own, the person who believes they are (or should be) the opposite sex should be seen as ambiguously sexed. The case fails, however, for it ignores the fact that a person's true sexed identity is biologically (not psychologically) determined and cannot, therefore, "be modified by surgical artifice." The *social case* argues that public acceptance of a transsexual's gender does not depend on their real sex but on their social role. But this case also fails, for it requires the public affirmation of an illusion.[6]

For O'Donovan, sexed identity is a divine gift revealed by the "non-negotiable biological datum" of our bodies. It cannot be changed, therefore; "it can only be either welcomed or resented."[7] While he does not explore how the problem of gender incongruence may best be addressed, O'Donovan is clear that SRS goes beyond the bounds of what it is legitimate for humans to do with their bodies.

DAVID HORTON, *CHANGING CHANNELS?*

In 1994, English evangelical David Horton also produced a small booklet in the Grove series titled *Changing Channels? A Christian Response to the Transvestite and Transsexual.*[8] The question driving Horton's booklet is this: "So is the transvestite, who periodically crosses the gender divide, and the transsexual who identifies with the opposite gender role, part of a breakdown in our social order, or merely a reminder of the variety that has always existed among men and women?"[9]

In answering this question, Horton rejects O'Donovan's contention that "we should not think of gender as a spectrum," despite conceding that "his 'bi-morphic' model" is in line with Genesis 1:27. In support, Horton draws attention to the possibility of various biological explanations for

6. O'Donovan, "Transsexualism," 135, 145, 153, 154.

7. O'Donovan, "Transsexualism," 141. O'Donovan is sensitive to the important distinction between forms of "physical sex-indeterminacy" (i.e., intersex conditions) and transsexualism, writing that the former can be "traced to a malfunction at some point in the outworking of the either-or of chromosomal endowment" (143), whereas "transsexuals present no physical ambiguity of sex, but are phenotypically completely normal members of the sex into which they were born" (136).

8. David Horton, *Changing Channels? A Christian Response to the Transvestite and Transsexual* (Nottingham: Grove Books, 1994).

9. Horton, *Changing Channels?*, 17.

trans phenomena (e.g., "Brain Sex") and, despite admitting that the "question of cause remains unclear," contends "that there are people who are *psychologically intersex*, as well as those with an in-between physiology."[10]

As to the Bible's "clear condemnation of transvestitism" in Deuteronomy 22:5, Horton believes that this is either "aimed at women who wished to infiltrate the assembly of Israel, or like so much of the Law of Moses, condemns an aspect of Canaanite fertility worship." His conclusion, then, is that the "psychologically intersexed" are not a result of "a breakdown in our social order," but "a reminder of the variety that has always existed among men and women."[11] Consequently, anything that helps a person achieve a sense of unity—be it cross-dressing or SRS—is ethically acceptable.

THE EVANGELICAL ALLIANCE, *TRANSSEXUALITY*

In 2000, the Evangelical Alliance in the UK produced *Transsexuality: A Report by the Evangelical Alliance Policy Commission.*[12] It addresses both current and historical contexts, medical and legal considerations, theological and ethical perspectives, and practical and pastoral issues. Its biblical chapter, however, is brief (a mere ten pages in total) and, while offering a helpful outline of "The Perspective of Scripture," contains little detailed exegesis or sustained commentary.[13]

The report's main argument is that it is the duty of every Christian to live in obedience to God and that natal gender (i.e., biological sex) should be seen as a clear indication of God's will. Wise pastoral care, therefore,

10. Horton, *Changing Channels?*, 17, 9, 17 (emphasis added).

11. Horton, *Changing Channels?*, 13, 17. Horton is also of the view that "no one, including the transgendered, are [*sic*] uninvolved in the causes of their own distress. Unresolved inner turmoil can affect behaviour and the way life is viewed" (16).

12. *Transsexuality: A Report by the Evangelical Alliance Policy Commission* (London: Evangelical Alliance, 2000).

13. The one exception is Deuteronomy 22:5. The report initially suggests that whatever "the significance of this particular verse, it is probably doing a disservice to reasonable hermeneutics to apply it directly to transsexuals" (47). However, it then argues that it likely signifies "a reaffirmation of divine intent, in that the sanctity of the distinctiveness between the two created sexes is to be maintained." This point is then further strengthened in a footnote that argues that "Yahweh was presumably unlikely to have been comfortable with his people cross-dressing if only it could have been freed from unfortunate religious associations, and we need to be careful not to dilute Scripture at this point" (47n5).

"will seek gently to restore the skewed perception of a transsexual person to a biblical view of maleness and femaleness." However, the report also acknowledges that the "pathway of growth, sanctification and change can be expected to be slow and painful" and that "struggle and relapse can be anticipated." It is also honest about the difficulties faced by "people who have determined to restore their birth sex identity as a consequence of biblical conviction."[14]

The report concludes with nine "Affirmations and Recommendations," which the authors believe "summarise a sensible and mainstream evangelical Christian response to transsexuality." Of particular significance is the statement contained in "Affirmation 2"—that "God creates human beings as *either* male *or* female" and that, as a consequence, "authentic change from a person's given sex is not possible and an ongoing transsexual lifestyle is incompatible with God's will as revealed in Scripture and in creation." For this reason, the report recommends against "gender reassignment surgery as a normal valid option for people suffering from gender dysphoria."[15]

MARK YARHOUSE, *UNDERSTANDING GENDER DYSPHORIA*

Since the arrival of the transgender moment in 2013, a number of significant treatments of trans issues have also been produced by American evangelicals. The first of these is *Understanding Gender Dysphoria* by psychologist Mark Yarhouse.[16] Yarhouse's book is particularly helpful in describing the nature, prevalence, prevention, and treatment of GD, and in mapping out the main lines of a pastorally sensitive Christian response to the phenomenon.[17]

In terms of biblical and theological engagement with the issues raised by GD (the subject of his second chapter), Yarhouse begins by addressing

14. *Transsexuality*, 82 (x2), 86, 83.

15. *Transsexuality*, 84, 84–85 (emphasis original), 85.

16. Mark Yarhouse, *Understanding Gender Dysphoria: Navigating Transgender Issues in a Changing Culture* (Downers Grove, IL: InterVarsity Press, 2015).

17. In ch. 3 ("What Causes Gender Dysphoria?"), he also addresses the difficult question of etiology. He does not, however, go to any great lengths to explore the origins and character of the transgender movement, or those within it who do not suffer from GD.

some "frequently cited biblical passages" (e.g., 1 Cor 6:9–10; Deut 22:5; 23:1; Matt 19:12 and Acts 8:26–39). He then proceeds to examine "the four acts of the biblical drama: *creation, fall, redemption* and *glorification*" before outlining "three different frameworks for understanding gender identity concerns": integrity, disability, and diversity. However, his treatment of the relevant biblical texts is disappointingly brief (a mere four and a half pages). Moreover, while he believes that the texts cited (esp. Deut 22:5) reveal that "cross-dressing for the purposes of deconstructing sex and gender should be a concern to the Christian," he concludes that it is difficult to get much more from these texts "without doing a fair amount of hermeneutical gymnastics."[18]

Yarhouse spends ten and a half pages thinking about "sexuality and gender in the context of God's redemptive plan for creation."[19] The results are certainly more fruitful, particularly due to his interactions with Christopher Roberts and Oliver O'Donovan's explorations of the teleology of human sexual difference.[20] Ethically, however, Yarhouse believes that "gender dysphoria is not the same as homosexuality." By this he means that in contrast to its condemnation of homosexual acts, the Bible does not clearly censure gender transitioning. Therefore, while he believes that the best way for the gender-dysphoric to resolve their distress is "in keeping with their birth sex," he does not rule out the possibility of Christians undergoing cross-hormonal treatment and sex reassignment surgery.[21]

VAUGHAN ROBERTS, *TRANSGENDER*

The year after Yarhouse's book appeared, English evangelical Anglican Vaughan Roberts produced *Transgender*,[22] which seeks to provide an accessible introduction to the transgender phenomenon from a Christian perspective, as well as a useful starting point for constructive and compassionate conversation both inside and outside the church.

---

18. Yarhouse, *Understanding Gender Dysphoria*, 35, 46, 35.

19. Yarhouse, *Understanding Gender Dysphoria*, 35.

20. Christopher C. Roberts, *Creation & Covenant: The Significance of Sexual Difference in the Moral Theology of Marriage* (New York: T&T Clark, 2007); Oliver O'Donovan, *Resurrection and Moral Order: An Outline for Evangelical Ethics*, 2nd ed. (Grand Rapids: Eerdmans, 1994).

21. Yarhouse, *Understanding Gender Dysphoria*, 160, 25.

22. Vaughan Roberts, *Transgender* (Epsom, UK: The Good Book Company, 2016).

In chapters 3–5, Roberts explores the relevance of the Bible's teaching to a number of the complex questions surrounding the issue of gender identity, especially the experience of GD. His aim is to "hold our questions up to the big story of the Bible: the story of creation, fall, redemption and eternity" in order to "understand what the Bible has to say on our subject."[23] Roberts ably fulfills this aim, but the book's brevity (at just seventy-four pages) means that his exposition and application of the Bible's teaching is necessarily cursory. Nevertheless, his conclusions are both clear and compassionate: "We are *created* but *fallen*. We are *made* but *marred*. And those who experience gender dysphoria, along with all of us, are both victims of the fall, and therefore to be sympathised with, and also, to some degree, sinners with disordered hearts who need to be both forgiven and rescued."[24]

In his final chapter, Roberts pushes further into the realm of implications, providing succinct but helpful answers to a range of important pastoral questions. His overriding concern, however, is that all people come to know the liberating truth about who they truly are through the gospel of Jesus Christ.[25]

ANDREW WALKER, *GOD AND THE TRANSGENDER DEBATE*

Arguing a similar case to Roberts but doing so at greater length (174 pages), Andrew Walker's *God and the Transgender Debate* was first published in 2017.[26] Building on the declared assumption that "the Bible is God's Word," Walker's ultimate purpose is "to let God's voice be heard." Before turning to the Bible's teaching, however, he first takes time to explain "How We Got to Where We Are" (ch. 2) and also to unpack "The Language" (ch. 3) of "the gender-identity revolution."[27]

---

23. Roberts, *Transgender*, 9, 20.

24. Roberts, *Transgender*, 53–54 (emphasis original).

25. Roberts, *Transgender*, 73–74.

26. Andrew T. Walker, *God and the Transgender Debate: What Does the Bible Actually Say About Gender Identity* (Epsom, UK: The Good Book Company, 2017). A second edition appeared in 2022. Citations and page numbers are from the second edition.

27. Walker, *Transgender Debate*, 18, 21, 31.

In chapters 5–7, Walker steps his way through the Bible's story line and, in subsequent chapters, applies its teaching to the questions raised by gender incongruence. His foundational insight is that, because our bodies matter, their sex is "not arbitrary; it is intentional." Consequently, any attempt to deny or disguise one's sex is an attempt "to nullify God's revelation both in nature and in Scripture." For this reason, adopting a trans identity is "not compatible with following Christ."[28] But while the path of discipleship may not be easy for the gender dysphoric, Walker affirms that the gospel is good news for trans-identified people, and that Scripture is more than able to equip the church for the task of loving and bearing witness to the transgender community.[29]

The book concludes with a helpful chapter on "Speaking to Children" (ch. 11) and a "Tough Questions" section (ch. 12)—which deals with a range of issues including restrooms, pronouns, and the difference between transgender experience and intersex conditions. Because of the breadth of Walker's coverage, he is not able to engage in a detailed exegesis of the relevant biblical texts or an in-depth treatment of the key theological issues, but that is not his purpose. His purpose is to introduce "what God has to say about sex and gender in his word" and to commend "a compassionate grace-and-truth response" to an often-heated debate.[30]

MARTIN DAVIE, *TRANSGENDER LITURGIES*

Martin Davie's *Transgender Liturgies* was written in response to a 2015 motion passed by the Blackburn Diocesan Synod of the Church of England.[31] The motion not only asserted that trans-identified people "be welcomed and affirmed in their parish church," but called upon the House of Bishops "to consider whether some nationally commended liturgical materials might be prepared to mark a person's gender transition."[32]

Davie's first chapter "explains in more detail what the motion proposes and the theological implications of passing it"—the chief one being "that

28. Walker, *Transgender Debate*, 154.

29. Walker, *Transgender Debate*, 115–27.

30. Walker, *Transgender Debate*, 18–19.

31. Martin Davie, *Transgender Liturgies: Should the Church of England Develop Liturgical Materials to Mark Gender Transition?* (London: The Latimer Trust, 2017).

32. Davie, *Transgender Liturgies*, 1.

someone can be a woman with male biology and vice versa."[33] Via an exposition of the arguments of three trans-affirming authors (Christina Beardsley, Chris Dowd, and Justin Tanis[34]), chapter 2 sets out the case in support of the claim that some people have "a self or spirit that is of one sex and a body that is another."[35] Chapter 3 then offers an incisive biblical and theological critique of this case, and concludes that "we have been created by God as part of a dimorphic sexual structure within which human beings exist as embodied creatures who are determined by their biology as either male or female."[36] Chapter 4 then sets out an alternative approach for the care and nurture of transgender people, and the final chapter argues that it would be a mistake to support the Blackburn motion.[37]

Davie's study is a model of careful evangelical scholarship. He engages fairly with the trans-affirming case while providing a clear and compelling critique of its weaknesses. His exposition of key scriptural texts (e.g., Gen 1:26–27; Deut 22:5; Gal 3:28), while concise, displays both theological depth and philosophical insight. His grasp of the medical issues and scientific arguments, as well as the pastoral implications of his conclusions, is likewise judicious and thoughtful. I intend to build on his work.

J. ALAN BRANCH, *AFFIRMING GOD'S IMAGE*[38]

With the goal of joining "conviction and compassion in an evaluation of transgenderism," J. Alan Branch's *Affirming God's Image: Addressing the Transgender Question with Science and Scripture* is a wide-ranging

33. Davie, *Transgender Liturgies*, 1, 10.

34. Christina Beardsley, *The Transsexual Person Is My Neighbour: Pastoral Guidelines for Christian Clergy, Pastors and Congregations* (with an Appendix on Intersex by Michelle O'Brien) (Brighton: Gender Trust, 2007), https://sibyls.co.uk/wp-content/uploads/2021/05/The-Transexual-Person-is-my-Neighbour-2007.pdf; Chris Dowd, "Five Things Cis Folk Don't Know About Trans Folk Because It Isn't on Trashy TV—My Right of Reply," in *This Is My Body: Hearing the Theology of Transgender Christians*, ed. Christina Beardsley and Michelle O'Brien (London: Darton, Longman & Todd, 2016), 101–7; Justin Tanis, *Trans-Gender: Theology, Ministry, and Communities of Faith* (Eugene, OR: Wipf & Stock, 2018).

35. Davie, *Transgender Liturgies*, 33.

36. Davie, *Transgender Liturgies*, 53.

37. In July 2017, the General Synod of the Church of England voted in favor of the Blackburn motion in all three houses (bishops: 30 for, 2 against, 2 recorded abstentions; clergy: 127 for, 28 against, 16 recorded abstentions; laity 127 for, 48 against, 8 recorded abstentions).

38. For a more substantial review of Branch's book, see Robert S. Smith, "Review of J. Alan Branch, *Affirming God's Image: Addressing the Transgender Question with Science and Scripture*.

investigation of the transgender phenomenon.[39] While Branch is convinced that a transgender identity is "completely inconsistent with Christian ethics," he is also concerned that "a Christian response should always be expressed with a tone of mercy."[40]

The theological heart of Branch's argument is found in chapter 3. Here he briefly examines the meaning of humanity's creation in the divine image as male and female, the impact of the fall, and the reality of disorders of sex development. He also explores the Old Testament's teaching on the importance of gender-appropriate distinctions (e.g., Deut 22:5), Jesus's teaching about eunuchs (Matt 19:12), and the apostolic reaffirmations of sex-based gender roles (e.g., Eph 5:21–33; Col 3:18–21; 1 Pet 3:1–7). In regard to the body and soul relationship, Branch concludes that because "we are a body-soul unity," the claim "to have the soul of one gender trapped in the body of another gender" is "a false claim based on an inadequate understanding of Christian anthropology."[41]

In his final chapter, Branch addresses a range of pastoral challenges, including pronoun use, bathroom use, how to support parents with a gender dysphoric child, and how to counsel someone who has undergone gender reassignment surgery and has now come to faith in Christ.[42] Like Davie's book, *Affirming God's Image* offers a model of thoughtful evangelical ethical reflection with a keen pastoral edge. In terms of the balance between scientific investigation and scriptural exploration, however, it is (deliberately) weighted toward the first. This again highlights the need for the kind of in-depth exegetical study and theological analysis that I am seeking to provide.

Bellingham, WA: Lexham, 2018," *Themelios* 44 (2019): 401–3.

39. J. Alan Branch, *Affirming God's Image: Addressing the Transgender Question with Science and Scripture* (Bellingham, WA: Lexham, 2018), 4.

40. Branch, *Affirming God's Image*, 4, 130.

41. Branch, *Affirming God's Image*, 41, 50.

42. While surgical steps will normally be irreversible, Branch's guiding principle is that "genuine repentance will find a way to embrace one's natal sex in an appropriate way" (*Affirming God's Image*, 140).

SHARON JAMES, *GENDER IDEOLOGY*[43]

The purpose of Sharon James's *Gender Ideology: What Do Christians Need to Know?* is to provide a brief critical analysis of contemporary gender ideology, or what the book elsewhere calls "gender theory." After initial chapters on "The Global Sexual Revolution" and "'Can we really Change Sex?' and other FAQs," chapter 3 identifies and critiques four false claims entailed in gender theory,[44] followed by several examples of "misleading vocabulary" that seek to bolster gender theory.[45] She concludes this chapter by highlighting a range of contradictions in gender theory.[46]

Having provided an answer to the historical question, "Where Did 'Gender Theory' Come From?" (ch. 4), chapter 5 turns in a more overtly theological direction. Here, James registers some important biblical insights—for example, that gender confusion "is a tragic outworking of living in a world 'groaning' because of the effects of sin (Rom. 8:19–22)." At the same time, she is emphatic that "God specifically designs and determines our body. It reflects His intent."[47] She also highlights the implications of Jesus being raised as a man and as the firstfruits (i.e., the one who guarantees our bodily resurrection). Consequently, "when we disparage the physical body, we disparage Christ."[48]

The book's penultimate chapter, "The 'Transgendering' of Children," includes helpful discussions of both child-onset GD and ROGD and an answer to the question, "What can parents do?"[49] The final chapter argues that gender theory shows a profound disrespect for the natural ecology of human beings, the Hippocratic commitment of medical professionals, the vulnerability of children, the rights of parents, the safety of women and girls, freedom of speech, those who detransition and, ultimately, God

---

43. For a more substantial review of James's book, see Robert S. Smith, "Review of Sharon James, *Gender Ideology: What Do Christians Need to Know?* Fearn: Christian Focus Publications, 2019," *Themelios* 46 (2021): 714–16.

44. These are: "1. Binary is bad"; "2. Gender is a spectrum"; "3. Boy/girl; man/woman are just social constructs"; and "4. "We all have a 'gender identity' which may be different from our biological sex" (James, *Gender Ideology*, 40).

45. These are: "1. 'Assigned' at birth"; "2. 'Transphobia' "; "3. 'Cisgender' "; "4. 'Gender' "; "5. 'Gender Neutral Pronouns' such as 'ze' or 'hir' " (James, *Gender Ideology*, 43–46).

46. E.g., that gender identity is both fluid and immutable.

47. James, *Gender Ideology*, 74–75, 78.

48. James, *Gender Ideology*, 75.

49. James, *Gender Ideology*, 98–114.

himself. As will become evident as my own evaluation proceeds, I am in strong agreement with James's critique of gender theory. But because of the book's brevity, it cannot provide what I hope to provide: a more substantial scriptural basis for its conclusions.

OWEN STRACHAN & GAVIN PEACOCK, *WHAT DOES THE BIBLE TEACH ABOUT TRANSGENDERISM?*

Owen Strachan and Gavin Peacock's *What Does the Bible Teach About Transgenderism?* goes some way toward supplying what is lacking in James's book. Indeed, as "a work of theology aimed at everyday transformation," its "first goal is to give biblical clarity on this subject."[50] Thus, while noting the public accessibility of *general revelation* and the way in which "the human body points to divine design," the authors are at pains to stress the need for *special revelation* (preserved in the form of Scripture) to truly understand God's mind on gender and identity. It is Scripture, then, that not only confirms that our body "tells us who we are: either a boy or a girl, a man or a woman" but "expressly forbids what some call 'gender bending.' "[51]

Turning to Genesis 1–2, the authors observe that there are "men and women in the world because God desired that two sexes would bear His image and glorify His name together." The historic fall, however, spoils the harmony of this partnership. One consequence of this is that they now "regard their bodies as a problem. ... Now they must cover themselves." Herein lies the root of all attempts to separate body and soul, and the drive to "create our own identity." The opposition of Deuteronomy 22:5 to any "presentation of an opposite sex identity" likewise reveals gender transitioning to be "a new term for an old sin."[52] The authors thus conclude by issuing a call to their readers "to reject cross-gender thinking, desiring, feeling, and acting."[53]

---

50. Owen Strachan & Gavin Peacock, *What Does the Bible Teach About Transgenderism?* (Fearn: Christian Focus Publications, 2020), 25.

51. Strachan & Peacock, *Transgenderism*, 28, 30, 31–32.

52. Strachan & Peacock, *Transgenderism*, 35, 43, 45, 48, 52.

53. Strachan & Peacock, *Transgenderism*, 63.

There is a refreshing straightforwardness to Strachan and Peacock's treatment of transgender issues. There is also much biblical wisdom to be found in their outline of the related subjects of sex, sexuality, temptation, and sanctification. The popular nature of the book, however, means that the authors do not quite deliver on their promise to sketch a "comprehensive biblical picture."[54] Although they identify (and in varying degrees engage with) the main biblical texts that require attention, they do not plumb the depths of these passages or answer the objections of those who use the same texts to make a very different case.[55]

PRESTON SPRINKLE, *EMBODIED*[56]

Of all the evangelical attempts to engage transgender questions, Preston Sprinkle's *Embodied: Transgender Identities, the Church & What the Bible Has to Say* is, arguably, the most thorough.[57] The book not only addresses the cultural, medical, psychological, and social angles of the transgender phenomenon, but contains several chapters of biblical exposition of the relevant texts and theological exploration of the key issues. Commendably, Sprinkle sets the work in a decidedly pastoral frame and endeavors to maintain a compassionate tone throughout.

In the book's early chapters, Sprinkle attends to matters of definition and the broad range of possible meanings that attach to the label "trans*."[58] His biblical exploration starts by stressing the importance not only of human physicality but of the fact that "we bear God's image as male and

---

54. Strachan & Peacock, *Transgenderism*, 63.

55. These weaknesses are compensated for in Strachan's more scholarly writings. See, e.g., Owen Strachan, "The Clarity of Complementarity: Gender Dysphoria in Biblical Perspective," *JBMW* (Fall 2016): 31–43; "Transgender Identity in Theological and Moral Perspective," in *Scripture and the People of God: Essays in Honor of Wayne Grudem*, ed. John DelHousaye, Jeff T. Purswell, and John J. Hughes (Wheaton, IL: Crossway, 2018), 316–30; "Transition or Transformation? A Moral-Theological Exploration of Christianity and Gender Dysphoria," in *Understanding Transgender Identities: Four Views*, ed. James K. Beilby and Paul Rhodes Eddy (Grand Rapids: Baker Academic, 2019), 55–83.

56. For a more substantial review of Sprinkle's book, see Robert S. Smith, "Review of Preston Sprinkle, *Embodied: Transgender Identities, the Church & What the Bible Has to Say*. Colorado Springs: David C. Cook, 2021," *Themelios* 46 (2021): 235–37.

57. Preston Sprinkle, *Embodied: Transgender Identities, the Church & What the Bible Has to Say* (Colorado Springs: David C. Cook, 2021).

58. Sprinkle adopts the practice of putting an asterisk after "trans" to indicate when he is using it "as a broad umbrella term to include a whole range of identities that aren't strictly transgender, such as nonbinary, genderqueer, and the like" (*Embodied*, 33).

female." He thus affirms Phyllis Bird's insight that biological sex is "an essential datum in any attempt to define the human being and the nature of humankind."[59] For Sprinkle, this explains why "Jesus views Genesis 1–2 as normative," why Paul "correlates the body with personhood," why "Scripture prohibits cross-sex behavior," and why "sex difference probably remains after the resurrection." It is also the reason why, according to Scripture, "men and women should maintain distinctions in how they present themselves" (e.g., Deut 22:5; 1 Cor 11:2–16).[60]

One of the strengths of Sprinkle's book is his willingness to address several trans-affirming interpretations of Scripture. For instance, in response to the idea that "the binaries of Genesis 1 are polar ends of a spectrum, allowing for hybrids and variations in between," he points out that we "simply don't encounter humans identified as something other than male or female in Scripture." He likewise answers the curious claim that Jesus's reference to "eunuchs from birth" means that "a person's internal sense of self is more definitive than their biological sex when there is incongruence between the two." Regarding the view that a person can have a female soul in a male body (or vice versa), Sprinkle suggests that the only way an affirmative case can be made is either by assuming an unbiblical form of substance dualism or by "relying on modern, stereotypical assumptions about what constitutes femaleness and maleness."[61]

However, when it comes to the question of whether intersex is caused by the fall, he (oddly and, to my mind, needlessly) declares himself to be agnostic.[62] Nevertheless, Sprinkle is clear that trans* and intersex are "two different ontological realities" that "shouldn't be quickly mapped onto each other." He is likewise unequivocal in his conviction that there are "good biblical and ethical reasons why a disciple of Jesus should not transition."[63]

The remainder of *Embodied* deals with a range of relevant questions and is completed by an important appendix on "Suicidality and Trans*

---

59. Sprinkle, *Embodied*, 67, 68 (citing Phyllis Bird, "'Bone of My Bone and Flesh of My Flesh,'" *Theology Today* 50 [1994]: 531).

60. Sprinkle, *Embodied*, 70, 71, 72, 75, 94.

61. Sprinkle, *Embodied*, 98, 99. 104, 153.

62. For a fuller explanation and critique of Sprinkle's agnosticism on this point, see Smith, "Review of Preston Sprinkle, *Embodied*," 237.

63. Sprinkle, *Embodied*, 126, 189.

People," which is both compassionate and judicious.[64] The book combines the strengths of the various evangelical attempts to address the transgender phenomenon in the last decade. It thus provides a further model of responsible biblical scholarship and substantial theological analysis.

CONCLUDING REFLECTIONS

In 2003, the Church of England's House of Bishops' Report, *Some Issues in Human Sexuality*, observed that "the amount of literature generated by the Christian debate about transsexualism has so far been quite small."[65] Twenty-one years on, this is no longer the case—especially if we consider contributions from non-affirming Catholic authors[66] and non-evangelical trans-affirming authors.[67] Moreover, in addition to the works just reviewed,

64. Sprinkle acknowledges both the high suicidality rate (probably 22 percent) and that "minority stress plays at least some role in mental health issues like anxiety and depression among trans*-identified people" (*Embodied*, 236). However, he also recognizes that "the presence of co-occurring mental health concerns" may largely explain the high rate and that "weaponizing suicidality to push a particular ideological point might actually increase suicide attempts among trans* people rather than reducing them" (239).

65. House of Bishops, *Some Issues in Human Sexuality*, 228.

66. E.g., Abigail Favale, *The Genesis of Gender: A Christian Theory* (San Francisco: Ignatius Press, 2022); Richard P. Fitzgibbons, Philip M. Sutton, and Dale O'Leary, "The Psychopathology of 'Sex Reassignment' Surgery: Assessing Its Medical, Psychological, and Ethical Appropriateness," *The National Catholic Bioethics Quarterly* 9:1 (2009): 97–125; Gabrielle Kuby, *The Global Sexual Revolution: Destruction of Freedom in the Name of Freedom*, trans. James Patrick Kirchner (Kettering: LifeSite, 2015); Margaret H. McCarthy, "Gender Ideology and the Humanum," *Communio* 43 (2016): 274–98; Melissa Moschella, "Sexual Identity, Gender, and Human Fulfillment: Analyzing the 'Middle Way' Between Liberal and Traditionalist Approaches," *Christian Bioethics* 25, no. 2 (2019): 192–215; Michele M. Schumacher, *Metaphysics and Gender: The Normative Art of Nature and Its Human Imitations* (Steubenville, OH: Emmaus Academic, 2023).

67. E.g., Marcella Althaus-Reid and Lisa Isherwood, eds., *Trans/Formations* (London: SCM, 2009); Beardsley and O'Brien, eds., *This Is My Body*; Susannah Cornwall, *Sex and Uncertainty in the Body of Christ: Intersex Conditions and Christian Theology* (Oakville: Equinox, 2010); Robert E. Goss and Mona West, eds., *Take Back the Word: A Queer Reading of the Bible* (Cleveland: Pilgrim, 2000); Austen Hartke, *Transforming: The Bible and the Lives of Transgender Christians* (Louisville: Westminster John Knox, 2018); Herzer, *Transgender Experience*; Teresa J. Hornsby and Deryn Guest, eds., *Transgender, Intersex, and Biblical Interpretation* (Atlanta: SBL, 2016); Victoria S. Kolakowski, "Toward a Christian Ethical Response to Transsexual Persons," *Theology and Sexuality* 6 (1997): 10–31; Heather Looy and Hessell Bouma III, "The Nature of Gender: Gender Identity in Persons Who Are Intersexed or Transgendered," *Journal of Psychology and Theology* 33 (2005): 166–78; L. McCall Tigert and M. C. Tirabassi, eds., *Transgendering Faith: Identity, Sexuality and Spirituality* (Cleveland: Pilgrim, 2004); Virginia Ramey Mollenkott, *Omnigender: A Trans-Religious Approach* (Cleveland: Pilgrim, 2007); Tanis, *Trans-Gender.*

evangelicals have produced short booklets,[68] contributed chapters to books,[69] published numerous articles,[70] and produced several broader treatments of human sexuality that address the transgender question.[71] Additionally, evangelical dioceses, denominations, and conventions have also written a range of policy and position statements.[72]

Nevertheless, in many of the works reviewed, three things are often lacking: first, a detailed exploration of the meaning and implications of the key biblical texts that speak to transgender claims; second, a thorough theological analysis of the relationship between identity and embodiment; and third, a careful engagement with the trans-affirming literature. This is not a criticism of these works, particularly as most of them do not intend to provide these things. Nor is it to deny that each of them, at different points and in differing degrees, makes a valuable contribution to the exegetical, theological, and hermeneutical task. It is simply to observe that with a few notable exceptions (e.g., Sprinkle's *Embodied*), the contributions

68. E.g., Andrew Bunt, *People Not Pronouns: Reflections on Transgender Experience* (Cambridge: Grove Books, 2021); Samuel D. Ferguson, *Does God Care about Gender and Identity?* (Wheaton, IL: Crossway, 2023); Smith, *How Should We Think about Gender and Identity?*

69. E.g., Denny Burk, "The Transgender Test," in *Beauty, Order, and Mystery: A Christian Vision of Human Sexuality*, ed. Gerald Hiestand and Todd Wilson (Downers Grove, IL: InterVarsity Press, 2017), 87–99; Matthew Mason, "The Wounded It Heals: Gender Dysphoria and the Resurrection of the Body," in *Beauty, Order, and Mystery*, 135–47; Andrew Sloane, "'Male and Female He Created Them'? Theological Reflections on Gender, Biology and Identity," in *Marriage, Family and Relationships: Biblical, Doctrinal and Contemporary Perspectives*, ed. Thomas A. Noble, Sarah K. Whittle, and Philip S. Johnston (London: Apollos, 2017), 223–36.

70. E.g., James N. Anderson, "Transgenderism: A Christian Perspective," *Reformed Faith & Practice* 2 (2017): 51–71: https://journal.rts.edu/article/transgenderism-christian-perspective; Martin Davie, "Transgender, Reality and Pastoral Care," *Reflections of an Anglican Theologian* (March 15, 2018), https://mbarrattdavie.wordpress.com/2018/03/16/transgender-reality-and-pastoral-care; Jason DeRouchie, "Confronting the Transgender Storm: New Covenant Reflections on Deuteronomy 22:5," *JBMW* 21 (2016): 58–69; Russell D. Moore, "The Transgender Revolution and the Rubble of Empty Promises," *TGC: U.S. Edition* (June 6, 2017), https://www.thegospelcoalition.org/article/transgender-revolution-and-rubble-of-empty-promises; Preston Sprinkle, "A Biblical Conversation About Transgender Identities" (The Center for Faith, Sexuality & Gender, 2018), https://www.centerforfaith.com/resources/pastoral-papers/a-biblical-conversation-about-transgender-identities.

71. E.g., Glynn Harrison, *A Better Story: God, Sex and Human Flourishing* (London: Inter-Varsity Press, 2017); R. Albert Mohler Jr., *We Cannot Be Silent: Speaking Truth to a Culture Redefining Sex, Marriage, and the Very Meaning of Right and Wrong* (Nashville: Nelson, 2015); Nancy R. Pearcey, *Love Thy Body: Answering Hard Questions about Life and Sexuality* (Grand Rapids: Baker, 2018).

72. E.g., Anglican Church Diocese of Sydney, "Gender Identity: A Report from the Social Issues Committee" (revised November 21, 2017), https://www.sds.asn.au/sites/default/files/Gender%20Identity.Report2017.FINAL.v2.pdf?doc_id=NTU0NDg=.

are either brief or address a wider range of questions or are written for a broad audience.

There is, then, a significant gap in evangelical scholarship regarding the relationship between identity and embodiment as it relates to the transgender phenomenon. There is likewise an urgent need for a more rigorous biblical and theological engagement with the central claim of trans theory that the sexed body does not signify the gendered self. For while the literature reviewed in this chapter generally concludes (sometimes by arguing, sometimes by assuming) that sexed embodiment is intended to ground gender identity, this needs to be examined more thoroughly and established more securely.

Moreover, there is a further need to resolve some of the tensions observed in this chapter, such as that between Horton and O'Donovan over whether gender is a spectrum and between Yarhouse and Sprinkle over the ethics of transitioning. Finally, the case being made by trans-affirming authors, that "transgendered individuals are an integral part of creation, a creation that God declared was good,"[73] needs to be thoughtfully and carefully answered.

In order to prepare the ground for the work of biblical and theological exposition, however, I first need to explain and defend the theological method I will employ in part 3. This is the task of the following chapter.

73. Tanis, *Trans-Gender*, 138; see also Hartke, *Transforming*, 1–5.

CHAPTER 3

EVANGELICAL THEOLOGICAL METHOD

Since then we are to discourse of the things of God, let us assume that God has full knowledge of Himself, and bow with humble reverence to His words. For He whom we can know only through his own utterances is a fitting witness concerning himself.[1]

—Hilary of Poitiers

Theological anthropology is an implicit and derivative, not explicit and foundational, doctrine. We only reach the stage of theological anthropology when we affirm that man is a being who has to do with God, or rather, when we affirm that God is the one who has to do with human being.[2]

—Kevin J. Vanhoozer

The transgender phenomenon could legitimately be approached from a range of different perspectives, each requiring its own methodology.

First, it could be approached from a sociopolitical perspective—as a feature of contemporary (mostly Western) societies that has various personal and cultural expressions, social causes and political outworkings. Second, it

1. Hilary of Poitiers, *On the Trinity*, 1.18 (*NPNF*[2] 9:45).

2. Kevin J. Vanhoozer, "Human Being, Individual and Social," in *The Cambridge Companion to Christian Doctrine*, ed. C. E. Gunton (Cambridge: Cambridge University Press, 1997), 159.

could be approached from a psycho-medical perspective—as a condition that has generally been regarded as a psychiatric disorder with agreed diagnostic criteria and is increasingly being treated medically by cross-sex hormone therapy (CHT) and SRS. Third, it could be approached from a historico-philosophical perspective—as a late twentieth century ideology that has a particular genealogy, assumes a particular metaphysic, and promotes a particular worldview. Fourth, it could be approached from a theo-anthropological perspective—as a claim about the ontology of (some of) those made in God's image, which requires understanding and evaluation in the light of divine revelation. Finally, as an extension of the theo-anthropological perspective, it could be approached from a theo-ethical perspective—in order to ascertain the will of God for those who experience gender incongruence and what it might mean for them to live in a manner that is glorifying to God, and good for themselves and others.

While the final two perspectives are my ultimate concern in this book (and so will govern the theological exposition of Scripture in chs. 7–11), the others must not be lost from view. The first, as seen in chapter 1, illumines the present context in which the questions about identity and embodiment are being raised, while also stressing their urgency. The second, which I will touch on briefly in chapter 6, highlights the need to clarify the nature of transgender experience and the appropriateness of different approaches to the treatment of GD. And the third, as we shall see in some detail in chapters 4–6, will not only help to map the intellectual history that has led to contemporary trans theory but will also provide us with a number of the conceptual categories and conceptual tools that enable it to be both articulated and evaluated.

However, as we shall see in this chapter, the primary reason why the theo-anthropological and theo-ethical perspectives must be our ultimate concern has to do with their unique authority and ability: *authority* over all the other perspectives and *ability* to correct or confirm insights gleaned from them. For a theo-perspective is a divine perspective, and "the word of our God will stand forever" (Isa 40:8).

FOUNDATIONS FOR EVANGELICAL THEOLOGY

DEPENDENCE ON DIVINE REVELATION

The primacy of the theo-anthropological and theo-ethical tasks is a direct implication of one of the basic tenets of traditional Christian theism: all human knowledge is necessarily dependent on divine revelation.[3] In fact, because he is the one who "gives to all mankind life and breath and everything" (Acts 17:25), "we are no less dependent on God for our knowledge than we are for our existence."[4] Moreover, this dependence is not simply a consequence of the fall; it "is part of what it means to be a creature rather than the Creator."[5] Consequently, epistemology cannot begin with the human knower but must begin with God, the source of all true knowledge (so Augustine).[6] Practically speaking, this means that "the starting point of inquiry for the Christian is not self-consciousness, but awareness of the reality of God, who is creator and redeemer of all things. Not 'I think, therefore I am,' but 'God is, therefore we are.' "[7]

Added to the fact of human dependence is the reality of divine transcendence; for "God is incomprehensible in His transcendence and voluntary hiddenness, and therefore is unknown to man unless He makes Himself known to him."[8] This rules out any notion of divine discovery, as if it were possible "to ascend to heaven by our own reason, will, and works."[9] Rather, as the Christian tradition from Irenaeus through Hilary to Calvin and Barth has repeatedly affirmed, "God is known through God

---

3. Alvin Plantinga, *Warranted Christian Belief* (New York: Oxford University Press, 2000), 182–368; "Is Belief in God Properly Basic?," *Noûs* 15 (1981): 41–51.

4. Michael S. Horton, *The Christian Faith: A Systematic Theology for Pilgrims on the Way* (Grand Rapids: Zondervan, 2011), 49.

5. Mark D. Thompson, "The Generous Gift of a Gracious Father: Toward a Theological Account of the Clarity of Scripture," in *The Enduring Authority of the Christian Scriptures*, ed. D. A. Carson (Grand Rapids: Eerdmans, 2016), 624.

6. Lydia Schumacher, "The 'Theo-Logic' of Augustine's Theory of Knowledge by Divine Illumination," *Augustinian Studies* 41 (2010): 375–99.

7. Daniel L. Migliore, *Faith Seeking Understanding: An Introduction to Christian Theology* (Grand Rapids: Eerdmans, 2004), 5.

8. T. H. L. Parker, *The Doctrine of the Knowledge of God: A Study in the Theology of John Calvin* (Edinburgh: Oliver & Boyd, 1952), 12.

9. Horton, *The Christian Faith*, 49.

and through God alone."[10] This is why the proper human response to divine revelation is to adopt the posture of a humble hearer and grateful receiver (Deut 5:1; Ps 85:8; Isa 1:2; Heb 12:28).

THE PRIMACY OF THE KNOWLEDGE OF GOD

Divine revelation generates a responsibility not merely to think God's thoughts after him but to seek *first* the knowledge of God, rather than knowledge of ourselves. For, as Calvin writes, "it is certain that man never achieves a clear knowledge of himself unless he has first looked upon God's face, and then descends from contemplating him to scrutinize himself."[11] This is why the whole enterprise of systematic theology aims to provide, first, "a conceptual articulation of Christian claims about God" and, second, an articulation of "everything else in relation to God."[12]

Moreover, it is also clear that no theology can truly be called *Christian theology* unless it is a faithful and disciplined discourse about *the God of the Christian gospel*—the God and Father of our Lord Jesus Christ.[13] Indeed, as the New Testament affirms (Matt 11:27; John 14:6–7; 1 Cor 12:3; 1 John 4:13–15), we may only finally know this God by "sharing in the knowledge of the Son by the Father and of the Father by the Son, and the testimony he gives us of himself through his Spirit."[14]

Therefore, while the area of this book's inquiry is primarily *anthropological*, it cannot help but be *theological*, *christological*, and *pneumatological*. For true knowledge of the creature is contingent on true knowledge of the *Triune* Creator (hence the need for *theo*-anthropology), with Christ constituting the revelatory center of our knowledge of God by the power of the Holy Spirit.[15] Colin Gunton expresses the point well: "We cannot

10. Barth, *CD*, 2/1, 44.

11. Calvin, *Institutes*, 1.1.2.

12. John Webster, "Introduction: Systematic Theology," in *Oxford Handbook of Systematic Theology*, ed. K. Tanner, J. Webster, and I. Torrance (Oxford: Oxford University Press, 2007), 2.

13. D. A. Carson, "The Role of Exegesis in Systematic Theology," in *Doing Theology in Today's World: Essays in Honor of Kenneth S. Kantzer*, ed. J. D. Woodbridge and T. E. McComiskey (Grand Rapids: Zondervan, 1991), 41 (emphasis original).

14. Thomas F. Torrance, *The Christian Doctrine of God, One Being Three Persons* (Edinburgh: T&T Clark, 1996), 11.

15. Torrance, *Christian Doctrine of God*, 2. As we shall see, Christ (as the *God*-Man) is not only the key to our knowledge of the Triune God, but (as the God-*Man*) the key to knowledge of ourselves.

understand our likeness to God apart from our continuing relation with God, through Christ and the perfecting Spirit."[16]

None of this diminishes the fact that there is an interrelationship between knowledge of God and knowledge of ourselves, nor does it deny the existence of a flexible pedagogical order between the two (as Calvin saw).[17] However, it does affirm an irreversible ontological order. Human beings are made in the image of the Triune Creator, not the other way around (Gen 1:26–27).[18] This is why "without knowledge of God there is no knowledge of self."[19]

THE SOURCES OF DIVINE SELF-DISCLOSURE

Having established that "the fundamental starting point for the systematized knowledge of God and his world must be God's self-disclosure,"[20] it is necessary briefly to clarify the sources or media through which this self-disclosure comes.

Christian theology has traditionally distinguished between general revelation (i.e., God's self-disclosure in his *works*) and special revelation (i.e., God's self-disclosure in his *words*). The differences between the two are several and significant, but for practical purposes may be summarized as follows: the former plays a vital but limited and (due to the noetic effects of sin) largely ineffective role in making God known, whereas the latter not only interprets the former but contains a clearer, more detailed and (by the power of the Holy Spirit) effective means of divine self-revelation. This contrast does not negate the value of general revelation; it simply highlights the need for the *oracula Dei* (the words of God) to illumine and interpret the *opera Dei* (the works of God). For there is "an interdependence between the *oracula Dei* and the *opera Dei*," writes T. H. L. Parker,

---

16. Colin E. Gunton, *The Triune Creator: A Historical and Systematic Study* (Grand Rapids: Eerdmans, 1998), 207.

17. Calvin, *Institutes*, 1.1.1–2. At the same time, Calvin insists that the *proper* pedagogical order (or "the order of right teaching") is that we must discuss knowledge of God first (1.1.3).

18. So, "the idol-maker is the theological opposite of the image bearer" (Richard Lints, *Identity and Idolatry: The Image of God and its Inversion* [Downers Grove, IL: InterVarsity Press, 2015], 35).

19. Calvin, *Institutes*, 1.1.2.

20. Harold O. J. Brown, "On Method and Means in Theology," in Woodbridge and McComiskey, eds., *Doing Theology in Today's World*, 161.

"with the primacy given decisively to the Word of God. The universe is a dark mystery to us unless the *lumen verbi* shines upon it."[21]

Furthermore, while the words by which God has revealed his nature, character, promises, and purposes have been spoken by his prophets "at many times and in various ways" (Heb 1:1), "in these last days" they have been "spoken to us by his Son" (Heb. 1:2)—the one whom John's Gospel calls "the Word" (John 1:1, 14), who is both "God's eternal Fellow" (for "the Word was *with* God") and "God's own Self" (for "the Word *was* God").[22] In short, special revelation comes to its culmination in Jesus Christ and the gospel that bears witness to him. As F. F. Bruce has memorably put it: "The story of divine revelation is a story of progression up to Christ. But there is no progression beyond Him."[23] Therefore, while special revelation is *inescapably verbal* (as it always involves words), as well as being *irreducibly personal* (so Emil Brunner) and *necessarily historical* (so Wolfhart Pannenberg), it is *finally Christological* (so Karl Barth).[24]

Furthermore, because Christ is both Son of God and Son of Man (or, in Chalcedonian thought, one person with both divine and human natures in hypostatic union), "His deity *encloses humanity in itself*."[25] In other words, "in Jesus Christ, as He is attested in the Holy Scripture, genuine deity includes in itself genuine humanity."[26] Consequently, writes Barth, theology

> must occupy itself neither with God in Himself nor with man in himself but with the man-encountering God and the God-encountering man and with their dialogue and history, in which their communion takes place and comes to its fulfilment. For this

21. Parker, *Knowledge of God*, 50.

22. Edmund P. Clowney, "A Biblical Theology of Prayer," in *Teach Us to Pray: Prayer in the Bible and the World*, ed. D. A. Carson (Exeter: Paternoster, 1990), 157.

23. F. F. Bruce, *The Epistle to the Hebrews* (Grand Rapids: Eerdmans, 1964), 46.

24. See Peter F. Jensen, "God and the Bible," in Carson, *Enduring Authority*, 486; Emil Brunner, *The Divine-Human Encounter*, trans. A. W. Loos (London: SCM, 1944); Barth, *CD*, II/1, 3–254; Wolfhart Pannenberg, "Dogmatic Theses on the Doctrine of Revelation," in *Revelation as History*, trans. David Granskou (New York: Macmillan, 1968), 123–58.

25. Karl Barth, *The Humanity of God*, trans. Thomas Wieser and John Newton Thomas (Richmond: John Knox, 1960), 50.

26. Barth, *Humanity of God*, 51.

> reason theology can think and speak only as it looks at Jesus Christ and from the vantage point of what He is.[27]

The significance of this christological insight for theo-anthropology will be explored later in this book. The point here is this: not only is true knowledge of God obtained through Christ alone (2 Cor 4:6), but also true knowledge of creation (in general) and humanity (in particular). As Gunton writes: "Knowledge of general revelation is the fruit of the gospel, christologically centred as that is. Without that, we do not see the world for what it truly is."[28]

THE AUTHORITY AND NECESSITY OF SCRIPTURE

In terms of our access to special revelation, I stand with the central Christian tradition of the last two millennia in accepting Scripture's self-testimony as to its own inspired character and divine authority (e.g., 2 Tim 3:16–17). This means that the Bible is far more than a human witness to divine revelation; it is "revelation itself in human words."[29] In terms of access, then, "the locus of God's special revelation is the Bible, the sixty-six canonical books, reliable and truthful as originally given."[30] As D. A. Carson writes, "Although it is entirely proper to speak of God's disclosing himself to us in the events and people of Scripture, and supremely in the person of his Son, in practice this forces us back to Scripture, the written revelation of God, for we have little or no access to the events and people apart from Scripture."[31]

This highlights two aspects of what in classical Reformed thought is referred to as *the necessity of Scripture*. The first is that we can only have assured knowledge of God and his purposes if we have his special revelation in an objective, written, and reliable form.[32] This, according to the Westminster Confession of Faith, is why God committed his word "wholly

---

27. Barth, *Humanity of God*, 55.

28. Colin E. Gunton, *A Brief Theology of Revelation* (Edinburgh: T&T Clark, 1995), 55.

29. Donald G. Bloesch, *A Theology of Word and Spirit: Authority & Method in Theology* (Downers Grove, IL: InterVarsity Press, 1992), 197.

30. Carson, "Role of Exegesis," 44.

31. Carson, "Role of Exegesis," 43–44. It is not my purpose to argue *for* this view of Scripture, but *from* it.

32. John M. Frame, *The Doctrine of the Word of God* (Phillipsburg, NJ: P&R, 2010), 211–13.

unto writing"; that is, "for the better preserving and propagating of the truth, and for the more sure establishment and comfort of the Church" (I.1). The necessity of Scripture, then, is not of an absolute kind, but is "consequent upon certain decisions of God."[33] That is, *it is God who has made Scripture necessary for his people*. The epistemological implication of this is that "the gospel of God is not given to us directly but comes to us through the Bible and through the church proclamation, insofar as this proclamation rests upon the Bible."[34] Similarly, in terms of Christian ethics, the only way to arrive at a sure and certain knowledge of God's will is through the study of Scripture.

Second, if the objective, written form of special revelation is found in Scripture *alone*, then what applies to theology (knowledge of God) applies also to theo-anthropology (knowledge of those made in God's image); that is, *Scripture is also necessary for us to gain true knowledge of ourselves*. As a result, theological anthropology is "the attempt to think through the meaning of the human story, as it unfolds from Genesis through the Gospels to the Apocalypse and as it is lived out before, with and by God."[35] In short, we need the Bible to teach us the truth about ourselves.

THE NATURE OF THE THEOLOGICAL TASK

The theological task involves building on this scriptural foundation in two ways. First, by exploring (what Augustine called) *scientia*—the science of God. This refers to the "disciplined activity in which the church reflects on the nature, will, and ways of the Creator."[36] Second, by seeking (what Augustine again called) *sapientia*—the wisdom of God. This involves understanding that "the definite purpose of theology is the formation of God's life and character in human believers and communities."[37]

In sum, the *task* of theology is twofold: (1) to grow in knowledge of God, his ways, and his will (orthodoxy-a); and (2) to grow in knowledge

33. J. F. Peter, "The Reformed View of the Scriptures," *EQ* 31 (1959): 197.

34. Bloesch, *Word and Spirit*, 196–97.

35. Vanhoozer, "Human Being," 159. As Barth remarks: "Theological anthropology expounds the knowledge of man which is made possible and needful by the fact that man stands in the light of the Word of God. The Word of God is thus its foundation" (*CD*, III/2, 20).

36. David K. Clark, *To Know and Love God: Method for Theology* (Wheaton, IL: Crossway, 2003), 87.

37. Clark, *To Know and Love God*, 87.

of ourselves, our needs, and our responsibilities (orthodoxy-b). The *purpose* of such growth is likewise twofold: (1) to love God and others truly (*orthokardia*), and (2) to live faithfully and wisely in his world (*orthopraxis*). In short, theology is *scientia* in the service of *sapientia*.

DOING EVANGELICAL THEOLOGY

Sola Scriptura in Practice

Given the nature and purpose of the theo-anthropological and theo-ethical tasks, and the authoritative role that special revelation plays in accomplishing them, it is essential that Scripture be allowed to govern and guide, illumine and evaluate, confirm and correct the interpretation and application of all other sources of knowledge. Only in this way can the Bible function effectively as the "fundamental, regulative 'control belief' for theology."[38] For, as Donald Bloesch writes: "Theology is not an analysis of the vagaries of universal religious experience nor an exploration of the possibility of meaning in a meaningless world but an exposition of the particularities of Scripture that bring meaning to the otherwise desolate landscape of human existence."[39]

Implicit in such an understanding is the idea that while "Christian theology may include more (but certainly not less) in its subject matter than the fundamental datum of Christian revelation, ... whatever further data are introduced it is the Christian revelation that must utterly control the discourse."[40] That is, all rational deductions, philosophical speculations, empirical findings, and experiential perceptions (e.g., information gleaned from both the hard and soft sciences) must, ultimately, be understood and assessed in the light of the knowledge of both God and ourselves revealed in Scripture.

This does not mean that the relationship between (say) theology and science is such that, at the slightest sign of the tension, the latter needs to be dragooned into slick harmonization with the former. Rather both of God's books, at least in the first instance, should be read on their own terms. Better, then, is the perspectival approach of C. Stephen

---

38. Clark, *To Know and Love God*, 87.

39. Bloesch, *Word and Spirit*, 115.

40. Carson, "Role of Exegesis," 44.

Evans, which acknowledges both "the possibility of a plurality of different descriptions of an object" and also "the different functions and purposes of the biblical and scientific accounts."[41] This creates space for interdisciplinary dialogue and mutual interrogation. Moreover, rather than leading to a false amalgam or forced compromise, it tends to produce *complementation*—an outcome where the essential components of the different sources of knowledge enrich and illumine each other.[42]

Nevertheless, there is more to be said. For not only do questions regarding the correct interpretation and integration of scientific data remain, but the magisterial role of Scripture needs to be honored in the relationship.[43] That is, *sola Scriptura* must operate *in practice*, not just *in theory*—the *norma normans* (the ruling norm) exercising its hermeneutical authority over the *norma normata* (the ruled norms).[44] This means that, when engaging theologically with an issue about which the Bible says little directly or nothing explicitly (e.g., trans theory or gender incongruence),

> the *control* must be with Scripture, even though the *substance* may largely derive from other sources. In other words, Christian theology properly addresses more than those subjects explicitly treated in Scripture, but where it does so it remains Christian theology only where the truths of Scripture have a bearing on the subject and remain uncompromised.[45]

THE DISCIPLINES OF THEOLOGY

Furthermore, if the task of theology is to be undertaken responsibly, the written form of special revelation must be engaged with in ways that are respectful of its nature, content, and form. This not only requires us to take seriously the dual authorship of Scripture, but also Augustine's insight

---

41. C. Stephen Evans, *Preserving the Person: A Look at the Human Sciences* (Vancouver: Regent College, 1977), 106.

42. Malcolm A. Jeeves and R. J. Berry, *Science, Life and Christian Belief: A Survey and Assessment* (Leicester: Apollos, 1998), 245.

43. Cornelius Van Til, "Introduction," in Benjamin B. Warfield, *The Inspiration and Authority of the Bible* (Phillipsburg, NJ: P&R, 1948), 29–33; John M. Frame, *The Doctrine of the Knowledge of God* (Phillipsburg, NJ: P&R, 1987), 86–87; Clark, *Know and Love God*, 287–94.

44. Graham A. Cole, "Sola Scriptura: Some Historical and Contemporary Perspectives," *Churchman* 104 (1990): 26.

45. Carson, "Role of Exegesis," 45 (emphasis original).

that in "speaking through a man, [God] speaks as a man" (*Deus per hominem more homino loquitur*).[46] This means that *the parts* will need to be interpreted in an appropriate manner (i.e., in their literary-historical contexts) and *the whole* understood both with an appreciation of the unfolding nature of biblical revelation and in relation to its central theme and focus, Jesus Christ.[47]

Systematic theology, then, will necessarily be grounded in biblical exegesis and guided by biblical theology.[48] Furthermore, all three disciplines will need to be informed by historical theology (which, in my view, includes contemporary insights) and likewise bear fruit in pastoral theology (which encompasses worship, ethics, and mission). What follows is a brief description of each of these disciplines.

Biblical exegesis

By "biblical exegesis" I mean the philological and historical analysis of the final form of the text of Scripture. Traditionally, this has been referred to as grammatico-historical exegesis and has generally been understood to involve an examination of a text's literary form, historical background, cultural setting, and authorial purpose.[49] Others prefer to speak of literary approaches to the text, as this foregrounds the need for genre sensitivity and affirms that the Bible is much more than "a theological outline with proof texts."[50] Combining these insights and emphases, Carson writes:

> Responsible exegesis will certainly resort to linguistic analysis, both lexis (analysis of the vocabulary) and syntax (analysis of the way words are related to each other). But it will also analyze the text at the level of the clause, the level of the sentence, the level of the discourse, and the level of the genre. It will seek to be sensitive

46. Augustine, *The City of God*, 17.6 (*NPNF*[1] 2:346).

47. Brian Rosner, "Biblical Theology," in *New Dictionary of Biblical Theology*, ed. T. D. Alexander and Brian S. Rosner (Leicester: Inter-Varsity Press, 2000), 10.

48. B. B. Warfield, "The Idea of Systematic Theology," in *Studies in Theology* (New York: Oxford University Press, 1932), 66.

49. Ralph P. Martin, "Approaches to New Testament Exegesis," in *New Testament Interpretation*, ed. I. Howard Marshall (Exeter: Paternoster, 1979), 226–29.

50. Leland Ryken, *How to Read the Bible as Literature ... and Get More Out of It* (Grand Rapids: Zondervan, 1984), 18.

to idiom, literary technique, metaphor, and lines of argument. It will ask how truth is conveyed in the rich plethora of literary genres found in the Bible.[51]

Biblical theology

"Biblical theology" is a term that has been used in a number of ways.[52] Writing in the Reformed tradition, Geerhardus Vos describes it as occupying a position "*between* Exegesis and Systematic Theology" and defines it as "that branch of Exegetical Theology which deals with the process of the self-revelation of God deposited in the Bible."[53] In a similar vein, I use it to refer to an approach to biblical interpretation that "proceeds with historical and literary sensitivity and seeks to analyse and synthesise the Bible's teaching about God and his relations to the world on its own terms, maintaining sight of the Bible's overarching narrative and Christocentric focus."[54] Biblical theology, then, not only assists interpreters in reading all of Scripture "with Christian eyes," but also functions as a bridging discipline, linking exegesis with systematic theology.[55]

Systematic theology

Systematic theology may be defined as "a rational and orderly account of the content of Christian belief."[56] It differs from biblical theology not by being less concerned with either the text or arc of Scripture, but because its primary principle of arranging the biblical material is logical rather than historical. As Vos explains: "Systematic Theology takes the Bible as a completed whole and endeavours to exhibit its total teaching in an orderly, systematic form."[57] In this sense, systematic theology is best seen

---

51. Carson, "Role of Exegesis," 47.

52. See the example given in Edward W. Klink III and Darian R. Lockett, *Understanding Biblical Theology: A Comparison of Theory and Practice* (Grand Rapids: Zondervan, 2012).

53. Geerhardus Vos, *Biblical Theology: Old and New Testaments* (Grand Rapids: Eerdmans, 1948), 5 (emphasis added), 11.

54. Rosner, "Biblical Theology," 10.

55. D. A. Carson, "Current Issues in Biblical Theology: A New Testament Perspective," *BBR* 5 (1995): 40–41.

56. S. W. Sykes, "Systematic Theology," in *A New Dictionary of Christian Theology*, ed. Alan Richardson and John Bowden (London: SCM, 1983), 560.

57. Vos, *Biblical Theology*, 5.

as a *culminating discipline*, whereas biblical theology is a *mediating discipline*. And yet, each requires the other. For in discerning what "the total redemptive and revealing activity of God means for us now," it is vital to recognize that while "all texts do not stand in the same relationship to us now ... in view of the unity of revelation they do stand in some identifiable relationship to all other texts and therefore to us."[58]

Pastoral theology

The concern for *scientia* (true knowledge) to issue in *sapientia* (wise living) gives rise to a fourth discipline: pastoral theology. This is because the final aim of systematic theology, like that of Scripture itself, "is practical and functional, not purely speculative."[59] Consequently, pastoral theology is not so much a separate discipline as that aspect of the theological task that helps us to see *how* and *in what ways* Scripture is "profitable for teaching, for reproof, for correction, and for training in righteousness" (2 Tim 3:16–17). It is worth noting, however, that when it comes to contemporary issues (like transgender questions), the application of Scripture will be found sometimes at the surface level of the text and other times "at the principial level underlying the passage (with the surface situation or command applying mainly to the ancient setting)."[60]

Historical theology

Consistent with the Reformed tradition, I regard historical theology as the study of the history of Christian thought.[61] As such, it includes "not only dogmas or doctrines but ethics and the Christian reflection upon other problems both of thought and society."[62] Historical theology, then, is a broad-ranging discipline that inevitably serves the other theological

---

58. Graeme Goldsworthy, "'Thus says the Lord!'—The Dogmatic Basis of Biblical Theology," in *God Who Is Rich in Mercy: Essays Presented to D. B. Knox*, ed. P. T. O'Brien and D. G. Peterson (Sydney: Anzea, 1986), 37.

59. James Leo Garrett, *Systematic Theology: Biblical, Historical & Evangelical: Volume 1* (Grand Rapids: Eerdmans, 1990), 9.

60. Grant R. Osborne, *The Hermeneutical Spiral: A Comprehensive Introduction to Biblical Interpretation* (Downers Grove, IL: InterVarsity Press, 1991), 327.

61. A. N. S. Lane, "Historical Theology," in *New Dictionary of Theology*, ed. Sinclair B. Ferguson and David F. Wright (Leicester: Inter-Varsity Press, 1988), 306.

62. Jaroslav Pelikan, *Historical Theology: Continuity and Change* (Eugene, OR: Wipf & Stock, 2014), xvii.

disciplines—even if not always to the same degree. While essentially *descriptive* (explaining what the church *has* believed) rather than *prescriptive* (advising what the church *should* believe), it also acts as a helpful check on the other disciplines, reminding interpreters that "one never steps outside the hermeneutical circle, simply exegetes Scripture, and discovers its doctrines in abstraction from a communal history of interpretation."[63] For this reason, I will take a number of historical theological soundings in later chapters of this book.

Disciplines in dialogue

Evangelicals have often viewed the relationship between the theological disciplines in a linear fashion—that is, exegesis leads to biblical theology, biblical theology to systematic theology, and systematic theology to pastoral theology. This is not altogether wrong, especially in view of the priority that is rightly given to exegesis.[64] However, no exegete comes to the task as a *tabula rasa*; rather, "the systematic theology one has adopted up to any particular point in the exegetical process exerts profound influence on the exegesis itself."[65] Thus, the lines of dialogue run in all directions. As Carson writes:

> Although in terms of authority status there needs to be an outward-tracing line from Scripture through exegesis towards biblical theology to systematic theology (with historical theology providing some guidance along the way), in reality various "back loops" are generated, each discipline influencing the others, and few disciplines influencing the others more than systematic theology, precisely because it is so worldview forming.[66]

This dynamic is not inherently problematic—indeed, it is unavoidable. Nevertheless, evangelical interpreters should appreciate it, and always

63. Michael S. Horton, "Historical Theology," in *Dictionary for Theological Interpretation of the Bible*, ed. Kevin J. Vanhoozer (Grand Rapids: Baker Academic, 2005), 293.

64. Clark, *Know and Love God*, 190.

65. Carson, "Role of Exegesis," 51.

66. D. A. Carson, "Systematic Theology and Biblical Theology," in Alexander and Rosner, eds., *New Dictionary of Biblical Theology*, 102.

be open to revisiting their exegesis and, where necessary, revising their systematic theological conclusions.

A METHODOLOGICAL MODEL

I have outlined the practice of evangelical theology to explain the kind of approach I will be taking in part 3 (chs. 7–11) of this book. For while my goal is to offer theo-anthropological and theo-ethical answers of a systematic kind, I will do so on a firm exegetical basis, sensitive to biblical theological development, with an eye to pastoral theological application, and attuned to historical theological insights. Also, while I will focus on the first of "the four major plot movements" of "the grand biblical narrative" (creation),[67] the significance of the other three (fall, redemption, and consummation) will never be far from view and will be addressed directly in the final two chapters.

In the search for a methodological paradigm to guide in this endeavor, I have found Kevin Vanhoozer's "Drama-of-Redemption Model" to be a fruitful way of "moving beyond the Bible to theology"—of progressing *from* exegesis *through* biblical and historical theology *to* systematic and pastoral theology.[68] Vanhoozer's approach not only upholds the primacy of holy Scripture for holy theology and holy living, but also "affirms God's actions in history, preserves the emphasis on story, and incorporates a canonically attuned, wisdom-oriented 'chastened' principlizing, while better integrating the interpreters into the action."[69] Otherwise put, "going beyond the Bible biblically is ultimately a matter of participating in the great drama of redemption of which Scripture is the authoritative testimony and holy script."[70]

---

67. Bruce Riley Ashford and David P. Nelson, "The Story of Mission: The Grand Biblical Narrative," in *Theology and Practice of Mission: God, the Church and the Nations*, ed. Bruce Riley Ashford (Nashville: Broadman & Holman, 2011), 6.

68. Vanhoozer, "Drama of Redemption," 151–99; Vanhoozer, *The Drama of Doctrine: A Canonical Linguistic Approach to Christian Theology* (Louisville: Westminster John Knox, 2005). Indeed, Vanhoozer insists that "we need all the theological disciplines working together in order to think and live biblically" ("Drama of Redemption," 155).

69. Vanhoozer, "Drama of Redemption," 153, 159.

70. Vanhoozer, "Drama of Redemption," 155–56. Importantly, Vanhoozer makes clear that his use of theatrical language does not commit him to any particular theory of drama (155). Its purpose, rather, is to stress that "theology involves not only theoretical but *theatrical* reasoning: *practical*

Of additional interest, and of special relevance to this book, is the fact that Vanhoozer demonstrates how his model might be applied to the transgender phenomenon (although he uses the older term "transsexuality"). He begins by defining sex as "something biological (chromosomal marker)," gender as "something sociological (cultural marker)," and gender identity as "something psychological (consciousness marker)." At the same time, he rightly acknowledges that one of the difficulties in theologizing about transgenderism is that "the Bible maintains a discrete silence with regard to the modern distinctions between 'sex,' 'gender,' and 'gender identity.' "[71] Nevertheless, in contrast to "a social constructivism that sees identity and roles as social creations only," Vanhoozer insists that, from a biblical perspective, "the body is integral to who we are. Human beings are psychosomatic unities. ... One's true self, therefore, is not hovering above or within one's body," nor is the person (i.e., "what makes me 'me' ") to be found in "one 'part' only (e.g., the body, the soul)." Rather, we are "embodied souls and ensouled bodies," for "it is embodied persons, not mere bodies, who are male or female." He thus concludes that the "belief that male souls are trapped in female bodies and vice-versa has little to justify it other than one's own subjective feeling."[72]

Placing this anthropological understanding within his theodramatic framework, Vanhoozer writes:

> It all begins with Act One, God's good creation: "male and female he created them" (Gen. 1:27). When viewed in theodramatic perspective, we see that we are but actors who have received divine casting calls. To be or not to be male or female is not for us to decide. ... It is the producer's call. Our task is to respond to our vocation as embodied creatures and to play our parts as well as we can to God's glory.[73]

In light of this, Vanhoozer concludes that sex-reassignment surgery is an instance of "a bad improvisation"—a form of (self) destructive

reasoning about what to say and do in particular situations in light of the gospel of Jesus Christ" (156, emphasis original).

71. Vanhoozer, "Drama of Redemption," 192, 194.

72. Vanhoozer, "Drama of Redemption," 195–96.

73. Vanhoozer, "Drama of Redemption," 197.

performance that not only forgets "what happened in Act One (creation)," but results in "the worst kind of playacting: hypocrisy." As a consequence, "those who seek to rewrite their roles make God a bit player in a drama that exchanges the gospel for the pottage of self-determination." True theodramatic participation moves in a more humble and obedient direction. Rather than fighting embodied reality, it seeks "to discern, deliberate on, and do those possibilities that are given to us with our biological sex."[74]

CONCLUDING REFLECTIONS

I do not intend to slavishly employ Vanhoozer's model (or his theatrical language) in part 3 (chs. 7–11) of this book. Nevertheless, there are obvious strengths to a dramatic conception of the theological task. Not only does it highlight the need for systematic theological synthesis to be sensitive to biblical theological development (and so to issues of continuity and discontinuity), but it sets out "a theological and hermeneutical program that takes its focusing point within the story and the community that God has graciously summoned to live it out."[75] In short, it is a model that encourages an integration of the theological disciplines and a marriage of theory and practice.

What is particularly noteworthy is the fact that Vanhoozer's conclusions about transgender questions are consistent with the thinking of many of the evangelical authors reviewed in the previous chapter. If he and they are correct, then it is not only true that "the body has an important part to play in all Acts of the theodrama," but, crucially, that "one's personhood cannot be divorced from one's sex."[76] For this insight, contrary to trans theory, affirms that the sexed body *does* signify the gendered self and so *should* ground gender identity, guide gender roles, and govern gender expression.

It is precisely this affirmation that part 3 of this book will seek to evaluate both in detail and from an evangelical perspective—that is, from the conviction that "Scripture alone is the authoritative script for right participation in the life and love of the Triune God because it alone is

74. Vanhoozer, "Drama of Redemption," 196–97.

75. Michael D. Williams, "Theology as Witness: Reading Scripture in a New Era of Evangelical Thought. Part II: Kevin Vanhoozer, The Drama of Doctrine," *Presbyterion* 37 (2011): 29.

76. Vanhoozer, "Drama of Redemption," 195–96.

the authorized text of the only true God."[77] As we shall see, this does not mean engaging only with evangelical theologians or biblical scholars who share this conviction—for all insights into the meaning and implications of Scripture's teaching should be heard and evaluated.[78] What it does mean is that I will proceed by way of literary-historical exegesis of Scripture to systematic-theological synthesis of Scripture, and do so in a way that is alert to biblical-theological development, engages with relevant historical-theological insights, and issues in pastoral-theological wisdom.

This brings part 1 of this book to an end. In part 2 (chs. 4–6), we turn to examine the history of and changes in conceptions of sex and gender over the past seventy-five years. This will not only help to sharpen our understanding of the questions that need to be resolved and the disputes that need to be settled, but will highlight why, ultimately, it is only the word of God that can do this.

---

77. Kevin J. Vanhoozer, "May We Go Beyond What Is Written After All?," in Carson, *Enduring Authority*, 754.

78. Daniel I. Block and Richard L. Schultz, "How Evangelical Biblical Scholars Treat Scripture," *CT* (February 28, 2018), https://www.christianitytoday.com/ct/2018/february-web-only/how-evangelical-biblical-scholars-treat-scripture.html.

PART 2

SEX, GENDER, AND TRANSGENDER IN HISTORICAL PERSPECTIVE

CHAPTER 4

THE CREATION AND CONSTRUCTION OF SEX

"Sex" is an ideal construct which is forcibly materialized through time. It is not a simple fact or static condition of a body, but a process whereby regulatory norms materialize "sex" and achieve this materialization through a forcible reiteration of those norms.[1]

—Judith Butler

As binaries in nature go, the sex division is one of the most stable and predictable there is.[2]

—Kathleen Stock

Contemporary understanding of both sex and gender, and especially of the distinction and relationship between them, is not only considerably varied but also constantly changing. Ever since the late 1950s, when the term "gender" first started to shed its strict grammatical sense, it has generally been assumed that sex is "the real" (being fixed by biology) and that gender is "the epiphenomenal" (i.e., the psychological, cultural, and linguistic effect or by-product of the real). Accordingly, the pairing has come to be viewed in terms of a distinction between the *natural* and the *social*, with the social

1. Judith Butler, *Bodies that Matter: On the Discursive Limits of "Sex"* (New York: Routledge, 1993), xii.
2. Stock, *Material Girls*, 75.

dichotomy of men and women seen as a reflection or manifestation of the natural dichotomy of human males and females.

However, subsequent developments in feminist thought,[3] combined with insights drawn from the sociology of knowledge,[4] have led to a questioning of this paradigm and to the proposal of an alternative conception of sex and gender—one in which *both* are viewed, at least to a large extent, as socially constructed entities.[5] According to this view, in comparing gender and sex, we are not comparing something social with something natural; rather, we are "comparing something social with something which is *also* social (in this case, the way a given society represents 'biology' to itself)."[6]

Taking this constructionist line of thought a step further, Judith Butler proposed the idea of gender as a "performative accomplishment," arguing that the gendered self does not exist "prior to its acts" but is grounded in "the stylized repetition of acts through time."[7] As her thought developed, she pushed further still, asking whether sex is "as culturally constructed as is gender" and, if so, whether "it was always already gender, with the consequence that the distinction between sex and gender turns out to be no distinction at all."[8] We shall explore her answer to this question in due course.

---

3. Especially the rise of "Social Construction Feminism," which not only sees gender as a "society-wide institution," imposed on men and women to justify treating them differently, but also sees "the dichotomies of male and female biological sex" as being "produced and maintained by social processes" (Judith Lorber, *The Variety of Feminisms and Their Contributions to Gender Equality* [Oldenburg: Bibliotheks- und Informationssystem, 1997], 29–30).

4. The sociology of knowledge, which is a subfield within sociology, (1) investigates the relationship between human thought and the social context within which it emerges; (2) examines the impact of that context on both the form and content of thought; and (3) explores the effects that prevailing ideas, in turn, have on human societies. Although the discipline can be traced back to the works of Émile Durkheim and Karl Mannheim, it was both clarified and popularized through Peter L. Berger and Thomas Luckmann's *The Social Construction of Reality: A Treatise in the Sociology of Knowledge* (New York: Anchor, 1966).

5. See, e.g., Dorothy E. Smith, *The Conceptual Practices of Power: A Feminist Sociology of Knowledge* (Boston: Northeastern University Press, 1990).

6. Christine Delphy, "Rethinking Sex and Gender," in *Sex in Question: French Materialist Feminism*, ed. Diana Leonard and Lisa Adkins (London: Taylor & Francis, 1996), 37 (emphasis original).

7. Judith Butler, "Performative Acts and Gender Constitution: An Essay in Phenomenology and Feminist Theory," *Theatre Journal* 40 (1988): 520.

8. Judith Butler, *Gender Trouble: Feminism and the Subversion of Identity* (New York: Routledge, 2007; first published 1990), 9–10.

More recently, additional questions have been raised by the phenomenon of intersex conditions, where a person's biological sex is, in some way and to some degree, either phenotypically or genotypically ambiguous. The key question is whether such variations should continue to be regarded as pathological (i.e., as disorders) and, if not, what effect this has on binary notions of both sex and gender.

The purpose of this chapter, as well as the two that follow it, is to explore these developments and to identify the key issues raised by them. I want also, at least provisionally, to suggest a way of resolving the tensions that exist between differing conceptions of both sex and gender, and differing understandings of the relationship between them. We begin with the question: How many sexes are there?

HOW MANY SEXES ARE THERE?

When Simone de Beauvoir famously proffered that "One is not born, but rather becomes, [a] woman," she was not suggesting that persons are born sexless.[9] Indeed, as Butler acknowledges, Beauvoir understood a woman's sex in terms of "the invariant, anatomically distinct, and factic aspects of the female body."[10] The title of *The Second Sex*, then, is an unequivocal reference to those who are biologically female. Beauvoir's point was not a *biological* one but a *sociological* one—that "the 'real woman' is an artificial product that civilization produces" and that "supposed 'instincts' of coquetry or docility are inculcated in her just as phallic pride is for man."[11] Positing this idea not only allowed her to challenge the assumption that a woman's biology justified her place in the social sphere, but to argue that "biological facts are just facts, brute facts," and, as such, "do not entail an answer to the normative question."[12]

---

9. Simone de Beauvoir, *The Second Sex*, trans. Constance Borde and Sheila Malovany-Chevallier (London: Vintage, 2011), 294. First published in French in 1949 as *Le Deuxième Sexe*. Beauvoir's original expression—"*On ne naît pas femme: on le devient*"—has been variously translated. "You are not born a woman: you become one," is another possible rendering.

10. Judith Butler, "Sex and Gender in Simone de Beauvoir's *Second Sex*," *Yale French Studies* 72: *Simone de Beauvoir: Witness to a Century* (1986): 35.

11. Beauvoir, *The Second Sex*, 433.

12. Ásta Kristjana Sveinsdóttir, "The Metaphysics of Sex and Gender," in *Feminist Metaphysics: Explorations in the Ontology of Sex, Gender and Self*, ed. Charlotte Witt (Dordrecht: Springer, 2011), 48.

Whether and to what extent this conclusion necessarily follows is a question to which we shall also return. But first things first. What are the brute biological facts? And how should we conceive of the biological differences between male and female? To answer these questions, it will help us to critically interact with the thinking of two highly influential authors—the historian and sexologist Thomas Laqueur (1945–) and the professor of biology and gender studies Anne Fausto-Sterling (1944–)—before turning to explore the significance of intersex conditions.

THOMAS LAQUEUR'S ONE-SEX MODEL

Laqueur's thesis explained

According to Laqueur, prior to the late eighteenth century, men and women were generally regarded as two different forms of the one sex. In fact, writes Laqueur, "for thousands of years it had been a commonplace that women had the same genitals as men except that, as Nemesius, bishop of Emesa in the fourth century, put it, 'theirs are on the inside of the body and not outside it.' "[13] To be specific, the vagina was thought to be an inverted penis, the uterus an interior scrotum and the ovaries internalized testes. Laqueur traces this particular anatomical understanding back through the Greek physician and philosopher Aelius Galenus (AD 129–c. 210), better known as Galen of Pergamon, to the Alexandrian anatomist Herophilus (325–255 BC).

For these ancient thinkers, the reason why female sexual anatomy was thought to be the inverse of male sexual anatomy was due to a lack of vital heat in fetal development. Moreover, because of this deficiency, females were often deemed to be imperfect and incomplete males. As Galen wrote, "just as mankind is the most perfect of all animals, so within mankind the man is more perfect than the woman, and the reason for his perfection is his excess of heat, for heat is Nature's primary instrument."[14] It was also thought that the presence of such heat was what produced in men a certain toughness or hardness (Latin: *duritia* or *robur*)—terms that

13. Thomas Laqueur, *Making Sex: Body and Gender from the Greeks to Freud* (Cambridge: Harvard University Press, 1990), 4.

14. Galen, *Galen on the Usefulness of the Parts of the Body* (*De usu partium*), trans. with comm. Margaret Tallmadge May (Ithaca, NY: Cornell University Press, 1968), 2:630.

referred not so much to phallic capacity as to "the muscularity of the ideal male body." Such robustness also "symbolized the moral uprightness and self-discipline that men were presumed to embody."[15] Women, conversely, were characterized by softness (Latin: *mollitia*), and so were thought to embody humanity's weaker and gentler qualities.[16]

For these reasons, Laqueur (and those who have followed him[17]) claims that the dominant conception of sex, from classical antiquity to the Enlightenment, was that "two genders correspond to but one sex" and "the boundaries between male and female are of degree and not of kind."[18] In Greco-Roman times, this generated a fear of "gender slippage, particularly from male to female." For if women were "not different in kind, but simply a lesser, incomplete version of men, what was there to keep men from sliding down the axis into the female realm?"[19] That such a slide was thought possible was (supposedly) evidenced not only by the existence of "hermaphroditic people, but in lapses in the routine behavior of dominating males."[20] Consequently, as classical historian Maud Gleason explains, "manhood was not a state to be definitively and irrefutably achieved" but was "always under construction and constantly open to scrutiny."[21]

Problems with the one-sex model

There are several problems with this thesis, however. First, at a conceptual level, it often involves a confusion of sex and gender—at least as they are now commonly distinguished. Gleason's claim above, for example, is not

---

15. Mathew Kuefler, *The Manly Eunuch: Masculinity, Gender Ambiguity and Christian Ideology in Late Antiquity* (Chicago: University of Chicago Press, 2001), 21.

16. Diana M. Swancutt, "'The Disease of Effemination': The Charge of Effeminacy and the Verdict of God (Romans 1:18–2:16)," in *New Testament Masculinities*, ed. S. D. Moore and J. C. Anderson (Atlanta: Society of Biblical Literature, 2003), 174.

17. See, e.g., Londa Schiebinger, *The Mind Has No Sex? Women and the Origins of Modern Science* (Cambridge: Harvard University Press, 1989); Faramerz Dabhoiwala, *The Origins of Sex: A History of the First Sexual Revolution* (London: Penguin, 2013).

18. Laqueur, *Making Sex*, 25. For example, Adrian Thatcher makes the claim that "for the greater part of Christian history, *it did not occur to anyone even to think that there were two distinct sexes*" (*God, Sex, and Gender: An Introduction* [Oxford: Wiley-Blackwell, 2011], 7) (emphasis original).

19. Colleen M. Conway, *Behold the Man: Jesus and Greco-Roman Masculinity* (Oxford: Oxford University Press, 2008), 18.

20. Thatcher, *God, Sex, and Gender*, 31.

21. Maud W. Gleason, *Making Men: Sophists and Self-Presentation in Ancient Rome* (Princeton, NJ: Princeton University Press, 1995), xxii.

about *biological maleness* but about *social manhood*. In that sense, she is saying no more than Beauvoir (except that she is saying it about the *first* sex); that is, one is not born, but becomes, a man—and, in the classical world, needed to develop and maintain one's manhood! Such an understanding is confirmed by Colleen Conway's work on Greco-Roman masculinity. "It was not enough to be clear that one was a man rather than a woman," writes Conway. "One also needed to be a *manly* man rather than a *womanly* man."[22] In other words, a person needed to align their (social) gender expression with their (biological) sex. The point to note, then, is this: whatever might be said of the boundary between masculinity and femininity (gender) and the possibility of social slippage between the two, the difference between male and female (sex) was not seen as a difference of *degree* but as a difference of *kind*. In the classical world, an unmanly man was still a male, not a female.[23] This means that Laqueur's insistence that the ancient model had "an unstable idea of sex and a stable idea of gender" is not so much overstated as it is back-to-front.[24]

Second, at a larger historical level, while numerous scholars have questioned elements of Laqueur's work (e.g., by showing that it doesn't hold true for this or that writer or period),[25] Helen King's 2013 study *The One-Sex Body on Trial: The Classical and Early Modern Evidence*, has provided the first wide-ranging critique of Laqueur's entire thesis. By dealing with both "the sources Laqueur omits, and the lack of care with which he uses those sources which he does bring into play,"[26] King demonstrates that wherever one looks (from the fifth century BC to the nineteenth

22. Conway, *Behold the Man*, 18 (emphasis added).

23. Although slightly overstating the point, Carlin Barton also confirms that this was the classical view when he writes that "in Roman culture, as in very many cultures, a male was not necessarily a man. One was ontologically a male but existentially a man. Born a male (*mas*) or a human (*homo*), one made oneself a man (*vir*)" (Carlin A. Barton, *Roman Honor: The Fire in the Bones* [Berkeley: University of California Press, 2001], 38).

24. See Brooke Holmes's critique of Laqueur's thesis in *Gender: Antiquity and Its Legacy* (Oxford: Oxford University Press, 2012), 50–55.

25. See, e.g., Annick Jaulin's devastating critique of Laqueur's elision of Aristotle and Galen in "La fabrique du sexe, Thomas Laqueur et Aristote," *Clio* 14 (2001): 195–205; Winfried Schleiner, "Early Modern Controversies about the One-Sex Model," *Renaissance Quarterly* 53 (2000): 180–91; Michael Stolberg, "A Woman Down to Her Bones: The Anatomy of Sexual Difference in the Sixteenth and Early Seventeenth Centuries," *Isis* 94 (2003): 274–99.

26. Helen King, *The One-Sex Body on Trial: The Classical and Early Modern Evidence*, The History of Medicine in Context (Burlington, VT: Ashgate, 2013), xi.

century AD) it is "difficult to identify any historical period in which the one-sex model dominated."[27] Rather, ever since antiquity, the two different ways of understanding the distinction between male and female bodies not only seem to have coexisted, but both are sometimes found within the same authors![28] Galen, for example, in the very treatise where he puts forward his (so named) one-sex model, also states that "the male animal differs from the female in its entire body."[29] The fact that Laqueur makes no mention of this dimension of Galen's thought touches on one of the main weaknesses of his project: his penchant for reducing complexity to simplicity.[30] Similar, if not more serious, problems emerge in Laqueur's treatment of Aristotle. For although he admits that Aristotle is "deeply committed to the existence of two radically different and distinct sexes," he then insists that he "offered the western tradition a still more austere version of the one-sex model than did Galen."[31] With good reason, Annick Jaulin calls this "rhetorical sleight of hand" ("tour de passe-passe rhétorique"),[32] for as Richard Posner has demonstrated and Laqueur's own quotations from Aristotle reveal, whatever else might be said of Aristotle, he was most definitely "a two-sex man."[33] This exposes another problem in Laqueur's work: his "selective use of 'evidence', and his lack of close reading of the material he does use."[34]

---

27. King, *One-Sex Body*, 7.

28. This is conceded in the preface to *Making Sex*, where Laqueur admits that "a two-sex and a one-sex model had always been available to those who thought about difference and that there was no scientific way to choose between them" (viii). Yet this is downplayed in the body of the book, which repeatedly claims that, by the late eighteenth century, "an anatomy and physiology of incommensurability replaced a metaphysics of hierarchy in the representation of woman in relation to man" (6).

29. See Galen, *On Semen*, 5.3.1, Corpus Medicorum Graecorum, ed., trans., and comm. Phillip de Lacy (Berlin: Akademie Verlag, 1992), 180. Cited in King, *One-Sex Body*, 37.

30. King, *One-Sex Body*, xi.

31. Laqueur, *Making Sex*, 28.

32. Jaulin, "La fabrique du sexe," 203 (translation mine). For Laqueur's rejoinder, see Thomas W. Lacquer, "L'usage de la catégorie de genre. Réponse de Thomas Laqueur à Annick Jaulin," *Clio* 15 (2002): 209–11.

33. Richard A. Posner, *Sex and Reason* (Cambridge: Harvard University Press, 1994), 28. For Laqueur's quotations of Aristotle, see *Making Sex*, 47–48. See also Prudence Allen's discussion of Aristotle's "sex polarity theory" (and rejection of Plato's "sex unity theory") in *The Concept of Woman: The Aristotelian Revolution, 750 b.c. – a.d. 1250*, 2nd ed. (Grand Rapids: Eerdmans, 1997), 83–88.

34. King, *One-Sex Body*, xi–xii.

Third, at a terminological level, the language of "one-sex" is misleading. For despite Laqueur's conviction that it accurately represents the thought of the classical authors (especially Galen and Aristotle), the model that these authors, at times, advocate is better described as an inversion model—that is, one in which female sex organs are regarded as internalized versions of their male counterparts. Consequently, if there is a unity to be discerned in the texts Laqueur examines, it is that of a single *flesh* (i.e., a common humanity), not that of a single *sex*.[35] For this reason, Matthew Kueffler contends that the inversion model was not seeking to reduce the two sexes to one; rather, it sought to explain the reality of human sexual dimorphism in a particular (and, we can now say, anatomically inaccurate) way. In other words, even on the inversion model, male and female were not "a single sex" but, quite literally, "opposite sexes."[36] Jaulin, then, is right to conclude "that it is inappropriate to label the ancient model 'one sex' " ("qu'il est abusif de nommer 'unisexe' le modèle antique").[37] It is simply "a different way of expressing physical sexual difference on the basis of the prevailing understanding of human anatomy."[38]

Deconstructing the one-sex model

While these criticisms raise serious questions about the validity of Laqueur's thesis, his one-sex model is not entirely without support. It is just that it is a rather clumsy way of capturing "a specific idea contained in a couple of paragraphs of a single book of a single work of Galen."[39] But it is not Galen's only idea (as we have seen), nor did it dominate subsequent centuries in the way that Laqueur claims.[40] During the Middle Ages, for example, male and female genitals were commonly presented "not as spatially inverted, but as distinct in function and form."[41] Similarly, after

35. Adrian Thatcher further compounds Laqueur's confusion when he claims that it is "probable that Greeks, Romans, Jews, and Christians actually held that there was one sex, not two. That sex was called 'man' " (Thatcher, *God, Sex, and Gender*, 7).

36. Kuefler, *Manly Eunuch*, 20.

37. Jaulin, "La fabrique du sexe," 204 (translation mine).

38. House of Bishops, *Some Issues in Human Sexuality*, 182.

39. Katharine Park, "Cadden, Laqueur, and the 'One-Sex Body,' " *MFF* 46 (2010): 99.

40. See further Joan Cadden, *Meanings of Sex Difference in the Middle Ages: Medicine, Science, and Culture* (Cambridge: Cambridge University Press, 1995).

41. Park, "Cadden, Laqueur," 99.

the publication of Latin translations of the *Hippocratic Diseases of Women* (1524–25), not only was there a heightened appreciation of the differences between male and female bodies, and with it an increase in knowledge as to how to treat them differently, but also irrefutable evidence that the greatest of classical physicians believed that the female body "cannot be understood by reference to the organs of the male body."[42]

Given Laqueur's "taste for Foucauldian schemas,"[43] his attempt to divide the history of thought about sex difference into two periods—one pre-Enlightenment and one post-Enlightenment—is unsurprising.[44] The problems identified above, however, suggest that his larger project is best seen as an ideologically driven protest against a certain type of *biologically based gender essentialism* in which "biology—the stable, ahistorical, sexed body—is understood to be the epistemic foundation for prescriptive claims about the social order."[45] Doubtless, this protest fitted comfortably into the cultural and academic context from which Laqueur's book emerged—for, as King points out, the 1980s was a time when "the primacy of social construction" was *de rigueur*.[46] But it is simply not the case that "what we call sex and gender were in the 'one-sex model' explicitly bound up in a circle of meanings from which escape to a supposed biological substrate—the strategy of the Enlightenment—was impossible." Nor does the evidence support Laqueur's claim that, prior to the seventeenth century, sex was "a sociological and not an ontological category."[47] The opposite is the case.

Therefore, the end point of Laqueur's thesis—that "sex, as much as gender, is made"[48]—is less reflective of a serious attempt to grapple with

---

42. King, *One-Sex Body*, 48.

43. Park, "Cadden, Laqueur," 97.

44. Foucault characteristically divided Western thinking about sex differences into two distinct periods: pre- and post- the invention of the idea of "true sex" in the mid-nineteenth century. See his introduction to the English translation of *Herculine Barbin: Being the Recently Discovered Memoirs of a Nineteenth-Century French Hermaphrodite*, trans. Richard McDougall (New York: Pantheon, 1980), vii–xvii.

45. Laqueur, *Making Sex*, 6.

46. King, *One-Sex Body*, 6.

47. Laqueur, *Making Sex*, 8. Even Adrian Thatcher, who is strongly supportive of Laqueur's larger thesis, concedes that the history leading up to the seventeenth century "may be more complicated than Laqueur initially allowed" (*Redeeming Gender* [Oxford: Oxford University Press, 2016], 57).

48. Laqueur, *Making Sex*, ix.

the complexities of sexological history and more reflective of a commitment to poststructuralism and a strong form of social constructionism.[49] He is claiming that sex differences are *subjective mental constructs* ("unfettered by fact" and "as free as mind's play"), not *objective physical realities.*[50] Furthermore, this claim, and the philosophical commitments that undergird it, becomes even more manifest in Laqueur's exploration of the development and dominance of the two-sex model in the post-Enlightenment period.

THE DEVELOPMENT OF THE TWO-SEX MODEL

Laqueur's account of the two-sex model

In Laqueur's account, the year 1800 marks the transition from the one-sex model to the two-sex model. From this point, he avers, "writers of all sorts were determined to base what they insisted were fundamental differences between the male and female sexes, and thus between man and woman, on discoverable biological distinctions and to express these in a radically different rhetoric." The result was "a new model of radical dimorphism, of biological divergence."[51] Woman was no longer seen as "a lesser version of man along a vertical axis of infinite gradations, but rather as an altogether different creature along a horizontal axis whose middle ground was largely empty."[52]

Laqueur posits an epistemological and a political reason for this change. Epistemologically, he claims that although skepticism was not invented at this point in history, "fact comes to be more clearly distinguished from fiction, science from religion, reason from credulity." As a consequence, "the cultural work that had in the one-flesh model been done by gender devolved now onto sex." Politically, he argues that the eighteenth and nineteenth centuries witnessed "endless new struggles for

49. Given the deconstruction of binaries that is central to the poststructuralist enterprise and the anti-realism that is inherent in most stronger forms of social constructionism, both terms are appropriate. On the former, see Réda Bensmaïa, "Poststructuralism," in *The Columbia History of Twentieth-Century French Thought*, ed. Lawrence Kritzman (New York: Columbia University Press, 2006), 92–95. On the latter, see Tom Andrews, "What Is Social Constructionism?," *The Grounded Theory Review* 11 (2012): 39–46.

50. Laqueur, *Making Sex*, 243.

51. Laqueur, *Making Sex*, 5–6.

52. Laqueur, *Making Sex*, 148.

power and position in the enormously enlarged public sphere"—struggles, in particular, "between men and women" and "between and among feminists and antifeminists." These conflicts helped fuel a desire to ground the moral, social, and sexual order in the objective facts of biology. For this reason, differences that had once "been expressed with reference to gender now came to be expressed with reference to sex, to biology."[53]

In presenting the history this way, Laqueur is again seeking to make the case that our supposed knowledge of nature is, in fact, a "richly complicated construction based not only on observation, and on a variety of social and cultural constraints on the practice of science, but on an aesthetics of representation as well."[54] He even goes so far as to claim that "the nature of sexual difference is not susceptible to empirical testing." His reasoning is that "already embedded in the language of science, at least when applied to any culturally resonant construal of sexual difference, is the language of gender."[55] Put more simply, the notion of two distinct and opposite sexes has been read into nature, not out of nature. This leads him to conclude that "despite the accumulation of facts about sex, sexual difference in the centuries after the scientific revolution was no more stable than it had been before."[56] For this reason, *Making Sex* has been described (perhaps sarcastically but not inaccurately) as an attempt to show "how the theory of biological sex was socially constructed *in* the sciences *by* nonscientific factors."[57]

Problems with the two-sex model

Laqueur's account of both *why* and *when* the two-sex model developed and came to dominate has not gone unchallenged.[58] While not taking issue with the broad arc of his thesis, Diarmaid MacCulloch sees the changes

---

53. Laqueur, *Making Sex*, 151–53. It has long been argued by feminist scholars that empirical science has often been used by men to subjugate women. See, e.g., Ruth H. Bleier, *Science and Gender: A Critique of Biology and Its Theories on Women* (New York: Pergamon, 1984).

54. Laqueur, *Making Sex*, 163–64.

55. Laqueur, *Making Sex*, 153, 148.

56. Laqueur, *Making Sex*, 153.

57. Alan Soble, "The History of Sexual Anatomy and Self-Referential Philosophy of Science," *Metaphilosophy* 34 (2003): 234 (emphasis original).

58. For example, Katharine Park and Robert A. Nye, "Destiny Is Anatomy, Review of Laqueur's *Making Sex: Body and Gender from the Greeks to Freud*," *The New Republic* 18 (1991): 53–57.

of which Laqueur speaks taking place in the seventeenth century (not the eighteenth and nineteenth centuries).[59] Without denying that greater biomedical understanding of sex differences was later used to legitimize female subordination, Michael Stolberg likewise provides ample evidence that by the year 1600 many leading physicians were insisting on "the unique and purposeful features of the female skeleton and the female genital organs and illustrated them visually."[60] Historically speaking, then, Laqueur's insistence that "sex as we know it" was "invented"[61] sometime in the eighteenth century is simply mistaken.[62] Similarly, his claim that sustained interest in the sex binary "was *a response to* the collapse of religion and metaphysics as the final authority for social arrangements" is, at best, anachronistic.[63] Doubtless, scientific progress never takes place in a social or ideological vacuum, but a less tendentious reading of the history reveals that the advances that led to a more accurate understanding of human sexual dimorphism were not driven by a war between the sexes but, as Stolberg argues, were the result of

> a growing preference for empirical observation and discovery, the blending of Galenic teleology with pious belief in the value and purpose of every creature, the gradual shift from more humoral to more solid conceptions of the body, and the "gynecologists' " professional interest in "difference," as well as changing notions of woman within the urban upper classes among whom the physicians moved and whose support they sought.[64]

---

59. Diarmaid MacCulloch, *The Reformation: A History* (New York: Penguin, 2004), 590.

60. Stolberg, "Woman Down to Her Bones," 274.

61. Laqueur, *Making Sex*, 149–51.

62. Park and Nye, "Destiny Is Anatomy," 54. For further criticisms, see Laura Gowing, "Women's Bodies and the Making of Sex in Seventeenth-Century England," *Signs* 37 (2012): 813–22; Brooke Holmes, "Let Go of Laqueur: Towards New Histories of the Sexed Body," *Eugesta: Journal on Gender Studies in Antiquity* 9 (2019): 136–75.

63. Thomas W. Laqueur, "Sex in the Flesh," *Isis* 94 (2003): 306 (emphasis added). Even as recently as 2012, Laqueur has maintained that "sometime during the Enlightenment physics took over from metaphysics, and social differentiation, in this case gender hierarchy, had to be defended on empirical grounds" (Thomas W. Laqueur, "The Rise of Sex in the Eighteenth Century: Historical Context and Historiographical Implications," *Signs* 37 [2012]: 806).

64. Stolberg, "Woman Down to Her Bones," 299.

More problematic still is Laqueur's determination to put what philosopher Alan Soble calls "a substantial philosophical spin on his historical studies."[65] This spin is a form of anti-empirical social constructionism. Laqueur seeks to defend his approach by appeal to "the Quine-Duhem thesis,"[66] according to which "no physical observation can ever decide between two theories, because each theory can be revised to accommodate the new evidence by adding new auxiliary hypotheses."[67] It is worth noting, however, that Willard Quine himself believed that this problem applies to *all* knowledge claims in *any* field, including philosophy and history.[68] Thus, the very thesis that Laqueur uses to establish the underdetermination of scientific theories can also be applied to his own historical and philosophical theories. Nevertheless, he goes on to insist that "new knowledge about sex did *not in any way* entail the claims about sexual difference made in its name. *No discovery or group of discoveries* dictated the rise of the two-sex model." This specific claim is then bolstered by the more general and perpetual claim that "*no set of facts ever entails any particular account of difference*."[69] How can such extraordinary claims be maintained? Because, Laqueur avers, the nature of sexual difference is "logically independent of biological facts." This is what enables him to conclude that "the more general shift in the interpretation of male and female bodies *cannot have been due*, even in principle, to scientific progress."[70]

Soble helpfully puts his finger on the central flaw in this mode of argument:

---

65. Soble, "History of Sexual Anatomy," 239.

66. Laqueur, *Making Sex*, 69. The thesis derives from a combination of the quite independent and somewhat differing insights of the French theoretical physicist Pierre Duhem (1861–1916) and the American philosopher and logician Willard Quine (1908–2000).

67. Stephen Thornton, "Popper, Basic Statements and the Quine-Duhem Thesis," *Yearbook of the Irish Philosophical Society* 9 (2007): 6.

68. See Donald Gilles, *Philosophy of Science in the Twentieth Century* (Oxford: Blackwell Publishers, 1993), especially ch. 5: "The Duhem Thesis and the Quine Thesis," 98–116; Alan Sokal, *Beyond the Hoax: Science, Philosophy and Culture* (Oxford: Oxford University Press, 2008), especially ch. 6: "Cognitive Relativism in the Philosophy of Science," 171–227.

69. Laqueur, *Making Sex*, 153, 19 (emphasis added).

70. Laqueur, *Making Sex*, 153, 9 (emphasis added).

> If the transition from the one-sex to the two-sex model could *not even in principle* have been the result of advances in the empirical data, would that not make Laqueur's historical conclusion, that the empirical was in fact irrelevant in this area, uninteresting? If something is impossible, then of course it did not happen. If, as a matter of the logic of science, empirical data are impotent or irrelevant, then we would seem to know in advance, by this philosophy of science, what any historical study of the theory of anatomical sex would eventually tell us about that specific history, that the empirical was in fact irrelevant.[71]

Laqueur, however, displays little awareness of the risk faced by anyone "who already thinks he knows the fact that the social, the political, and the metaphysical trump the empirical when much is 'at stake' and who thinks that theories are socially constructed, invented or concocted, to meet various social and personal needs."[72] The inescapable result is self-referential incoherence—with Laqueur's thesis falling by its own sword.[73] As Meryl Altman and Keith Nightenhelser remark, "there is something paradoxical—even when Foucault does it—about 'marshalling evidence' for the conclusion that the facts didn't matter."[74] A further casualty of Laqueur's approach is that biological science is changed "from an empirical discipline to a kind of phantasmic literature."[75] For when it comes to deciding which of the models (the one-sex or the two-sex) is correct, Laqueur concludes that "there is no scientific way to choose between them."[76]

In the introduction to her critique of *Making Sex*, Helen King remarks that Laqueur's book is "by far the most influential work on the history

71. Soble, "History of Sexual Anatomy," 239 (emphasis original).

72. Soble, "History of Sexual Anatomy," 244 (emphasis original).

73. For a discussion of the types and features of this characterization, see George I. Mavrode, "Self-Referential Incoherence," *American Philosophical Quarterly* 22 (1985): 65–72; John M. Frame, "Self-Refuting Statements," *New Dictionary of Christian Apologetics*, ed. W. C. Campbell-Jack and Gavin J. McGrath (Leicester: Inter-Varsity Press, 2006), 660–62.

74. Meryl Altman and Keith Nightenhelser, "Book Review of *Making Sex: Body and Gender From the Greeks to Freud by Thomas Laqueur*," *Postmodern Culture* 2 (1992): http://www.pomoculture.org/2013/09/26/book-review-of-making-sex.

75. Soble, "History of Sexual Anatomy," 244.

76. Laqueur, *Making Sex*, viii.

of the body, across a range of academic disciplines."[77] This is why it has been important to analyze its arguments and assess their cogency. As we have seen, because of his philosophical commitments, Laqueur lands in a place of epistemological (and biological) agnosticism. Unsurprisingly, then, his conclusion is noncommittal: "two sexes are not the necessary, natural consequence of corporeal difference. Nor, for that matter is one sex."[78]

So how many sexes are there? While Laqueur is ultimately unable to answer this question, others have been less agnostic.

FIVE-SEX AND THREE-SEX MODELS

The five-sex model

The five-sex model is most readily associated with Anne Fausto-Sterling, emeritus professor of biology and women's studies at Brown University. In a landmark article written in 1993, she argued that "there are many gradations running from male to female; and depending on how one calls the shots, one can argue that along that spectrum lie at least five sexes—and perhaps even more."[79] She then went on to explain that while the standard medical literature tends to use the term *intersex* for all who have some mixture of male and female characteristics, there are, in fact, three major subgroups that can be distinguished:

> the so-called true hermaphrodites, whom I call herms, who possess one testis and one ovary (the sperm- and egg-producing vessels, or gonads); the male pseudohermaphrodites (the "merms"), who have testes and some aspects of the female genitalia but no ovaries; and the female pseudohermaphrodites (the "ferms"), who have ovaries and some aspects of the male genitalia but lack testes.[80]

In a follow up article written in 2000, Fausto-Sterling admitted that her original piece was "intended to be provocative" and had been "written with tongue firmly in cheek." She also revised her claim that 4 percent of

---

77. King, *One-Sex Body*, 1.

78. Laqueur, *Making Sex*, 243.

79. Anne Fausto-Sterling: "The Five Sexes: Why Male and Female Are Not Enough," *The Sciences* (March/April 1993): 21.

80. Fausto-Sterling, "Five Sexes," 21.

children are born "intersexual in some form" to 1.7 percent, making clear that this new figure, while more accurate, was still "a ballpark estimate, not a precise count."[81] Most significantly, she suggested that since 1993, "society has moved beyond five sexes to a recognition that gender variation is normal and, for some people, an arena for playful exploration." As a consequence, it would be "better for intersexuals and their supporters to turn everyone's focus away from genitals." Fausto-Sterling concluded her article by clarifying that she was not arguing for "a pastel world in which androgyny reigns and men and women are boringly the same." Rather, in her vision of the sexes, "strong colors coexist with pastels."[82]

These ideas were both developed and deepened in her larger monograph, also published in 2000, *Sexing the Body: Gender Politics and the Construction of Sexuality*. Central to the book's thesis is the claim that labeling someone either a man or a woman is not a scientific decision but a social decision. This, she clarifies, is not to deny that we "may use scientific knowledge to help us make the decision, but only our beliefs about gender—not science—can define our sex."[83] In a way that strongly suggests the influence of Foucault (as well as a number of his disciples),[84] Fausto-Sterling insists that "our beliefs about gender affect what kinds of knowledge scientists produce about sex in the first place." She is thus strongly critical of second-wave feminists for assuming that physical sex was "hardwired"—an assumption that left them open to claims that "male/female differences in cognitive function and behavior could *result* from sex differences."[85]

Fausto-Sterling's thesis, however, goes far beyond claiming that the "bodily signals and functions we define as male or female come already entangled in our ideas about gender." She also believes that "components

81. Anne Fausto-Sterling, "The Five Sexes, Revisited," *The Sciences* 40, no. 4 (2000): 19–20.

82. Fausto-Sterling, "Five Sexes, Revisited," 22–23.

83. Anne Fausto-Sterling, *Sexing the Body: Gender Politics and the Construction of Sexuality* (New York: Basic Books, 2000), 3.

84. In the opening chapter of *Sexing the Body*, Fausto-Sterling not only cites and interacts with Foucault (especially *The History of Sexuality: The Will to Knowledge: Volume I*, trans. Robert Hurley [New York: Pantheon, 1978]), but also with Jana Sawicki (*Disciplining Foucault: Feminism, Power, and the Body* [New York: Routledge, 1991]) and Lois McNay (*Foucault and Feminism: Power, Gender, and the Self* [Boston: Northeastern University Press, 1993]).

85. Fausto-Sterling, *Sexing the Body*, 3–4 (emphasis original).

of our political, social, and moral struggles become, quite literally, embodied, incorporated into our very physiological being." Otherwise put, our bodies absorb and exhibit scientific theories about sex that have been "sculpted by the social milieu in which biologists practice their trade."[86] This, then, is no mere *epistemological* claim; it is an *ontological* claim: *ideas affect anatomy*! Nor is it a passing piece of rhetoric; it is a persistent theme of her book. Furthermore, Fausto-Sterling is not simply referring to surgeries that are performed (perhaps needlessly) on those with intersex conditions—although this is a major concern of chapters 2–4. She is also making a claim for bodily pliability and a transcending of the nature/culture divide: "As we grow and develop, we literally, not just 'discursively' (that is, through language and cultural practices), construct our bodies, incorporating experience into our very flesh. To understand this claim, we must erode the distinctions between the physical and the social body."[87]

This does not mean that Fausto-Sterling denies the reality of materiality or the objectivity of sexual anatomy. "There *are* hormones, genes, prostates, uteri, and other body parts and physiologies," she writes, "that we use to differentiate male from female." What she is challenging is the idea that materiality is "that which can support construction but cannot itself be constructed."[88] Human sex, then, is not only a biological reality that produces a certain cultural effect, but is also "a somatic fact, *created by* a cultural effect." This enables her to speak of the human body as "a biocultural system in which cells and culture mutually construct each other."[89]

So how does the social become material, the theoretical physiological? Suggesting that it would "require a book-length essay" to do justice to her claim, Fausto-Sterling refrains from giving concrete examples of how "the production of gendered knowledge about the body" effects "the materialization of gender within the body."[90] In more recent writings, however,

86. Fausto-Sterling, *Sexing the Body*, 4–5.

87. Fausto-Sterling, *Sexing the Body*, 20. To make her case, Fausto-Sterling draws on the work of the philosopher and feminist theorist Elizabeth A. Grosz (*Volatile Bodies: Towards a Corporeal Feminism* [Bloomington: Indiana University Press, 1994]).

88. Fausto-Sterling, *Sexing the Body*, 22.

89. Fausto-Sterling, *Sexing the Body*, 21, 242 (emphasis original).

90. Fausto-Sterling, *Sexing the Body*, 253. The closest Fausto-Sterling comes to substantiating her claim is in her brief comments (on 242) regarding (1) human growth—"how one experiences one's sexual body changes over time"—and (2) the way in which athletes "reshape their bodies through

she has sought to provide an account of "how the material body both acts upon and is acted upon by culture."[91] In a 2014 essay, titled "Nature," she begins by pointing to surgeries on the intersexed to show how "medical scientists literally create sex, while at the same time policing the boundaries of the sexed body."[92] Then, drawing on the works of Elizabeth Grosz, Donna Haraway, and Elizabeth Wilson,[93] she identifies body-part replacements, tattoos and jewelry, diet and exercise, and even the concept of the cyborg as ways in which we "sculpt our bodies" and reconfigure "the relations between nature/culture and human/machine."[94] Finally, she notes that newer understandings of the nervous system indicate that it "*requires* environmental input to help shape and refine the quantity and quality of connections between cells within the brain and with the peripheral nervous system."[95] In addition to these points, in a 2019 article, "Gender/Sex, Sexual Orientation, and Identity Are in the Body: How Did They Get There?," she points to phenomena such as "manspreading," the ability to "retrain our voices," and the embodied nature of memory as further instances of the way cultural features of gender "embed new bodily habits into our sensorimotor (neuromuscular) system."[96]

Many of these examples are uncontroversial. It is not in dispute that psychosocial forces produce a wide range of somatic (including

---

a process that is at once natural and artificial." She then attempts to connect such changes to "the transformations under-gone by surgical transsexuals." However, on her own terms, it is clear that such transformations are "artificial" and not "natural" changes. Fausto-Sterling, then, offers no examples of males *naturally* turning into females or vice versa.

91. Anne Fausto-Sterling, "Nature," in *Critical Terms for the Study of Gender*, ed. Catharine R. Stimpson and Gilbert Herdt (Chicago: University of Chicago Press, 2014), 313 (294–319); "The Problem with Sex/Gender and Nature/Nurture," in *Debating Biology: Sociological Reflections on Health, Medicine and Society*, ed. S. J. Williams, L. Birke, and G. A. Bendelow (New York: Routledge, 2003), 123–32; "The Bare Bones of Sex: Part 1—Sex and Gender," *Signs* 30 (2005): 1491–527; *Sex/Gender: Biology in a Social World* (London: Routledge, 2012).

92. Fausto-Sterling, "Nature," 314.

93. Grosz, *Volatile Bodies*; Donna J. Haraway, *Simians, Cyborgs, and Women: The Reinvention of Nature* (New York: Routledge, 1991); Elizabeth A. Wilson, *Psychosomatic: Feminism and the Neurological Body* (Durham, NC: Duke University Press, 2004).

94. Fausto-Sterling, "Nature," 314.

95. Fausto-Sterling, "Nature," 315.

96. Anne Fausto-Sterling, "Gender/Sex, Sexual Orientation, and Identity Are in the Body: How Did They Get There?," *The Journal of Sex Research* (2019): 5–6.

neurological) effects.[97] What has not been demonstrated, however, is that such forces are able to modify chromosomes, alter gonads, or change genitalia. Culture, for all its gender-defining and body-influencing power, does not bring about spontaneous sex change in individuals.[98] The reason for this, as I will argue further below, is that human sex (however it might be interpreted and whatever epigenetics might yet reveal) is "formed through a complex, multi-stage development in the mother's womb."[99] That is, sex is a *given biological fact* determined at conception and developed in utero, not a *socially constructed effect* produced post-partum. Contrary to Fausto-Sterling, then, the differences between the physical and the social cannot be eroded, or the nature/culture distinction dissolved.[100]

The main element of Fausto-Sterling's thesis that warrants further exploration is the phenomenon of intersex conditions and, in particular, whether such variations constitute an additional sex category to male and female.

The phenomenon of intersex conditions

The term "intersexuality" was coined by the German geneticist Richard Goldschmidt in 1917.[101] It replaced two older terms, "hermaphrodite" and "pseudo-hermaphrodite," but has since been superseded by the more clinical categories, "Disorders of Sex Development" (DSD[1]) and/or "Disorders

97. See Richard J. Davidson and Bruce S. McEwen, "Social Influences on Neuroplasticity: Stress and Interventions to Promote Well-Being," *Nature Neuroscience* 15 (2012): 689–95; Jenny Gu and Ryota Kanai, "What Contributes to Individual Differences in Brain Structure?," *Frontiers in Human Neuroscience* 8, art. 262 (2014): 1–6, https://www.ncbi.nlm.nih.gov/pmc/articles/PMC4009419.

98. The one instance of (apparent) spontaneous sex change that Fausto-Sterling discusses briefly is that of XY newborns with 5-alpha reductase deficiency, who are sometimes mistaken for girls—given that they usually have "a tiny penis or clitoris, undescended testes, and a divided scrotum" (*Sexing the Body*, 109). During adolescence, however, a surge of naturally produced testosterone causes the penis to grow, the testes to descend and the scrotum to fuse. This change, needless to say, has nothing to do with culture.

99. Patricia Weerakoon and Kamal Weerakoon, "The Biology of Sex and Gender," in *The Gender Conversation: Evangelical Perspectives on Gender, Scripture, and the Christian Life*, ed. Edwina Murphy and David Starling (Eugene, OR: Wipf & Stock, 2016), 321.

100. Steven Pinker, "Why Nature & Nurture Won't Go Away," *Dædalus* (Fall 2002): 1–13.

101. Richard B. Goldschmidt, "Intersexuality and the Endocrine Aspect of Sex," *Endocrinology* 1 (1917): 433–56.

of Sex Differentiation" (DSD^{2}).[102] The introduction of this nomenclature has not gone without controversy. This is mainly due to the fact that the word "disorder" carries overtones of "medical conditions in need of repair, when some intersex anatomies, though atypical, do not necessarily need surgical or hormonal correction."[103] Consequently, alternative nomenclature—e.g., "Differences of Sex Development" (DSD^{3}) or "Divergences of Sex Development" (DSD^{4})—has also been suggested.[104] Many, however, still wish to retain the word "intersex"—some for deeply personal reasons,[105] others because of its utility as "an umbrella concept used to cover a wide range of variations in sex development."[106]

Without here pausing to weigh up the various terminological options, and mostly for the sake of simplicity, I will retain the word "intersex" and intend it to include DSD^{1} and DSD^{2} (but not DSD^{3} and DSD^{4}).[107] In my usage, then, "intersex" embraces (what Abigail Favale terms) "'congenital conditions of sexual development' (CCSDs)";[108] that is, the full range of "inborn somatic deviations of the reproductive tract from the norm and/or discrepancies among the biological indicators of male and female."[109]

As the major intersex conditions are listed and explained in the relevant literature, it is not my purpose to describe them in any detail here.[110] Nevertheless, the main variants are shown in the following table:

---

102. Jennifer Anne Cox, *Intersex in Christ: Ambiguous Biology and the Gospel* (Eugene, OR: Cascade, 2018), 10–11.

103. Elizabeth Reis, "Divergence or Disorder," *Perspectives in Biology and Medicine* 50 (2007): 535.

104. Claudia Wiesmann, Susanne Ude-Koeller, Gernot H. G. Sinnecker, and Ute Thyen, "Ethical Principles and Recommendations for the Medical Management of Differences of Sex Development (DSD)/Intersex in Children and Adolescents," *European Journal of Pediatrics* 169 (2010): 671–79.

105. See, e.g., Michelle O'Brien, "Intersex, Medicine, Diversity, Identity and Spirituality," in Beardsley and O'Brien, *This Is My Body*, 45–56.

106. Megan K. DeFranza, *Sex Difference in Christian Theology: Male, Female, and Intersex in the Image of God* (Grand Rapids: Eerdmans, 2015), 24.

107. My main reason for excluding these latter categories is because they are often used to include differences that are normal variations among members of the same sex (e.g., size of genitalia).

108. Favale, *Genesis of Gender*, 125.

109. *DSM-5*, 451.

110. For example, Gerald N. Callahan, *Between XX and XY: Intersexuality and the Myth of Two Sexes* (Chicago: Chicago Review Press, 2009); Cornwall, *Sex and Uncertainty*, 237–46; Cox, *Intersex in Christ*, 12–17; DeFranza, *Sex Difference*, 24–44.

TABLE 2: MAPPING INTERSEX VARIATIONS

Subcategories	*Male*	*Intersex Variations*	*Female*
Chromosomes	XY	XXY, XYY, XO, XX/XY mosaicism	XX
Hormones	higher testosterone, dihydroxytestosterone	variable hormone levels and responsiveness	higher estrogen and progesterone, low testosterone
Internal genitalia	vas deferens, seminal vesicles, bulbourethral glands, prostate gland	female ↔ ambiguous ↔ male	ovaries, oviducts, uterus, cervix, upper vagina
External genitalia	penis, testes, scrotal sacs	female ↔ ambiguous ↔ male	clitoris, labia, vagina
Reproductive function	semen, ejaculation	absent or variable	ovulation, menses

As the table[111] seeks to illustrate, intersex conditions can involve abnormalities at one or more levels: irregular chromosomal patterns, unusual hormone levels, ineffective hormone reception, mixed internal genitalia, and ambiguous external genitalia. In some cases, "genitalia will appear to be typically male or typically female but will be discordant with the 'sex' of the chromosomes, the gonads, or both."[112] Depending on the precise condition, reproductive function may also be impaired.

Due to the dispute about which variations ought to be categorized as intersex conditions, the question of prevalence is also a matter of significant debate. In 2000, Fausto-Sterling and a number of her colleagues surveyed the medical literature from 1955 to the (then) present and, as noted earlier, concluded that "approximately 1.7% of all live births do not conform to a Platonic ideal of absolute sex chromosome, gonadal, genital, and hormonal dimorphism."[113] In 2003, however, philosopher Carrie Hull drew attention to numerous errors and omissions in the collection and

111. Table adapted from Looy and Bouma, "Nature of Gender," 167.

112. Sharon E. Sytsma, "Introduction," in *Ethics and Intersex*, ed. Sharon E. Sytsma (Dordrecht: Springer, 2006), xvii.

113. Melanie Blackless, Anthony Charuvastra, Amanda Derryck, Anne Fausto-Sterling, Karl Lauzanne, and Ellen Lee, "How Sexually Dimorphic Are We? Review and Synthesis," *American Journal of Human Biology* 12 (2000): 161.

interpretation of the data used in Fausto-Sterling's study. After making the necessary adjustments, and without questioning the study's definition of intersex or the number of conditions included in its purview, she suggested a much-reduced figure of 0.37 percent.[114]

Interestingly, Hull was (apparently) unaware of the questions raised the previous year by physician and psychologist Leonard Sax. In Sax's estimation, it is more clinically appropriate to restrict the category of intersex to conditions in which genotypic (i.e., chromosomal) sex is inconsistent with phenotypic (i.e., genital) sex, or in which the phenotype is not classifiable as either male or female (i.e., Disorders of Sex *Differentiation*/DSD[2]). He thus concluded that a number of Disorders of Sex *Development*/DSD[1]—for example, late-onset congenital adrenal hyperplasia, Klinefelter's syndrome (XXY), Turner's syndrome (XO), vaginal agenesis and chromosomal variants such as XXX and XYY—cannot be described as intersex in any "meaningful clinical sense."[115] Subtracting these conditions reduced the frequency rate to 0.018 percent. Moreover, if Hull's adjustments are applied to Sax's figure, the percentage drops to 0.015 percent.[116]

Do intersex conditions constitute a third sex?

While debates concerning definition and frequency are bound to continue, the more important question is whether intersexuality should be regarded as a third sex. One champion of such an idea is Gilbert Herdt, Emeritus Professor of Human Sexuality Studies and Anthropology at San Francisco State University. In his editor's preface to *Third Sex, Third Gender* (1993), a multi-authored collection of historical and cross-cultural essays, Herdt strongly criticized "the one-dimensional ideology of sexual dimorphism."[117] This ideology, he believes, has meant that "cross-cultural variations in sexual and gender patterns have been downplayed when it

---

114. Carrie L. Hull, "Letter to the Editor: How Sexually Dimorphic Are We? Review and Synthesis," *American Journal of Human Biology* 15 (2003): 112–15.

115. Sax, "How Common Is Intersex?," 175.

116. Alex Byrne, "Is Sex Binary?," *ARC Digital* (November 2, 2018), https://medium.com/arc-digital/is-sex-binary-16bec97d161e.

117. Gilbert Herdt, "Preface," in *Third Sex, Third Gender: Beyond Sexual Dimorphism in Culture and History*, ed. Gilbert Herdt (New York: Zone Books, 1993), 13. See also Gerard Loughlin, "Gender Ideology: For a 'Third Sex' Without Reserve," *Studies in Christian Ethics* 31 (2018): 471–82.

comes to discussions of 'normal' reproductive sexuality and kinship; that is, when it comes to thinking about whether there are only two sexes and genders in the nature of human groups."[118]

The interpretation of such cross-cultural variations is, of course, precarious. Consequently, Karen Lebacqz's question is critical: "Are liminal individuals actually accorded a third sex status within their own cultures, or is the claim that there is a third sex really a Western imposition?"[119] The difficulty of giving a definitive answer to this question (at least in many cases) means that the claimed connections between third gender roles in other cultures and the fact of intersex conditions are often "speculative and tenuous."[120] But this uncertainly need not detain us. Given the empirical reality of intersex conditions, the more important question is whether they should be regarded as *natural divergences* or *pathological deviations*; that is, are they an instance of healthy *biological diversity* or a form of *anatomical disability*?

In answer to this question, we begin by noting that while a small number of intersex conditions are potentially life-threatening,[121] the majority are not.[122] For this reason, some argue that the pathology is not in the bodies of those with atypical anatomy but in the social expectations and restrictions placed on them or "the way in which cultures narrate and organize the world."[123] Megan DeFranza, for example, believes it is "the unnecessary assumption of the binary that leads to the mistreatment of intersex children"; that is, to "attempts to 'correct' their bodies through medically unnecessary castration and plastic surgery."[124] DeFranza is surely right to protest unnecessary and irreversible cosmetic interventions (particularly where consent is lacking), as she is to champion "a

118. Herdt, "Preface," 12.

119. Karen Lebacqz, "Difference or Defect? Intersexuality and the Politics of Difference," *Annual of the Society of Christian Ethics* 17 (1997): 217.

120. Lebacqz, "Difference or Defect?," 217.

121. For example, Congenital Adrenal Hyperplasia (CAH). See further Cox, *Intersex in Christ*, 12–13. In such cases, it may well be wise to remove "any vestigial gonadal tissue that might become cancerous" (Lebacqz, "Difference or Defect?," 224).

122. Looy and Bouma, "Nature of Gender," 175.

123. Cox, *Intersex in Christ*, 134. This, however, is not Cox's own view. She affirms the importance of the medical model, as well as seeing a measure of validity in the social and cultural models.

124. Megan K. DeFranza, "Response to Mark A. Yarhouse and Julia Sadusky," in Beilby and Eddy, *Understanding Transgender Identities*, 139.

patient-centered model" instead of a "concealment-centered model."[125] But her assault on sexual dimorphism fails to treat with sufficient seriousness the fact that "human bodies must be either male or female to reproduce."[126]

The problem comes clearly into focus if we ask the question that has been hovering over this entire discussion: What defines sex? As is highlighted by the fact that the whole conversation surrounding intersexuality largely concerns *reproductive anatomy*, the question is best answered in terms of actual *reproductive structures* and potential *reproductive roles*. Beauvoir understood this, emphasizing that "male and female organisms ... are basically defined by the gametes they produce."[127] It is also important to recognize that organisms remain male or female even when their "root capacity for reproductive function" is "immature or damaged."[128] For "while a reproductive system structured to serve a particular reproductive role may be impaired in such a way that it cannot perform its function, the system is still recognizably structured for that role, so that biological sex can still be defined strictly in terms of the structure of reproductive systems."[129]

None of this is to deny that certain Disorders of Sex *Differentiation* (e.g., Mixed Gonadal Dysgenesis) may obscure a person's reproductive structure and so make sex determination difficult.[130] Nor is it surprising that some, because of the ambiguities arising from their condition, feel that "neither category fits adequately, and who prefer to claim a liminal

---

125. These terms were introduced by Alice D. Dreger, "Shifting the Paradigm of Intersex Treatment," *Intersex Society of North America* (2003), https://isna.org/pdf/compare.pdf.

126. Scott E. Stiegemeyer, "How Do You Know Whether You Are a Man or a Woman?," *CTQ* 79 (2015): 26.

127. Beauvoir, *The Second Sex*, 26.

128. Christopher O. Tollefsen, "Sex Identity," *The Public Discourse* (July 13, 2015), http://www.thepublicdiscourse.com/2015/07/15306.

129. Lawrence S. Mayer and Paul R. McHugh, "Sexuality and Gender: Findings from the Biological, Psychological, and Social Sciences," *The New Atlantis* 50 (Fall 2016): 90. It is important to recognize that the chromosomal and gamete accounts of sex are not in conflict. The reason why a male may be defined as someone who has "advanced some way down the developmental pathway that results in the production of small gametes" (Byrne, "Is Sex Binary?") is precisely because he has XY chromosomes.

130. A person with Mixed Gonadal Dysgenesis has a combination of sex chromosomes, some cells being XY and others XO. This form of chromosomal mosaicism usually results in the formation of two different gonads: an undescended testis on one side, and an improperly developed gonad on the other. This, in turn, can result in a highly diverse body and genital presentation, ranging from female to someone with ambiguous external genitalia to male.

or 'third' gender identity."[131] But difficulty in discerning whether someone is male or female does not mean they are neither.[132] Occasional epistemological uncertainty, therefore, is not a reason to abandon the sex binary. As Sprinkle writes: "Variations within two categories, or even a blend of two categories, doesn't mean more than two categories exist."[133] Indeed, there is no third type of gamete, just as there is no third type of gonad or third type of genitalia.[134] It is also not possible for a person to have fully functioning sex organs of both sexes.[135] As Kathy Scarbrough, a specialist in female reproductive neuroendocrinology, explains:

> There are only two types of gametes and there are no intermediate forms. Gonads (ovaries and testes) and gametes don't get mismatched in the natural world because the gamete is dependent on the gonad for its maturation. This means that there are no examples of human beings born with an ovary that produces sperm or vice versa.[136]

To claim that there are more than two sexes, then, "would require a radical re-formulation of what 'sex' means in Biology as a discipline."[137] Precisely because "there are no intrinsically-ordered states between male and female reproductive anatomies," biological sex "does not meet the defining criteria for a spectrum."[138] It is necessarily binary. Intersex conditions, therefore, do not represent an additional sex category.[139]

---

131. Susannah Cornwall, "Recognizing the Full Spectrum of Gender? Transgender, Intersex and the Futures of Feminist Theology," *Feminist Theology* 20 (2012): 239.

132. John Skalko, "Why There Are Only Two Sexes," *The Public Discourse* (June 5, 2017), http://www.thepublicdiscourse.com/2017/06/19389.

133. Sprinkle, *Embodied*, 98.

134. Anderson, *When Harry Became Sally*, 88; Favale, *Genesis of Gender*, 124.

135. Skalko, "Only Two Sexes."

136. Kathy Scarbrough, "The Difference Between Sex and Gender and Why It Matters," in *Female Erasure: What You Need to Know About Gender Politics' War on Women, the Female Sex and Human Right*, ed. Ruth Barrett (Pacific Palisades: Tidal Time Publishing, 2016), 29.

137. Emi Koyama, "From 'Intersex' to 'DSD': Toward a Queer Disability Politics of Gender," *Intersex Initiative* (2006), http://www.intersexinitiative.org/articles/intersextodsd.html.

138. Emma Hilton and Jenny Whyte, "Project Nettie: Scientists Supporting Biological Sex," *Project Nettie: Scientists Supporting Biological Sex*, https://projectnettie.wordpress.com. Contra Jenell Williams Paris, *The End of Sexual Identity: Why Sex Is Too Important to Define Who We Are* (Downers Grove, IL: Intervarsity Press, 2011), 33–34.

139. *Pace* Callahan, *Between XX and XY*, 8, 77–78, 163.

IS SEX SOCIALLY CONSTRUCTED?

As we have seen, thinking about the making and meaning of biological sex, at least since the early 1980s, has become increasingly complicated by two interrelated developments: an increased awareness of intersex conditions (just discussed) and the rise of radical social constructionism.[140] Because of the significance of the second of these developments, and in order to prepare the ground for our exploration of the changes in thinking about gender in the following chapter, it is necessary to offer a number of further reflections on the epistemology that has helped to produce it.[141]

THE POSTMODERN CHALLENGE

From social constructionism to queer theory

Few disciplines (if any) have escaped the influence of postmodern thought, with its thorough-going questioning of all taken-for-granted perspectives and its "incredulity toward meta-narratives."[142] Although "postmodernism" is a somewhat sweeping term that is not simply defined,[143] central to postmodern epistemology is the idea that "human emotions, conceptual categories, and patterns of behaviour (such as those characterizing men and women or homosexuals and heterosexuals) are social constructions."[144] Epistemologically, this means the replacement of an *exogenic perspective* (in which knowledge conforms to the objective contours of the world) with an *endogenic perspective* (in which knowledge is fashioned by subjective

---

140. In 1999, Ian Hacking sought to track the first of these developments by examining the publication dates of the various "The Social Construction of X" book titles. He listed two titles from 1979, eight from the 1980s, and twenty-one from the 1990s. See Ian Hacking, *The Social Construction of What?* (Cambridge: Harvard University Press, 1999), 1–2.

141. It is important not to confuse social constructionism with postmodernism, particularly as it has its own intellectual roots (e.g., Comte, Marx, Durkheim, Weber, and Mannheim) and developmental history (e.g., Mead, Spencer, Blumer, Berger, and Luckmann). Nevertheless, it has been profoundly influenced by the anti-structuralism, subjectivism, relativism, and pluralism that characterize much postmodern thought.

142. Jean-François Lyotard, *The Postmodern Condition: A Report on Knowledge*, trans. Geoff Bennington and Brian Massumi (Minneapolis: University of Minnesota Press, 1984), xxiv. See Christopher Butler, *Postmodernism: A Very Short Introduction* (Oxford: Oxford University Press, 2002) for an overview of postmodernism's impact on a wide range of fields.

143. Christopher Watkin, *From Plato to Postmodernism: The Story of Western Culture Through Philosophy, Literature and Art* (London: Bristol Classical Press, 2011), 186.

144. Pinker, "Why Nature & Nurture," 4.

factors within us).[145] Vivien Burr explains the consequences of this shift for our understanding of the sex binary:

> Our observations of the world suggest to us that there are two categories of human being, men and women. Social constructionism bids us to seriously question whether the categories "man" and "woman" are simply a reflection of naturally occurring distinct types of human being. This may seem a bizarre idea at first, and of course differences in reproductive organs are present in many species. But we become aware of the greyness of such categories when we look at practices such as gender re-assignment surgery and the surrounding debate about how to classify people as unambiguously male or female. We can thus begin to consider that these seemingly natural categories may be inevitably bound with gender, the normative prescriptions of masculinity and femininity in a culture, so that these two categories of personhood have been built upon them.[146]

It is not surprising that the natural sciences have also come under sustained attack from the stronger forms of social constructionism, which claim that what passes for hard fact "typically depends on a subtle but potent array of social microprocesses."[147] The upshot of this claim is that scientists "do not so much 'discover' the nature of reality as 'construct' it."[148] Moreover, due to unconscious bias, they do so in ways that are unavoidably prejudiced, if not self-serving. This highlights the central noetic claim of postmodernism: that "the subject is not a neutral suprahuman observer but what Kierkegaard called an 'existing person,' a finite human person with desires, intentions, perspectives, and prejudices that shape their understanding."[149] *Consequently, all human knowing is profoundly conditioned, if not determined, by our situatedness.* Furthermore, for more radical

---

145. Kenneth J. Gergen, "The Social Constructionist Movement in Modern Psychology," *American Psychologist* 40 (1985): 269.

146. Vivien Burr, *Social Constructionism*, 3rd ed. (London: Routledge, 2015), 3.

147. Gergen, "Social Constructionist Movement," 268.

148. Butler, *Postmodernism*, 38.

149. J. De Waal Dryden, *A Hermeneutic of Wisdom: Recovering the Formative Agency of Scripture* (Grand Rapids: Baker Academic, 2018), 7–8.

social constructionists, "language does not mirror reality; rather, it constitutes it."[150] In fact, for some, we have no access to the world, not even biomedical reality, beyond language.[151] This means that "it is through language, rather than through perceptual experience, that our conception of the world is formed"[152]—a view increasingly referred to as "the discursive construction of reality."[153]

Catalyzed by Foucault's ideas concerning the construction of sex by means of historically contingent discourse, queer theory builds on this epistemological premise.[154] It assumes that all aspects of humanity, but especially sex and gender, are not only historically variable but are a result of (what Foucault called) "discursive formation."[155] In other words, *things do not have meaning in themselves; meaning is supplied by speech.* Indeed, discourse can even be said to summon things into being "by identifying, specifying, and defining them."[156] Consequently, queer theory "sets itself against the tendency within the hard sciences to understand phenomena, including sexual phenomena, in terms of definable essences (essentialism) with a 'nature,' often rooted in biology, that preexists and transcends language."[157] Hence, David Halperin's famous declaration that a queer identity is "an identity without an essence."[158] At the same time, queer theorists also make a point of exposing language for its inadequacy.[159] Accordingly,

---

150. Gail T. Fairhurst and David Grant, "The Social Construction of Leadership: A Sailing Guide," *Management Communication Quarterly* 24 (2010): 174.

151. Michael R. Bury, "Social Construction and the Development of Medical Sociology," *Sociology of Health and Illness* 8 (1986): 137–69.

152. Dave Elder-Vass, *The Reality of Social Construction* (Cambridge: Cambridge University Press, 2012), 78.

153. See, e.g., David Pujante, "The Discursive Construction of Reality in the Context of Rhetoric," in *Developing New Identities in Social Conflicts: Constructivist Perspectives*, ed. Esperanza Morales-López and Alan Floyd, Discourse Approaches to Politics, Society and Culture 71 (Amsterdam: John Benjamins Publishing Co, 2017), 42–65.

154. Tamsin Spargo, *Foucault and Queer Theory* (Cambridge: Icon Books, 1999), 26.

155. William Turner, *A Genealogy of Queer Theory* (Philadelphia: Temple University Press, 2000), 29. For Foucault's own exposition of "discursive formation," see Michel Foucault, *The Archaeology of Knowledge*, trans. A. M. Sheridan Smith (1969; Abingdon: Routledge, 2002), 34–43.

156. Stanley J. Grenz, *A Primer on Postmodernism* (Grand Rapids: Eerdmans, 1996), 132.

157. Paul Rhodes Eddy and James K. Beilby, "Understanding Transgender Experiences and Identities: An Introduction," in Beilby and Eddy, *Understanding Transgender Identities*, 11.

158. David M. Halperin, *Saint Foucault: Towards a Gay Hagiography* (New York: Oxford University Press, 1995), 62.

159. Giffney, "Introduction," 7.

their work is characteristically marked by an emphasis on "fluidity, über-inclusivity, indeterminacy, indefinability, unknowability, the preposterous, impossibility, unthinkability, unintelligibility, meaninglessness and that which is unrepresentable or incommunicable."[160]

Queer theory, then, is not only complex but highly paradoxical. On the one hand, it asserts that language has immense constructive powers.[161] For example, the "naming" of a child's sex is thought to both create and legislate social reality "by requiring the discursive/perceptual construction of bodies in accord with principles of sexual difference."[162] And yet, on the other hand, queer theory concedes that the powers of language are severely limited. For although language "casts sheaves of reality upon the social body," the appearance is ultimately deceptive.[163] What this means for the sex binary is that the differences that distinguish male and female are more a product of sociolinguistic construction than they are a matter of objective biological reality.[164]

Standing squarely in this stream, Judith Butler asserts that the notion of sex as "the raw" and gender as "the cooked" is not only a reified illusion of a defunct structuralist anthropology, but a "discursive formation that acts as a naturalized foundation for the nature/culture distinction and the strategies of domination that that distinction supports."[165] In other words, despite having a façade of naturalness and objectivity, the sex binary is a discursive formation in the service of an oppressive *masculinist* and *heterosexist* ideology.[166]

---

160. Giffney, "Introduction," 8.

161. L. Zimman, "The Discursive Construction of Sex: Remaking and Reclaiming the Gendered Body in Talk About Genitals Among Trans Men," in *Queer Excursions: Retheorizing Binaries in Language, Gender, and Sexuality*, ed. L. Zimman, J. Davis, and J. Raclaw (New York: Oxford University Press, 2014), 13–34. In Foucault's thought, for example, even the self is constructed through language (Grenz, *Primer on Postmodernism*, 130).

162. Butler, *Gender Trouble*, 157. The words quoted here are Butler's, but the idea comes from Monique Wittig, "One Is Not Born a Woman," *Feminist Issues* 1, no. 2 (1981): 48.

163. Monique Wittig, "The Mark of Gender," *Feminist Issues* 5, no. 2 (1985): 4.

164. Eddy and Beilby, "Understanding Transgender Experiences," 11.

165. Butler, *Gender Trouble*, 50.

166. Butler, "Performative Acts," 524–25; see Butler, *Bodies that Matter*, xi–xii.

Evaluating social constructionism

As was observed regarding Laqueur's work, *radical* social constructionism (like hard postmodernism) is beset with a crippling contradiction. If all truth claims are historically and culturally specific (and so hostage to limiting and prejudicial social forces), then this also applies to the claim that *all truth claims are historically and culturally specific*. Indeed, if statements of fact are always a form of fiction, reading always a form of misreading, and language always metaphorical and never literal, then there is no reliable vantage point from which to make such determinations and no stable basis upon which to maintain a distinction between truth and falsehood.[167] As Christopher Butler points out, "if anyone says that everything is 'really' just constituted by a deceiving image, and not by reality, how does he or she *know*?" Hard postmodernism, then, either collapses under its own weight or is exposed as duplicitous—for "it is logically obvious that you can't demonstrate how language always 'goes astray' without *at the same time* having a secret and contradictory trust in it."[168]

This is not to deny the validity of a more *moderate* form of social constructionism (or soft postmodernism), particularly if it maintains a focus on epistemological formation and resists making ontological assertions. In fact, the founding text of the discipline, Peter Berger and Thomas Luckmann's *The Social Construction of Reality: A Treatise in the Sociology of Knowledge*, was (as its subtitle makes clear) a study in *epistemology*, not *ontology*. It could be argued then that the entire edifice of radical social constructionism is built on a misunderstanding of the very work "which introduced the term social construction to sociologists and began the trajectory that has led to its current ubiquity."[169]

It also needs to be said that if there is a genuinely *social* dimension to our construction of knowledge, then the pluralistic relativism that pervades the postmodern project is unwarranted.[170] For it is impossible to

---

167. And yet, this was precisely Foucault's view. As Paul Rabinow comments: "For Foucault, there is no external position of certainty, no universal understanding that is beyond history and society" ("Introduction," in *The Foucault Reader: An Introduction to Foucault's Thought*, ed. Paul Rabinow [London: Penguin, 1984], 4).

168. Butler, *Postmodernism*, 118 (emphasis original), 18.

169. Elder-Vass, *Social Construction*, 7.

170. John W. Cooper, "Reformed Apologetics and the Challenge of Post-Modern Relativism," *CTJ* 28 (1993): 109.

maintain that "we cannot have access to the external world independently of our beliefs about it unless we retreat into solipsism: the belief that I am the only thing that exists."[171] But if we allow that our *knowledge* of reality is (to some degree) *socially* constructed and *socially* confirmed, then we have conceded that genuine interpersonal communication is possible and, in so doing, have revealed that we are open to an outside reality (i.e., the thoughts of others). Solipsism is thereby ruled out, for, as Anthony Giddens observes, "the individual's biography, if she is to maintain regular interaction with others in the day-to-day world, cannot be wholly fictive."[172] So then, once we accept that we are able to communicate with others, albeit imperfectly, "we implicitly accept that those communications are something external to us and that we have access to them, even if that access is mediated by our existing beliefs."[173]

This demonstrates that realism (i.e., the view that an external world exists independently of our thinking and speaking about it), particularly of a more *critical* kind (i.e., that recognizes that all human knowledge is perspectival and fallible), is not irreconcilable with a more moderate form of social constructionism. Otherwise put, the fact that our knowledge of the world is always subjectively interpreted does not "force us to adopt a promiscuous and unbridled relativism."[174] As Roger Scruton illustrates: "The distinction between red and green, is an objective distinction, even though it is, in Colin McGinn's words, 'subjectively constituted.' "[175] Therefore, it is *relativism* (i.e., the view that we have no unmediated access to the external world and so cannot make objective claims about it) that is the true enemy of a properly conceived social constructionism. Relativism inevitably fractionates into what Hilary Putnam calls "first-person relativism," which, in turn, devolves into solipsism.[176] For this reason, D. A. Carson is right to conclude that "all our understandings are interpretive,

---

171. Elder-Vass, *Social Construction*, 13.

172. Anthony Giddens, *Modernity and Self-Identity: Self and Society in the Late Modern Age* (Oxford: Polity Press, 1991), 54.

173. Elder-Vass, *Social Construction*, 13.

174. John Cromby and David J. Nightingale, "What's Wrong with Social Constructionism?," in *Social Constructionist Psychology: A Critical Analysis of Theory and Practice*, ed. David J. Nightingale and John Cromby (Buckingham: Open University Press 1999), 9.

175. Roger Scruton, *Sexual Desire: A Philosophical Investigation* (London: Continuum, 2006), 275.

176. Hilary Putnam, *Renewing Philosophy* (Cambridge: Harvard University Press, 1992), 75–76.

and that the interpretive communities in which we find ourselves are extremely influential. But this does not mean, on the one hand, that we cannot articulate objective truth, and on the other that our interpretive communities bind us utterly."[177]

It follows from this that while Foucault had good reason to reject the idea of the transcendent, disinterested knower as a Western invention,[178] his claim that it is "warped and twisted" to ask questions "about what man is in his essence" is needlessly pessimistic, if not hypocritical.[179] Similarly, while Butler may be right to say that "gender is the cultural significance that the sexed body assumes" and that this significance is "codetermined through various acts and their cultural perception," it does not follow that it is impossible "to know sex as distinct from gender."[180] To the contrary,

> to not give the extra-discursive body causal powers is to produce a form of the epistemic fallacy, that is, the belief that statements about being can be reduced to statements about knowledge. It is perfectly true that unmediated knowledge of the body is impossible, but that does not mean that its powers are limited to those humans themselves construct.[181]

Nonetheless, queer theorists are insistent that when (say) a doctor announces that a child is a boy or a girl "they are not simply *reporting* on what they see (this would be a constative utterance), they are actually *assigning* a sex and a gender to a body that can have *no existence outside discourse*."[182] Again, such a view is not only self-contradictory but, as will be explained further in chapter 6, stems from a basic misunderstanding

177. D. A. Carson, *The Gagging of God: Christianity Confronts Pluralism* (Grand Rapids: Zondervan, 1996), 129.

178. So Grenz, *Primer on Postmodernism*, 130.

179. Michel Foucault, *The Order of Things: An Archaeology of the Human Sciences*, trans. Alan Sheridan (New York: Vintage, 1973), 342–43. For a critique of Foucault, see Jürgen Habermas, *The Philosophical Discourse of Modernity*, trans. Frederick Lawrence (Cambridge: Cambridge University Press, 1987), 282–86.

180. Butler, "Performative Acts," 524.

181. Kathryn Dean, Jonathan Joseph, and Alan Norrie, "New Essays in Critical Realism," *New Formations* 56 (Autumn 2005): 20.

182. Sara Salih, *Judith Butler* (Oxford: Routledge, 2003), 89.

of the nature of speech acts.[183] While bodily sex might be *socially conceived*, it is not *socially constructed*—not if this means "there is no 'natural body' that pre-exists its cultural inscription."[184] We, therefore, have good reason to reject the view that

> language constitutes, rather than represents, reality; that the autonomous and stable subject of modernity has been replaced by a postmodern agent whose identity is largely other-determined and always in process; that meaning has become social and provisional; or that knowledge only counts as such within a given discursive formation, that is a given power situation.[185]

CONCLUDING REFLECTIONS

THE LIMITS OF SOCIAL CONSTRUCTIONISM

Social constructionism, in all its forms, falls firmly on the culture side of the traditional nature/culture divide.[186] How far it falls depends on how radical it is. But the further it falls, the more ontology is swallowed up by epistemology, objectivity by subjectivity. The net result is an undervaluing of materiality and, in particular, the objective reality of our physicality. For by "either ignoring the body or treating it as mere metaphor or text, social constructionism obscures and downplays the significance of its functional, physiological, hormonal, anatomical and phenomenological aspects."[187] The facticity of the body is thereby obscured as the naming of its sex ceases to be an act of *recognition* and becomes one of *assignation*. We have seen how such a view plays itself out in the approach of both Laqueur and (in a less consistent way) Fausto-Sterling.[188]

---

183. Alex Byrne, "Is Sex Socially Constructed?," *ARC Digital* (December 1, 2018), https://medium.com/arc-digital/is-sex-socially-constructed-81cf3ef79f07.

184. Salih, *Judith Butler*, 62 (emphasis added).

185. Hans Bertens, *The Idea of the Postmodern: A History* (London: Routledge, 1995), 6.

186. Indeed, in social constructionism, the divide itself is regarded as a social construction.

187. Cromby and Nightingale, "What's Wrong with Social Constructionism?," 10.

188. I say "less consistent" because Fausto-Sterling the social constructionist appears to be in a constant tussle with Fausto-Sterling the biological scientist. For example, as early as 2000, she claimed to have abandoned her original five-sex model, instead speaking of men and women as coming in a "wider assortment" (*Sexing the Body*, 110). And yet, in 2012, she insisted that "our bodies are too complex to provide clear-cut answers about sexual difference" (*Sex/Gender*, 21). As recently as 2018, she has insisted that "two sexes have never been enough to describe human variety. Not in

None of this means that it is inappropriate to speak of certain entities (like languages, monetary systems, notions of citizenship, etc.) as having been socially constructed. Everything depends on *what* these entities are, and *whether* or *in what way* and *to what extent* they have been constructed. Crucially, for something to be a social construct it must be more than a social category; it must only exist within a social matrix.[189] Conversely, it must cease to exist (or, at least, become something else) if it is taken out of that matrix. As we have seen, biological sex is no such entity. Putting a person in solitary confinement may well affect their sanity, but it will not change their sex.

THE CHALLENGE OF INTERSEXUALITY

However, as we have also seen, social constructionism is not the only force feeding the contemporary penchant to deconstruct and denaturalize human sexual dimorphism. Intersex conditions are also frequently used as a kind of "trump card … to erase the fundamental and stable reality of biological sex, in order to justify the idea that sex is a construct and open the door to limitless self-identification."[190] This, of course, is not always the intention behind intersex advocacy (even if it is almost always the effect). DeFranza, for example, is motivated (at least in part) by compassion for those "whose presence among us has been overlooked, marginalised, and outright oppressed."[191] Nevertheless, while this concern is commendable, her proposed solution (to modify the sex binary) fails to take account of two important facts.

First, as Emi Koyama, founder of Intersex Initiative Portland, points out, "most people born with intersex conditions … simply see themselves as a man (or a woman) with a birth condition like any other."[192] This does

biblical times and not now" (Anne Fausto-Sterling, "Why Sex Is Not Binary: The Complexity Is More Than Cultural. It's Biological, Too," *The New York Times* [Oct 25, 2018], https://www.nytimes.com/2018/10/25/opinion/sex-biology-binary.html).

189. Haslanger, *Resisting Reality*, 131.

190. Favale, *Genesis of Gender*, 125.

191. DeFranza, *Sex Difference*, 286. We shall examine DeFranza's biblical and theological case in later chapters.

192. Koyama, "From 'Intersex' to 'DSD.'"

not mean that we should be unconcerned for outliers.[193] But it does mean that the large majority of people with intersex conditions are not asking for an adjustment to the binary model.

Second, as argued earlier in this chapter, all people are *either* male *or* female—even if not always straightforwardly so, and despite the fact that, in very rare instances, sex-determination may prove elusive. Accordingly, those with intersex conditions are best advised to embrace their sex "insofar as it may be known."[194] Moreover, far from excluding or marginalizing those with intersex conditions, such counsel is aimed at communicating *belonging*. For such conditions are embraced by, and only comprehensible within, the male-female binary. There is thus no need to "open up space" for the inclusion of the intersexed, as DeFranza urges.[195] The need, rather, is *to better appreciate and more effectively communicate that they are already included.*

THE SPECTER OF "HETEROSEXISM"

The other major source of protest against the sex binary is what Butler calls "heterosexism" (or "compulsory heterosexuality" or "heterosexual hegemony").[196] Coined in 1972,[197] "heterosexism" refers to a form of "systematic social bias, in which society rewards heterosexuals (in the form of economic benefits and civil rights) and punishes all other sexualities."[198] Behind heterosexism lies *heteronormativity*—the assumption that "there are only two naturally occurring and opposite sexes, and each is, naturally, attracted to the other."[199] (Heteronormatively also assumes what is increasingly referred to a *cisnormativity*—the idea that there is a natural

193. Contra Rachel Held Evans, "The False Gospel of Gender Binaries," *RachelHeldEvans.com* (November 19, 2014), http://rachelheldevans.com/blog/gender-binaries.

194. "The Nashville Statement," Article 6.

195. DeFranza, *Sex Difference*, 17.

196. Butler, "Preface (1999)," in *Gender Trouble*, vii, xii, and passim.

197. The term "heteronormativity" first appeared in Craig Rodwell, "The Tarnished Golden Rule," *Queen's Quarterly* 3 (1971): 5. The language of "compulsory heterosexuality," first appears in Adrienne Rich, "Compulsory Heterosexuality and Lesbian Existence," *Signs: Journal of Women in Culture and Society* 5 (1980): 631–60.

198. Teresa J. Hornsby, "The Dance of Gender: David, Jesus, and Paul," *Neotestamentica* 48 (2014): 79. For a more developed definition, see also Patricia Beattie Jung and Ralph F. Smith, *Heterosexism: An Ethical Challenge* (Albany: State University of New York Press, 1993), 13–14.

199. Hornsby, "Dance of Gender," 79.

alignment between biological sex, gender identity, gender roles and gender expression.) But not only does homosexuality challenge these assumptions, intersexuality does too. As Susannah Cornwall writes: "Essentialist male-female demarcations falter when faced with a body or identity which pushes their boundaries."[200] Virginia Ramey Mollenkott is even stronger: "Intersexual people are the best biological evidence we have that the binary gender construct is totally inadequate and is causing injustice and unnecessary suffering."[201]

The use of the intersexed to contest the validity of heteronormativity is a common feature of queer writing. The reason for this, as Butler explains, is that one of the ways compulsory heterosexuality is imposed and perpetuated "is through the cultivation of bodies into discrete sexes."[202] But if the sex binary can be shown to be a needless and oppressive social construction, then heteronormativity is undermined. This subversive strategy can be traced back at least to Foucault's publication of *Herculine Barbin* (1980). As the opening paragraph of his introduction makes clear, Foucault's aim in publishing *The Recently Discovered Memoirs of a Nineteenth-Century French Hermaphrodite* was to show how "the categories of heterosexual and homosexual ... are themselves dependent on a sexually dimorphic conception of the human body."[203] This is why Butler contends that, in editing and publishing Barbin's journals, "Foucault is clearly trying to show how an hermaphroditic or intersexed body implicitly exposes and refutes the regulative strategies of sexual categorization."[204]

THE REALITY OF THE SEX BINARY

As we have seen, such claims misconstrue the challenge that intersex conditions pose to the sex binary. The gonads and genitals of those with even the most ambiguous of conditions "are not ordered to some different sexual end of their own, but are abnormally and/or defectively lacking in the typical functional male or female form, imperfectly related to the

200. Cornwall, *Sex and Uncertainty*, 12.

201. Mollenkott, *Omnigender*, 51; Fausto-Sterling, *Sexing the Body*, 71–73.

202. Butler, "Performative Acts," 524.

203. Marc Lafrance, "The Struggle for True Sex: *Herculine Barbin dite Alexina B* and the Work of Michel Foucault," *Canadian Review of Comparative Literature* 32 (2005): 269n8.

204. Butler, *Gender Trouble*, 130.

ends of male and female sexual organs."[205] Simply put, intersex conditions do not constitute a third natural kind of sex.[206]

While definitive answers to the questions raised by the preceding discussion cannot be provided independently of epistemological commitments (ideally, as we have seen, a critical realist epistemology and, ultimately, an anthropology derived from biblical revelation), the primary contention of this chapter is that, unless one adopts a *radical* (and necessarily self-refuting) social constructionist epistemology, there is no reason to doubt and every reason to affirm that *sex is an objective biological reality that is binary in nature*. In short, there are two and only two sexes.

But can the same be said of gender? What precisely is gender? How is it different from sex? And what is the relationship between sex and gender? These are questions I will take up in the following chapter.

---

205. Alastair Roberts, "Podcast: Intersex," *Alastair's Adversaria* (August 25, 2015), https://alastairadversaria.com/2015/08/25/podcast-intersex.

206. The reason male and female are the only "natural kinds" of sex is because "'natural kinds' are so called because they tell us something about the causal structures of the world." See Caroline New, "Sex and Gender: A Critical Realist Approach," *New Formations* 56 (Autumn 2005): 63; Carrie L. Hull, *The Ontology of Sex: A Critical Inquiry into the Deconstruction and Reconstruction of Categories* (London: Routledge, 2006), 105.

CHAPTER 5

THE INVENTION AND SUBVERSION OF GENDER

What is now called the nature of women is an eminently artificial thing—the result of forced repression in some directions, unnatural stimulation in others.[1]

—John Stuart Mill

There is no "being" behind doing, effecting, becoming; "the doer" is merely a fiction added to the deed—the deed is everything.[2]

—Friedrich Nietzsche

Since the fourteenth century, the English word "gender" has been a common grammatical term. Although there is evidence from as early as the fifteenth century of a sexological application of the term (to refer to either of the two biological forms of a species),[3] this extended use is rare and most instances appear to be either humorous or ironic. During the second half of the twentieth century, however, things changed rather dramatically. In fact, the journey of gender, both linguistically and conceptually, from the late 1950s to

1. John Stuart Mill, *The Subjection of Women* (New York: D. Appleton and Company, 1869), 38–39.

2. Friedrich Wilhelm Nietzsche, *On the Genealogy of Morals*, trans. Walter Kaufmann (New York: Vintage, 1969), 45.

3. *The Merriam-Webster.com Dictionary*, s.v. "gender (n.)," https://www.merriam-webster.com/dictionary/gender.

the present day, is as surprising as it is complex. In some domains, gender can be said to have replaced sex linguistically and eclipsed it conceptually, which has led one researcher to speak of "The Inexorable Rise of Gender and the Decline of Sex."[4] At the same time, gender has also come to be distinguished from sex and, for some, completely disconnected from it. Others have sought to absorb sex into gender, effectively dissolving nature into culture. Without appreciating something of the contours, complexities, and consequences of this journey, it is impossible to understand either the contemporary gender debates or the central claim of transgender theory.

The purpose of this chapter is to trace the main developments in gender theory from the publication of Beauvoir's *The Second Sex* to the work of Judith Butler. In the course of this journey, I will also examine the origin and meaning(s) of several related terms—notably, gender roles and gender identity. The nature of this exercise is primarily descriptive rather than evaluative. In the following chapter, however, I will not only offer an assessment of Butler's proposal but articulate a view of gender as both distinct from sex but inextricably connected to it and necessarily grounded on it.

DISTINGUISHING GENDER AND SEX

GRAMMATICAL ORIGINS

In terms of its etymology, "gender" is a late Middle English term with its roots in the Latin word *genus*, meaning the kind, type, or class of a thing. Some time prior to the fourteenth century, it found its way into English via the Old French word *gendre* (now *genre*).[5] In most Indo-European languages, it is not only nouns, adjectives, or pronouns that refer to sexed beings that take masculine or feminine form (i.e., grammatical gender), but many words for things, concepts, and mental states are masculine or feminine also. The gender of a word, then, is not necessarily associated with the sex (or lack thereof) of the object it denotes. For example, the

4. David Haig, "The Inexorable Rise of Gender and the Decline of Sex: Social Change in Academic Titles, 1945–2001," *Archives of Sexual Behavior* 33 (2004): 87–96.

5. Donald A. Ringe, *From Proto-Indo-European to Proto-Germanic* (Oxford: Oxford University Press, 2006), 61.

German word for "manliness" (*männlichkeit*) is grammatically feminine and the French word for "tree" (*arbre*) is masculine.

In the English language, however, the gender of a word does usually correspond to the sex (or otherwise) of the object denoted by it.[6] Thus, masculine nouns (e.g., boy or ram) and pronouns (e.g., he/him) refer to male humans or animals, feminine nouns (e.g., girl or ewe) and pronouns (e.g., she/her) refer to female humans or animals, and neuter nouns (e.g., rock or house) and pronouns (e.g., it/its) refer to things to which the categories of maleness or femaleness do not apply.

THE RAPID ASCENT OF GENDER

Evidence of dramatic change

As already noted, prior to 1960, extant instances of gender being substituted for sex are scarce. As David Haig's analysis of 1,162,909 scientific article titles published between 1945 and 1959 has shown, only five contained the word "gender"—three in a grammatical sense and two in a sexological sense.[7] Between 1960 and 1980, however, "there was a dramatic increase in the proportion of titles containing sex and/or gender."[8] The main reason for this "was the adoption of gender in the 1970s by feminist scholars as a way of distinguishing 'socially constructed' aspects of male-female differences (gender) from 'biologically determined' aspects (sex)."[9] Then, notes Haig, during the 1980s, "gender began a rapid rise in frequency at the expense of sex" and, as a consequence, gender has come to function as a synonym, even a euphemism, for sex.[10]

6. Connell and Pearse, *Gender*, 9.

7. Haig, "Inexorable Rise," 89. Similarly, in a comprehensive bibliography of 12,000 titles that covered the marriage and family literature from 1900–1964, not a single occurrence of gender was found. See J. Aldous and R. Hill, *International Bibliography of Research in Marriage and the Family Vol. 1: 1900–1964* (Minneapolis: University of Minnesota Press, 1967).

8. Haig, "Inexorable Rise," 90.

9. Haig, "Inexorable Rise," 87.

10. Haig, "Inexorable Rise," 90, 95. This is evident both in popular speech and practice (e.g., gender reveal parties) and on numerous official forms.

The influence of Simone de Beauvoir

What set these changes in motion? In large measure, the story begins with Beauvoir. As we saw in the previous chapter, when she averred that "one is not born, but rather becomes, [a] woman," her point was that no "biological, psychical or economic destiny defines the figure that the human female *takes on in society*."[11] In other words, the distinction she was making was between *given biological sex* (being born female) and *acquired social sex* (becoming a woman). On this view, "the term 'female' designates a fixed and self-identical set of natural corporeal facts ..., and the term 'woman' designates a variety of modes through which those facts acquire cultural meaning."[12] Beauvoir's purpose in making such a distinction, however, was not only analytical but also emancipatory. It enabled her to argue against the view that "social reality was determined by natural reality."[13] Otherwise put, the possession of *female anatomy* did not (and so ought not) dictate any particular *feminine destiny*.

Beauvoir was not the first to make such a distinction or to present such an argument. Since the early part of the twentieth century, a variety of first-wave feminists and post-Freudian psychoanalysts had questioned biological essentialism and the natural determinism it implied.[14] Consequently, by the mid-twentieth century, "anthropologists and sociologists wrote of 'sex roles' to refer to the culturally determined expected behavior of women and men and 'sexual status' to acknowledge that different cultures accorded different rankings to men and women."[15] In fact, in 1949 (the same year that *The Second Sex* first appeared in French), Margaret Mead had posed the question, "How are men and women to think about their maleness and their femaleness in this twentieth century, in which so many of our old ideas must be made new?"[16]

---

11. Beauvoir, *The Second Sex*, 294 (emphasis added).

12. Butler, "Beauvoir's *Second Sex*," 36.

13. Sveinsdóttir, "Metaphysics of Sex and Gender," 48.

14. See, e.g., Rosalind Rosenberg, *Beyond Separate Spheres: Intellectual Roots of Modern Feminism* (New Haven: Yale University Press, 1982); Mari Jo Buhle, *Feminism and Its Discontents: A Century of Struggle* (Cambridge: Harvard University Press, 1998).

15. Joanne Meyerowitz, "A History of 'Gender,' " *American Historical Review* 113 (2008): 1354.

16. Margaret Mead, *Male and Female: A Study of the Sexes in a Changing World* (New York: William Morrow & Co., 1949), 27.

Beauvoir, then, was not the progenitor of this line of thinking. Nor did she coin the terminological distinction between sex and gender. Nevertheless, by arguing with unparalleled rigor that "social reality" need not be determined by "natural reality," while at the same time protesting "against the physical, psychological and intellectual confinement of women,"[17] she successfully challenged the long-held assumption that "women's biological features explained and justified women's place and function within the social sphere."[18] As a result, *she effectively cemented the conceptual distinction between sex and gender*. She thereby provided a vital plank in the case for the social construction of the latter, despite the fact that, at this point in the journey, the notion of "socially constructed sex differences did not yet have a word to connote it."[19]

THE MEN WHO "INVENTED" GENDER

John Money (1921–2006)

In 1955, the missing word—"gender"—was supplied by John Money, a professor of pediatrics and medical psychology at Johns Hopkins University Hospital. The context of Money's linguistic innovation was his treatment of children with intersex conditions (his language was "hermaphroditism").[20] From a series of case studies, he and a number of colleagues came to reject the idea that masculinity and femininity are innate characteristics of males and females, and to embrace "a conception that psychologically, sexuality is undifferentiated at birth and that it becomes differentiated as masculine or feminine in the course of the various experiences of growing up."[21] In 1965, he elaborated on this notion of early psychosexual plasticity as follows:

---

17. Sheila Rowbotham, foreword to Beauvoir, *The Second Sex*, x.

18. Sveinsdóttir, "Metaphysics of Sex and Gender," 48.

19. Meyerowitz, "History of 'Gender,' " 1353.

20. John Money, "Hermaphroditism, Gender and Precocity in Hyperadrenocorticism: Psychologic Findings," *Bulletin of the Johns Hopkins Hospital* 96 (1955): 253–64; "Linguistic Resources and Psychodynamic Theory," *British Journal of Medical Psychology* 28 (1955): 264–66.

21. John Money, J. G. Hampson, and J. L. Hampson, "An Examination of Some Basic Sexual Concepts: The Evidence of Human Hermaphroditism," *Bulletin of the Johns Hopkins Hospital* 97 (1955): 308.

> The condition existing at birth and for several months thereafter is one of psychosexual undifferentiation. Just as in the embryo, morphologic sexual differentiation passes from a plastic stage to one of fixed immutability, so also does psychosexual differentiation become fixed and immutable—so much so, that mankind has traditionally assumed that so strong and fixed a feeling as personal sexual identity must stem from something innate, instinctive, and not subject to postnatal experience and learning. The error of this traditional assumption is that the power and permanence of something learned has been underestimated.[22]

The nature of Money's linguistic innovation was twofold: first, he restricted the language of sex purely to biology and, second, he applied the term "gender role" to what had previously been called "sex role." By "gender role," Money meant "all those things that a person says or does to disclose himself or herself as having the status of boy or man, girl or woman." He further argued that a person's gender role is not determined by their biology but is revealed by their "general mannerisms, behaviors and attitudes; preference in games and recreational interests; spontaneous themes of conversation, content of dreams, ramblings and fantasies; response to oblique surveys and projective tests; evidence of erotic practices and, finally, the person's own responses when asked."[23] In short, *gender role has nothing necessarily to do with biological sex.*

As later writings confirm, Money clearly thought of himself as the man who invented gender, and repeatedly claimed to have coined the term "*gender role,* from which gender identity later became a spin-off."[24] In 1998, Money put it this way:

> In 1955 I coined the term *gender role*. It is defined as *everything* that one says and does to indicate that one is either male or female, or androgyne. The other side of the same coin is gender identity. It

22. John Money, "Psychosexual Differentiation," in *Sex Research, New Developments*, ed. John Money (New York: Holt, Rinehart, and Winston, 1965), 12.

23. Money et al., "An Examination," 302.

24. John Money, "This Week's Citation Classic," *Current Contents* 11 (March 16, 1987): 12, http://garfield.library.upenn.edu/classics1987/A1987G240300001.pdf.

> is defined as the persistence of one's individuality as male, female, or ambivalent, as it is experienced in self-awareness and behavior. Gender identity is the private experience of gender role, and gender role is the public manifestation of gender identity.[25]

The implications of this linguistic innovation, for both expressing human experience and expanding human thought, have proved to be revolutionary. Moreover, Money was clearly cognizant of the power of words to help break new conceptual ground and to validate the experience of those whose biology and psychology do not align.[26]

Robert J. Stoller (1924–1991)

Without wishing to detract from Money's ingenuity, however, it is probably more accurate to see his contribution less in terms of linguistic invention and more as having "popularized a usage that already existed."[27] Part of the evidence for this is that, as early as 1945, American psychologist Madison Bentley had used "gender" to signal "the socialized obverse of sex."[28] Of particular significance is the fact that it was Robert J. Stoller, professor of psychiatry at UCLA Medical School and a researcher at the UCLA Gender Identity Clinic, who first distinguished *gender role* from *gender identity*—"*gender identity* being interpsychic and *gender role* being behavioural and socially prescribed as well as socially and historically stereotyped."[29] This, then, led him to articulate the hypothesis that "the two realms (sex and gender) are not at all inevitably bound in anything like a one-to-one relationship, but each may go in its quite independent

25. John Money, *Sin, Science and Sex Police: Essays on Sexology & Sexosophy* (Amherst, NY: Prometheus Books, 1998), 347.

26. According to Terry Goldie, Money's "obsession with his achievement in establishing that word, *gender*, was about the importance of language in our understanding of bodies and sexuality." See Terry Goldie, *The Man Who Invented Gender: Engaging the Ideas of John Money* (Vancouver: UBC Press, 2014), 8 (emphasis original).

27. Goldie, *Man Who Invented Gender*, 6.

28. Madison Bentley, "Sanity and Hazard in Childhood," *American Journal of Psychology* 58 (1945): 228.

29. Vern L. Bullough, "The Contributions of John Money: A Personal View," *The Journal of Sex Research* 40 (2003): 232 (emphasis added). For Stoller, the advantage of the phrase "gender identity" was that "it clearly refers to one's self-image as regard to belonging to a specific sex" (Robert J. Stoller, "A Contribution to the Study of Gender Identity," *International Journal of Psycho-Analysis* 45 [1964]: 220).

way."[30] This, in turn, allowed Stoller to provide a more thorough account of *transsexualism*, which he defined as "the conviction in a biologically normal person of being a member of the opposite sex."[31] The implication of these insights, at least in Stoller's mind, was that one can not only "speak of the male sex or the female sex, but one can also talk about masculinity and femininity and not necessarily be implying anything about anatomy or physiology."[32]

Therefore, while Stoller clearly followed Money and built on his insights, his contribution to contemporary understandings of gender is not only as important as Money's but, arguably, more enduring.[33] For it was Stoller who parsed out the differences between "gender" ("a term that has psychological or cultural rather than biological connotations"), "gender role" ("the overt behavior one displays in society") and "gender identity" (a person's "knowledge and awareness, whether conscious or unconscious, that one belongs to one sex and not the other").[34] Furthermore, by establishing sex and gender as "two independent orders of knowledge," Stoller not only deepened Money's theory, but identified gender "as a grid of intelligibility with its own dominion of unconscious rules and mechanisms that governed human sexual behavior."[35] This, as we shall see shortly, not only opened the way for an emergent second-wave feminist movement, but effectively "circumscribed the ways in which it was possible to think about gender."[36]

The gender identity paradigm

The significance of Money's initial innovation/popularization ought not to be lost from view, however. In helping to forge a new definition of gender, he not only "discovered or uncovered its possibility," but "used his

30. Robert J. Stoller, *Sex and Gender: The Development of Masculinity and Femininity* (New York: Science House, 1968), vii.

31. Robert J. Stoller, "Male Childhood Transsexualism," *Journal of the American Academy of Child Psychiatry* 7 (1968): 193.

32. Stoller, *Sex and Gender*, ix.

33. This is evident in the definitions given in *DSM*-5's entry on "Gender Dysphoria" (451–59).

34. Stoller, *Sex and Gender*, 9–10.

35. Jemima Repo, *The Biopolitics of Gender* (Oxford: Oxford University Press, 2016), 54, 56.

36. Jennifer Germon, *Gender: A Genealogy of an Idea* (New York: Palgrave MacMillan, 2009), 64.

authority to institute and appoint it."[37] It is little wonder, then, that on the basis of his quantitative analysis of the terminological changes in the titles of academic journal articles, Haig concludes that "the increase in the use of gender, and the associated decline of sex," was "derived by descent and with modification from Money."[38] Furthermore, Money is also frequently credited with having pioneered (what Donna Haraway calls) "the interactionist version of the gender identity paradigm"—that is, one in which "the functionalist mix of biological and social causations made room for a myriad of 'sex/gender differences' research and therapeutic programmes, including surgery, counselling, pedagogy, social services, and so on."[39]

Nevertheless, Money and Stoller's respective contributions should not be played off against each other.[40] Indeed, the "gender identity paradigm" might equally be dubbed the "Money-Stoller paradigm," since from the late 1960s onward feminist writers have routinely made reference to their respective bodies of work, sometimes focusing on one more than the other but often interacting with both jointly.[41]

THE BIOPOLITICS OF THE SEX/GENDER DISTINCTION

The foregoing discussion highlights a point of considerable historical significance: the contemporary concept of gender originated not in the domains of feminism or the social sciences but in the biomedical domain.[42]

---

37. Goldie, *Man Who Invented Gender*, 7.

38. Haig, "Inexorable Rise," 95.

39. Haraway, *Simians, Cyborgs, and Women*, 133.

40. In highlighting the significance of Money and Stoller, the contribution of the German-American endocrinologist and sexologist Harry Benjamin (1885–1986) to the development of "transsexual medicine" should not be overlooked. Indeed, in the late 1940s/early 1950s, Benjamin was already working with transsexuals (Christine Jorgensen being his most famous patient) and publishing in the field. In his magnum opus, *The Transsexual Phenomenon* (New York: The Julian Press, 1966), Benjamin argued that transsexualism could not be cured by psychotherapeutic means. Rather, if requested, transsexuals should be given cross-sex hormones and sex-reassignment surgery in order to change the body to fit the mind.

41. See, e.g., Kate Millett, *Sexual Politics* (New York: Doubleday, 1970); Jessie Bernard, *Women and the Public Interest: Policy and Protest in American Life* (Chicago: Aldine, 1971); Ann Oakley, *Sex, Gender, and Society* (New York: Harper Colophon, 1972), 158–69; Andrea Dworkin, *Woman Hating: A Radical Look at Sexuality* (New York: Plume Penguin Books, 1974), 182; Marcia Yudkin, "Transsexualism and Women: A Critical Perspective," *Feminist Studies* 4, no. 3 (1978): 97–106.

42. Marina Cortez, Paula Gaudenzi, and Ivia Maksud, "Gender: Pathways and Dialogues between Feminist and Biomedical Studies from the 1950s to 1970s," *Physis: Revista de Saúde Coletiva* 29 (2019): 3, http://www.scielo.br/pdf/physis/v29n1/0103-7331-physis-29-01-e290103.pdf.

Consequently, the feminist debates of the 1970s, particularly over the respective roles of biological determinism and social constructionism, all occurred "within discursive fields pre-structured by the gender identity paradigm crystallized in the 1950s and 60s."[43] In addition to this, the Money-Stoller paradigm implicitly embraced a strongly dualistic conception of the mind-body relation: sex being grounded in the body (and so immutable) and gender identity being generated by the mind (and so mutable).

While many feminists later came to reject this paradigm (particularly due to its Cartesianism), it was initially deemed to be an effective way of combating the various forms of biological determinism that were "constantly deployed against feminists in urgent 'sex differences' political struggles."[44] Differentiating gender from sex, then, provided "a way of arguing that social roles were 'culturally constructed' and therefore open to question."[45] For while gender identity and gender roles were distinct, the uniting thought was this: if gender is constructed, it can also be deconstructed!

Diagnosing the problem

Adoption of the Money-Stoller paradigm is evident is Kate Millett's *Sexual Politics* (1970)—the first major feminist work to employ the terminological distinction between sex and gender, and also to credit Money and Stoller with having established it.[46] Accordingly, she writes of "important new research" (meaning Money and Stoller's) that has not only suggested that "the possibilities of innate temperamental differences seem more remote than ever," but has provided "fairly concrete positive evidence of the overwhelmingly cultural character of gender." The major sociopolitical implication of this, as Millett saw it, was that there is "insufficient evidence for the thesis that the present social distinctions of patriarchy (status, role, temperament) are physical in origin."[47]

---

43. Haraway, *Simians, Cyborgs, and Women*, 133.

44. Germon, *Gender*, 134.

45. Joan Wallach Scott, "Gender: Still a Useful Category of Analysis?," *Diogenes* 225 (2010): 79.

46. Millett, *Sexual Politics*, 29–31.

47. Millett, *Sexual Politics*, 29.

"Patriarchy" was the name that Millett (and others) gave to the social system that, in Beauvoir's thought, defined man as "the One" (the "essential") and woman as "the Other" (the "inessential").[48] It was also regarded as the cause of the general sense of emptiness (felt, at least, by many American women) that Betty Friedan called "the problem that has no name."[49] For Millett, however, it was nothing less than "the institution whereby that half of the populace which is female is controlled by that half which is male." Patriarchy, she believed, was governed by a twofold principle: that "male shall dominate female" and that "elder male shall dominate younger." It was also seen to express itself in a range of "cruelties and barbarities"—notably, suttee, foot-binding, veiling, purdah, genital mutilation, involuntary marriage, child marriage, concubinage and prostitution.[50] In short, patriarchy "rewarded men for being men and punished women for being women."[51]

For Millett, then, the goal of sexual revolution was clear: "to bring the institution of patriarchy to an end, and the traditional socialization by which it is upheld." This was the only way to liberate "half the race from its immemorial subordination."[52] Furthermore, freedom would require not only the "abolition of sex role and the complete economic independence of women," but also a "re-examination of the traits categorized as 'masculine' and 'feminine,' with a reassessment of their human desirability."[53]

Dismantling the system

While in furious agreement with Millett's diagnosis, other feminist thinkers of the period wished to follow her prescription to (what they saw as) its logical conclusion: *androgyny*—that is, the development of an equal blend of both masculine and feminine traits in all people.[54] Shulamith

48. Beauvoir, *The Second Sex*, 6–7.

49. Betty Friedan, *The Feminine Mystique* (New York: Norton, 1963).

50. Millett, *Sexual Politics*, 25, 46.

51. Elaine Storkey, *Created or Constructed?: The Great Gender Debate* (Carlisle: Paternoster, 2000), 28.

52. Millett, *Sexual Politics*, 62, 363.

53. Millett, *Sexual Politics*, 62.

54. See, e.g., Carolyn G. Heilbrun, *Toward A Recognition of Androgyny* (New York: Knopf, 1973); June Singer, *Androgyny: Toward a New Theory of Sexuality* (New York: Anchor, 1976); Ann Ferguson, "Androgyny as an Ideal for Human Development," in *Feminism and Philosophy*, ed. Mary

Firestone, for instance, had already gestured in this direction, declaring that the "end goal of feminist revolution must be, unlike that of the first feminist movement, not just the elimination of male *privilege* but of the sex *distinction* itself: genital differences between human beings would no longer matter culturally."[55] Andrea Dworkin was even more explicit: because "'man' and 'woman' are fictions, caricatures, cultural constructs," the best way to bring an end to "gynocide" (the destruction of women) is to "accomplish the transformation into androgyny."[56] For Gayle Rubin, the realization of such a goal would require a complete demolition of the entire "sex/gender system"—that is, that "set of arrangements by which a society transforms biological sexuality into products of human activity, and in which these transformed sexual needs are satisfied."[57] Accordingly,

> the feminist movement must dream of even more than the elimination of the oppression of women. It must dream of the elimination of obligatory sexualities and sex roles. The dream I find most compelling is one of an androgynous and genderless (though not sexless) society, in which one's sexual anatomy is irrelevant to who one is, what one does, and with whom one makes love.[58]

According to Rubin, the conviction behind such thinking was that gender identity is not in fact "an expression of natural differences" but "the suppression of natural similarities." That is, discrete gender identity formation was not a *spontaneously occurring phenomenon* but something that was *achieved by means of repression*—"in men, of whatever is the local version of 'feminine' traits; in women, of the local definition of 'masculine' traits." Consequently, she argued, "a thoroughgoing feminist revolution would liberate more than women. It would liberate forms of sexual expression, and it would liberate human personality from the straightjacket of gender."[59]

Vetterling-Braggin, Frederick A. Ellison, and Jane English (Totowa, NJ: Littlefield, Adams, 1977), 45–69.

55. Shulamith Firestone, *The Dialectic of Sex: The Case for Feminist Revolution* (New York: Farrar, Straus and Giroux, 1970), 11 (emphasis original).

56. Dworkin, *Woman Hating*, 174, 191.

57. Gayle Rubin, "The Traffic in Women: Notes on the Political Economy of Sex," in *Toward an Anthropology of Women*, ed. Rayna R. Reiter (New York: Monthly Review Press, 1975), 159.

58. Rubin, "Traffic in Women," 204.

59. Rubin, "Traffic in Women," 180, 200.

In the journey of gender, then, Rubin can be seen to be taking a significant step beyond Beauvoir. But she goes further still. For her, gender is not only a needless "identification with one sex; it also entails that sexual desire be directed toward the other sex." Thus, the suppression of homosexuality (and likewise the oppression of homosexuals) is "a product of the same system whose rules and relations oppress women."[60] While she was by no means the first to make such a claim, Rubin was here forging a link between the feminist and homosexual (especially lesbian) revolutions.[61] As we shall see shortly, this connection would become a feature of (as well as a source of confusion and conflict within) the feminist movement of the 1980s.[62] It is nonetheless a connection that persists to the present day.[63]

Changing the terms of the gender binary

During the late 1970s and early 1980s, the attempt to liberate women from the constraints of traditional femininity "represented a conscious, sustained, and explicit effort to change the terms of the gender binary."[64] Indeed, if gender is nothing more than a cultural construction (or worse, an oppressive patriarchal imposition), it is not surprising that many feminists were deeply suspicious of it, "especially when it played a part in subordinating women."[65] In short, while sex might need to remain (provided its significance was seen as minimal), *gender needed to be either overhauled or overthrown.*

For the majority of second-wave feminists, then, the problem was that "the history of an almost universal force called the patriarchy had compelled the division of humans into male and female, with all aspects of our cultures the products of that compulsory separation."[66] The solution, therefore, was major gender reform. Germain Greer helpfully sums up this stream of feminist thought:

---

60. Rubin, "Traffic in Women," 180.

61. See Jill Johnston, *Lesbian Nation: The Feminist Solution* (New York: Simon and Schuster, 1973).

62. For a helpful discussion of these tensions, see Patricia Elliot, *Debates in Transgender, Queer, and Feminist Theory: Contested Sites* (Abingdon: Ashgate, 2010), 1–30.

63. Ilana Eloit and Clare Hemmings, "Lesbian Ghosts Feminism: An Introduction," *Feminist Theory* 20 (2019): 351–60.

64. Joy Ladin, "The Genesis of Gender," *Tikkun* 30, no. 3 (2015): 48.

65. Meyerowitz, "History of 'Gender,' " 1355.

66. Goldie, *Man Who Invented Gender*, 6.

> Masculinity is to maleness as femininity is to femaleness. That is to say that maleness is the natural condition, the sex if you like, and masculinity is the cultural construct, the gender. Where feminists once talked of sex discrimination, they now usually refer to gender roles, because the cultural construct is what can and should be changed; sex, as a biological given, is less susceptible.[67]

But, as we are about to see, other feminist thinkers were far from happy with such an understanding.

DISCONNECTING GENDER FROM SEX

RETHINKING SECOND-WAVE FEMINISM

Due, in part, to the impact of post-structuralism and post-colonialism on feminist thought (in particular, the challenge put to the notion that there is "some golden nugget of womanness all women have as women"), the path pioneered by Millett, Firestone, Rubin, and others was increasingly problematized throughout the 1980s.[68] The main concern was this: by distinguishing gender from sex, and then shifting the focus from sex to gender, second-wave feminists had simply replaced a *natural* form of categorization with a *social* form of categorization.[69] These changes, writes Elaine Storkey, inadvertently "opened up a different form of absolutism. Cultural roles, patterns of learning and socially imposed norms became, rather than biology, the new constituents of gender identity."[70]

By reifying gender in this way, feminists appeared to have locked themselves into a parallel binary system that was just as oppressive as the one they were trying to escape. Furthermore, by assuming that sex difference was more or less immutable, "the essentialism inherent in the categories man and woman and male and female was left unexamined."[71] This omission was a particular sticking point for some lesbian feminists. Indeed,

67. Germaine Greer, *The Whole Woman* (London: Doubleday, 1999), 288.

68. Elizabeth V. Spelman, *Inessential Woman: Problems of Exclusion in Feminist Thought* (Boston: Beacon, 1988), 159. Her broader protest was against white, middle-class bias in feminist theory.

69. Elaine Graham, *Making the Difference: Gender, Personhood and Theology* (London: Mowbray, 1995), 124.

70. Storkey, *Created or Constructed?*, 42.

71. Germon, *Gender*, 86.

the French theorist Monique Wittig not only made the provocative claim that "lesbians are not women,"[72] but even went so far as to suggest that

> our survival demands that we contribute all our strength to the destruction of the class of women within which men appropriate women. This can be accomplished only by the destruction of heterosexuality as a social system which is based on the oppression of women by men and which produces the doctrine of the difference between the sexes to justify this oppression.[73]

At the same time, the goal of androgyny also came in for heavy criticism.[74] According to psychologist Sandra Bem (who in the early 1980s had been one of androgyny's chief proponents),[75] the central problem was that it "focuses more on the individual's being both masculine and feminine than on the culture's having created the concepts of masculinity and femininity in the first place. Hence androgyny can legitimately be said to reproduce precisely the gender polarization that it seeks to undercut."[76]

QUE(E)RYING GENDER

Reconceptualizing gender: De Lauretis

Not surprisingly, then, by the mid-1980s feminist scholars were becoming increasingly convinced that the Money-Stoller paradigm had "now become a limitation, something of a liability to feminist thought." Indeed, far from helping the cause of women's liberation, it seemed to tie feminist thought "to the terms of Western patriarchy itself," thus imprisoning

---

72. Monique Wittig, "The Straight Mind," in *The Straight Mind and Other Essays* (Boston: Beacon, 1992), 32. Her argument is that "what makes a woman is a specific social relation to a man, a relation which implies personal and physical obligation as well as economic obligation ... a relation which lesbians escape by refusing to become or stay heterosexual" ("One Is Not Born a Woman," 54).

73. Wittig, "One Is Not Born a Woman," 54.

74. See the list of criticisms (which includes its "implicitly dualistic" and "essentially apolitical" nature) in Graham, *Making the Difference*, 20–22.

75. Sandra Lipsitz Bem, "The Measurement of Psychological Androgyny," *Journal of Consulting and Clinical Psychology* 42 (1974): 155–62; "On the Utility of Alternative Procedures for Assessing Psychological Androgyny," *Journal of Consulting and Clinical Psychology* 45 (1977): 196–205.

76. Sandra Lipsitz Bem, *The Lenses of Gender: Transforming the Debate on Sexual Inequality* (New Haven: Yale University Press, 1993), 125. The shift in Bem's views is evident in her "Gender Schema Theory: A Cognitive Account of Sex Typing," *Psychological Review* 88 (1981): 354–64.

it "within a conceptual frame of a universal sex opposition."[77] To address this problem, Teresa de Lauretis (who coined the term "queer theory") argued that

> we need a notion of gender that is not so bound up with sexual difference as to be virtually coterminous with it and such that, on the one hand, gender is assumed to derive unproblematically from sexual difference while, on the other, gender can be subsumed in sexual differences as an effect of language, or as pure imaginary—nothing to do with the real.[78]

In short, for women to be released from "the patriarchal contract," the link between gender and sexual difference needed to be "unraveled and deconstructed."[79]

But how might this be done?

De Lauretis's suggestion involved reconceptualizing gender not as "a property of bodies or something originally existent in human beings," but as "'the set of effects produced in bodies, behaviors, and social relations,' in Foucault's words, by the deployment of 'a complex political technology.' "[80] For de Lauretis, then, it is imperative to move away from the idea that gender is "the representation of each individual in terms of a particular social relation which pre-exists the individual and is predicated on the conceptual and rigid (structural) opposition of two biological sexes." It needs to be reconceptualized as a form of personal, cultural, and rhetorical production "whose status (truth value, epistemological or moral weight, etc.) and degree of 'reality' (objective to subjective) vary according to the social hierarchy of discourses and representations."[81]

---

77. Teresa de Lauretis, *Technologies of Gender: Essays on Theory, Film, and Fiction* (Bloomington: Indiana University Press, 1987), 1–2.

78. De Lauretis, *Technologies of Gender*, 2.

79. De Lauretis, *Technologies of Gender*, 17, 2.

80. De Lauretis, *Technologies of Gender*, 3. The quote is from Foucault's *History of Sexuality*, 1:127..

81. De Lauretis, *Technologies of Gender*, 5, 96. See further Sarah Gamble, "Gender and Transgender Criticism," in *Criticism in the 21st Century*, ed. Julian Wolfreys, 2nd ed. (Edinburgh: Edinburgh University Press, 2015), 29–31.

Doing gender: West and Zimmerman

Coming from an adjacent angle, Candice West and Don Zimmerman sought "to advance a new understanding of gender as a routine accomplishment embedded in everyday interaction."[82] In this conception, gender "is not simply an aspect of *what one is*, but, more fundamentally, it is something *that one does*, and does recurrently, in interaction with others."[83] In short, *action* (specially, social interaction over time) produces *being*. Gender is thus "an achieved property of situated conduct" which, at a societal level, is enacted in a variety of cultural forms and institutional frameworks (e.g., sex-segregated sports). In fact, it is the relationship between a person's sex category and their enacted gender that "links the institutional and interactional levels, a coupling that legitimates social arrangements based on sex category and reproduces their asymmetry in face-to-face interaction."[84]

However, precisely because it is "the interactional validation of those distinctions that confers upon them their sense of 'naturalness' and 'rightness,' " the institutional forces that effectively maintain the distinctions between women and men are not irresistible. This is important, for what it means is that by challenging "existing arrangements" (like gender norms and expectations) social change becomes possible, provided that (West and Zimmerman were quick to add) these changes are "pursued *both* at the institutional and cultural level of sex category *and* at the interactional level of gender." Therefore, if the connection between sex category and gender relationship can be recast (and effectively decoupled), and gender itself reconceptualized (so that it no longer "produces, reproduces, and legitimates the choices and limits that are predicated on sex category"), then it is not only possible for gender to be *done differently* but for "a new perspective on the entire network of gender relations" to be developed.[85]

82. Candice West and Don H. Zimmerman, "Doing Gender," *Gender & Society* 1 (1987): 125. An earlier version of West and Zimmerman's article had been presented to the American Sociological Association in 1977. They then spent the next decade refining it and trying to get it published. See Candice West and Don H. Zimmerman, "Accounting for Doing Gender," *Gender and Society* 23 (2009): 112.

83. West and Zimmerman, "Doing Gender," 140 (emphasis added).

84. West and Zimmerman, "Doing Gender," 126, 147.

85. West and Zimmerman, "Doing Gender," 140, 146–47 (emphasis added).

DISSOLVING SEX INTO GENDER

JUDITH BUTLER'S INNOVATION

We have already begun to engage with the gender theorist who is best known for the kind of radical recasting and reconceptualizing of gender proposed by de Lauretis, West, and Zimmerman: Judith Butler.[86] Due to the impact of her thought on all subsequent gender theorizing (including trans theory), a more thoroughgoing exposition of her work is both appropriate and, indeed, necessary at this point.

In contrast to the view that gender roles and identities are cultural manifestations of biological givens, Butler claims that cultural assumptions about gender "determine our conception of biological sex as the origin of gender identity."[87] She thus calls into question the idea of an innate or precultural ground for gender identity and argues instead that gender is "tenuously constituted in time, instituted in an exterior space through a *stylized repetition of acts*."[88] Consequently, a gender identity is nothing more than "a constructed identity, a performative accomplishment." Moreover, because "there is no preexisting identity by which an act or attribute might be measured," there are "no true or false, real or distorted acts of gender, and the postulation of a true gender identity would be revealed as a regulatory fiction."[89] In Sartrean terms, there is no gendered *essence* that precedes gendered *existence*. Or in Butler's own terms, "there is no 'one' who takes on a gender norm. On the contrary, this citation of the gender norm is necessary in order to qualify as a 'one,' to become viable as a 'one.' "[90]

---

86. Curiously, Butler nowhere references West and Zimmerman in her writings, despite clearly playing on their article title in the title of her book *Undoing Gender* (New York & London: Routledge, 2004), and de Lauretis appears only once in an endnote in *Gender Trouble* (214n49) and in two endnotes in *Bodies That Matter* (202n33 and 204n6).

87. Turner, *Queer Theory*, 109

88. Butler, *Gender Trouble*, 191.

89. Butler, *Gender Trouble*, 192.

90. Butler, *Bodies that Matter*, 177.

INFLUENCES ON BUTLER'S THOUGHT

Butler's indebtedness to the existentialism of Sartre and Beauvoir is everywhere apparent in her writings.[91] Her engagement with them, however, is far from uncritical. In fact, she complains that there are "many occasions in both Sartre's and Beauvoir's work where 'the body' is figured as a mute facticity, anticipating some meaning that can be attributed only by a transcendent consciousness, understood in Cartesian terms as radically immaterial."[92] She also charges that Beauvoir's theory of embodiment is fatally "limited by the uncritical reproduction of the Cartesian distinction between freedom and the body," a distinction she believes is irredeemably "phallogocentric."[93]

By way of contrast, Butler is more favorably disposed toward Maurice Merleau-Ponty's exposition of the phenomenological tradition with its stress on "the *meanings* that embodied existence assumes in the context of lived experience."[94] She is particularly impressed by its "doctrine of constitution" which holds (on the one hand) that "social agents *constitute* social reality through language, gesture, and all manner of symbolic social signs," and yet (on the other) takes "the social agent as an *object* rather than the subject of constitutive acts." She nonetheless finds fault with phenomenology for assuming "the existence of a choosing and constituting agent prior to language."[95]

Butler's familiarity with (what William Turner calls) "Feminist uses of Foucault" is likewise evident throughout her work.[96] Indeed, her description of *Gender Trouble* as "*a feminist genealogy* of the category of woman"

---

91. See, e.g., Geoff Boucher, "Judith Butler's Postmodern Existentialism: A Critical Analysis," *Philosophy Today* 48 (2004): 355–69; Kathleen Lennon, "Judith Butler and the Sartrean Imaginary," *Sartre Studies International* 23 (2017): 22–37.

92. Butler, *Gender Trouble*, 164; see also 196n21.

93. Butler, *Gender Trouble*, 17. "Phallogocentrism" is a portmanteau word coined by Jacques Derrida that first appeared in his "Le Facteur de la verite," *Poetique* 21 (1975): 96–147; trans. Willis Domingo et al., "The Purveyor of Truth," *Graphesis: Perspectives in Literature and Philosophy, Yale French Studies* 52 (1975): 31–113. It is a blend of "phallocentrism" (which refers to the masculine point of view) and "logocentrism" (which refers to the meaning-assigning role of language).

94. Butler, "Performative Acts," 520 (emphasis original). See further Maurice Merleau-Ponty, "The Body in its Sexual Being," ch. 5 in *The Phenomenology of Perception*, trans. Colin Smith (Boston: Routledge and Kegan Paul, 1962), 154–73.

95. Butler, "Performative Acts," 519 (emphasis original).

96. Turner, *Queer Theory*, 84, 109.

is overtly Foucauldian.[97] The many connections between Foucault's oeuvre and the larger project of second-wave feminism are, of course, well-recognized: both, for example, "bring to the fore the crucial role of discourse in its capacity to produce and sustain hegemonic power."[98] Butler, however, also sees a significant difference between feminism and Foucault:

> Where feminist analysis takes the category of sex and, thus, according to him, the binary restriction on gender, as its point of departure, Foucault understands his own project to be an inquiry into how the category of "sex" and sexual difference are constructed within discourse as necessary features of bodily identity.[99]

Moreover, this construction is far from benign. "To be sexed, for Foucault, is to be subjected to a set of social regulations," which not only operates as "the formative principle of one's sex, gender, pleasures, and desires," but also functions as "the hermeneutic principle of self-interpretation." This highlights Foucault's basic problem with second-wave feminism: because the category of sex is inevitably regulative, "any analysis which makes that category presuppositional uncritically extends and further legitimates that regulative strategy as a power/knowledge regime."[100] Butler agrees: second-wave feminism had not only reified gender, it had assumed an objective, prediscursive, and (inherently) oppressive notion of sex. By so doing, it had needlessly constrained "the very cultural possibilities that feminism is supposed to open up."[101]

THE LOGIC OF BUTLER'S THOUGHT

Decoupling sex and gender

In terms of the logic of her gender theory, *Butler's first step is to decouple sex and gender* (or, in her mind, expose the lack of inherent connection between them). Taking Beauvoir's dictum as her starting point, she insists

---

97. Butler, *Gender Trouble*, 9 (emphasis original).

98. Irene Diamond and Lee Quinby, eds., *Introduction to Feminism and Foucault: Reflections on Resistance* (Boston: Northeastern University Press, 1988), x.

99. Butler, *Gender Trouble*, 130.

100. Butler, *Gender Trouble*, 130.

101. Butler, *Gender Trouble*, 201.

that "the sex/gender distinction implies a radical heteronomy of natural bodies and constructed genders with the consequence that 'being' female and 'being' a woman are two very different sorts of being." She then argues that if the distinction is consistently applied, being a woman is only "one cultural interpretation of being female," and the female body is thereby revealed as "the arbitrary locus of the gender 'woman.' "[102] Early in *Gender Trouble* she expresses it this way: "When the constructed status of gender is theorized as radically independent of sex, gender itself becomes a free-floating artifice, with the consequence that *man* and *masculine* might just as easily signify a female body as a male one, and *woman* and *feminine* a male body as easily as a female one."[103]

This leads Butler to two conclusions. The first is that there is no reason why the same body, at different points, could not become "the locus of other constructions of gender."[104] In short, gender is *fluid*. The second is that even if sex could be shown to be "unproblematically binary" (which she disputes), "there is no reason to assume that genders ought also to remain as two."[105] In short, gender is *diverse*.

Displacing sex by gender

Having decoupled sex and gender, *Butler's next step is to displace sex by gender*. As noted in the previous chapter, the very concept of "sex-as-matter, sex-as-instrument-of-cultural signification" is, for her, really only "a discursive formation that acts as a naturalized foundation for the nature/culture distinction and the strategies of domination that that distinction supports."[106] One implication of this is that gender should not be thought of "merely as the cultural inscription of meaning on a pregiven sex"; rather, it is "the very apparatus of production whereby the sexes themselves are established." Otherwise put, "gender is not to culture as sex is to nature; gender is also the discursive/cultural means by which 'sexed nature' or 'a natural sex' is produced and established as 'prediscursive,'

102. Butler, "Beauvoir's *Second Sex*," 35.

103. Butler, *Gender Trouble*, 10 (emphasis original).

104. Butler, "Beauvoir's *Second Sex*," 35.

105. Butler, *Gender Trouble*, 10.

106. Butler, *Gender Trouble*, 47–48.

prior to culture."[107] Gender, then, supplants sex; for, ultimately, there is no sex, only gender. In *Bodies That Matter*, Butler explains it this way:

> If gender consists of the social meanings that sex assumes, then sex does not *accrue* social meanings as additive properties, but rather *is replaced by* the social meanings it takes on; sex is relinquished in the course of that assumption, and gender emerges, not as a term in a continued relationship of opposition to sex, but as the term which absorbs and displaces "sex."[108]

This does not mean that the body's sex is nonexistent, but simply that it is inaccessible, incomprehensible, and unutterable apart from notions of gender—so much so that what we think of as "sex" is revealed "to have been gender all along."[109]

The construction of sex via gender

All of this highlights the significant epistemological difference between second-wave feminist theory (as represented by Rubin) and third-wave feminist theory (as represented by Butler)—a difference that is largely due to the influence of poststructuralism (especially Derridean deconstruction) on feminist intellectuals.[110] David Halperin captures the difference this way: "According to Rubin, human societies begin with sexed bodies and produce gender. According to Butler, human societies begin with gender and impose it on human bodies as sex."[111] This is why it makes no sense for Butler "to define gender as the cultural interpretation of sex"; for, to her mind, "sex itself is a gendered category."[112] As Sara Salih, summarizing Butler's thought, writes: "All bodies are gendered from the beginning of

---

107. Butler, *Gender Trouble*, 10–11.

108. Butler, *Bodies That Matter*, xiv (emphasis original).

109. Butler, *Gender Trouble*, 12. See further Daniel R. Patterson, *Reforming a Theology of Gender: Constructive Reflections on Judith Butler and Queer Theory* (Eugene, OR: Cascade, 2022), 105–6.

110. See further Susan Archer Mann and Douglas J. Huffman, "The Decentering of Second Wave Feminism and the Rise of the Third Wave," *Science & Society* 69 (2005): 56–91; Joan Wallach Scott, "Deconstructing Equality-versus-Difference: Or, the Uses of Poststructuralist Theory for Feminism," *Feminist Studies* 14 (1988): 32–50.

111. David M. Halperin, "Sex/Sexuality/Sexual Classification," in *Critical Terms for The Study of Gender*, ed. C. R. Stimpson and G. Herdt (Chicago: University of Chicago Press, 2014), 452.

112. Butler, *Gender Trouble*, 11.

their social existence (and there is no existence that is not social), which means that there is no 'natural body' that pre-exists cultural inscription."[113] In short, gender is constructed first; sex is constructed via gender.

BUTLER'S NOTION OF PERFORMATIVITY

How, then, is gender constructed? Butler's answer is that gender is "performatively constituted."[114] But what exactly does this mean and how is it achieved? Her answer is twofold: gender is (1) *discursively constructed in language* and (2) *dramatically reiterated in life*. We shall briefly explore each of these ideas in turn.

The discursive construction of gender

Taking Wittig's claim (that "there is a plasticity of the real to language: language has a plastic action upon the real"[115]) as her starting point, Butler contends that language shapes bodies through a variety of illocutionary acts, which, when repeated, "become entrenched practices and, ultimately, institutions."[116] As she makes clear in both *Bodies That Matter* (1993) and a 1994 interview, "Gender as Performance,"[117] her particular understanding of this interplay derives from the "Speech Act Theory" of J. L. Austin and John Searle, and also from Jacques Derrida's notion of "citationality" or "iterability."[118] The result is a view of gender performativity that sees it "as the reiterative and citational practice by which discourse produces the effects that it names."[119] Put more simply, it is not that *gender does language* but that *language does gender*.[120] So when a child is declared to be a "girl," the very use of "the term or, rather, its symbolic power, governs the

113. Salih, *Judith Butler*, 62.

114. Butler, *Gender Trouble*, 33.

115. Wittig, "The Mark of Gender," 4.

116. Butler, *Gender Trouble*, 158.

117. Judith Butler, "Gender as Performance: An Interview with Judith Butler," *Radical Philosophy: A Journal of Socialist and Feminist Philosophy* 67 (Summer, 1994): 32–39.

118. See John Langshaw Austin, *How to Do Things with Words* (Cambridge: Harvard University Press, 1955); John Searle, *Speech Acts: An Essay in the Philosophy of Language* (Cambridge: Cambridge University Press, 1969); Jacques Derrida, "Signature Event Context" ("Signature Evénement Contexte"), in *A Derrida Reader: Between the Blinds*, ed. Peggy Kamuf (New York: Columbia University Press, 1999), 80–111.

119. Butler, *Gender Trouble*, xii.

120. Salih, *Judith Butler*, 64.

formation of a corporeally enacted femininity."[121] There is, then, no such thing as pre-discursive gender; gender is an effect of language, not its cause.[122]

But what kind of effect? Butler contends that gender is "an ideal which is constituted but which *does not exist*."[123] In other words, it is a linguistic artifice, an ontological illusion conjured up by the performative powers of discourse. Consequently, "If the inner truth of gender is a fabrication and if a true gender is a fantasy instituted and inscribed on the surface of bodies, then it seems that genders can be neither true nor false, but are only produced as the truth effects of a discourse of primary and stable identity."[124]

In sum, gender has neither a priori nor a posteriori actuality. As a result, "the psychoanalytic notion of gender identification is constituted by a fantasy of a fantasy."[125]

The dramatic reiteration of gender

The same can be said of *gendered acts*—the dramatic reiterations of gender in daily life. Like the linguistic construction of gender, the "doing" of gender, for Butler, is the recitation of "a corporeal style, an 'act,' as it were, which is both intentional and performative, where 'performative' suggests a dramatic and contingent construction of meaning."[126] This leads her to the controversial conclusion that "all gender is like drag, or is drag."[127] Her reasoning is this: "*In imitating gender, drag implicitly reveals the imitative structure of gender itself—as well as its contingency.*" Gender is thus "a parodic repetition that exposes the phantasmatic effect of abiding identity as a politically tenuous construction."[128] Put differently, "there is neither an 'essence' that gender expresses or externalizes nor an objective ideal to which gender aspires." Rather, it is repeated *acts* of gender that create

121. Butler, *Bodies That Matter*, 177.

122. Salih, *Judith Butler*, 64.

123. Butler, *Bodies That Matter*, 215n11 (emphasis added).

124. Butler, *Gender Trouble*, 186.

125. Butler, *Gender Trouble*, 188.

126. Butler, *Gender Trouble*, 177.

127. Butler, *Bodies That Matter*, 85.

128. Butler, *Gender Trouble*, 187 (emphasis original), 192.

the *idea* of gender, and with it a "belief in its necessity and naturalness." But Butler is clear that "without those acts, there would be no gender at all. Gender is, thus, a construction that regularly conceals its genesis."[129]

It follows from this that gender is not a given reality and that

> In the place of an original identification which serves as a determining cause, gender identity might be reconceived as a personal/cultural history of received meanings subject to a set of imitative practices which refer laterally to other imitations and which, jointly, construct the illusion of a primary and interior gendered self or parody the mechanism of that construction.[130]

BUTLER'S UNDERSTANDING OF GENDER IDENTITY

What, then, remains of gender identity? As we have seen, the notion of a *gendered self* is, for Butler, a "fictive production," for gender identity is grounded on "the stylized repetition of acts through time and not a seemingly seamless identity." Moreover, because of the "arbitrary relation between such acts," as well as their "internally discontinuous" nature, what they reveal is "the temporal and contingent groundlessness of this 'ground.' "[131] This view both closes the door on any possibility of "naturalized or essentialist gender identities," and opens the door to a person having "a fluidity of identities" with "the performative possibilities for proliferating gender configurations outside the restricting frames of masculinist domination and compulsory heterosexuality."[132]

Yet it is not only the stability of gender identity that Butler seeks to challenge; *identity itself is subverted*—as the subtitle of *Gender Trouble* (i.e., *Feminism and the Subversion of Identity*) indicates. For just as "gender produces the misnomer of a prediscursive 'sex,' "[133] so it exposes the illusion of a prediscursive "I."[134] This is a consistent theme throughout Butler's

129. Butler, "Performative Acts," 273.

130. Butler, *Gender Trouble*, 188; Butler, "Performative Acts," 273.

131. Butler, *Gender Trouble*, 33, 192.

132. Butler, *Gender Trouble*, 188, 192–93.

133. Butler, *Bodies That Matter*, xv.

134. Butler, *Gender Trouble*, 195. This point is crucial for Butler. Gendered acts are "not performed by a subject"; rather, it is their repetition that "*enables* a subject and *constitutes* the temporal condition for the subject" (*Bodies That Matter*, 95, emphasis added).

oeuvre. Thus, toward the end of *Gender Trouble,* and echoing Nietzsche, she writes: "There need not be a 'doer behind the deed' "; rather "the 'doer' is variably constructed in and through the deed."[135] In *Bodies That Matter*, she likewise asserts that the idea of a subject who precedes or activates its "various identifications" is nothing more than "a grammatical fiction."[136] On the final page of *The Psychic Life of Power*, she similarly avers that "there appears to be no 'one' without ambivalence, which is to say that the fictive redoubling necessary to become a self rules out the possibility of strict identity."[137] And in *Giving an Account of Oneself*, she maintains that "The 'I' is always to some extent dispossessed by the social conditions of its emergence."[138]

Furthermore, just as there is no "doer *behind* the deed," so there is no doer *beyond* the deed: "the 'I' neither precedes *nor follows* the process of this gendering, but emerges only within and as the matrix of gender relations themselves."[139] Thus, the question posed at the beginning of *Gender Trouble*—"To what extent do regulatory practices of gender formation and division constitute identity, the internal coherence of the subject, indeed, the self-identical status of the person?"[140]—has its answer: the identity constituted by one's gendered acts (and, for Butler, all acts are gendered) is not just ephemeral but, ultimately, chimerical. As Butler confirms, "what the person 'is,' and, indeed, what gender 'is,' is always relative to the constructed relations in which it is determined"; that is, "gender does not denote a substantive being."[141]

---

135. Butler, *Gender Trouble*, 195.

136. Butler, *Bodies That Matter*, 63.

137. Judith Butler, *The Psychic Life of Power: Theories in Subjection* (Stanford: Stanford University Press, 1997), 198.

138. Judith Butler, *Giving an Account of Oneself* (New York: Fordham University Press, 2005), 8.

139. Butler, *Bodies That Matter*, xvi (emphasis added).

140. Butler, *Gender Trouble*, 23.

141. Butler, *Gender Trouble*, 14.

CONCLUDING REFLECTIONS

The journey of gender (which by no means ends with Butler) is both a part and a result of a much larger series of developments in Western intellectual and civilizational history.[142] Its beginnings can be traced to the seventeenth century (at least) and its watershed moments are typically characterized as a series of *turns*: for example, the *subjective* turn (Descartes), the *expressivist* turn (Rousseau), the *autonomous* turn (Kant), the *economic* turn (Marx), the *linguistic* turn (Wittgenstein), the *psychological* turn (Freud), the *existential* turn (Sartre), the *poststructural* turn (Derrida), the *postmodern* turn (Foucault),[143] and the *queer* turn (Butler). Although it has not been my purpose to sketch this larger story, several observations are in order at this point.

First, it is generally recognized that it was the turn toward subjectivity and the self, initiated by Descartes, that led to the subsequent turns and effectively sowed the seeds of the modern crisis of identity.[144] Descartes, of course, could not have predicted (and nor should he be blamed for) all that has happened to *the self* in subsequent centuries—especially as several of the *turns* have been explicitly anti-Cartesian.[145] Nevertheless, it is not claiming too much to say that the zeitgeist of the contemporary West (with its expressive individualism and culture of narcissism) is an outworking of the attempt to prove "the objectivity of our experience and knowledge from the first-person standpoint."[146] Nor is it surprising that if one "begins from the subjective self, one ends by losing any reason for thinking there is a subjective self."[147]

---

142. See, e.g., James H. Billington, *Fire in the Minds of Men: Origins of the Revolutionary Faith* (New York: Basic Books, 1980), 482–503; Trueman, *Rise and Triumph*, 35–71.

143. Although Foucault disavowed the label "postmodernist," by rejecting the Baconian idea that knowledge produces power, and insisting instead that "power produces knowledge" and that it is those who are in power (whether social, political, educational, or ideological) who decide what is and is not genuine "knowledge," he affirmed what many would see as the fundamental postmodern claim. See, e.g., Foucault, *Discipline and Punish*, 27.

144. Robert C. Solomon, *Continental Philosophy since 1750: The Rise and Fall of the Self* (Oxford: Oxford University Press, 1988), 5; Trueman, *Rise and Triumph*, 57.

145. We have seen this in Butler, but the roots of her protest stem from Nietzsche. See Friedrich Wilhelm Nietzsche, *Beyond Good and Evil*, trans. Walter Kaufmann (New York: Vintage, 1989), 66–67.

146. Charles Taylor, *Sources of the Self: The Making of the Modern Identity* (Cambridge: Harvard University Press, 1989), 6.

147. James W. Sire, *Naming the Elephant: Worldview as a Concept*, 2nd ed. (Downers Grove, IL: InterVarsity Press, 2015), 87.

Second, there are, of course, other factors and forces that need to be appreciated, particularly if we are to understand the feminist movement of the last seventy-five years. Twentieth-century feminism is a particular manifestation of a wider revolt against the hierarchical and logical structures of Western thought and culture—a revolt that stands opposed to any notion of natural essences and, consequently, privileges *becoming* over *being*.[148] In particular, modern feminism derives much of its impetus, structure, and intellectual underpinnings from Marxian conflict theory—except that women are substituted for the oppressed proletarian class and men for the oppressive bourgeoisie. Indeed, so deeply is the root system of second-wave feminism entwined with that of Marxism that when Beauvoir wrote *The Second Sex*, "she still pinned her hopes for sexual equality on a Marxist revolution."[149] By the early 1970s, however, Firestone saw things rather differently. Indeed, the reason the socialist dream was never realized, she believed, was because Marx had not dug deeply enough into "the psychosexual roots of class."[150] In her mind, the only way "to truly eradicate all class systems" was via a much larger sexual revolution—one that would involve a reversion to what Freud had called "polymorphous perversity" or what she termed "unobstructed *pansexuality*."[151]

Third, in terms of more recent developments in gender theory, it also needs to be noted that there would likely have been no queer turn (at least as we know it) without Foucault. He, like no other before him, prosecuted the case that what we think of as *natural* is, in fact, *cultural*; what we think of as *objective* is, in fact, *subjective*; what we think of as *freedom* is, in fact, another form of *oppression*. Furthermore, because "what counts as knowledge is constituted within networks of power,"[152] and because this power

---

148. See the discussion in Watkin, *From Plato to Postmodernism*, 179–84.

149. Watkin, *From Plato to Postmodernism*, 181. See further Margaret A. Simons, "*The Second Sex*: From Marxism to Radical Feminism," in *Feminist Interpretations of Simone de Beauvoir*, ed. Margaret A. Simons (Pennsylvania: Pennsylvania University Press, 1995), 243–62.

150. Firestone, *Dialectic of Sex*, 11.

151. Firestone, *Dialectic of Sex*, 11–12 (emphasis original). Here Firestone reveals her indebtedness to Herbert Marcuse's *Eros and Civilization: A Philosophical Inquiry into Freud* (Boston: Beacon, 1955).

152. James K. A. Smith, *Who's Afraid of Postmodernism?: Taking Derrida, Lyotard, and Foucault to Church* (Grand Rapids: Baker, 2006), 85.

"is everywhere" and "comes from everywhere,"[153] what is required is "an attitude of perpetual suspicion and critique," as well as a posture of resistance toward all "models of rationalized identity."[154] The key here is the capture of language and the dismantling of categories. David Crawford helpfully summarizes the logic and goal of this approach: "When social groups and institutions can tell others who and what they are, they wield vast power. The control of language is the first and most important weapon in this veiled struggle. Liberation therefore entails above all else the disclosure of the vast lie contained in categories, types, and natures."[155] In short, because categorization is a form of control, the best way for control to be resisted is for categories to be denaturalized and deconstructed: that is, unmasked as false "totalizations"—contingent and alterable, rather than timeless and immutable.[156]

Finally, Butler's radical gender project needs to be understood against this background and, in particular, as an extension of the trajectory set by Foucault. For while we have no reason to doubt Butler's claim that *Gender Trouble* was driven by a desire to resolve an impasse in feminist theorizing about "the category of women,"[157] only a pronounced Foucauldian fear of categorization can account for the shape her theory takes and for the following personal admission:

> The prospect of being anything, even for pay, has always produced in me a certain anxiety, "to be" gay, "to be" lesbian seems to be more than a simple injunction to become who or what I already am.... I am not at ease with lesbian theories, gay theories, for identity categories tend to be instruments of regulatory regimes. ... Indeed, a Foucauldian perspective might argue that the affirmation of "homosexuality" is itself an extension of a homophobic discourse.[158]

---

153. Foucault, *History of Sexuality*, 1:93.

154. Turner, *Queer Theory*, 176.

155. David S. Crawford, "Liberal Androgyny: 'Gay Marriage' and the Meaning of Sexuality in Our Time," *Communio* 33 (2006): 250.

156. Watkin, *From Plato to Postmodernism*, 187.

157. Butler, *Gender Trouble*, 2.

158. Judith Butler, "Imitation and Gender Insubordination," in *Lesbian and Gay Studies Reader*, ed. Henry Abelove, Michele Aina Barale, and David M. Halperin (New York: Routledge, 1993), 308.

It is not difficult, then, to appreciate why Butler characterizes her troubling of gender as a form of resistance against the hegemony of "the heterosexual matrix."[159] However, it could equally be seen as an implicit rejection of the homosexual matrix. For if sex is "always already gender," and gender (being "performatively produced") has no ontological status either before or after its discursive construction, then all we are left with is "the phantasmatic nature of sexual identity."[160]

As we shall see in the following chapter, Butler has not always resisted the conclusion that follows from this line of logic. For if gender really is nothing more than "the repeated stylization of the body, a set of repeated acts within a highly rigid regulatory frame that congeal over time to produce the appearance of substance,"[161] then *there is neither male nor female, neither heterosexual nor homosexual, apart from such acts*.[162] All that can really be said to exist are beings who are "not yet 'subjects,' but who form the constitutive outside to the domain of the subject," and will, in due course, become discursively constituted by their performativity.[163] As Butler summarizes: "The univocity of sex, the internal coherence of gender, and the binary framework for both sex and gender" are nothing more than "regulatory fictions that consolidate and naturalize the convergent power regimes of masculine and heterosexist oppression."[164]

Having now expounded the key elements of Butler's gender theory, the main task of the following chapter is to provide a critical evaluation of this theory. But before I embark on this task, Butler's project first needs to be set within a further context: the intra-feminist debate regarding trans-identities (i.e., whether trans women *are* women). Then, after evaluating Butler's gender project, I will endeavor to articulate a more coherent conception of gender—one that maintains an inextricable link to biological sex while, at the same time, making room for different sociocultural manifestations and flexible forms of personal expression.

---

159. Butler, *Gender Trouble*, 46–106.

160. Butler, *Gender Trouble*, 9, 34, 76 (compare 38–39).

161. Butler, *Gender Trouble*, 43–44.

162. Indeed, such entities "exist *only* within the heterosexual matrix" (Butler, *Gender Trouble*, 150, emphasis original).

163. Butler, *Bodies That Matter*, xiii.

164. Butler, *Gender Trouble*, 46.

CHAPTER 6

RECLAIMING SEX AND RESCUING GENDER

The real crisis is not that gender non-conforming people exist, it's that we have been taught to believe in only two genders in the first place.[1]

—Alok Vaid-Menon

The problem with gender, as we now have it, is the violence—both real and metaphorical—we do by generalizing. No woman or man fits the universal gender stereotype.[2]

—Anne Fausto-Sterling

To assess the coherence of Butler's gender theory (and to propose a more cogent and coherent alternative), it is necessary to set her contribution within the intra-feminist debate regarding trans identities. For the question of whether *trans women* (i.e., biological males who identify as women) should be regarded *as women* (with all the legal rights and protections granted to women) is not just a major point of tension within Western societies but

1. Alok Vaid-Menon, *Beyond the Gender Binary* (New York: Penguin, 2020), 5.
2. Fausto-Sterling, *Sexing the Body*, 108.

a major source of division within feminism.[3] As we saw in chapter 1, the acronym TERF is applied, often as a slur, to those who insist either that trans women are different from natal women or that they are not women at all.[4] Non-trans feminists or gender-critical feminists are more neutral labels for those who hold this view.

By way of contrast, those who affirm that trans women are women are either called trans-inclusive feminists or, simply, transfeminists—a term given currency by Emi Koyama's "The Transfeminist Manifesto" (2001).[5] The division between non-trans feminists and transfeminists is often characterized as a conflict between (on one side) second-wave feminists and (on the other) third-wave feminists, who have generally embraced "the fight for trans rights as a fundamental part of intersectional feminism," coupled with fourth-wave feminists, who tend to be "queer, sex-positive, trans-inclusive, body-positive, and digitally driven."[6] The reality on the ground, however, is not always quite so neat.

In fact, historically, the division has existed *within* second-wave feminism almost from its inception. For example, as early as 1974, Dworkin was arguing that an androgynous future would "mean the end of transsexuality as we know it. Either the transsexual will be able to expand his/her sexuality into a fluid androgyny, or, as roles disappear, the phenomenon of transsexuality will disappear and that energy will be transformed into new modes of sexual identity and behavior."[7] Few shared her optimism, however, and (as we saw in our last chapter) support for such a prospect was relatively short-lived. Since the late 1970s, then, the question has tended to boil down to this: Should trans women be seen as "innocent

---

3. For an illuminating account of the current controversy (focused mainly on the UK), see Douglas Murray, *The Madness of Crowds: Gender, Race and Identity* (London: Bloomsbury, 2019), 210–17.

4. Colleen Flaherty, "'TERF' War," *Inside Higher Ed* (August 19, 2018), https://www.insidehighered.com/news/2018/08/29/philosophers-object-journals-publication-terf-reference-some-feminists-it-really.

5. Emi Koyama, "The Transfeminist Manifesto" (2001), in *Catching a Wave: Reclaiming Feminism for the 21st Century*, ed. Rory Cooke Dicker and Alison Piepmeier (Boston: Northeastern University Press, 2003), 244–59.

6. Constance Grady, "The Waves of Feminism, and Why People Keep Fighting over Them, Explained," *Vox* (July 20, 2018), https://www.vox.com/2018/3/20/16955588/feminism-waves-explained-first-second-third-fourth.

7. Dworkin, *Woman Hating*, 186–87.

victims" of patriarchy's hegemonic control of oppressive sex and gender norms, or should they be regarded as "co-conspirators" in an attempt by men to possess women "and to remake them in a mould that suits them"?[8]

Writing in 1979, Janice Raymond (as noted in ch. 1) very much took the latter view. While sympathetic to trans women's "specific form of gender agony," the way to address it, she argued, was not by joining "the women's community," but by coming to terms with "the particular life history that produced such distress."[9] Nor did she deem "sex-conversion surgery" to be a viable therapeutic option, as this only reinforces "the foundation of sex-role oppression, which is sex-role stereotyping, by encouraging the transsexual to conform to these stereotypes." In other words, by reifying the very "social norms that produced transsexualism to begin with," the medical-technical solution to "gender agony" perpetuates the very problem it seeks to solve.[10]

In 1987, however, trans woman Sandy Stone (who had been both named and criticized in Raymond's book) penned an essay titled, "The *Empire* Strikes Back: A Posttranssexual Manifesto."[11] In what has since been described as "the protean text from which contemporary transgender studies emerged," Stone responded "not by waging an anti-feminist counterattack on Raymond" but by challenging the assumptions undergirding her concept of womanhood.[12] Complaining of the ways in which "the medicalization of transsexuality" had produced "acquiescence to a strict gender binary,"[13] Stone regarded "born in the wrong body" explanations

---

8. Stephen Whittle, "Where Did We Go Wrong? Feminism and Trans Theory—Two Teams on the Same Side?," in *The Transgender Studies Reader*, ed. Susan Stryker and Stephen Whittle (New York: Routledge, 2006), 196.

9. Raymond, *Transsexual Empire*, 116.

10. Raymond, *Transsexual Empire*, 18. Raymond further (and provocatively) claimed that all MtF transsexuals "rape women's bodies by reducing the real female form to an artifact, appropriating this body for themselves" (104).

11. The manifesto was first presented at "Other Voices, Other Worlds: Questioning Gender and Ethnicity," Santa Cruz, CA, in 1988 and first published in *Body Guards: The Cultural Politics of Gender Ambiguity*, ed. Kristina Straub and Julia Epstein (New York: Routledge, 1991). Stone's approach was significantly influenced by Donna Haraway's "A Manifesto for Cyborgs: Science, Technology, and Socialist Feminism in the 1980s," *Socialist Review* 80 (1985): 65–108.

12. Susan Stryker and Stephen Whittle, in their editorial introduction to Sandy Stone's "The *Empire* Strikes Back: A Posttranssexual Manifesto," in Stryker and Whittle, eds., *Transgender Studies Reader*, 221.

13. Bettcher, "Feminist Perspectives on Trans Issues."

of transsexuality as a remnant of "the binary phallocratic founding myth" of the West, which claims that "only one body per gendered subject is 'right.' " What was needed instead was "a deeper analytical language for transsexual theory," one that accounted for "the sorts of ambiguities and polyvocalities which have already so productively informed and enriched feminist theory."[14]

Despite the pleas of trans women that their oppression be recognized as "gender-based oppression," many feminists dismissed the trans cause and were openly hostile toward the intrusion of genetic males (even post-operative trans women) into women-only spaces. Tensions came to a head in 1991, when the National Lesbian Conference in Atlanta banned all "nongenetic women" and the Michigan Womyn's Music Festival expelled all who were not "womyn-born-womyn."[15]

Not all feminists agreed with this response, however. Gayle Rubin, for instance, regarded it as both hypocritical and unjust. Invoking the specter of Beauvoir and other key feminist slogans, her pushback was firm: "After decades of feminist insistence that women are 'made, not born,' after fighting to establish that 'anatomy is not destiny,' it is astounding that ostensibly progressive events can get away with discriminatory policies based so blatantly on recycled biological determinism."[16]

Practically, then, it appeared that the options were two only: either *accept* biological determinism and *exclude* trans women from the category of "woman" or *reject* biological determinism and *include* trans women within the category of "woman"—or, at the very least, "allow room for a third space between man and woman."[17]

Queer theory stepped into the middle of this divide and presented itself as a third (and superior) way. According to queer theorists, both

---

14. Sandy Stone, "The *Empire* Strikes Back: A Posttranssexual Manifesto," in Stryker and Whittle, eds., *Transgender Studies Reader*, 229, 231. Interestingly, most of those who took up Stone's challenge have not abandoned "wrong body" explanations. Indeed, according to Jay Prosser, the distinction between immutable gender identity and (surgically) mutable bodily sex "serves as the logic of transsexuality" (Jay Prosser, *Second Skins: The Body Narratives of Transsexuality* [New York: Columbia University Press, 1998], 43).

15. Gayle Rubin, "Of Catamites and Kings: Reflections on Butch, Gender, and Boundaries," in *The Persistent Desire: A Femme-Butch Reader*, ed. Joan Nestle (Boston: Alyson, 1991), 475.

16. Rubin, "Catamites and Kings," 475.

17. Bettcher, "Feminist Perspectives."

transfeminists and non-trans feminists had fallen prey to a false determinism. For trans theory (in both its forms) holds that gender is determined by gender identity and non-trans theory holds that gender is determined by biological sex.[18] Queer theory, however, holds that gender is performatively constituted and that sex (as it is "always already gender") is determined by gender. As we saw in chapter 1, the four positions may be contrasted as follows:

TABLE 3: NON-TRANS, TRANS & QUEER THEORIES CONTRASTED

Type of Theory	*Sex is*	*Gender is*
Non-trans Theory	Determined by biology	Socially constructed upon sex
Soft Trans Theory	Determined by biology	Determined by gender identity
Hard Trans Theory	Determined by gender identity	Determined by gender identity
Queer Theory	Determined by gender	Performatively constituted

Queer theory, then, not only agrees with Bernice Hausman's charge that "transsexuals are the dupes of gender,"[19] but also regards both non-trans and soft-trans theorists as the dupes of sex!

In order to adjudicate between the feminist, trans, and queer alternatives, and having now set Butler's philosophical project in its immediate context, the remainder of this chapter will be given over to two tasks: first, an evaluation of Butlerian gender theory; and second, an articulation of a view of gender that, contrary to both queer theory and trans theory, sees it as necessarily anchored in biological sex (while not being identical with it) and as open to different cultural constructions and flexible (albeit bounded) personal expression.

PROBLEMATIZING BUTLER

The influence of Judith Butler's gender theorizing over the last thirty years is difficult to overstate. Her thought has not only provided "the critical underpinning of much subsequent Queer thought and practice,"[20] but has

18. This does not mean that non-trans feminists believe that sex determines any particular set of gender roles or gender expressions, but simply that it determines whether one is a man or a woman.

19. Bernice L. Hausman, *Changing Sex: Transsexualism, Technology, and the Idea of Gender* (Durham, NC: Duke University Press, 1995), 140.

20. Lynne Segal, "After Judith Butler: Identities, Who Needs Them?," *Subjectivity* 25 (2008): 384.

profoundly influenced contemporary understandings of "the relationship between sex, gender and desire."[21] Although Butler has since claimed that *Gender Trouble* was only written "for a few friends" and that she "imagined maybe one or two hundred people might read it,"[22] the book's revolutionary aim was never in doubt: to expose gender not merely as a discursively constituted fabrication, but as one "maintained for the purposes of the regulation of sexuality within the obligatory frame of reproductive heterosexuality."[23] Moreover, as she reveals in the preface to the 1999 edition of *Gender Trouble*, her larger moral and political goal was (and still is) "to undermine any and all efforts to wield a discourse of truth to delegitimate minority gendered and sexual practices."[24]

Alongside the adulation she has received, Butler's work has been strongly criticized from various angles and for a variety of reasons. Regarding her style, for instance, Martha Nussbaum complains that her excessive verbosity and opacity "causes the reader to expend so much effort in deciphering her prose that little energy is left for assessing the truth of the claims."[25] James Heartfield also wonders whether some of Butler's more paradoxical conclusions are due to her being "carried away with her own dialectical skills."[26] While such criticisms are not without validity, as Butler herself concedes,[27] my own view is that her claims are not only discernible (even if not always on first reading) but are worthy of engagement and, most especially, careful evaluation.

---

21. Susan A. Spear and Jonathan Potter, "From Performances to Practices: Judith Butler, Discursive Psychology and the Management of Heterosexist Talk," in *Talking Gender and Sexuality*, ed. Paul McIlvenny (Philadelphia: John Benjamin Publishing Company, 2002), 151.

22. Butler, *Undoing Gender*, 207.

23. Butler, *Gender Trouble*, 185.

24. Butler, *Gender Trouble*, viii.

25. Martha C. Nussbaum, "The Professor of Parody: The Hip Defeatism of Judith Butler," *New Republic* 220 (February 22, 1999): 39.

26. James Heartfield, *The "Death of the Subject" Explained* (Sheffield: Sheffield Hallam University, 2006), 43.

27. For instance, Butler herself acknowledges the difficulty of her prose (*Bodies That Matter*, 64).

RESPONSES TO BUTLER'S ATTEMPT TO DENATURALIZE GENDER

What, then, can be said of Butler's radical attempt to denaturalize gender—that is, to separate sex and gender and subsume sex into gender?

Feminist responses

First, Butler's approach has left many second-wave feminists deeply disturbed. For if we accept her claim that "to identify as a woman is a culturally enforced effect,"[28] what does this do to the *category* of woman and, indeed, the *cause* of women? Indeed, what does it say to "the material suffering of women who are hungry, illiterate, violated, beaten"? Nussbaum's answer is that Butler's view mocks the plight of women, narcissistically focusing on "the self rather than thinking in a way that helps the material condition of others." So, she surmises, Butlerian feminism (at best) offers a false hope and (at worst) "collaborates with evil"![29] Other critics have been less damning but equally doubtful that one can embrace the kind of poststructuralist approach to gender that Butler advocates and still retain a genuine commitment to female liberation.[30]

Gay and lesbian responses

Second, and somewhat ironically (given that she has historically identified as a lesbian),[31] a number of gay and lesbian theorists have also expressed concern that Butler's denaturalization of gender and (apparent) dematerialization of sex undermines "many of the cherished assumptions of gay liberation and lesbian feminism, including their appeals to commonality and collectivity."[32] Indeed, her denial of a precultural ground for identity

---

28. Liz Kotz and Judith Butler, "The Body You Want: Liz Kotz Interviews Judith Butler," *Artforum International* 31, no. 3 (1992): 88, https://www.artforum.com/print/previews/199209/the-body-you-want-an-inteview-with-judith-butler-33505.

29. Nussbaum, "Professor of Parody," 44–45.

30. Seyla Benhabib, "Feminism and Postmodernism: An Uneasy Alliance" in *Feminist Contentions: A Philosophical Exchange*, ed. Seyla Benhabib, Judith Butler, Drucilla Cornell, and Nancy Fraser (London: Routledge, 1995), 24.

31. However, she has more recently indicated that she is legally non-binary. See "Judith Butler on her Philosophy and Current Events," *Interviews by Kian* (December 27, 2019), https://interviewsbykian.wordpress.com/2019/12/27/judith-butler-on-her-philosophy-and-current-events.

32. Annamarie Rustom Jagose, *Queer Theory: An Introduction* (Melbourne: Melbourne University Press, 1996), 85.

has provoked Michael Warner to wonder how a lesbian could coherently be defined on Butler's terms.[33] This is not an unwarranted jibe, for Butler herself is not at all certain "that lesbians can be said to be 'of' the same sex or that homosexuality in general ought to be construed as love of the same."[34] Moreover, given her contention that we need to invert the thought that "there is first a sex that is expressed through a gender and then through a sexuality,"[35] it is hardly surprising that Butler's framework has been deemed "inadequate to comprehend the complexities of the gendering of lesbian relationships."[36]

Trans responses

Third, several trans critiques of Butler have also been forthcoming.[37] This too is not surprising, as Butler's theory "leaves the charges of gender replication entirely applicable to those trans people who see themselves and who behave as 'real' men and women."[38] Accordingly, Viviane Namaste not only accuses Butler of distorting transgendered reality and denying transgendered identities,[39] but of contributing to the existence of an ever widening gap between the lived experience of transsexuals and the theoretical explanations offered by Anglo-American feminists.[40]

---

33. Michael Warner, "From Queer to Eternity: An Army of Theorists Cannot Fail," *Village Voice Literary Supplement* (June 1992), 19. He suggests (tongue in cheek) that a lesbian, for Butler, might be defined as "the incoherence of gender binarism and heterosexuality condensed to the point of parody."

34. Butler, *Bodies That Matter*, 35.

35. Butler, "Imitation and Gender Insubordination," 318.

36. Kath Weston, "Do Clothes Make the Woman?: Gender, Performance Theory, and Lesbian Eroticism," *Genders* 17 (1993): 5.

37. See Viviane K. Namaste, "'Tragic Misreadings': Queer Theory's Erasure of Transgender Subjectivity," in *Queer Studies: A Lesbian, Gay, Bisexual, and Transgender Anthology*, ed. Brett Beemyn and Mickey Eliason (New York: New York University Press, 1996), 183–206; Henry Rubin, "Phenomenology as Method in Trans Studies," *GLQ: A Journal of Lesbian and Gay Studies* 4 (1998): 263–82.

38. Bettcher, "Feminist Perspectives," 5.3.

39. Viviane K. Namaste, *Invisible Lives: The Erasure of Transsexual and Transgendered People* (Chicago: The University of Chicago Press, 2000), 13–14. For a defense of Butler, from a trans perspective, see Tobias Raun, "Trans as Contested Intelligibility: Interrogating How to Conduct Trans Analysis with Respectful Curiosity," *lambda nordica* 1 (2014): 13–37 (esp. 32–33).

40. Viviane K. Namaste, "Undoing Theory: The 'Transgender Question' and the Epistemic Violence of Anglo-American Feminist Theory," *Hypatia: A Journal of Feminist Philosophy* 24, no. 3 (2009): 28.

Jay Prosser takes issue with Butler at a more theoretical level. Butler's "deliteralization of sex," Prosser alleges, is not only based on a false conception of "the body as the psychic projection of a surface," but stems from a misreading of "Freud's description of the bodily ego in *The Ego and the Id*." In Freud's understanding, "bodily ego is designed not to dematerialize the body into phantasmatic effect but to materialize the psyche, to argue its corporeal dependence." Butler, however, "collapses bodily surface into the psychic projection of the body," thus neutralizing the body as "a discernible referential category" and negating Freud's concern "to articulate the bodily origins of the ego."[41] Prosser's point, then, is that Butler is wrong, and Freud is right: *the body is not a product of the ego, but the ego is a product of the body*.

Prosser also sees an irreconcilable conflict between Butler's "refiguration of sex into gender" and "the logic of transsexuality."[42] Determined to locate "a bodily mooring for transsexual identity,"[43] Prosser offers two arguments for the centrality of embodiment to transsexual experience. The first is that the somatic feeling of being at odds with one's natal sex "demands some recognition of the category of corporeal interiority (internal bodily sensations)." The second is that the transsexual's desire to reconfigure their physical body to align with their body image "reveals that it is the ability to feel the bodily ego in conjunction and conformity with the material body parts that matters in a transsexual context." Prosser thus upholds "the material reality of the imaginary and not, as Butler would have it, the imaginariness of material reality."[44]

Philosophical responses

Fourth, Butler's ideological commitment to downplaying the epistemological significance of the sexed body has also led to various lines of philosophical critique. Justin Erik Halldór Smith, for example, accuses her

---

41. Prosser, *Second Skins*, 40–42.

42. Prosser, *Second Skins*, 43.

43. Gayle Salamon, *Assuming a Body: Transgender and Rhetorics of Materiality* (New York: Columbia University Press, 2010), 37.

44. Prosser, *Second Skins*, 43–44. This, as we have seen, is not a fair criticism. Butler does not believe that materiality is illusory. Prosser's affirmation of "the material reality of the imaginary" is also highly questionable. For a critical appraisal of Prosser's view, see Salamon, *Assuming a Body*, 37–42.

of being *either* a classical philosophical idealist (who believes that "there is no concrete external world without human categories to interpret it") *or* an anthropocentrist human-exceptionalist (who believes "that human beings are not animals alongside others, but that their essence is non-natural in origin").[45] Either way, if one considers a simple biological fact like the respective pelvis sizes of males and females, it cannot follow that "the perception of an anatomical difference so deep as to be immediately evident in the skeleton is nothing more than an illusion." He concludes: "Biology may not be exclusive destiny, but it does dictate the terms under which the will is free to do its work."[46]

In a similar vein, even Ásta Kristjana Sveinsdóttir, who is largely sympathetic to Butler's project, believes it is necessary to reject her quasi-Kantian "transcendental idealism" and to accept that there are "properties that are biologically given and that put constraints on what sex assignment is possible." In short, it is simply not the case that "the gender matrix dictates the materialization of sex, as Butler would have it."[47]

Each of these lines of critique highlights the same basic problem: Butler's "critical genealogy of the naturalization of sex and of bodies in general" leads her to render "the figure of the body as mute, prior to culture, awaiting signification."[48] This does not mean that she denies the extralinguistic reality of bodies. Her point, rather, is that it is impossible to think about our bodies in a discursively unmediated way.[49] But she is also claiming considerably more than this. In Butler's schema, "the body loses its inherent significance, thereby relinquishing its capacity to tell society how each member of society should understand him or herself,

---

45. Justin Erik Halldór Smith, "The Anthropocentric Idealism of Judith Butler," *Justin Erik Halldór Smith* (January 6, 2018), https://www.jehsmith.com/1/2018/01/gender-trouble-as-anthropocentric-idealism.html.

46. Justin Erik Halldór Smith, *Irrationality: A History of the Dark Side of Reason* (Princeton: Princeton University Press, 2019), 218–20.

47. Sveinsdóttir, "Metaphysics of Sex and Gender," 64. Although an improvement on Butler's view, Sveinsdóttir's alternative—that sex is "a conferred property where the aim is to track certain *physical* properties, but where the resulting property is a *social* property, in fact a legal one" (63, emphasis original)—falls prey to a similar subordination of the physical to the social.

48. Butler, *Gender Trouble*, 202.

49. Heiko Motschenbacher, *Language, Gender and Sexual Identity: Poststructuralist Perspectives* (Philadelphia: John Benjamins Publishing Company, 2010), 13.

and how each should act socially and sexually."[50] Thus, Sveinsdóttir is right to call this proposal "a Kantian 'Copernican Revolution' of sorts"; for rather than our thought and practices conforming to the nature of the world, in Butler's view, "the world conforms to our thought and practices."[51]

Butler's admission of incoherence

Having critiqued the self-refuting and solipsistic nature of this kind of radical social constructionism in the previous chapter, I will not repeat that critique here. I will, however, draw attention to Butler's own tacit admission about the incoherence of the revolution she proposes. In her attempt to rethink "the category of women," she suggests that "we must use this language to assert an entitlement to conditions of life in ways that affirm the constitutive role of sexuality and gender in political life, and we must also subject our very categories to critical scrutiny." She even confesses that she does not yet know the ways in which our anthropological categories "must be expanded, destroyed, or reworked both to encompass and open up what it is to be human and gendered."[52] What she does claim to know is that "there is no necessary reason for [sex] to remain the same for all women."[53] In short, although Butler is determined to champion the rights of women, she has no definitive answer to Patricia Elliot's question, "Who gets to be a woman?"[54] Unsurprisingly, then, her theory has not settled the debate between transfeminists and non-trans feminists.

EVALUATING BUTLER'S APPROACH TO GENDER PERFORMATIVITY

As we have seen, the reason for Butler's equivocation on basic questions of identity is her conviction that gender "is real only to the extent that it is performed."[55] Moreover, at the heart of this lived accomplishment is "discursive performativity"—the idea that gender is, first and foremost,

50. Dan Patterson, "A Brief History of Gender and Its Significance," *Essentials* (Spring 2016): 8.

51. Sveinsdóttir, "Metaphysics of Sex and Gender," 57.

52. Butler, *Undoing Gender*, 37–38.

53. Butler, *Bodies That Matter*, 35.

54. Patricia Elliot, "Who Gets to Be a Woman?: Feminist Politics and the Question of Trans-Inclusion," *Atlantis* 29 (2004): 13–20.

55. Butler, "Performative Acts," 527.

"constructed and constituted by language."[56] This is why the thought of a person having a gendered essence or "organizing gender core" is, for her, nothing more than "an illusion discursively maintained." The notion of a "gendered body" is, likewise, something that has "no ontological status apart from the various acts which constitute its reality."[57] In my estimation, Annamarie Jagose is right to describe such a view "as a naive rendering of more complex material conditions."[58]

Butler, of course, should not be faulted for exploring the performative powers of speech or the discursive effects of language on gender conceptions, roles, identity formation, and bodily acts. She is to be faulted, however, for her reductionism. Seyla Benhabib draws attention to the problem with the following series of questions:

> Are linguistic practices the primary site where we should be searching for an explication of gender constitution? What about other practices like family structures, child-rearing patterns, children's games, children's dress habits, schooling, cultural habitus etc? Not to mention of course the significance of the words, deeds, gestures, phantasies, and the bodily language of parents, and particularly of the mother in the constitution of the gender identity of the child.[59]

While some of Butler's later writings might be seen as providing partial answers to such questions,[60] her conviction that the attribution of qualities (like sex or gender) to human bodies has effect only through language not only betrays a kind of "linguistic monism or determinism," but verges on the supernatural, effectively granting God-like, body-forming powers to human words.[61]

---

56. Salih, *Judith Butler*, 64. "If one wonders how a linguistic theory of the speech act relates to bodily gestures," writes Butler, "one need only consider that speech itself is a bodily act with specific linguistic consequences" (*Gender Trouble*, xxvii).

57. Butler, *Gender Trouble*, 185.

58. Jagose, *Queer Theory*, 87.

59. Seyla Benhabib, "Subjectivity, Historiography, and Politics: Reflections on the 'Feminism/Postmodernism Exchange,' " in Benhabib, Butler, Cornell and Fraser, eds., *Feminist Contentions: A Philosophical Exchange*, 109.

60. See, e.g., Judith Butler, *Antigone's Claim: Kinship Between Life and Death* (New York: Columbia University Press, 2000); Butler, *Giving an Account of Oneself*.

61. Turner, *Queer Theory*, 112. Butler's view is clear from the parallel she draws between the divine performative "Let there be light" (Gen 1:3) and human speech acts—even though (with Derrida) she

What accounts for this curious apotheosizing of language in Butler's thought? The answer is a misappropriation of speech act theory based on a misapplication (if not an intentional blurring) of Austin's linguistic categories. For while Austin makes a clear distinction between *constative* statements (which *describe* states of affairs) and *performative* statements (which *create* states of affairs)—the former being either "true or false" and the latter either "happy or unhappy" (i.e., effective or ineffective)[62]—Butler believes that "the constative claim is always to some degree performative."[63] Thus, in her reckoning, the declaration, "It's a girl" (announced, say, when a female child is born), "shifts an infant from an 'it' to a 'she' " and "in that naming, the girl is 'girled,' brought into the domain of language and kinship through the interpellation of gender."[64]

The problem here, as philosopher Alex Byrne explains, is that such appellations are neither explicit nor implicit performatives:

> Explicit performatives contain an action-verb like "apologize," "thank" ("I thank you"), or "bet" ("I bet $100"), and "It's a girl" does not. That sentence is therefore not an *explicit* performative. And if it is an *implicit* one, then we should be able to make what is implicit, explicit. Just as we can roughly paraphrase the implicit performative "I'm sorry" by the explicit performative "I apologize," we should be able to find an explicit performative that corresponds to "It's a girl." Explicit performatives are typically in the first-person present indicative: "I apologize," "I thank you," and so on; their performative character can be further highlighted with the adverb "hereby"—"Hereby, I apologize." So is the doctor or other medical authority in effect saying "Hereby, I make the baby a girl"?[65]

If so, Byrne continues, "then provided the doctor had the appropriate authority and sincerely proclaimed 'It's a girl,' then the baby *would* be a girl, with no possibility of error."[66] This, however, cannot be the case, for

sees the latter as "derivative" and "citational," not "originating" (*Bodies That Matter*, xxi).

62. Austin, *How to Do Things*, 54.

63. Butler, *Bodies That Matter*, xix.

64. Butler, *Bodies That Matter*, xvii.

65. Byrne, "Is Sex Socially Constructed?" (emphasis original).

66. Byrne, "Is Sex Socially Constructed?" (emphasis original).

the doctor could always be mistaken. (Hence the relevance of intersex conditions to the broader discussion.) But assuming the infant has been correctly identified, it also cannot be the case that the child is *turned into* a female by the doctor's declaration. Rather, and despite Butler's claims to the contrary, she is simply being *recognized* (and so *described*) as a girl.[67]

Therefore, irrespective of whatever social or cultural expectations may follow from the declaration of a child's sex, such statements are clearly and strictly constative (not performative) utterances. Butler has confused naming with making, appellation with interpellation, discourse with creation. As those philosophers who embrace the "new materialism" rightly insist, *although our access to metaphysical reality is mediated through discourse, it is not reducible to discourse.*[68] As Susan Hekman remarks, "our language structures how we apprehend the ontological but it does not constitute it."[69]

ASSESSING BUTLER'S NOTION OF THE SUBJECTED SUBJECT

The freedom of the subject is a further casualty of Butler's more developed understanding of gender. While she is right to challenge the pretension of "an autonomous and self-grounding subject,"[70] her reason for doing so is her conviction that "there is no subject who decides on its gender"; to the contrary, "gender is part of what decides the subject."[71] Such a view would make sense if Butler simply wished to affirm that sex is biologically determined and that gender naturally and necessarily "mirrors sex or is otherwise restricted by it." But Butler, as we have seen, flatly rejects such propositions. At the same time, she insists that "being a man" or "being a woman" is "the forcible approximation of a norm one never chooses"; in

---

67. For example, in *Bodies That Matter,* Butler insists that "the discursive condition of social recognition *precedes and conditions* the formation of the subject: recognition is not conferred on a subject, but forms that subject" (171, emphasis original).

68. Coined in the 1990s, the "new materialism" describes a turn in philosophy away from the dualism characteristic of modernism and toward a recognition of the ontological importance of matter. It thus seeks to correct the almost exclusive focus on epistemology occasioned by the linguistic turn. See Diana Coole and Samantha Frost, "Introducing the New Materialisms," in *New Materialisms: Ontology, Agency, and Politics,* ed. Diana Coole and Samantha Frost (Durham, NC: Duke University Press, 2010), 1–43.

69. Susan J. Hekman, "Constructing the Ballast: An Ontology for Feminism," in *Material Feminisms,* ed. Stacy Alaimo and Susan J. Hekman (Bloomington: Indiana University Press, 2008), 98.

70. Butler, *Gender Trouble,* 60.

71. Butler, *Bodies That Matter,* ix.

fact, it is "a norm that chooses us." That such statements are to be taken at face value is clear from the fact that she even criticizes Beauvoir's notion of gender construction for implying the existence of an agent "who somehow takes on or appropriates that gender and could, in principle, take on some other gender."[72] Such an idea is far too autonomous and voluntaristic for Butler.

Admittedly, it is difficult to reconcile such avowedly deterministic statements with Butler's earlier claim that gender is "a free-floating artifice" with "the performative possibilities for proliferating gender configurations." In fact, Butler's only solution to this paradox, as she indicates in the preface to the 1999 edition of *Gender Trouble,* is to deny "the occasional voluntarism" articulated in *Gender Trouble* and to admit that the book "sometimes reads as if gender is simply a self-invention."[73] Consequently, in subsequent writings, she has been careful to distinguish the concept of *performance* (which "presumes a subject") from that of *performativity* (which "contests the very notion of the subject"),[74] and to insist that "gender is not an artifice to be taken on or taken off at will."[75]

Despite this modification (or reversal) of her earlier thought, Butler still thinks that it is possible to salvage "a more general theory of agency."[76] She attempts this by arguing that gender's hegemonic discourse can be altered or, at least, subverted. This explains why her discussions of drag are so crucial to her larger theory.[77] Drag "effectively mocks both the expressive model of gender and the notion of a true gender identity," and in so doing it destabilizes "the naturalized categories of identity and desire."[78] There is a problem, however. For Butler, gendered acts, even subversive ones, are always citational (i.e., reiterative or rearticulatory) and necessarily involve "an originary complicity with power in the formation of the 'I.' " This not only rules out "any notion of a voluntarist

---

72. Butler, *Gender Trouble,* 9, 86, 11.

73. Butler, *Gender Trouble,* 10, 92–93, xxvi.

74. Butler, "Gender as Performance," 33.

75. Butler, *Bodies That Matter,* ix.

76. Butler, *Gender Trouble,* xxvi.

77. Kathleen Lennon and Rachel Alsop, *Gender Theory in Troubled Times* (Cambridge: Polity Press, 2020), 157.

78. Butler, *Gender Trouble,* 186, 189; see further *Bodies That Matter,* ch. 4: "Gender Is Burning: Questions of Appropriation and Subversion" (81–97).

subject who exists quite apart from the regulatory norms which she/he opposes," but it also means that "the subject who would resist such norms is itself enabled, if not produced, by such norms."[79] Thus, Butler's attempt to escape from the Scylla of biological determinism plunges her headlong into the Charybdis of cultural/linguistic determinism.[80] On either account, the agent is not free.[81]

By her own admission, then, Butler's notion of agency "in no way presupposes a choosing subject."[82] There can be "no 'being' behind doing" (Nietzsche) and thus "no doer behind the deed."[83] Moreover, as we noted earlier, there is no "I" produced by the gendering process either; such an entity "emerges only within and as the matrix of gender relations themselves."[84] So then, the only kind of subject possible on Butler's account is one that is forced into being "via subjection to social norms."[85] This explains why Benhabib charges Butler with bidding farewell to "the self as the subject of a life-narrative,"[86] and why Salih describes her "subject" as being "trapped within a discourse it has no power to evade or to alter."[87] For Butler's belief in "the subjected status of the subject" inevitably means "the evacuation or displacement of human agency" and an unavoidable paralyzing of the self.[88] So, what began "as a criticism of the monopoly over freedom exercised by men has turned, paradoxically, into a criticism of freedom as such."[89]

To conclude: Butler's attempt to articulate a purely performative view of gender constitution, based partly on a radical appropriation of Nietzsche's idea of "the self as a masquerading performer" (who does

---

79. Butler, *Bodies That Matter*, xxiii.

80. Turner, *Queer Theory*, 114.

81. Even in her more recent work, Butler does not appear to have found a satisfactory way out of this dilemma. See, e.g., Judith Butler, *Senses of the Subject* (New York: Fordham University Press, 2015), 1–16.

82. Butler, *Bodies That Matter*, xxiii.

83. Butler, *Gender Trouble*, 195, citing Nietzsche, *Genealogy of Morals*, 45.

84. Butler, *Bodies That Matter*, xvi (emphasis added).

85. Lennon and Alsop, *Gender Theory*, 155.

86. Benhabib, "Feminism and Postmodernism," 21.

87. Salih, *Judith Butler*, 67.

88. Butler, *Bodies That Matter*, 82, xvi–xviii.

89. Heartfield, *'Death of the Subject' Explained*, 43.

not exist behind its mask) and partly on a Derridean deconstruction of speech act theory, ultimately leads to incoherence.[90] It neither does justice to "the complexities of the ontogenetic origins of gender in the human person," nor does it provide "a sufficiently thick and rich account of gender formation that would also explain the capacities of human agents for self-determination."[91] All Butler manages to leave us with is a thoroughly subjected subject who is helpless to escape the hegemonic constraints of the gender matrix.

POSTSCRIPT: BUTLER'S EVOLUTION

As we have seen, Butler's thought is not only difficult to pin down, but has also developed over time.[92] In fact, as Lynne Segal points out, since the publication of *Gender Trouble* in 1990, there have been significant shifts observable on five interconnected fronts:

> from primarily semiotic analysis to stressing the significance of the socio-cultural moment; from political abstractions to ethical reasoning; from pivotal concern with gender and sexuality to a general interest in alterity and the face/place of the other; from a Foucauldian engagement with exteriority and performativity to a more psychodynamic interest in interiority and stress upon the formative early years of life; from a rejection of identities into the specific embrace of several very distinct ones, articulated—with a suitable plethora of caveats—in the form of an identity politics.[93]

Although it is not my purpose to track and unpack these shifts in detail, I will provide four brief illustrations of how Butler's thought has evolved in regard to some of the issues highlighted in the foregoing evaluation.

First, in *Undoing Gender* (2004), while Butler is candid about the fact that the purpose of her earlier work was "to disturb—fundamentally—the way in which feminist and social theory think gender," she also admits that *Gender Trouble* was "a text I probably wrote too quickly, a text whose

---

90. Benhabib, "Feminism and Postmodernism," 21–22.

91. Benhabib, "Subjectivity, Historiography, and Politics," 108, 110.

92. Regrettably, I have not been able to engage with Butler's latest work on gender, *Who's Afraid of Gender?* (New York: Farrar, Straus and Giroux, 2024), as it was not yet available at time of publication.

93. Segal, "After Judith Butler," 384.

future I did not anticipate at the time." Apparently, all she really wished to do was to "combat forms of essentialism which claimed that gender is a truth that is somehow there, interior to the body, as a core or as an internal essence, something that we cannot deny, something which, natural or not, is treated as given." She did not wish to deny that what "operates at the level of cultural fantasy [gender] is not finally dissociable from the ways in which material life is organized [sex]."[94]

Second, in a 2006 interview, Butler further explained that one of the weaknesses of *Gender Trouble* is that it overemphasized "the priority of culture over nature" and "did not take account of a nature that might be, as it were, beyond the nature/culture divide, one that is not immediately harnessed for the aims of certain kinds of cultural legitimation practices." Consequently, she now finds Fausto-Sterling's interactionist model—in which "biology conditions cultural life and contributes to its forms" and "cultural life enters into the reproduction of our bodies at a biological level"—more compelling.[95]

Third, in a 2015 interview with trans historian Cristan Williams, Butler also admits that at the time *Gender Trouble* was written she "did not think well enough about trans issues," especially the way in which "the primary experience of the body is registered." She now accepts that "some people really love the gender that they have claimed for themselves" and so has little time for "the feminist police force who rejects the lived embodiment of trans women." This may well be true. But it is straining credulity for her to say that she never meant that trans identities are "all a fiction, and that a person's felt sense of gender was therefore 'unreal.' "[96] For not only is that precisely what she claimed but also what her theory demands. Similarly, it is only slightly less incredible for her to insist that she "did not mean to

94. Butler, *Undoing Gender*, 207, 212–14.

95. Vicki Kirby and Judith Butler, "Butler Live" (interview), in *Judith Butler: Live Theory*, ed. Vicki Kirby (London: Continuum, 2006), 144–45.

96. Cristan Williams and Judith Butler, "Judith Butler on Gender and the Trans Experience: 'One Should Be Free to Determine the Course of One's Gendered Life' " (interview), *Verso* (May 26, 2015), https://www.versobooks.com/blogs/2009-judith-butler-on-gender-and-the-trans-experience-one-should-be-free-to-determine-the-course-of-one-s-gendered-life.

argue that gender is fluid and changeable."[97] The truth, it would seem, is that she has now abandoned some of her earlier views.

Fourth, in the same interview with Williams (and consistent with certain aspects of her earlier view), Butler makes clear that she has "no problem" with a woman having a penis or a man having a vagina. In fact, anyone "can have whatever primary characteristics they have (whether given or acquired) and that does not necessarily imply what gender they will be, or want to be." At the same time, she also believes that, for others, "primary sexual characteristics signify gender more directly." How these two contrary affirmations can be harmonized is unclear. What is clear is that Butler now believes "we have to accept a wide variety of positions on gender. Some want to be gender-free, but others want to be free really to be a gender that is crucial to who they are."[98] What all this amounts to is an approach to gender in which trans theory applies to some and queer theory applies to others.

HOW, THEN, SHOULD WE CONCEIVE OF GENDER?

The conceptual and political journey taken by gender over the last seventy-five years has brought us to a place not of clarity and consensus, but of confusion and contradiction. Can a person's gender be at odds with their sex? It all depends on what gender is or, at least, how the term is being used. (And, of course, if sex is "always already gender," then the question is moot.) Is it possible for a person to change their gender or, perhaps against their will, for their gender to change? Again, it all depends on what gender is.

97. Williams and Butler, "Judith Butler on Gender." Certainly, by the time she wrote *Bodies That Matter*, Butler sought to clarify that her references (in *Gender Trouble*) to multiple gender identifications were not meant "to suggest that everyone is compelled by being or having such identificatory fluidity" (64). Nevertheless, the question is not whether people do or do not experience or pursue perpetual fluidity, but whether this is even possible. On her account of gender, it most certainly is.

98. Williams and Butler, "Judith Butler on Gender."

FIVE COMPETING CONCEPTIONS OF GENDER

In an attempt to bring much-needed clarity to the current debate, British philosopher Kathleen Stock has helpfully differentiated five distinct conceptions of gender, asking of each, in turn, "whether one can change gender, in that particular sense."[99]

Gender as a synonym for biological sex

The first conception that Stock considers is that of *gender as a synonym for biological sex*. As we have seen, this reappropriation of the term's (original) grammatical meaning not only has a long history but is now ubiquitous—as is evidenced by the identity categories on numerous official forms and in expressions like "the gender pay gap" or "gender-based violence." On this understanding, asking whether someone can change their gender is simply another way of asking whether they can change their sex.

This latter question leads Stock to consider the nature of intersex conditions and to contend that while a person need not possess all of the typical sex characteristics normally required to be either male or female, they "do still need to possess some of them." She further maintains that while some with intersex conditions undergo surgical or hormonal interventions, this should not be confused with a person attempting "to change their underlying biological nature."[100] The conclusion to be drawn is that because sex cannot change (as it is chromosomally determined), gender cannot change either (as it is nothing more than a synonym for sex).

Gender as the culturally accepted manifestation of sex

Second, Stock considers the view that *gender is the cultural manifestation of sex*. On this account, gender is a way of referring to "the collection of stereotypical characteristics, behaviours, and attitudes, culturally approved of as 'normal,' 'right' or 'appropriate' (etc.) for male- and female-sexed people,

99. Kathleen Stock, "Can You Change Your Gender?," *The Philosopher* 107, no. 3 (2019): 19–23. In her more recent monograph *Material Girls* (2021), Stock not only reduces these five conceptions to four (38) but, because of the confusion the term "gender" generates, has sought to avoid it wherever possible (39). She opts instead for less ambiguous language—e.g., *sex-based stereotypes* (rather than gender stereotypes), *sex nonconforming* (rather than gender nonconforming), and *gender identity* for "whether you related to yourself as a boy or man, girl or woman, or neither" (40).

100. Stock, "Can You Change," 20 (emphasis original). The goal, rather, is "to give an appearance more typical of one category."

respectively."[101] These norms may be radically divergent in different historical epochs and may (and invariably do) vary widely across cultures. But none of these differences change what gender is: *gender is whatever the agreed norms happen to be at a particular time and place.*

Can a person change their gender, on this view? Stock's answer is ambivalent. She certainly believes that people can protest, resist, and even subvert prevailing gender norms—for example, by adopting "an appearance, behaviour or attitude, culturally approved of as normal-for-the-opposite-sex." What a person cannot do, however (at least, not single-handedly), "is change the cultural fact that such characteristics are deemed abnormal for your sex by others, and perhaps on some level even by yourself."[102] On this view, then, it is possible to *challenge* gender but not (or, at least, not easily) to *change* gender.

Gender is the occupation of masculine or feminine social roles

In the third view Stock examines, gender is defined in purely functional terms—that is, as *the occupation of masculine or feminine social roles.* As per the previous view, these roles are determined by whatever "set of sex-based stereotypes" prevails in the surrounding culture.[103] On this view, sex and gender are theoretically separable as gender is something that is *performed* by individuals and *perceived* by society. This means that by adopting a different set of roles, a person could potentially change genders.

Stock illustrates how this might occur by suggesting that "a male could, in certain circumstances, socially transition to the point of being perceived as either enacting, or as becoming subject to, the stereotypes associated with femininity, or both."[104] If this were to happen, then a male could be said to have ceased being a man (socially), yet he would still be a male (biologically). In short, his gender would have changed but not his sex.

---

101. Stock, "Can You Change," 20.
102. Stock, "Can You Change," 20–21.
103. Stock, "Can You Change," 21.
104. Stock, "Can You Change," 21.

Gender is sex because sex is a projection of gender

The fourth conception Stock considers again regards gender as a synonym for sex but does so by conceiving of *sex as a projection of gender.* On this view, "gender (and so sex) is understood as wholly non-material and socially constructed. That is, there are no discernible material facts about biological sex, detached from the ways in which society codes it." This, as we have seen, was the view Judith Butler articulated in *Gender Trouble*. However, given the evident capacity of humans to reproduce as a species, Stock has little time for the idea that "there are no underlying material facts about maleness and femaleness to which humans can have reliable epistemic access."[105]

Nevertheless, for the sake of argument, Stock grants the conception in order to see whether it would enable a person to change their gender. In her view, it is not obvious that it can. She explains why: "As individuals, we might play with social norms, parody them, attempt to subvert them: but we can't thereby control how the wider collective is culturally primed to read us."[106] Social symbols, as Butler herself now acknowledges, are not things an individual can either create or control. On this view, then, while an individual may seek to change their gender, there is no guarantee that they will succeed.

Gender as equivalent to gender-identity

Stock's fifth and final conception is that of *gender as gender-identity.* Defining gender-identity as "a person's individual feelings of ease, or lack of ease, with their sex, and with the sociocultural expectations placed upon that sex," Stock suggests that most of those who are content with their sex are not aware of having a gender-identity. For this reason, "it would seem false to say that everyone has one."[107] In her view, the notion is most salient for people who are gender dysphoric—that is, those who experience a persistent and distressing level of incongruence between their (subjective) psychological sex and their (objective) biological sex.

105. Stock, "Can You Change," 22.

106. Stock, "Can You Change," 22.

107. Stock, "Can You Change," 22.

The deeper question, however, is whether one's gender-identity can be changed. In answer to this question, Stock begins by clarifying that since gender-identity is "grounded in a set of feelings," it is not only "detached from the question of one's actual sex," but also "from the issue of one's gender, in the socially constructed sense." Neither of these realities can be changed. In regard to gender dysphoric feelings, however, Stock notes that these can sometimes be "temporary, particularly when they occur in childhood and teens, and can be changed simply by the acquisition of new experiences, altering one's self-conception." She also notes that various therapeutic approaches may produce change, but that this "will depend on individual factors, such as personality, history, and how deeply psychologically-rooted and prolonged the feelings are."[108]

TOWARD A COHERENT CONCEPTION OF GENDER

Stock's analysis is immensely helpful in distinguishing the major conceptions of gender that are currently vying for supremacy within feminism (particularly) and Western culture (generally). But clarifying the alternatives does not itself decide between them. How, then, should we conceive of gender? Is it a necessary category? Is it a helpful supplement to sex? Or does it create more problems than it solves?

These questions cannot finally be answered without appealing to a transcendent authority capable of providing an objective and infallible standard of the true, the good, and the beautiful. Moreover, any answer that does not make such an appeal inevitably begs the question that lurks behind all normative claims—"the grand sez who" (to use Arthur Allen Leff's memorable phrase).[109] For, ultimately, there can be no moral or metaphysical evaluation that is beyond challenge, unless it comes from one who is "the unjudged judge, the unruled legislator, the premise maker who rests on no premises, the uncreated creator of values."[110]

---

108. Stock, "Can You Change," 22–23. "In cases of severely distressing, prolonged dysphoria," Stock concedes, "A person can reasonably seek social and/or legal transition as a therapeutic strategy to alleviate such feelings, by acquiring an outward presentation which 'matches' their gender-identity" (22).

109. Arthur Allen Leff, "Unspeakable Ethics, Unnatural Law," *1979 Duke Law Journal* 6 (December 1979): 1230.

110. Leff, "Unspeakable Ethics," 1230.

Although I clearly believe in such a being—"the God and Father of our Lord Jesus Christ," as the New Testament repeatedly calls him (Rom 15:6; 2 Cor 1:3; Eph 1:3; 1 Pet 1:3)—it is not my purpose here to make the case for his existence. However, not only can such a case be made (and made convincingly!),[111] but, as was outlined in chapter 3, there are equally compelling reasons to view the Bible as the written and inspired form of God's self-revelation. But our exploration of Scripture awaits part 3 of this book. At this point, I simply wish to make two points of a logical and practical nature, each with several implications.

It is advantageous to distinguish gender from sex

First, despite the questionable origins and checkered history of the distinction between sex and gender, *it is advantageous to distinguish gender from sex.*

Before explaining why this is so, it is worth noting that "gender's history as an ontological category is very specific and relatively recent in English."[112] This means that the English language has long functioned (and quite successfully) without giving *gender* a sexological sense or treating it as anything other than a synonym for *sex*. It is also clear that the linguistic innovations pioneered and popularized by Money and Stoller were neither inevitable nor essential; that is, "sex role" and "sex identity" could just as easily have done the work of "gender role" and "gender identity."

So then, my reasons for affirming the sex-gender distinction ought not to be confused with those of Stoller. To recap: Stoller regarded "gender" as having "psychological or cultural rather than biological connotations." This not only enabled him to distinguish "male" and "female" (sex) from "masculine" and "feminine" (gender), but also to assert that "these latter may be quite independent of (biological) sex."[113] So although Stoller was quick to insist that "the normal male has a preponderance of masculinity and the normal female a preponderance of femininity," he tacitly affirmed that *no one's gender is actually determined by their biological sex*. This, of

111. Timothy Keller, *Making Sense of God: An Invitation to the Skeptical* (New York: Viking, 2016); Plantinga, *Warranted Christian Belief*, 182–368; Plantinga, "Is Belief in God Properly Basic?," 41–51; Richard Swinburne, *The Existence of God*, 2nd ed. (Oxford: Clarendon, 2004).

112. Germon, *Gender*, 85.

113. Stoller, *Sex and Gender*, 10.

course, follows if gender means nothing more than "the amount of masculinity or femininity" possessed or exhibited by an individual.[114] But here is the question: How is it possible for notions of masculinity and femininity to come into being independently of biological sex?

The short answer is they cannot. Consequently, insoluble problems emerge if gender is defined without refence to sex. And yet such definitions are now commonplace, and not just in the trans-affirming literature. For example, no less a luminary than Hilary Lips defines "gender" as the "culturally-mediated expectations and roles associated with *masculinity and femininity*."[115] But not only is such a definition viciously circular, but by associating gender with masculinity and femininity rather than sex, the influence of the biological upon the social is badly obscured.

Better, then, is Raewyn Connell and Rebecca Pearse's definition of gender as "the structure of social relations that centres on the reproductive arena, and the set of practices that bring reproductive distinctions between bodies into social processes."[116] This definition not only takes the way societies recognize and express sex differences with far greater seriousness, but provides *a bodily basis* for the other dimensions of gender that Lips rightly acknowledges—namely, *gender identity* ("thinking of oneself as male or female") and *gender role* ("behaving in ways considered appropriate for women and men in the surrounding culture").[117] In light of this, Lips's definition could (and, in my view, should) be rewritten as follows: *gender is the culturally mediated set of conceptions, expectations, and roles associated with being either male or female*. Such a definition distinguishes gender from sex without disconnecting gender from sex.[118]

---

114. Stoller, *Sex and Gender*, 10.

115. Hilary M. Lips, *Gender: The Basics*, 2nd ed. (London: Routledge, 2018), 2 (emphasis added).

116. Connell and Pearse, *Gender*, 11.

117. Lips, *Gender*, 2–3. While Lips (somewhat confusingly) adds *sexual orientation* as a third dimension of gender, a better case can be made for regarding *gender expression*—i.e., the cultural signals and symbols that indicates whether one is male or female (e.g., dress, hair styles, grooming, and demeanor)—as a third dimension of gender.

118. Distinguishing sex and gender in this way has the additional advantage of clarifying "the old ambiguity in meaning between sex and sexuality" *and* "sex as the broader corpus of male–female differences" (Joan Busfield, *Men, Women and Madness: Understanding Gender and Mental Disorder* [London: Palgrave, 1996], 32), and it also preserves what is valid in the feminist protest against excessive or uncritical notions of biological determinism.

Three implications follow from such an understanding.

Implication 1. Drawing a distinction between sex and gender is useful for combating overblown notions of gender essentialism and rigid gender stereotypes. If sex and gender are conceptually conflated, then it is much easier for certain distributional facts or statistical findings (e.g., 60 percent of men prefer *x*) to be essentialized (i.e., a preference for *x* is an essential male property). Restrictive and oppressive gender stereotypes are thereby created or perpetuated (e.g., any male who does not prefer *x* is not a real man). The resulting confusion is well illustrated by Sam Killermann's remarkable claim that, although he identifies as a man, the fact that he is "sensitive, kind, familial" and really loves "dark chocolate and red wine and romcoms" means that he also identifies "with a lot of what it means to be a woman."[119] In sum, one way to combat a false gender essentialism produced by a hard biological determinism is to distinguish gender from sex without disconnecting gender from sex.[120]

Implication 2. What we have previously said of sex (i.e., that it is determined at conception and established in utero) cannot be said of gender—at least, not to the same extent. That is, in both its social and psychological aspects, gender is not simply a *given biological fact,* but also a *culturally constructed and personally produced effect.*[121] Lips, therefore, is right to aver that both "biology and environment interact in complicated processes to produce gender identity," even while admitting that the details of this interaction (i.e., *what* contributes *what* and *how*) are "not yet fully understood."[122] Likewise, in the development of many gender roles there is "an inextricable mix of biological sex and social gender constructions."[123] In short, there is a *gravenness* to gender that contrasts with the *givenness* of sex. So then, because it is necessary to distinguish sex and gender conceptually, it is helpful to distinguish them terminologically.

---

119. Sam Killermann, *Guide to Gender: The Social Justice Advocate's Handbook*, 2nd ed. (Austin, TX: Impetus Books, 2017), 90–91.

120. Hull, *Ontology of Sex*, 105.

121. For a helpful survey of the history of theories, as well as a discussion of the various contributors to the development of both gender identity and gender roles, see Lips, *Gender*, 3–14.

122. Lips, *Gender*, 18.

123. Cordelia Fine, *Testosterone Rex: Unmaking the Myths of our Gendered Minds* (New York: Norton, 2017), 26. See also Vicki Kirby, "Natural Convers(at)ions: Or, What If Culture Was Really Nature All Along?," in Alaimo and Hekman, *Material Feminisms*, 214–36.

Implication 3. Failing to preserve the sex/gender distinction tends to lead to a relativizing of other important distinctions. These include the distinction between the natural and the social *sciences* (e.g., anatomy v. anthropology) and natural and social *kinds* (e.g., biological facts v. cultural artefacts).[124] Moreover, as Carrie Hull argues, "if all ways of grouping items are equally relative to language and culture, correlation and causation are effectively equated."[125] One potential (indeed likely) result of this equation is the further reinforcement of arbitrary gender stereotypes, since the only way to define or discern a person's gender would be on the basis of who exercises certain *tasks*, exhibits certain *traits*, or enjoys certain *tastes*. As feminist philosopher Linda Alcoff rightly sees, this would mean the disintegration of the category of *woman* (and, of course, man too!), for while all women have a common biological essence (i.e., femaleness), "there is no gender essence all women share."[126]

A further casualty is the collapse of the distinction between *actuality* and *potentiality*, with the result that "there is no real difference between individuals who have a potential yet do not exercise it, and those who never possessed the potential to begin with."[127] This necessarily disconnects the category of woman from that of female (and, likewise, the category of man from that of male), with the entailment that anyone who sincerely self-declares to be a woman should be regarded as a woman, irrespective of their biology.[128] The social and political ramifications of this (as we shall see shortly) are immense. Not surprisingly, Hull concludes, "The deconstruction of the sex/gender distinction may permit the wholesale dismissal of attempts at biological theorizing about gender roles. But

124. What distinguishes "natural kinds" from "social kinds," according to Muhammad Ali Khalidi, is that "the former are associated with properties that are *causally related* whereas the latter are associated with properties that are *conventionally related*" ("Three Kinds of Social Kinds," *Philosophy and Phenomenological Research* 90 [2015]: 111 [emphasis added]).

125. Hull, *Ontology of Sex*, 98.

126. Linda M. Alcoff, *Visible Identities: Race, Gender and the Self* (Oxford: Oxford University Press, 2006), 147–48. However, Alcoff rightly asserts that "maintaining a distinction between the objective category of sexed identity and the varied and culturally contingent practices of gender does not presume an absolute distinction of the old-fashioned sort between culture and a reified nature" (175).

127. Hull, *Ontology of Sex*, 98.

128. Kathleen Stock, "Changing the Concept of 'Woman' Will Cause Unintended Harms," *The Economist* (July 6, 2018), https://www.economist.com/open-future/2018/07/06/changing-the-concept-of-woman-will-cause-unintended-harms.

in giving up the distinctions between potential and actual, correlation and causation, and the natural and social sciences, we concede too much."[129]

It is necessary to anchor gender in sex

Second, for the distinction between sex and gender to remain meaningful and useful, *it is necessary to anchor gender in sex.*

Our exploration of sex (in ch. 4) not only sought to show its objective and extra-discursive reality, but also that there are only two biological sexes, "albeit with some anomalies."[130] Furthermore, in view of the critique of Butler's attempt to denaturalize gender in this chapter, as well as her own backpedaling in more recent years, the claim that there is no sex that precedes gender should now be laid to rest. That no human being is born into an a-cultural, pre-linguistic void does not change the fact that *bodies* (with their biological sex) pre-exist *identities* (with their psychosocial gender). Thus, as Caroline New observes, wherever one goes in the world, it is possible to "identify female human beings, women, even though the meanings of femaleness are culturally variable." Why so? Because the "socio-cultural structures of gender ontologically presuppose the physiological structures of sexual difference."[131]

This is why all attempts to "do away with the idea that sex comes first" and deny that sex "logically and chronologically precedes any interpretation of it" are inevitably doomed to failure.[132] *Every cultural interpretation of sex requires the transcultural and pre-hermeneutical existence of sex.* Consequently, Joan Wallach Scott's claim that "there is not only no distinction between sex and gender, but gender is the key to sex" is not merely confused (for if there is no distinction between sex and gender, then neither can be said to be "the key" to the other) but has inverted the true order of the nature/culture relationship. For while it is undoubtedly true that gender "produces *meanings* for sex and sexual difference,"[133] just

---

129. Hull, *Ontology of Sex*, 105.

130. Hull, *Ontology of Sex*, 96–97. See further Tom Chivers, "Of Course Biological Sex Exists," *UnHerd* (December 10, 2019), https://unherd.com/2019/12/yes-of-course-biological-sex-exists.

131. Caroline New, "Feminism, Critical Realism, and the Linguistic Turn," in *Critical Realism: The Difference It Makes*, ed. Justin Cruickshank (London: Routledge, 2003), 65–66.

132. Tina Chanter, *Gender: Key Concepts in Philosophy* (London: Continuum, 2006), 6.

133. Scott, "Gender," 13 (emphasis added).

as inherited gender conceptions inevitably color the way that sex is read, metaphysics and hermeneutics must not be confused: the former precedes the latter, logically speaking. Consequently, *because sex is the ontological foundation of gender, it is necessary to anchor gender in sex.*

Three implications flow from this conclusion.

Implication 1. The purpose of gender expression is to reveal sex. As Roger Scruton explains, the function of gender in human interactions is as "an elaborate social prelude," but "when the curtain rises, what is disclosed is not gender, but sex." Sex-specific clothing, he notes, provides a striking illustration of this, for such clothing "dramatizes the sexuality of the body in the act of concealing it." Scruton thus concludes: "Sex is hidden so that it might be revealed as gender. Men and women are able to perceive each other sexually in the veils which hide their sex." It follows, then, that any form of gender expression that intentionally obscures the reality or clarity of one's sex cannot be deemed authentic, for sex is "the 'truth' of gender."[134] Beauvoir understood this, which is why she insisted that "no woman can claim without bad faith to be situated beyond her sex"—meaning that no woman can genuinely profess to be a man.[135]

Implication 2. Inverting the sex/gender relationship disastrously undermines the significance of personal embodiment and historical embeddedness. Elaine Graham offers two reasons why this is the case:

> Firstly, gender is perceived as a matter of behaviour and consciousness, presupposing disembodied minds as the primary and determinant sites of gender: a perpetuation of, rather than a challenge to, Cartesian dualism. Secondly, the privileging of consciousness universalizes and abstracts the material and historical aspects of "lived experience." Such a theory of gender thereby posits a rationalist, ahistorical account involving neutral, passive bodies.[136]

Graham, therefore, is right to insist that "bodies are crucial actors in the cultural rendition of gender."[137] They are anything but passive in the

---

134. Scruton, *Sexual Desire*, 265, 268, 266.

135. Beauvoir, *The Second Sex*, 4.

136. Graham, *Making the Difference*, 124.

137. Graham, *Making the Difference*, 145.

formation of personal identity and utterly foundational to interpersonal (especially familial) relationships. For it is ultimately a person's body that determines whether they are a son or a daughter, a brother or a sister, a husband or a wife, a mother or a father, and so on. Moreover, as Stock's analysis of gender has identified, the cultural form that each of these relational roles takes is never entirely a matter of individual choice. Rather, it is "something accomplished in interaction with others" and "in relation to normative conceptions of appropriate attitudes and activities *for particular sex categories*."[138]

A properly grounded conception of gender, then, demands that we view "bodies as social, not atomistic or individual" and recognize that "the ontology of the body always pre-exists individual consciousness and reflects wider social forces."[139] For this reason, Moira Gatens is right to contest the "alleged *neutrality* of the body" and "the postulated *arbitrary* connection between femininity and the female body, masculinity and the male body."[140] There is nothing neutral about sexed embodiment and nothing arbitrary about the sex-and-gender connection. Consequently, even if we allow for a considerable degree of gender construction, unless our assertions about gender are grounded in the body, they become idiosyncratic, confusing, and, ultimately, meaningless.

Implication 3. If sex is the foundation of gender, then the central transgender claim—that the sexed body neither signifies nor determines the gendered self—cannot be sustained. As Scruton explains, the transgender person mistakenly "identifies his sex through his gender, and his gender not through his body but through his conception of himself. His body, he feels, belongs to a kind to which he himself does not belong."[141] Doubtless, the distress that such feelings produce is painfully real. But the feelings are not grounded in objective reality; they are, rather, the product of mistaken identification,

---

138. Candice West and Sarah Fenstermaker, "Doing Difference," *Gender and Society* 9 (1995): 21 (emphasis added).

139. Graham, *Making the Difference*, 130.

140. Moira Gatens, *Imaginary Bodies: Ethics, Power, and Corporeality* (London: Routledge, 1996), 4 (emphasis original).

141. Scruton, *Sexual Desire*, 274.

somatic disaffection, or false hope.[142] For, in reality, there is no essential conflict between the body and the self.

Brubaker, however, begs to differ. In his view, gender identity—which he defines as "an inner essence of which each individual is the sole legitimate interpreter"—is the key to one's gender. Sensing the specter of self-reference in such a highly subjective and disembodied contention, he then proceeds to modify it with two paradoxical assertions. He first states that "while gender identity is understood as independent of the visible morphological features of the sexed body, it is *at the same time* widely understood as grounded in other—*as yet unknown*—properties of the body."[143] He then insists that gender identity should be understood "*both* as a subjective inner essence, accessible to and knowable by the individual, *and* as an objective constitutional fact over which the individual has no control." These assertions are question-begging in the extreme, and the second irreconcilable with the first. Gender identity cannot "be both disembodied and re-embodied," as Brubaker claims.[144]

Equally unpersuasive is the transgender theory of Julie Nagoshi and Stephan/ie Brzuzy, which attempts to incorporate "*both* a fluid self-embodiment *and* a self-construction of identity that dynamically interacts with this embodiment in the context of social expectations and lived experiences."[145] While the authors assure us that such an approach delivers "a more complete and inclusive understanding of gender and sexual identity," it is far from clear that this is the case or what fluid self-embodiment even means, let alone how it is possible. Prima facie, the claim that gender identity is simultaneously "fluid, embodied, and socially and self-constructed" is beset with contradictions. Thus, the authors' hope of reconciling feminist and queer theories in a place "beyond essentialism and constructivism" is neither realized nor realizable.[146]

142. For further discussion of this point, and a comparison of different explanatory models, see Stock, *Material Girls*, 109–41.

143. Brubaker, *Trans*, 136 (emphasis added).

144. Brubaker, *Trans*, 136–37 (emphasis original).

145. Julie L. Nagoshi, Craig T. Nagoshi, and Stephan/ie Brzuzy, *Gender and Sexual Identity: Transcending Feminist and Queer Theory* (G. Filip-Crawford, A. Varley & R. Hess III, Contributors. New York: Springer Science+Business Media, 2014), 77 (emphasis added).

146. Julie L. Nagoshi and Stephan/ie Brzuzy, "Transgender Theory: Embodying Research and Practice," *Affilia: Journal of Women and Social Work* 25 (2010): 432, 437, 435.

To recap: Whether someone is a man or woman is either determined by their sex (i.e., by whether they are male or female) or it is "radically independent of sex."[147] It cannot be both. If it is the latter (as Butler maintains), then gender is ultimately a mix of individual traits, subjective tastes, personal desires, and self-perceptions—that is, it is a synonym for personality. If, however, gender is the former (determined by sex)—which, as I have argued, is the only way a notion of gender can coherently be maintained—then neither form of trans theory (let alone queer theory) can be sustained.

THE CHALLENGE POSED BY TRANSGENDER THEORY

Despite the overwhelming problems (philosophical, psychological, medical, and social) faced by transgender theory, it is increasingly common for gender identity (i.e., one's "internal sense of being male, female, both, or neither"[148]) to be accepted as the infallible gauge of a person's gender and, in the harder form of trans theory, for it to be regarded as the appropriate determinant of sex. So then, while in popular parlance it is often said that "gender is between your ears, and sex is between your legs,"[149] hard trans theory claims that what is "between your ears" (i.e., one's subjective gender identity) reveals your *true sex*—regardless of what is "between your legs." More than that, what is between your ears reclassifies what is between your legs. Hence the memes noted in chapter 1: "some men menstruate" and "some women do have penises."

Behind this way of thinking, as the legal scholar and trans activist Stephen Whittle acknowledges, lies the fact that "transgendered people have questioned the whole notion of objectivity—they do not try to claim it and instead they have built upon the tradition the community has of autobiographical writing to give a voice to their self-acknowledged subjectivity."[150] Angela Jones puts the point even more forcefully: "Subjectivities

147. Butler, *Gender Trouble*, 10.

148. Hartke, *Transforming*, 21.

149. See, e.g., Breanne L. Heldman, "Chaz Bono: Gender Is Between Your Ears, Not Legs," *ENews* (November 19, 2009), https://www.eonline.com/au/news/154524/chaz-bono-gender-is-between-your-ears-not-legs.

150. Whittle, "Where Did We Go Wrong?," 199.

are ours to craft, and while it is arduous to escape the hegemonic discursive power regimes that imprison our bodies, it is an exercise of agency, empowerment, and queerness to challenge such discursive power regimes."[151] Such an approach to identity, however, effectively nullifies the role of the body in both sex determination and gender identity formation. Sheila Jeffreys, therefore, is entirely correct to say that the "idea of 'gender identity' disappears biology."[152]

Despite this, trans theory appears to have no shortage of advocates in the medical arena.[153] Dr. Deanna Adkins, for example, a pediatric endocrinologist at Duke University School of Medicine and the director of the Duke Center for Child and Adolescent Gender Care, claims that from "a medical perspective" gender identity is "the appropriate determinant of sex."[154] The result of such a stance is

> a radical redefinition of our words "man" and "woman," and of the political entities those words describe. Rather than referring to members of biological classes, who can generally speaking be distinguished from one another by sight, the words will now refer to subjective mental states, feelings in a person's head, indistinguishable from one another except by self-declaration.[155]

While Patricia Elliot may be right to say that "*problematizing* the question of identity—what it means to be a woman, a man, or some other

---

151. Angela Jones, "Rachel Dolezal Is Really Queer: Transracial Politics and Queer Futurity," *Social (In)Queery* (June 17, 2015), https://socialinqueery.com/2015/06/17/rachel-dolezal-is-really-queer-transracial-politics-and-queer-futurity.

152. Jeffreys, *Gender Hurts*, 6.

153. Since 2007, e.g., "the number of gender clinics treating children in the United States has grown from zero to more than 100" (Chad Terhune, Robin Respaut, and Michelle Conlin, "As More Transgender Children Seek Medical Care, Families Confront Many Unknowns," *Reuters* [October 6, 2022], https://www.reuters.com/investigates/special-report/usa-transyouth-care).

154. Deanna Adkins, "Expert Declaration of Deanna Adkins, M.D.," *U.S. District Court, Middle District of North Carolina*, Case 1:16-cv-00236-TDS-JEP (13 May, 2016), 5 (para. 23); compare 11 (para 39): https://www.aclu.org/sites/default/files/field_document/AdkinsDecl.pdf. Adkins reached this conclusion, first, by assuming that a person's gender identity is unalterable (para. 30) and then, by equating GD and DSD/intersex conditions (para. 32). It is on the basis of these demonstrably false premises that she then drew the conclusion that defining "biological sex" as "the physical condition of being male or female" is "counter to medical science" and "inherently flawed" (para. 35).

155. Rebecca Reilly-Cooper, "Why Self-Identification Shouldn't Be the Only Thing That Defines Our Gender," *The Conversation* (May 13, 2016), https://theconversation.com/why-self-identification-shouldnt-be-the-only-thing-that-defines-our-gender-57924.

identity—is not necessarily the same thing as *politicizing* the feminine, at least not in the narrow sense of prescribing who gets to be a woman," the second inevitably follows the first. Consequently, trans women, regardless of their intentions, pose a direct challenge "to mainstream feminist conceptions of sex as a stable and immutable basis of gender."[156]

The challenge, of course, is more than conceptual. Failing to distinguish between trans women and natal women, and granting the former the rights of the latter, also presents a risk (both potential and actual) to the physical and emotional safety of women and girls. This is why non-trans feminists frequently draw attention to a range of harms faced by biological females, and contend that such dangers are likely to increase if trans women are given "unrestricted access to protected spaces originally introduced to shield females from sexual violence from males." Their argument is not that trans women are "particularly dangerous or more prone to sexual violence," but that the category of "self-declared trans women" includes "many with postpubescent male strength, no surgical alteration of genitalia, and a sexual orientation towards females."[157] Furthermore, opening women's spaces to trans women is making it exceedingly difficult to prevent sexual predators from taking advantage of the situation.[158]

THE CHALLENGE POSED *TO* TRANSGENDER THEORY

Although other dimensions of the sociopolitical challenge presented by the medico-legal acceptance of transgender theory could be considered,[159] we return to explore further the philosophical challenge presented to transgender theory.

---

156. Elliot, *Debates in Transgender*, 18, 21.

157. Stock, "Changing the Concept."

158. See the cases documented in chapter 16 ("Abolishing Women's Safe Spaces") of Byrne et al., *Transgender: One Shade of Grey*, 268–87, and those discussed in chapter 8 ("We Just Need to Pee: Why Female-Only Spaces Matter So Much to Women") in Joyce, *Trans*, 149–73. See also the following Facebook group for an archive of global incidents of violent and sexual crimes committed by males posing as or claiming to be women: "This Never Happens," *facebook.com* (created on October 22, 2016).

159. As well as the debate over whether medicine and law actually construct, rather than diagnose, the "transgender child" (Heather Brunskell-Evans, "The Medico-Legal 'Making' of 'The Transgender Child,'" *Medical Law Review* 27 [2019]: 640–57), the question of trans women competing against natal women in sports is another area of significant controversy (e.g.,

At the heart of trans theory lies the extraordinary claim that subjective feelings possess a greater authority than objective reality. But why should this claim be accepted? Why is a person's *true sex* determined by an inner *gender identity*, when their "age and height and race and species are not determined by an inner sense of identity"?[160] Interestingly, Brubaker attempts to answer this question (at least, with respect to race) by arguing that because race is fundamentally determined by one's ancestry, it is "located outside the self and open to inspection by others." But when it comes to gender, he argues, this is determined by "the individual's monopolistic access to the inner sense of self that is understood to be constitutive of gender identity."[161]

But what is the basis for this view? Why should a person's gender be determined by their psychology rather than their biology? As we have seen, Brubaker's answer to this question reveals the supposition that lies at the base of most formulations of trans theory: "one's subjective gender identity is grounded in and caused by *some unknown constitutional factor* and is thus unchosen and unchanging."[162] However, the evidence in support of this hypothesis (especially for the existence of some kind of body-brain mismatch) is, at best, correlational rather than causational and, more likely, demonstrates either that human brains are not "sex dimorphic,"[163] or that "even quite marked sex differences in the brain may have little consequence for behaviour."[164] So even if a biological contributor to gender identity could be identified, its role would only be

Rodrigo Pérez Ortega, "World Athletics Banned Transgender Women from Competing. Does Science Support the Rule?," *Science* (April 4, 2023), https://www.science.org/content/article/world-athletics-banned-transgender-women-competing-does-science-support-rule.

160. Anderson, *When Harry Became Sally*, 47–48.

161. Brubaker, *Trans*, 141.

162. Brubaker, *Trans*, 141 (emphasis added).

163. See B. P. Kreukels and A. Guillamon, "Neuroimaging Studies in People with Gender Incongruence," *International Review of Psychiatry* 28 (2016): 120–28; Lise Eliot, Adnan Ahmed, Hiba Khan, and Julie Patel, "Dump the 'Dimorphism': Comprehensive Synthesis of Human Brain Studies Reveals Few Male-Female Differences Beyond Size," *Neuroscience & Biobehavioral Reviews* 125 (2021): 667–97, doi.org/10.1016/j.neubiorev.2021.02.026.

164. Fine, *Testosterone Rex*, 92–93; see also Mohammad Reza Mohammadi and Ali Khaleghi, "Transsexualism: A Different Viewpoint to Brain Changes," *Clinical Psychopharmacology Neuroscience* 16 (2018), 136–43.

influential, not determinative.[165] Despite these widely recognized realities, Brubaker remains committed to a notion of gender identity as "an unchosen, unchanging inner essence and the sexed body as its choosable and changeable expression."[166] Solid reasons to believe in such an essence are, however, problematically absent.

Therefore, proponents of transgender ideology are faced with an array of insuperable challenges. Ryan Anderson identifies some of the more obvious: (1) "to offer a plausible definition of gender and gender identity that is independent of bodily sex"; (2) to explain how it might be possible for a person to even "know if he or she 'feels like' the opposite sex, or neither, or both"; (3) "to explain why the mere feeling of being male or female (or both or neither) *makes* someone male or female (or both or neither)"; and (4) "to present an argument for why transgender beliefs determine reality."[167]

For want of a coherent response to these challenges, transgender theorists tend either to revert to gender voluntarism (e.g., by insisting that because gender is a social construct gender identity is both chosen and changeable),[168] or, as we have seen with Brubaker, collapse into self-contradiction (e.g., by insisting that gender identity is both "a subjective inner state that is independent of the sexed body" and is "grounded in other—as yet unknown—properties of the body").[169] Such incoherence only highlights the deeper paradox at the heart of trans theory: that, on the one hand, it "depends for its very existence on the idea that there is an 'essence' of gender, a psychology and pattern of behaviour, which is suited to persons with particular bodies and identities," and, on the other, that an essential gender can "end up in the minds and bodies of persons with inappropriate body parts that need to be corrected."[170] This paradox is intolerable and irresolvable. How can a woman be defined as someone who, regardless of their biology, feels the way other women feel precisely

165. See fn. 85 in ch. 1 of this book for a further discussion of this point.

166. Brubaker, *Trans*, 137.

167. Anderson, *When Harry Became Sally*, 46–47 (emphasis original).

168. Bornstein, *Gender Outlaw*, 51–52.

169. Brubaker, *Trans*, 136.

170. Jeffreys, *Gender Hurts*, 1–2.

because of their biology? Indeed, how can any person know what it feels like to be another person—of either sex? They cannot.

ACCOUNTING FOR CROSS-GENDER IDENTIFICATION

The preceding critique of trans theory is not intended to minimize the anguish felt by many who experience gender incongruence. Such identity conflicts (particularly if they are pronounced and persistent) can be deeply distressing and ought to evoke a response of heartfelt compassion.[171] I am also well aware that while some who suffer from GD desire to alter their bodies (or perhaps believe, anatomy notwithstanding, they are the opposite sex), others have no illusions about their sex and no desire to transition.[172] Either way, the critique I am offering here is not of people with identity conflicts, but of the idea that *subjective feelings transcend objective facts*—that is, that gender identity (*how* I feel) determines gender (*who* I am) and that gender either determines sex (*what* I am) or legitimates attempts to change it. It is this claim that has been found wanting. With reference to the softer form of trans theory, Robert George explains why:

> What is a pre-operative "male-to-female" transgender individual *saying* when he says he's "really a woman" and desires surgery to confirm that fact? ... It is clearly *false* to say that this biological male is *already* perceived as a woman. He wants to be perceived this way. Yet the pre-operative claim that he is "really a woman" is the premise of his plea for surgery. So it has to be prior. What, then, does it refer to? The answer cannot be his inner sense. For

171. It is not my purpose, in this chapter, to articulate an ethical framework to guide appropriate treatment of this (often debilitating) condition. Because such a framework is inevitably worldview dependent, it will arise (in principle) from the theological method outlined in chapter 3 and take shape (in practice) from the biblical survey undertaken in chapters 7 to 11.

172. Anderson, *When Harry Became Sally*, 45. See also Christine Overall, "Sex/Gender Transitions and Life-Changing Aspirations," in *You've Changed: Sex Reassignment and Personal Identity*, ed. Laurie Shrage (Oxford: Oxford University Press, 2009), 11–27; "Trans Persons, Cisgender Persons, and Gender Identities," in *Philosophy of Sex: Contemporary Readings*, ed. Nicholas Power, Raja Halwani, and Alan Soble, 6th ed. (New York: Rowman & Littlefield, 2012), 251–67.

that would still have to be an inner sense of *something*—but there seems to be no "something" for it to be the sense of.[173]

How, then, might we account for cross-gender identification? In the view of psychologist and MtF transsexual Anne Lawrence, "transsexualism represents a fundamental disorder in a person's sense of self."[174] Sexologist Ray Blanchard similarly suggests that the "concept of cross-gender identity is really not a normal gender identity which has found itself lodged in the wrong body. Cross-gender identity is a constant preoccupation with, and unhappiness about, the individual's gender" (i.e., sex).[175]

But what gives rise to this "preoccupation" and "unhappiness" with one's sex? As we have seen, there is little reason to think that the answer lies in the biological/neurological realm.[176] This leaves the psychosocial or psychosexual realms.[177] Yet even here a wide range of plausible (but not always compatible) hypotheses have been put forward.[178] Consequently, "many who propose some form of a psychological causation theory hold that it is merely one piece of the puzzle."[179] This seems wise.

---

173. Robert P. George, "Gnostic Liberalism," *First Things* (December 2016), https://www.firstthings.com/article/2016/12/gnostic-liberalism.

174. Anne A. Lawrence, "Shame and Narcissistic Rage in Autogynephilic Transsexualism," *Archives of Sexual Behavior* (2008): 458.

175. Cited (via interview) in Madeleine Kearns, "Has Trans Orthodoxy Conquered the World?," *UnHerd* (January 6, 2020), https://unherd.com/2020/01/how-the-trans-orthodoxy-conquered-the-world.

176. Unless, of course, a person's gender distress is due to an intersex condition (possibly undiagnosed). This is why *DSM-5* is careful to distinguish between GD "*without* a disorder of sex development" and GD "*in association with* a disorder of sex development" (455–56, emphasis added). Its conclusion regarding the former is that "current evidence is insufficient to label gender dysphoria without a disorder of sex development as a form of intersexuality limited to the central nervous system" (457).

177. For a helpful survey of the range of theories and models, including "The Blanchard Typology," see Eddy and Beilby, "Understanding Transgender Experiences," 21–34.

178. For example, an overly enmeshed relationship with the parent of the opposite sex, an overly distant relationship of the parent of the same sex, an internalized belief that one's parents wanted a child of the opposite sex, childhood sexual trauma, false gender stereotypes, a personality disorder, androphilia (i.e., the desire of a man to be attractive to other men as a woman), or autogynephilia (i.e., a man's attraction to the idea of himself as a woman). On these latter two theories, see Ray Blanchard, "Typology of Male-to-Female Transsexualism," *Archives of Sexual Behavior* 14 (1985): 247–61.

179. Eddy and Beilby, "Understanding Transgender Experiences," 24.

Furthermore, the uniqueness of each person's circumstances and susceptibilities, along with the realities of equifinality (multiple paths leading to the same outcome) and multifinality (the same path leading to different outcomes) would suggest that *the precise etiology of gender incongruence is necessarily person-specific, even where common contributors are at play.* These considerations point toward one or more "multifactorial models with an emphasis on psychosocial factors."[180] Of course, in many cases, "the specific causal mechanisms of transgender experience are exceedingly complex," and, in some, may prove to be inscrutable.[181] Nevertheless, the resulting condition is clear: a misaligned gender identity produced by a psychological identification with the opposite sex (or perhaps a non-identification with either sex).

RESCUING GENDER FROM TRANS THEORY AND QUEER THEORY

The absence of easy answers regarding the etiology of gender incongruence does nothing to salvage the credibility of trans theory. *Nobody is born in the wrong body* (metaphysically speaking), even if such a statement accurately conveys how some people feel. The problem necessarily lies elsewhere. Therefore, contrary to Ann Travers's charge, it is not the case that "questioning the authenticity of anyone's gender self-determination is oppressive."[182] Nor should *doubting* the validity of a trans person's self-conception (that they *are* in the wrong body) be equated with a *denial* of their self-perception (that they *feel like they are* in the wrong body). What is being challenged is the belief that *subjective perceptions determine objective reality,* and what is being queried is *whether a person's experience has been rightly interpreted.*

Therefore, while there may be scope for a variety of different personal gender conceptions (just as there is for different cultural gender expressions), unless the categories of man and woman are anchored in the objective realities of male and female bodies, gender becomes a private, solipsistic, incommunicable attribute, akin to Ludwig Wittgenstein's

180. Yarhouse, *Understanding Gender Dysphoria,* 76.

181. Eddy and Beilby, "Understanding Transgender Experiences," 34.

182. Ann Travers, *The Trans Generation: How Trans Kids (and Their Parents) Are Creating a Gender Revolution* (New York: New York University Press, 2018), 119.

"beetle in a box."[183] For not only is sexed embodiment "sufficiently important, and sufficiently vivid, to make an indelible impact upon our experience,"[184] but, as we have seen in this chapter (as well as the two preceding it), *gender is permeable to sex in a way that sex is not to gender*. Sex, then, is the foundation; gender is the construction that rests on (and can only rest on) that foundation.

Nor does it follow that the best way to resolve the conundrum of gender incongruence is to eliminate gender altogether, as some feminists have opined.[185] Doubtless, needlessly narrow and rigid gender stereotypes generate a certain amount of confusion and protest, if not actual cases of GD.[186] But, once again, the better solution is surely to challenge and change such stereotypes, not to "use whatever means we have to give up on gender."[187] So, although there is a grain of truth in Bernice Hausman's provocative claim that "transsexualism is gender's alibi—seeming to prove its facticity in the demand to be recognized as the other sex," it does not follow that it is impossible "for any subject to authentically or finally 'be' a sex."[188] To the contrary, *because all people are embodied and all bodies are sexed, it is impossible for any person not to be a sex*. For sex, as I have argued in this part of the book, is an extra-discursive, pre-hermeneutical, biological given; gender, by contrast, while experienced and expressed in different ways, is objectively and immutably determined by sex. That is, an adult human male *is* a man, however he might experience or express

---

183. In his *Philosophical Investigations* (1.293), Wittgenstein suggested we imagine that each of us has a box with something in it that we call a "beetle." But no one can look into anyone else's box, so the only knowledge anyone has of what a beetle is, is derived from looking at their own beetle. The result is that it is impossible for anyone to ever know if they are talking about the same thing. See Ludwig Wittgenstein, *Philosophical Investigations*, trans. G. E. M. Anscombe, 3rd ed. (Oxford: Basil Blackwell, 1986), 100. For a discussion of Wittgenstein's point, see Richard Floyd, "The Private Language Argument," *Philosophy Now* 58 (November/December 2006): 19–21, https://philosophynow.org/issues/58/The_Private_Language_Argument.

184. Scruton, *Sexual Desire*, 265.

185. Reilly-Cooper, "Gender Is Not a Spectrum." Jeffreys similarly argues that "without 'gender,' transgenderism could not exist" (*Gender Hurts*, 2).

186. See further Anna I. R. van der Miesen, Annelou. L. C. de Vries, Thomas D. Steensma, and Catharina A. Hartman, "Autistic Symptoms in Children and Adolescents with Gender Dysphoria," *Journal of Autism and Developmental Disorders* 48 (2018): 1537–48.

187. Suzanne J. Kessler, *Lessons from the Intersexed* (New Brunswick: Rutgers University Press, 1998), 132.

188. Hausman, *Changing Sex*, 140.

his manhood, and an adult human female *is* a woman, however she might experience or express her womanhood.[189]

CONCLUDING REFLECTIONS

The conclusion to be drawn from this exploration of the various understandings of sex and gender that are currently vying for supremacy is that the non-trans theorists are correct. Given that sex is a matter of biology (established fundamentally and immutably by a person's genotype), the only way a distinct notion of gender (i.e., the psycho-social aspects of sex) can coherently be maintained is for it to be rooted in the sexed body. In other words, *because the sexed body determines the gendered self, it is sex that should ground gender identity, govern gender roles, and guide gender expression.*

As we have seen, any other conception, especially one that anchors a person's gender in their gender identity, ultimately turns gender into an idiosyncratic attribute and gender identity into a placeholder for personality. As this results in there currently being a little over eight billion genders in the world (since every person is unique), it effectively renders gender a superfluous term, if not also a meaningless concept. This helps to explain why "the sex/gender binary, which defined gender as the social assignment of meaning to biologically-given sex differences, remains in place despite a generation of scholarship aimed at deconstructing that opposition."[190] It is also why neither queer theory nor trans theory (in either form) is sustainable.

And yet such a conclusion continues to be resisted by numerous thinkers and writers in a variety of domains—not least in the fields of biblical scholarship and Christian theology. This highlights the need for what part 3 of this book will endeavor to provide: a biblical and theological assessment of trans theory from an evangelical perspective.

There is, however, a deeper reason why such an approach is necessary. Because there is, in fact, no "autonomous secular realm, completely

189. This does not mean that every expression of manhood (or womanhood) is equally authentic or equally clear. Some may be confusing (perhaps even intentionally so). This is where cultural gender norms not only play an important role but are, in fact, inevitable. For, like a shared language, they establish a set of boundaries for gender expression so that sex is rightly perceived.

190. Scott, "Gender," 10–11. Scott, it should be noted, is not at all pleased with this state of affairs.

transparent to rational understanding,"[191] a biblical and theological assessment is *the only way to resolve the current transgender debate*. For unless we hear from "the unjudged judge, the unruled legislator, the premise maker who rests on no premises, the uncreated creator of values,"[192] all we are left with is a set of competing claims, undergirded by competing epistemologies, and a situation where, in Christopher Watkins's chilling words, "only power and violence are left to arbitrate between competing interpretations."[193]

Thankfully, this is not the case. Therefore, to Scripture we now turn.

---

191. John Milbank, *Theology and Social Theory: Beyond Secular Reason*, 2nd ed. (New York: Wiley-Blackwell, 2008), 1.

192. Leff, "Unspeakable Ethics," 120.

193. Christopher Watkin, *Biblical Critical Theory: How the Bible's Unfolding Story Makes Sense of Modern Life and Culture* (Grand Rapids: Zondervan, 2022), 77.

PART 3

SEX, GENDER, AND TRANSGENDER IN BIBLICAL PERSPECTIVE

CHAPTER 7

MALE AND FEMALE IN THE BEGINNING

For nature never can be forced to change. What once has been impressed on it, may not be transformed into the opposite by passion. For passion is not nature, and passion is wont to deface the form, not to cast it into a new shape. Though many birds are said to change with the seasons, both in color and voice, ... they do not alter their nature itself, so as in the transformation to become female from male.[1]

—Clement of Alexandria

Belief in Genesis 1:27, lack of belief in transgenderism and conscientious objection to transgenderism in our judgment are incompatible with human dignity and conflict with the fundamental rights of ... transgender individuals.[2]

—David Alan Perry

As was signaled toward the end of part 1, in this third part of the book, I will devote a (seemingly) disproportionate amount of attention to Genesis 1 and 2 —three whole chapters, in fact! This is for three important reasons: first,

1. Clement of Alexandria, *The Instructor*, 2.10 (*ANF* 2:259).

2. Employment Judge, David Alan Perry, "Dr David Mackereth v The Department for Work and Pensions and Advanced Personnel Management Group (UK) Ltd: 1304602/2018," GOV.UK (October 7, 2019), https://assets.publishing.service.gov.uk/media/5d9b0c8aed915d35cff2225d/Dr_David_Mackereth_v_The_Department_for_Work_and_Pensions___Advanced_Personnel_Management_Group__UK__Ltd_1304602_-_2018_-_Judgment_and_reasons.pdf.

because of the foundational significance of these chapters for the Bible's sexual anthropology; second, because of the way in which the other acts of the biblical drama build on and interact with these chapters; and third, because of the attention given to (and the interpretations that have arisen from) these chapters by queer scholars and trans-affirming authors.

Accordingly, the purpose of this and the following two chapters is to explore the sexed nature of humanity *as it was in the beginning*; that is, prior to the entrance of sin into the world.[3] While Genesis 1 will be the primary focus of the present chapter, several other scriptural passages (which in various ways engage, develop, or illuminate its teaching) will occupy our attention, as will the anthropological dimension of the doctrine of the creation more broadly. At every point in the investigation, the key questions raised by trans theory—How many sexes are there? What is the relationship of gender to sex? Is it possible for a person's gendered self to conflict with their bodily sex?—will be kept in mind and, at appropriate points, addressed directly.

The obvious starting point is Genesis 1:27 and the relationship it reveals between humanity's creation "in the image of God" (בְּצֶלֶם אֱלֹהִים, *betselem 'elohim*) and our being made "male and female" (זָכָר וּנְקֵבָה, *zakhar uneqevah*). To properly understand this relationship, Genesis 1:27 needs to be read in context—both the immediate context of verses 26–28 and the larger context of 1:1–2:3. Furthermore, however one regards the compositional history of the Bible's opening chapters, the final form of the text indicates that Genesis 1 and 2 are to be read together "as part of the same story of creation, albeit told from different perspectives."[4] For this reason, they should not only be seen as "synoptic accounts of the same events," but allowed to complement, supplement, and interpret one another.

3. I share Fellipe do Vale's concern that, when it comes to theologizing about human sexuality, there is a risk in invoking the doctrine of creation "without recognition of the ways it has been distorted by sin and without seeing eschatology as a surplus to it' (Fellipe M. do Vale, *Gender as Love: A Theological Account of Human Identity, Embodied Desire, and Our Social Worlds* [Grand Rapids: Baker Academic, 2023], 181). I will seek to provide that "recognition" in chapters 10–11.

4. Marc Cortez, *Theological Anthropology: A Guide for the Perplexed* (London: T&T Clark, 2010), 27.

While it is not my purpose to rehearse the complex history of debate regarding the genre of the biblical creation accounts,[5] I find John Sailhamer's term "mega history" to be an apt descriptor and, because of the way the biblical authors speak of Adam, I hold that he (like Eve) is "both an archetype and a historical figure."[6] However, my primary concern—which is to discern what Genesis 1 and 2 teach about sex and gender—largely transcends the genre question. Indeed, the task of rightly deducing the sexual anthropology of these chapters is shared by biblical scholars across the convictional spectrum.[7] For not only is it clear that they teach a mixture of theology, anthropology and ethics ("just as much as do the laws and sermons found elsewhere in the Pentateuch"),[8] but it is broadly recognized—even by many who do not hold to an evangelical doctrine of Scripture—that "the Bible's first statement concerning humankind remains the normative statement that governs all others."[9]

"GOD CREATED MAN IN HIS OWN IMAGE"

HUMANITY'S CREATION IN THE CONTEXT OF GENESIS 1:1–2:3

Within the opening chapters of Genesis, 1:1–2:3 form a discrete section. This is indicated by the way 2:1–3 repeats and reverses the main terms of 1:1—"the heavens and the earth" (2:1), "God" (2:2) "created" (2:3)—so forming an obvious *inclusio*, and by the repetition of the expression "God created" (בָּרָא אֱלֹהִים, *bara' 'elohim*) in 1:1 and 2:3. In terms of its function, the section "introduces the two main subjects of Holy Scripture, God

5. For a useful survey of the genre debate, see Richard M. Davidson, "The Genesis Account of Origins," in *The Genesis Creation Account and Its Reverberations in the Old Testament*, ed. Gerald A. Klingbeil (Berrien Springs, MI: Andrews University Press, 2015), 69–87.

6. John H. Sailhamer, *Genesis Unbounded: A Provocative New Look at the Creation Account* (Sisters, OR: Multnomah Books, 1996), 239; Darrell L. Bock, "Thinking Backwards about Adam and History" *TRINJ* 40 (2019): 139.

7. In Paul Jewett's view, for example, taking a non-literal approach to Genesis 2 "in no way alters the significance of the narrative as a divine revelation" (Paul K. Jewett, *Man as Male and Female: A Study in Sexual Relationships from a Theological Point of View* [Grand Rapids: Eerdmans, 1975], 122).

8. Gordon J. Wenham, *Genesis 1–15*, WBC 1 (Waco, TX: Word, 1987), 5.

9. Bird, "Bone of My Bone," 528.

the Creator and man his creature, and sets the scene for the long tale of their relationship."[10]

As outlined in Genesis 1, the six days of creation are characterized by a number of recurrent (although not rigidly applied) literary formulae:[11]

1. Introduction: "And God said"
2. Volitive command: "Let there be"
3. Indicative result or commentary: "and it was so" or "and God made"
4. Divine evaluation: "God saw that it was good"
5. Naming of created object: "God called"
6. Concluding merism: "there was evening and there was morning"
7. Enumerative summary: "day [X]"

Not only do these features speak of "a God who creates order by his very word of command,"[12] but as it is God *alone* who creates (5x), speaks (10x), separates (3x), calls (5x), makes (5x), lets (15x), sees (7x), and blesses (3x), they also reveal that everything in creation is reliant on him for its existence, significance, identity, function, and direction. Horton, therefore, is right to see the creation account as both a declaration of "God's historical act and claim upon all of reality" and "the preamble and historical prologue for the Law (Torah), with its stipulations and sanctions."[13] In short, the *way* of creation is determined by and dependent on the *word* of its creator.[14]

The ramifications of this for anthropology are significant. Not only is our origin in God, but since he has formed and fashioned us according

10. Wenham, *Genesis 1–15*, 5.

11. Adapted from Bill T. Arnold, *Genesis*, NCBC (Cambridge: Cambridge University Press, 2009), 31.

12. Wenham, *Genesis 1–15*, 10.

13. Horton, *The Christian Faith*, 325.

14. Phyllis A. Bird, "'Male and Female He Created Them': Gen 1:27b in the Context of the Priestly Account of Creation," *Harvard Theological Review* 74 (1981): 136.

to his purpose, God alone "has the right to declare what it means to be human."[15] As we shall see in the chapters ahead, this has both *ethical implications*—for humanity has been made to live "by every word that comes from the mouth of the LORD" (Deut 8:3)—and, as we saw in chapter 3, *epistemological implications*. As Christoph Schwöbel explains, "adequate and complete knowledge of what it means to be human can neither be read off the empirical findings of the different anthropological disciplines, nor developed from the reflexive character of human self-consciousness."[16] What is required, rather, is a sola Scriptura approach with a christological focus: the first because we are dependent on biblical revelation for objective and infallible knowledge of God, humanity, and the relationship between them; the second because, ultimately, it is only in Jesus Christ that we see what it means to be truly human.[17]

One final observation regarding Genesis 1:1–2:3 is in order. The successive divine evaluations—"it was *good*" (טוֹב, *tov*) in 1:4, 10, 12, 18, 21 and 25, and "it was *very good*" (טוֹב מְאֹד, *tov me'od*) in v. 31—do more than speak of creation's construction and completion; they build toward the unveiling of creation's ultimate goal: divine rest (2:2–3).[18] The identification of this goal is not in conflict with the biblical author's depiction of humanity's creation as "the climax of the six days' work."[19] Rather, it points to the fact that humanity, as "the agent through whom the aims of creation will be realised," shares the *telos* of entering God's Sabbath.[20] In Claus Westermann's words, "the work which has been laid on man is not his goal. His goal is the eternal rest which has been suggested by the rest of

---

15. Stanley Grenz, *Theology for the Community of God* (Grand Rapids: Eerdmans, 1994), 127 (compare 142).

16. Christoph Schwöbel, "Human Being as Relational Being: Twelve Theses for a Christian Anthropology," in *Persons, Divine and Human*, ed. Christoph Schwöbel and Colin E. Gunton (Edinburgh: T&T Clark, 1991), 145.

17. Marc Cortez, *ReSourcing Theological Anthropology: A Constructive Account of Humanity in the Light of Christ* (Grand Rapids: Zondervan, 2017), 169.

18. Arnold, *Genesis*, 40; compare Bruce Riley Ashford and Craig G. Bartholomew, *The Doctrine of Creation: A Constructive Kuyperian Approach* (Downers Grove, IL: InterVarsity Press, 2020), 225.

19. Wenham, *Genesis 1–15*, 37. This point is highlighted by the threefold use of *bara'* (ברא) in 1:27, as well as by the addition of the definite article *he* (ה, lit: "day *the* sixth") in v. 31.

20. William J. Dumbrell, *Covenant and Creation: An Old Testament Covenant Theology*, 2nd ed. (Milton Keynes: Paternoster, 2013), 34.

the seventh day."[21] We shall return to this insight in chapter 11, for what it suggests is that humanity's protological existence has always been directed toward a greater eschatological end: transfiguration or glorification.

THE MEANING OF THE *IMAGO DEI*

That humanity should be created for such a destiny raises the question of Psalm 8:4: "What is man that you are mindful of him, and the son of man that you care for him?" The answer, as the psalm itself indicates, is found in Genesis 1:26: "Then God said, 'Let us make *man* [אָדָם, *'adam*][22] *in our image* [בְּצַלְמֵנוּ, *betsalmenu*], *after our likeness* [כִּדְמוּתֵנוּ, *kidmuthenu*]. And let them have dominion over the fish of the sea and over the birds of the heavens and over the livestock and over all the earth and over every creeping thing that creeps on the earth.' "

The debate over meaning

As the history of its interpretation reveals, the meaning of the divine image is highly contested. Part of the reason for this is that many explanations have been overly influenced by "whatever emphasis happened to be current in psychology, or philosophy, or sociology, or theology."[23] It has also been suggested that Scripture itself does not fully elucidate the expression.[24] For David Kelsey, this explains why even "the most careful and most influential exegeses seem to cancel out each other."[25] While this may be a somewhat pessimistic view of the exegetical status quo, it is now generally agreed that the question cannot be settled by reference to Genesis 1 alone, and is only finally answered by a broader canonical (and ultimately christological) approach.[26]

---

21. Claus Westermann, *Creation*, trans. John J. Scullion (London: SPCK, 1974), 65.

22. When *'adam* is being used generically (i.e., as a collective singular), as it is here (compare "let *them* have dominion"), I will use the term "humanity" or (when quoting sources) "man."

23. Edward M. Curtis, "Image of God (OT)," in *The Anchor Bible Dictionary*, Volume 3: H–J, ed. David Noel Freedman (New York: Doubleday, 1992), 389–90.

24. James Barr, for instance, thinks that it is likely that the author of Genesis lacked "any definite idea about the content and location of the image of God" (Barr, "The Image of God in the Book of Genesis: A Study of Terminology," *BJRL* 51 [1968]: 13).

25. David H. Kelsey, *Eccentric Existence: A Theological Anthropology* (Philadelphia: Westminster, 2009), 2:900.

26. Anthony Hoekema, e.g., arrives at his theological conclusions by refracting a full biblical survey through a critical historical survey. See Hoekema, *Created in God's Image* (Grand Rapids:

Exegetically, debate has centered around three main questions, all of which have been variously answered: (1) Why does God speak in plural terms ("let *us* make" / "in *our* image" / "after *our* likeness")? (2) What is the respective force of the prepositions "in" (בְּ, *b*) and "after" (כְּ, *k*)? And (3) is there a difference in meaning between "image" (צֶלֶם, *tselem*) and "likeness" (דְּמוּת, *demuth*)?[27] Regarding the nature of the image, interpretations have tended to fall into four broad categories: (1) *structural* views (e.g., the image consists in the possession of a rational soul);[28] (2) *functional* views (e.g., the image equates to the exercise of dominion);[29] (3) *ethical* views (e.g., the image is humanity's original righteousness);[30] and (4) *relational* views (e.g., the image is seen in human fellowship).[31]

Nevertheless, the complexity and uncertainty of the situation should not be overstated. Not only are many of the proposals compatible or complementary, but the following six conclusions now command widespread scholarly agreement:[32]

1. To image God means to reflect and represent him.
2. "Image" and "likeness" are virtual synonyms.
3. "In" and "after" are also virtual synonyms.
4. The image of God is a dynamic concept.
5. The image of God includes all human beings.
6. The image of God is, ultimately, a christological concept.

Eerdmans, 1986), 11–101. Kelsey, by way of contrast, develops his theological anthropology by starting with the Old Testament Wisdom literature (*Eccentric Existence*, 1:176–89).

27. The third of these questions would seem to be answered by the interchangeability of the terms within the book of Genesis itself (compare 5:1–3; 9:6). This suggests that the second question can be answered similarly—a conclusion supported by the fact that the LXX translates both Hebrew prepositions by the same Greek preposition (κατα, *kata*). Along these lines, Wenham concludes that "according to our likeness" functions as "an explanatory gloss indicating the precise sense of 'in our image'" (*Genesis 1–15*, 29). The first question is answered in fn. 32.

28. E.g., Thomas Aquinas, *Summa Theologiae: Latin Text and English Translation, Introductions, Notes, Appendices, and Glossaries*, ed. T. Gilby and T. C. O'Brien, 60 vols. (New York: McGraw Hill, 1963–1976), 1a.90.2–4.

29. E.g., David J. A. Clines, "The Image of God in Man," *TB* 19 (1968): 53–103.

30. E.g., Martin Luther, *Lectures on Genesis Chapters 1–5*, *LW* 1, 65.

31. E.g., Stanley J. Grenz, "The Social God and the Relational Self: Toward a Theology of the *Imago Dei* in the Postmodern Context," in *Personal Identity in Theological Perspective*, ed. Richard Lints, Michael S. Horton, and Mark R. Talbot (Grand Rapids: Eerdmans, 2006), 70–92.

32. These points have been adapted from Cortez, *Theological Anthropology*, 16–17. Point 3, however, is not included in Cortez's list.

Building on these six points of consensus, six observations of an exegetical nature further enhance the clarity of the larger picture.

Six exegetical observations

First, however one interprets the divine plurals in Genesis 1:26, it is evident that *humanity stands in a unique relationship to God.*[33] This is initially signaled by the change from impersonal words of divine declaration ("Let there be") to personal words of divine deliberation ("Let *us* make").[34] But it is primarily an entailment of the fact that no other creature is said to be the *imago Dei*. In making humanity, then, God has created "a real partner; which is capable of action and relation to him."[35] Herein lies the biblical basis not only for the doctrine of human exceptionalism, but also for an affirmation of the dignity and sanctity of *all* human life (compare Gen 9:5–6).[36] Every human being, as the psalmist insists, has been crowned with glory and honor (Ps 8:5–8). Humanity, then, is uniquely privileged and, as a result, uniquely accountable.

Second, syntactically, Genesis 1:26b ("and let them have dominion") functions as a purpose statement.[37] That is, *the reason humanity has been created in the divine image is to serve as God's vicegerent on earth*. Although this task does not define the image, it does depict humanity as "a physical manifestation of divine (or royal) essence that bears the function of that which it represents."[38] This is borne out by the command of verse 28 ("fill the earth and subdue it"), where humanity is called to imitate God's twofold work of forming and filling by "populating and organizing (in a

33. In context, the plural cohortative is best seen as "an especially emphatic exhortation of self-deliberation or determination, expressing the measured and intentional action God is about to take" (Arnold, *Genesis*, 44). Contra Arnold, however, this does not rule out the possibility of "an intradivine conversation," with all the trinitarian possibilities that such an expression entails (Kenneth A. Mathews, *Genesis 1–11:26*, NAC 1A [Nashville: Broadman & Holman, 1996], 163).

34. Mathews, *Genesis 1–11:26*, 160.

35. Barth, *CD*, III/1, 184.

36. Christopher Watkin, *Thinking Through Creation: Genesis 1 and 2 as Tools of Cultural Critique* (Phillipsburg, NJ: P&R, 2017), 95–98.

37. Richard J. Middleton, *The Liberating Image: The* Imago Dei *in Genesis 1* (Grand Rapids: Brazos, 2005), 53.

38. John H. Walton, *Genesis: The NIV Application Commentary* (Grand Rapids: Zondervan, 2001), 131.

manner appropriate to humans) the unformed and unfilled earth."[39] In the first instance, then, the text presents humans less as *formal representations of the divine being*, and more as *functional representatives of the divine rule.*[40]

Third, representation, however, is also a key part of the picture. Hence, *the physicality of humanity is highly significant.* Indeed, "visibility and bodiliness" are irreducible elements of the word "image" (*tselem*).[41] This does not mean that "the bodily form of man was made after the pattern of the bodily form of God."[42] But it does mean that "it is only as embodied beings that we can function as God's representatives in a physical world."[43] Moreover, when we consider the Old Testament's use of *image* with reference to idols (e.g., Num 33:52; 2 Kgs 11:18), and with it the fact that idols were thought to be united to the (supposed) reality behind them, it is clear that God created humanity "to be the physical means through which he would manifest his own divine presence in the world."[44] Therefore, whatever else might be said about the nature of the *imago Dei*, embodiment (including *sexed* embodiment) is integral to the biblical presentation.

Fourth, all of this suggests that *humanity has been created not so much* after *God's image but* as *God's image.*[45] As David Clines explains, "according to Genesis 1 man does not have the image of God, nor is he made *in* the image of God, but is himself the image of God."[46] Not all commentators agree, however; many believing that the prepositions in verse 26 express *norm* rather than *essence*, and so should both be translated "according to"

---

39. Middleton, *Liberating Image*, 89.

40. This resolves the dilemma of Howard Eilberg-Schwartz, who sees "a fundamental tension between being made in God's image and being obliged to reproduce" ("People of the Body: The Problem of the Body for the People of the Book," *Journal of the History of Sexuality* 2 [1991]: 7).

41. Middleton, *Liberating Image*, 25.

42. H. Wheeler Robinson, "Hebrew Psychology," in *The People and the Book*, ed. A. S. Peake (Oxford: Clarendon, 1925), 369. Indeed, such a view not only confuses representation with resemblance, but ignores Scripture's testimony that God is spiritual and invisible (Deut 4:15; John 1:18; 4:24; Luke 24:39; Rom 1:20; 1 Tim 1:17; 6:16). For a helpful discussion and defence of divine incorporeality, see John M. Frame, *The Doctrine of God* (Phillipsburg, NJ: P&R Publishing, 2002), 583–91.

43. Cortez, *Theological Anthropology*, 40.

44. Cortez, *ReSourcing Theological Anthropology*, 109; compare Andreas Schüle, "Made in the 'Image of God': The Concepts of Divine Images in Gen 1–3," *ZAW* 117 (2005): 1–20.

45. Henri Blocher, *In the Beginning: The Opening Chapters of Genesis*, trans. David G. Preston (Downers Grove, IL: InterVarsity Press, 1984), 84–85.

46. Clines, "Image of God," 80 (emphasis original).

(the LXX renders both as *kata*) rather than either "in" or "after."[47] On this view, "man is a copy of something that had the divine image, not necessarily the image itself."[48] John Kilner, a recent proponent of this view, thus posits a distinction between God, his image, and humanity.[49] Moreover, by drawing on the New Testament's christological teaching (e.g., 2 Cor 4:4; Col 1:15), he not only distinguishes Christ as God's "imprint-image" from human beings as his "likeness-image," but argues that "God's intention from the beginning has been to conform people to God's image—to Christ (Rom 8:29)."[50]

There are strengths to this approach. As the New Testament makes plain, Christ is the *imago Dei* par excellence. Furthermore, as we have seen already (in chapter 3) and will see further (in chapter 11), there are good reasons for grounding anthropology in Christology.[51] Nonetheless, the prepositional argument (on which Kilner's distinction relies) is difficult to reconcile with both Genesis 5:3—where Adam is said to father Seth "after his image" (כְּצַלְמוֹ, *ketslamo*)—and 1 Corinthians 11:7—where Paul declares that man *is* (ὑπάρχων, *hyparchōn*) the image of God.[52] These texts depict the *imago Dei* as a status that is *actually* (rather than *potentially*) possessed by all people—even post-fall (compare Gen 9:3; Jas 3:9).

Clines's view, then, is to be preferred. But on either view, the reality of being made *in* God's image is one that pertains to every stage and condition of human life.[53] It is thus unaffected by whether a person is unsure or confused about their biological sex or gender identity. The reason for this is plain: created identity is determined not by the creature but "by the

---

47. John F. Kilner, *Dignity and Destiny: Humanity in the Image of God* (Grand Rapids: Eerdmans, 2015), 91, esp. fn. 26.

48. Wenham, *Genesis 1–15*, 32.

49. Kilner, *Dignity and Destiny*, 91.

50. Kilner, *Dignity and Destiny*, 59, 91.

51. Marc Cortez, "Nature, Grace, and the Christological Ground of Humanity," in *The Christian Doctrine of Humanity: Explorations in Constructive Dogmatics*, ed. Oliver D. Crisp and Fred Sanders (Grand Rapids: Zondervan, 2018), 23–40.

52. Blocher, *In the Beginning*, 85.

53. On the importance of this understanding for those with severe cognitive disabilities, see George C. Hammond, *It Has Not Yet Appeared What We Shall Be: A Reconsideration of the* Imago Dei *in Light of Those with Severe Cognitive Disabilities* (Phillipsburg, NJ: P&R, 2017).

transcendent God who makes creation what it is."[54] However we might develop our identity, then, who and what we are is, first and foremost, a divine gift.

Fifth, this last point highlights the validity of Millard Erickson's insight that the *imago Dei* is not, in fact, correlated with any variable whatsoever but "refers to something a human *is* rather than something a human *has* or *does*."[55] Barth puts it this way: "There is no point in asking in which of man's peculiar attributes and attitudes" the image is to be located; it consists, rather, "as man himself consists as the creature of God. He would not be man if he were not the image of God. He is the image of God in the fact that he is man."[56] In short, the *imago Dei* is ontological before it is functional; doing arises from being, existence from essence.

Finally, in contrast to Genesis 1:26, which "speaks less of the nature of God's image than of its purpose,"[57] Genesis 5:3 ("When Adam had lived 130 years, he *fathered a son* [יוֹלֶד, *yoled*] in his own *likeness* [*demuth*], after his *image* [*tselem*], and named him Seth") links *image* with *sonship*. For Henri Blocher, this is a vital clue to the deeper meaning of 1:26 (and also 5:1b–2), indicating that "God created man as a sort of earthly son, who represents him and responds to him."[58] In other words, *image* and *sonship* are "mutually explanatory concepts. To be the image of God is to be the son of God."[59]

Turning to the New Testament, this conclusion gains further support from Luke 3:38, where Seth is called "the son of Adam, the son of God" (υἱός … τοῦ Ἀδὰμ τοῦ θεοῦ, *huios … tou Adam tou theou*), and from Acts 17:29, where Paul refers to all human beings as "God's offspring" (γένcς … τοῦ

54. Ryan S. Peterson, *The* Imago Dei *as Human Identity: A Theological Interpretation*, JTI Supplement 14 (Winona Lake, IN: Eisenbrauns, 2016), 65.

55. Millard J. Erickson, *Christian Theology*, 2nd ed. (Grand Rapids: Baker, 1998), 532.

56. Barth, *CD*, III/1, 184.

57. Gerhard von Rad, *Genesis*, trans. J. H. Marks & J. Bowden (London: SCM, 1972), 59.

58. Blocher, *In the Beginning*, 89; compare Catherine McDowell, "In the Image of God He Created Them: How Genesis 1:26–27 Defines the Divine-Human Relationship and Why It Matters," in *The Image of God in an Image Driven Age: Explorations in Theological Anthropology*, ed. Beth Felker Jones and Jeffrey W. Barbeau (Downers Grove, IL: InterVarsity Press, 2016), 29–46.

59. Meredith G. Kline, *Kingdom Prologue: Genesis Foundations for a Covenantal Worldview* (Overland Park, KS: Two Age, 2002), 46.

θεοῦ, *genos ... tou theou*).[60] For this reason, Gavin Ortlund is right to contend that "greater recognition should be given to the metaphor of begottenness in discussions concerning the meaning of the *imago Dei* in the Bible. ... At its core, the *imago Dei* suggests that humans are like God: and the analogy of children seems quite apt for communicating this idea."[61]

We shall have cause to revisit this link between *image* and *sonship* (in particular, what it means to be conformed to Christ's image) in a later chapter. As we are about to see, however, one thing that *cannot* be inferred from it is that the male is *more* (or *more directly*) the image of God than the female.

"MALE AND FEMALE HE CREATED THEM"

This brings us to the central anthropological question of this chapter: What is the relationship between humanity's creation in the divine image and its sexual dimorphism?

PRELIMINARY EXEGETICAL OBSERVATIONS

Genesis 1:27a ("So God created man in his own image") directly answers the statement of divine deliberation in verse 26a ("Let us make man in our image"). This is evident from the fact that the key terms are repeated—although "man" (*'adam*) has the definite article (*he*)[62] and "image" (*tselem*) lacks the corresponding term "likeness" (*demuth*).[63] The only other difference is that verse 27 uses "create" (*bara'*) rather than "make" (עָשָׂה, *'asah*),

---

60. Brian Rosner, *Known by God: A Biblical Theology of Personal Identity*, Biblical Theology for Life (Grand Rapids: Zondervan, 2017), 82–83.

61. Gavin Ortlund, "Image of Adam, Son of God: Genesis 5:3 and Luke 3:38 in Intercanonical Dialogue," *JETS* 57 (2014): 687.

62. It is likely that "man" (*'adam*) lacks the article in v. 26 not only to match "God" (*'elohim*), which is also anarthrous, but because it is generic humanity that is on view. In light of this, the addition of the article in v. 27a appears to be anomalous (particularly as the near repetition of the same language in 5:1b lacks the article). Most likely, "the definite article is used because the subject, *'ādām*, has already been introduced in the last verse" (John H. Walton with a contribution by N. T. Wright, *The Lost World of Adam and Eve: Genesis 2–3 and the Human Origins Debate* [Downers Grove, IL: InterVarsity Press, 2015], 60).

63. As already noted, "image" and "likeness" are virtual synonyms. Consequently, in v. 27, "image" alone stands in for both terms, just as "likeness" does in Genesis 5:1.

but this is almost certainly stylistic, as both terms are used interchangeably throughout Genesis 1.[64]

TABLE 4: GENESIS 1:27 — ENGLISH AND HEBREW

English Standard Version	*Biblia Hebraica Stuttgartensia*
a. So God created man in his own image,	וַיִּבְרָ֨א אֱלֹהִ֤ים ׀ אֶת־הָֽאָדָם֙ בְּצַלְמ֔וֹ
b. in the image of God he created him;	בְּצֶ֥לֶם אֱלֹהִ֖ים בָּרָ֣א אֹת֑וֹ
c. male and female he created them.	זָכָ֥ר וּנְקֵבָ֖ה בָּרָ֥א אֹתָֽם

Structurally, the whole verse forms a three-line poem, with lines one and two standing in a chiastic relationship—line two repeating and inverting the thought of line one. Line three then explicates the nature of "the man" (*ha'adam*), revealing that *he* is not only a *plural entity* (humanity)—the "them" (אֹתָם, *'otham*) in 27c explicating the "him" (אֹתוֹ, *'otho*) in 27b—but a *sexually dimorphic species*—the "male and female" (*zakhar uneqevah*) in 27c explicating "the image of God" (*tselem 'elohim*) in 27b. Contextually, this plurality was already hinted at in verse 26—in the plural form of the verb רָדָה (*radah*, "let *them* have dominion" [וְיִרְדּוּ, *weyirdu*])—and its purpose further clarified in the command "be fruitful and multiply" (פְּרוּ וּרְבוּ, *peru urevu*) in verse 28.

From an exegetical standpoint, then, the meaning of Genesis 1:27 would appear to be straightforward: the *imago Dei* is both male and female, and human beings are either male or female. As Barth summarizes: "We cannot say man without having to say male or female and also male and female. Man exists in this differentiation, in this duality."[65]

However, several intersex scholars and trans-affirming authors have challenged this understanding. Some suggest that "the Genesis emphasis on the pairing of male and female (including Gen 5:1–2) reflects a cultural understanding that has subsequently been modified by human experience and research."[66] Others claim that the Bible itself gives reasons for thinking that "the original created being is either hermaphroditic or sexually

64. "Create" is used in vv. 1, 14 and 27[x3]; "make" is used in vv. 7, 16, 25, 26 and 31. Moreover, Genesis 2:4, which uses both words in parallel, also shows that they function as virtual synonyms.

65. Barth, *CD*, III/2, 286.

66. Mollenkott, *Omnigender*, 103. Mollenkott attributes this view to Rabbi Robert Saks (n. 14).

undifferentiated, a 'gender outlaw' by modern terms, closer to a transgender identity than to half of a binary gender construct."[67] Others still claim that Scripture's depiction of created variety is by no means exhaustive; that is, "just because Genesis 1 does not make a statement about a particular aspect of creation" (e.g., intersexuality), this does not mean that "it is not part of God's *good* creation."[68] Along these lines, Austen Hartke confidently declares that "for as long as there have been humans, there have been people who fall outside of the male/female binary."[69]

To evaluate these claims, and to clarify the significance of Genesis 1:27 for theological anthropology (in general) and what it indicates about the relationship between biological sex and personal identity (in particular), three questions require further exploration: (1) Does Genesis 1:27 teach that humanity was initially androgynous? (2) Does Genesis 1:27 allow for additional sexes? (3) What is the relationship between "the image of God" and "male and female"?

DOES GENESIS 1:27 TEACH THAT HUMANITY WAS INITIALLY ANDROGYNOUS?

Androgyne myths were common in antiquity.[70] For Plato (or, at least, his character Aristophanes), "there were not merely two sexes as there are now, male and female, but three, and the third was a combination of the other two."[71] By the end of the first century of the Christian era, the androgyne myth was even being used by some Christians to make sense of the creation accounts in Genesis 1 and 2: "Genesis 1:27 detailed the creation of an original androgynous progenitor of the human race, and Genesis 2:22 expressed the tragic bifurcation of that being into two distinct sexes."[72] By the third century, such ideas had found their way into Jewish thought.[73]

---

67. Mollenkott, *Omnigender*, 99.

68. Herzer, *Transgender Experience*, 52 (emphasis original).

69. Hartke, *Transforming*, 51.

70. Wayne A. Meeks, "The Image of the Androgyne: Some Uses of a Symbol in Earliest Christianity," *History of Religions* 13 (1974): 185.

71. Plato, *The Symposium*, ed. M. C. Howatson and Frisbee C. C. Sheffield, trans. M. C. Howatson (Cambridge: Cambridge University Press, 2008), 22, §189e.

72. Colleen Conway, "The Construction of Gender in the New Testament," in Thatcher, *Oxford Handbook of Theology, Sexuality, and Gender*, 228.

73. E.g., Bereshit Rabba 8:1.

Rabbis in the early Talmudic period, for example, make reference to a version of the Septuagint which renders both Genesis 1:27c and Genesis 5:2a as "male and female he created *him*"—inferring original androgyny.[74]

Gregory of Nyssa's interpretation of Genesis 1:27

Such ideas persisted over the ensuing centuries, not only in the hands of the Gnostics, who "were particularly entranced by the androgynous character of the primal man,"[75] but also in the minds of certain Nicene and post-Nicene fathers—notably, Gregory of Nyssa. For Gregory, not only did "the distinction of male and female" have "no reference to the Divine Archetype," but the creation of male and female in Genesis 1:27c is "a departure from the Prototype" of 1:26–27b.[76] In his treatise *De hominis opificio* (*On the Making of Man*), he explains as follows:

> While two natures—the Divine and incorporeal nature, and the irrational life of brutes—are separated from each other as extremes, human nature is the mean between them: for in the compound nature of man we may behold a part of each of the natures I have mentioned—of the Divine, the rational and intelligent element, which does not admit the distinction of male and female; of the irrational, our bodily form and structure, divided into male and female: for each of these elements is certainly to be found in all that partakes of human life. That *the intellectual element, however, precedes* [προτερεύειν, *protereuein*] *the other*, we learn as from one who gives in order an account of the making of man; and we learn also that his community and kindred with the irrational is for man a provision for reproduction. For he says first that "God created man in the image of God" (showing by these words, as the Apostle says, that in such a being there is no male or female): then he adds the peculiar attributes of human nature, "male and female created He them."[77]

74. Babylonian Talmud, Megillah 9a, 13.
75. Meeks, "Image of the Androgyne," 188.
76. Gregory of Nyssa, *On the Making of Man*, XVI.7 (*NPNF*[2] 5:405–6).
77. Gregory of Nyssa, *On the Making of Man*, XVI.9 (*NPNF*[2] 5:405, emphasis added).

What Gregory appears to be arguing here is that humanity's creation takes place in two stages: initially as *non-genitalized intellectual beings* ("in the image of God") and subsequently as *genitalized biological beings* ("male and female").[78] However, according to J. Warren Smith, Gregory "does not mean that God performed two separate acts of creation"; rather, the order is "only at the level of God's intention."[79] Whether or not this is correct, a deeper question remains: Why would God dilute his pure image with the irrationality of sex distinctions? Gregory's answer in this paragraph is that it is "a provision for reproduction." Later in his treatise, however, a more disturbing reason emerges:

> But as He perceived in our created nature *the bias towards evil,* and the fact that *after its voluntary fall* from equality with the angels it would acquire a fellowship with the lower nature, He mingled, *for this reason,* with His own image, an element of the irrational (for the distinction of male and female does not exist in the Divine and blessed nature);—transferring, I say, to man the special attribute of the irrational formation, He bestowed increase upon our race not according to the lofty character of our creation; for it was not when He made that which was in His own image that He bestowed on man the power of increasing and multiplying; but when He divided it by sexual distinctions, then He said, "Increase and multiply, and replenish the earth."[80]

Gregory is unambiguous: human sex distinctions are not merely part of our (stage two) *createdness,* enabling us to reproduce, but they anticipate our *fallenness.*[81] Indeed, they are a consequence of a supposed "bias

78. Sarah Coakley, "The Eschatological Body: Gender, Transformation, and God," *Modern Theology* 16 (2000): 68.

79. J. Warren Smith, "The Body of Paradise and the Body of the Resurrection: Gender and the Angelic Life in Gregory of Nyssa's *De hominis opificio*," *HTR* 92 (2006): 212.

80. Gregory of Nyssa, *Making of Man*, XXII.4 (*NPNF*² 5:411–12, emphasis added).

81. For this reason, some interpreters have argued that Gregory sees "the garments of skin" (Gen 3:21) given to Adam and Eve in their postlapsarian state in terms of human sex distinctions (e.g., Hans Boersma, "Putting on Clothes: Body, Sex, and Gender in Gregory of Nyssa," *CRUX* 54 [2018]: 27–34). On the problems with this way of reading Gregory, see John Behr, "The Rational Animal: A Rereading of Gregory of Nyssa's *De hominis opificio*," *JECS* 7 (1999): 219–47; Mark D. Hart, "Reconciliation of Body and Soul: Gregory of Nyssa's Deeper Theology of Marriage," *Theological Studies* 51 (1990): 450–78.

toward evil" within our created natures! As Smith rightly sees, this means that "had God foreseen that humanity would not fall, he would not have gendered human beings for a sexual mode of reproduction."[82] It is also noteworthy that, contra Smith, Gregory does appear to affirm that God created human nature in two sequential steps: first, "*when* He made that which was in His own image" and, second, "*when* He divided it by sexual distinctions." Moreover, insists Gregory, since "male and female does not exist in the Divine and blessed nature," they do not truly belong to the *imago Dei* either.

Admittedly, Gregory's anthropological thought is not easily synthesized, and may well be described as "kaleidoscopic."[83] Nevertheless, Christopher Roberts is right to conclude that "sexual difference has a lower status in Gregory's protology, for it appears that, like clothes or 'garments of skin,' it would not have existed without sin."[84]

As a point of clarification, Gregory is not so much arguing for original *androgyny* (or *bisexuality*) as he is for original *asexuality* (or *presexuality*). In Sarah Coakley's words, the primal human person "is what one might call 'humanoid' (or perhaps 'angeloid')—neither male nor female in any commonly accepted sense."[85] This, she is quick to add, does not mean that Gregory can be co-opted by postmodern theorists who wish to promote contemporary notions of *gender fluidity*: "His understanding of what constitutes authentic human existence before God, eludes even these 'transgressive' categories."[86] Nevertheless, Gregory's interpretation of Genesis 1:27 does focus the question we are seeking to resolve: "Is human unity, 'humankind,' the fundamental ontological 'fact' prior to sexual difference, or is sexual difference equally fundamental?"[87]

82. Smith, "Body of Paradise," 209.

83. Smith, "Body of Paradise," 228.

84. Roberts, *Creation & Covenant*, 26.

85. Sarah Coakley, *God, Sexuality and the Self: An Essay "On the Trinity"* (Cambridge: Cambridge University Press, 2013), 281.

86. Coakley, *God, Sexuality and the Self*, 282.

87. Thatcher, *Redeeming Gender*, 143.

Problems with Gregory's interpretation

As I have already noted, both the grammar and structure of the Hebrew text indicate that to be human is to be *either* male *or* female. The syntactical shift from the singular pronoun *him* (in v. 27b) to the plural pronoun *them* (in 27c) reveals that *man* (in 27a) "is not one single creature who is both male and female but rather two creatures, one male and one female."[88] Augustine saw this clearly, insisting that human beings "were corporeal and heterogeneous from the beginning, and sexuality was in no way at odds with the original innocence of Eden."[89] Thus, at the end of chapter 22 of book III of *The Literal Meaning of Genesis*, he writes:

> Lest anyone suppose that this creation took place in such a way that both sexes appeared in one single human being (as happens in some births, in the case of what we call hermaphrodites), the sacred writer shows that he used the singular number [i.e., he made *him*] because of the bond of unity between man and woman, and because woman was made from man. ... Hence he immediately added the plural number when he said, *He made them ... and He blessed them.*[90]

Suffice it to say that the syntax of Genesis 1:27 "prevents one from assuming the creation of an originally androgynous man."[91]

The same applies to claims of original asexuality and bisexuality. As queer theologian Ken Stone concedes, "the structure and content of the text as it stands do seem to encourage interpretations that grant a foundational status to binary sexual division as a crucial defining feature of humankind."[92] In fact, John Skinner is right to put the point more strongly,

---

88. Phyllis Trible, *God and the Rhetoric of Sexuality* (Philadelphia: Fortress, 1978), 18.

89. Leah DeVun, "Heavenly Hermaphrodites: Sexual Difference at the Beginning and End of Time," *Postmedieval: A Journal of Medieval Cultural Studies* 9 (2018): 134.

90. Augustine, *The Literal Meaning of Genesis: Book 1–6*, trans. and annotated by John Hammond Taylor (New York: Newman, 1982), 1:99.

91. Von Rad, *Genesis*, 60.

92. Ken Stone, "The Garden of Eden and the Heterosexual Contract," in *Bodily Citations: Religion and Judith Butler*, ed. Ellen T. Armour and Susan M. St. Ville (New York: Columbia University Press, 2006), 53.

insisting that the midrashic claim that "man as first created was bisexual and the sexes separated afterwards is *far from the thought of this passage*."[93]

Further confirmation of this interpretation of Genesis 1:27 is found in 5:1b–2:

TABLE 5: GENESIS 5:1b–2 — ENGLISH AND HEBREW

English Standard Version	*Biblia Hebraica Stuttgartensia*
1b When God created man,	בְּיוֹם בְּרֹא אֱלֹהִים֙ אָדָ֔ם
he made him in the likeness of God.	בִּדְמ֥וּת אֱלֹהִ֖ים עָשָׂ֥ה אֹתֽוֹ׃
2 Male and female he created them,	זָכָ֥ר וּנְקֵבָ֖ה בְּרָאָ֑ם
and he blessed them and named them	וַיְבָ֣רֶךְ אֹתָ֗ם וַיִּקְרָ֤א אֶת־שְׁמָם֙ אָדָ֔ם
Man when they were created.	בְּי֖וֹם הִבָּֽרְאָֽם

Here, in what is a transparent reformulation of Genesis 1:26–27, we see that the "man" made "in the likeness of God" (5:1b) is a community of persons, not an androgynous, asexual, or bisexual individual. For "God blessed *them* (*'otham*) and named *them* (*'otham*) Man" (5:2). In other words, unlike the uses of "man" (*'adam*) in verse 1a and verse 3 (where *'adam* clearly functions as a personal name), the uses in verse 1b and verse 2 are generic. In its generic sense, writes Phyllis Trible, "the word humankind is synonymous with the phrase 'male and female,' though the components of this phrase are not synonymous with each other. Unity embraces sexual differentiation; it does not impose sexual identicalness."[94]

So then, while we have yet to consider the teaching of Genesis 2, the conclusion to be drawn from the evidence of Genesis 1 is that the initial androgyny interpretation of verse 27 is (as Brunner puts it) "an impossibility for Christian thought."[95] The rabbinical gloss that suggests that Adam was initially a hermaphrodite is based on a misconstrual of the biblical author's meaning and should not be used to cast doubt on the clarity of the created distinction between male and female. There is likewise no support for regarding intersexuality "as a reminder of the 'original innocence'

93. John Skinner, *A Critical and Exegetical Commentary on Genesis*, ICC (Edinburgh: T&T Clark, 1934), 33 (emphasis added).

94. Trible, *Rhetoric of Sexuality*, 18.

95. Emil Brunner, *Man in Revolt: A Christian Anthropology*, trans. O. Wyon (London: Lutterworth, 1939), 348.

and perfection before sin distorted it" or for the extraordinary claim that "it is the birth of people who are not hermaphrodites which might be 'the consequence of Adam's sin.' "[96]

The picture that emerges from both Genesis 1:27 and 5:1b–3 is unambiguous: in the beginning as well as after it, God created "an original duality of the sexes and not an androgynous creature."[97]

DOES GENESIS 1:27 ALLOW FOR ADDITIONAL SEXES?

The case for additional sexes

But how complete is that picture? Does the creation of male and female in Genesis 1:27 mean *only* male and female? Or is it possible that male and female are the *two poles* at either end of a *broader spectrum*?

A number of intersex advocates and trans-affirming authors believe so.[98] They argue that intersex conditions should be understood "not as pathological, or as something which has gone wrong with the male-and-female divine plan for creation, but as evidence that the diversity of creation is broader than we can easily understand."[99] A similar suggestion is made regarding those who identify as transgender.[100] The claim, then, is that *variations in sex presentation and gender experience are manifestations not of postlapsarian disorder but of prelapsarian diversity*. As Justin Tanis reasons:

> While in the Genesis account, God separates the day from the night, the sea from the land, and the plant from the animal, our own observations of the creation reveal less differentiation than the text seems to imply. Day and night are not fixed entities with

96. Sally Gross, "Intersexuality and Scripture," *Theology & Sexuality* 11 (1999): 74.

97. Richard M. Davidson, *Flame of Yahweh: Sexuality in the Old Testament* (Peabody, MA: Hendrickson, 2007), 19.

98. E.g., Tara Soughers, *Beyond a Binary God: A Theology for Trans* Allies* (New York: Church, 2018); Cheryl Evans, *What Does God Think: Transgender People and the Bible* (Cheryl Evans, 2017); O'Brien, "Intersex, Medicine, Diversity," 45–56; Virginia Ramey Mollenkott, "We Come Bearing Gifts: Seven Lessons Religious Congregations Can Learn from Transpeople," in Althaus-Reid and Isherwood, *Trans/Formations*, 46–58.

99. Susannah Cornwall, "Intersex Conditions/DSDs: Some Christian Theological Implications," Intersex, Identity and Disability: Issues for Public Policy, Healthcare and the Church, *Briefing Paper 4, Lincoln Theological Institute* (2012), 15, http://www.klinefelter.se/wp-content/uploads/Briefing-paper-4-UPDATED-APR-2013.pdf.

100. E.g., Justin Sabia-Tanis, "Holy Creation, Wholly Creative," in Beilby and Eddy, *Understanding Transgender Identities*, 195–222.

> clear boundaries where one ends and the other begins; every day contains both dawn and dusk, which creates a time in which day and night exist together in the same moment as one moves into the next. … In the story of Genesis, even while God was creating apparent opposites, God also created liminal spaces in which the elements of creation overlap and merge. Surely the same could be said about the creation of humanity with people occupying many places between the poles of female and male in a way similar to the rest of creation.[101]

Tanis's point is that "the act of creation, even while differentiating between elements of creation, still leaves space for 'in between' things: dusk, dawn, intersexed persons."[102] In her *Sex Difference in Christian Theology*, Megan DeFranza similarly argues that Genesis 1 does not provide "a comprehensive list of all the good things God has made"; it makes no mention, for example, of the hybrid species or mixed forms found in creation, such as "rivers, asteroids, planets, amphibians, dusk, dawn, etc."[103] She then extends her thought to humanity, concluding that "rather than identifying male and female as the paradigmatic forms of otherness, they can be interpreted as the fountainhead of others who may become more 'other' than their parents could have ever conceived."[104]

This argument can be characterized as both *an argument from silence* (i.e., "just because Genesis 1 does not make a statement about a particular aspect of creation, this does not mean that reality does not exist in creation, nor that it is not part of God's *good* creation") and *one that attempts to draw an inference from parallel evidence* (i.e., given that we see numerous instances of hybridity in nature, "might there not be a dawn and dusk, a shoreline and a marshland, another classification kingdom in the realm of male and female?"[105]). As such, it prompts the questions:

---

101. Tanis, *Trans-Gender*, 57–58.

102. Tanis, *Trans-Gender*, 59; compare Hartke, *Transforming*, 51.

103. Megan K. DeFranza, *Sex Difference in Christian Theology: Male, Female, and Intersex in the Image of God* (Grand Rapids: Eerdmans, 2015), 177.

104. DeFranza, *Sex Difference*, 178.

105. Herzer, *Transgender Experience*, 52 (emphasis original), 53.

What are we meant to make of this silence? and What inference should we draw from hybridity?

For Hartke, answers are provided not by Scripture but by private revelation: "Instead of asking the text to define and label all that is, *we can ask God to speak into the space between the words*, between biblical times and our time, and between categories we see as opposites."[106] For Linda Tatro Herzer, it is "modern medicine" that clarifies that "intersex conditions are the dusk and dawn of God's male and female creations." This, then, enables her to conclude that "we can no longer argue that being any of the gender variant expressions under the transgender umbrella is 'a sin' based on the notion that God creates only male and female."[107] DeFranza, too, acknowledges that "Genesis does not answer the question for us." But, for her, a wider and more eschatologically-oriented reading of Scripture does.[108] What is not clear, however, is whether she thinks sex and gender variance are implicitly part of the Edenic pattern (as her references to created hybrid forms suggest) or whether the sex binary functions only as "the fountainhead of human difference without requiring the male-female pattern to become the paradigmatic form of the other." Either way, she is highly critical of the view that intersex conditions "are a result of the Fall, or that they stray from God's creational intent."[109]

The case against additional sexes

In response to such arguments, seven points can be made.

First, on closer inspection of Genesis 1, it is apparent that DeFranza (et al.) have overstated the number of created forms not encompassed by the text. Dawn and dusk, for example, are clearly implied in the sixfold expression "there was evening and there was morning" (vv. 5, 8, 13, 19, 23 and 31), and planets, if not asteroids too, are included in the reference

106. Hartke, *Transforming*, 53 (emphasis added).

107. Herzer, *Transgender Experience*, 56–57.

108. Megan K. DeFranza, "Good News for Gender Minorities," in Beilby and Eddy, *Understanding Transgender Identities*, 173. In particular, she notes that Isa 56:5 promises eunuchs "a place in God's house *as they are*, not after some kind of restoration to an Edenic pattern" ("Good News for Gender Minorities," 174, emphasis original).

109. DeFranza, *Sex Difference*, 179–80, 177 (compare 11–12, 104, 164, 173).

to "the stars" (הַכּוֹכָבִים, *hakkokhavim*) in verse 16 (compare 2:1).[110] What is more, one need only read on into Genesis 2 to discover the existence of rivers (2:10–14).

Second, while Genesis 1 is not seeking to provide an *exhaustive* list of all that God has made, there are several indicators in the text that it is seeking to be *comprehensive*. For example, verse 21 speaks of "*every* living creature that moves, with which the waters swarm" and "*every* winged bird according to its kind," and verse 25 speaks of God making "*everything* that creeps on the ground" (כָּל רֶמֶשׂ הָאֲדָמָה, *kol-remes ha'adamah*)—a statement that would, doubtless, include amphibians and other dual-environmental creatures.[111]

Third, that "male and female" (*zakhar uneqevah*) are to be understood as a strict binary is confirmed by the command of 1:28: "Be fruitful and multiply" (*peru urevu*)—a command that not only requires *both* male and female, but *only* male and female. Indeed, as many commentators have observed, in the sequence of thought that develops through verses 26–28, the reference to male and female in verse 27 is preparatory for understanding the nature and purpose of God's command and blessing in verse 28.[112]

Fourth, given the way that Genesis regularly links divine blessing and reproductive fecundity (12:2–3; 17:16; 22:17; 26:24; 39:5; 48:3–4), it is not surprising that after the flood the same command is given to Noah and his sons (and their respective wives) in Genesis 9:1 (compare v. 7)—particularly after Noah has succeeded in rescuing "two and two (שְׁנַיִם שְׁנַיִם, *shenayim shenayim*) … male and female (*zakhar uneqevah*) of all flesh" (7:15–16; compare v. 9).[113] In regard to the *number* of created sexes, then, and the fact that sex is defined in terms of reproductive structure and function, the biblical text here could not be more explicit.

---

110. In Old Testament thought, "the sun and the moon and the stars" refers to "all the host of heaven" (Deut 4:19; compare Ps 8:3; 136:7–9; Isa 13:10). See Reimund Leicht, "Planets in Ancient Hebrew Literature," in *Giving a Diamond: Essays in Honor of Joseph Yahalom on the Occasion of His Seventieth Birthday*, ed. Wout van Bekkum and Naoya Katsumata (Leiden: Brill, 2011), 15–38.

111. Brian Neil Peterson, "Does Genesis 2 Support Same-Sex Marriage? An Evangelical Response," *JETS* 60 (2017): 693.

112. Mathews, *Genesis 1–11:26*, 173; compare Wenham, *Genesis 1–15*, 33; Bird, "Male and Female," 155.

113. The pairing of "male and female" (*zakhar uneqevah*) also occurs in Gen 5:2; Lev 12:2–7; 15:33; 27:2–7; Num 5:3 and Deut 4:16 (with reference to humans) and in Gen 6:19; 7:3, 9, 16; Lev 3:1, 6 (with reference to animals).

Fifth, the link between the sex binary and reproduction also points to another theme of Genesis: the importance of healthy male-female fertility for the multiplication of "the generations" (תּוֹלְדֹת, *toledoth*).[114] This theme, as Augustine saw, provides further confirmation that "the human sexes, as the result of which there exist such generations, are two, male and female."[115] It also explains why reproductive incapacity is seen as a cause for grief, and not as an alternate form of blessing (Gen 11:30; 25:21; 29:31).

Sixth, the need for both male and female in order to fulfill the procreative dimension of the creational mandate (and, as we shall see in Gen 2, the establishment of man-woman marriage as the context for its fulfillment) clearly shows heterosexuality "to be the order of creation."[116] It thus follows that there is "no place in God's good order for unisexuality or for any diminishing or confusion of sexual identity."[117] Such confusion may be a feature of postlapsarian existence, but it is not an indicator of healthy created variety.

Seventh, the reality of the sex binary does not mean that God's creative intention was a series of identikit males and identikit females. Nor, as we shall see in chapter 10, does it imply that the bodies of those with intersex conditions "are more 'fallen' than anyone else's."[118] All bodies born outside of Eden are prone to disease, disability, and death. The point is, rather, that the many forms of disorder with which we are now familiar—physiological and psychological—were not present "in the beginning."

---

114. Walton, *Genesis*, 135 (compare 39 and 53). This expression occurs eleven times in Genesis: 2:4; 5:1; 6:9; 10:1; 11:10; 11:27; 25:12; 25:19; 36:1; 36:9; 37:2.

115. Saint Augustine, *On Genesis: "Two Books on Genesis against the Manichees" and "On the Literal Interpretation of Genesis: An Unfinished Book,"* trans. Roland J. Teske; The Fathers of the Church: A New Translation, vol. 84 (Washington, DC: Catholic University of America Press, 1991), 88, §1.24.42.

116. Samuel H. Dresner, "Homosexuality and the Order of Creation," *Judaism* 40 (1991): 309.

117. Mathews, *Genesis 1–11:26*, 173.

118. Susannah Cornwall, "Introduction," in *Intersex, Theology and the Bible: Troubling Bodies in Church, Text and Society*, ed. Susannah Cornwall (New York: Palgrave Macmillan, 2015), 6.

The binary model in the beginning

Despite Patricia Beattie Jung's confident assertion that "nowhere does the Bible specify that God created people only either male or female,"[119] this is precisely what is specified in Genesis 1:27 (and in 5:1b–3 also). Moreover, the reason why no additional sex-forms were created is because none are needed—neither for *humans* (to function and fulfill our responsibilities as divine image bearers), nor for *animals* (to reproduce "according to their kinds"). Indeed, even amphibians, as Brian Peterson wryly notes, "still breed within male-female categories."[120]

Therefore, while DeFranza may have some grounds for complaining of the "naïve repetition" of a "simplistic binary model" (particularly in sexual anthropologies that display no awareness of the reality of intersex conditions), it is misleading to describe the binary model itself as "dishonest to the diversity of persons created in the image of God."[121] For, as we have seen, whether one adopts a chromosome, gamete, or cluster account of sex, intersex conditions do not constitute a third sex.[122] Moreover, as we shall see, the binary nature of sex is repeatedly affirmed in Scripture—not only by the author of Genesis, but also by the Lord Jesus: "He who created them from the beginning made them male and female" (Matt 19:4; compare Mark 10:6).

THE RELATIONSHIP BETWEEN "THE IMAGE OF GOD" AND "MALE AND FEMALE"

This bring us to a much-discussed question: What is the relationship between "the image of God" and "male and female"?

Three possible answers

In his 1975 publication *Man as Male and Female*, Paul Jewett helpfully maps out three contrasting answers to the above question. The first views the male-female distinction as *oppositional* to the meaning of the *imago Dei*. Consequently, we must "think in terms of oneness, not diversity, in terms

---

119. Patricia Beattie Jung, "Christianity and Human Sexual Polymorphism: Are They Compatible?," in *Ethics and Intersex*, ed. Sharon E. Sytsma (Dordrecht: Springer, 2006), 307.

120. Peterson, "Same-Sex Marriage?," 693.

121. DeFranza, *Sex Difference*, 268, 270.

122. Stock, *Material Girls*, 45–60; Soh, *End of Gender*, 15–38.

of unity, not polarity, if we would think rightly about Man." The second views the male-female distinction as *incidental* to the *imago Dei*. That is, while both men and women possess the divine image, the sex binary is not a necessary part of that image. The third views the male-female distinction as *essential* to the *imago Dei*—that is, "fellowship as male and female is what it *means* to be in the image of God." On this understanding, "to talk about Man as such is precisely to talk about Man as man and woman."[123]

The first of these views, at least historically, has often appealed to the androgyne myth and has also tended "to relate Man's sexual polarity to his fallen condition rather than his original condition." From this it follows that "Man cannot live in peace and harmony while he remains a sexual being."[124] An asexual future is thus to be both desired and anticipated. While a more "sex positive" version of this view has been developed by intersex advocates and trans-affirming authors, its androgynous premise (as we have seen) is not supported by Genesis 1:27, and nor (as we will see) is it found in Genesis 2. Therefore, as Barth counsels, "we have to make our choice between mythology and the Word of God."[125] For the evangelical, the choice is clear.

This leaves us with the second and third views. As a way of adjudicating between them, I will expound the third view more fully and then consider two objections against it—objections that have convinced some that the words "male and female he created them" (Gen 1:27c) provide "a democratizing clarification rather than an indication of the meaning of the image."[126] In other words, they demarcate rather than define the *imago Dei*.

Karl Barth's answer to the question

Karl Barth is the name most readily associated with the idea that the male and female relationship is the key to the *imago*. Barth, however, makes no claim to be the originator of this view—crediting it to Dietrich Bonhoeffer's provocative (but undeveloped) suggestion that "the likeness,

123. Jewett, *Male and Female*, 23–24 (emphasis original).

124. Jewett, *Male and Female*, 25–26.

125. Barth, *CD*, III/4, 161.

126. Peterson, *Human Identity*, 48.

the analogia, of humankind to God is not *analogia entis* but *analogia relationalis*."[127] For Barth, this gives rise to the thought that humanity was created to correspond to the "relationship and differentiation in God Himself," the fellowship between male and female being some kind of analogue of the fellowship within the Triune Godhead. From this it follows that "man can and will always be man before God and among his fellows only as he is man in relationship to woman and woman in relationship to man. And as he is one or the other he *is* man."[128]

This, for Barth, is no dogmatic supposition but the necessary result of a contextual exegesis of Genesis 1:27. Both the *concept* of the divine image (which is "inseparable from the idea of a prototype and copy, of a counterpart realized in free differentiation and relationship") and the *content* of the verse (with the threefold application of "created" [*bara'*] linking the clauses together) led him to ask: "Could anything be more obvious than to conclude from this clear indication that the image and likeness of the being created by God signifies existence in confrontation, i.e., in this confrontation, in the juxtaposition and conjunction of man and man which is that of male and female?"[129]

In Barth's view, the answer to this question is plain: "The text itself says that it consists in a differentiation and relationship between man and man"—that is, "man and woman."[130] Moreover, because the relationship between man and woman "rests on a structural and functional distinction," humanity never exists as "an abstract and neutral humanity ... but always as the human male or the human female."[131]

Barth is not alone in interpreting Genesis 1:27 this way. Westermann, too, believes that "there can be no question of an 'essence of man' apart from existence as two sexes. Humanity exists in community, as one beside the other, and there can only be anything like humanity and human relations

---

127. Dietrich Bonhoeffer, *Creation and Fall: A Theological Exposition of Genesis 1–3*, ed. John W. De Gruchy, trans. Douglas S. Bax (Minneapolis: Fortress, 2004), 65 (emphasis original).

128. Barth, *CD*, III/1, 196, 198, 186 (emphasis original).

129. Barth, *CD*, III/1, 195.

130. Barth, *CD*, III/1, 195. Elsewhere Barth writes: "By the divine likeness of man in Genesis 1:27ff. there is understood the fact that God created them male and female, corresponding to the fact that God Himself exists in relationship and not in isolation" (*CD*, III/4, 117).

131. Barth, *CD*, III/4, 117.

where the human species exists in twos."[132] Clines also agrees, asserting that "the most basic statement about man, according to Genesis 1, that he is the image of God, does not find its full meaning in man alone, but in man and woman."[133]

Objections to the Barthian view

As we consider a number of objections to this view, it is worth noting that some of the criticisms leveled against Barth fail to understand his thought on its own terms. For example, Graham Ward's charge that Barth's treatment of man and woman "returns to a natural theology his theological system is set up to refute" reveals a basic confusion between *natural theology* and *a theology of nature*.[134] Barth is constructing the latter, not doing the former.[135] Others have engaged in an openly hostile reading of Barth, usually due to their own precommitments.[136] Cornwall, for instance, having already judged that the binary sex model is "a golden calf," charges that "Barth's whole system of male-and-female cosmic interaction, mirroring God-and-humanity interaction, is based on a desire which possesses and incorporates, which *eliminates* difference." In particular, she believes that it renders intersex conditions "literally nonsensical."[137] This, of course, would only follow if such conditions constituted a third sex. As we have seen, they do not.

However, other criticisms of Barth's view—especially those of a more exegetical nature—are more penetrating. Two warrant our attention.

Objection 1. According to Phyllis Bird, the relationship between being created in "the image of God" and "male and female" is "progressive, not synonymous. The second statement adds to the first; it does not explicate it." The two clauses thus "contain two essential and distinct statements

---

132. Claus Westermann, *Genesis 1–11: A Commentary*, trans. John J. Scullion (Minneapolis: Augsburg House, 1984), 160.

133. Clines, "Image of God," 95; see also Bruce Waltke with Cathi J. Fredricks, *Genesis: A Commentary* (Grand Rapids: Zondervan, 2001), 66.

134. Graham Ward, "The Erotics of Redemption—After Karl Barth," *Theology & Sexuality* 8 (1998): 65.

135. Barth could not be clearer on this point (*CD*, III/1, 194–96).

136. E.g., John Blevins, "Broadening the Family of God: Debating Same-Sex Marriage and Queer Family in America," *Theology & Sexuality* 12 (2005): 73–77.

137. Cornwall, *Sex and Uncertainty*, 84–85 (emphasis original), 86.

about the nature of humanity: *adam* is created *like* (i.e., resembling) God, but *as* creature, and hence male and female." Consequently, "the statement, 'male and female he created them' ... "relates only to the blessing of fertility, making explicit its necessary presupposition."[138] To this, Richard Middleton adds that because "the third line in three-line Hebrew poetic units typically does not repeat a previous idea, but more usually serves a progressive function, introducing a new thought," it is unlikely "that 'male and female' specifies in any way the nature of the image."[139]

Phyllis Trible, however, is not persuaded by these arguments. In her view,

> "Male and female" correspond structurally to "the image of God," and this formal parallelism indicates a semantic correspondence. Likewise, the switch from the singular pronoun "him" to the plural pronoun "them" at the end of these two parallel lines provides a key for interpreting humanity (*hā-ʾādām*) in the first line. The plural form reinforces sexual differentiation within the unity of humanity.[140]

Moreover, the threefold repetition of "created" in verse 27 also supports the view that line three explicates (rather than develops) lines one and two. So if there is a sequence to be observed, it is "between (not within) verses: from verse 26 ('Let us make ...') to verse 27 ('God created ...') and then to verse 28 ('God blessed them and said ...')."[141] A further counterargument is this: the explicit accentuating of sexual difference in the creation of humanity (as opposed to the creation of the animals, where it is implicit) would seem to indicate that the blessing of fertility (in v. 28) is "something given in addition to this creation."[142] The implication of this is that "sexual difference and community belong to the very image of God itself; they are not merely related to human fertility."[143]

---

138. Bird, "Male and Female," 149–50, 155.

139. Middleton, *Liberating Image*, 49–50.

140. Trible, *Rhetoric of Sexuality*, 17.

141. Gagnon, *Homosexual Practice*, 59n42.

142. Jürgen Moltmann, *God in Creation: An Ecological Doctrine of Creation*, trans. Margaret Kohl (London: SCM, 1985), 222; Trible, *Rhetoric of Sexuality*; von Rad, *Genesis*, 60.

143. Moltmann, *God in Creation*, 222.

While Middleton challenges this last point, reasoning that because male and female are *biological* terms, they do "not define the content of the image in social-relational terms at all," this needlessly splits human *sexuality* from human *sociality*.[144] It also ignores the relationality implied in the words that preface the command of verse 28 ("God said *to them* [לָהֶם, *lahem*]") and risks equating human sexuality with animal sexuality. The problem here, as Kenneth Mathews perceptively remarks, is that "human life, unlike the lower orders, is not instructed specifically to produce 'after its kind.' This omission elevates the sexual experience and goal of the human family as distinctive."[145] Human sexuality, in other words, is more than animalistic.

Does this, then, mean that the Barthian view stands vindicated?

Not entirely. Although Barth is right to stress the connection between Genesis 1:27c and clauses a and b, his critics are also right to highlight its relationship to verse 28. This suggests that "male and female" *both* explains *and* develops "the image of God"—that is, it "continues the idea of the preceding context (Gen. 1:26–27a, b) while bringing in the new idea for transitioning to the commandment given in verse 28."[146] Nevertheless, as Meredith Kline helpfully cautions, "even if Genesis 1:27c and 5:2a were taken with the preceding image statements in 1:27a and b and in 5:1b and c respectively, it could not be simply assumed that the intention was to define the content of the image idea. The purpose might rather be to identify men and women alike as being individually the image of God."[147]

Kline's comment focuses the question that remains: Does "male and female" *define the content* of the divine image? To answer this question, a second exegetical objection to Barth's view needs to be considered.

Objection 2. The objection is that Barth's interpretation of Genesis 1:27 (that the image consists in the relationship between man and woman) is irreconcilable with Genesis 5:3. Ryan Peterson, for example, argues that

---

144. Middleton, *Liberating Image*, 50. Middleton's objection also sits oddly with his assertion that imaging God involves representing and extending his rule "through the ordinary communal practices of human sociocultural life" (60).

145. Mathews, *Genesis 1–11:26*, 174.

146. Hongyi Yang, *A Development, Not a Departure: The Lacunae in the Debate of the Doctrine of the Trinity and Gender Roles* (Phillipsburg, NJ: P&R, 2018), 50.

147. Meredith G. Kline, *Images of the Spirit* (Eugene, OR: Wipf & Stock, 1991), 30.

Adam's fathering of Seth "after his image" also involves "the transmission of humanity's divine likeness."[148] John Frame similarly contends that "Adam transmits his 'image' (the image of God, according to verse 1) to his son Seth."[149] In other words, given that *image* in Genesis 5:3 refers to a "him" (*homo solitarius*) rather than a "them" (*humana relationes*), being made in God's image seems to speak of an individual, rather than communal, reality.[150]

Anticipating this objection, Barth points out that Genesis 5:3 does not say that Adam begat Seth in *God's* image, but in *his* image. It is not an extension of 1:27, therefore, but an outworking of 1:28. So, writes Barth, it is "not at all the case that God's activity now finds as it were renewal and continuation in Adam's procreation." In saying this, he is not denying that Seth too bears the divine likeness. His point, rather, is that all image bearing is "the realisation of a hope which can be fulfilled only in a direct decision and action on the part of God Himself." Otherwise put, coming to bear the image of God is a *divine gift*, not a *human accomplishment*. So, although Barth acknowledges the importance of the "the physical sequence of the generations" in God's purposes, he is insistent that *human procreation*, while being "the place where divine decision and action are continually realised," *does not of itself transmit the image.*[151]

Few have found this reading convincing. As Nathan McDonald reflects, such an "interpretation of Genesis 5:3 appears very strained, an impression that Barth's two pages of detailed discussion serve only to reinforce."[152] The primary reason for this is that Barth seems determined to resist the logical implication of the text; for if Adam bears God's image, then his fathering of Seth in his own image (which is also God's image) would surely mean that Seth too bears God's image.

What then explains Barth's refusal to draw this conclusion? It appears to be a result of his desire to affirm (on the one hand) that human beings

---

148. Peterson, *Human Identity*, 48.

149. John M. Frame, "Men and Women in the Image of God," in *Recovering Biblical Manhood and Womanhood: A Response to Evangelical Feminism*, ed. John Piper and Wayne Grudem (Wheaton, IL: Crossway, 1991), 229; compare Wenham, *Genesis 1–15*, 127.

150. Blocher, *In the Beginning*, 89.

151. Barth, *CD*, III/1, 198–99.

152. Nathan McDonald, "The *Imago Dei* and Election: Reading Genesis 1:26–28 and Old Testament Scholarship with Karl Barth," *IJST* 10 (2008): 321.

are beings-in-relation, and so not images in isolation, and (on the other) that the most fundamental of all human relationships—that which is both prior to and gives rise to all others (e.g., marriage, family, society)—is the male-female relationship.[153] But what he does not seem to appreciate is that there is no inherent conflict between these important affirmations and the teaching of Genesis 5:3. Seth, as an individual image bearer, is simultaneously a being-in-relation and the product of a male-female relationship.

A modified Barthian response to the question

What, then, is the relationship between "the image of God" and "male and female"? And how should we regard Barth's answer to this question? In my view, it is as unwarranted to label Barth's view arbitrary, as it is to claim that "nothing indicates" that male and female is "the explanation of the-being-in-the-image-of-God."[154] While his rather forced interpretation of Genesis 5:3 suggest that he has overread Genesis 1:27, he has rightly seen the two statements—"God created man in his own image" and "male and female he created them"—as being deeply connected. As to the precise nature of that connection, however, we are on firmer ground to conclude that

> the latter is brought into such close connection with the former as to imply the most intimate relation between Man's existence in the image of God and his fellowship as male and female. The two, therefore, should never be discussed separately. So far as Man is concerned, being in the divine image and being male and female, though not synonymous, are yet so closely related that one cannot speak biblically about the one without speaking also about the other.[155]

What, then, of the claim that the relationship between male and female *defines the content* of the divine image? Not only is this saying more than Genesis 1:27 permits, but Genesis 5:3 (compare 9:6; 1 Cor 11:7; Jas 3:9) stands against it. Therefore, rather than saying (as does Barth) that the

153. Barth, *CD*, III/4, 117.

154. Blocher, *In the Beginning*, 92.

155. Jewett, *Male and Female*, 46.

image consists in "the differentiation and relationship between man and woman,"[156] it is more defensible to say (as does Jewett) that "Man's existence in the fellowship of male and female is the mode of his existence as created in the image of God."[157] The difference between these two statements is that the first conceives of male-female duality as *the essence of the image* (making it necessarily corporate), whereas the second sees it as *expressive of the image* (allowing it to be both corporate and individual). Thus, the latter statement not only affirms all the various social manifestations of the image, but more easily integrates those texts that either state or imply that individuals are image bearers. Moreover, it also affirms that *both* male *and* female are "characterized equally by the image,"[158] as well as the fact that the image comes in only two forms: *either* male *or* female.

In short, the *imago Dei* is *both* personal *and* communal. Neither should be thought to take precedence over the other, for, as Genesis 1:26–28 reveals, "person and community are two sides of one and the same life process."[159] Matthew Levering's conclusion, then, is apt: "Conceiving of the image of God as expressed communally should be paired with the insistence that *each* individual human is in the image of God."[160]

Barth, of course, never denied this latter point. Recall his statement that man never exists as "an abstract and neutral humanity ... but always as the human male or the human female."[161] This means that *the Barthian view requires modification rather than rejection*; it needs to clarify (or affirm more consistently) that sexual dimorphism is the *mode* of the divine image, rather than its *meaning*. With this adjustment made, we are better able to appreciate the relationship between "the image of God" and "male and female," and the "him" and "them" in Genesis 1:27. We are also helped to see why the gift of divine likeness has been instantiated in two (and only two) sexes. For while the *imago Dei* is on display in every kind of human

---

156. Barth, *CD*, III/1, 195.

157. Jewett, *Male and Female*, 45.

158. Bird, "Male and Female," 159 (emphasis original).

159. Moltmann, *God in Creation*, 223.

160. Matthew Levering, *Engaging the Doctrine of Creation: Cosmos, Creatures, and the Wise and Good Creator* (Grand Rapids: Baker Academic, 2017), 155 (emphasis original).

161. Barth, *CD*, III/4, 117.

relationship, it is "the radical, sexual duality of man which is the root of all other fellowship."[162]

Therefore, while each human being is "the image of God," the dimorphic combination of "male and female" is necessary for the fullness and fruitfulness of that image. This reality, as we shall see further in the exposition of Genesis 2:24–25 in chapter 9, points to the significance of marriage, where husband and wife "are images of God separately, and they are also the image of God together, procreating as he created."[163]

CONCLUDING REFLECTIONS

PROBLEMATIZING A TRANS-AFFIRMATIVE READING OF GENESIS 1

Although we are only at the beginning of our journey through Scripture, it is important to pause at this point and tease out the implications of what we have seen so far. How then does Genesis 1 (and especially verse 27) help us in our evaluation of the central claim of trans theory?

In her study of Genesis 1, queer theologian Deryn Guest acknowledges that the divine purpose appears to be "entirely about creating boundaries" and that "to argue differently seems perverse."[164] But because she believes that reading "with the grain of the text" enshrines "genderism" (i.e., cisnormativity) and inspires "trans intolerance," she hopes to find another way of interpreting Genesis 1—one that does not endorse "a heteronormative sex/gender system and condemn trans people to the realm of the abject."[165] That way begins by perceiving God "in the qualities of formlessness and fluidity" that characterized the earth prior to "the subsequent feats of creation." Finding the divine "within the deep, dark, fluid presences that are not all about order and boundaries" enables her to propose a different kind of God: a queer God whose being is "fluid, unstable and multiple." Such a God makes "trans lives more liveable," for recognizing

162. Bavinck, *Reformed Dogmatics: God and Creation: Volume Two*, ed. John Bolt; trans. John Vriend (Grand Rapids: Baker, 2004), 587.

163. Blocher, *In the Beginning*, 93.

164. Deryn Guest, "Troubling the Waters: תהום, Transgender, and Reading Genesis Backwards," in *Transgender, Intersex, and Biblical Interpretation*, ed. Teresa J. Hornsby and Deryn Guest (Atlanta: SBL, 2016), 38.

165. Guest, "Troubling the Waters," 21–22, 40.

"the Deity's presence" in chaos and disorder, allows us to accept "our own unbecoming."[166]

It is difficult to imagine an interpretation of Genesis 1 more at odds with the tenor of the text itself. Not only is the language of "without form and void" (תֹהוּ וָבֹהוּ, *thohu wavohu*) in verse 2 a description of the pre-formed earth (not God), but it is a state that is presented as the very antithesis of the ordered creation declared "very good" in verse 31. Moreover, contrary to the affirmation of verse 26 (that humanity has been created in *God's* image), Guest intentionally reads the chapter backwards in order to recast God in the image of primordial chaos. She thus presents "an inherently unstable Deity, complex and unruly, itching to be free, longing to break out of the boundaries humans have erected." This is not simply *eisegesis* (as opposed to *exegesis*) but, from a biblical standpoint, an exercise in idolatry—a fashioning of God in the likeness of unformed created things (Rom 1:22–23). Genesis 1 provides no reason for thinking that God's true nature is revealed in "the nonnormative sexual stories" of gender outlaws, or that "God, the ambivalent, not easily classified sexuality" is an appropriate way to name him.[167]

In sum, Guest's attempt to render Genesis 1 amenable to a trans-affirmative reading is singularly unconvincing.

WHAT THEN IS REVEALED IN THE BEGINNING?

The following four points provide a summary conclusion to our exploration of the sexual anthropology of the Bible's opening chapter.

First, there is no basis in Genesis 1 for belief in an original androgynous progenitor of the human race. Rather, "sexual dimorphism, the fact that we come in these two distinct kinds, is a fundamental fact about humanity."[168] While sexual duality does not define God's image, the sex binary is basic to the divine design. As Barth writes, "there is no being of man above the being of male and female."[169] The unavoidable implication

---

166. Guest, "Troubling the Waters," 40–41.

167. Guest, "Troubling the Waters," 22, 41.

168. Alastair Roberts, "The Music and the Meaning of Male and Female," in *True to Form: Primer 03 – Gender and Sexuality*, ed. David Shaw (Market Harborough: The Fellowship of Independent Evangelical Churches, 2016), 36.

169. Barth, *CD*, III/2, 289.

of this is that all image bearers are *either* male *or* female. This is not to ignore the postlapsarian realities of intersex conditions and gender incongruence (or the challenges they present), but it is to acknowledge that one of the chief purposes of Genesis 1 is "to describe the order established within creation—as an order determined by God, from the beginning."[170] As such, it is an order that is without confusion and, as verse 31 affirms, it is "very good."

Second, because this God-given order *reveals created nature* (the true), it *establishes created norms* (the good). In so doing, it clarifies what is and is not the way of blessing. It likewise confirms that blessing cannot truly be known apart from a recognition of and respect for the *givenness* of created nature—including human nature. The reason for this, as Bird identifies, is that "there is a corollary to the idea that all of creation is derived from God and dependent upon God. It is the idea of the permanence and immutability of the created orders."[171] Thus, in regard to the differences between the sexes, these are clearly "intended by God and thus are not malleable or interchangeable."[172]

Third, these insights highlight the importance of the human body for the biblical presentation of the *imago Dei*. As we have seen, the divine image cannot be confined to "certain 'higher' qualities" (e.g., rationality or spirituality); rather, "the whole man is the image of God."[173] Consequently,

> The body cannot be left out of the meaning of the image; man is a totality, and his "solid flesh" is as much the image of God as his spiritual capacity, creativeness or personality, since none of these "higher" aspects of the human being can exist in isolation from the body. ... In so far as man is a body and a bodiless man is not man, the body is the image of God; for man is the image of God.[174]

Moreover, it is not simply our *embodied* nature that is crucial to the *imago Dei*, but our *sexed* bodies: "We bear God's image as male and

---

170. Bird, "Male and Female," 136.

171. Bird, "Male and Female," 146.

172. Ashford and Bartholomew, *Doctrine of Creation*, 361.

173. Gerrit C. Berkouwer, *Man: The Image of God*, trans. D. W. Jellema (Grand Rapids: Eerdmans, 1962), 75.

174. Clines, "Image of God," 86.

female."[175] The fact that these sexually dimorphic terms are the only distinguishing identifiers given in Genesis 1 tells us that *sexed embodiment is foundational to personal identity*. Matthew Mason expresses it this way: "Just as I am not a person who happens to have a body, so I am not a fundamentally asexual person who happens to have a male body. I am a man."[176] Sexed embodiment, then, not only enables us to represent God and exercise dominion in his world, but it determines our *sexed identity* (as male or female), establishes our *gendered relationships* (as son or daughter, brother or sister, etc.), and signals our potential *marital* and *reproductive roles* (as husband or wife, father or mother).

Fourth, while personal and social gender construction is an inevitable part of this task, faithfulness requires that it be undertaken in a way that is congruent with "the sexuate form of our male and female bodies."[177] In other words, we are called to work *with* (rather than *against*) the grain of created nature. As we shall see in a more developed way in the chapters that follow, in biblical anthropology (as in human experience) the biological always precedes the psycho-sociocultural. This means that *the sex of the body* (male or female) *determines the gender of the person* (boy or girl, man or woman). Craig Gay helpfully draws out the implication of this connection:

> Although it is possible to read the words "male" and "female" in [Genesis 1:27] and similar texts as referring only to the biological aspects of sex, the suggestion that our experience of maleness and femaleness is socially constructed seems to imply a good deal more plasticity in human nature than this text permits. It also tends to replace God's creative agency with our own, or at least with that of society.[178]

---

175. Sprinkle, *Embodied*, 67.

176. Matthew Mason, "The Authority of the Body: Discovering Natural Manhood and Womanhood," *BET* 4 (2017): 50.

177. Mason, "Authority of the Body," 57.

178. Craig M. Gay, "'Gender' and the Idea of the Social Construction of Reality," in *Christian Perspectives on Gender, Sexuality and Community*, ed. Maxine Hancock (Vancouver: Regent College, 2003), 168.

Gay's point is that the various facets of gender are (or, at least, ought to be) the natural extensions of biological sex into the psychological, social, and cultural realms. This insight helps to explain why Scripture, as noted in chapter 3, does not clearly distinguish sex, gender, and gender identity, as is now commonly done.[179] This does not invalidate the drawing of these distinctions, however, for arguably they are implicit in the scriptural account. Moreover, as the psycho-sociocultural extensions of sex are not automatically *given* by the Creator but are (in part) *graven* by the creature, they may quite legitimately be viewed as *constructions*—or, in theodramatic terms, *improvisations*. The question, then, is whether our gender conceptions and constructions are *faithful*—that is, in harmony with our God-given bodies. As I have argued in this chapter, and will demonstrate further in those that follow, blessing will elude us if they are not. The reason for this is clear: it is the sexed body that provides the foundation (and so determines the boundaries and direction) for authentic gender cultivation.

179. Vanhoozer, "Drama of Redemption," 194.

CHAPTER 8

THE MAKING OF MAN AND WOMAN

God divided mankind into two classes, namely, male and female, or a he and a she. ... Therefore each of us must have the kind of body God has created for us. I cannot make myself a woman, nor can you make yourself a man; we do not have that power. But we are exactly as he created us; I am a man and you a woman.[1]

—Martin Luther

The great controlling myth of our time has been the belief that within each one of us there is a real, inner, private "self," long buried beneath layers of socialization and attempted cultural and religious control, and needing to be rediscovered if we are to live authentic lives.[2]

—N. T. Wright

The primary purpose of this chapter is to explore the contribution of Genesis 2 (particularly vv. 7, 18, and 20–23) to sexual anthropology. As with our study of Genesis 1 in the previous chapter, a range of other biblical texts—which either illuminate or develop the thought of Genesis 2—will be

1. Martin Luther, *The Estate of Marriage* (1522), *LW* 45, 17–18.

2. N. T. Wright, *Creation, Power and Truth: The Gospel in a World of Cultural Confusion* (London: SPCK, 2013), 9.

discussed in the process, especially in terms of their contribution to our understanding of human constitution. For this reason, it will be necessary (at times) to consider the impact of the fall on human persons and their bodies. And, once again, the central questions raised by trans theory (How many sexes are there? What is the relationship of gender to sex? Can a person have a gendered self at odds with their bodily sex?) will be addressed at key points.

Although there are obvious differences between Genesis 1 and 2 (in style, focus, and detail), rhetorical analysis suggests that the two accounts present "a congruent narrative," the latter providing "a thematic elaboration" of the main features of the former.[3] In fact, not only can Genesis 2 be seen roughly to follow the pattern of Genesis 1, but the events of days three and six are now expanded and their meaning expounded.[4] Genesis 2, then, "is much more than a simple tale relating how the first couple had their beginning in the Garden."[5] It takes us from the broad, cosmic canvas of creation and brings us "into the realm of concrete and particular social, economic, and cultural realities, moving us into the arena of history, where all of our questions about the nature and destiny of the human being are formulated, and must be answered."[6]

In broad terms, Genesis 2 reveals *how* man and woman were originally created, *why* both their sameness and their distinctness are vital, and *what* their relationship means for the future and flourishing of human society.[7] Therefore, although Barth's remark that the chapter has "only one theme—the completion of the creation of man by the adding to the male of the female"—is unnecessarily reductionistic, he is right to observe

3. Mathews, *Genesis 1–11:26*, 188–89; C. John Collins, *Reading Genesis Well: Navigating History, Poetry, Science, and Truth in Genesis 1–11* (Grand Rapids: Zondervan, 2018), 160–75. Others, however, have argued that the two creation accounts are to be read sequentially (e.g., Walton, *Adam and Eve*, 63–69). For a critique of the sequentialist view, see William Lane Craig, *In Quest of the Historical Adam: A Biblical and Scientific Exploration* (Grand Rapids: Eerdmans, 2021), 88–93.

4. Roberts, "Male and Female," 30–31.

5. Brian Neil Peterson, "Postmodernism's Deconstruction of the Creation Mandates," *JETS* 62 (2019): 128.

6. Bird, "Bone of My Bone," 523.

7. Peterson, "Postmodernism's Deconstruction," 128.

that "what was said in one short sentence [in 1:27] is now developed at large [in 2:4–25]."[8]

This chapter is divided into two sections: first, the forming of the man; and second, the building of the woman. The implications for trans theory will be considered at the end of each section. Verses 24 and 25 will be the subject of the following chapter.

THE FORMING OF THE MAN (GENESIS 2:7)

In marked contrast to Genesis 1, where, as Peter Miscall observes, there is "not a no, a not, a never, or such in the story,"[9] Genesis 2 portrays a situation where "*no* bush of the field was yet in the land and *no* small plant of the field had yet sprung up—for the LORD God had *not* caused it to rain on the land, and there was *no* man to work the ground" (v. 5). The divine remedy for this fourfold lack is twofold: first, the LORD forms a man (v. 7); then, he plants a garden for the man to inhabit and work in (v. 8). I will touch only briefly on the man's location and vocation, as my primary concern in this section is with the first of these divine acts—the man's formation.

THE MANNER OF THE MAN'S FORMATION

The manner of the man's creation in stated laconically in verse 7:

> then the LORD God formed *the man* [*ha'adam*] of dust from *the ground* [הָאֲדָמָה, *ha'adamah*] and breathed into his nostrils the *breath of life* [נִשְׁמַת חַיִּים, *nishmath khayyim*], and the man became a *living creature* [נֶפֶשׁ חַיָּה, *nephesh khayyah*].

Three points of significance warrant brief comment.

The presence of paronomasia

The first is the paronomasia or wordplay between "the man" (*ha'adam*) and "the ground" (*ha'adamah*), the latter being the grammatically feminine form of the former. The effect (and, doubtless, intention) of this pun is to emphasize the man's connection to the earth. As Gordon Wenham

8. Barth, *CD*, III/1, 288.

9. Peter D. Miscall, "Jacques Derrida in the Garden of Eden," *USQR* 44 (1990): 3.

reflects, "He was created from it; his job is to cultivate it (2:5, 15); and on death he is to return to it."[10] Significantly, it also reveals his *basic materiality*. That said, there is little reason to follow Trible's penchant for translating *ha'adam* as "the earth creature," and even less to support her contention that he is a sexually undifferentiated "it."[11] The man's title reflects his origin, nature, task, and (potential) destiny, but, as we are about to see, it does not diminish either his humanity or his sexed nature.

The man's body is formed first

Second, the LORD God's forming of the man from the dust of the ground directly involves him in the shaping of the man's *body*. This not only highlights *the goodness of bodies* (in that embodiment is the result of deliberate divine creative construction) but indicates that *embodiment is basic to human identity*.[12] This is further confirmed by the fact that the man's body is formed *first*—before he receives "the breath of life." The significance of this is that the "materiality, the objectivity, and the givenness of the body precedes and grounds our self-consciousness, activity, and self-determination."[13]

Interestingly, however, the text does not *say* "the LORD God formed the man's *body*" (although this is clearly implied), but that "the LORD God formed *the man*." The import of this is that *the man was formed by the forming of his body*. This again reveals "the priority and irreducibility of the man's bodily composition," as well as its significance for his personhood.[14]

Moreover, as I will argue more fully when we come to verse 23, the body that was formed was a *male body*. This explains why "the man" (*ha'adam*) is given the name that, in due course, will be revealed to be his personal *male* name.[15] Otherwise put, "the man" is male from the beginning—his maleness determined and revealed by his God-given bodily

---

10. Wenham, *Genesis 1–15*, 59.

11. Trible, *Rhetoric of Sexuality*, 80 (compare 140n8).

12. David Atkinson, *The Message of Genesis 1–11* (Downers Grove, IL: InterVarsity Press, 1990), 57. It thus matters to God how bodies are treated (compare Lev 19:28; 21:5; 1 Cor 6:13–20; Eph 5:28–30).

13. Roberts, "Male and Female," 40.

14. Colin J. Smothers, "On the Body and Its Meaning," *Eikon* 3, no. 1 (2021): 100.

15. Lawson G. Stone, "The Soul: Possession, Part, or Person?," in *What About the Soul? Neuroscience and Christian Anthropology*, ed. Joel B. Green (Nashville: Abingdon, 2004), 49.

form. Genesis 2:7 thus reinforces a key insight gleaned from Genesis 1: *to be human is to be embodied and to be embodied is to be sexed.*

The breath of life is given second

Third, the man only becomes *a living being* (*nephesh khayyah*) when *the breath of life* (*nishmath khayyim*) is *breathed* (נָפַח, *naphakh*) into his nostrils. "The breath of life" (*nishmath khayyim*) is thus a metonym for animation, signifying "the sustaining life principle embodied in man that comes from God."[16] In accord with the idea of divine donation, the verbal root "to breathe" (*naphakh*), as Derek Kidner explains, "is warmly personal, with the face-to-face intimacy of a kiss and the significance that this was giving as well as making; and self-giving at that."[17] It is not surprising that upon receipt of this gift, the man becomes "fully alive."[18]

We shall look more deeply into *what* was given in the next section. But what this second divine act reveals is that *embodiment is a necessary but not sufficient condition for human life*. Something more is required. It is also worth noting that the status "living being" (*nephesh khayyah*) is not unique to humanity; the same expression is used of sea creatures in 1:20 and of land animals and birds in 2:19 (compare 1:24, 30). The term thus emphasizes not human uniqueness, but creaturely dependence. All life is a divine gift.

REFLECTIONS ON HUMAN CONSTITUTION

I turn now to reflect on the contribution of Genesis 2:7 to the broader canonical understanding of human constitution.

Genesis 2:7 has been referred to as "the *locus classicus* of Old Testament anthropology."[19] It is generally thought to offer the paradigmatic formula for human constitution: "'dust' + 'breath of life' = 'soul.' "[20] Furthermore,

---

16. Mathews, *Genesis 1–11:26*, 197.

17. Derek Kidner, *Genesis: An Introduction and Commentary*, TOTC (Leicester: Inter-Varsity Press, 1967), 60 (emphasis original).

18. This is how Joel Green glosses *nephesh khayyah* (*Body, Soul and Human Life: The Nature of Humanity in the Bible* [Milton Keynes: Paternoster, 2008], 64).

19. Green, *Body, Soul and Human Life*, 64.

20. Richard M. Davidson, "The Nature of the Human Being from the Beginning: Genesis 1–11," in *"What Are Human Beings that You Remember Them?": Proceedings of the Third International Bible Conference Nof Ginosar and Jerusalem June 11–21, 2012*, ed. Clinton Wahlen (Silver Spring, MD: Review and Herald, 2015), 23.

because it offers little direct support to the idea that the soul is an immaterial entity, distinct from the body, it appears to stand opposed to most forms of dualism.[21] Indeed, if Scripture yielded no further anthropological insights beyond this point, a case might be made for a monistic conception of the human person. But Scripture, of course, has considerably more to say. It would thus be procrustean to read Genesis 2:7 in a way that prevents additional revelation from clarifying or developing our anthropological understanding. At the same time, it would be foolish to ignore its significance, particularly in view of its canonical placement and the archetypal features of the pattern it lays down.[22]

What then can be affirmed when Genesis 2:7 is considered in light of further scriptural revelation?

An animated body, not an incarnated soul

Exegetically, as Gerrit Berkouwer notes, "it is hardly permissible to impose the idea of two substances on the text."[23] Even if we were to translate "living being" (*nephesh khayyah*; LXX: ψυχὴν ζῶσαν, *psychēn zōsan*) as "living soul" (KJV), the man is not *bequeathed* a "soul" (*nephesh*); rather, he *becomes* a "soul" (*nephesh*) upon receipt of the "breath of life" (*nishmath khayyim*; LXX: πνοὴν ζωῆς, *pnoēn zōēs*). This does not rule out the possibility of a duality within his being, as Berkouwer acknowledges,[24] but it does present the man as "an animated body, and not an incarnated soul."[25] As Gerhard von Rad remarks, the text "distinguishes not body and 'soul' but more realistically body and life."[26] Joel Green's conclusion is therefore apt: "'Soul' is not for the Genesis story a unique characteristic of the human person; humans are not distinctively *human* on account of their purported possession of a 'soul.'"[27]

21. John W. Cooper, *Body, Soul & Life Everlasting: Biblical Anthropology and the Monism-Dualism Debate* (Grand Rapids: Eerdmans, 1989), 42.

22. Walton, *Adam and Eve*, 74–77.

23. Berkouwer, *Man*, 215.

24. In fact, adds Berkouwer, "It is important to make the simple observation that duality and dualism are not at all identical" (*Man*, 211).

25. Robinson, "Hebrew Psychology," 362.

26. Von Rad, *Genesis*, 77.

27. Green, *Body, Soul and Human Life*, 64 (emphasis original).

"Living creature" refers to the man in totality

Whether it is translated "living soul" (KJV), "living person" (NASB), "living being" (NIV) or "living creature" (ESV), what is the meaning of *nephesh khayyah* in Genesis 2:7?

As is well recognized, *nephesh* is a polysemic term—sometimes bearing an *anatomical* meaning (e.g., "throat" [Hab 2:5] or "neck" [1 Sam 28:9]), sometimes an *animating* meaning (e.g., "breath" [Job 41:21] or "vitality" [Gen 9:4]), sometimes an *internal* meaning (e.g., "desire" [Hos 4:8] or "soul" [Isa 10:18]), and sometimes a *holistic* meaning (e.g., "person" [Lev 23:30] or "self" [Gen 12:13]).[28] In Genesis 2:7, it clearly "denotes the totality of Adam's being."[29] As I have noted, the man does not so much *have* a *nephesh* as he *is* a *nephesh*. Consequently, Calvin is mistaken when he argues that *nephesh* here refers to "the very essence of the soul."[30] And while Thomas Aquinas's view, that "the soul is united to the body as its form,"[31] has considerably more to commend it (as we shall see shortly), it is difficult to delineate a subsistent soul distinct from the man's body in Genesis 2:7. What this means, as Daniel Fredericks cautions, is that care is needed "not to import a Greek paradigm of psychology to *nephesh*; though at times it refers to the inner person, it seldom denotes a 'soul' in any full sense."[32]

Indications of duality within holism

How then should we understand what happens to the man when the Lord God breathes "the breath of life" (*nishmath khayyim*) into him?

The connections between Genesis 2:7 and Ezekiel 37:9–10 (seen in both the structural parallels and the repetition of *nephesh*) suggest that the "breath of life" that enters into the man in the garden is synonymous with the "spirit" (רוּחַ, *ruakh*) that enters into the dry bones in Ezekiel's valley (compare Gen 6:17; 7:22; Job 33:4; 34:14; Isa 42:5). Such an

---

28. On the various senses of *nephesh*, see Hans Walter Wolff, *Anthropology of the Old Testament*, trans. Margaret Kohl (Philadelphia: Fortress, 1974; repr., Mifflintown, PA: Sigler, 1996), 10–25.

29. Stone, "The Soul," 53.

30. John Calvin, *Genesis*, trans. and ed. John King (Edinburgh: Banner of Truth Trust, 1847), 112.

31. Thomas Aquinas, *Summa Contra Gentiles*, trans. Anton C. Pegis, James F. Anderson, Vernon J. Bourke and Charles J. O'Neil (Notre Dame: University of Notre Dame Press, 1975), 2:300.

32. Daniel C. Fredericks, "נֶפֶשׁ," in *NIDOTTE*, 3:133–34.

understanding is supported by numerous Old Testament passages where, as a result of the action of God's *ruakh*, human beings (and animals too) can be described as possessing a *ruakh* of their own (Gen 41:8; Job 17:1; Ps 31:5; 77:6)—albeit contingently so (Ps 104:29–30).[33] Thus, Zechariah 12:1 states that the LORD "formed the spirit [*ruakh*] of man within him." Moreover, if we include those texts that speak of human death, it is apparent that "the body is what is placed in the grave, and soul and spirit refer to man's ongoing life."[34] Consequently, as Ecclesiastes 12:7 declares, upon the death of the body, "the spirit [*ruakh*] returns to God who gave it."

So then, while Genesis 2:7 makes no explicit mention of a discrete human spirit corresponding to or created by the divine breath, the existence of such an element can be inferred from the broader Old Testament witness. Thus, it is not inherently problematic that, in the domain of theo-anthropological discourse, the inner, immaterial aspect of the human person should come to be referred to as *the soul* (or *the spirit*)—even though this is not the meaning of *ruakh* in Genesis 2:7.[35]

In sum, while not stating it explicitly, Genesis 2:7 leaves room for, if not gestures toward, an *elemental duality* (as opposed to an *ontological dualism*) within the holism of the man's being.[36] The nature of this duality is not only clarified within the Old Testament but comes to even sharper expression in the New.[37]

---

33. For this reason, Wolff insists that *ruakh* "must from the beginning properly be called a theo-anthropological term" (*Anthropology of the Old Testament*, 32). For a helpful survey of the various anthropological denotations of *ruakh* in the Old Testament, see Bruce K. Waltke, *An Old Testament Theology: An Exegetical, Canonical, and Thematic Approach* (Grand Rapids: Zondervan, 2007), 227–28.

34. John M. Frame, *Systematic Theology: An Introduction to Christian Belief* (Phillipsburg, NJ: P&R, 2013), 798.

35. We should not, then, be overly critical of Tertullian for claiming that "from the breath of God first came the soul" (*A Treatise on the Soul*, 27 [*ANF* 3:208]).

36. It is essential to "make a distinction between a 'duality' of being in which a modality of differentiation is constituted as a fundamental unity, and a 'dualism' which works against that unity" (Ray S. Anderson, *On Being Human: Essays in Theological Anthropology* [Grand Rapids: Eerdmans, 1982], 209).

37. See, e.g., Matt 10:28; 1 Cor 7:34; 2 Cor 7:1; Heb 12:22–23; Jas 2:26; Rev 6:9; 20:4. Furthermore, the New Testament writers display a variety of different ways of speaking about these two anthropological aspects. As Robert Gundry writes: "'Inner man,' 'spirit,' 'soul,' 'mind,' 'heart,'—all do duty for the incorporeal part of man and different functions thereof. 'Outer man,' 'flesh,' 'body,' 'members,' 'mouth,' 'face,' and several metaphors do similar duty for the corporeal part of man" (Robert H. Gundry, *Sōma in Biblical Theology: With Emphasis on Pauline Anthropology* [Grand Rapids: Zondervan, 1987], 156).

The stress on psychosomatic integration

There are various ways to label the resulting anthropological picture. Erickson, for example, speaks of *conditional unity*,[38] Anthony Hoekema uses the language of *psychosomatic unity*,[39] and John Cooper suggests that "*dualistic holism* best captures the presentation of Scripture as a whole."[40] These proposals all have comparable merit, for what they share in common is a rejection of both (1) strong forms of *metaphysical monism* (e.g., materialism or physicalism) and (2) hard forms of *substance dualism* (e.g., Platonism or Cartesianism).[41] The stress in each case is on *integration*, on the fact that human beings have been created "as integral personal-spiritual-physical wholes—single beings consisting of different parts, aspects, dimensions, and abilities that are not naturally independent or separable." In succinct philosophical terms, "a human being is one substance, entity, or thing constituted of two distinct ingredients or components."[42] Or as Bonhoeffer expresses it: "A human being does not 'have' a body—or 'have' a soul; instead a human being 'is' body and soul."[43]

Human constitution outside of Eden

When it comes to the fashioning of human beings outside of Eden, "the description of Adam's creation in Genesis 2:7," writes Vern Poythress, "has only limited parallels with passages elsewhere in Scripture about God's subsequent providential work of creating new human beings."[44] Nevertheless, there are several important conceptual and terminological connections—especially those related to God's forming of human beings out of clay made from (and, at death, returning to) the dust. For example,

---

38. Erickson, *Christian Theology*, 554–57.

39. Hoekema, *Created in God's Image*, 217.

40. John W. Cooper, "The Current Body-Soul Debate: A Case for Dualistic Holism," *SBJT* 13 (2009): 35 (emphasis original).

41. On the relationship between the Platonic and Cartesian conceptions, see Green, *Body, Soul, and Human Life*, 48–51.

42. Cooper, "Current Body-Soul Debate," 35–36.

43. Bonhoeffer, *Creation and Fall*, 77.

44. Vern S. Poythress, *Interpreting Eden: A Guide to Faithfully Reading and Understanding Genesis 1–3* (Wheaton, IL: Crossway, 2019), 207.

how much more those who dwell in houses of *clay* [חֹמֶר, *khomer*],
whose foundation is in the *dust* [עָפָר, *ʿaphar*]. (Job 4:19a–b)

Your hands fashioned and made me,
and now you have destroyed me altogether.
Remember that you have made me like *clay* [*khomer*];
and will you return me to the *dust* [*ʿaphar*]? (Job 10:8–9)

For he knows how we are *formed* [יֵצֶר, *yetser*];[45]
he remembers that we are *dust* [*ʿaphar*]. (Ps 103:14, ESV mg.)

So, despite the uniqueness of the man's creation in Genesis 2:7, Poythress is right to conclude that there is a clear "relation of analogy to later instances when God brings human beings into existence."[46] Not surprisingly, as the following verses of Psalm 139 illustrate (and the italicized words highlight), Scripture continues to understand "human beings holistically as single entities which are psychosomatic unities":[47]

13 For you formed *my* inward parts;
you knitted *me* together in my mother's womb.
14 I praise you, for *I* am fearfully and wonderfully made.
Wonderful are your works;
my soul knows it very well.
15 *My* frame was not hidden from you,
when *I* was being made in secret,
intricately woven together in the depths of the earth.
16 Your eyes saw *my* unformed substance;
in your book were written, every one of them,
the days that were formed for *me*
when as yet there was none of them. (Ps 139:14–16)

Evidently, David sees no disjunction between body and self. As the LORD formed his "inward parts" (כִּלְיָה, *kilyah*),[48] *he* was "knitted

45. *yetser* here is the nominal form of the verb used in Gen 2:7.

46. Poythress, *Interpreting Eden*, 192.

47. Cooper, *Body, Soul, and Life Everlasting*, 78.

48. "Inward parts" or, more literally, "kidneys" (compare Ps 16:7; Jer 12:2) refers to "the highly sensitive organ of self-knowledge" (Wolff, *Anthropology of the Old Testament*, 96).

together" (v. 13); as his "frame" (עֹצֶם, *ʿotsem*)[49] was "intricately woven together in the depths of the earth,"[50] *he* was "made in secret" (v. 15). Such descriptions confirm what we have already seen: "The body isn't just something that clothes the self, but is itself the self."[51] Moreover, in contrast to the two-step creation of "the man" (*haʾadam*) in the garden, we are here presented with a single act of creation. While this does not make body and person coterminous, it does mean that *there is no body that precedes the person or person that precedes the body*; the forming of the one is simultaneous with the making of the other. As Carl Trueman writes:

> There is no "I" behind or before the body. There is no "us" that exists (logically, let alone chronologically) independently of our flesh and that is then randomly assigned to the bodies we have. Our bodies are an integral part of who we are. And I do not "occupy" my body as I might occupy a house or a space suit or a deck chair at the beach. On the contrary, it is an integral part of me, inseparable from who I am.[52]

IMPLICATIONS FOR TRANS THEORY[53]

How then does this picture of human constitution assist us in our assessment of trans theory—especially the claim that a person can have the soul of one sex in the body of the other?

The implausibility of a body-soul mismatch

Despite its affirmation of duality, the holism of the scriptural presentation of anthropological constitution leaves no room for a conception of human beings as "composed of two separate entities joined together in an uneasy alliance."[54] Accordingly, writes Cooper, it is "anti-scriptural" to

---

49. "Frame" (*ʿotsem*) quite literally means "bones" or "bone structure" (see Leslie C. Allen, *Psalm 101–150*, WBC 21 [Waco, TX: Word, 1987], 249) but may also, by extension, refer to the whole body.

50. As the parallel between verse 15c and verse 13b reveals, "the depths of the earth" is a metaphor for the womb (Derek Kidner, *Psalms 73-150*, TOTC [Leicester: Inter-Varsity Press, 1975], 466).

51. Roberts, "Male and Female," 40.

52. Carl R. Trueman, "The Triumph of the Social Scientific Method," *First Things* (June 15, 2020), https://www.firstthings.com/web-exclusives/2020/06/the-triumph-of-the-social-scientific-method.

53. With permission, the following section has been adapted from Robert S. Smith, "Body, Soul, and Gender Identity: Thinking Theologically About Human Constitution," *Eikon* 3 no. 2 (2021): 27–37.

54. Anderson, *On Being Human*, 209.

think of the soul as being "in tension with the body."[55] The reason for this, as we have seen, is that body and soul, although distinct, inter-penetrate one another—we are as much ensouled bodies as we are embodied souls. Consequently, "biological processes are not just functions of the body as distinct from the soul or spirit, and mental and spiritual capacities are not seated exclusively in the soul or spirit. All capacities and functions belong to the human being as a whole, a fleshly-spiritual totality."[56] Such synthetic integration necessarily excludes the possibility of an ontological mismatch between the (visible) body and the (invisible) soul. So, if a person's body is unambiguously sexed as male, it is simply not conceivable that their soul could be female. Indeed, a radical elemental disjunction of this kind would effectively "destroy the unity of the human person which is at the heart of a biblical anthropology."[57]

Terrance Tiessen's hypothesis

Nevertheless, it is precisely this kind of disconnection that has been proposed (albeit tentatively) by Terrance Tiessen.[58] To make his case, Tiessen relies on a particular version of Thomistic dualism drawn from the work of J. P. Moreland and Scott Rae.[59] According to Moreland and Rae, "the human person is identical to its soul, and the soul comes into existence at the point of conception." From that moment on, the soul "begins to direct the development of a body" guided by "the various teleological functions latent within the soul." Therefore, not only is the soul "ontologically prior to the body," but "the various biological operations of the body have their roots in the internal structure of the soul, which forms a body to facilitate those operations."[60] On the basis of such an understanding, Tiessen

55. John W. Cooper, "Dualism and the Biblical View of Human Beings (2)," *The Reformed Journal* (October 1982): 18.

56. Cooper, *Body, Soul & Life Everlasting*, 78.

57. Anderson, *On Being Human*, 209.

58. Terrance Tiessen, "A Female Soul in a Male Body? A Theological Proposal," *Theological Thoughts* (June 20, 2015), https://www.thoughtstheological.com/a-female-soul-in-a-male-body-a-theological-proposal.

59. In particular, J. P. Moreland and Scott B. Rae, *Body & Soul: Human Nature & the Crisis in Ethics* (Downers Grove, IL: InterVarsity Press, 2000), 199–224.

60. Moreland and Rae, *Body & Soul*, 204–6.

draws the conclusion that the "maleness or femaleness of human beings is an aspect of the soul."[61]

He then considers the impact of the fall in order to hypothesize "the possibility of soul/body disjunction." He begins by drawing attention to the phenomenon of intersexuality. His argument is that while each person's soul is either male or female, in some cases "abnormalities occur in the development of the person's body so that doctors find it extremely difficult to say whether the person who has just been born is female or male." Then, by extension, he suggests that perhaps others (he cites Bruce/Caitlyn Jenner as an example), whose bodies are unambiguously male or female, might experience a total "incongruence between the sex of their soul and the sex of their body." So, while Tiessen rejects the idea that "sexual identity is a social construct" and affirms that our goal should be "to live as God has created us," his contention is that the truth of our created sex is not ultimately found in the body but in the soul.[62]

Responding to Tiessen's hypothesis

In response to this proposal, four points can be made.

First, Tiessen appears to have overlooked a vital aspect of Moreland and Rae's position. While their view is avowedly Thomistic and dualistic, they not only regard *the body as being in the soul* ("in that the body is a spatially extended set of internally related heterogeneous parts that is an external expression of the soul's 'exigency' for a body"), but *the soul as being in the body* ("as the individuated essence that stands under, informs, animates, develops and unifies all the body's parts and functions"). This means that as a body develops and matures, "the soul's internal structure for a body is progressively realized in a lawlike way," with the result that "the soul is fully present in every body part."[63] So assuming, for the moment, that the body's sex is derived from the soul, the implication of this is that the sex of the body *reveals* the sex of the soul. Therefore, while some intersex conditions may cloud this revelation (and so make sex-determination difficult), it does not follow that a female soul can

61. Tiessen, "A Female Soul."

62. Tiessen, "A Female Soul."

63. Moreland and Rae, *Body & Soul*, 205–6, 201.

be *hidden* inside an unambiguously male body or vice versa. To suggest otherwise, is to move away from the organicism advocated by Moreland and Rae and to embrace a considerably stronger form of substance dualism—one these authors reject.[64]

Second, despite its internal coherence, Moreland and Rae's particular version of Thomistic dualism is difficult to reconcile with Scripture's dualistic holism. For while they acknowledge that "a human being is a unity of two distinct entities—body and soul," the kind of unity they affirm is functional, not ontological. That is, rather than being body-soul composites, "human persons are identical to immaterial substances, namely, to souls."[65] Therefore, although Moreland and Rae support a one-substance anthropology, they are insistent that "the one substance is the soul, and the body is an ensouled biological and physical structure that depends on the soul for its existence."[66] Arguably, this conception is more Platonic than biblical.

It is also interesting to reflect that, historically, such a view stands in contrast to that of Irenaeus, who held that the soul, while certainly *part* of the man, was not *the* man: "For the perfect man consists in the commingling and the union of the soul receiving the spirit of the Father, and the admixture of that fleshly nature which was moulded after the image of God."[67] Moreover, when the sequence of Genesis 2:7 is borne in mind (with the man's body being formed *first*) and, behind this, the fact that Genesis 1:27 defines human beings by reference to their bodily sex (male and female), it is clear that embodiment is basic to human ontology. Therefore, to insist, as Moreland and Rae do, that "the organism as a whole (the soul) is ontologically prior to its parts" is not merely to speculate beyond Scripture, but to push against it.[68] Michael Williams, then, is right to conclude that it is "not materialist, but rather fully biblical, to say

64. Moreland and Rae, *Body & Soul*, 199–201.

65. Moreland and Rae, *Body & Soul*, 17, 21, 11. For a more recent statement of this view, see J. P. Moreland, "In Defense of Thomistic-Like Dualism," in *The Blackwell Companion to Substance Dualism*, ed. Jonathan J. Loose, Angus J. L. Menuge, and J. P. Moreland (Oxford: Oxford University Press, 2018), 103.

66. Moreland and Rae, *Body & Soul*, 201.

67. Irenaeus, *Against Heresies*, 5.6.1 (*ANF* 1:531).

68. Moreland and Rae, *Body & Soul*, 206.

that we might be more than our bodies, but we are not something other than our embodied selves."[69]

Third, Moreland and Rae's particular version of Thomistic dualism is also difficult to reconcile with Thomas's own hylomorphic view of human persons.[70] Developed from Aristotle, hylomorphism maintains that all substances are composed of both *matter* (Gk. *hylē*) and *form* (Gk. *morphē*).[71] This means that "substances are not just things that *have* material and formal *components*. Rather, substances are those things that *are* material and formal *composites*."[72] As Thomas writes: "The being that a composite substance has is not the being of the form alone nor of the matter alone but of the composite."[73] When such an understanding is applied to human beings, it leads to "an ontologically holist view of human persons that maintains that we are a composite of body and soul."[74] Consequently, Thomas understands that "man is not a soul, nor a mere body; but both soul and body."[75] So then, in contrast to Moreland and Rae's person-soul identity view (i.e., that we *are* souls who *have* bodies), Thomas holds that each human person is a hylomorphic psychosomatic union—that is, a body-soul synthesis.

Furthermore, Thomas regards the particularity of each human body (including its biological sex) as "the principle of existence of that particular human being."[76] In other words, what differentiates persons from one another is "the particular set of matter that composes their respective

---

69. Michael D. Williams, "'For You Are with Me': Physical Anthropology and the Intermediate State," *Presbyterion* 45 (2019): 23.

70. Moreland and Rae readily acknowledge that "Thomas Aquinas may not have accepted all aspects of our version of Thomistic substance dualism" (*Body & Soul*, 199).

71. Hylomorphism is not Thomas's own term, but first appears in the nineteenth century. For an account of its origins and various meanings, see Gideon Manning, "The History of 'Hylomorphism,'" *Journal of the History of Ideas* 74 (2013): 173–87.

72. James K. Dew Jr., "In Defense of Modified Thomistic Holism: A Proposal for Christian Anthropology" (diss., University of Birmingham, UK, 2019), 140, https://etheses.bham.ac.uk//id/eprint/9396/1/Dew2019PhD.pdf (emphasis added).

73. Thomas Aquinas, *On Being and Essence*, trans. A. Maurer (Toronto: Pontifical Institute of Medieval Studies, 1968), 36.

74. Dew, *Modified Thomistic Holism*, 141.

75. Aquinas, *Summa Theologiae*, 1a.75.4. Thomas is here citing Augustine (*The City of God*, 19.3 [*NPNF*[1] 2:400]) who, in turn, is citing the Roman philosopher Varro (116–27 BC).

76. Andrzej Maryniarczyk, "Is the Human Soul Sexed? In Search for the Truth on Human Sexuality," *Studia Gilsoniana* 9 (2020): 108.

bodies."[77] As Jewett remarks, "this soul that is 'I' is the soul of my particular body and of no others."[78] In short, it is this body that makes me *me*. For Thomas, then, *the sex of a person's body is integral to their identity*. This is not to ignore the fact that outside of Eden bodies can be badly damaged—by disease, disability, disfigurement, and so on. But it is to say that they cannot be entirely *wrong*. For if I were to take possession of a different body (as opposed to having my body restored), I would no longer be the same person. In this sense, Bonhoeffer was right to insist that those "who reject their bodies reject their existence before God the Creator."[79]

Fourth, there is good reason to question the idea that the body takes its sex from the soul. For Sprinkle, this is because "the categories of 'male' and 'female' are by definition descriptions of our bodies, not our souls or any other immaterial aspect of our being. Sex is a material, biological category. Accordingly, immaterial souls can't be sexed."[80] What leads some advocates of hylomorphism to think otherwise, however, is the following Thomistic principle: "Since the form is not for the matter, but rather the matter for the form, we must gather from the form the reason why the matter is such as it is; and not conversely."[81] From this it follows that the soul (as the body's form) is the cause of the body's sex.[82] Nevertheless, other Thomistic interpreters see matters differently.[83] Because Thomas insists that the body is the principle of the soul's *individuation*, it is the soul that takes its sex (or, at least, its gender identity) from the body, not the other way around.[84] As Elliott Bedford and Jason Eberl explain:

> While strictly speaking the soul, which is immaterial, is not sexed, each soul is created by God as the vivifying principle of sexed bodies and is thereby individuated and sexed as an inseparable

77. Aquinas, *On Being and Essence*, 143.

78. Paul K. Jewett with Marguerite Shuster, *Who We Are: Our Dignity as Human: A Neo-Evangelical Theology* (Grand Rapids: Eerdmans, 1996), 42.

79. Bonhoeffer, *Creation and Fall*, 77.

80. Sprinkle, *Embodied*, 150.

81. Aquinas, *Summa Theologiae*, 1.76.5.

82. Maryniarczyk, "Is the Human Soul Sexed?," 121.

83. Elliott Louis Bedford and Jason T. Eberl, "Is the Soul Sexed? Anthropology, Transgenderism, and Disorders of Sex Development," *Health Care Ethics USA* 24, no. 3 (2016): 20–23.

84. Bedford and Eberl, "Is the Soul Sexed?," 20. If gender is understood to encompass the psycho-social aspects of personal identity, then it may be the better term to apply to souls.

> accidental quality of the human being. In short, as the vivifying principle of actually existing human beings, the human soul is properly characterised as sexed.[85]

It is also worth noting that on this view (no less than the alternative) there is no difficulty accounting for the scriptural indications that departed spirits remain male or female in the intermediate state (e.g., Samuel remains Samuel in Sheol and even appears as "an old man" [אִישׁ זָקֵן, *'ish zaqen*], 1 Sam 28:14). This is because the soul retains the sex/gender derived from the body, even after the body has returned to the dust.

It is difficult to determine which of these interpretations most faithfully represents Thomas's thought. It may even be that he is at odds with himself on this point.[86] However, the second interpretation is not only plausible but, in light of what we have seen, better reflects the biblical presentation. For as Genesis 1:27 and 2:7 make plain, *sex is*, first and foremost, *a property of bodies*. That sex is also a property of human *persons* is testimony to the significance of the body for personal identity. Consequently, although I am more than my body, I am my body and my body is me. Indeed, to "assert otherwise," write Bedford and Eberl, "is to bifurcate the essential integral nature of our body-soul unity, laying the foundation for a problematic body-self dualism."[87]

Hylomorphism rules out trans theory

On either of the above accounts, trans theory is ruled out. For on both accounts, *the sex of the body reveals the sex/gender of the person*. In light of this, the claim that "a discrepancy between the perceiving mind and the existing body" is reflective of a genuine ontological divide can only be made on the basis of an unbiblical form of "body-self dualism." Such a view, therefore, is "incompatible with a Christian anthropology and so is any justification built upon it."[88] This does not mean denying that "the deep-seated patterns of feeling and experience involved in gender

---

85. Bedford and Eberl, "Is the Soul Sexed?," 21.

86. Dew, *Modified Thomistic Holism*, 195.

87. Bedford and Eberl, "Is the Soul Sexed?," 22.

88. Bedford and Eberl, "Is the Soul Sexed?," 24, 26; compare Edmund Fong, "Gender Dysphoria and the Body-Soul Relationship," *Themelios* 47 (2022): 348–65.

dysphoria are themselves bodily," as Mike Higton alleges, for all mental states are necessarily bodily states also.[89] But it does mean that gender dysphoric individuals "are not experiencing an ontological disintegration, even if they perceive themselves to be."[90] In other words, gender incongruence (whatever factors may have given rise to it in any particular case) is not an experience of *ontological misalignment*.[91] There is no actual mismatch between body and soul.

In sum, whether God establishes the sex of the body *immediately* (independently of the soul) or *mediately* (via the soul), the net result is the same—a hylomorphic, body-soul composite. It is not accurate, then, to "speak of the soul as if it were the real person and the body only its garment or vehicle"; we are, rather, "embodied persons and personalized bodies."[92] Consequently, if a person's body is unambiguously sexed as male, it is simply not possible for their soul to be female.[93]

THE BUILDING OF THE WOMAN (GENESIS 2:18, 21–23)

We turn now to consider the significance of the creation of woman in Genesis 2:21–23, beginning with the divine declaration of verse 18: "It is not good that the man should be alone; I will make him a helper fit for him."

Before embarking on an exposition of this statement, however, it is important to note three developments that precede it. The first (in vv. 8–14) is the Lord God's planting of a garden in Eden. The second (in v. 15; compare v. 8b) is the placing of the man in the garden "to serve [עָבַד, *'avad*] it and keep it"—language that, because of its connection to the duties

89. Mike Higton, "A Critique of 'Transformed' 4," *kai euthùs* (February 28, 2019), https://mikehigton.org.uk/a-critique-of-transformed-4.

90. Bedford and Eberl, "Is the Soul Sexed?," 27.

91. As Stock has convincingly argued (*Material Girls*, 109–41), gender incongruence is more helpfully regarded as a form of *epistemological misidentification* (rather than *ontological misalignment*).

92. Gilbert Meilaender, *Faith and Faithfulness: Basic Themes in Christian Ethics* (Notre Dame: University of Notre Dame Press, 1991), 41.

93. Having sent Professor Tiessen my critique of his proposal, he has graciously indicated that he has been persuaded to abandon it. He has also written a fresh article explaining how he now thinks about these matters. See Tiessen, "Body, Soul, and Transgenderism: A Revision of My Earlier, Tentative, Theological Proposal," https://www.thoughtstheological.com/body-soul-and-transgenderism-a-revision-of-my-earlier-tentative-theological-proposal.

of the Levites in the tabernacle, suggests we see the man as "exercising a priestly function."[94] The third (in vv. 16–17) is the words of permission and prohibition regarding what the man can and cannot eat—words that indicate a boundary to the man's extensive freedom.

Three significant developments also follow verse 18. The first (in v. 19a) is the LORD God's forming of "every beast of the field and every bird of the heavens" (compare Gen 1:20–25). The second (in vv. 19b–20a) is the man's naming of the beasts and the birds—a responsibility that allows him a share in the creative process.[95] The third is the way in which the man's need for a *suitable* companion is heightened by this process. For despite the array of animals brought to him, "there was not found a helper fit for him" (v. 20b).

A PROBLEM AND ITS SOLUTION (V. 18)

Verse 18 begins by drawing attention to a problem in the paradisical scene: "It is not good that the man should be alone." By placing the words "not good" (לֹא־טוֹב, *lo'-tov*) at the head of the statement, the Hebrew text emphasizes the *significance* of the problem. But what is the *nature* of the problem? To properly understand the divinely proposed solution (the making of "a helper fit for him"), this question must first be answered.

The nature of the man's aloneness

Given the orderly and purposeful sense of the word "good" (*tov*) in Genesis 1, it is generally agreed that the diagnosis of 2:18a "has nothing to do with moral perfection or quality of workmanship—it is a comment concerning function."[96] Nor is it simply that the man is lonely—in need of companionship or sexual fulfilment. Rather, in view of the purpose for which the man was placed in the garden (v. 15), the immediate problem the LORD God identifies "is connected with the need for man to be a

---

94. William J. Dumbrell, *The Faith of Israel: Its Expression in the Books of the Old Testament* (Leicester: Inter-Varsity Press, 1988), 19; Paul F. Scotchmer, "Lessons from Paradise on Work, Marriage, and Freedom: A Study of Genesis 2:4–3:24," *Evangelical Review of Theology* 28 (2004): 80–85.

95. Arnold, *Genesis*, 60.

96. John H. Walton, *The Lost World of Genesis 1: Ancient Cosmology and the Origins Debate* (Downers Grove, IL: InterVarsity Press, 2009), 51.

'worker' or 'servant.' "[97] In other words, the man has a task to accomplish, and he cannot do it alone.

Interestingly, it was common in the patristic period to view the man's need primarily in procreative terms.[98] This is understandable, for producing progeny is clearly *one reason* (indeed a vital one) why he requires "a helper fit for him" (compare 1:28). It is also important to note that motherhood is not just a key aspect of the woman's calling (as 3:16 indicates), but a responsibility that only she, as a female, can fulfill (3:20).[99] Nevertheless, because Genesis 2:18 makes no *explicit* mention of childbearing, Werner Neuer suggests that it "diminishes the text if the idea of help is limited to the process of procreation, in which the woman conceives, carries and gives birth for the man."[100] The point is well taken. At the same time, when chapters 1–3 are read together, it is clear that "procreation is a central feature of the help provided, and it cannot be excluded from the purposes for which the woman is given as a help."[101]

The point, then, is simply this: the man not only needs a *human other* (a companion); he needs a *sexual other* (a mate). To rightly understand the nature of his aloneness (v. 18), then, humanity's larger calling must be kept in view (v. 15; compare 1:26–28).

The meaning of "a helper fit for him"

What, then, is the precise meaning of the expression "a helper fit for him" (עֵזֶר כְּנֶגְדּוֹ, *'ezer kenegdow*; LXX: βοηθὸν κατ' αὐτόν, *boēthon kat' auton*)?

Entirely appropriately, *'ezer* is translated "helper" in most contemporary English versions. Although it often refers to divine assistance (e.g., Exod 18:4; Deut 33:7; Ps 30:10), it can also be used of human aid—rendered either by equals (e.g., Isa 30:5) or by subordinates (e.g., 1 Kgs 20:16; 1 Chr

97. Christopher Ash, *Marriage: Sex in the Service of God* (Leicester: Inter-Varsity Press, 2003), 119.

98. E.g., Tobit 8:6; Clement of Alexandria, *Stromata* 2.23 (*ANF* 2:377–78); Augustine, *On Genesis*, 376–80; Ambrose, *Dogmatic Treatises, Ethical Works, and Sermons* (*NPNF*[2] 7:256).

99. Accordingly, the name Eve (חַוָּה, *khawwah*), which resembles the Hebrew word for *living* (חָיָה, *khayah*), is given to the woman precisely because she is "the mother of all living" ([אֵם כָּל חָי, *'em kol-khay*] 3:20; compare 4:1–2).

100. Werner Neuer, *Man and Woman in Christian Perspective*, trans. Gordon J. Wenham (Wheaton, IL: Crossway, 1991), 69.

101. Ken Magnuson, *Invitation to Christian Ethics: Moral Reasoning and Contemporary Issues* (Grand Rapids: Kregel, 2020), 232.

12:1, 22–23; 22:17; 2 Chr 26:13; Ezek 12:14).[102] So while "helper" is clearly a relational term (describing a relationship of benefit), the word itself "does not imply that the helper is stronger than the helped; simply that the latter's strength is inadequate by itself (e.g. Josh 1:14; 10:4, 6; 1 Chron 12:17, 19, 21, 22)."[103] For this reason, it "does not specify position or rank, whether of superiority or inferiority."[104] Such connotations, if present, must be gleaned from the context.

The compound phrase "fit for him" (*kenegdow*)—which means, literally, "like opposite him"[105]—expresses "the notion of similarity as well as supplementation."[106] As such, it emphasizes correspondence rather than identicality. It thus anticipates what will be disclosed even more clearly in verses 22–23: the woman is both *like* the man (being of the *same kind*), yet *different* from the man (being of the *opposite sex*). In this way, "Genesis 2 shows that there are real differences between men and women. These serve to supply the lacks and needs of the one sex through the gifts of the other."[107] While I will have more to say about the significance of the *difference* implied by *kenegdow* in the next chapter, it is important to recognize that the expression also connotes *equality*. Indeed, *kenegdow* has been translated "equal and adequate to himself."[108] So, although clearly made "for" (לוֹ, *lo*) the man (compare 1 Cor 11:9), the helper is not inferior to the man.

What conclusions may be deduced from these observations? Although drawing in aspects of the narrative yet to be explored, Christopher Ash's summary is insightful:

> When we read Genesis 2:18 in the context that precedes (both from 2:4 and also 1:1–2:3) and in the wider context of all Scripture, we are therefore led to recognize that both the procreational and relational benefits of marriage are set before the fall in the context of an

102. As Terrance Wardlaw Jr. has shown, Ezek 12:14 "clearly refers to officials who are subordinate to the prince in Jerusalem" (*Created Male and Female* [Eugene, OR: Wipf & Stock, 2021], 14).

103. Wenham, *Genesis 1–15*, 68.

104. Davidson, *Flame of Yahweh*, 29.

105. Wenham, *Genesis 1–15*, 68.

106. Von Rad, *Genesis*, 82.

107. Neuer, *Man and Woman*, 70.

108. Francis Brown, S. R. Driver, and Charles A. Briggs, *A Hebrew and English Lexicon of the Old Testament* (Oxford: Clarendon, 1968), 617.

overarching purpose, the achievement of a task calling humankind into an awesome dignity. Any creation ethic of marriage must set it in this outward-looking context of task, and not simply (or even predominantly) as God's answer to human loneliness.[109]

THE TAKING OF THE WOMAN FROM THE MAN (VV. 21–23)

This brings us to the event of the woman's creation, which the author of Genesis narrates as follows:

> [21] So the LORD God caused a deep sleep to fall upon *the man* [*ha'adam*], and while he slept took one of his *ribs* [צֵלָע, *tsela'*] and closed up its place with flesh. [22] And the *rib* [*tsela'*] that the LORD God had taken from *the man* [*ha'adam*] he *made* [בָּנָה, *banah*] into a *woman* [אִשָּׁה, *'ishah*] and brought her to *the man* [*ha'adam*]. [23] Then *the man* [*ha'adam*] said,

> "This at last is bone of my bones
> and flesh of my flesh;
> she shall be called *Woman* [*'ishah*],
> because she was taken out of *Man* [אִישׁ, *'ish*]."

For our purposes, three features of these verses require probing. The first is the meaning and significance of "rib" (*tsela'*; LXX: πλευρά, *pleura*). The second is the meaning and significance of "made" (*bnh*; LXX: οἰκοδομέω, *oikodomeō*). The third is the similarity and differences between the man and the woman. To conclude this section, I will explore the relevance of these verses for trans theory—giving particular attention to the charge of Gnosticism that is sometimes leveled against it.

The meaning and significance of tsela'

The first term to examine is *tsela'*. As we have noted, there are several terminological connections between the Edenic scene and later depictions of the tabernacle.[110] This word is another. Although contemporary English translations routinely render it *rib* (e.g., ESV, NIV, CSB, HCSB),

---

109. Ash, *Marriage*, 121–22.

110. For an elaborated list of seventeen intertexual parallels, see Richard M. Davidson, "Cosmic Metanarrative for the Coming Millennium," *JATS* 11 (2000): 108–11.

in virtually every other Old Testament occurrence, *tsela'* refers to "the 'side' of sacred architecture: the ark, tabernacle, incense altar, temple rooms."[111] We shall return to the significance of this association later. The point to note here is that *side* (rather than *rib*) is the more likely meaning and therefore a better translation (so NET). This is not to suggest that we are meant to envisage the LORD God removing the entirety of the man's side, but that a single rib is too specific (compare NIV footnote: "part of the man's side"). This is supported by the man's language in verse 23 ("bone of my bones *and* flesh of my flesh"), which suggests that both bone and flesh were taken.[112]

These observations have led some scholars to the speculate that *ha'adam* was "an originally binary human, or one sexually undifferentiated, who is split down the side to form two sexually differentiated counterparts."[113] As we saw in the previous chapter, such an interpretation appears in a number of the early Christian (especially Gnostic) writings, and in certain rabbinic sources like Bereshit Rabba 8:1.[114]

However, as we have also seen, Genesis 1 does not support the notion of an androgynous progenitor of the race. Nevertheless, queer commentator Michael Carden believes that "the androgyne's trace is found *more clearly* in the second creation account in Genesis 2–3."[115] In support of this claim, Carden suggests the words of Genesis 2:23–24 "echo Aristophanes's tale in Plato's *Symposium* according to which humans were originally dyads of three sexes—male, female and hermaphrodite."[116] However, *Symposium* was written around 385 BC, whereas Genesis (most likely) took its final form somewhere between 1250 BC and 950 BC.[117] So an *echo* of the former

111. Robert A. J. Gagnon, "Transsexuality and Ordination," *Dr Robert A. J. Gagnon* (August 2007), http://www.robgagnon.net/articles/TranssexualityOrdination.pdf. Of the thirty-nine instances of the term (outside of Gen 2), the only exception is in 2 Sam 16:13, where it refers to a hillside.

112. The use of *pleura* in the LXX (e.g., Dan 7:5; Jdt 6:6; Sir 30:12; 42:5; 4 Macc 18:7) also suggests that *side* is the likely meaning, although not in a way that excludes the removal of a *rib*.

113. Robert A. J. Gagnon, "The Old Testament and Homosexuality: A Critical Review of the Case Made by Phyllis Bird," *ZAW* 117 (2005): 388; compare A. T. Reisenberger, "The Creation of Adam as Hermaphrodite—and Its Implications for Feminist Theology," *Judaica* 42 (1993): 447–52.

114. Bereshit Rabbah is a talmudic-era midrash on Genesis (c. AD 300–500).

115. Michael Carden, "Genesis/Bereshit," in *The Queer Bible Commentary*, ed. Deryn Guest, Bob Goss, Mona West, and Tom Bohache (London: SCM, 2006), 27 (emphasis added).

116. Carden, "Genesis/Bereshit," 28.

117. Wenham, *Genesis 1–15*, xliv.

text in the latter is simply not possible. The only other piece of evidence Carden mentions is the rabbinic interpretation noted above.

To engage with this interpretation, it will help us to revisit Trible's claim that, prior to verse 22, "the man" is neither male nor androgynous but a sexually undifferentiated (i.e., asexual or presexual) *it*.[118] The claim rests on three assumptions: (1) that the grammatically masculine form of *ha'adam* does not indicate that the referent is a male; (2) that the meaning of *ha'adam* changes as the narrative unfolds; and (3) that it is only with the creation of the female that *ha'adam* becomes a male—a change supposedly indicated by the introduction of the new term *'ish* at the end of verse 23.[119] Along similar lines, David Tabb Stewart states that Genesis 2:20–21 presents us with a "three-gender system": "male, female and androgyne or *ha'adam*, 'the human.' "[120]

Notwithstanding his stated desire to discover and exploit "tensions and contradictions" in the text, Ken Stone identifies the main difficulties with this view:

> For example, the term *'adam* continues to be used with reference to the male character even after the creation of the woman. This continuity between *'adam* and the man implies perhaps that *'adam* was understood to have been male already before that time. Indeed, the speech given by *'adam* in 2:23 seems to assume a continuity of identity between *'adam* and the "man" when it notes that "woman" was taken "from man" just after verse 21 has specified that God caused the *'adam* to fall asleep and then took "one from its ribs" in order to create the second human.[121]

This last observation is decisive. Verse 23 reveals that *ha'adam* and *'ish* have one and the same referent ("the man")—a conclusion confirmed by verses 24–25, where *'ish* and *'ishah* (in v. 24) parallel *ha'adam* and *'ishah* (in v. 25). Not only does this negate Trible's first assumption (for, in this case, the gender of *ha'adam* does match the sex of its referent), but it shows

118. Trible, *Rhetoric of Sexuality*, 80

119. Trible, *Rhetoric of Sexuality*, 80, 98.

120. David Tabb Stewart, "Leviticus," in Guest, Goss, West, and Bohache, *The Queer Bible Commentary*, 92.

121. Stone, "Garden of Eden," 50, 57.

her second and third assumptions to be without foundation. It thus rules out the possibility that *ha'adam* was originally a two-faced, double-sided being. Richard Davidson, then, is correct: "Nothing has changed in the makeup of 'the human' during his sleep except the loss of a rib. There is no hint in the text of an originally bisexual or sexually undifferentiated being split into two different sexes."[122] Like Genesis 1, then, Genesis 2 offers no support to the idea of protological androgyny or to the view that *ha'adam* was originally an indeterminate "it."

The meaning and significance of banah

We turn next to examine the meaning and significance of the verb *banah*—usually translated "made" (e.g., ESV, NIV, CSB, HCSB), but occasionally "fashioned" (e.g., NASB) or "built" (e.g., DRB). The term appears frequently in the book of Genesis and in virtually every other instance refers to the building of an edifice: a city (4:17; 10:11; 11:4–5, 8), an altar (8:20; 12:7–8; 13:18; 22:9; 26:25; 35:7) or a house (33:17).[123] It is, therefore, a construction word, which is why it is used elsewhere of the building of both the earthly temple (Ps 78:69) and the heavenly sanctuary (Amos 9:6). Accordingly, the LXX routinely translates it by *oikodomeō*.

For Robert Alter, the deployment of "built" not only complements the potter's term, "fashioned" (in 2:7), but is "more appropriate because the LORD is now working with hard material, not soft clay."[124] This insight takes on added significance when paired with the fact that *tzela'*, as we noted earlier, typically refers to the *side* of sacred architecture. It thus intimates "an aesthetic intent and connotes also the idea of reliability and permanence."[125] All of this suggests that in *building* the woman from the *side* of the man, the LORD God is engaging in a specific act of *sacred construction*.

The woman, then, is a discrete and complete being in herself—a fact emphasized by the LORD God's presentation of her *to* the man (v. 22). So,

---

122. Davidson, *Flame of Yahweh*, 20.

123. In two instances (Gen 16:2; 30:3), it is used metaphorically of the building up of descendants.

124. Robert Alter, *Genesis: Translation and Commentary* (New York: Norton, 1996), 9.

125. Samuel L. Terrien, "Toward a Biblical Theology of Womanhood," in *Male and Female: Christian Approaches to Sexuality*, ed. Ruth T. Barnhouse and Urban T. Holmes (New York: Seabury, 1976), 18.

while her substance is taken from the man, she is not a sub-species of the man. She is an equal and comparable human being, no less the image of God than he. Moreover, her sex (already named in 1:27), while different from that of the man, has its own uniqueness, glory, integrity, and purpose. Barth, then, is correct: "Woman could not have been introduced with greater honour."[126]

The similarity and differences between the man and the woman

We now come to consider the similarity and differences between the man and the woman—especially as these are reflected in verse 23. Unsurprisingly, the man's first response to the woman is one of grateful and uninhibited delight: "This at last is bone of my bones and flesh of my flesh" (v. 23b). This is precisely what could not be said of any of the animals previously brought to him. But now he recognizes one who is *consubstantial* with him—made of the same stuff! This explains the note of relief in his opening exclamation: "This at last" (זֹאת הַפַּעַם, *zo'th happa'am*) or, as the HCSB has it, "This one, at last" or, as the GNB glosses, "At last, here is one of my own kind."

"Bone of my bones and flesh of my flesh" (עֶצֶם מֵעֲצָמַי וּבָשָׂר מִבְּשָׂרִי, *'etsem me'atsamay uvasar mibbesari*) is a typical Hebrew way of conveying a kinship relationship (e.g., Gen 29:14; Judg 9:2; 2 Sam 5:1; 19:12–13; 1 Chron 11:1). Within the narrative of Genesis 2, however, the words have a literalness that sets them apart from other similar expressions.[127] This is reinforced by the remainder of the man's poem: "she shall be called *Woman* (*'ishah*), because she was *taken out of Man* (מֵאִישׁ לֻקֳחָה, *me'ish luqokhah*)." In locating the origin of the woman in himself, the man is doing more than remarking on the closeness of their kinship; he is pointing to "their possession of an identical essence."[128] Blocher, then, is right to aver that "the first truth about man and woman remains that of their common human nature, with much in their activity having little reference to their sex."[129]

126. Barth, *CD*, III/1, 299.

127. Umberto Cassuto, *A Commentary on the Book of Genesis 1–11: Part 1: From Adam to Noah*, trans. Israel Abrahams (Jerusalem: Magnes Press, 1961; repr., Skokie, IL: Varda, 2005), 136.

128. Blocher, *In the Beginning*, 98.

129. Henri Blocher, "Women, Ministry and the Gospel: Hints for a New Paradigm?," in *Women, Ministry and the Gospel: Exploring New Paradigms*, ed. Mark Husbands and Timothy Larson (Downers

At the same time, there are important differences between them—not least to do with their sex. As we have already seen, the problem of the man's aloneness is solved neither by a creature alien to him (i.e., an animal), nor by one who is identical to him (i.e., another man), but by one who is "essentially like him but opposite to him. His other half. His complement."[130] Therefore, while James Brownson rightly sees a movement "from the isolation of an individual to the deep blessing of shared kinship and community," his claim that "the text doesn't really explore gender differences at all" is erroneous.[131] Both unity and distinction are equally on view.

This is first apparent in the different *origins* of the two—the man being taken from the *ground* (2:7), the woman from the man's *flesh* (2:21). As the larger narrative confirms (e.g., 3:16–19), these differing "modes of creation" match their different orientations: the man being primarily turned toward "the world of things" and the woman primarily turned toward "the world of persons."[132] As Alastair Roberts expresses: "The man is formed from the earth to till the ground, to serve and rule the earth. The woman is built from the man's side to bring life and communion through union."[133] These differing orientations, however, should not be viewed in a rigid or totalizing fashion. Genesis 1:28 has already made clear that the responsibility of dominion and multiplication is given to *both sexes*. Consequently, both man and woman are to be involved in *both spheres*. The point, then, is not that the sexes should occupy separate domains, but that they will each make distinct but complementary contributions to both domains.

Difference is also indicated by the terms *'ish* and *'ishah*, which, in the broader context, map onto "male and female" (1:27), respectively. While an etymological link between them is uncertain, like *'adam* and *'adamah* (in 2:7), the pairing of *'ish* and *'ishah* is a form of sound play.[134] The purpose of the pun is likewise clear: to indicate the woman's source (that she

---

Grove, IL: InterVarsity Press, 2007), 245.

130. Claire S. Smith, *God's Good Design: What the Bible Really Says About Men and Women*, 2nd ed. (Sydney: Matthias Media, 2019), 176.

131. James V. Brownson, *Bible, Gender, Sexuality: Reframing the Church's Debate on Same-Sex Relationships* (Grand Rapids: Eerdmans, 2013), 30–31.

132. Neuer, *Man and Woman*, 70.

133. Roberts, "Male and Female," 36.

134. Mathews, *Genesis 1–11:26*, 219.

was "taken out of man") and, therefore, the profundity of her connection to the man. And yet, as we have already seen, she does not so much stand *next to* him (as a copy) but *opposite* him (as a counterpart).

It follows from this that Beauvoir's claim—that the woman "determines and differentiates herself in relation to the man," but "he does not in relation to her"—is mistaken. Not only are both determined and differentiated with reference to each other, but when the woman is presented to the man, she is not at all "the inessential in front of the essential."[135] Rather, she is the utterly and equally essential—and that precisely because of her difference. Therefore, to the degree that it is helpful to speak of her as *other* to him, this is only because he also is *other* to her. Still, such language risks obscuring the emphasis of the text. For in the theology of Genesis 2 (as in Genesis 1), genuine difference is necessary for true unity. As Phyllis Bird remarks: differentiation is "the precondition for community, and sexual differentiation is the basis for the primary community."[136] Put differently, the man and the woman "are appropriately and distinctly individual, so as to be able to procreate, but also alike enough to be singly human."[137]

Finally, the man's naming of himself as *'ish* (in contrast to *'ishah*) intimates that "it is through encountering her nature that he is able truly to understand his own."[138] At the same time, it is clear that he was "a self-aware man in soul and body before he knew himself to be, properly speaking, male."[139] In this sense, we can affirm Gunton's insight that "men and women are what they are only by virtue of the otherness of one to the other."[140] This does not mean, however, that Trible's claim—that it is only with the creation of the woman that the man becomes sexed—has merit after all. For, as we have seen, Trible mistakes the *clarification* of the man's sex (which takes place in v. 23) with the *creation* of the man's sex (which

135. Beauvoir, *The Second Sex*, 6.

136. Bird, "Bone of My Bone," 524.

137. Arnold, *Genesis*, 61.

138. Favale, *Genesis of Gender*, 43.

139. Smothers, "On the Body," 100.

140. Colin E. Gunton, "Proteus and Procrustes: A Study in the Dialectic of Language in Disagreement with Sallie McFague," in *Speaking the Christian God: The Holy Trinity and the Challenge of Feminism*, ed. Alvin F. Kimel, Jr. (Grand Rapids: Eerdmans, 1992), 79.

took place in v. 7). In so doing, she confuses epistemology with ontology, knowing with being.

The man's act of naming, then, is a linguistic response to preexisting realities; it does not create those realities.[141] Moreover, the biblical sequence, is clear: "Adam was formed first, then Eve" (1 Tim 2:13). So, while the presentation of the woman to the man grants him insight into the significance of his own maleness, it does not establish it. His sex (like hers) is objectively determined by the God-given form of his body and consequently remains stable throughout the narrative.

IMPLICATIONS FOR TRANS THEORY

Embodiment and sexed identity

For Augustine, "the body is not an extraneous ornament or aid, but part of the man's nature."142 Expressed otherwise, your body is "not a vehicle driven by the 'real' you, your mind; nor a mere costume you must don";143 it *is* the real you (even if there is more to you) and, in particular, *it is the God-given indicator of your divinely determined sexed identity*. Thus, the sex of the *body* reveals the sex (and so gender) of the *person*. Or to put the point in the language of the opening chapters of Genesis, the reason Adam is a "man" (*'ish*) is because he has a "male" (*zakhar*) body; the reason Eve is a "woman" (*'ishah*) is because she has a "female" (*neqevah*) body. In this sense, the anthropology of Genesis 1 and 2 straightforwardly affirms not only the sex-and-gender binary, but also the sex-and-gender connection. It is, in that sense, unapologetically cisnormative.

As we have also seen, such an understanding of sexed identity stands in direct opposition to both forms of trans theory. For *soft trans theory* holds that gender identity determines gender but not sex (so for a person's sex to align with their true self, their body needs to be altered) and *hard trans theory* holds that gender identity determines both gender and sex (so for a person's sex to align with their true self, their body does not need to be altered). On either view, both the ontological and the

141. Favale, *Genesis of Gender*, 43.

142. Augustine, *The City of God*, 1.13 (*NPNF*[1] 10).

143. Sherif Girgis, Ryan T. Anderson, and Robert P. George, *What Is Marriage?: Man and Woman: A Defense* (New York: Encounter, 2012), 24.

epistemological significance of the body is profoundly diminished, if not outrightly denied. Biblical anthropology is likewise rejected, for in biblical thought, "maleness and femaleness are physically grounded, not psychologically determined."[144]

The charge of Gnosticism

This explains why a number of evangelical writers have described trans theory as a species of Gnosticism. Andrew Walker, for example, argues that because "Gnosticism says that there is an inherent tension between our true selves and the bodies we inhabit," the idea that "our gender can be different than our biological sex is a modern form of the old Gnostic idea."[145] Craig Carter levels a parallel charge: "The essence of modern gender theory is the teaching that sex is merely incidental to identity. ... In this way we see the return of ancient Gnosticism."[146] The 2018 Evangelical Alliance report, *Transformed*, argues similarly: "Any form of Christianity that devalues the body and the physical creation in general is deeply problematic. These ideas have more to do with Gnosticism, or ancient Greek Platonism, than following Jesus."[147] J. Alan Branch likewise avers that "the modern claims that 'I am a man trapped in a woman's body' or 'I am a woman trapped in a man's body' have strong Gnostic overtones."[148] And, finally, Nancy Pearcey calls transgender ideology "ancient Gnosticism in new garb."[149]

To be clear, none of these writers are arguing that trans theory *is* Gnosticism *simpliciter*. Their point, rather, is that trans theory and Gnosticism "share a revolt against the external, against the body, against nature itself," and also "a deep-rooted conviction that the source of the self is found by looking within." Moreover, in several Gnostic texts, as in much gender theorizing, "the difference between male and female, or the notion of there being a natural order to human sexual relations—are at best

144. Sam Allberry, *What God Has to Say about Our Bodies: How the Gospel Is Good News for Our Physical Selves* (Wheaton, IL: Crossway, 2021), 58.

145. Walker, *Transgender Debate*, 28.

146. Craig A. Carter, "The New Gender Gnostics," *Eikon* 2, no. 1 (2020): 37.

147. Evangelical Alliance, *Transformed*, 12.

148. Branch, *Affirming God's Image*, 108.

149. Pearcey, *Love Thy Body*, 196.

illusory and at worst corrupted deceptions."[150] It is also noteworthy that in many trans narratives, the human body is "likened to a cage that constrains a good spirit."[151] Thus, in both worldviews, observes O'Donovan, the body is effectively reduced to "undifferentiated matter, on which the spirit proposes to exercise unlimited freedom."[152]

Adjudicating the validity of the charge

Many trans-affirming authors object to this critique. Beardsley, for instance, not only draws attention to the fact that "Gnosticism was a notoriously varied and complex phenomenon," but believes that "there is something disturbing" about attempts to equate transgender experience with an ancient heresy.[153] Rodney Holder, likewise, takes issue with O'Donovan's comparison, arguing that trans people are not objecting to embodiment as such, but insisting that their natal sex is "wrong."[154] Inasmuch as "many transgender individuals say that a sense of peace and freedom only emerges when they feel unity and harmony in bodymind," Mary Elise Lowe also contends that the desire for SRS is decidedly anti-Gnostic![155] And, finally, Scott Bader-Saye insists that gender transitioning "avoids the charge of Gnosticism" because its goal "is not the punishment, torment, or destruction of the flesh but rather its metamorphosis for the sake of participating in gendered reciprocity."[156]

These responses deserve careful consideration, as does Sprinkle's caution that it can be "lazy and unthoughtful to simply write off every trans* claim as Gnostic and anti-body."[157] But it is far from clear that this

---

150. Harrison, *Better Story*, 17. On the various conceptions of sex in the Gnostic texts, see Jonathan Cahana, "Gnostically Queer: Gender Trouble in Gnosticism," *Biblical Theology Bulletin* 41 (2011): 24–35.

151. Branch, *Affirming God's Image*, 108.

152. O'Donovan, "Transsexualism and Christian Marriage," 151.

153. See Kurt Rudolph, *Gnosis: The Nature and History of an Ancient Religion* (Edinburgh: T&T Clark, 1983), 9, 53; Beardsley, "Taking Issue," 75.

154. Rodney Holder, "The Ethics of Transsexualism, Part 2: A Christian Response to the Issues Raised," *Crucible* 37, no. 3 (1998): 128.

155. Mary Elise Lowe, "From the Same Spirit: Receiving the Theological Gifts of Transgender Christians," *Dialog: A Journal of Theology* 56 (2017): 33.

156. Scott Bader-Saye, "The Transgender Body's Grace," *Journal of the Society of Christian Ethics* 39 (2019): 88.

157. Sprinkle, *Embodied*, 148–49.

is what those who have made such comparisons have done. O'Donovan, for instance, is more than alert to the fact that those who seek SRS "do not retreat from their bodies into a Gnostic spirituality; if anything, they are preoccupied with them." And yet, he is also right to insist that for a person to claim that their "real sex" is independent of their embodied sex is to engage (even if unwittingly) in "a kind of Gnostic withdrawal from material creation."[158] For in moving the seat of one's sexed identity entirely into the realm of the spiritual or psychological, the revelatory significance of the body is more than reduced; it is rejected.

It is here that the key point of connection with ancient Gnosticism lies. For, as Lesley-Anne Dyer Williams identifies, at the heart of Gnosticism is the rejection of the idea that our bodies "reveal the good intent of the maker of the universe."[159] This rejection is illustrated (albeit inadvertently) in the following admission by Tanis:

> The information that our bodies convey about us is relevant, but it is not the only perspective. This information is not all there is to know. We learn, too, how important it is that our bodies tell the truth about who we are and that we need our bodies to be congruent with our identities. Precisely because we value our bodies, we need them to express—through our clothes or our physical form—what we know about ourselves. We love our bodies into new forms and new ways of moving in the world.[160]

Here Tanis is claiming that the "information" of the trans-identified person's given (i.e., unmodified) body is, in fact, false. It does not reveal the truth about their identity. This truth, as Tanis goes on to explain, is known in a way that is "independent of the body."[161] Epistemologically, then, the charge of Gnosticism is upheld.

In sum, trans theory, in both its forms, contradicts biblical anthropology "not by directly questioning the goodness of embodiment as such,

158. O'Donovan, "Transsexualism and Christian Marriage," 147.

159. Lesley-Anne Dyer Williams, "Beautiful Bodies and Shameful Embodiment in Plotinus's *Enneads*," in *Embodiment: A History*, Oxford Philosophical Concepts, ed. Justin E. H. Smith (Oxford: Oxford University Press, 2017), 81.

160. Tanis, *Trans-Gender*, 183–84.

161. Tanis, *Trans-Gender*, 184.

but by challenging the goodness of this particular body vis-à-vis one's 'true' identity."[162] Whether we describe such a challenge as quasi-Gnostic (or in some other way) is less important than the fact that it cannot be reconciled with Scripture. Being a man or a woman is a divine gift—a gift revealed by the reality of our natal sex.

CONCLUDING REFLECTIONS

The central finding of this chapter is that psychosomatic unity characterizes not only the original Edenic couple, but also their post-fall progeny—all who bear "the image of the man of dust" (1 Cor 15:49). As Samuel Ferguson writes, "There is no sense in Genesis 1 and 2 that gender identity can be divorced from human embodiment. Therefore, there is no sense in these chapters that manhood and womanhood are merely psychological realities separable from maleness and femaleness. In a profound sense, one's body *is* one's gender."[163]

What this means *ontologically*, as Andrzej Maryniarczyk identifies, is that "a human being is not an asexual soul confined to a sexual body. What we are dealing here with is the ontic, psychological and physical unity."[164] What this means *epistemologically*, as Abigail Favale discerns, is that our bodies are "the visible reality through which we manifest our hidden, inner life."[165] What this means *ethically*, as Matthew Mason perceives, is that we are "called to responsible stewardship of our bodies with their structural integrity as male and female."[166]

This last point requires further elaboration, as it contains a range of important entailments and also requires some necessary nuancing, particularly for life outside of Eden. But as our exploration of Genesis 2 is not yet complete, this task will be deferred until we have engaged with verses 24 and 25. This is the purpose of the following chapter.

---

162. Todd T. W. Daly, "Gender Dysphoria and the Ethics of Transsexual (i.e., Gender Reassignment) Surgery," *Ethics & Medicine: An International Journal of Bioethics* 32 (2016): 39.

163. Ferguson, *Does God Care about Gender and Identity?*, 21 (emphasis original).

164. Maryniarczyk, "Is the Human Soul Sexed?," 122.

165. Favale, *Genesis of Gender*, 40.

166. Mason, "Authority of the Body," 46.

CHAPTER 9

THE MEANING AND MYSTERY OF MARRIAGE

Subject to several centuries of interpretation, the meanings associated with the statements "Therefore a man leaves his father and his mother and clings to his wife," and "in the image of God he created them, male and female he created them" can and do change. Neither statement has settled the question of God's plan for human sexuality, nor have they provided a fixed definition of human marriage.[1]

—Jennifer Wright Knust

Marriage fulfills, and so makes sense of, a feature of our common human biological nature. Human beings come into existence with a dimorphically differentiated sexuality, clearly ordered at the biological level towards heterosexual union as the human mode of procreation.[2]

—Oliver O'Donovan

The primary purpose of this chapter is to complete the theological exposition of Genesis 2 begun in the previous chapter by focusing on what its two final verses disclose about the meaning and mystery of the marriage of

1. Jennifer Wright Knust, *Unprotected Texts: The Bible's Surprising Contradictions about Sex and Desire* (New York: HarperOne, 2011), 56.

2. O'Donovan, "Transsexualism and Christian Marriage," 141.

man and woman, and to see what this, in turn, reveals about the purpose of sex and the nature of gender.

This chapter is divided into three sections. In the first, "The Meaning of Marriage," four matters will occupy our attention: (1) the purpose of Genesis 2:24–25; (2) the nature of the "one flesh" union of verse 24; (3) the importance of the two sexes for this union; and (4) the significance of the statement of verse 25 ("the man and his wife were both naked and were not ashamed"), particularly in the light of 3:7. In the second section, "The Mystery of Marriage," we shall step outside the book of Genesis to explore the typological and eschatological significance of marriage. In the final section, "Implications for Trans Theory and Practice," the relevance of both the sex-and-gender binary and the sex-and-gender connection will be teased out.

THE MEANING OF MARRIAGE

THE PURPOSE OF GENESIS 2:24–25

The etiology of marriage

In Genesis 2:24–25, the narrator, whom Jesus identifies as God (Matt 19:4–5), resumes his role. The purpose of the verses, as most commentators recognize, is to highlight the normative nature of the preceding account by "applying the principles of the first marriage to every marriage."[3] In this way, they bring the story of the making of the man and the woman to a natural and fitting denouement.[4]

TABLE 6: GENESIS 2:24–25 — ENGLISH AND HEBREW

English Standard Version	*Biblia Hebraica Stuttgartensia*
[24] Therefore a man shall leave his father and his mother and hold fast to his wife, and they shall become one flesh.	עַל־כֵּן֙ יַֽעֲזָב־אִ֔ישׁ אֶת־אָבִ֖יו וְאֶת־אִמּ֑וֹ וְדָבַ֣ק בְּאִשְׁתּ֔וֹ וְהָי֖וּ לְבָשָׂ֥ר אֶחָֽד׃
[25] And the man and his wife were both naked and were not ashamed.	וַיִּֽהְי֤וּ שְׁנֵיהֶם֙ עֲרוּמִּ֔ים הָֽאָדָ֖ם וְאִשְׁתּ֑וֹ וְלֹ֖א יִתְבֹּשָֽׁשׁוּ

3. Wenham, *Genesis 1–15*, 70; compare Mathews, *Genesis 1–11:26*, 222; Arnold, *Genesis*, 61.

4. Von Rad, *Genesis*, 84.

Not all accept this interpretation, however. Andrew Sloane, for instance, regards verses 24–25 as "parenthetic in nature," with marriage functioning only as "a tangible 'application' of the nature of God's intentions for human community."[5] This, however, misses the force of the "therefore" (עַל־כֵּן, *ʿal ken* = "because of this" or "for this reason") that begins verse 24, which indicates that what follows is *etiological*—that is, intended "to explain something that exists today, referring it back to the creative work of God (narrated in vv. 18–23) as its causal antecedent."[6] The point, then, is that the historic phenomenon of marriage is a direct result of the creative acts depicted in the previous verses and, more broadly, of God's summons for humanity to reproduce (1:28)—marriage being the divinely ordained context for the fulfillment of the procreational mandate.

This interpretation is confirmed in Matthew 19:4–5 (compare Mark 10:6–7). By directly linking Genesis 1:27 and 2:24, Jesus shows that *man-woman marriage* is an immediate implication of *male-female creation*. Even James Brownson, despite his desire to downplay gender complementarity in Genesis 2, affirms that "the story envisions marriage as the most basic form of this community, and it assumes that marriage is constituted by a husband and wife."[7] Consequently, von Rad's verdict is both valid and astute:

> In this statement the entire narrative so far arrives at the primary purpose toward which it was oriented from the beginning. This shows what is actually intended. The story is entirely aetiological, i.e., it was told to answer a quite definite question. A fact needs explanation, namely, the extremely powerful drive of the sexes to each other. ... The recognition of this narrative as aetiological is theologically important. Its point of departure, the thing to be explained, is for the narrator something in existence, present, not something "paradisiacal" and thus lost![8]

---

5. Andrew Sloane, "'And he shall rule over you': Evangelicals, Feminists, and Genesis 2–3," in *Tamar's Tears: Evangelical Engagements with Feminist Old Testament Hermeneutics*, ed. Andrew Sloane (Eugene, OR: Wipf & Stock, 2012), 21–22.

6. Angelo Tosato, "On Genesis 2:24," *CBQ* 52 (1990): 40n26.

7. Brownson, *Bible, Gender, Sexuality*, 30–31.

8. Von Rad, *Genesis*, 84–85.

Three necessary clarifications

Before exploring the nature of the *one-flesh* union of marriage, I will offer three clarifications in light of the above interpretation of Genesis 2:24.

First, the fact that *the language of marriage* is lacking in the verse does not mean that *the concept of marriage* is absent. As is well recognized, the Old Testament has no technical language for marriage or marrying. The terms commonly translated as "marry" (*laqakh* and *'ishah*) mean, respectively, "to take" (Gen 19:14; Lev 21:7, 14) and "woman/wife" (Num 36:6; Deut 22:16; Ezek 44:22). Jesus and Paul, then, have rightly discerned the intention of the verse (Matt 19:3–6; Mark 10:6–9; Eph 5:31), which is "to show the origin of this form of life that is known to all peoples, whether in a greater or lesser degree of conformity to God's design."[9]

Second, the fact that Genesis 2:24 is etiological does not mean that it is *descriptive only* and not *normative also*. As Angelo Tosato has demonstrated, the verse functions both at the factual level (what *does* take place) and at the juridical level (what *should* take place).[10] Megan Warner disagrees, however, insisting that rather than defining marriage as heterosexual the text depicts "the powerful attraction that causes human beings to seek relationship in opposition to the wishes of their parents, society, and religion."[11] But not only does such an interpretation ignore the repeated prohibitions against homosexual relations in both testaments (e.g., Lev 18:22; 20:13; Rom 1:26–27; 1 Cor 6:9; 1 Tim 1:10), it fails to appreciate that the "very fact that same-sex intimate relationships are not included in this picture is an instance where absence is evidence that same-sex relationships are not to be part of the norm for God's covenant community."[12] In short, Genesis 2:24 is *both* descriptive *and* normative.

Third, the fact that Genesis 2 presents marriage as "the *telos* or focal point of the whole relationship between male and female" does not mean

9. Blocher, *In the Beginning*, 105.

10. Tosato, "On Genesis 2:24," 405–6; compare Gagnon, "Old Testament and Homosexuality," 386; Brevard S. Childs, "The Etiological Tale Re-Examined," *VT* 24 (1974): 393.

11. Megan Warner, "'Therefore a Man Leaves His Father and His Mother and Clings to His Wife': Marriage and Intermarriage in Genesis 2:24," *JBL* 136 (2017): 269.

12. Katherine M. Smith, "Belonging to God in Relational Wholeness: A Conservative Perspective on the Old Testament's View of Marriage and Same-Sex Intimate Relationships," in *Marriage, Same-Sex Marriage and the Anglican Church of Australia: Essays from the Doctrine Commission* (Mulgrave: Broughton, 2019), 108–9.

that every human being is obligated to marry and have children. Marriage, as we saw in chapter 7, is not essential for becoming a complete person. If it were, individuals would bear only half the *imago Dei*, and the unmarried would be consigned to "a permanent state of deficiency with no hope of remedy apart from marriage."[13] Moreover, while the Old Testament clearly presents marriage as the norm, the New Testament views both "marriage and singleness as alternative vocations, each a worthy form of life, the two together comprising the whole Christian witness to the nature of affectionate community."[14] As Paul writes: "Each has his own gift from God, one of one kind and one of another" (1 Cor 7:7). The obligation to marry and multiply, then, lies on the entire race, not on each individual. As Christopher Roberts states: "It is at the level of the whole species where the teleology of sexual difference demands to be fulfilled. This creates some space for a potential division of labor; not every man or woman must procreate."[15] Nor must they marry, and those who do not are no less man or woman than those who do.

THE NATURE OF THE "ONE-FLESH" UNION

Three prerequisites for becoming "one flesh"

We turn now to the nature of the *one-flesh* union. According to verse 24, the forming of such a union entails three prerequisites: first, a *man* (*'ish*) and a *woman* (*'ishah*) are required; second, the man must "*leave* (עָזַב, *'azav*) his *father* (אָב, *'av*) and his *mother* (אֵם, *'em*)"; third, the man must "*hold fast* (דָּבַק, *davaq*) to his *wife* (*'ishah*)." We shall explore the first of these elements in the next section, but a brief comment on the second and third is important here.

The language of the man *leaving* his father and mother has sometimes been a source of confusion. The typical pattern of Jewish marriage was *patrilocal*, with the couple living in or near the husband's family home.[16] Mollenkott, however, believes that verse 24 pictures a *matrilocal* custom,

13. Brownson, *Bible, Gender, Sexuality*, 29.

14. O'Donovan, *Resurrection and Moral Order*, 70.

15. Roberts, *Creation & Covenant*, 106–7 (summarizing the thought of Thomas Aquinas).

16. Joseph H. Hellerman, *The Ancient Church as Family* (Minneapolis: Fortress, 2001), 32–33; compare the marriages of Rebekah (Gen 24), Tamar (Gen 38), and the sons of Jacob (Gen 37).

thereby revealing its non-normative nature.[17] But this is to misunderstand the kind of "leaving" on view. While the verb *'azav* ("leave") can refer to geographical departure (Gen 39:12; 44:22), it is often used in covenantal contexts (Gen 24:27; 28:15), where it carries the relational sense of "forsake" (Deut 28:20; 29:25; 31:6, 8). This is more likely what is being envisaged in Genesis 2:24; a change of *allegiance,* not a change of *residence,* is what is on view.[18] As Wenham remarks: "On marriage a man's priorities change. Beforehand his first obligations are to his parents: afterwards they are to his wife."[19] Thus the married couple now form "a new cell" in the human community.[20]

This understanding is confirmed by the corresponding verb *davaq* ("hold fast" or "cleave") in the next phrase of Genesis 2:24. Again, we are dealing with a *relational* rather than *locational* term (compare Gen 34:3), although here a sexual connotation is also present (compare 1 Cor 6:16).[21] As such, *davaq* conveys both the passion and permanence that ought to characterize the marriage relationship. Moreover, it too is a common *covenantal* term, used of the Lord's summons for Israel to *hold fast* to him (Deut 10:20; 11:22; 13:4; 30:20). This, in turn, suggests that marriage too is as a form of covenant (Prov 2:17; Jer 31:32; Ezek 16:8; Mal 2:14).

The meaning of "one flesh"

What light does this shed on the meaning of *one flesh* (בָּשָׂר אֶחָד, *basar 'ekhad*)?

In answering this question, scholars often "vacillate between the idea of sexual activity and procreation and the resulting kinship bonds."[22] Some, however, take a both-and approach. Christopher Ash, for instance, suggests that *one flesh* signifies "the creation not merely of a sexual union but also of a public social unit. A new family unit is created by marriage." His argument is twofold: first, elsewhere in Genesis, *basar* ("flesh") is used of

17. Mollenkott, *Omnigender,* 101.

18. Mathews, *Genesis 1–11:26,* 222–23. As Westermann notes, the text does not say that the man leaves his parents' *house,* but that he leaves his *parents* (*Genesis 1–11,* 233).

19. Wenham, *Genesis 1–15,* 71.

20. Blocher, *In the Beginning,* 106.

21. See the discussion below regarding Paul's use of Gen 2:24 in 1 Cor 6:16.

22. Peterson, "Same-Sex Marriage?," 689.

family connection (e.g., 29:14; 37:27); second, the man's leaving of his parents suggests "a union which is both sexual and public."[23] Robert Gundry, however, while not denying that a more comprehensive union is on view, argues that *one flesh* refers to "physical [i.e., sexual] union alone." His reasoning is also twofold: first, the three uses of *basar* in verses 22–23 are all physical; second, both the man's words (v. 23) and the narrator's words (v. 25) encase the saying with "references to the human body."[24]

How might this debate be settled? Broader canonical observations suggest an answer. First, as commentators generally agree, the evident link between "one flesh" (v. 24) and "flesh of my flesh" (v. 23) indicates that the former expression entails physical union—the joining of two corresponding (i.e., differently sexed) *bodies*.

Second, that such a union is the result of sexual intercourse is confirmed by Paul's statement in 1 Corinthians 6:16: "Or do you not know that he who is joined [κολλάω, *kollaō*] to a prostitute becomes one body with her? For, as it is written, 'The two will become one flesh.' " Here the apostle makes plain that male-female sex, even outside of marriage, "creates a mysterious but real and enduring union between man and woman."[25]

Third, Paul's language in 1 Corinthians 6:16 also clarifies that is it the sexual *joining* (*kollaō*) of a man and a woman that *results* in the two becoming "one body" (ἓν σῶμά, *hen sōma*) or "one flesh" (σάρκα μίαν, *sarka mian*). This suggests that the scope of *one flesh* not only includes the *means* (sexual intercourse) but also the *end* (the bond it produces).

Fourth, this points to the contextual connotation of the Hebrew word *davaq* ("hold fast") in Genesis 2:24—a connotation confirmed by the fact that the LXX translates it by *proskollaō* (προσκολλάω, *proskollaō* is a synonym of the simpler form of the word used by Paul in 1 Corinthians 6:16).[26] Thus, "hold fast" (at least in Genesis 2:24) *connotes* sexual intercourse.[27]

---

23. Ash, *Marriage*, 348–49.

24. Gundry, *Sōma in Biblical Theology*, 64.

25. Richard B. Hays, *First Corinthians* (Louisville: Westminster John Knox, 2011), 105. Interestingly, Paul does not encourage the men of Corinth to maintain or formalize these unions, but to break them off. This suggests that he did not regard them as marriages (Ash, *Marriage*, 349).

26. Synonymity is evident from the fact that in citing Gen 2:24 in Matt 19:5, Jesus uses *kollaō*, whereas in Mark 10:7 (compare Eph 5:31), he uses *proskollaō*.

27. Brownson, *Bible, Gender, Sexuality*, 87.

Fifth, if Genesis 2 is read in the light of Genesis 1 (as Jesus's teaching indicates it should be), then it is difficult to avoid the conclusion that "the 'one flesh' notation also anticipates the bearing of children."[28] As Kline articulates: "Created male and female, man was to multiply through sexual fruitfulness. In Genesis 1 the procreation mandate is formulated in simple functional terms. Genesis 2 adds the institutional (i.e., the familial) aspect, so assigning human procreation to its proper context in the marital relationship."[29]

These observations suggest that the one-flesh union of marriage is *irreducibly sexual.* But given the prerequisites stated in Genesis 2:24 (and the fact that not all one-flesh relationships are marriages [compare 1 Cor 6:16]), the union on view is clearly *more than sexual.* Arguably, then, kinship relation is the bigger idea, but kinship of a unique kind: a *covenantal kinship* of a *heterosexual nature* that is preceded by *parental leaving* (separation), characterized by *interpersonal bonding* (dedication), established by *sexual coupling* (copulation), and intended to be *life creating* (procreation).

THE TWO SEXES AND "ONE FLESH"

Curiously, the necessity of the heterosexual nature of this covenant has been subjected to challenge by some evangelicals.[30] Even Preston Sprinkle (who opposes same-sex marriage on various grounds) expresses some doubt that the idea of one flesh "in itself demands that marital partners must be opposite sexes," and even suggests that "Genesis 2:24 doesn't inherently rule out homosexual marriages."[31]

How essential, then, are the two sexes for the one-flesh union of marriage?

---

28. Peterson, "Same-Sex Marriage?," 690.

29. Kline, *Kingdom Prologue*, 68–69.

30. E.g., Mark Achtemeier, *The Bible's Yes to Same-Sex Marriage: An Evangelical's Change of Heart* (Louisville: Westminster John Knox, 2014), 58.

31. Preston Sprinkle, *People to Be Loved: Why Homosexuality Is Not Just an Issue* (Grand Rapids: Zondervan, 2015), 31.

Indicators from the preceding context

The key to understanding the meaning of one flesh in Genesis 2:24 lies in the preceding verses, for there is no meaning of the expression *in itself*, only *in context*. The fact that there are no other instances of *basar 'ekhad* in the Old Testament and that the five New Testament occurrences of *sarka mian* are all quotations of the LXX of Genesis 2:24 (Matt 19:5–6 [x2]; Mark 10:8; 1 Cor 6:16; Eph 5:31) underscores the salience of this point.

As we saw in the previous chapter, the first indicator of sexual difference is found in the compound expression *kenegdow* (in vv. 18 and 20)—literally, "like opposite him." This announces that the woman is *like* (*k*) the man, being "bone of [his] bone and flesh of [his] flesh," but also *opposite* (*neged*) to the man and so "fit for him."[32] Thus, with "male and female" (1:27) and "be fruitful and multiply" (1:28) in the background, and "man" and "woman" (2:22–23) and "father" and "mother" (2:24) in the foreground, it is difficult to avoid the conclusion that what is conveyed by *'ezer kenegdow* (in 2:18 and 20) is *sexual complementarity*, "as opposed to the simple idea of a 'fitting helper,' which most translations present in a non-sexual way."[33] As Robert Gagnon writes, "the obvious complementarity (and concordant sexual attraction) of male and female witnesses to God's intent for human sexuality. Male and female are 'perfect fits' from the standpoint of divine design and blessing. Male and male, or female and female, are not."[34]

However, Gagnon then misstates matters when he describes marriage as "a *re*union that not only provides companionship but restores *'ādām* to his original wholeness," and, even more so, when he claims that the union of husband and wife "makes possible a single, composite human being."[35] As we have seen, the man was male *before* the woman was made (compare 1 Cor. 11:8), and the woman *qua* woman was not extracted from the man but built separately out of part of the man. Moreover, not only is one flesh primarily a kinship notion, but verse 25 makes clear that it cannot mean *one person*—evidenced by the expression *shenehem* (שְׁנֵיהֶם

32. Wenham, *Genesis 1–15*, 68; Sprinkle, *People to Be Loved*, 32–33.

33. Peterson, "Same-Sex Marriage?," 688.

34. Gagnon, *Homosexual Practice*, 62.

35. Gagnon, *Homosexual Practice*, 61 (emphasis original).

= "they both" or "the two of them"). Consequently, the coming together of man and woman is not "a reconstitution of the two constituent parts, male and female, that were the products of the splitting."[36] It is, rather, "the bringing together of two differentiated beings, with one made *from* and both made *for* the other."[37] So while Gagnon is correct that "only a being made from *'adam* can and ought to become someone with whom *'adam* longs to *re*unite in sexual intercourse and marriage,"[38] their union, as Brownson rightly discerns, does not reconstitute an "original, binary, or androgynous *'adam*."[39] Thus, even in the one-flesh union of marriage, the man and the woman remain distinct (and distinctly sexed) persons.

Why a "second sex" is needed

And yet, Brownson too misconstrues the text when he declares that Genesis "portrays marriage as a solution, not for 'incompleteness,' but for *aloneness*."[40] As we have seen, it is both. For without the man's incompleteness being resolved by the creation of a "like-opposite" helper, much of his aloneness would remain. This explains why *the one flesh union of marriage is necessarily heterosexual in character*. As Alastair Roberts writes: "That men and women can become 'one flesh' in marriage is a result of the fact that they are uniquely fitted for each other." Indeed, he continues, "each sex has one half of a single sexual and reproductive system and the natural offspring of a male-female union is a positive manifestation of the 'one flesh' that bond can constitute."[41]

Consequently, Brownson's claim that the "entire discussion of one flesh in Genesis (and indeed throughout the Bible) takes place without even a hint of concern with procreation" is to be rejected.[42] While not the sole purpose of marriage, procreation, as we have seen, is a key part of the

36. Gagnon, "Old Testament and Homosexuality," 388.

37. Kevin DeYoung, *What Does the Bible Really Teach About Homosexuality?* (Nottingham: InterVarsity Press, 2015), 28 (emphasis original).

38. Gagnon, *Homosexual Practice*, 61.

39. Brownson, *Bible, Gender, Sexuality*, 28.

40. Brownson, *Bible, Gender, Sexuality*, 29 (emphasis original).

41. Roberts, "Male and Female," 39–40.

42. Brownson, *Bible, Gender, Sexuality*, 89.

picture from the outset.[43] Moreover, natural kinship (i.e., blood relations) is only possible because of prior procreation, and covenantal kinship (i.e., man-woman marriage) is both the presupposition of all such bonds and the divinely intended context for the development of what John Walton calls "flesh-lines."[44]

For these reasons, two corresponding sexes are required for the establishment of a one-flesh union.[45] Genesis 2:24, where *'ish* and *'ishah* are the necessary prerequisite for everything that follows, including the binary relation of *'av* ("father") and *'em* ("mother"), makes this conclusion inescapable. Thus, despite his desire to find "potential openings for queer contestation of the heterosexual contract," even Stone concedes that we "can never turn Genesis into a queer manifesto."[46] The creation of the man's helper in the form of the woman was no arbitrary act on the Lord God's part. The union for which they were made and to which they were called was only possible because of their biological distinctions. For this reason, as O'Donovan points out,

> A conception of marriage that abstracts the personal from the biological leaves the meaning of the biological order ambiguous, even questionable, whereupon the temptation soon overtakes us to regard it as an arbitrary and pointless limitation on personal freedom which is better resisted. It is the first and decisive step in contemporary manifestations of the Manachaean spirit to regard nature, not as a gracious gift of the Creator, but as a problem to be overcome.[47]

43. In light of this, Blocher's categorization of procreation as "a purpose of marriage only indirectly" is too weak (*In the Beginning*, 108). See Andreas J. Köstenberger with David W. Jones, *God, Marriage and Family: Rebuilding the Biblical Foundations*, 2nd ed. (Wheaton, IL: Crossway, 2010), 85–90.

44. Walton, *Genesis*, 178.

45. Contra Sprinkle, who suggests that even if the Corinthian men had been visiting male (rather than female) prostitutes, Paul would still have applied the "one flesh" teaching of 1 Cor 6:16 to their behavior (*People to be Loved*, 30).

46. Stone, "Garden of Eden," 50.

47. O'Donovan, "Transsexualism and Christian Marriage," 142.

As we shall see further later in this chapter, herein lies one of the keys to understanding why the introduction of same-sex marriage has helped to facilitate the sundering of sex and gender.

NAKED BUT NOT ASHAMED

This brings us to Genesis 2:25: "And the man and his wife were both *naked* [עֲרוּמִּים, *ʿărummim*] and were *not ashamed* [לֹא יִתְבֹּשָׁשׁוּ, *lo' yithboshashu*]."

The narrative function of 2:25

In terms of the broader narrative, this verse performs an important bridging function, connecting the preceding scene of Edenic bliss with the account of the fall that is shortly to unfold.[48] This is highlighted by the way in which the word "crafty" (עָרוּם, *ʿārum*) in 3:1 plays on "naked" (*ʿărummim*) in 2:25 (compare 3:7). However, it would be a mistake to see the couple's naiveté as indicative of a problem or to regard their nakedness as a sign of neediness.[49] "They were not poor in their nakedness," writes Barth; "they were rich in things in which they later became poor."[50] John Paul II agrees: "The words of Genesis 2:25, 'they did not feel shame,' do not express a lack but, on the contrary, they serve to indicate a particular fullness of consciousness and experience, above all the fullness of understanding the meaning of the body connected with the fact that 'they were naked.' "[51]

Therefore, while the couple's want of embarrassment concerning their nakedness may permit a comparison to young children, they were not children (as the terms "man" and "woman" make plain). Their shamelessness, then, was not occasioned by ignorance or insensitivity but by pure innocence: "They had nothing to hide from each other, because as God created them both were right before God and therefore for one another."[52] By describing Edenic experience in this way, 2:25 presents the *before*

---

48. Mathews, *Genesis 1–11:26*, 224; Wenham, *Genesis 1–15*, 71; Westermann, *Genesis 1–11*, 234.

49. Contra Sarah G. Turner-Smith, "Naked but Not Ashamed: A Reading of Gen 2:25 in Textual and Cultural Context," *JTS* 69 (2018): 425–46.

50. Barth, *CD*, III/1, 329.

51. John Paul II, *Man and Woman He Created Them: A Theology of the Body*, trans. Michael Waldstein (Boston: Pauline Books & Media, 2006), 174.

52. Barth, *CD*, III/1, 309.

picture (of guilt-free delight) that is then contrasted with the *after* picture of 3:7 (of guilt-ridden anxiety).

The meaning of "not ashamed" in context

While English versions routinely translate the Hebrew root *bosh* (בוֹשׁ) by "shame," not all agree that this is the most accurate way to convey the sense of the term. For Wenham, part of the problem is that *bosh* often lacks "the overtones of personal guilt" that are normally bound up with the English word "shame," and so he suggests "they were unabashed" or "they were not disconcerted" as preferable translations.[53] Yael Avrahami, however, sees a different and deeper issue. From a study of the Psalms, she concludes that *bosh* refers not to shame but to "the experience of a disconnection between expectations and reality"—that is, "בוֹשׁ is the experience (or causing) of disappointment."[54] From a survey of its wider use in the Old Testament, Daniel Wu supports Avrahami's definition, but also finds that *bosh* can carry the senses of dismay/disillusionment/despair or failure/frustration/embarrassment, and, in certain contexts, mean precisely "what contemporary English speakers would define as 'shame.' "[55]

How then should *bosh* be understood in Genesis 2:25? While the translation "the man and his wife were both naked, and were not disappointed" is certainly not impossible,[56] several considerations favor a more traditional rendering.

The first is the social dimension of the text. This is seen in the fact that "*they* were *both* (*shenehem*) naked and were not ashamed," as it is in the contrasting picture of 3:7: "the eyes of *both of them* (*shenehem*) were opened, and *they* knew that *they* were naked." This dramatic change reveals a profound relational fracture; due to the entrance of sin, the two are now discomfited (if not threatened) by each other's presence. The fact that they immediately seek to cover themselves confirms this—self-concealment being a reflex response to shame. "For what is shame," asks Blocher, "other

53. Wenham, *Genesis 1–15*, 71.

54. Yael Avrahami, "בוֹשׁ in the Psalms: Shame or Disappointment?," *JSOT* 34 (2010): 303.

55. Daniel Y. Wu, *Honor, Shame, and Guilt: Social-Scientific Approaches to the Book of Ezekiel*, BBRS 14 (Winona Lake, IN: Eisenbrauns, 2016), 100, 103–4.

56. Wu, *Honor, Shame, and Guilt*, 177n24.

than a feeling of embarrassment which makes us hide?"[57] In Genesis 2:25, however, the unselfconscious nudity of the man and woman signals a freedom "not to be concealed from one another, but to be revealed and known without any cover."[58] Consequently, they "were not ashamed" (KJV/ESV) or "they felt no shame" (NIV/HCSB) are apposite translations.

A second consideration that supports this understanding is the fact that the Old Testament regularly connects nakedness with judgment and humiliation (e.g., Gen 3:7, 10–11; Ezek 16:22, 37, 39; Isa 20:4; 47:3; Hos 2:3; Amos 2:16; Nah 3:5 and Mic 1:8, 11).[59] Not surprisingly, the shift from a carefree experience of nakedness (in Genesis 2:25) to one that is anxiety-filled (in 3:7) is a direct consequence of the couple's disobedience. In 2:25, however, it is precisely their lack of guilt that makes their nakedness so unproblematic. In simple terms, *they have no shame before each other because they have no guilt before God*. Barth reflects on the implications of this phenomenon: "No shame can cling to the nature of man as created by God, to male and female as He created them, to the due sequence and order of their relationship. This can never be an object of shame."[60] This again suggests that "not ashamed" helpfully conveys the meaning of *lo' yithboshashu*.

A third element of the narrative that confirms this understanding is the reaction of the couple to the divine presence in 3:8, along with the explanation of their actions in 3:10. For as soon as they heard him walking in the garden, "they hid themselves from the presence of the LORD God among the trees of the garden" (3:8). Such a maneuver, as we have already noted, is a shame response. However, it is also a fear response, for it is not finally before each other that they feel most exposed, but before their maker. Indeed, as verse 10 explains, the reason they sought to hide

57. Blocher, *In the Beginning*, 173. On this point, Bonhoeffer is insightful: "Shame is a cover in which I hide myself from the other because of my own evil, that is, because of the dividedness that has come between us. Where one person accepts the other as the helper who is a partner given by God, where one is content with understanding-oneself-as-derived-from and destined-for-the-other, in belonging-to-the-other, there human beings are not ashamed. In the unity of unbroken obedience one human being stands naked before another, uncovered, revealed in body and in soul, and is not ashamed" (*Creation and Fall*, 101).

58. Barth, *CD*, III/1, 329.

59. See Victor P. Hamilton, *The Book of Genesis Chapters 1–17*, NICOT (Grand Rapids: Eerdmans, 1990), 181.

60. Barth, *CD*, III/4, 150.

was precisely because they were "afraid" (יָרֵא, *yare'*)—afraid of the LORD God! As Luther summarizes:

> Therefore after their conscience has been convicted by the Law and they feel their disgrace before God and themselves, Adam and Eve lose their confidence in God and are so filled with fear and terror that when they hear a breath or a wind, they immediately think God is approaching to punish them; and they hide.[61]

These considerations not only help resolve the translation question but highlight the significance of the couple's lack of shame. For just as the presence of shame (in 3:7) is "the sign of a grievous disruption,"[62] so its absence (in 2:25) is a sign of glorious freedom. Guiltless before God, the man and woman were guileless before each other. They had nothing to fear or conceal, for they had nothing of which to be ashamed.

Knowledge, nakedness, shame, and sexuality

This brings us to a further dimension of the text that is of especial relevance to our study. As the account of the fall unfolds in Genesis 3, it becomes clear that the couple's original want of shame is not due to a lack of *emotion* but a lack of *knowledge*—knowledge that is tied to the one tree from which they are forbidden to eat: "the tree of the *knowledge* [*yada'*] of good and evil" (2:9, 17). Although it has been variously interpreted,[63] the knowledge symbolized by this tree is best understood as "an exceptional possession of deity," and so a property "attributable only to God."[64] This is confirmed later in the chapter, where the LORD God says: "Behold, the man has become *like one of us* in *knowing* [*yada'*] good and evil" (3:22). To eat from this tree, then, is "to assert human autonomy ... deciding what is right without reference to God's revealed will."[65]

---

61. Luther, *Lectures on Genesis*, 170.

62. Von Rad, *Genesis*, 91.

63. For a detailed survey and assessment of eight different explanations of the meaning of "the knowledge of good and evil," see Westermann, *Genesis 1–11*, 242–48.

64. Mathews, *Genesis 1–11:26*, 203; compare Wenham, *Genesis 1–15*, 87; Ashford and Bartholomew, *Doctrine of Creation*, 227.

65. Wenham, *Genesis 1–15*, 63–64; Dumbrell, *Faith of Israel*, 20.

What is of particular interest is that as soon as the couple eat from the tree, the knowledge they gain is knowledge of their *nakedness*: "Then the eyes of both were opened, and they *knew* [*yada'*] that they were *naked* [עֵירֹם, *'erom*]" (3:7).

What, then, is the precise connection between knowledge, nakedness, and shame, and what does this connection reveal about the significance of human sexuality? Part of the answer to this question lies in the fact that just as 2:25 presents a direct link between *innocence and an absence of bodily shame*, so 3:7 reveals a parallel link between *guilt and the presence of bodily shame*—specifically, *genital* shame, as is indicated by their construction of "loincloths" (חֲגוֹרָה, *khagorah*).[66]

But why genital shame? One suggested answer is that the couple's knowledge of their nakedness refers to the awakening of their sexual consciousness.[67] The inference that some have then drawn is that "sexuality was not part of God's intention for humans in creation."[68] There are two main problems with this view, however.

First, 2:25 does not imply that the couple were *ignorant* of their nakedness but simply that they were *unperturbed* by it. What changes in 3:7 is that "their dispositional stance toward that knowledge is different, as is immediately evident in their attempt to cover themselves."[69] The cause of this change is the experience of guilt occasioned by their disobedience.[70] In other words, it is the loss of innocence that problematizes their nakedness and makes shame "a phenomenon that is inseparable from sexuality."[71] So then, the reason for the man and woman's original lack of embarrassment was neither sexual unawareness nor sexual inexperience; it was, rather, as Augustine rightly discerned, their "simplicity and chastity of soul."[72]

---

66. *khagorah* could also be translated "aprons" (Westermann, *Genesis 1–11*, 182; von Rad, *Genesis*, 83).

67. E.g., Sam Dragga, "Genesis 2–3: A Story of Liberation," *JSOT* 55 (1992): 5–8; Jacob Milgrom, "Sex and Wisdom: What the Garden of Eden Story Is Saying," *BRev* 10, no. 6 (1994): 21, 52. See also the references and citations compiled by Westermann (*Genesis 1–11*, 243, 250).

68. Stephen Sapp, *Sexuality, the Bible, and Science* (Philadelphia: Fortress, 1977), 18. This, however, is not Sapp's own view.

69. C. John Collins, "What Happened to Adam and Eve? A Literary-Theological Approach to Genesis 3," *Presbyterion* 27 (2001): 26.

70. Collins, "What Happened to Adam and Eve?," 30n61; contra Westermann, *Genesis 1–11*, 253.

71. Von Rad, *Genesis*, 85.

72. Augustine, *On Genesis*, 115.

Second, while the first explicit reference to sexual intercourse does not occur until 4:1 ("Adam *knew* [*yada'*] Eve his wife, and she conceived"), there is no reason to think the couple refrained from sexual activity prior to their fall (compare 1:28). Nor does the repetition of *yada'* in 3:5 and 3:7 mean that the temptation of the woman was "replete with sexual overtones."[73] For while *yada'* has a clear sexual connotation in 4:1, nothing in the context of chapter 3 supports such a meaning, and it is entirely inappropriate to 3:5 and 3:22. The knowledge gained from eating, then, was not sexual knowledge but, as we have seen, "the ability to become self-legislating."[74] So, writes Walton, "interpreters who point to the use of the verb 'to know' as referring to sexual intercourse will find no help here, because the verb does not mean that when connected to the merism 'good and evil.' "[75] The fall into *sin* should not be construed as a fall into *sex*!

What then is the relationship between shame and sexuality?

To begin, note that the words translated "naked" in 2:25 (*'arummim*) and 3:7 (עֵירֻמִּם, *'erummim*), while sharing the same root, are different in form. This does not necessarily signify a difference in meaning,[76] but the literary effect intimates that the knowledge acquired by the couple "seems somehow to have affected their perception of their nakedness."[77] They now see through what Augustine describes as "perverted eyes."[78] As a result, muses Luther, "the glory of the genitals was turned into the utmost disgrace." Why so? Because nothing "in all nature is nobler than the work of procreation," for it is this that "preserves the species." For Luther, then, it is the entrance of sin, with its attendant guilt, that explains why "the most honorable and most excellent part of our body" has "become the most shameful."[79]

Bonhoeffer, however, suggests another reason. While shame-free nakedness is "the essence of unity, of not being torn apart, of being for

73. Raymond Collins, *Christian Morality: Biblical Foundations* (Notre Dame: University of Notre Dame Press, 1986), 160.

74. Dumbrell, *Faith of Israel*, 20.

75. Walton, *Genesis*, 171.

76. Contra Davidson, who argues that the latter terms mean "utterly naked" (*Flame of Yahweh*, 57).

77. Elaine A. Phillips, "Serpent Intertexts: Tantalizing Twists in the Tales," *BBR* 10 (2000): 237.

78. Augustine, *On Genesis*, 119.

79. Luther, *Lectures on Genesis*, 167–68.

the other," the presence of shame speaks of division, of opposition, of a world rent asunder.[80] It thus signals "the loss of an inner unity, an unsurmountable contradiction at the basis of our existence."[81] Hence, as a result of their sin, the couple are alienated from each other; they no longer trust one another and each poses a risk to the other. Instinctively, they seek to hide the parts of their anatomy that at once distinguish them and yet make their union possible. Difference is now dangerous; rather than drawing them together, it threatens to drive them apart. They are now vulnerable to each other, as self-giving love is undermined by the *libido dominandi* (compare 3:16). As Blocher writes: "Since sexuality gives their impoverished relationship its specific form, each can be apprehensive of being no more than a sexual object for the other." Moreover, precisely because their sex distinctions testify to their need for one another (compare 2:18), they also pose a direct challenge to "the fundamental desire of sin: autonomy, self-sufficiency."[82] The war of the sexes has thus begun.

Concluding summary

Genesis 2:25 precludes the possibility that sexual awareness is occasioned by the fall. It thus stands against all attempts to recast human sexuality as intrinsically shameful. Indeed, the text "declares unequivocally that the necessity of shame, however great it may have become as a result of man's disobedience, does not derive from his nature as established by God but is contrary to it."[83] Put positively, the shame-free nakedness of the couple "signifies the original good of the divine vision."[84] Like Genesis 1, then, "Genesis 2 is free of every kind of disapproval or devaluation of the sexual."[85]

As we shall explore further in the following chapter, everything changes once the couple enters the experience of "knowing good and evil" in Genesis 3. While such knowing cannot be reduced to sexual knowledge, the fact that it immediately affects the sexual realm indicates the significance of sexuality for our nature and calling as divine image bearers (Gen

80. Bonhoeffer, *Creation and Fall*, 124.

81. Von Rad, *Genesis*, 85.

82. Blocher, *In the Beginning*, 175–76.

83. Barth, *CD*, III/1, 311.

84. John Paul II, *Theology of the Body*, 177.

85. Neuer, *Man and Woman*, 63.

1:27–28; compare Rom 1:24–27). Not surprisingly, after the fall, human sexuality is profoundly problematized: sexed embodiment is a source of anxiety and nakedness a cause of shame. As Luther remarks, "The parts of our body remain the same. But those which, when they were naked, were looked upon with glory are now covered up as shameful and dishonorable, as a result of the inner revolt."[86]

As a further consequence of humanity's fall, there is now also a *nakedness of soul*—a condition known not only by the primal couple but by the entirety of their progeny. This is a nakedness that no fig leaf, garment of skin, or gender transition can ever hope to cover. Indeed, as we shall see in later chapters, it can only be covered by being clothed with the Lord Jesus Christ (Rom 13:14; Gal 3:27).

THE MYSTERY OF MARRIAGE

In this section, we shall step outside of Genesis 2 (and so, to some extent, trespass on the following chapter), yet without leaving it behind. My primary aim is to explore the apostle Paul's teaching regarding marriage in Ephesians 5:22–33, especially the citation of Genesis 2:24 in verses 31–32. I will then engage with several revisionist interpretations of both Genesis 2:24 and Ephesians 5:22–33, showing why these cannot be sustained.

EPHESIANS 5:31–32 IN CONTEXT

The analogy between Christ and the church

In the closing verses of Ephesians 5, after having described Christ's care for his church (vv. 25–27), the apostle Paul writes: "*In the same way* (οὕτως, *houtōs*), husbands should love their wives *as their own bodies* (ὡς τὰ ἑαυτῶν σώματα, *hōs ta heautōn sōmata*). He who loves his wife loves himself. For no one ever hated *his own flesh* (τὴν ἑαυτοῦ σάρκα, *tēn heautou sarka*), but nourishes and cherishes it, just as Christ does the church, because we are members *of his body* (τοῦ σώματος αὐτοῦ, *tou sōmatos autou*)" (vv. 28–30). As is evident throughout the marital section of his "house table" (vv. 22–33), Paul's entire argument presupposes the existence of an analogy between man-woman marriage and the relationship of Christ and the church.

86. Luther, *Lectures on Genesis*, 167.

Paul's deployment of this analogy enables him to affirm both the distinction between and the unity of husband and wife. The distinction is seen in that while husbands are to model their headship on the pattern of Christ's love for his church (vv. 25–27), *wives* are to model their submission on the pattern of the church's response to Christ (vv. 22–24, 33b). The unity is seen in that husbands are to regard their wives as "their own bodies" (v. 28a) and their "own flesh" (v. 29), with the consequence that "he who loves his wife loves himself" (vv. 28b, 33a). Analogically, this oneness reflects the fact that the church is none other than Christ's own body (v. 30; compare 1:23; 2:16; 3:6; 4:4, 12, 16; 5:23). It is this parallel that then leads Paul to cite a version of the LXX of Genesis 2:24 in verse 31, with an explanatory comment in verse 32:

TABLE 7: EPHESIANS 5:31–32 — ENGLISH AND GREEK

English Standard Version	*Novum Testamentum Graece*
[31] "Therefore a man shall leave his father and mother and hold fast to his wife, and the two shall become one flesh." [32] This mystery is profound, and I am saying that it refers to Christ and the church.	[31] ἀντὶ τούτου καταλείψει ἄνθρωπος [τὸν] πατέρα καὶ [τὴν] μητέρα καὶ προσκολληθήσεται πρὸς τὴν γυναῖκα αὐτοῦ, καὶ ἔσονται οἱ δύο εἰς σάρκα μίαν. [32] τὸ μυστήριον τοῦτο μέγα ἐστίν· ἐγὼ δὲ λέγω εἰς Χριστὸν καὶ εἰς τὴν ἐκκλησίαν

The meaning and significance of the "mystery"

To grasp the meaning of verses 31–32, it is vital to understand the import of the word mystery (μυστήριον, *mystērion*). As its use throughout the letter to the Ephesians shows (compare 1:9; 3:3, 4, 9; 6:19), a mystery is not "something that is baffling and defies explanation. Rather, it refers to a truth whose explanation, clarification, and verification is contingent upon the coming and revelation of Christ."[87] So understood, what is being affirmed in verse 32 is that "the meaning of marriage is something that was once hidden in the Old Testament but that now has been revealed in the gospel."[88] But *what* has now been revealed? Given the "breathtaking

87. Hamilton, *Genesis 1–17*, 185.

88. Denny Burk, *What Is the Meaning of Sex?* (Wheaton, IL: Crossway, 2013), 87.

juxtaposition" of the citation of Genesis 2:24 (in v. 31),[89] the answer is unmissable: it is that "the one-flesh union of man and woman points to the union of Jesus Christ with his blood-bought bride, the church."[90]

Such a claim takes us beyond the realm of analogy into that of typology.[91] The *protological marriage* of Adam and Eve (at the beginning) is a type of the *eschatological marriage* of Christ and the church (at the end). This means that the "deepest meaning of marriage is that it is an enacted parable of another marriage—the marriage of Christ to his bride."[92] Of course, biblical antecedents to this particular form of typology can be found in the Old Testament's use of spousal imagery to depict the relationship between Yahweh and Israel (e.g., Isa 54:4–8; Ezek 16:1–14; Hos 2:19–20). Moreover, Jesus continues and focuses this practice, not only by referring to himself as "the bridegroom" (Matt 9:15; Mark 2:19–20; Luke 5:34–35; John 3:29), but by presenting himself "in the role of Yahweh in the divine marriage with the covenanted people."[93] Paul's teaching, then, is consistent with this tradition but also transcends it. In his view, Genesis 2:24 refers *directly* to Christ and the church.

The theological order of Paul's typology

Paul, however, is doing more than asserting a typological connection between the protological marriage and the eschatological marriage; he is affirming a particular theological order. By stating that Genesis 2:24 "refers to Christ and the church" (εἰς Χριστὸν καὶ εἰς τὴν ἐκκλησίαν, *eis Christon kai eis tēn ekklēsian*) he is making the point that "the marital relationship established in Genesis 2:24 is itself based on something more fundamental, namely the eternal relationship between Christ and his church to which

89. Raymond C. Ortlund Jr., *God's Unfaithful Wife: A Biblical Theology of Spiritual Adultery*, NSBT 2 (Downers Grove, IL: InterVarsity Press, 2002), 156.

90. Todd A. Wilson, *Mere Sexuality: Rediscovering the Christian Vision of Sexuality* (Grand Rapids: Zondervan, 2017), 90.

91. See James M. Hamilton Jr., *Typology—Understanding the Bible's Promise-Shaped Patterns: How Old Testament Expectations are Fulfilled in Christ* (Grand Rapids: Zondervan Academic, 2021), esp. 26–28 (for a helpful definition of typology) and 307–32 (for a detailed discussion of marriage).

92. Burk, *Meaning of Sex*, 87.

93. Ortlund Jr., *God's Unfaithful Wife*, 139.

human marriage points."[94] Otherwise put, the protological is the ectype (the copy) and the eschatological the archetype (the original), the former being grounded on the latter.

For Karl Barth, the christological foundation of marriage is related to the larger reality that "creation is the way and means to the covenant."[95] What he means by this, as Christopher Roberts explains, is that "creation is for the sake of covenant, that what God made in Genesis can only be understood on the basis of what Christ does second in sequence, although not in intention."[96] Barth expands as follows:

> When the Old Testament gives dignity to the sexual relationship, it has in view its prototype, the divine likeness of man as male and female which in the plan and election of God is primarily the relationship between Jesus Christ and His Church, secondarily the relationship between Yahweh and Israel, and only finally—although very directly in view of its origin—the relationship between the sexes.[97]

It is precisely because "Jesus Christ and His Church are the internal basis of creation" that the relationship between Christ and his bride (in both its distinction and unity) provides a fitting template for marriage.[98] This is what enables the apostle to argue as he does in Ephesians 5:22–33. As Ray Ortlund Jr. observes, "the typology serves Paul's pastoral purpose of providing a model for Christian marriage which is grounded in primeval human origins and reflective of ultimate divine reality."[99]

The deeper theological point, however, is this: while the union of husband and wife serves several divine purposes (the consummation of love, the procreation of children, social stability, etc.), chief among them is that it both reflects and anticipates God's ultimate purpose of union and cohabitation with his people (Rev 21:1–3). In other words, not only

---

94. Martin Davie, *What Does the Bible Really Say? Addressing Revisionist Arguments on Sexuality and the Bible* (London: The Latimer Trust, 2020), 20.

95. Barth, *CD*, III/1, 229.

96. Roberts, *Creation and Covenant*, 158. Roberts is here summarizing Barth's view.

97. Barth, *CD*, III/1, 322.

98. Barth, *CD*, III/1, 322.

99. Ortlund Jr., *God's Unfaithful Wife*, 156.

does man-woman marriage provide the world with a symbol of the relationship between God and his people, but the "covenantal creation ordinance of marriage exists to be fulfilled at the marriage feast of the Lamb."[100]

THE QUEERING OF MARRIAGE

On the basis of the preceding theological exposition of Genesis 2:24 and Ephesians 5:31–32, I turn now to consider and critique several revisionist interpretations of both texts.

Michael Carden's reading of Genesis 2

As the exegesis of Genesis 2 has revealed, males and females do not become men and women by entering marriage.[101] By marrying, rather, a man becomes a husband and a woman a wife. The categories of man and woman, then, are not first and foremost *social* categories but *sex* categories (i.e., a man is an adult human male, a woman an adult human female). And while husband and wife are social (or, better, relational) categories, they necessarily map onto sex (i.e., a husband is a married man, a wife a married woman). Given these connections, and the meaning of these terms, it is simply not possible for a man to become a wife or a woman a husband.

Michael Carden, however, argues that Genesis 2:24 takes us in a different direction altogether. Presupposing the correctness of the rabbinic tradition in which "the human couple of Genesis 2 was understood to originally have been two sides or faces of the one being," he argues that Genesis culminates with "the high, mythic, androgynous vision of sexuality as restoring the primal union of one flesh among humans." This implies that for the one-flesh union envisaged in Genesis 2:24 to be achieved, "a husband must give up his gender privilege and with his wife descend to the intermediate level, neither male nor female."[102] In other words, by entering marriage, man and woman cease to be man and woman; they both become agendered.

---

100. Hamilton Jr., *Typology*, 329.

101. Contra Daniel Boyarin, who asserts that rather than presupposing the natural differences between the sexes, "marriage produces such naturalized gender difference" ("Paul and the Genealogy of Gender," *Representations* 41 [Winter 1993]: 20).

102. Carden, "Genesis/Bereshit," 28–29.

Such a conclusion, however, is contradicted by verse 25: "the *man* [*'adam*] and his *wife* [*'ishah*] were both naked and were not ashamed." Evidently, the man and woman of verses 21–23 remain man and woman in and after verses 24–25. In becoming one flesh, neither loses their sex. In fact, their marital union depends on a continuing distinction; their unity requires diversity, and the diversity serves their unity. Moreover, Carden misapprehends the meaning of "one flesh." While the spousal bond is only possible because the woman was originally "taken out" (*laqakh*) of the man, and so shares in his bone and flesh (v. 23), the fact that "they are no longer two but one flesh" (Matt 19:6) does not mean a return to an original hermaphroditic state. Not only did such a state never exist, but, as I have argued in this chapter, one flesh denotes a unique form of covenantal kinship, which presupposes sexual difference and anticipates the bearing of children.

James Brownson's reading of Genesis 2 and Ephesians 5

This brings us to consider further James Brownson's interpretation of Genesis 2. While accepting that one flesh connotes "a kinship bond," Brownson rejects the idea that physical complementarity is necessary to that bond.[103] He thus dismisses von Rad's claim that Genesis 2:24 helps explain why the sexes are drawn to each other,[104] insisting instead that the only concern of the text is "the formation of the essential and foundational building blocks of human community." In making such an argument, his hope is to demonstrate that "Genesis 2 does not teach a normative form of gender complementarity, based on the biological differences between male and female." His larger aim is to build a biblical case for "committed, loving, consecrated same-sex relationships."[105]

Of additional interest is the way in which Ephesians 5:31–32 is then brought into his argument. Brownson contends that the sole point of correspondence between the human marital bond and the union between Christ and the church is that of "mutual care and kinship obligation." Gender complementary is not relevant to either relationship. If it were, he

103. Brownson, *Bible, Gender, Sexuality*, 38.

104. Von Rad, *Genesis*, 85

105. Brownson, *Bible, Gender, Sexuality*, 34, 38, 279.

argues, it would be impossible to conceive of the mixed-gendered church as Christ's wife (Eph 5:31–32) or to make sense of those texts that "speak of men as well as women as brides to Christ (e.g., 1 Cor. 11:2; Rev. 19:7ff)."[106]

The problems with Brownson's reading of both texts are manifold. Indeed, his approach is characterized not only by a series of false dichotomies but also by a determination to minimize "the theological and moral significance of human sexual differentiation in God's creation purposes."[107] For example, he insists that the focus in Genesis 2 "is not on the complementarity of male and female but on the similarity of male and female."[108] But as we have seen in our exposition of verse 18, *both* are equally necessary.

Furthermore, Brownson's claim that "the language of 'one flesh' in Genesis 2:24 does not refer to physical gender complementarity but to the common bond of shared kinship" is also unconvincing.[109] As the context makes clear, the particular kinship on view is entirely dependent on gender complementarity; *sexual otherness* is necessary for *spousal oneness*. Brownson's error, then, as Nate Collins discerns, is that he "fails to understand that the author is pointing out that the one-flesh union between the first man and woman was a particular *type* of kinship union, one that was unitive in a way that could be said only of a man and a woman."[110] Additionally, Brownson fails to acknowledge the paradigmatic nature of the primal union, despite the "therefore" (*ʿal-ken*) at the beginning of verse 24, which clearly links the narrator's words to the man's exclamation about the sameness and difference of the woman in verse 23.

I will address Brownson's thoughts about Ephesians 5 below. But the teaching of Genesis 2 is unambiguous: *only a man and woman are able to form a one-flesh union*. As Davidson writes, "The intrinsic human duality of male and female and the heterosexual marital form involving a sexual

106. Brownson, *Bible, Gender, Sexuality*, 38.

107. Andrew Goddard, "James V. Brownson, *Bible, Gender, Sexuality*: A Critical Engagement," *The Kirby Laing Institute for Christian Ethics* (2014), 67.

108. Brownson, *Bible, Gender, Sexuality*, 37.

109. Brownson, *Bible, Gender, Sexuality*, 35.

110. Nate Collins, *All But Invisible: Exploring Identity Questions at the Intersection of Faith, Gender & Sexuality* (Grand Rapids: Zondervan, 2017), 213n31 (emphasis original).

union of a man and woman (not man with man, or human with animal) constitute the divine paradigm for humanity from the beginning."[111]

Adrian Thatcher's reading of Genesis 2

In his 2016 publication *Redeeming Gender*, Adrian Thatcher argues that although Genesis 1 might be thought to suggest a two-sex model, "Genesis 2 massively supports the one-sex continuum." It does this, he believes, by teaching that "the woman comes from the flesh of the man," which (supposedly) rules out the idea of opposite sexes. From this he infers that neither "exclusive heterosexuality" nor "modern complementarity" can be found in the Bible's opening chapters. Even in marriage, he writes, "the man and the woman are not opposite sexes, but 'one flesh' (Gen. 2:24)." Despite this, he also contends that by introducing the woman as man's helper, Genesis 2 unequivocally presents women as inferior to men. This leads him to caution those concerned for sexual equality to look "not to disputed readings and questionable interpretations of Genesis, but to the person and work of Christ through whom the equality of all human beings becomes a possibility." Indeed, he even goes so far as to claim that "Christ is linked to the creation narratives only for them to be relativized in relation to him."[112]

Interestingly, Thatcher's interpretation of Genesis 2 contrasts sharply with that of Mollenkott, who insists that "the Hebrew makes clear that Adam and Eve are powers equal to one another, 'fitting helpers' for one another, equally placed in charge of the remainder of creation (Gen. 1:28–31)."[113] As my exposition has demonstrated, Mollenkott has the stronger case here.[114] Moreover, like Brownson, Thatcher has set up a false dichotomy. The woman is not "one sex" with the man; she is "like-opposite" (*kenegd*) the man—one of his *kind* yet corresponding to

111. Davidson, *Flame of Yahweh*, 21.

112. Thatcher, *Redeeming Gender*, 145–47.

113. Mollenkott, *Omnigender*, 102.

114. This is not to deny the evidence of asymmetry within their relationship. This is clear not only from the sequence of their creation (compare 1 Tim 2:13) but also from the fact that the woman has her source in the man (compare 1 Cor 11:7–10). Whether this asymmetry is described of in terms of order, authority, hierarchy, or responsibility, what is clear is that it threatens neither their unity nor their equality. To the contrary, it reflects their complementarity and serves their mutual interdependence (compare 1 Cor 11:11).

him in her *sex*. Finally, Thatcher's assertion that "exclusive heterosexuality" cannot be found in the text (and so, by implication, homosexuality can be) is sheer eisegesis. As William Loader states plainly: "The creation stories leave no room for notions of people being anything other than heterosexual and so imply that to depart from that order is sin."[115]

Thatcher's interpretation of Genesis 2, then, is entirely unpersuasive. Furthermore, it not only pits Scripture against Scripture, equality against difference, and unity against distinction, but also (as we shall explore further in the chapter 11) Christ against creation.

Virginia Mollenkott's reading of Ephesians 5

Writing under the heading "Transgender Imagery in the New Testament," Virginia Mollenkott has also drawn attention to the fact that "the New Testament depicts all believers, viewed collectively, both as the bride of Christ (Eph. 5:25–27) and as members of Christ's body (5:30)." From this she deduces that if Christ's body is assumed to be a male body, "then Christian women, by putting on Christ like a garment, are imaged as either androgynous he/shes or as transvestites." Alternatively, if the church is assumed to be female, then it is "a he/she, a transgender entity." She then adds a further thought that "since the men in Ephesus were called Christ's bride—and by extension, all Christian men were called Christ's bride—then the New Testament has used imagery of a same-sex marriage in which a 'male' Christ marries not only Christian women but millions of male brides." Mollenkott concludes by suggesting that "such biblical gender bending ought to encourage those who take Scripture seriously to become less rigid about gender identities, roles, and presentations."[116] Finally, as an extension of her thought, Robert Goss contends that what we have in Ephesians 5 "is a text that can be used to justify same-sex and transgendered marriages," and that "Christology realizes its ultimate queer potential in a transgendered Christ—full of fluid identities."[117]

---

115. William Loader, "Homosexuality and the Bible," in *Two Views on Homosexuality, the Bible, and the Church*, ed. Preston Sprinkle (Grand Rapids: Zondervan, 2016), 23.

116. Mollenkott, *Omnigender*, 126–27.

117. Robert E. Goss, "Ephesians," in Guest, Goss, West, and Bohache, *The Queer Bible Commentary*, 637.

What are we to make of such claims—including Brownson's contention that gender complementarity is irrelevant to Paul's analogy? Is it really the case that the "parody of a queer reading actually brings out the full intent of the text of Ephesians 5:21–30," as Goss avers?[118] Or have these authors misunderstood and misapplied the apostle's teaching?

Four comments should suffice to answer this question.

First, it is noteworthy that nowhere in Ephesians 5 does Paul speak of Christ as the *husband* of the church or of the church as the *bride* of Christ. While such a imagery is implied (and, as noted previously, can be found elsewhere in the New Testament), the main terminological links between the two relationships are through the terms "head" (κεφαλὴ, *kephalē*) and "body" (σώμα, *sōma*)/"flesh" (σάρξ, *sarx*). Just as Christ is the head of his church, so a husband is the head of his wife (v. 23), and just as the church is the body of Christ (v. 30), so a husband is to love his wife as his own body/flesh (vv. 28–29). It is via this parallel that both the distinction between husbands and wives and their differing responsibilities are affirmed. Against Brownson, then, gender complementarity (or, better, sex distinction) lies at the very heart of the passage.

Second, to the extent that Paul is depicting the relationship between Christ and the church as a marriage (particularly by his use of Gen 2:24 in v. 31), he is speaking metaphorically.[119] In this sense, his comment in verse 32 may be likened to Galatians 4:24, "where he informs the readers that he is going to allegorize an OT passage."[120] In other words, Christ is not *literally* the husband of the church (any more than he is *literally* the head of the church) and the church is not *literally* the bride of Christ (any more than it is *literally* the body of Christ). Rather, these images provide "a metaphorical picture of the relationship God desires to have with God's people."[121] They communicate vital truth about Christ's relationship to the church—that is, that he is her savior (v. 23) and sanctifier (v. 26), and that he nourishes and cherishes her (v. 29).

118. Goss, "Ephesians," 637.

119. Frank S. Thielman, "Ephesians," in *Commentary on the New Testament Use of the Old Testament*, ed. G. K. Beale and D. A. Carson (Grand Rapids: Baker Academic, 2007), 828.

120. Harold W. Hoehner, *Ephesians: An Exegetical Commentary* (Grand Rapids: Baker, 2002), 780.

121. Stanley J. Grenz, *The Social God and the Relational Self: A Trinitarian Theology of the* Imago Dei (Louisville: Westminster John Knox, 2001), 303.

Third, the metaphorical nature of this imagery explains why Paul is constrained in his use of it and why, contra Brownson and Mollenkott, he nowhere refers to individual Christians (female or male) as "brides of Christ."[122] It also rules out the kind of tendentious application exemplified by Mollenkott's claim that Paul depicts "a same-sex marriage in which a 'male' Christ marries not only Christian women but millions of male brides." For within Paul's use of the marriage metaphor, the church is consistently and collectively pictured as female—not as a he/she, a transgender entity. So, although Christ's (metaphorical) bride is composed of (literal) men and women, this hardly qualifies as biblical gender bending. And while it may go some way toward encouraging Christians "to become less rigid about gender identities, roles, and presentations," it does not mean that differences disappear or that there are no distinctions to be maintained.[123]

Fourth, while Paul's application of Genesis 2:24 to the heavenly-eschatological marriage shows that "*when God designed the original marriage He already had Christ and the church in mind*,"[124] his pastoral purpose is to show the relevance of the ultimate union for earthly marriages in the here and now. In other words, Paul is using Genesis 2:24 not only in a typological fashion but for a parenetic purpose: that is, "to support the exhortation of the husband's tender care of wife, his own body/flesh (vv. 28–30)."[125] Moreover, the kind of marriages Paul has in mind are *necessarily heterosexual*, as his binary language confirms, and the spouses *necessarily cisgendered*, as Genesis 2:24 (and indeed the entire biblical witness) makes clear.

---

122. Wherever the New Testament applies bride language to the church (e.g., Rev 19:7; 21:2, 9; 22:17; compare 2 Cor 11:2), it always does so collectively, as Mollenkott admits (*Omnigender*, 126).

123. Mollenkott, *Omnigender*, 126–27. Moreover, Westfall's claim that the responsibilities Paul assigns to husbands in Eph 5:26–27 "are domestic chores delineated as women's work in the culture" (*Paul and Gender*, 56) goes too far. Paul is not, in fact, using domestic imagery, but a mixture of baptismal and nuptial imagery (as Westfall acknowledges on p. 57). Moreover, the apostle's point is not literal but ethical (see Andrew T. Lincoln, *Ephesians*, WBC 42 [Waco, TX: Word, 1990], 375–78).

124. George W. Knight III, "Husbands and Wives as Analogues of Christ and the Church: Ephesians 5:21–33 and Colossians 3:18–19," in Piper and Grudem, *Recovering Biblical Manhood and Womanhood*, 176 (emphasis original).

125. Hoehner, *Ephesians*, 781.

IMPLICATIONS FOR TRANS THEORY AND PRACTICE

It remains, then, to tease out the implications of the preceding exposition for trans theory and practice.

As the French feminist philosopher Monique Wittig saw clearly, it is the sex binary (with its physiological complementarity and reproductive potential) "that founds society as heterosexual."[126] While not all human beings do or desire to marry and procreate, the purpose of the dimorphic pattern of creation is plain: "to have a male body is to have a body structurally ordered to loving union with a female body, and vice versa." Not surprisingly, it is precisely this gift that "enables us to form relationships of love, between husband and wife, parent and child."[127] It also explains why Scripture regards same-sex sexual relations as "contrary to nature" and therefore prohibited (Rom 1:26–27; compare Lev 18:22; 20:13; 1 Cor 6:9; 1 Tim 1:10).

Along with the sex-and-gender binary, the other element that has emerged from the above exposition of Genesis 2 is the sex-and-gender connection—that is, the fact that gender is nothing other than "the social appropriation of sex and its meaning at the level of conceptualisation, i.e. in the life of the mind."[128] This is not because the Bible clearly differentiates between sex and gender; in fact, it simply "assumes there are appropriate roles and behaviors corresponding to the sex with which we are born."[129] But in so doing, it testifies to the indivisibility of bodily sex and (what we today call) gender.

Such an understanding has profound implications for personal identity, for interpersonal relationships, and for marriage in particular.

---

126. Monique Wittig, "The Category of Sex," in *The Straight Mind and Other Essays* (Boston: Beacon, 1992), 5.

127. O'Donovan, "Transsexualism and Christian Marriage," 152, 141.

128. Evangelical Alliance, *Transsexuality*, 63.

129. J. Alan Branch, *50 Ethical Questions: Biblical Wisdom for Confusing Times* (Bellingham, WA: Lexham, 2022), 224.

PERSONAL IDENTITY

Gender identity is objectively grounded in sex

The indissolubility of the sex-and-gender connection means that authentic personal identity is necessarily *cisgendered*. Gender is not "radically independent of sex" (as Judith Butler would have it), but necessarily grounded in it.[130] As Miroslav Volf affirms: "men's and women's gender identities are rooted in the specificity of their distinct bodies."[131] This is why it is not possible for a male to (truly) be a woman or for a female to (truly) be a man, and why to claim as much is either an expression of confusion or, in Sartrean terms, an act of "bad faith"—that is, "an attempt to evade the responsibility of discovering and understanding one's authentic self."[132]

Behind this connection lies the fact that sex "permeates one's individual being to its very depth; it conditions every facet of one's life as a person." As such, it not only provides the biological basis from which gender norms develop but has unavoidable psychological effects. For just as "the self is always aware of itself as an 'I,' so this 'I' is always aware of itself as *himself* or *herself*. Our self-knowledge is indissolubly bound up not simply with our *human* being but with our *sexual* being."[133] In short, psychology is designed to be informed by biology, the perceiving mind by the objective body.

This, at least, is *how things should be*. But it is not always *how things are*. Outside of Eden, some males perceive themselves to be *herselves* and some females *himselves*. Others perceive themselves as *both* or *neither*.[134] The reasons for such misperceptions are many, varied, and often complex. But one archetypical element, highlighted by Genesis 3:7, is the universal human experience of bodily (especially genital) shame. The link between this reality and (at least in some instances) a desire to present as a gender

---

130. Butler, *Gender Trouble*, 10.

131. Miroslav Volf, *Exclusion and Embrace: A Theological Exploration of Identity, Otherness, and Reconciliation* (Nashville: Abingdon, 1996), 174.

132. Aakash Pydi, "Jean Paul Sartre: The Concept of Bad Faith and Its Role in Ethical Analysis," *Aakash Pydi* (March 11, 2018), https://medium.com/@aakashpydi/jean-paul-sartre-the-concept-of-bad-faith-and-its-role-in-ethical-analysis-93f4553fa242.

133. Jewett, *Male and Female*, 172 (emphasis original).

134. For a recent exploration of the history of gender nonconformity, see Leah DeVun, *The Shape of Sex: Nonbinary Gender from Genesis to the Renaissance* (New York: Columbia University Press, 2021).

contrary to one's sex is not difficult to discern. As Collins notes, "Shame robs us of our personhood, and the primary way we demonstrate this as fallen humanity is by presenting a false self, or an imposter, to the people around us."[135]

Gender identity is received, not chosen

The distressing nature of gender incongruence should arouse our sympathies and inform our care. But it does not change the creational pattern or alter ethical norms. For "God's intent for human sexuality is imbedded in the material creation of gendered beings."[136] Irrespective of our subjective perceptions, then, the objective reality of our sex "goes down to the very roots of our personal existence, and penetrates into the deepest 'metaphysical' grounds of our personality and our destiny."[137]

It follows from this that *gender identity is received before it is developed.* Necessarily wedded to the givenness of our sex, it is not something we decide to add. Moreover, our embodiment is a *deliberate divine donation,* not an *arbitrary developmental endowment.* For just as the LORD God established the gender identities of the first man and woman by the bodies he gave them, so my gender identity was determined by the sexed nature of the body formed for me in my mother's womb (Ps 139:13–16). In this way, "the dimorphic shape of our bodies as male or female has authority to shape our understanding of sex and gender."[138]

So then, to the extent that we can speak of gender identity and gender roles as *constructed,* faithfulness, as we saw in chapter 7, requires that all such constructions respect and reflect biological reality. For *God's desire for my gender*—that is, whether I should perceive and present myself as a man or a woman—is revealed by *the design of my body.* Our task, then, is to "learn to read the meaning that God has inscribed on our bodies and to live in its light."[139] This is the central finding of this book.

---

135. Collins, *All But Invisible,* 170.

136. Gagnon, *Homosexual Practice,* 58.

137. Brunner, *Man in Revolt,* 345.

138. Mason, "Authority of the Body," 46.

139. Mason, "Authority of the Body," 57.

Gender authenticity requires gender integrity

Such an understanding of gender's relationship to sex is in direct conflict with the contemporary zeitgeist, according to which "we find our identity not in any supposed status as creatures, but in our activity as creators."[140] It also stands opposed to the modified, quasi-Christian form of this idea, according to which the "creation narratives present gender as *our business to explore and to define and not just God's business to declare and to impose*."[141] Scott Cowdell, for example, makes the provocative claim that the man's naming of both the woman and himself shows that "God entrusted to the creature of earth a role in the defining of gender."[142] Going considerably further, Tanis speaks of surgical transition as "a collaboration between God and humanity in co-creating what our bodies are and what they become."[143]

However, no gender self-definition takes place in Genesis 2:23. The man's words are *a statement of recognition*; he sees the woman's connection to and difference from himself, and so applies to her the title *'ishah* given by the narrator in verse 22—the ה- (*-h*) ending signifying the feminine form of his own title *'ish*. Nor are attempts to change sex appropriate expressions of human dominion. As Robert George explains: "If we are body-mind (or body-soul) composites and not minds (or souls) inhabiting material bodies, then respect for the person demands respect for the body, which rules out mutilation and other direct attacks on human health."[144] Bodies are to be nourished and cherished (Eph 5:29).

The basic principle of medical ethics is also clear: the manipulation of created matter ought to be constrained by "the inherent structural integrity of that matter."[145] By this measure, medical transitioning is ethically

140. Grenz, *Community of God*, 129.

141. Scott Cowdell, "Gender and Identity: Freeing the Bible from Modern Western Anxieties," *ABC Religion & Ethics* (September 14, 2017), https://www.abc.net.au/religion/gender-and-identity-freeing-the-bible-from-modern-western-anxiet/10095390 (emphasis original).

142. Cowdell, "Gender and Identity."

143. Tanis, *Trans-Gender*, 166. Similar arguments are offered by Gerard Loughlin, "Being Creature, Becoming Human: Contesting Oliver O'Donovan on Transgender, Identity and the Body," *ABC Religion & Ethics* (September 5, 2018), https://www.abc.net.au/religion/being-creature-becoming-human-contesting-oliver-odonovan-on-tran/10214276.

144. George, "Gnostic Liberalism."

145. O'Donovan, "Transsexualism and Christian Marriage," 151.

indefensible. Attempts to change sex are not acts of human-divine co-creation, but false forms of gender construction (or, more accurately, destruction) that work *against*, rather than *with*, the grain of created nature. The path of *gender authenticity* is one of *gender integrity*. In psychosocial terms, this means being "fully conscious of our sex and thankful for it, living our lives before God as a man or a woman with a sober and good conscience."[146]

INTERPERSONAL RELATIONSHIPS

Bodily sex shapes our relationships

The sex-and-gender binary and the sex-and-gender connection likewise have implications for personal relationships. Bodily sex not only informs a person's *self-conception* (as girl or boy, man or woman), but our *modes of relation*: that is, "one's identity as father or mother, son or daughter, brother or sister and one's natural resonance and affinity with other members of one's sex."[147] Thus, the sex of my body determines the *form* (and perhaps much of the *content* too) of my relationships.[148]

Consequently, both men and women come to learn more about who and what they are by interacting not only with members of their own sex but also with members of the other sex. In that sense, the sexes illumine, define, and enrich each other—just as they did in the garden. As Barth notes: "It is always in relation to their opposite that man and woman are what they are in themselves."[149] Sex likewise determines whether our relationships are to be characterized as homosocial or heterosocial. Thus, the "unremittingly social" nature of the body is inseparable from the fact that it is irreducibly sexual.[150]

Therefore, sexed embodiment lies at the heart of all our relationships—starting with those within our immediate family. These relationships then

146. Jewett with Shuster, *Who We Are*, 132, summarizing Barth, *CD*, III/4, 156–57.

147. Roberts, "Male and Female," 41.

148. Sloane concurs: "our bodily existence shapes our relationships, making some relationships possible rather than others, and so shapes what identifies and defines us. I am son and brother and husband and father and friend; and both my maleness and the particular forms of masculinity that I express necessarily shape those relationships and the self that they form and inform ("Male and Female," 232).

149. Barth, *CD*, III/4, 163.

150. Matthew Lee Anderson, *Earthen Vessels: Why Our Bodies Matter to Our Faith* (Minneapolis: Bethany, 2011), 108.

provide a pattern for others. Indeed, with the exception of husband and wife, all the major family roles find analogous instantiations in both civil and ecclesiastical contexts.[151] This is why Deborah can describe herself as a "mother in Israel" (Judg 5:7) and why Paul instructs the young man Timothy, whom he repeatedly calls his "child" (τέκνον, *teknon*):[152] "Do not rebuke an older man but encourage him as you would a father, younger men as brothers, older women as mothers, younger women as sisters, in all purity" (1 Tim 5:1–2).

So then, the distinction of the sexes within the unity of humanity creates and colors an array of different forms of fellowship. On this point, Geoffrey Bromiley is insightful:

> Whether within marriage or outside of it, this distinction in unity forms an integral and inescapable part of human reality. It denotes the broader relation of the sexes in which no male can exist without the female and no female without the male. When humanity multiplies, people may live single lives or even lives segregated according to sex. They may avoid both marriage and sex itself in the narrow sense. Yet they cannot get outside the common structure of human life. Single men will have, or will have had, at least, a mother, and single women a father, along with the necessary grandmothers and grandfathers whom they might well have known in their early years. It is also highly probable that they will have, or will have had, sisters, brothers, aunts, uncles, nieces, nephews, cousins, and for a period at least, some friends or acquaintances of the opposite sex. God has made sexuality in this wider sense an essential element in being human. No one can escape it.[153]

151. Scott Swain, "More Thoughts on Theological Anthropology: Man as Male and Female," *Reformed Blogmatics* (May 14, 2020), https://www.scottrswain.com/2020/05/14/more-thoughts-on-theological-anthropology-man-as-male-and-female.

152. See 1 Cor 4:17; Phil 2:22; 1 Tim 1:2; 18; 2 Tim 1:2; 2:1.

153. Geoffrey W. Bromiley, *God and Marriage* (Grand Rapids: Eerdmans, 1980), 2.

Androgyny undermines relationality

The role that bodily sex plays in defining and shaping our relationships also explains why androgyny is both undesirable and unrealizable. As we have seen, sexual dimorphism "is a fundamental fact about humanity."[154] Moreover, because sex is determined by the chromosomal underpinnings of our respective reproductive structures, it is both ineradicable and immutable. Definitionally, then, as J. Budziszewksi observes, "a woman is a human being of that sex whose members are potentially mothers," and a man is "a human being of the sex whose members have a different potentiality than women do: the potentiality for fatherhood."[155]

As we have also seen, the postlapsarian fact that the process of sex differentiation can very occasionally go awry and, as a result, a small number of people exhibit characteristics of both sexes, does not mean that there are more than two sex categories. Thus, Sloane's observation that "male and female phenotypes exist as polar rather than binary phenomena" does not mean that sex is "a *spectrum*."[156] Indeed, such a conclusion not only confuses matters but "places preposterous over-demanding conditions on sex category membership."[157] Sloane is, of course, right that forcing "human bodies into *rigid* 'male' or 'female' types fails to do justice to the realities of the world as it is," but this does not mean that those whose bodies are not paradigmatically male or female are "neither-nor."[158] There are, quite literally, billions of different male and female bodies, a fact that testifies to the "complex expressions of the rich variety of God's creation."[159] And yet, on any account of sex, there are still only two sexes.

Androgyny, however, is more than physiologically unrealizable; it is ethically undesirable. Because it seeks to blend or blur the distinction

---

154. Roberts, "Male and Female," 36.

155. J. Budziszewksi, *On the Meaning of Sex* (Wilmington, DE: Intercollegiate Studies Institute, 2014), 58–59. As Stock clarifies, "when we talk about males and females, we are talking about a capacity that a given organism either *actually has* or at least *would have had under certain given circumstances* (e.g. had *that* particular variation not occurred; had *that* particular environmental factor not interfered, etc.)" (*Material Girls*, 46, emphasis original). So, for example, a post-menopausal woman is still a female.

156. Sloane, "Male and Female," 233–34 (see fn. 32, emphasis original).

157. Stock, *Material Girls*, 56.

158. Sloane, "Male and Female," 233 (emphasis added).

159. Sloane, "Male and Female," 234.

between the sexes, it militates against the divine intention for human relationships. Reflecting on the androgynous aims of second-wave feminism, Melanie Phillips writes: "Androgyny is the ultimate expression of individualism. It presupposes that one person alone can achieve human potential; there's no need for anyone else to be involved. Otherness is superfluous. We can each do otherness ourselves."[160] In light of the divine declaration in Genesis 2:18 ("It is not good that the man should be alone"), Blocher is even stronger:

> Immediately we can see the perversity of the androgyne myth; by conferring on the same individual the attributes of both sexes, it expresses the ideal of self-sufficient solitude, it rejects the duty towards one's neighbour that God has inscribed within mankind, and thereby it rejects the duty towards the Creator that neighbour-love both reflects and honours.[161]

As we have seen in the exposition of Genesis 2, it was not God's purpose to create sexually undifferentiated or nonbinary beings. Nor is it his purpose that we relate in a unisex or agendered fashion. In fact, attempting to do so not only suggests that our relationships, and the sex differences that define, delimit, and enhance them, are "not good," but also turns "what really is a construct—the abstract 'individual'—into a new natural, so as to turn what is really natural—constitutive relations—into a 'construct.' "[162]

Moreover, the effects of this inversion, which have been compounding since the early 1960s, along with accompanying attempts to minimize or ignore the reality of sexual difference, have, in Mary Eberstadt's words, led to a major "reconfiguring of the human ecosystem." By pathologizing traditional expressions of masculinity and femininity, the sexual revolution has effectively (and, for some, intentionally) subsidized and valorized androgyny. The results, however, have been relationally deleterious, for one of the effects of incentivizing women to behave in more masculine ways and men in more feminine ways has been an increasing number of

160. Melanie Phillips, "How Feminists Have Weaponised Androgyny," *MelaniePhillips.com* (January 19, 2018), https://www.melaniephillips.com/feminists-weaponised-androgyny.

161. Blocher, *In the Beginning*, 97.

162. McCarthy, "Gender Ideology," 294.

"ever more alienated women, reacting to ever more distant men."[163] It is unsurprising that gender confusion proliferates in such a climate.

Recovering healthy relationality

Reluctance to embrace the goodness of the sex binary is part of the legacy of the fall, and the deep-seated, shame-driven fears that so easily divide the sexes and threaten to frustrate all our relationships. Multiple manifestations of misogyny and misandry, both externalized and internalized, are one of the tragic outcomes. But sex-shaming is not God's intention. We are called by creation (and, as we shall see in the next chapter, enabled by redemption) not only to celebrate the goodness of our own sex, but also that of the other sex, and the good purposes our sex distinctions serve. For as Alastair Roberts rightly sees, the created differences between men and women "are not differences designed to polarise us or pit us against each other. Rather, these differences are to be expressed in unified yet differentiated activity within the world and the closest of bonds with each other. It is not about *difference from* each other so much as *difference for* each other."[164]

It is in this way, and for this reason, that socially developed gender differences "extend out from and symbolically highlight the primary differences of our created natures and purposes."[165] This is not to deny the many commonalities that testify to the equal worth and dignity of the sexes. But it is to insist that within our shared humanity "men and women are inherently different in the sexuate form of our male and female bodies that blossom into our gender as masculine and feminine."[166]

The way forward, then, is not to return to some version of what Dale Kuehne calls the "tWorld" (traditional world), in which men and women are pressured "to fit into preconceived, socially conditioned gender roles." Rather, it involves inhabiting the "rWorld" (relational world), where loving

163. Mary Eberstadt, "The Lure of Androgyny," *Commentary* (October 2019), https://www.commentary.org/articles/mary-eberstadt/the-lure-of-androgyny. For a more detailed discussion of the evidence supporting Eberstadt's claims, see Mary Eberstadt, *Adam and Eve after the Pill: Paradoxes of the Sexual Revolution* (San Francisco: Ignatius, 2012), 36–65.

164. Roberts, "Male and Female," 38 (emphasis added).

165. Roberts, "Male and Female," 37.

166. Mason, "Authority of the Body," 57.

relationships (with God and others) provide the context for personal, communal, and sexual wholeness. In such a "world," gender norms are not eschewed but allowed to emerge in ways that recognize that "women and men complement each other relationally."[167] In other words, men and women will be best placed to relate in culturally appropriate masculine and feminine ways as they embrace the reality of their biology in their imitation and service of Christ.[168]

MARRIAGE

The significance of heterosexual marriage

While the roles of husband and wife are "not sufficient to account for the full array of callings that God has given to human beings as men and women,"[169] the significance and centrality of marriage in God's purposes is clear from Genesis 2:24. As O'Donovan writes, "in the ordinance of marriage there was given an end for human relationships, a teleological structure which was a fact of creation and therefore not negotiable."[170] In other words, due to its binary form, unitive purpose, and procreative potential, marriage is able to do what no other relationship can: "disclose the goodness of biological nature by elevating it to its teleological fulfilment in personal relationship."[171]

For this reason, the biblical template for marriage is necessarily sexuate in form; man and woman, with their complementary reproductive organs and capacities, are indispensable to the design. In short, the one-flesh union is only possible between husband and wife. The reason is because husband and wife are not simply *social roles* but *sexual entities*. Scripture presents a consistent view of marriage: "namely, that marriage is the union of two people of opposing biological sex, and that this sexed

---

167. Dale S. Kuehne, *Sex and the iWorld: Rethinking Relationship beyond an Age of Individualism* (Grand Rapids: Baker, 2009), 184–85.

168. Steven Wedgeworth, "What Is Effeminacy?," *Desiring God* (October 17, 2023).

169. Swain, "More Thoughts."

170. O'Donovan, *Resurrection and Moral Order*, 69.

171. O'Donovan, "Transsexualism and Christian Marriage," 141.

complementarity is essential not incidental to the nature and purpose of marriage."[172]

This view necessarily excludes same-sex unions. Such marriages not only fail to fulfill God's creational intent but stand in clear violation of his expressed will (Lev 18:22; 20:13; Rom 1:26–27; 1 Cor 6:9–11; and 1 Tim 1:10). It also excludes the union of a man and a trans woman (i.e., a biological male who identifies as a woman) or that of a woman and a trans man (i.e., a biological female who identifies as a man). However they may appear, these are, in fact, same-sex relationships.[173] O'Donovan, therefore, is right to reject both *the psychological case* (that self-consciousness determines sex) and *the social case* (that social recognition determines sex) for such unions. The first fails because it ignores the fact that a person's true sexed identity is "conferred biologically," not psychologically; the second fails because it involves a form of "public fiction."[174]

The relevance of the eschatological marriage

As we saw in the exposition of Ephesians 5:31–32, Genesis 2:24 refers not only to the protological union of the couple in the garden, but to the eschatological union of Jesus Christ and his followers. Hence Paul instructs Christian husbands to love their wives not as Adam loved Eve, but "as Christ loved the church" (Eph 5:25). He likewise calls on Christian wives to submit themselves to their husbands not as Eve submitted to Adam, but "as the church submits to Christ" (Eph 5:22).

Of course, the two marital models should not be pitted against one another—for redemption means the liberation and restoration of creation, not its abolition. Nevertheless, in light of Ephesians 5:31–32, Davie's statement that "Christians are called to live within the pattern of marriage thus established by God at creation and, by so doing, reflect the eternal marriage between Christ and his church" could equally be reversed: Christians

---

172. Claire S. Smith, "Family Ties: Marriage, Sex, and Belonging in the New Testament," in *Marriage, Same-Sex Marriage and the Anglican Church of Australia*, 142.

173. The marriage of a man to a trans man (or vice versa) is slightly less problematic, as the marriage is, at the level of biology, heterosexual. Serious problems remain, however, due to the homosexual appearance of the marriage and the cross-gender identification and/or presentation of one of the spouses.

174. O'Donovan, "Transsexualism and Christian Marriage," 145, 153.

are called to model their marriages on Christ and the church and, by so doing, fulfill the pattern established in creation.[175]

Either way, the Christo-ecclesiological model has two further implications.

First, if a married man transitions genders (even if only socially), he is portraying Christ as having abandoned his role as the *husband* of his church. Likewise, if a wife transitions genders (again, even if only socially), she is portraying the church as having abandoned her role as the *bride* of Christ. These are serious acts of abdication, for both portrayals deny the nature and responsibilities of marriage and so dishonor the relationship they ought to reflect—Christ and the church. They likewise create the facade of a same-sex union (if not claim to be one) due to the cross-sex presentation and (perhaps also) cross-sex identification of one of the spouses.

Second, as we have seen, if a man marries a trans woman or a woman a trans man, they have, in fact, entered a same-sex union. The heterosexual appearance of such a "marriage" is illusory. The relationship, therefore, cannot truly model itself on Christ and the church, let alone fulfill the unitive and procreative purposes of marriage. I thus concur with O'Donovan that churches should neither perform nor bless the marriages of "postoperative transsexuals." To do so would be either to engage in or to affirm an act of public deception, promoting "the appearance of a marriage where no marriage can exist."[176]

The necessity of the sex-and-gender connection

It follows, then, that transgender marriages are contrary to both the creational ectype and the Christo-ecclesiological archetype. By imitating a same-sex union, either in form or in fact, they rob marriage of its soteriological shape and its gospel-testifying potential. As Claire Smith observes: "the ability of human marriage to explain or reflect rich theological truths—such as, the union of Christ and the church—demands that the sex and

175. Davie, *What Does the Bible Really Say?*, 26.

176. O'Donovan, "Transsexualism and Christian Marriage," 156.

gender differences within human marriage are real not illusory, stable not fluid, and fixed not interchangeable."[177]

The reason for this, as we have seen in this chapter, is that the "otherness of husband and wife, rooted in the proclamation that marriage is about Jesus and the church, is foundational to God's design."[178] But for this *otherness* to be enduring, the sex-and-gender connection in each of the spouses needs to be unwavering. In other words, for marriage to bear the witness it is intended to bear, it not only needs to be heterosexual, but the spouses need to express their gender in accord with their sex.

Moreover, although in marriage husband and wife are given "a tiny foretaste of the wonder of the coming union with Christ because both are united to one so very different than themselves,"[179] the witness of their relationship is primarily directed outward. For in the end, "marriage was not made for man; man, redeemed humanity, was made for marriage—the marriage of Christ and his church at the end of all time."[180] Human marriage not only points to this marriage; it calls others into it.

There is, then, no greater blessing than that of being "invited to the marriage supper of the Lamb" (Rev 19:9). There is likewise no greater service an earthly marriage can perform than to declare this invitation by faithfully reflecting the union of Christ and his church. This can only be done, however, if the marriage is marked by love and respect (Eph 5:33) and the connection between the sex and gender of both spouses is secure.

CONCLUDING REFLECTIONS

The conviction lying behind much trans-affirming literature is that "many behaviours often rejected by the mainstream Christian tradition (such as homosexual activity, gender-bending and intentionally child-free marriages) would not necessarily be seen as problematic if the sexually dimorphic model on which so-called gender complementarity supervenes were

177. Smith, "Family Ties," 143–44.

178. David White, *God, You, and Sex: A Profound Mystery* (Greensboro, NC: New Growth, 2019), 46.

179. White, *God, You, and Sex*, 46.

180. Owen Strachan, *Reenchanting Humanity: A Theology of Mankind* (Fearn: Christian Focus Publications, 2019), 155.

disturbed."[181] Trans-affirming authors attempt such a disturbance in a variety of ways. For Cornwall, the Bible is not only one of several sources of revelation but must be interpreted "in dialogue with the shifting social and cultural contexts in which its readers live." Therefore, those "who read its meaning as once established and never unchanging [*sic*] may miss promptings from other areas."[182] For Hartke, scriptural revelation is similarly deficient. Thus, we "shouldn't expect all humans to fit into the categories of 'male' and 'female,' just because those are the only two listed in Genesis 1."[183] For Mollenkott, the Bible is simply passé. Its affirmation of the sex-and-gender binary and the sex-and-gender connection "reflects a cultural understanding that has subsequently been modified by human experience and research."[184]

Such approaches are incompatible with an evangelical view of Scripture's authority and sufficiency. They also misunderstand the function of Genesis 1 and 2, which is to provide us with a divinely inspired depiction of "the order established within creation—as an order determined by God, from the beginning."[185] This order confirms created nature and establishes created norms (and so clarifies what are and are not postlapsarian deviations, afflictions, declensions, and temptations). In other words, the Bible's opening chapters not only depict how things *were originally* but how they *are essentially*—the distorting effects of sin notwithstanding.

Moreover, central to what is revealed is the fact that "to exist as a man or a woman is the concrete and necessary form of all human existence, and it is the biblical paradigm for human life as co-humanity or community."[186] While Cornwall complains that such a conclusion reifies "the twin idols of male-and-female and heteronormativity,"[187] Genesis shows that

---

181. Cornwall, *Sex and Uncertainty*, 7.

182. Susannah Cornwall, "Laws 'Needefull in Later to Be Abrogated': Intersex and the Sources of Christian Theology," in Cornwall, *Intersex, Theology and the Bible*, 149. I assume Cornwall meant to write either "unchanging" or "never changing."

183. Hartke, *Transforming*, 53.

184. Mollenkott, *Omnigender*, 103.

185. Bird, "Male and Female," 136.

186. Alistair Iain McFadyen, *The Call to Personhood: A Christian Theory of the Individual in Social Relationships* (Cambridge: Cambridge University Press, 1990), 31–32.

187. Cornwall, *Sex and Uncertainty*, 235.

these are not human idols but divine ideals. They are thus the God-given norms that not only inform our anthropology but establish the basis and boundaries of sexual ethics. Consequently, "being male and female is integral to our calling as image bearers, not least in that most basic of all human communities—the one known as marriage."[188]

Marriage, therefore, has been the central concern of this chapter—particularly as its meaning is disclosed in Genesis 2:24–25 and its mystery unveiled in Ephesians 5:31–32. What we have seen, in brief, is that what is true for both personal identity and interpersonal relationships generally is true for marriage specifically—that is, both the sex-and-gender binary (the fact that there are only two sexes and only two genders) and the sex-and-gender connection (the fact that gender is intended to exhibit and express sex) are essential to the divine design. To put the point plainly: according to Genesis 2, marriage is *necessarily heterosexual* and the spouses *necessarily cisgendered.*

This highlights one further issue raised by trans-affirming scholars. It has been argued that to ask the opening chapters of Genesis to provide a foundation for sexual ethics is to ask "primeval history to do something it is neither intended nor equipped to do."[189] But while there is wisdom in heeding Jane Shaw's caution against operating "as if there were a seamless line from the world of Genesis to the early twenty-first century,"[190] the fact of the matter, as we shall see further in the following chapters, is that "the opening chapters of Scripture may be seen as of 'seminal character' and 'determinative' for a biblical view of sexuality."[191] Poythress puts it this way: "These chapters have universal implications because the beginning is intrinsically universal in its scope and, according to God's determination, has effects on all of subsequent history."[192]

It is for this reason that the opening chapters of Genesis have been "fundamental to the Christian understanding of sex and gender across

---

188. Wilson, *Mere Sexuality*, 36.

189. John F. Tuohey, "The Gender Distinctions of Primeval History and a Christian Sexual Ethic," *Heythrop Journal* 36 (1995): 184–85.

190. Jane Shaw, "Reformed and Enlightened Church," in *Queer Theology: Rethinking the Western Body*, ed. Gerard Loughlin (Oxford: Blackwell, 2007), 277.

191. Davidson, *Flame of Yahweh*, 5.

192. Poythress, *Interpreting Eden*, 127.

denominational and historical boundaries."[193] While Genesis 2 presents us with a view of humanity as not only "rooted in nature and history (formed of the dust of the ground)," but also "self-aware and able to transcend to some extent natural and historical necessity (given the divine breath of life),"[194] we are neither autonomous self-creators nor semi-autonomous co-creators. Rather, we are accountable stewards, with a responsibility "to the natural order of creation, and so to the natural order of our bodies, which are dimorphic: male and female."[195] So then, although the psychosocial construction of gender is an important and inevitable human task, obedient cultivation "operates with the natural reality of difference between the sexes, rather than creating difference *ex nihilo*."[196]

This concludes our theological exposition of sex and gender in creation. It remains for us to explore briefly how these themes are addressed in the remaining movements of Scripture's grand narrative—fall, redemption, and consummation.

---

193. Tina Beattie, "The Theological Study of Gender," in Thatcher, *Oxford Handbook of Theology, Sexuality, and Gender*, 40.

194. Meilaender, *Faith and Faithfulness*, 41.

195. Mason, "Authority of the Body," 47.

196. Roberts, "Male and Female," 37.

CHAPTER 10

SEX AND GENDER OUTSIDE OF EDEN

We even find it difficult to be human beings, men with real flesh and blood of our own; we are ashamed of it, we think it a disgrace, and are always striving to be some unprecedented kind of generalized human being.[1]

—Fyodor Dostoyevsky

Once the knowledge of God is lost, mankind accuses finitude of causing his disorder, whereas that disorder is the fruit of disobedience. Once the communion is lost, mankind wants to replace it with confusion.[2]

—Henri Blocher

The previous three chapters have provided a theological exposition of Genesis 1 and 2, deliberately focusing on their foundational anthropological contribution and what they reveal about creational sexology. We have seen the following: (1) "in the beginning" God made humankind as two distinct yet complementary sexes (male and female); (2) sex is an immutable biological reality; and (3) the psychosocial-cultural dimensions of sex—what we today call *gender* (or, more precisely, *gender identity, gender roles,* and

1. Fyodor Dostoyevsky, *Notes from Underground,* trans. Jessie Coulson (Melbourne: Penguin, 2010), 152.

2. Blocher, *In the Beginning,* 73.

gender expression)—are, from the Bible's perspective, best seen as the psychological perception, social manifestation, and cultural communication of biological sex. Furthermore, due to the normative nature of Genesis 1 and 2, authentic gender identity, like faithful gender roles and expression, is grounded in sex.

The purpose of both this and the next chapter is to take a series of soundings from the remainder of the Bible to see how the anthropological and sexological picture we have observed in creation is damaged, restored, and transformed by the other major movements of Scripture's grand narrative—fall, redemption, and consummation. Although I will loosely structure these chapters around these movements, and address the main theological questions raised by them, much of what follows consists of a series of focused exegetical explorations. These will not only enable an engagement with the key texts that speak of the relationship of gender to sex, but assist in the assessment of the central claim of trans theory: that the sexed body has no necessary bearing on the gendered self.

THE FALL AND ITS CONSEQUENCES

THE NATURE OF THE FALL

In theological discourse, "the fall" is the term typically given to humanity's disobedience as depicted in Genesis 3. Although the Bible nowhere uses *fall* language to describe this event, the expression appears as early as the apocryphal book of 2 Esdras:

> O Adam, what have you done?
> For though it was you who sinned,
> the fall [Lat. *tuus casus*] was not yours alone,
> but ours also who are your descendants. (7:118 NRSA)[3]

Nevertheless, given the absence of the language and imagery of *falling* in Genesis 3, it has been argued that its deployment risks obscuring what is present—that is, willful disobedience to the divine command (Gen 2:17; 3:17). Indeed, for Bonhoeffer, even "the word *disobedience* fails to describe the situation adequately." For what we see is an unconscionable act of

3. For a helpful discussion of this text, see C. John Collins, "May We Say That Adam and Eve 'Fell'? A Study of a Term and Its Metaphoric Function," *Presbyterion* 46 (2020): 53–74.

"rebellion, the creature's stepping outside of the creature's only possible attitude, the creature's becoming creator, the destruction of creatureliness, a defection."[4]

While this insight is crucial, it is not necessary to abandon the traditional nomenclature to preserve it. What is necessary is to recognize that humanity's *fall* was not an accidental stumbling but an intentional and, ultimately, inscrutable act of treason. There was no preexisting flaw in the couple to account for their revolt—no "crack preceding the split," as Blocher puts it.[5] So, although transgression was clearly a *possibility* from the moment the command was issued, how possibility became *actuality* remains a mystery.

THE BIBLICAL ACCOUNT OF THE FALL

The account of the fall in Genesis 3 begins by highlighting the unparalleled craftiness (*ʿārum*) of the serpent (v. 1a). Although the Old Testament never discloses a link between the serpent and the Satan (1 Chr 21:1; Job 1:6–2:7; Zech 3:1–2), the book of Revelation does so directly, speaking of "that ancient serpent, who is called the devil and Satan, the deceiver of the whole world" (12:9; compare 20:2). Given that his patent purpose in Genesis 3 is to bring about the death of humanity (compare 2:17), Jesus rightly calls him "a murderer from the beginning" (John 8:44). So then, however we might finally categorize the precise literary form of the Genesis account (i.e., whether and to what degree it contains symbolic imagery), the snake is evidently "more than a literal snake; rather, it is Satan's personal presence in the garden."[6]

To achieve his malign purpose, the serpent begins by painting God "as a little harsh and repressive" (v. 1b).[7] Then, in response to the woman's answer, he not only accuses the LORD of lying (v. 4), but claims that God has an ulterior motive for deceiving the couple (v. 5). In this way, he undermines the woman's confidence in the wisdom and goodness of God and

---

4. Bonhoeffer, *Creation and Fall*, 120.

5. Blocher, *In the Beginning*, 138.

6. Mathews, *Genesis 1–11:26*, 234. In Blocher's view, "once the two issues of form and content are properly distinguished, the real problem is not to know if we have a historical account of the fall, but the account of a historical fall" (*In the Beginning*, 157).

7. Wenham, *Genesis 1–15*, 73.

his word. The fall is thus in motion: doubt has been planted, resentment cultivated, and unbelief has germinated. Verse 6 then describes the final stages of the birth of sin: covetousness is aroused (as the woman sees the tree is "good for food," "a delight to the eyes" and "desired to make one wise") and disobedience results: "she *took* ... and *ate*, and she also *gave* some to her husband ... and he *ate*."[8]

Given its foundational significance in the biblical narrative, it is not surprising that Genesis 3 contains several leitmotifs and other archetypical features that grant it a paradigmatic role both for several scriptural accounts of desire and for human experience more generally.[9] This in no way detracts from the historicity of the events it portrays, but instead points to the programmatic character of the original sin.

For this reason, it is not difficult to describe some forms of what we might call transgender temptation in terms of the stages identified above: (1) *doubt* about the goodness or reality of one's sexed body; (2) *resentment* regarding the fact or appearance of one's body; (3) *unbelief* regarding the rightness of the God-given body or one's ability to be reconciled to it; (4) *desire* for a different body or to be a different sex; and (5) *disobedience* in the form of cross-gender identification and cross-sex presentation. As I will discuss later in the chapter, the call of Scripture is to resist such a temptation.

THE EFFECTS OF THE FALL

What were the effects of "the transgression of Adam" (Rom 5:14)? I began to answer this question in the previous chapter as we examined the responses of the couple in Genesis 3:7–10. Charles Hodge's summary is incisive:

> The effects of this first sin upon our first parents themselves were, (1.) shame, a sense of degradation and pollution; (2.) dread of the displeasure of God, or a sense of guilt, and the consequent desire

---

8. These categories have been adapted from Hoekema, *Created in God's Image*, 130.

9. See Cephas T. A. Tushima, "The Paradigmatic Role of Genesis 3 for Reading Biblical Narratives about Desire," *Unio Cum Christo* 5 (2019): 87–102.

> to hide from his presence. These effects were unavoidable. They prove the loss not only of innocence but of original righteousness, and, with it, of the favour and fellowship of God.[10]

I also noted that the couple's shame was focused on their *nakedness*, particularly their *genitalia*. To understand this reaction (and in addition to the reasons suggested in the previous chapter), it is necessary to appreciate that in our sexuality "our whole self is at stake personally, emotionally, and physically." This clarifies why sexual shaming is not only profoundly humiliating but deeply destructive of a person's sense of self. It likewise reveals why "we identify that sense of shame with our genitalia," and instinctively take steps to "cover them up from visual violation" and "to protect ourselves from the shame of sexual dishonor and abuse."[11] It also has the potential to explain (even if only in part) why *some* who have been subjected to sexual shaming may desire to escape their sex.[12] There are, of course, many other reasons why a person may experience gender incongruence, but, tragically, there is no shortage of accounts of those who have "turned to a transgender identity to escape pain and trauma."[13]

Although these pastoral realities deserve deeper probing, my purpose, at this point, is to turn our attention to five other matters of significance: the first concerns what Genesis 3:16 reveals about the postlapsarian relationship between the man and the woman; the second concerns the wider wages of sin experienced by their progeny; the third concerns the relationship between the fall and human sexuality; the fourth concerns the somatic effects of sin; and the fifth clarifies what has not changed as a result of the fall.

---

10. Charles Hodge, *Systematic Theology: Volume II* (Ontario: Devoted, 2016), 64.

11. John Kleinig, *Wonderfully Made: A Protestant Theology of the Body* (Bellingham, WA: Lexham Press, 2021), 36.

12. Kenneth J. Zucker and Myra Kuksis, "Gender Dysphoria and Sexual Abuse: A Case Report," *Child Abuse & Neglect* 14 (1990): 281–83.

13. E.g., Walt Heyer, "Childhood Sexual Abuse, Gender Dysphoria, and Transition Regret: Billy's Story," *Public Discourse* (March 26, 2018), https://www.thepublicdiscourse.com/2018/03/21178.

The words of divine sentence in Genesis 3:16

The words of divine sentence recorded in Genesis 3:14–19 are addressed to the three agents responsible for the fall—the serpent (vv. 14–15), the woman (v. 16), and the man (vv. 17–19). Appropriately, all are held accountable for their own contribution—deception, desire, and disobedience, respectively. Moreover, in each case, the punishment is both *functional* and *relational*—the serpent is consigned to crawl on its belly and be at enmity with the woman and her seed; the woman will have pain in childbirth and (as I will argue below) experience a conflicted relationship with the man; and the man will know toil in his labor and have a vexed relationship with the ground.

The two aspects of the LORD God's words to the woman, which relate directly to her two primary roles, warrant special attention.

First, verse 16ab ("I will surely multiply your pain in childbearing; in pain you shall bring forth children") makes plain that childbearing itself is not the woman's punishment; rather, it is *the pangs of childbirth*—as Scripture often calls them (e.g., Isa 26:17; Jer 22:23; Hos 13:13)—that perform this function. Indeed, the sentence presupposes the goodness of motherhood and its centrality to the woman's vocation (compare Gen 1:28). The fall, then, has neither altered her sex nor changed her calling. The new element is the anguish involved in her becoming "the mother of all living" (3:20).

Before leaving this first point, it is also worth noting that the ESV translation ("I will surely *multiply* [רָבָה, *ravah*] your pain)," while paralleled in several English versions (e.g., "I will *intensify* your labor pains" [CSB]), seems to suggest that some amount of pain would have been part of the woman's experience even if sin had not entered the world. However, the verb *ravah* (which simply means "to cause to be numerous") carries no necessary implication of this kind.[14] The point, rather, is that what was to be a domain of unreserved blessing (Gen 1:28) is now "a perpetual reminder of sin and the woman's part in it."[15]

14. C. John Collins, *Genesis 1–4: A Linguistic, Literary and Theological Commentary* (Phillipsburg, NJ: P&R, 2006), 159n36.

15. Mathews, *Genesis 1–11:26*, 250.

The second part of the penalty pronounced on the woman is in verse 16cd: "Your *desire* [תְּשׁוּקָה, *teshuqah*] shall be *contrary to* [אֶל, *'el*] your husband, but he shall *rule* [מָשַׁל, *mashal*] over you." Because the precise denotation of several key terms in this sentence is contested, both its translation and interpretation are much debated. It should also be noted that by rendering *'el* as "contrary to," the ESV preempts the interpretive task. While this may well convey the meaning in context (see below), the preposition typically denotes *directed motion*. Consequently, either "for" (so NIV, CSB) or "toward" (so ISV, LSV) are more straightforward translations (as the ESV footnote indicates). The sense of *teshuqah* is also debated.[16] However, on the basis of its three occurrences in the Old Testament (Gen 3:16; 4:7; Song 7:10), it is generally thought to convey the idea of *stretching out after* and so is helpfully translated by "desire" (so most English versions), "longing," or "craving"—"with the context telling us what kind of craving is in view."[17]

The key hermeneutical question, then, turns on the kind of *desire* the author has in mind. The traditional view is that *affectionate* or *sexual desire* is intended (compare Song 7:10), particularly as this will ensure that children continue to be born (as v. 16ab anticipates). So, despite the pain that pregnancy will inevitably produce, the woman "will continue to desire the very relations with her husband that cause it."[18] The contemporary view, however, is that *adversarial* or *subversive desire* is what is meant.[19] While this reading is demanded neither by the noun *teshuqah* nor by the preposition *'el*, it seems likely in view of the parallel expression in Genesis 4:7cd: "Its *desire* [*teshuqah*] is *contrary to* [*'el*] you, but you must rule [*mashal*] over it." Here, as John Collins observes, "it is plain that 'desire for' someone is 'desire to master' that person."[20] Therefore, despite

16. E.g., Janson C. Condren, "Towards a Purge of the Battle of the Sexes and 'Return' for the Original Meaning of Genesis 3:16b," *JETS* 60 (2017): 227–45. Condren contends that the word carries the sense of "return," not "desire."

17. Collins, *Genesis 1–4*, 160; compare David Talley, "תְּשׁוּקָה," *NIDOTTE* 4:341–42.

18. Condren, "Towards a Purge," 229.

19. The origins of this view are usually traced to Susan T. Foh, "What Is the Woman's Desire?," *WTJ* 37 (1975): 376–83.

20. Collins, *Genesis 1–4*, 160.

several grammatical difficulties pertaining to 4:7,[21] its structural similarity and textual proximity to 3:16 not only suggest that the two verses should be read in concert, but also that the evident adversarial sense of 4:7c clarifies the meaning of 3:16c.[22]

This, in turn, illuminates the sense of "rule" (*mashal*) in 3:16d. While the *denotation* of the word is entirely neutral (compare Gen 1:16; 2 Sam 23:3), the context can supply it with a negative (or dominating) *connotation*.[23] This is likely the case here. Just as Cain must conquer that which seeks to control him, so the man will subdue the woman who seeks to subvert him. Domination, therefore, is the anticipated outcome.

At the same time, *description* should not be read as *prescription*. As Mathews elaborates: "We cannot understand the divine word 'he will rule over you' as a command to impose dominance any more than v. 16a is an exhortation for the woman to suffer as much as possible during childbirth. It is a distortion of the passage to find in it justification for male tyranny."[24] Nor does Genesis 3:16 mean that all marriages are consigned to perpetual conflict and bereft of divine blessing. The Old Testament provides numerous flawed-yet-positive portrayals of marriage (e.g., Abraham and Sarah, Isaac and Rebecca, Jacob and Rachel, Ruth and Boaz, Hannah and Elkanah, etc.) and continues to speak of "the beauty and joy of love between man and woman" (e.g., Deut 24:5, Prov 5:18–19; Song 4:1–7; Eccl 9:9).[25]

What we are given in Genesis 3:16, then, is insight into the etiology of common marital pathologies and fallen human proclivities. In both parts of the verse, we are dealing with a corruption or distortion of a created good. The good of marriage remains, but conflict is now introduced into it; the good of childbirth remains, but pain is now added to it. In this light, clauses c and d do not present a shift from an "egalitarian vision of sexuality to the utilitarian and hierarchical economics of procreative sexuality in the patriarchal social order," as Carden suggests. Nor is there

21. See Wenham, *Genesis 1–15*, 104–6; Mathews, *Genesis 1–11:26*, 269–71; Condren, "Towards a Purge," 231–34.

22. Hamilton, *Genesis 1–17*, 201.

23. Collins, *Genesis 1–4*, 159–60.

24. Mathews, *Genesis 1–11:26*, 251.

25. Neuer, *Man and Woman*, 82.

any basis for his claim that "the mythic androgynous realm remains as a dangerous memory critiquing, challenging the patriarchal procreative hierarchy of seed, field and womb."[26] What is on view, rather, is the forfeiture of the freedom and harmony that marked the prelapsarian relationship of the man and the woman in the garden (Gen 2:25). This state of innocence is now lost.

The wages of sin—original and actual

The words spoken to the man in Genesis 3:19 confirm the threat of 2:17. Physical death is now an inevitability: "for you are dust, and to dust you shall return." In the account of Genesis 3, this outcome is secured by the expulsion of the man and woman from Eden. Their banishment means that they are now no longer able to "take also of the tree of life and eat, and live forever" (v. 22). To prevent their return, the Lord God places, at the east of the garden, "the cherubim and a flaming sword that turned every way to guard the way to the tree of life" (v. 24). In this way, death is assured not only for Adam and Eve but also for their posterity.

However, Scripture sees a deeper connection between the event of the first sin and the universality of human death. The apostle Paul expresses it succinctly in 1 Corinthians 15:22: "in Adam all die" (ἐν τῷ Ἀδὰμ πάντες ἀποθνῄσκουσιν, *en tō Adam pantes apothnēskousin*). As is generally recognized, the thought here is one of *corporate solidarity*; that is, because Adam stands at the head of the entire human race, what he did "plunged not only himself but the whole human race into ruin."[27] Additional insights emerge from Romans 5:12–19, where Paul argues that Adam's transgression, while unique (v. 14), "led to condemnation for all people" (v. 18). The question, however, is whether this verdict is immediate or mediate—that is, a consequence of the *original sin* of Adam or of the *actual sins* of his descendants. While this is a vexed question, the parallels between Adam's "one trespass" and Christ's "one act of righteousness" (v. 18), along with the forensic terms Paul uses (e.g., κατάκριμα, *katakrima* [v. 18] and καθίστημι, *kathistēmi* [v. 19]), strongly suggest the former: the condemnation was

---

26. Carden, "Genesis/Bereshit," 30.

27. Donald Macleod, "Original Sin in Reformed Theology," in *Adam, the Fall, and Original Sin: Theological, Biblical, and Scientific Perspectives*, ed. Hans Madueme and Michael Reeves (Grand Rapids: Baker, 2014), 137.

immediate.[28] This, then, clarifies the meaning of verse 12: "so death spread to all men *because all sinned*" (ἐφ᾽ ᾧ πάντες ἥμαρτον, *eph' hō pantes hēmarton*). Paul is not here saying that all have sinned *actually* (although that too is true), but that all sinned *originally*—that is, "in Adam."[29]

Whether the participation of the race in Adam's sin is best explained in terms of representationalism, realism, or a combination of both, our adamic inheritance is evidently comprised of two components: *inherited guilt* (condemnation) and *inherited corruption* (concupiscence). As Calvin writes: "Not only has punishment fallen upon us from Adam, but a contagion imparted by him resides in us, which justly deserves punishment."[30] Indeed, so extensive is sin's pollution that our problem goes beyond an absence of original righteousness; we are infected with "a definite in-built bias to sin."[31] Therefore, both the *totus homo* ("the whole man") and the *totum hominus* ("the whole of man") have been sullied by sin. Moreover, as Calvin elaborates, "we are so vitiated and perverted in every part of our nature by this great corruption ... that this perversity never ceases in us, but continually bears new fruits—the works of the flesh."[32]

In this sense, *original sin* is the source of *actual sin*; the latter inevitably following from the former.

The fall and human sexuality

For this reason, David had good reason to declare, "I was brought forth in iniquity, and in sin did my mother conceive me" (Ps 51:5). The meaning of his statement has, of course, been much debated, with some seeing a reference to sexual passion or the act of intercourse itself. But this misses the obvious: *David is not confessing anyone's sins but his own* (vv. 1–4).[33]

---

28. See Thomas R. Schreiner, "Original Sin and Original Death: Romans 5:12–19," in Madueme and Reeves, *Adam, the Fall, and Original Sin*, 271–88.

29. This judgment interprets v. 12 in the light of vv. 18–19. However, given the summary nature of the latter verses (note the ἄρα οὖν, *ara oun* at the beginning of v. 18), this is entirely defensible. See Douglas J. Moo, *The Letter to the Romans*, NICNT, 2nd ed. (Grand Rapids: Eerdmans, 2018), 344–56. For an alternative interpretation, see James D. G. Dunn, *Romans 1–8*, WBC 38A (Dallas: Word, 1988), 273–74.

30. Calvin, *Institutes*, 2.1.8.

31. Robert Letham, *Systematic Theology* (Wheaton, IL: Crossway, 2019), 381.

32. Calvin, *Institutes*, 2.1.8.

33. Marvin E. Tate, *Psalms 51–100*, WBC 20 (Waco, TX: Word, 1990), 19.

Consequently, his words are best understood as an acknowledgment of *his own fallen nature manifested in his adultery*. So understood, his sin was "no freak event: it was in character; an extreme expression of the warped creature he had always been, and of the faulty stock he sprang from."[34] Psalm 51:5, then, affirms what we have already seen: while we are responsible for our actual sins, "one is a sinner simply as a result of one's natural human descent."[35]

What does not follow from this is any pathologizing of sex per se. For while all aspects of human sexuality and sexed identity have been distorted by the fall (as Rom 1:21–27 amply bears witness), "accounting for the propagation of original sin by the disorder of human sexual life has no sufficient warrant from the Bible."[36] Despite this, the attempt to find an inherent link between sex and sin has a long history to it. Clement of Alexandria, for example, thought the fall involved premature sexual intercourse between Adam and Eve.[37] And, as noted in chapter 4, Gregory of Nyssa believed that human sex distinctions were created in anticipation of the fall. But, as we have also seen, neither of these interpretations finds any secure basis in the biblical text.

Care is needed, then, to rightly articulate the relationship between sex and the fall. For while instances of fallen sexuality proliferate after Genesis 3 (e.g., Gen 6:1–2; 9:22; 19:4–11), the goodness of created sexuality remains (e.g., Prov 18:22; compare 1 Tim 4:1–5). Thus, to so accent the brokenness of creation that its essential integrity is obscured is to slide into an unbiblical form of dualism.[38] Not surprisingly, as the story of human existence outside the garden unfolds, two contrasting forms of sexual understanding and gender expression emerge: "on the one hand, the positive affirmations of sexuality, upholding and amplifying the Edenic pattern, and, on the other hand, the portrayals of departure from the Edenic plan through

34. Derek Kidner, *Psalms 1–72*, TOTC (Leicester: Inter-Varsity Press, 1973), 190–91.

35. Walther Eichrodt, *Theology of the Old Testament*, trans. J. A. Baker, OTL (Philadelphia: Westminster, 1961), 1:268.

36. Henri Blocher, *Original Sin: Illuminating the Riddle*, NSBT 5 (Leicester: Apollos, 1997), 114.

37. Clement of Alexandria, *Stromata* 3.14.94, in *Alexandrian Christianity: Selected Translations of Clement and Origen*, ed. Henry Chadwick and J. E. L. Oulton (London: SCM, 1954), 84.

38. Brian Brock, *Disability: Living into the Diversity of Christ's Body* (Grand Rapids: Baker Academic, 2021), 105.

the exploitation and distortion of God's intent for sexuality."[39] So while the book of Genesis contains numerous accounts of the latter—not only recording the sins of men against women but also those of men against men, women against women, and women against men[40]—it is not the case that "without sin there is no sexuality," as Kierkegaard held.[41] As we have seen, *sexuality preceded sin*. What the fall introduced is corrupted forms of sexuality and disordered experiences of sexed identity. Gender incongruence is simply one instance of the latter.

The somatic effects of sin

The fall also creates problems for sexed bodies. Because sin has entered the world, human beings are beset with a range of disorders of sex development and various forms of sexual dysfunction. So, while Christopher Morgan is right to say that sin "is ethical, not physical or tied to the cosmos,"[42] *the effects of sin are undeniably physical and unavoidably cosmic* (Rom 8:20–21). The words of divine sentence spoken to man in Genesis 3 makes this plain: "cursed is the ground because of you" (v. 17) and "to dust you shall return" (v. 19). Thus, disease and disability, which are the natural precursors to death, are our common companions throughout life. As Jürgen Moltmann observes: "In truth, there is no such thing as a life without disabilities."[43]

The individual reality, however, is that different bodies are afflicted differently, and some more profoundly than others. In light of this, it is not true to say that "sin impacts every human life equally."[44] Not only can particular sinful actions do irreparable damage to particular human bodies but, as Peter Comensoli observes, "some people appear not to have

39. Davidson, *Flame of Yahweh*, 83.

40. See Brian Neil Peterson, "Male and Female Sexual Exploitation in Light of the Book of Genesis," *JETS* 62 (2019): 693–703.

41. Søren Kierkegaard, *The Concept of Anxiety: A Simple Psychologically Orienting Deliberation on the Dogmatic Issue of Hereditary Sin*, ed. and trans. Reidar Thomte and Albert B. Anderson (Princeton, NJ: Princeton University Press), 49.

42. Christopher W. Morgan, "Sin in the Biblical Story," in *Fallen: A Theology of Sin*, ed. Robert A. Peterson and Christopher W. Morgan (Wheaton, IL: Crossway, 2013), 138.

43. Jürgen Moltmann, "Liberate Yourselves by Accepting One Another," in *Human Disability and the Service of God: Reassessing Religious Practice*, ed. Nancy L. Eisland and Don E. Saliers (Nashville: Abingdon, 1998), 110.

44. Brock, *Disability*, 104.

been properly 'knit together in their mother's womb' or apparently their humanity has subsequently become unraveled (Ps 139:13)."[45] Theologically, such disorders are regarded as forms of "natural evil" (as opposed to "moral evil") and a result of the fall.[46] In regard to intersex conditions specifically, I agree with Jennifer Cox that there is "no explanation for congenital defects of bodies and sex organs other than the fact that human sin has changed the nature of the world and the nature of human bodies." This, of course, does not mean that it is "the individual sin of intersex people that resulted in their unusual biology"; rather, "it is the result of every person's sin."[47] In short, intersex conditions are one of the many consequences of living outside of Eden.

Consequently, I cannot concur with Sally Gross's claim that it is "a grave sin against revelation to view intersexuality as 'unnatural' or as 'the consequence of Adam's sin.' "[48] Every type of disease, dysfunction, and disability must, of necessity, be characterized this way. Scripture "gives no other explanation for the brokenness of the world and the fragility of human bodies."[49] Moreover, to read postlapsarian disorder back into prelapsarian order is not only to succumb to a version of the is-ought fallacy, but to ignore the somatic effects of sin. What the fall means, in practical terms, is that our present experience of embodied life has been "radically altered for the worse, so that its actual state is very different from that purposed for it by the Creator."[50] It is no surprise, then, that some people are afflicted by a disorder of sex development, just as others are afflicted by somatic disorders of many and various kinds.

---

45. Peter A. Comensoli, *In God's Image: Recognizing the Profoundly Impaired as Persons* (Eugene, OR: Cascade, 2018), 18.

46. I agree with Fraser Watts, therefore, that it would be "theologically unsound to assume that the physical is good, but that the psychological is defective" (Fraser Watts, "Transsexualism and the Church," *Theology and Sexuality* 9 [2002]: 80). It does not follow from this, however, that where a gender dysphoric person's sex is unambiguous that gender transitioning can be justified.

47. Cox, *Intersex in Christ*, 47.

48. Gross, "Intersexuality and Scripture," 74.

49. Cox, *Intersex in Christ*, 44.

50. "Fall, the," in *The Oxford Dictionary of the Christian Church*, ed. F. L. Cross and E. A. Livingstone, 2nd ed. (Oxford: Oxford University Press, 1997), 597.

What has not changed as a result of the fall

The fall has not altered the fact of sexual dimorphism; the two sexes of Genesis 1 and 2 remain. This is everywhere apparent in Scripture, not only from the wide range of binary sex terms applied to humans, including the various ways in which the two sexes are differentiated, but also from the way that male and female animals are described and distinguished. Even the category of the eunuch (Heb: סָרִיס, *saris*/Gk: εὐνοῦχος, *eunouchos*), for all its social liminality, is not presented in Scripture as a third sex. Eunuchs, rather, "were biological males who were infertile, most often as a result of some impairment in their sexual anatomy from birth or through castration."[51] Therefore, irrespective of how eunuchs were sometimes regarded in later Christian reflection, for the biblical authors, male and female are the only two existing sex categories.

This does not mean that the existence of those with intersex conditions "is not recognized in the male-female absolute dichotomy of the Bible," as Marc Brettler charges.[52] It means, rather, that *all people*, regardless of their sexual clarity or reproductive capacity, *are included within the binary categories of male and female*—even if not always straightforwardly so. Pastorally and theologically, then, Denny Burk's conclusion is apt: "The phenomenon of intersex should call forth our compassion and our love for our neighbors who carry in their persons a painful reminder of the groaning creation. It should not call forth from us a revision of the binary ideal of Scripture."[53]

Furthermore, while marriage outside of Eden is invariably affected by the fall, its heterosexual nature and unitive and procreative purposes remain. What is added, however, is *a new redemptive dimension*. Genesis 3:15 makes clear that procreation will be the means by which the tempter is finally overcome: the serpent's head will be crushed by the woman's

51. Sprinkle, *Embodied*, 102. In the later rabbinic literature, the female parallel to the eunuch was known as the *aylonith*. This word was applied to women who typically had under-developed genitalia, found intercourse painful, were infertile and, instead of menstruation, experienced monthly abdominal pain. See John Hare, "Hermaphrodites, Eunuchs, and Intersex People: The Witness of Medical Science in Biblical Times and Today," in Cornwall, *Intersex, Theology and the Bible*, 85.

52. Marc Zvi Brettler, "Happy Is the Man Who Fills His Quiver with Them (Ps. 127:5): Construction of Masculinities in the Psalms," in *Being a Man: Negotiating Ancient Constructs of Masculinity*, ed. Ilona Zsolnay (London: Routledge, 2017), 199.

53. Burk, *Meaning of Sex*, 180–81; contra William Loader, *Sex, Then and Now: Sexualities and the Bible* (Eugene, OR: Cascade, 2022), 21.

seed (זֶרַע, *zera‘*). Adam and Eve are thus given hope that "despite their sin there will be a fulfilment of the blessing through progeny as foreseen at creation (1:26–28)."[54] This hope is renewed after Abel's death by the birth of Seth (called "another seed" [זֶרַע אַחֵר, *zera‘ 'akher*] in 4:25) and continues through Noah's "seed" (9:9) and the promise made to Abram's "seed" in 12:7. In fact, as an examination of the fifty-nine uses of "seed" in the book of Genesis reveals, "the entire book highlights the existence of a unique line of 'seed' which will eventually become a royal dynasty."[55] From Genesis 3:15 on, then, the woman's *collective seed* (i.e., those who "call on the name of the LORD" [4:26]) looked forward to and provided the lineage for the coming of her *individual seed*—"the man who would achieve the ultimate victory over the serpent."[56] This seed, as the New Testament makes plain, is none other than Jesus of Nazareth, the son of David, the son of Abraham, the son of Adam, the son of God (Luke 3:23–38; Gal 3:16, 19; 2 Tim 2:8).

Therefore, although there is no sexual desire that is unsullied by concupiscence, spousal union and the birth of children are not only a cause for rejoicing but are central to God's plan to redeem his people and "destroy the one who has the power of death, that is, the devil" (Heb 2:14; compare Gal 4:4). This, again, highlights the reality of the sex-and-gender binary and the importance of sex-and-gender connection. As Alastair Roberts writes:

> Possession of a womb is not something that can be detached from what it means to be a woman in Genesis, nor possession of a penis from what it means to be a man. It is not insignificant that circumcision and the opening of wombs are such central themes in the book [of Genesis]: the conception, bearing, and raising of children are integral to the fulfilment of God's purpose.[57]

In sum, the sex-and-gender binary and the sex-and-gender connection not only persist after the fall, but also remain necessary for human

---

54. Mathews, *Genesis 1–11:26*, 246.

55. T. Desmond Alexander, "Genealogies, Seed and the Compositional Unity of Genesis," *TB* 44 (1993): 269.

56. James M. Hamilton, "The Skull Crushing Seed of the Woman: Inner-Biblical Interpretation of Genesis 3:15," *SBJT* 10 (2006): 43.

57. Roberts, "Male and Female," 37.

marriage, the creation of human family, and, most significantly, the divine plan of salvation. This, then, brings us to consider more directly what Scripture reveals about the redemption of sex and gender.

THE REDEMPTION OF SEX AND GENDER

THE COVENANT OF GRACE

The *protoevangelium* of Genesis 3:15 naturally raises the larger question as to how its promise of deliverance will be fulfilled in the course of human history. The answer, according to the Reformed tradition, is through the covenant of grace. In this covenant, according to the Westminster Confession of Faith, God "freely offers unto sinners life and salvation by Jesus Christ; requiring of them faith in Him, that they may be saved, and promising to give unto all those that are ordained unto eternal life His Holy Spirit, to make them willing, and able to believe" (VII.3). Importantly, however, as the Confession goes on to explain, the covenant of grace has been "differently administered" in different historical epochs. For example, in its Sinaitic (or old covenant) form, "it was administered by promises, prophecies, sacrifices, circumcision, the paschal lamb, and other types and ordinances delivered to the people of the Jews, all foresignifying Christ to come" (VII.5). So understood, the covenant of grace is the foundation of all the major biblical covenants (e.g., with Noah, Abraham, Moses, and David) and comes to its final expression in the new covenant inaugurated by Jesus's blood (Jer 31:31–34; Luke 22:20; 1 Cor 11:25; 2 Cor 3:6; Heb 8:8; 9:15; 12:24). Thus, despite important contrasts and clear elements of discontinuity between old and new covenants, there are not "two covenants of grace, differing in substance, but one and the same, under various dispensations" (VII.7).[58]

For our purposes, two aspects of this one covenant are of particular relevance: its restorative purpose and the place of law within it.

58. See M. Eugene Osterhaven, "Covenant Theology," in *Evangelical Dictionary of Theology*, ed. Walter A. Elwell (Grand Rapids: Baker, 2001), 303; compare Robert L. Reymond, *A New Systematic Theology of the Christian Faith* (Nashville: Nelson, 1998), 512–35.

The restorative purpose of the covenant of grace

As to the first of these aspects, Michael Horton offers the following insight: "In the covenant of grace God restores in his new creation what was lost in the old creation and could not be recovered according to the original principle that was established in nature."[59] Redemption, then, far from abandoning creation, is aimed at its rescue and rehabilitation. This is not to deny the possibility that Adam's original state was "provisional and temporary, and could not remain as it was." Indeed, as we shall explore further when we turn to 1 Corinthians 15, it is likely that Adam was always intended to "pass on to higher glory."[60] The main point, however, has to do with the *continuity* between creation and new creation. As Oliver O'Donovan has memorably phrased it: "New creation is creation renewed, a restoration and enhancement, not an abolition."[61]

Becoming a new creation in Christ (2 Cor 5:17), however, does not mean the restoration of paradisical perfection—at least, not yet. *For full deliverance from the law of sin and death to be realized, bodily resurrection is required.* Thus, in our present state "we groan, longing to put on our heavenly dwelling" (2 Cor 5:2). Given this state of eschatological tension, Daniel Patterson is quite right to point out that "Adam and Eve in the beginning function like a universal law that teaches humanity, in its entirety, that it has been dislocated from Eden and now exists in a fallen embodied state out of which it needs to be saved."[62] Genesis 1 and 2, then, ought to make us yearn for the day when "what is mortal may be swallowed up by life" (2 Cor 5:4). Patterson is also correct to say that it makes "no theological sense" to present "Adam and Eve as a means to life"—particularly as this diverts attention from "the one true way to life, who for good reason is referred to in scripture as the second Adam."[63]

---

59. Michael S. Horton, "Post Reformation Reformed Anthropology," in *Personal Identity in Theological Perspective*, ed. Richard Lints, Michael S. Horton, and Mark R. Talbot (Grand Rapids: Eerdmans, 2006), 59.

60. Bavinck, *God and Creation*, 564.

61. Oliver O'Donovan, *Crisis in the Church: The Gay Controversy and the Anglican Communion* (Eugene, OR: Cascade, 2008), 99.

62. Daniel R. Patterson, "The Law of Adam and Eve: Judith Butler Matters, and so Does the Fall and Jesus," in *1968: Culture and Counterculture*, ed. Thomas V. Gourlay and Daniel Matthys (Eugene, OR: Pickwick, 2020), 303.

63. Patterson, "Law of Adam and Eve," 295.

Nevertheless, rejecting "the law of Adam and Eve" as *the way to life* does not mean that the primal couple have nothing to teach us about *the way of life*. In fact, Patterson confirms as much, acknowledging that "Jesus holds up Adam and Eve as God's ordained order."[64] Consequently, as we saw in the previous chapter, there is no need to play off the first Adam and his bride (Eve) against the second Adam and his bride (the church), as if only the latter "are paradigmatic for learning how to embrace the body."[65] To the contrary, as Bruce Waltke argues, Genesis 1 and 2 continue to "serve as God's founding charter for humanity. The rest of Scripture recounts the sacred story that, to a large extent, moves toward the restoration of that charter."[66]

It follows, then, that "the law of Adam and Eve" does not simply function as a measure of our defects but, like the law of God more generally, provides Christians with "a rule of life informing them of the will of God" and "directs and binds them to walk accordingly."[67] This brings us to consider the place of law in the covenant of grace.

The place of law in the covenant of grace

In Reformed thought, grace and law (when rightly construed) are not alternative pathways to salvation; rather, "they fulfill different functions: grace constitutes, law regulates."[68] The law does more than this, according to Calvin: first, it "warns, informs, convicts, and lastly condemns, every man in his own unrighteousness" and, second, it restrains those "who

---

64. Patterson, "Law of Adam and Eve," 307. Curiously, Patterson problematizes this fact by suggesting that because "Adam and Eve manifest as a vision of life that operates as a law that condemns," Jesus's reference to them creates an "ethical paradox" for the Christian (307). But the paradox is overstated. Only if the connection between creation and commandment is denied, a third use of the law rejected, and a form of antinomianism embraced, is there a conflict between "perfect vision *and* perfect law" (301, emphasis original).

65. Patterson, "Law of Adam and Eve," 293.

66. Waltke, *Old Testament Theology*, 233–34.

67. WCF, XIX.6. That the apostle Paul sees matters this way is also apparent from 1 Corinthians 14:34, where "what the law says," as most recent commentators recognize, refers to "the same text he used in his discussion of women praying and prophesying (1 Cor. 11:3–16), namely the creation narratives (Gen. 1–2)" (Claire S. Smith, *Pauline Communities as 'Scholastic Communities': A Study of the Vocabulary of 'Teaching' in 1 Corinthians, 1 and 2 Timothy and Titus* [Tübingen: Mohr Siebeck, 2012], 90; compare Roy E. Ciampa and Brian S. Rosner, *The First Letter to the Corinthians*, PNTC [Grand Rapids: Eerdmans, 2010], 727–28).

68. Letham, *Systematic Theology*, 356.

are untouched by any care for what is just and right unless compelled by hearing the dire threats in the law." But its "third and principal use"—to teach us God's will and exhort us to obey it—"pertains more closely to the proper purpose of the law." So then, while true obedience is only possible for "believers in whose hearts the Spirit of God already lives and reigns," the law remains "the best instrument for them to learn more thoroughly each day the nature of the Lord's will to which they aspire."[69] In this sense, the law is vital for sanctification.

However, as the New Testament makes plain, there are elements of Old Testament law (notably, the ceremonial and civil commands) that are either "now abrogated" or "not obliging any other now, further than the general equity thereof may require."[70] At the same time, as Article VII of the Thirty-Nine Articles of Religion insists, "no Christian man whatsoever is free from the obedience of the commandments which are called moral." In short, *the moral law alone is trans-covenantal; the civil and ceremonial laws are not*. And yet, while this tripartite division of old covenant law is a standard feature of Reformed thought, it has not gone uncriticized.[71] Its main weakness, notes D. A. Carson, "is that it attempts to construct an *a priori* grid to sort out what parts of the law Christians must keep or do, and holds that Paul must have adopted some such grid, even if he does not explicitly identify it." Nevertheless, provided we pay attention to the continuities and discontinuities established by the New Testament, he continues, "we may still usefully speak of the tripartite division from an *a posteriori* perspective."[72]

My purpose in raising this issue is not only to highlight the importance of the moral law for the covenant of grace (in all of its forms of administration) but, in light of the previous section, to endorse Christopher

---

69. Calvin, *Institutes*, 2.7.6, 10, 12.

70. WCF, XIX.3–4.

71. E.g., J. Daniel Hays, "Applying the Old Testament Law Today," *Bibliotheca Sacra* 158 (2001): 21–35.

72. D. A. Carson, "Mystery and Fulfillment: Toward a More Comprehensive Paradigm of Paul's Understanding of the Old and New," in *The Paradoxes of Paul*, vol. 2 of *Justification and Variegated Nomism*, ed. D. A. Carson, Peter T. O'Brien, and Mark A. Seifrid (Grand Rapids: Baker Academic, 2004), 429 (emphasis original); compare Ronald M. Rothenberg, "Relation of the Tripartite Division of the Law and the Public/Private Distinction: Examining the Streams of Thought Behind Them," *JETS* 61 (2018): 805–23.

Wright's claim that "the purpose of the ethical provisions given in redemption, which include both the covenant law of the Old Testament and the ethics of the kingdom of God in the New, is to restore to humans the desire and the ability to conform to the creational pattern—God's original purpose for them."[73] In this sense, the "biblical commands are not arbitrary decrees but correspond to the way the world is and will be."[74] This is why there is no ultimate conflict between biblical law and natural law (properly understood). As we are about to see, this is particularly important to appreciate when it comes to commands that give shape to the Bible's sexual ethics.

DEUTERONOMY 22:5

We turn then to the first of two prohibitions relevant to our study of sex and gender in old covenant law: Deuteronomy 22:5: "A *woman* [*'ishah*] shall not wear a *man's garment* [כְּלִי- גֶבֶר, *keli-gever*], nor shall a *man* [גֶּבֶר, *gever*] put on a *woman's cloak* [שִׂמְלַת אִשָּׁה, *simlath 'ishah*], for whoever does these things is an *abomination* [תּוֹעֵבָה, *to'evah*] to the LORD your God."

Revisionist interpretations of the verse

This text has frequently been regarded as a straightforward injunction against transvestitism and, by inference, all forms of gender-bending or cross-sex identification. As such, it is typically termed "a text of terror" by those who identify "as butch lesbians, or drag queens/kings, or are transsexuals."[75]

However, queer commentators and trans-affirming authors have not only disputed this reading but have argued that applying the verse to transgenderism "is neither exegetically nor hermeneutically sound."[76] Susannah Cornwall, for example, is particularly critical of interpretations that merge "travestitism (changing clothes) and transsexualism (changing

73. Christopher J. H. Wright, *Walking in the Ways of the Lord: The Ethical Authority of the Old Testament* (Downers Grove, IL: InterVarsity Press, 1995), 44.

74. Richard Bauckham, *God and the Crisis of Freedom: Biblical and Contemporary Perspectives* (Louisville: Westminster John Knox, 2002), 70.

75. Deryn Guest, "Deuteronomy," in Guest, Goss, West, and Bohache, *The Queer Bible Commentary*, 133.

76. Cornwall, *Sex and Uncertainty*, 134.

body)," contending that there is "no suggestion that, by wearing a woman's garment, a man *becomes* a woman; the issue is that he could be *mistaken* for a woman, which matters very much in a context where women and men operate in clearly-defined and segregated spaces." For her, then, the prohibition arises solely from the Hebrew concern "with not 'mixing' (or mixing-up) things which should remain distinct."[77]

Similarly, on the basis of William Countryman's blanket dismissal of the contemporary relevance of all of the mixing prohibitions in Israel's holiness code, Virginia Mollenkott deems it "ludicrously selective to invoke Deuteronomy 22:5 against cross-dressers."[78] Justin Tanis too concurs, claiming that "the most compelling argument against this passage as a prohibition against cross-dressing is that we fail to follow any of the other directives around it."[79] Taking a rather different approach, Linda Tatro Herzer sees the verse as an enduring warning to people "to *not* dress in a way that would hide their true identity and deceive others in a harmful way." But what this means, she argues, is that it is "an exhortation to modern-day gender variant individuals not to hide themselves, but to dress in the clothes that truly reflect their internal sense of themselves!"[80]

The meaning and implications of the verse

Rather than engaging in a direct critique of these interpretations, I offer the following nine points in order to clarify the meaning and implications of Deuteronomy 22:5.

First, while the verse appears to sit oddly in its immediate context (i.e., vv. 1–4 and 6–8), it is not the case that the "broader context of the verse is of little help."[81] Indeed, from a literary perspective, verse 5 anticipates the prohibitions against a range of other mixtures (in vv. 9–11), as well as the laws governing sexual relations between men and women (in vv. 13–30).

---

77. Cornwall, *Sex and Uncertainty*, 134–35 (emphasis original).

78. Mollenkott, *Omnigender*, 104 (referencing L. William Countryman, *Dirt, Greed, and Sex: Sexual Ethics in the New Testament and their Implications for Today* [Philadelphia: Fortress, 1988], 26–27).

79. Tanis, *Trans-gender*, 66.

80. Herzer, *Transgender Experience*, 38–39 (emphasis original).

81. Harold Torger Vedeler, "Reconstructing Meaning in Deuteronomy 22:5: Gender, Society, and Transvestitism in Israel and the Ancient Near East," *JBL* 127 (2008): 460.

This fact alone suggests that the text's primary concern is "the breaking of God's order for gender distinction."[82]

Second, while the word translated *man* (*gever*) is not the more common term (*'ish*), to argue that it bears the specific meaning of *warrior*, as some commentators have,[83] is not only to confuse the noun with the adjective (which means *mighty* [Gen 10:8–9; Deut 10:17]), but to ignore the fact that "within the Pentateuch all other instances of *gever* simply overlap in meaning with *'ish*, showing up in contexts that distinguish the men from the young (Exod 10:7, 11) or from women and children (12:37)."[84]

Third, as for the word translated *garment* (*keli*), although this too is not the typical word for male clothing (but means, more broadly, *implement* or *vessel*), it is again needlessly restrictive to translate it as the "gear of a warrior."[85] As its use in the Old Testament makes clear, it is a word that could be applied to virtually "any object associated with men."[86] This means that while it can refer to weapons (compare Deut 1:41), it more likely refers to "anything that is worn as a symbol of maleness."[87]

Fourth, by way of contrast, the word translated *cloak* (*simlah*) refers unambiguously to clothing—either "a cloak, mantle, wrap, or other garment that a woman wears."[88] This, then, tells against restricting the meaning of *keli* and suggests that it too is primarily a reference to clothing. This further strengthens the case that the prohibition is against cross-dressing and "aimed at deliberate attempts to confuse genders," regarding such acts as violations of "the clear sexual distinctions created by God."[89]

Fifth, the seriousness of the prohibition is highlighted by the application of the Hebrew word *to'evah* ("abominable, detestable, offensive

---

82. Ajith Fernando, *Deuteronomy: Loving Obedience to a Loving God* (Wheaton, IL: Crossway, 2012), 508.

83. E.g., J. Gordon McConville, *Deuteronomy*, AOTC (Downers Grove, IL: InterVarsity Press, 2002), 337.

84. DeRouchie, "Transgender Storm," 63.

85. Duane L. Christensen, *Deuteronomy 21:10-34:12*, WBC 6B (Waco, TX: Word, 2002), 494.

86. DeRouchie, "Transgender Storm," 63.

87. Gary Harlan Hall, *Deuteronomy: The College Press NIV Commentary* (Joplin, MO: The College Press, 2000), 330.

88. Hilary Lipka, "The Prohibition of Cross-Dressing: What does Deuteronomy 22:5 Prohibit and Why?," *TheTorah.com – A Historical and Contextual Approach* (N.D.), 2, https://thetorah.com/the-prohibition-of-cross-dressing.

89. Hall, *Deuteronomy*, 330.

thing"[90]) to "whoever does these things." Within Deuteronomy, this term is most often applied to idolatrous practices (7:25–26; 12:31; 13:14; 17:1, 4; 20:18; 27:15; 32:16). However, it is noteworthy that it is also applied to both male and female prostitution (23:18) and, in the book of Leviticus, to male homosexual intercourse (Lev 18:22; 20:13).

Sixth, the use of *toʿevah* in Deuteronomy 22:5 has led some scholars to argue that the reason cross-dressing is forbidden is because "some form of serious immorality or idolatry was involved."[91] For Gordon McConville, the prohibition is intended "either to discourage homosexuality, or to prohibit transvestite practices found in Canaanite and Mesopotamian worship."[92] For Wright, it relates to either "orgiastic rites involving transvestitism," or "some form of pagan worship, or both."[93] Without disputing the relevance of this background, not only is there no reference to it anywhere in the chapter, but the general nature of the wording of verse 5 indicates, as Davidson rightly discerns, that it "goes beyond a cult setting to include any and all circumstances of men dressing like women and vice versa."[94] This is evident from the expression "whoever does *these things* [אֵלֶּה, *ʾelleh*]," where the "things" on view are, specifically, the *actions* of cross-dressing, not the *reasons* for or *consequences* of such behavior.

Seventh, these observations strongly suggest that the principal purpose of the command is "to preserve the order built into creation, specifically the fundamental distinction between male and female."[95] As Davidson writes: "cross-dressing is morally/cultically repugnant to God ... primarily ... because it mixes/blurs the basic distinctions of gender duality (male and female) set forth in creation."[96] This explains why anyone who "blurs these divinely ordered distinctions" is deemed "an abomination to the Lord."[97]

---

90. Michael A. Grisanti, "תָּעַב," *NIDOTTE* 4:314.

91. E.g., J. Gary Millar, *Now Choose Life: Theology and Ethics in Deuteronomy*, NSBT 6 (Leicester: Apollos, 1998), 135.

92. McConville, *Deuteronomy*, 337.

93. Christopher J. H. Wright, *Deuteronomy*, UBC (Grand Rapids: Baker, 1996), 241.

94. Davidson, *Flame of Yahweh*, 171.

95. Daniel I. Block, *Deuteronomy: The NIV Application Commentary* (Grand Rapids: Zondervan, 2012), 512.

96. Davidson, *Flame of Yahweh*, 172.

97. Eugene H. Merrill, *Deuteronomy*, NAC (Nashville: Broadman & Holman, 1994), 297.

Eighth, it follows, then, that Deuteronomy 22:5 has abiding moral significance and cannot be dismissed as a bygone irrelevance. Even those who are less persuaded of the tripartism of the Reformed tradition, and who take a more principlist approach to the present application of old covenant law, hold that the verse is "instructive for the church in helping us recognize the appropriate path for gender expression and the sinfulness of gender confusion, which includes cross-dressing and transgender practice."[98]

Ninth, as Jason DeRouchie argues, Deuteronomy 22:5 would seem to have two clear implications for contemporary Christians: (1) "to let their gender expression align with their biological sex"; and (2) "to guard against gender confusion, wherein others could wrongly perceive a man to be a woman and a woman to be a man based on dress."[99] To this end, the Christian's aim should be to "present himself or herself in such a way that represents the appropriate gender expression of biological sex."[100]

In sum, irrespective of the particular historico-cultural form that gender expression takes, biologically grounded gender differences "are part of God's good creation and should be celebrated rather than confused." As a creation-based command given within the context of the covenant of redemption, "Deuteronomy 22:5 gives us a biblical admonition to maintain such gender differences in our outward expressions to society."[101] Therefore, while care must be taken in applying this text (and needlessly narrow gender stereotypes ought to be resisted), it is not "doing a disservice to reasonable hermeneutics" to acknowledge its implications for transgender expression today.[102]

---

98. DeRouchie, "Transgender Storm," 66.

99. DeRouchie, "Transgender Storm," 63.

100. Mark D. Liederbach and Evan Lenow, *Ethics as Worship: The Pursuit of Moral Discipleship* (Phillipsburg, NJ: P&R, 2021), 598.

101. Liederbach and Lenow, *Ethics as Worship*, 599.

102. Contra Evangelical Alliance, *Transsexuality*, 47. However, see fn. 5, which modifies this verdict.

DEUTERONOMY 23:1 (MT 23:2)

We come now to the second of the prohibitions relevant to our study of sex and gender in old covenant law: Deuteronomy 23:1: "No one whose testicles [פְּצוּעַ, *phetsua'*] are crushed [דַּכָּא, *dakka*] or whose male organ [שָׁפְכָה, *shophkah*] is cut off [כְּרוּת, *kheruth*] shall enter the assembly of the LORD."

Trans-affirming reactions to the command

This text is not only frequently discussed in the trans-affirming literature, but more than one author admits to wrestling personally with whether it stands as an abiding prohibition "against any kind of bodily modification of sex characteristics."[103] The (self-described) "Jewish, transgender, working-class revolutionary" Leslie Feinberg initially believed this to be the case, but eventually came to view the command as "trans-phobic and gender-phobic," the product of wealthy Hebrew males "trying to consolidate their patriarchal rule."[104] Tanis, who appears to take the authority of the text more seriously, confesses to taking refuge in the fact that "the vast majority of modern people of faith clearly do not heed the prohibitions from this section of Deuteronomy."[105] Nevertheless, "the Big Question," as Mollenkott rightly espies, is not whether the verse is currently being heeded, but whether it "forbids gender reassignment surgery and, if so, whether that law should be applied to contemporary transsexuals."[106]

To answer this question, I will, first, clarify the nature of the command; second, attempt to discern its rationale; third, assess its abiding significance in the light of subsequent revelation; and fourth, explore its relevance to the practice of GRS.

The nature of the command

As to *the nature of the command,* while not excluding emasculated males from the nation, Deuteronomy 23:1 clearly prohibits their attendance at all formal gatherings of the people of Israel (e.g., "festival occasions and other times of public worship").[107] Interestingly, Peter Craigie suggests

---

103. Hartke, *Transforming,* 88.

104. Feinberg, *Transgender Warriors,* 53, 50.

105. Tanis, *Trans-gender,* 68.

106. Mollenkott, *Omnigender,* 134.

107. Merrill, *Deuteronomy,* 307.

that the command was most likely aimed at those who had engaged in self-castration for idolatrous purposes, and so was "probably not intended to bar from the community those whose state of emasculation had been brought on by accident or illness."[108] But the text makes no discrimination of this kind. Moreover, in view of Deuteronomy's earlier proscription on sacrificing animals with any kind of injury, defect, or blemish (15:21; compare Lev 22:24–25), as well as the injunctions in Leviticus 21:16–24 against those with disfigurements or disabilities (including "crushed testicles" [v. 20]) performing priestly duties, the cause of emasculation would appear to be immaterial. In other words, whether the damage to a man's genitalia was intentional or accidental, the outcome was identical: exclusion from the LORD's assembly.

The rationale of the command

As to *the command's rationale,* those who see a reference to idolatrous self-mutilation have often viewed it as a protest against the castration rituals that are thought to have been part of Canaanite religion. Thus, Eugene Merrill suggests that the text is designed "to underscore the principle of separation from paganism, where such deformities were not only acceptable but frequently central to the practice of the cult."[109] Again, while this is possible, nothing in the verse or its context suggests as much. What is more likely is that the command arises from the conviction that defacing the human body is "inconsistent with the character of Jehovah's people."[110] This is certainly the basis for the related prohibition in 14:1–2a: "You shall not cut yourselves or make any baldness on your foreheads for the dead. *For you are a people holy to the LORD your God*" (compare 23:14). Furthermore, given the link forged in Leviticus between holiness and wholeness,[111] Deuteronomy 23:1 appears to be a way of urging "a concrete statement of this wholeness in unmutilated members of the covenant

---

108. Peter C. Craigie, *The Book of Deuteronomy,* NICOT (Grand Rapids: Eerdmans, 1976), 296–97.

109. Merrill, *Deuteronomy,* 307.

110. Samuel Rolles Driver, *A Critical Commentary on Deuteronomy,* ICC (New York: Scribner's Sons, 1902), 260.

111. E.g., Saul M. Olyan, "Mary Douglas's Holiness/Wholeness Paradigm: Its Potential for Insight and its Limitations," *Journal of Hebrew Scriptures* 8 (2008): art. 10, 1–9 , https://doi.org/10.5508/jhs.2008.v8.a10.

tribal assembly."[112] Wright takes this a step further, concluding that the command expresses *both* "a concern for wholeness *and* a rejection of that which appeared to mutilate nature and God's design for creation (compare 14:1)."[113]

The command's focus on male genitalia, however, indicates that its intent is even more precise: it is not concerned with a general disfiguring of a man's bodily integrity but with a particular deficit in a man's sexual anatomy. For Cornwall, this shows the main problem to be an inability to "participate in procreation or ritual circumcision."[114] Gagnon disagrees: for him, the command has "everything to do with maintaining gender distinctions."[115] Philo, similarly, argues that it is aimed at "men who belie their sex and are affected with effemination" (literally, "female androgyne disease" [*τήν θήλειαν νόσον ανδρογύνων, tēn thēleian noson androgynōn*])." It thus "expels those whose generative organs are fractured or mutilated, who husband the flower of their youthful bloom, lest it should quickly wither, and restamp the masculine cast into a feminine form."[116] In ascribing a particular motive to a self-inflicted act, however, Philo speculates beyond the text. As I have noted, the verse itself makes no mention of either intention or self-castration; the fact of genital damage is the problem, the cause is left open: anyone "whose testicles are crushed or whose male organ is cut off."[117] In other words, the rationale for excluding eunuchs from the assembly lies solely in their bodily condition, not in how or why it has come about. While the reason this is deemed problematic is less certain, a combined concern for genital integrity, sexual clarity, and procreative ability seems likely.

The abiding significance of the command

As to *the command's abiding significance*, the first point to be made is one on which trans-affirming and non-affirming scholars agree. The Evangelical Alliance Report (2000) expresses it this way: "In relation

112. Davidson, *Flame of Yahweh*, 326.

113. Wright, *Deuteronomy*, 247 (emphasis added).

114. Cornwall, *Sex and Uncertainty*, 136.

115. Gagnon, *Homosexual Practice*, 135, compare 175–76n21.

116. Philo, *On the Special Laws*, I.325, in *On the Decalogue. On the Special Laws, Books 1–3*, trans. F. H. Colson, LCL (Cambridge: Harvard University Press, 1937), 289.

117. The fact that כְּרוּת is a passive Qal participle highlights the indeterminacy of the agent.

to Deuteronomy 23:1, there is a clear progression in Scripture which culminates in the implied acceptance of the genitally-mutilated by Jesus in Matthew 19:12, and the conversion, baptism and acceptance into the kingdom of God of the Ethiopian eunuch in Acts 8:26–39."[118] This development, as Megan DeFranza correctly discerns, is part of the broader "movement from the Old to the New Testament"—a movement that allows, if not requires, certain laws to be made redundant (e.g., "laws about mixing things that should be distinct, laws guarding the boundaries of Israel's identity").[119] We shall return to the reasons for this development shortly.

It is also agreed that Isaiah 56:3–5 prophesies this change:

> 3 Let not the foreigner who has joined himself to the LORD say,
> "The LORD will surely separate me from his people";
> and let not the eunuch say,
> "Behold, I am a dry tree."
> 4 For thus says the LORD:
> "To the eunuchs who keep my Sabbaths,
> who choose the things that please me
> and hold fast my covenant,
> 5 I will give in my house and within my walls
> a monument and a name
> better than sons and daughters;
> I will give them an everlasting name
> that shall not be cut off.

As verse 4 confirms, this oracle functions as a word of comfort to "those Israelites who without becoming unfaithful to YHWH have been 'cut' against their will in foreign courts and now fear they will be judged as dry trees, unworthy to dwell among God's people in Israel."[120] In this sense, McConville is right to see the eunuchs here addressed as being in a "different category" to those whose mutilation was "a mark of a particular religious commitment."[121] And yet, as we have seen, the exclusion

118. Evangelical Alliance, *Transsexuality*, 46.

119. DeFranza, "Good News," 165.

120. Herman Bavinck, *Reformed Ethics: The Duties of the Christian Life: Volume Two*, ed. John Bolt (Grand Rapids: Baker, 2021), 24–25.

121. McConville, *Deuteronomy*, 348–49.

demanded by Deuteronomy 23:1 is broader than this. Therefore, what is being promised by Isaiah is not only a reward for faithfulness but an inclusion that was previously not possible even for the faithful. In short, a day is coming when Deuteronomy 23:1 will be abrogated.

Interestingly, the concern put into the mouth of the eunuch in verse 3 "is not explicitly related to God excluding him from temple worship but is connected to his status as a 'dry tree' "—that is, as one who is unable to produce descendants.[122] Nevertheless, verse 5 not only addresses this lack (guaranteeing something "better than sons and daughters") but also promises permanent access to God's *house* (i.e., his temple [בַּיִת, *bayith*]), where an eternal memorial will be established and a name given that will never be "cut off" (כָּרַת, *karath,* compare Deut 23:1).[123] It is difficult to overstate the extraordinary nature of this promise to covenant-keeping eunuchs. As Alec Motyer expresses, in Isaiah's vision of postexilic Israel gathered in the new temple, every faithful eunuch "is there in his own person (*name*) and is enriched with blessings far beyond those which even an earthly family (*sons and daughters*) might have brought."[124]

How, then, do we best explain what Westermann calls "the revolutionary nature of the change here made on the Deuteronomic regulation"?[125] The answer lies in the eschatological realization of the Isaianic promise. The gathering of "the outcasts of Israel" and the "yet others" (i.e., gentiles!) "besides those already gathered" (v. 8) is what creates a "house of prayer for all peoples" (v. 7). This, according to Isaiah 2, is a reality that "shall come to pass in the latter days," when "the mountain of the house of the Lord shall be established as the highest of the mountains" and "all the nations shall flow to it" (2:2). In other words, the inclusion of eunuchs is tied to the exaltation of the new temple, the restoration of Israel, and the salvation of the gentiles.

---

122. Gary V. Smith, *Isaiah 40–66*, NAC 15B (Nashville: Broadman & Holman, 2009), 533.

123. The clear intertexual reference to Deuteronomy 23:1, underscored by the repetition of כרת, further supports John Watts's insight that the "prohibition is now removed on Yahweh's authority" (John D. W. Watts, *Isaiah 34–66*, WBC 25 [Waco, TX: Word, 1987], 249).

124. Alec Motyer, *The Prophecy of Isaiah* (Leicester: Inter-Varsity Press, 1993), 466 (emphasis original).

125. Claus Westermann, *Isaiah 40–66: A Commentary* (Philadelphia: Westminster, 1969), 313.

Most importantly, however, for this future to be realized, it must be preceded by the atoning work of the suffering servant (42:1–4; 49:1–6; 50:4–11; 52:13–53:12). This is why it is not surprising that in the account of the fulfillment of this prophecy in Acts 8, a citation from Isaiah 53 is at the heart of the narrative. Moreover, by repeatedly identifying the Ethiopian official as a *eunouchos* (vv. 27, 34, 36, 38 and 39), it is likely that Luke "intentionally echoed Isaiah 56:1–8 in order to suggest its fulfillment through Jesus Christ."[126] In other words, it is because Christ has brought this promise to pass that "nothing hindered the eunuch from being a full-fledged follower of the one in whom Isaiah's promises were being fulfilled."[127] This is why the answer to his question in verse 36—"What prevents me from being baptized?"—is simple: nothing whatsoever. His believing response to Philip's message is all that is required for "inclusion within the new community inaugurated by the risen suffering servant, Jesus Christ."[128]

Deuteronomy 23:1, then, like the ceremonial laws of the old covenant more generally, was one of the "*regulations for the body* [*δικαιώματα σαρκὸς, dikaiōmata sarkos*] imposed until the time of reformation" (Heb 9:10)—that is, the inauguration of the new covenant. Now that time has come and, "through the greater and more perfect tent (not made with hands, that is, not of this creation)" (9:11), Christ has "entered once for all into the holy places ... by means of his own blood," he has not only secured "an eternal redemption" for all who are called (9:12, 15), but "has perfected for all time those who are being sanctified" (10:14). Consequently, no bodily deformity, including genital mutilation, can prevent those who "draw near with a true heart in full assurance of faith" from entering "the holy places by the blood of Jesus" (10:19, 22). Hallelujah!

126. Sarah J. Melcher, "A Tale of Two Eunuchs: Isaiah 56:1–8 and Acts 8:26–40," in *Disability Studies and Biblical Literature*, ed. Candida R. Moss and Jeremy Schipper (New York: Palgrave MacMillan, 2011), 126.

127. Ben Witherington III, *The Acts of the Apostles: A Socio-Rhetorical Commentary* (Grand Rapids: Eerdmans, 1998), 296.

128. Cox, *Intersex in Christ*, 85.

The contemporary relevance of the command

Given that Deuteronomy 23:1 has been thought to provide grounds not only "for the rejection of sex reassignment as a viable treatment for transsexuals, but further, for rejection of post-operative transsexuals from the community of faith,"[129] what can be said about *its relevance to the practice of GRS today*?

The first point that needs to be made is that the abrogation of Deuteronomy 23:1 in the new covenant is good news for anyone who (to employ the broad rabbinic categories referenced by Jesus in Matthew 19:12) is either a eunuch "from birth" (סְרִיס חַמָּה, *saris khama*) or has been made a eunuch "by men" (סְרִיס אָדָם, *saris 'adam*).[130] This, then, includes *both* those with intersex conditions that render them infertile *and* those who, for one reason or another, have undergone sterilization or castration (including for reasons of gender dysphoria). The prohibition that once applied, does so no longer.

However, it is important to recognize that *the promise of Isaiah 56 is not made to all without distinction.* It is applicable only to those who "choose the things that please [the LORD] and hold fast [his] covenant" (v. 4). Similarly, its fulfillment in Acts 8 is dependent on the eunuch's repentant and believing response to "the good news about Jesus," evidenced by his request for baptism (vv. 35–36). This raises the question as to what it means for a person who has engaged in cross-sex identification or has undertaken GRS to "bear fruits in keeping with repentance" (Matt 3:8; Luke 3:8) and to live in a way that pleases the Lord (Eph 5:10; Col 1:10; 1 Thess 4:1).

As Genesis 1–2 establishes, and Deuteronomy 22:5 confirms, "what is gender normative in God's world is that one's biological sex should govern both one's gender identity and expression."[131] The relaxing of Deuteronomy 23:1 does nothing to alter this. Furthermore, given that the purpose of redemption is to restore "what we have corrupted and distorted, including

---

129. Kolakowski, "Transsexual Persons," 20.

130. See further Charlotte Elisheva Fonrobert, "Gender Identity in Halakhic Discourse," *Shalvi/Hyman Encyclopedia of Jewish Women* (December 31, 1999), https://jwa.org/encyclopedia/article/gender-identity-in-halakhic-discourse.

131. DeRouchie, "Transgender Storm," 62.

what we have distorted in our sexuality,"[132] the abrogation of the prohibition cannot be taken as an encouragement to engage in cross-sex identification or genital surgery aimed at approximating the appearance of the opposite sex.

Of course, for those who have undergone GRS, there may be little that can be done to reverse the steps that have been taken. If so, as Russell Moore counsels, a former trans woman may need to learn to see himself as the equivalent of a self-made eunuch—that is, "someone wounded physically by his past sin, but awaiting wholeness in the resurrection from the dead."[133] Nevertheless, ceasing CHT, cross-dressing, and identifying contrary to their biological sex is the way of honesty. Therefore, while I agree with DeFranza that "people should not be judged by whether they had had an operation on their genitals but by their relationship with God—a relationship based on grace through faith,"[134] *pursuing faithfulness means living (as much as is possible) in harmony with one's God-given sex.*

CONCLUDING REFLECTIONS

Because the scriptural survey begun in this chapter will be continued in the next, only a brief concluding reflection is required at this point.

We have seen thus far that while the fall has introduced a distortion into human nature that has a direct effect on all aspects and expressions of human sexuality (including gender identity, roles, and expression), "redemption does not turn us from sexuality; it illumines the goodness of it."[135] It does this not simply by reaffirming its created nature and intended purpose, but by protecting and promoting holy and healthy sexuality—notably through the sanctifying gift of the law, which reveals the way *of* life. Moreover, as we shall see in the next chapter, redemption moves us toward God's final purpose—the full restoration and total transformation of the created order.

Outside of Eden, then, things have not changed essentially: the sexed body continues to determine the gendered self. Accordingly, *our present*

---

132. Lewis B. Smedes, *Sex for Christians* (Grand Rapids: Eerdmans, 1976), 104.

133. Russell D. Moore, "Joan or John? An Ethical Dilemma," *SBJT* 13, no. 2 (2009): 52–56.

134. DeFranza, "Good News," 173.

135. Smedes, *Sex for Christians*, 104.

task is to work with the grain of creation toward the goal of new creation. In practice, this means that

> whatever we are by creation, we must affirm: our rationality, our sense of moral obligation, our masculinity and femininity. ... All this is part of our created humanness. ... But whatever we are by the Fall, we must deny or repudiate: our irrationality; our moral perversity; our loss of sexual distinctives. ... All this is part of our fallen humanness.[136]

Given the legacy of original sin, however, pursuing such a course is not only exceedingly difficult (indeed it is impossible without the new birth promised in the new covenant) but also contains a fundamental epistemological challenge. O'Donovan states it this way:

> In speaking of man's fallenness we point to an inescapable confusion in his perceptions of it. This does not permit us to follow the Stoic recipe for "life in accord with nature" without a measure of epistemological guardedness. ... Together with man's essential involvement in created order and his rebellious discontent with it, we must reckon also upon the opacity and obscurity of that order to the human mind which has rejected the knowledge of its Creator.[137]

O'Donovan's point is that fallen human beings are not readily able to deduce the true nature and purpose of creation simply by means of empirical observation and rational reflection. Special revelation is required. This does not mean that "there is no *ontological* ground for an 'ethic of nature' "; it means, rather, that our *epistemological* certainty "about the order which God has made depends upon God's own disclosure of himself and of his works."[138] This highlights our need to listen carefully to Scripture so that, despite the disruption and distortion that sin's entrance into the world has wrought, the significance of our embodied sex might be rightly discerned and the psychosocial dimensions of that sex (i.e., our gender identity,

---

136. John R. W. Stott, "Am I Supposed to Love Myself or Hate Myself?: The Cross Points the Way between Self-Love and Self-Denial," in *Christ the Cornerstone: Collected Essays of John Stott* (Bellingham, WA: Lexham, 2019), 70. First published in *CT* 28, no. 7 (April 20, 1984): 26–28.

137. O'Donovan, *Resurrection and Moral Order*, 19.

138. O'Donovan, *Resurrection and Moral Order*, 19 (emphasis original).

gender roles and gender expression) might be accurately perceived and authentically expressed.

In this way, scriptural revelation serves the goal of redemption. The creator's purpose is not to abandon or abolish the created order but to rehabilitate and reintegrate that which has been wounded and fragmented by sin. However, because the experience of God's saving mercies is *both now and not-yet*, much of the damage borne by our mortal bodies (whether congenital or acquired) will not be undone in this present age. Nevertheless, there is both a promise of present inclusion and the prospect of future resurrection for all who repent and believe in Jesus Christ. This, then, brings us to the final chapter, where we shall explore the importance of Jesus's person and work, the nature of life in Christ, and the hope of bodily resurrection.

CHAPTER 11

SEX AND GENDER IN THE END

Humankind no longer lives in the beginning; instead it has lost the beginning. Now it finds itself in the middle, knowing neither the end nor the beginning, and yet knowing that it is in the middle.[1]

—Dietrich Bonhoeffer

The authors of Gen. 2 and the Song of Songs speak of man and woman as they do because they know that the broken covenant is still for God the unbroken covenant, intact and fulfilled on both sides; that as such it was already the inner basis of creation, and that as such it will again be revealed at the end.[2]

—Karl Barth

The aim of this final chapter is to complete the task commenced in the previous one, focusing especially on the relevant aspects of the doctrines of redemption and consummation as these are expounded at key points in the New Testament.

The chapter is divided into three main sections. The first examines the importance of Christology and some of the issues that arise from Jesus's

1. Bonhoeffer, *Creation and Fall*, 28.

2. Barth, *CD*, III/1, 314–15.

person, work, and teaching. The second explores a number of key aspects of soteriology—notably, the nature of the Christian life and what it means to be a man or woman "in Christ." The third expounds the most relevant element of biblical eschatology: the resurrection of the body. Once again, the bulk of the chapter will be composed of a series of brief exegetical explorations of the key texts that illumine the relationship between identity and embodiment, not only in the present age but also in the age to come. Discerning what Scripture reveals about sex and gender in the end will help to bring our evaluation of trans theory to completion.

THE PERSON, WORK, AND TEACHING OF CHRIST

THE HUMANITY OF JESUS

The Niceno-Constantinopolitan Creed summarizes what the New Testament teaches: that "the only Son of God, eternally begotten of the Father ... was incarnate of the Virgin Mary, and became man."[3] As the apostle John expresses it: "the Word became flesh and dwelt among us" (John 1:14). In becoming flesh, however, the Word did not cease to be divine (John 1:1); rather, "the Son or Logos remained who he eternally was and is."[4] The church fathers, then, were right to affirm that in the one person of Jesus Christ, the divine nature of the eternal Son exists in hypostatic union with his human nature. Consequently, as the Athanasian Creed asserts, he is *both* "God, of the Substance of the Father, begotten before the worlds; *and* Man, of the Substance of his Mother, born in the world." Indeed, it is this dual reality that enables him to serve as the "one mediator between God and men [εἷς μεσίτης θεοῦ καὶ ἀνθρώπων, *heis mesitēs theou kai anthrōpōn*]" (1 Tim 2:5).[5]

My primary interest in the points that follow is the reality of Jesus's humanity and the particularity of his embodied sex. My wider concern, however, is not only christological but anthropological. For if there is one

3. Douglas McCready, *He Came Down from Heaven: The Preexistence of Christ and the Christian Faith* (Downers Grove, IL: IVP Academic, 2005), 313–15.

4. Letham, *Systematic Theology*, 471.

5. A. T. B. McGowan, *The Person and Work of Christ: Understanding Jesus* (Milton Keynes: Paternoster, 2012), 58.

thing that the last century of biblical reflection on theological anthropology has revealed, it is that "the mystery of man reveals itself fully only in the light of Christ."[6] Or as Bonhoeffer laconically states it: "Man becomes man because God becomes man."[7]

Three points are briefly explored here: the first concerns the way in which the process of the incarnation affirms the goodness of female sexuality; the second concerns the reality and significance of Jesus's male body; the third addresses the question: Can a male Messiah save females?

Born of a woman

The incarnation means that *for the Son of God to become a human person, he needed to become a human body*. Unlike the first Adam, however, he did not arrive in the world as a fully formed adult male. Rather, he developed in the same way that all children of Adam do: he had "to become a fetus in the womb, a baby in a cot, a toddler stumbling about as he learned to walk, a teenager going through puberty, a fully grown man."[8] This does not mean that Jesus passed through "every age, becoming an infant for infants" and "an old man for old men" (even living into his fifties), as Irenaeus taught.[9] It simply means that his experience of embodiment encompassed the key stages of human life—from childhood to adulthood.

The beginning of Jesus's embodiment process was, of course, utterly and miraculously unique. According to the Gospels, he was divinely conceived in the womb of his mother, Mary (Matt 1:23; Luke 1:31, 35). But once conceived, his body was entirely dependent on hers. This not only highlights the reality of Jesus's humanity but the importance of Mary's—particularly her sex, with all its exclusively female reproductive and nurturing capacities. Indeed, one is hard pressed, writes Eric Johnson, "to think of a more profound way of underscoring the unique gift of childbearing. Mary as woman illustrates the essential link of biology and gender

6. John D. Zizioulas, "Human Capacity and Human Incapacity: A Theological Exploration of Personhood," *Scottish Journal of Theology* 28 (1975): 433.

7. Dietrich Bonhoeffer, *Ethics*, ed. Eberhard Bethge (New York: Macmillan, 1962), 20.

8. Allberry, *What God Has to Say*, 20.

9. Irenaeus, *Against Heresies*, 2.22.4 (*ANF* 1:391).

that is often minimized in feminist discussions"[10]—and, we might add, outrightly denied by transgender theory.

By his incarnation, then, the Son of God affirms not only the goodness of human embodiment (including his own male body), but the goodness of female sexuality. Both pre- and post-partum, the Son of God depended for his human life on the reality and integrity of Mary's sex. As Johnson again remarks: "Possessing a womb and breasts provides the biological basis for a singular interpersonal experience that in turn paves the way for a special relationship with and ministry to one's children."[11]

So, precisely because Mary's sex enabled her to serve the Son of God in this way, Jesus was truly "the *son* of Mary" (Mark 6:3) and Mary was truly "the *mother* of Jesus" (John 2:1, 3; Acts 1:14). The incarnation, then, reinforces what Scripture everywhere makes plain (e.g., Gen 4:1–2; 1 Cor 11:11–12): "there is no male sexuality without female sexuality."[12]

But it does more than this; it honors the particular glory of womanhood (generally) and motherhood (specifically). It is not merely that the Son of God "did not abhor the virgin's womb";[13] he exalts female sexuality and venerates the unique God-given powers of the female body. It is difficult to imagine a more potent antidote to the long, ugly history of misogyny and to low views of the female body.

The maleness of Jesus

We turn now to consider the reality and significance of Jesus's maleness. The Messiah did not come as a bigendered being, nor did God send male and female twins to save sinners. Rather, the eternal Word became flesh as *a human male*. This, of course, was foreshadowed by numerous prophetic predictions that "the one who is to come" (Matt 11:3; Luke 17:19) will be born as "a *son*" (בֵּן, *ben*, Isa 7:14; 9:6), become a "*man* of sorrows" (אִישׁ מַכְאֹבוֹת, *'ish makh'ovoth*, Isa 53:3), and will reign as an

10. Eric L. Johnson, "Playing Games and Living Metaphors: The Incarnation and the End of Gender," *JETS* 40 (1997): 272–73.

11. Johnson, "Playing Games," 273.

12. Wilson, *Mere Sexuality*, 46.

13. The Latin expression *non horruisti virginis uterum* first appears in the fourth-century hymn *Te Deum laudamus* (Lat. "God, We Praise You").

explicitly *male* savior and ruler (Gen 3:15; 49:10; 2 Sam 7:12–13; Ps 2:6–7; Isa 11:1–5). At a deeper metaphysical level, it is also consonant with Jesus's identity as the incarnate *Son*—that is, the preexistent Son who became a man. Otherwise put, the reason Jesus is called the Son is not because he was born as a male; rather, he was born as a male because he was (and is) the Son. Christ's sex, then, was not arbitrary, nor was it left to chance; rather, "in the divine overshadowing of Mary, God supplied the precise chromosome that determined the child's gender."[14]

With the exception of the Docetists (who, by casting doubt on the reality of Jesus's humanity, provoked the ire of Ignatius),[15] Jesus's sex has rarely been seriously questioned in the history of Christian thought.[16] It is a testament to this that the maleness of Jesus has long been regarded as the central problem of feminist theology.[17] Not only has it been thought "to justify patriarchy and thereby defeat feminist struggles,"[18] but because Jesus is and remains a man, women (it is claimed) "cannot see themselves as liberated through him."[19] Due to the significance of this concern, we shall return to the question of how a male savior can redeem, restore, and affirm females shortly.

Interestingly, however, the reality and integrity of Jesus's sex has been challenged in recent times. In 2012, Susannah Cornwall made the following pronouncement:

> It is not possible to assert with any degree of certainty that Jesus was male as we now define maleness. There is no way of knowing for sure that Jesus did not have one of the intersex conditions which would give him a body which appeared externally to be

---

14. Johnson, "Playing Games," 277. By "gender" here, Johnson means "sex."

15. See Ignatius, *Letter to the Ephesians*, 7 (*ANF* 1:48); *Letter to the Trallians*, 9-10 (*ANF* 1:70).

16. The same cannot be said for Jesus's *gender*, however. See Eleanor McLaughlin, "Feminist Christologies: Re-Dressing the Tradition," in *Reconstructing the Christ Symbol: Essays in Feminist Christology*, ed. Mary Anne Stevens (New York: Paulist, 1993), 138.

17. E.g., Mary Daly, *Beyond God the Father: Toward a Philosophy of Women's Liberation* (Boston: Beacon, 1973); Elizabeth Johnson, "Wisdom Was Made Flesh and Pitched Her Tent Among Us," in Stevens, *Reconstructing the Christ Symbol*, 95–117.

18. Delfo Canceran, "Image of God: A Theological Reconstruction of the Beginning," *The Asia Journal of Theology* 25 (2011): 14.

19. Rosemary Radford Ruether, *To Change the World: Christology and Cultural Criticism* (New York: Crossroad, 1981), 47.

> unremarkably male, but which might nonetheless have had some "hidden" female physical features.[20]

Cornwall later clarified that she was "not suggesting that Jesus did not live as a man, interact with others as a man, identify as a man, and so on. But that is not the same thing as saying he was male in biological terms." At the same time, she not only admits that there is no evidence that Jesus was intersex, but that the chances of him being so are, statistically speaking, "extremely *un*likely." So why even raise the possibility? By her own admission, her motivation stems from the fact that Jesus's maleness has sometimes been used to exclude women from certain ministry roles. The logic of her challenge, then, is this: if doubt can be cast on Jesus's maleness, then (at least potentially) "a set of justifications for opposing women's priestly and episcopal ministry fall away."[21]

The question of which ministerial functions and ecclesial offices should be open to women will not be pursued further here. Nor will I pause to critique the nature of Cornwall's theological method. The pertinent question concerns Jesus's maleness and whether the New Testament gives us any reason to doubt its reality or integrity. The short answer is that it does not. For while the anthropological term most commonly applied to Jesus (and self-applied by him) is the general masculine term *anthrōpos* (ἄνθρωπος, e.g., John 8:40; 19:5), Jesus is also referred to by the more specific masculine term *anēr* (ἀνὴρ, *anēr*, e.g., Luke 24:19; John 1:30). These appellations, along with the fact that some eighty-one times in the four Gospels, Jesus either refers to himself or is referred to by others as "the Son of Man" (ὁ υἱὸς τοῦ ἀνθρώπου, *ho huios tou anthrōpou*), all suggest that Jesus was straightforwardly male. In addition to this, and as feminist scholars have long acknowledged, "Jesus is addressed in dominantly masculine names such as teacher, master and lord."[22]

---

20. Susannah Cornwall, "Intersex and Ontology: A Response to *The Church, Women Bishops and Provision*" (Manchester: Lincoln Theological Institute, 2012), 15 (online).

21. Susannah Cornwall, "Sex Otherwise: Intersex, Christology and the Maleness of Jesus," *JFSR* 30, no. 2 (2014): 26–27 (emphasis original).

22. Canceran, "Image of God," 14.

Cornwall, of course, is not disputing these facts. So, is there further evidence that Jesus not only identified as a man (psychologically) and presented as a man (socially) but was, in fact, a male (biologically)?

The most conclusive pieces of testimony are found in the second chapter of Luke's Gospel. Here we are told that Mary "gave birth to *her firstborn son* [*τὸν υἱὸν αὐτῆς τὸν πρωτότοκον, ton huion autēs ton prōtotokon*] wrapped *him* [*αὐτὸν, auton*] in swaddling cloths and laid *him* [*auton*] in a manger" (v. 7). Then, by recording that "at the end of eight days, when he was circumcised, he was called Jesus" (v. 21a), Luke makes plain that the child had male genitalia and that calling him by the male name, "Jesus"—"the name given by the angel before he was conceived in the womb" (v. 21b; compare 1:31)—was not only entirely appropriate but divinely required. Finally, Luke reports that when the prescribed time for their purification came, they brought Jesus up to Jerusalem "to present him to the Lord" (v. 22). This involved the offering of "a sacrifice according to what is said in the Law of the Lord, 'a pair of turtledoves, or two young pigeons' " (v. 24; compare Lev 12:8). But what was the rationale behind this sacrifice? The explanation is given in verse 23, via a summary citation of Exodus 13:2, 12 and 15: "Every *male* [*ἄρσεν, arsen*] who first opens the womb shall be called holy to the Lord."[23] While it is *arsenika* (ἀρσενικά) rather than *arsen* (ἄρσεν) that appears in the LXX of Exodus 13:12 and 15, both terms translate the Hebrew noun *zakhar* and the meaning of both terms is identical: *male*.

Contrary to Cornwall, then, Jesus not only *appeared* to be male but *was* (and indeed *remains*) male. Thus, in becoming incarnate, the eternal Son "took upon himself a male body, which in its resurrected form he has and will have forever."[24] Moreover, precisely because it is the male body of Jesus that determines his identity as a man, *Jesus is the ultimate example of the goodness and necessity of the sex-and-gender connection.*

23. On the origins of Luke's citation, see Darrell L. Bock, *Proclamation from Prophecy and Pattern: Lucan Old Testament Christology*, JSNT Sup 12 (Sheffield: JSOT, 1987), 82–83.

24. Johnson, "Playing Games," 278.

The savior of all

We come, then, to the question of how a male Messiah can save females. As I have just established, "Jesus became like us, not only in our humanity, but also in our sexuality—that is, his body is a biologically sexed body just like ours."[25] But given that not all bodies are sexed as *male*, some have raised concerns about the aptness or adequacy of the Son's incarnation (or, at least, the orthodox understanding of it).[26] Indeed, on the basis of the patristic insight that *the unassumed is the unhealed*, the possibility has been mooted that if the savior of the world is nothing more than male, "then his human nature is the wrong kind of thing to perform his soteriological task."[27]

In response to this challenge, three points need to be made.

The first concerns the *anhypostatic* nature of Jesus's humanity. In orthodox christological understanding, the divine Son takes to himself an impersonal human *nature*, not a particular human *person*. What this means is that "the person who personalizes the human nature of Christ is not a created human person (like all the other persons personalizing the other human natures we encounter); rather it is the eternal second person of the Trinity."[28] His humanity, therefore, is a *shared humanity*. As the writer of the letter to the Hebrews testifies: "Since therefore the children *share in flesh and blood*, he himself likewise *partook of the same things*" (Heb 2:14).

The second point concerns the *enhypostatic* (or in-personal) nature of Jesus's humanity. This idea highlights the fact that "the human nature of Christ, although not itself an individual, is individualized as the human nature of the Son of God. It does not, for a single instant, exist as *anhypostasis* or non-personal."[29] For this reason, the specific features of Jesus's humanity (especially his sex and his race) are vital for his role as the second Adam and the Jewish Messiah. In addition to this, as Rosemary

25. Wilson, *Mere Sexuality*, 44.

26. E.g., Carter Heyward, *Our Passion for Justice: Image of Power, Sexuality, and Liberation* (New York: Beacon, 1984), 212.

27. Fellipe M. do Vale, "Can a Male Savior Save Women?: The Metaphysics of Gender and Christ's Ability to Save," *Philosophia Christi* 21 (2019): 310.

28. Fred Sanders, *Jesus in Trinitarian Perspective: An Intermediate Christology* (Nashville: Broadman & Holman Academic, 2007), 31.

29. Donald Macleod, *The Person of Christ* (Downers Grove, IL: InterVarsity Press, 1998), 202.

Radford Ruether affirms, "the historical particularity of his maleness is essential to his ongoing representation."[30] That is, for Jesus to continue to function as our great high priest (as Hebrews 7:25 insists he does), he must continue to be human and continue to be male. So then, *it is precisely because he is a particular male person that Jesus is able to represent humanity generally*. His maleness is not a problem to be solved, but a necessary part of the divine solution to the problem of sin—a problem faced by men and women alike.

Third, the fact that Jesus is *truly human* does not require him to possess *all* the attributes or properties possessed by *every human*. Indeed, such a conclusion, in philosophical terms, blurs the distinction between *kind essentialism* (i.e., "properties definitive of membership in that kind") and *individual essentialism* (i.e., "properties that an object *must* have if it exists at all").[31] The point is this: for Jesus to represent and redeem (say) Mary Magdalene, he need only share her *kind essence*, not her *individual essence*. For although "the fact that the Son became incarnate as a gendered individual would seem to require us to affirm that sexuality is an essential feature of human existence,"[32] this does not make maleness into an essential *human* property—one that *all* humans must share. As Genesis 1:27 makes clear, humankind comes in two forms. But while biological sex is an essential attribute of *humankind*, maleness and femaleness are essential attributes only of *particular individuals*.

In sum, there are reasons why only a male Messiah can save, but there is no reason why a male Messiah cannot save females. He is "the savior of *all people* [*άντων ἀνθρώπων, antōn anthrōpōn*]" (1 Tim 4:10) because he shares our humanity.

30. Rosemary Radford Ruether, "The Liberation of Christology from Patriarchy," *Religion and Intellectual Life* 2, no. 3 (1985): 127.

31. Charlotte Witt, "What Is Gender Essentialism?," in *Feminist Metaphysics: Explorations in the Ontology of Sex, Gender and Self*, ed. Charlotte Witt (Dordrecht: Springer, 2011), 12, 21. It does not follow from this, however, that each person has two distinct essences: (1) a generic human essence and (2) an individual personal essence.

32. Cortez, *ReSourcing Theological Anthropology*, 198.

Concluding reflection on Jesus's humanity

By being born of a woman as a male, the Son of God affirms the essential nature of sexuality for all people. Moreover, as we have seen, the incarnation esteems both forms of the *imago Dei*—male and female. This is not surprising, for *Jesus did not come to save us from our sex, but from our sins.* Consequently, as we shall explore shortly, being conformed to his image means being conformed to his *character*, not his *gender*. Nonetheless, as the New Testament makes plain, christoformity includes learning to see ourselves and express ourselves sexually in ways that accord with God's creational purpose for the particular sex given to each of us. There is thus neither need nor warrant to look for "a larger Christ outside binary boundaries" (as Marcella Althaus-Reid advocates),[33] or to invent a "Bi/Transvestite Christ" in order to "play with gender constructions intersected with diverse sexual attractions" (as Robert Goss has sought to do).[34] Indeed, such maneuvers not only miss what it means for us to be remade into Christ's (perfect) image, but are blatant attempts to remake him into our (fallen) likeness.

THE TEACHING OF JESUS

The final task in this first section is to engage in a brief exposition of Jesus's teaching in Matthew 19:4–12. The relevance of this teaching is twofold: first, what it reveals about the ongoing applicability of Genesis 1 and 2; second, how Jesus sees eunuchs fitting into the sex-and-gender binary.

The occasion for Jesus's teaching

The occasion for Jesus's teaching is the question put to him by the Pharisees in verse 3: "Is it lawful to divorce one's wife for any cause?" While the question was not genuinely inquisitive—for, as Matthew discloses, the Pharisees were *testing him* (πειράζοντες αὐτὸν, *peirazontes auton*)—behind it was a longstanding debate between the major rabbinical schools within Palestinian Judaism as to the meaning and application of Deuteronomy 24:1. As is clear from his response, Jesus sides with the stricter Shammaite

33. Marcella Althaus-Reid, *Indecent Theology: Theological Perversions in Sex, Gender and Politics* (London: Routledge, 2000), 114.

34. Robert E. Goss, *Queering Christ: Beyond Jesus Acted Up* (Cleveland: Pilgrim, 2002), 176.

interpretation of the expression "some indecency" (דְּבַר עֶרְוָה, *devar 'erwah*), rather than the more lenient Hillelite interpretation.[35] At the same time, by restricting the grounds of legitimate divorce and non-adulterous remarriage to "sexual immorality" alone (πορνείᾳ, *porneia* v. 9), Jesus evidently "cuts his own swathe."[36] For while the school of Shammai sanctioned divorce and remarriage on a variety of other grounds, Jesus does not. This indicates "a huge gulf between the teaching of Jesus and the rest of Jewish society."[37] The standards of his kingdom are higher.

The theological basis for Jesus's reply

The theological basis for Jesus's view of marriage is his understanding of the intimate relationship between Genesis 1:27 and 2:24. He thus begins his reply to the Pharisees with a partial citation of the first text: "He who created them from the beginning made them male and female" (v. 4). He then follows immediately with a direct citation of the second: "Therefore a man shall leave his father and his mother and hold fast to his wife, and the two shall become one flesh" (v. 5).

Three features of verse 4 are of particular significance. The first is Jesus's description of God as "the creator" (ὁ κτίσας, *ho ktisas*). This title is not only unique to Matthew's account of this interchange, but is also absent from the LXX of Genesis 1.[38] By deliberately speaking of God in this way, Jesus was likely employing a typical rabbinic form of argument—namely, "the more original, the weightier."[39] His point, then, is that the later concession of Moses must be understood in the light of the original creative act of God. As Leon Morris writes: "Our sexuality is of divine

35. In the Shammaite view, it referred to "a matter of forbidden sexual intercourse." In the Hillelite view, it also covered trivial offenses, like ruining a meal (*Mishnah*, Gittin 9:10).

36. Carson, "Matthew," 411. It is generally agreed that *porneia* covers "every kind of unlawful sexual intercourse" (William F. Arndt, Walter Bauer, and F. Wilbur Gingrich, *A Greek-English Lexicon of the New Testament and Other Early Christian Literature*, 3rd ed. [Chicago: University of Chicago Press, 2001], 693).

37. David Instone-Brewer, *Divorce and Remarriage in the Bible: The Social and Literary Context* (Grand Rapids: Eerdmans, 2002), 183.

38. In Genesis 1:27, the LXX translates *'elohim* by ὁ θεὸς, *ho theos*.

39. Leon Morris, *The Gospel According to Matthew*, PNTC (Grand Rapids: Eerdmans, 1992), 481.

ordinance; it is intended to be exercised in monogamous relationships."[40] Divorce, then, was never the creator's will (v. 6).

A second difference between Jesus's language and that of Genesis 1 is found in his partial citation of Genesis 1:27 (in v. 4), which incorporates an allusion to Genesis 1:1. However, whereas the LXX of Genesis 1:1 has "*in* the beginning" (ἐν ἀρχῇ, *en archē*), Jesus says "*from* the beginning" (ἀπ' ἀρχῆς, *ap' archēs*). The significance of this change is that, in contrast to ἐν (*en*), ἀπὸ (*apo*) indicates "the beginning point of an action that continued for some time after: 'from the beginning on.' " In other words, Jesus is saying that this is not simply *how things once were*; it is *how things still are*. In practical terms, the construction implies that "God's creative work continues through procreation."[41]

Third, in stating "male and female he *made* them [ἄρσεν καὶ θῆλυ ἐποίησεν αὐτούς, *arsen kai thēly epoiēsen autous*]," Jesus's intention is to draw out the present implications of this originary fact—that is, *the creator continues to make males and females, continues to call them into man-woman marriage, and continues to join them together as one flesh.* As Carson writes: "the 'one flesh' in every marriage between a man and a woman is a reenactment of and testimony to the very structure of humanity as God created it."[42] Here, then, is confirmation of the continuation of both the sex-and-gender binary and the sex-and-gender connection.

A final comment pertains to verse 8, where Jesus answers a further question: "Why then did Moses *command* [ἐνετείλατο, *eneteilato*] one to give a certificate of divorce and to send her away?" In response, Jesus begins by correcting the Pharisees' mischaracterization of Moses's action: "Because of your hardness of heart Moses *allowed* [ἐπέτρεψεν, *epetrepsen*] you to divorce your wives." Divorce, then, "is never to be thought of as a God-ordained, morally neutral option but as evidence of sin."[43] It is a concession reflective not of God's purpose but of humanity's stubbornness. This is why Jesus again says, "*from the beginning* [*ap' archēs*] it was not so." The point, then, is clear: because the kingdom of God "is ultimately to

40. Morris, *Matthew*, 481.

41. Charles L. Quarles, *Matthew*, EGGNT (Nashville: Broadman & Holman, 2017), 221.

42. Carson, "Matthew," 412.

43. Carson, "Matthew," 413.

involve the restoration of the perfection of the pre-fall creation," writes Donald Hagner, "the ethics of the kingdom as taught by Jesus reflect this fact."[44] Thus, the only (potentially) valid ground for divorce is "sexual immorality" (v. 9).

The meaning of verse 12

This brings us to verse 12, which forms a key part of Jesus's response to his disciples' exclamation: "If such is the case *of a man with his wife* [τοῦ ἀνθρώπου μετὰ τῆς γυναικός, *tou anthrōpou meta tēs gynaikos*], it is better not to marry" (v. 10). Jesus begins by indicating the normality of marriage and the fact that refraining from marriage is not for everyone, "but only those to whom it is given" (v. 11). This raises the question: To whom has such an ability been given? The short answer is *to eunuchs*. However, Jesus then distinguishes three types of eunuchs—the first two literal, the third metaphorical: "For there are eunuchs who have been so from birth, and there are eunuchs who have been made eunuchs by men, and there are eunuchs who have made themselves eunuchs for the sake of the kingdom of heaven. Let the one who is able to receive this receive it" (Matt 19:12).

As noted in chapter 7, Jesus's *first type* of eunuch—literally "eunuchs who from the womb of their mother were born that way [εὐνοῦχοι οἵτινες ἐκ κοιλίας μητρὸς ἐγεννήθησαν οὕτως, *eunouchoi hoitines ek koilias mētros egennēthēsan houtōs*]"—was a standard rabbinic category (Heb. *saris khama*). We also saw that a *saris khama* was a male "born without the ability to be a husband and father because of a defect in his physiology."[45] Jesus's *second type*—"eunuchs who have been made eunuchs by men"—was likewise common (Heb. *saris 'adam*), referring to "a male who had either been literally castrated or who had, sometimes after birth, lost the power to reproduce, whether through a disease, an injury, or some other debilitating factor."[46]

Jesus, however, speaks of a *third type* of eunuch: those "who have made themselves eunuchs for the sake of the kingdom of heaven." As the

44. Donald A. Hagner, *Matthew 14–28*, WBC 33B (Waco, TX: Word, 1995), 550.

45. Jeffrey A. Gibbs, *Matthew 11:2–20:34*, Concordia Commentary (St. Louis: Concordia, 2010), 954.

46. W. D. Davies and Dale C. Allison, *A Critical and Exegetical Commentary on the Gospel According to Saint Matthew: Volume III: XIX–XXVIII*, ICC (Edinburgh: T&T Clark, 1997), 22.

overwhelming majority of commentators recognize, his meaning here is not literal (or biological) but metaphorical (or social), for in the context of a discussion of marriage and divorce, it is clear that "to make oneself a eunuch means to voluntarily remain single and celibate."[47]

Against Linda Tatro Herzer, then, Jesus's third type of eunuch does not refer to "people who would be defined today as gay or transgender."[48] Rather, it refers to "those who have renounced marriage (such as John the Baptist and Jesus himself) to give priority to the work of the kingdom (compare 1 Cor 7:32–34)."[49] Indeed, given the wording of the disciples' statement in verse 10 ("If such is the case of a *man* with his wife"), it refers explicitly to *men* who have made such a decision. This reinforces what we have already seen: all three categories of eunuch refer to *males*. Jesus, then, is not differentiating eunuchs from *men and women* (as if they were a third sex), but from *married men*.

The queering of Jesus's categories

So understood, Matthew 19:12 resists a variety of alternative interpretations found in trans-affirming literature. For example, claiming that the kingdom of heaven is "located within us (Luke 17:21)," Mollenkott suggests that "what Jesus means by being eunuchs 'for the sake of the kingdom of heaven' is the Jewish counsel of being true to one's deepest nature." This, then, enables her to argue that Jesus's third category includes "not only pre-operative and non-operative transsexuals but all other transgenderists, celibates, and homosexuals who do not engage in reproductive sex."[50] However, with the exception of "celibates," not only is such a conclusion ruled out by a contextual exegesis of Matthew 19 (let alone the Bible's sexual ethical teaching), but it is based on a misreading of Luke 17:21. For despite a long history of misinterpretation, Jesus did not say that the

---

47. Gibbs, *Matthew 11:2–20:34*, 955; compare John Nolland, *The Gospel of Matthew*, NIGTC (Grand Rapids: Eerdmans, 2005), 780–82; Carson, "Matthew," 419; Morris, *Matthew*, 485–86; R. T. France, *The Gospel According to Matthew*, NICNT (Grand Rapids: Eerdmans, 2007), 725.

48. Herzer, *Transgender Experience*, 46.

49. Hagner, *Matthew 14–28*, 550.

50. Mollenkott, *Omnigender*, 136.

kingdom of God is located *within each one of you*, but that "the kingdom of God is *in your* [pl.] *midst* [ἐντὸς ὑμῶν ἐστιν, *entos hymōn estin*]."[51]

Equally problematic is Lewis Reay's claim that Jesus's second type of eunuch refers to "those who are transgender in the broadest sense of this word," and his third type to "those who are gender different, or gender queer, that is, not conforming to normative definitions of gender roles and identities."[52] Yet Reay goes even further. Building on Halvor Moxnes's claim that by applying the term "eunuch" to himself Jesus puts himself "permanently out of place, in a liminal position,"[53] Reay insists that Jesus identifies as "truly gender queer" and so functions as the ultimate "transcestor"—Reay's term for historical figures who prove that "transpeople" have "always been here."[54] However, such conclusions are not only without foundation in the text itself, but involve a basic confusion of categories. On this score, even Megan DeFranza acknowledges that we must "be careful to differentiate between castrated eunuchs and transgender people who choose surgical transition."[55] None of Jesus's categories includes the latter.

It is simply not plausible, then, that Jesus's third category of eunuch refers to those who have "chosen a life outside of their assigned sex," as Hartke proposes.[56] That is not what a commitment to celibacy and singleness involves. And DeFranza's suggestion that Jesus's words overturn the Old Testament idea that "the distinctions between male and female were of ultimate importance" is at odds with verse 4. Nor is Jesus holding up eunuchs "as models of radical discipleship," as she claims.[57] He is simply likening men who have chosen not to marry *for kingdom reasons* to those who cannot marry *for biological reasons*. Doubtless, given the Jews' high regard for marriage and childbearing and low regard for those

51. See I. Howard Marshall, *The Gospel of Luke: A Commentary on the Greek Text* (Exeter: Paternoster, 1978), 655–56; Darrell L. Bock, *Luke 9:51–24:53*, BECNT (Grand Rapids: Baker, 1996), 1414–17.

52. Lewis Reay, "Towards a Transgender Theology: Que(e)rying the Eunuchs," in Althaus-Reid and Isherwood, *Trans/Formations*, 150.

53. Halvor Moxnes, *Putting Jesus in His Place: A Radical Vision of Household and Kingdom* (Louisville: Westminster John Knox, 2003), 89.

54. Reay, "Transgender Theology," 157, 149n1.

55. DeFranza, "Good News," 164.

56. Hartke, *Transforming*, 106.

57. DeFranza, "Good News," 165. See the discussion of *ap' archēs* earlier in this section.

who (quite literally) "made themselves eunuchs," Jesus's language would have contained a certain shock value. Nevertheless, as Morris concludes:

> Jesus is not saying that this [i.e., denying oneself marriage] is a higher calling than others or that all his followers should seek to serve in this way; that would be a contradiction of his appeal to Genesis 1–2. He is simply saying that the claims of the kingdom override all other claims and that some are called to serve in the path of celibacy (just as others are called to serve in marriage).[58]

Concluding comment on Matthew 19:4–12

In Matthew 19:4–12, Jesus is neither "validating a choice to live outside the typical gender norms and expressions of the day," nor is he "defending a genderless expression of humanity"; rather, he is simply "highlighting the willingness of the kingdom-centered eunuch to sacrifice that which was deemed by many to be an essential part of human expression in the service of a higher cause."[59] Most importantly, Jesus's starting point must not be lost from view, nor its significance minimized. *Whatever one's marital status or reproductive capacity, the sex binary remains*: "From the beginning the creator made them male and female" (v. 4). While this does not guarantee that everyone fits neatly into these categories, either socially or physiologically, as far as Jesus is concerned there is no third sex category. Eunuchs of all types were male.

SEX, GENDER, AND LIFE IN CHRIST

We turn next to a brief examination of several texts from the Pauline epistles—two from 1 Corinthians (6:9–10 and 11:3–16) and a third from Galatians (3:28). While these are not the only Pauline passages of relevance to our subject, they are the main texts that are commonly discussed in both the trans-affirming and non-affirming literature. My purpose is to see what light they shed on both the reality of the sex-and-gender binary and the importance of the sex-and-gender connection and, as a result, how they may assist in our assessment of trans theory. Before engaging in

58. Morris, *Matthew*, 485–86.

59. Eddy and Beilby, "Understanding Transgender," 49.

my exegesis, however, a comment on Paul's understanding of the nature of the Christian life is in order.

THE NATURE OF THE CHRISTIAN LIFE

In his letter to the Romans, the apostle Paul is unequivocal that in the saving purpose of God, all who believe that Jesus was "delivered up for our trespasses and raised for our justification" are "justified by faith" and "have peace with God" (Rom 4:24–25; 5:1–2). Indeed, so completely has God's grace in Christ triumphed over human sin that it prompts the question: Are we to continue in sin that grace may abound? (Rom 6:1). Paul's answer is negative and emphatic: "By no means! How can we who died to sin still live in it?" (Rom 6:2). This, of course, is consistent with the general shape of the New Testament's teaching (e.g., 1 Pet 2:24; 4:1–2): "ethical transformation is the end in view for the one encountering God through Jesus Christ."[60] In short, release from sin's *penalty* is with a view to release from sin's *power*.

But how is the latter possible? Paul's answer is that by the Holy Spirit those who trust in Christ are brought into union with him and so become "sharers with him in the gifts with which he is endowed."[61] As he writes to the Corinthians: "If anyone is in Christ, he (or she) is a new creation. The old has passed away; behold, the new has come" (2 Cor 5:17). It is because of this new reality that believers are to consider themselves "dead to sin and alive to God in Christ Jesus" (Rom 6:11). What this means in practice is, rather than presenting our "members to sin as instruments for unrighteousness," we are to present ourselves to God "as those who have been brought from death to life" and our "members to God as instruments for righteousness" (Rom 6:13).

Change of this kind, however, is normally a slow and staggered process, as believers learn gradually to put off the "old self, which … is corrupt through deceitful desires" (Eph 4:22) and "put on the new self, created after the likeness of God in true righteousness and holiness" (Eph 4:24). Furthermore, as Andrew Cameron remarks, in this process our old identity stories "can function as a kind of prison"; although Christ has opened

---

60. Mark Saucy, "Personal Ethics of the New Covenant," *EQ* 86 (2014): 355.

61. Calvin, *Institutes*, 3.11.10.

wide the door, "it can take us quite a while to inhabit freedom."[62] It is necessary, then, for those in Christ to be able to discern the difference between slavery and freedom, learning the ways of the latter while avoiding the snares of the former.

What will this mean for the believer's sex and sexuality, gender, and gender identity? The following texts help answer this question.

1 CORINTHIANS 6:9–10

> Or do you not know that the unrighteous will not inherit the kingdom of God? Do not be deceived; neither fornicators, nor idolaters, nor adulterers, nor *effeminate* [μαλακοὶ, *malakoi*], nor *homosexuals* [ἀρσενοκοῖται, *arsenokoitai*], nor thieves, nor the covetous, nor drunkards, nor revilers, nor swindlers, will inherit the kingdom of God. (NASB 1995)

These verses contain a vice list and constitute a warning. They follow immediately on the heels of Paul's rebuke of the Corinthians for taking each other to court before unbelievers rather than enduring being wronged and defrauded (vv. 6–7). In context, then, their aim is to "provide encouragement to the Corinthians to follow Paul's difficult advice in vv. 7–8 (not to dispute with one another, even if it means you suffer)."[63] At the same time, a number of the vices also point forward to verses 12–20 and supply extra reasons to "flee from sexual immorality" (v. 18).

The meaning of malakoi

For our purposes, the key clause of interest is "neither effeminate nor homosexuals" (οὔτε μαλακοὶ οὔτε ἀρσενοκοῖται, *oute malakoi oute arsenokoitai*), and the particular term of interest is that translated "effeminate" (*malakos* = "soft"; compare Matt 11:8; Luke 7:25).[64]

---

62. Andrew J. Cameron, *Joined-Up Life: A Christian Account of How Ethics Works* (Nottingham: Inter-Varsity Press, 2011), 98.

63. Ciampa and Rosner, *Corinthians*, 240. Similarly, David E. Garland translates *malakoi* as "those who are penetrated sexually by males" and *arsenokoitai* as "those males who sexually penetrate males" (*1 Corinthians*, BECNT [Grand Rapids: Baker Academic, 2003], 214).

64. Apart from NASB 1995 (and NASB 1977), Berean Literal Bible, KJV, Legacy Standard Bible, Amplified Bible, ASV, English Revised Version, Literal Standard Version, New Heart English Bible,

As most commentators see it, the pairing of "effeminate" (*malakoi*) with "homosexuals" (*arsenokoitai*) suggests that Paul is referring to "those who willingly play the passive and active roles in homosexual acts."[65] The reason he regards such behavior as immoral is twofold: first, it is prohibited by Old Testament law (Lev 18:22; 20:13); second, it is deemed a violation of the created order. As Wenham explains:

> Israel's repudiation of homosexual intercourse arises out of its doctrine of creation. God created humanity in two sexes, so that they could be fruitful and multiply and fill the earth. Woman was man's perfect companion, like man created in the divine image. To allow the legitimacy of homosexual acts would frustrate the divine purpose and deny the perfection of God's provision of two sexes to support and complement one another.[66]

That Paul shared this understanding is confirmed by his description of homosexual desires and acts as "against nature" (παρὰ φύσιν, *para physin*) in Romans 1:26.[67]

However, while Paul's use of the term *malakoi* clearly includes men who play the female role in homosexual encounters, the general meaning of the term is considerably more wide-ranging. Throughout the Greco-Roman literature it refers to men who behaved, spoke, dressed, and groomed themselves like women, and so was essentially a term for "men who confused gender distinctions."[68] Dale Martin puts the point bluntly: "all penetrated men were *malakoi*, but not all *malakoi* were penetrated men."[69] The implication of this, as William Loader notes, is that had Paul wished to identify only one particular form of sexual self-feminization,

---

Webster's Bible Translation, and Young's Literal Translation, all translate *malakoi* by "effeminate."

65. Ciampa and Rosner, *Corinthians*, 241.

66. Gordon J. Wenham, "The Old Testament Attitude to Homosexuality," *Expository Times* 102 (1990–91): 363.

67. As Gagnon rightly points out, *para physin* does not mean against "the way things are usually done," but against "the material shape of the created order" (*Homosexual Practice*, 256).

68. Sprinkle, *People to Be Loved*, 106. See the literature cited on p. 107n12.

69. Dale B. Martin, *Sex and the Single Savior: Gender and Sexuality in Biblical Interpretation* (Louisville: Westminster John Knox, 2006), 45.

he "could have used one of the more usual designations" rather than "a word with a broad meaning."[70]

This suggests that Paul's use of *malakoi* not only covers men who allow themselves to be sodomized, but also "those who engage in a process of feminization to erase further their masculine appearance and manner."[71] Consequently, if the Deuteronomic prohibition against cross-dressing continues to apply to God's people, and both homosexual behavior and cross-sex identification are here problematized by Paul, then how much more would he have opposed medical and surgical "gender transitioning"?

The significance of verse 11

Having delivered his warning against engaging in behaviors that will result in exclusion from God's kingdom (v. 9), Paul concludes this section of his argument on a more positive note: "And such were some of you. But you were washed, [but] you were sanctified, [but] you were justified in the name of the Lord Jesus Christ and by the Spirit of our God" (v. 11). Here Paul's emphasis is not so much on the *need* for behavioral change or the *possibility* of such change taking place, but on the fact that *the decisive change has already occurred.*[72] Indeed, his opening expression—"and these things some [of you] were" (καὶ ταῦτά τινες ἦτε, *kai tauta tines ēte*)—stresses the transformative effects of the Corinthians' conversion to Christ. David Garland captures the logic of Paul's thought helpfully: "In 5:7, he juxtaposes the indicative with the imperative, 'You are ..., now be,' to make his case. Here, he juxtaposes the past and the present, 'You once were ..., but now are,' to make his case. Their former life was to be just that, their former life."[73] As a consequence, believers are to be and behave differently, for "God in his mercy has already removed the stains of their past sins, has already begun the work of ethical transformation, and has already given them forgiveness and right standing with himself."[74]

70. William Loader, *The New Testament on Sexuality* (Grand Rapids: Eerdmans, 2012), 328.

71. Gagnon, *Homosexual Practice*, 312.

72. As my parenthetical additions to the ESV indicate, the conjunction ἀλλὰ, *alla* ("but") occurs three times in the Greek text, emphasizing the radical nature of conversion and the newness of life in Christ.

73. Garland, *1 Corinthians*, 215.

74. Gordon D. Fee, *The First Epistle to the Corinthians*, rev. ed., NICNT (Grand Rapids: Eerdmans, 2014), 273.

The relevance of Paul's words for the subject of this book is straightforward: believers who were formerly *malakoi* (whatever form their cross-sex identification or behavior took) are such no longer. They have been made new in Christ and so must *be what they are* (compare 5:7). This means recognizing that the body is "for the Lord and the Lord for the body" (6:13) and so heeding the call to "glorify the Lord with your body" (6:20). Martin Davie helpfully teases out the practical implications of this call:

> This means that in the case of a transgender person who is a baptised believer the call to put off the old nature and put on the new one has to mean, among other things, being willing to accept and live out their true, God given, sexual identity. For those going through gender transition this will mean stopping the process and for those who have gone through gender transition this will mean undergoing de-transition and reverting to living according to their birth sex.[75]

The alternative, it would seem, is to risk falling under the disciplinary measures outlined by Paul in 1 Corinthians 5:4–13 and, in the worst case, failing to inherit the kingdom of God (6:9). This is not to suggest that all forms of cross-sex identification are of equal seriousness or that all steps taken along the path of gender transitioning can be easily or entirely reversed. It is to insist that "God is in the business not of whitewashing sins but of transforming sinners."[76] In short, new life means new lifestyle.

1 CORINTHIANS 11:2–16

Our second Pauline text is 1 Corinthians 11:2–16. It is neither my purpose nor is it possible to attempt a detailed exposition of this rich and complex passage. Nor will I endeavor to adjudicate some of its more contested elements—for example, whether Paul is speaking about veils, hairstyles, or head coverings (although I will assume the latter),[77] and

75. Davie, *Transgender Liturgies*, 79–80.

76. Garland, *1 Corinthians*, 215.

77. See Joan E. Taylor, "'The Woman Ought to Have Control over Her Head because of the Angels' (1 Corinthians 11.10)," in *Gospel and Gender: A Trinitarian Engagement with Being Male and Female in Christ*, ed. Douglas A. Campbell (New York: T&T Clark, 2003), 48–49. For a detailed defense of the view that Paul is referring to hairstyles, see Philip B. Payne, *Man and Woman, One in Christ: An Exegetical and Theological Study of Paul's Letters* (Grand Rapids: Zondervan, 2009), 141–73.

whether his teaching applies to all men and women or only to husbands and wives (although I will assume the former).[78] My main point of interest is the apostle's concern that the members of the Corinthian church "keep their physical appearances different according to their sex (vv. 14–15)."[79] What this meant in the context of their assemblies was that when praying or prophesying (key forms of congregational speech that likely "serve together as a general reference to active participation in worship"), the men were not to cover their heads but the women were (vv. 4–5). However, the deeper concern behind this particular practice is the need to "maintain and even celebrate the gender distinctions with which we have been created."[80]

The rationale for Paul's instruction

The primary reason for Paul's practical directive has to do with the God-given differences between the sexes. These are highlighted in several ways in the course of his argument. First, there is a difference in terms of *headship*: "the head of every man is Christ, the head of the woman, the man" (v. 3).[81] Second, there is a related difference in terms of *glory*: "man ... is the image and glory of God, but woman is the glory of man" (v. 7).[82] Third, there is a difference in terms of *creation order and created purpose*: "For man was not made from woman, but woman from man. Neither was man created for woman, but woman for man" (vv. 8–9).[83] Finally, there is an observable physiological difference between men and women's *hair*: "Does not nature itself teach you that if a man wears long hair it is a disgrace for him,

---

78. Anthony C. Thiselton, *The First Epistle to the Corinthians*, NIGTC (Grand Rapids: Eerdmans, 2000), 822. I will also assume what Lucy Peppiatt calls a "traditional reading" of the passage (Peppiatt, *Women and Worship at Corinth: Paul's Rhetorical Arguments in 1 Corinthians* [Eugene, OR: Cascade, 2015], 24), as opposed to her "rhetorical reading," which holds that in vv. 4–5 and 7–10 Paul is "citing his opponents in order to refute their views" (12).

79. Brad Klassen, "The Pauline Response to Today's Sexual and Gender Confusion," *MSJ* 28 (2017): 152.

80. Ciampa and Rosner, *Corinthians*, 515, 503.

81. For a compelling case that "head" (*kephalē*) denotes "authority over," see Paul Gardner, *1 Corinthians*, ZECNT (Grand Rapids: Zondervan, 2018), 480–85.

82. As 15:49 clarifies, Paul's language does not imply that woman is not the image of God.

83. For Paul, these differences diminish neither the equality nor interdependency of the sexes. See Gardner, *1 Corinthians*, 494.

but if a woman has long hair, it is her glory? For her hair is given to her for a covering" (vv. 14–15).[84]

The apostle nominates these divinely designed distinctions because interpersonal responsibilities flow from them, and these cannot be properly discharged if they are obscured. This explains why they require visible manifestation in gender presentation—particularly in the context of public worship. So, when praying or prophesying, the way for a man to honor his *relational head* (Christ) is to not cover his *literal head* (v. 4), and the way for a woman to honor her *relational head* (man) is to cover her *literal head* (v. 5). By such actions, the Corinthian believers will reflect and respect God-given "glory" (*δόξα, doxa*; vv. 7, 15)—not just their own and each other's but, above all, Christ's—and will likewise avoid "disgrace" (*ἀτιμία, atimia*, vv. 6, 14). This latter concern highlights a societal dimension to the Corinthians' actions. For, as Rachel Gilson notes, "the way that Christians related to and represent sex in their public spaces is open to public judgment, both positive and negative."[85] In this sense, the church, like its apostle, is not only accountable to the Lord (4:5), but is on display "to the world, to angels, and to men" (4:9).

The abiding significance of Paul's instruction

What is of especial relevance is the fact that Paul's directive is not motivated by "the desire to appease cultural norms" but is based on "distinctions in the creation record of Genesis 2, referring both to the order and to the purpose of God's creation of man as male and female (compare 1 Cor. 11:7–9 with Gen. 2:21–24)."[86] Indeed, there is some Greco-Roman evidence that suggests that head coverings in worship were usual for men and optional for women.[87] And yet, even if Paul was aware of such a practice, his teaching is not presented as a form of anti-pagan protest. While

84. On vv. 14–15, see Michael Lakey, *Image and Glory of God: 1 Corinthians 11:2–16 as a Case Study in Bible, Gender and Hermeneutics*, LNTS 418 (New York: T&T Clark, 2010), 117–21.

85. Rachel Gilson, "Male and Female in Distinction and Glory: First Corinthians 11:2–16 and Contemporary Questions of Sex, Gender and Transgender Identities," *EQ* 93 (2022): 50.

86. Klassen, "The Pauline Response," 152.

87. See Richard Oster, "When Men Wore Veils to Worship: The Historical Context of 1 Corinthians 11.4," *NST* 34 (1988): 481–505; Mark T. Finney, "Honour, Head-Coverings and Headship: 1 Corinthians 11.2–16 in Its Social Context," *JSNT* 33 (2010): 31–58.

evidently critical of the Corinthian Christians, he is not engaging in a wider cultural critique. As we have seen, the main reasons for his instruction are grounded on creation. The point, then, is that the ultimate guide for Christians is not *culture* (or its negation) but *nature* (φύσις, *physis*)—and nature, not as interpreted by culture, but as revealed in *Scripture*.[88]

This is not to deny that culture can influence how nature is read and that such readings inevitably change as cultures change. It is thus generally recognized that in contemporary Western cultures the presence (or absence) of a head covering does not signify what it does in other places and has at other times—that is, "uncovered women are not generally received as abnormal, disgraceful, or gender-bending at home or at worship services."[89] Nevertheless, the difficulty this creates for discerning the abiding significance of Paul's words should not be overstated. For while there may well be "no piece of clothing that functions as a cultural equivalent to the first-century Graeco-Roman head covering,"[90] the deeper concern of the text is unaffected: *Christians are to "do gender" (particularly, but not only, in public worship) in a way that signals their grateful recognition of both God-given sex differences and the particularity of their own biologically determined sex.* Moreover, as Thomas Schreiner recognizes, "in every culture there are certain kinds of adornment which become culturally acceptable norms of dress for men and women."[91] Faithful gender expression, then, will take note of these norms and will operate in a way that is culturally intelligible rather than culturally confusing.

The contemporary relevance of Paul's instruction

Paul's instruction has obvious application to the way that Christian men and women present themselves in the assemblies of God's people, particularly in terms of hairstyle, dress, and general demeanor. As Gilson

---

88. For a thorough and convincing argument that Paul's use of "nature" (*physis*) is rooted in creation rather than custom, see Branson L. Parler, "Hair Length and Human Sexuality: The Underlying Moral Logic of Paul's Appeal to Nature in 1 Corinthians 11:14," *CTJ* 51 (2016): 112–36.

89. Gilson, "Male and Female," 53.

90. Smith, *God's Good Design*, 78.

91. Thomas R. Schreiner, "Head Coverings, Prophecies and the Trinity," in Piper and Grudem, *Recovering Biblical Manhood and Womanhood*, 138.

again comments: "God encourages us to hold to and hold up the goodness of humanity as male and female, and to seek to orient our display of this reality in ways that speak truth and radiate glory."[92] As I have noted previously, this does not mean conforming ourselves to restrictive gender stereotypes—particularly as "the Bible doesn't give us narrow mandates for how all men and women must behave."[93] But it does mean accepting and delighting in sex differences, rather than seeking to deny, diminish, or disguise them.

Most pointedly, Paul's teaching has implications for those who are tempted to engage in a range of "transgender expressions"—attempts to flout gender norms, blur gender distinctions, or transgress gender boundaries, often in the name of "culture-making." On this score, Branson Parler's reflection is helpful: "Our culture-making with respect to gender should not erase the proper creational diversity and difference given in creation nor should it erase the givenness of who we are. Rather, our culture-making is always a response to the gift of who we are as male and female, not something we invent ex nihilo."[94] Others, of course, have more deeply-felt reasons for desiring to obscure their sex—many to escape profound gender distress. Nevertheless, as O'Donovan gently reminds, growing in maturity involves not only recognizing our body as a divine gift, but "accepting this gift and learning to love it, even though we may have to acknowledge that it does not come to us without problems." He continues:

> Responsibility in sexual development implies a responsibility to nature—to the ordered good of the bodily form which we have been given. And that implies that we must make the necessary distinction between the good of the bodily form as such and the various problems that it poses to us personally in our individual experience. This is a comment that applies not only to this very

92. Gilson, "Male and Female," 60.

93. Sprinkle, *Embodied*, 86.

94. Parler, "Hair Length," 134.

striking and unusually distressing problem [GD], but to a whole range of other sexual problems too.[95]

In sum, for all its complexity, 1 Corinthians 11:2–16 constitutes a clear summons to contemporary Christian men and women "to embrace the gender sovereignly determined by God at conception and revealed through anatomy, to understand its distinct vertical and horizontal responsibilities, and to live it out for one's entire life."[96]

GALATIANS 3:28

We come now to the so-called Magna Carta of humanity: Galatians 3:28.[97] The verse, of course, can only truly be understood in the context of Paul's entire letter and is unintelligible apart from its immediate context, verses 26–29:

TABLE 8: GALATIANS 3:26–29 — ENGLISH AND GREEK

English Standard Version	*Novum Testamentum Graece*
[26] for in Christ Jesus you are all sons of God, through faith. [27] For as many of you as were baptized into Christ have put on Christ. [28] There is neither Jew nor Greek, there is neither slave nor free, there is no male and female, for you are all one in Christ Jesus. [29] And if you are Christ's, then you are Abraham's offspring, heirs according to promise.	[62] Πάντες γὰρ υἱοὶ θεοῦ ἐστε διὰ τῆς πίστεως ἐν Χριστῷ Ἰησοῦ· [72] ὅσοι γὰρ εἰς Χριστὸν ἐβαπτίσθητε, Χριστὸν ἐνεδύσασθε. [28] οὐκ ἔνι Ἰουδαῖος οὐδὲ Ἕλλην, οὐκ ἔνι δοῦλος οὐδὲ ἐλεύθερος, οὐκ ἔνι ἄρσεν καὶ θῆλυ· πάντες γὰρ ὑμεῖς εἷς ἐστε ἐν Χριστῷ Ἰησοῦ. [29] εἰ δὲ ὑμεῖς Χριστοῦ, ἄρα τοῦ Ἀβραὰμ σπέρμα ἐστέ, κατ' ἐπαγγελίαν κληρονόμοι.

While there is much to be explored in this text, for the purpose of this book, my primary interest lies in what Paul means by the phrase, "there is no male and female [οὐκ ἔνι ἄρσεν καὶ θῆλυ, *ouk eni arsen kai thēly*]" (v. 28c). Is this simply a statement regarding the spiritual equality of all who are "in Christ Jesus"? Or does it have repercussions for ministry roles and gender presentation? Is Paul transcending Genesis 1:27 and negating the ongoing relevance of sexual dimorphism? Is he pointing toward an

95. O'Donovan, *Begotten or Made?*, 2nd ed. (Landrum, SC: Davenant Press, 2022), 29.

96. Klassen, "The Pauline Response," 153.

97. Jewett, *Male and Female*, 142.

androgynous future? How do his words apply to those who wish to claim a transgender (or perhaps nonbinary) identity? These are merely some of the questions generated by this phrase.

Egalitarian readings of the text

Prior to the twentieth century, commentators generally took the view that Galatians 3:28 applies "[o]nly to sex as affecting our relation to Christ."[98] In other words, it affirms that *all* who are "in Christ" are *equally* "sons of God" (v. 26) and "Abraham's offspring" (v. 29), but it "changes nothing in the domain of this world and this natural life."[99]

By the second half of the twentieth century, however, such an interpretation was increasingly coming under challenge. Krister Stendahl, for example, argued that Paul's statement constitutes a "breakthrough" which "points beyond and even 'against' the prevailing practice of the New Testament church," and so must "manifest itself in the social dimensions of the church."[100] While rejecting Stendahl's characterization of Galatians 3:28 as a "breakthrough" (and arguing instead that it represents the status quo of the New Testament church), Elisabeth Schüssler Fiorenza drew a comparable conclusion: "in the Christian community all distinctions of religion, race, class, nationality, and gender are insignificant."[101] The key implication of this, for her, was that all ministry functions and all church offices should be open to women.

In recent decades, a host of commentators and feminist scholars have voiced similar sentiments. James Dunn, for instance, suggests that it is "highly unlikely" that Paul "would have allowed gender or social status as such, any more than race, to constitute a barrier against any service in the gospel."[102] Kirsten Guidero likewise claims that because "through baptism into Christ, women as well as men, slaves as well as free, Gentiles as

98. Joseph Agar Beet, *A Commentary on St. Paul's Epistle to the Galatians*, 4th ed. (London: Hodder and Stoughton, 1893), 100.

99. R. C. H. Lenski, *The Interpretation of St. Paul's Epistles to the Galatians, to the Ephesians, and to the Philippians* (Columbus, OH: Wartburg, 1946), 189.

100. Krister Stendahl, *The Bible and the Role of Women: A Case Study in Hermeneutics*, trans. E. T. Sander (Philadelphia: Fortress, 1966), 32–35.

101. Elisabeth Schüssler Fiorenza, *In Memory of Her: A Feminist Theological Reconstruction of Christian Origins*, 2nd ed. (New York: Crossroad, 1994), 213.

102. James D. G. Dunn, *The Epistle to the Galatians* (London: Black, 1993), 207.

well as Jews, receive both equal entrance *and* equal standing within the community of Christ ... no one can hold special offices on the basis of any of these distinctions."[103]

At the same time, in making their case, egalitarian interpreters have not wished to dispute either the reality or importance of male and female sex distinctions.[104] Dunn, for example, insists that Paul's point in Galatians 3:28 is not that sex distinctions have been *removed*, but that they have been *relativized*—that is, they no longer imply "relative worth or value."[105] Even Schüssler Fiorenza is adamant that Galatians 3:28 "does not assert that there are no longer men and women in Christ, but that patriarchal marriage ... is no longer constitutive of the new community in Christ."[106]

Queer readings of the text

However, what egalitarian writers *affirm* (the enduring nature of sex difference) is the very thing that queer authors *deny*—or, at least, *query*. For instance, on the basis of the grammatical shift from *nor* to *and* in Galatians 3:28 ("neither Jew *nor* Greek, neither slave *nor* free, no male *and* female"), Mollenkott postulates that this points toward "a time when instead of separate gender obligations, both physical maleness-femaleness and masculine-feminine social roles will be recognized as a continuum on which individuals may locate themselves comfortably and without fear of reprisal."[107]

Cornwall, too, sees Paul's grammatical variation as opening up space for "an erasure of the binarism." What she means by this is "the end of an exclusive, heteronormative system wherein humans are completed as humans only by so-called sexual complementarity." While she is quick to clarify that this does not mean the disappearance of "male and female as gamete possibilities," it does mean the end of "male-and-female as a

---

103. Kirsten Lauren Guidero, "'No Longer any Male and Female'? Galatians 3, Baptismal Identity, and the Question of an Evangelical Hermeneutic," *Priscilla Papers* 33, no. 3 (2019): 24, 19–27 (emphasis original).

104. There are exceptions, of course. Hans Betz, for example, argues that the text nullifies both "*social* differences" and "*biological* distinctions" (Hans Dieter Betz, *Galatians: A Commentary on Paul's Letter to the Churches in Galatia*, Hermeneia [Minneapolis: Fortress, 1989], 195, emphasis original).

105. Dunn, *Galatians*, 207.

106. Schüssler Fiorenza, *In Memory of Her*, 211.

107. Mollenkott, *Omnigender*, xii.

socially limiting construct." One implication of this is that the bodies of those with intersex conditions "need not be altered to 'fit' it." At base, however, is her conviction that Galatians 3:28 signals the ultimate cessation of male-and-female and that this, therefore, is "the end—the *telos*—for humanity."[108]

According to Dale Martin, however, if the text is translated more literally, it is open to a wide range of interpretive possibilities. For instance, "no male and *female*" could mean that the "inferior female has been swallowed up into the eschatologically perfected male form." Or, if the emphasis is instead placed the word *male*, then it could mean that "the male is now *female*"—because "the masculine side is what needs to be taken up into the feminine." Alternatively, if we emphasize *and*, it might mean that "in Christ everyone is both: masculifeminine or feminimascupersons." Martin's preferred option, however, is to "destabilize the duality," admit that "gender is multiplex, not duplex," and "dispense with the dichotomy, the dualism, the dimorphism entirely." The goal is to invent "all sorts of new ways of being human, not just two" and to open the door to "as yet unknowable ways of gendering human experience." After chiding those who believe that "one must be *either* male *or* female," he concludes by suggesting that we should recognize "just how queer a text Galatians 3:28 is. And that we should use its queerness to help us get along with the task of queering our Christian selves."[109]

Finally, while perhaps not "queer readings" (strictly speaking), androgynous interpretations of Galatians 3:28 also abound. For instance, drawing on Philo's reading of Genesis, Wayne Meeks has proposed that the text is a "baptismal reunification formula" that not only "presupposes an interpretation of the creation story in which the divine image after which Adam was modeled was masculofeminine," but also proclaims that "the act of Christian initiation reverses the fateful division of Genesis 2:21–22."[110] In a similar vein, Daniel Boyarin argues that the text is both "a reflection of the primal androgyne interpretation of Genesis 1.28" and "a representation

---

108. Cornwall, *Sex and Uncertainty*, 72–74 (emphasis original).

109. Martin, *Single Savior*, 89–90 (emphasis original).

110. Meeks, "Image of the Androgyne," 185.

of an androgyny that exists on the level of the spirit."[111] In favor of such interpretations, writes Jeremy Punt, is his claim that "a one-body or one-sex model reigned in the ancient world."[112]

A contextual reading of the text

However, a contextual reading of Galatians 3:28 leads to very different conclusions to the queer (and androgynous) readings noted above and, to a lesser extent, many egalitarian readings also. Indeed, despite his attempt to commandeer Paul's statement for queer and postcolonial purposes, Punt concedes that, at the level of authorial intent, "Paul did not invest Gal 3:28 with emancipatory or egalitarian meaning."[113] Moreover, as Pauline Hogan's historical-critical study of the reception of Galatians 3:28 in the early patristic period has demonstrated, the text was not regarded as a charter text for egalitarian liberation, nor was it seen as depicting Christ as an androgynous Savior, nor was his church viewed as the recreation of an original androgynous humanity.[114]

What, then, is the meaning and import of Paul's statement? As Douglas Moo rightly recognizes, Galatians 3:26–29 lies at the heart of Paul's argument in chapters 3–4 (if not the entire letter) and forms a fitting climax to 3:7–25.[115] Having established that "it is those of faith who are the sons of Abraham" (v. 7) and that it is only "in Christ Jesus" that "the blessing of Abraham" can come to the gentiles (v. 14), Paul now confirms that *all* who have been "baptized into Christ have put on Christ" (v. 27) and so *all* are "sons of God, through faith" (v. 26). This leads him to conclude that "if you are Christ's, then you are Abraham's offspring, heirs according to promise" (v. 29).

Within this train of thought, verse 28 serves to clarify *who* are included in the "all" of verse 26 and the "many" of verse 27—that is, *every believer without distinction*—and to insist on the spiritual equality and ecclesial

111. Boyarin, "Genealogy of Gender," 32n91, 16.

112. Jeremy Punt, "Power and Liminality, Sex and Gender, and Gal 3:28. A Postcolonial, Queer Reading of an Influential Text," *Neotestamentica* 44 (2010): 151. As we saw in ch. 4, however, this is a highly dubious supposition!

113. Punt, "Power and Liminality," 162.

114. Pauline N. Hogan, *"No Longer Male and Female": Interpreting Galatians 3.28 in Early Christianity*, LNTS 380 (New York: T&T Clark, 2008), 193–95.

115. Douglas J. Moo, *Galatians*, BECNT (Grand Rapids: Baker Academic, 2013), 248.

unity of all who have been justified by faith (v. 24) and received the promised Holy Spirit (v. 14). Thus, the force of Paul's neither-nor formula is, in fact, both-and: *both* Jew *and* Gentile, *both* slave *and* free, *both* male *and* female are Abraham's seed and God's children. There is no gradation, no distinction, and no division, "for you [are] all one in Christ Jesus" (πάντες γὰρ ὑμεῖς εἷς ἐν Χριστῷ Ἰησοῦ, *pantes gar hymeis heis en Christō Iēsou*).

The reason why Paul slightly varies his construction in his third couplet (shifting from neither-nor to not-and) is almost certainly because he is citing verbatim the LXX of Genesis 1:27c (ἄρσεν καὶ θῆλυ ἐποίησεν αὐτούς, *arsen kai thēly epoiēsen autous*). The slight change of form, then, "implies no real change of meaning."[116] In other words, Paul is no more claiming that sexual dimorphism has disappeared than he is that racial or social distinctions have disappeared. What he is claiming is that "Jews are not superior to Gentiles, those who are free are not more important than slaves, and men are not worth more than women."[117] Galatians 3:28, then, is not announcing "the absolute abolition of these distinctions but only their irrelevance for participation in Christian baptism and full membership in the Christian community."[118] In regard to sex difference specifically, Judith Gundry-Volf helpfully remarks:

> Gal 3,28 does not declare sex difference in any sense abolished in a new creation of a unified, sexually undifferentiated humanity. Rather, it refers to the adiaphorization of sex difference in a new creation where being male or female is no advantage or disadvantage in relation to God and other and where man and woman are reconciled and united as equals. Christ is not portrayed as amalgamizing Christians into a new "one" above fleshly distinctions by virtue of being himself genderless or androgynous.[119]

116. Richard N. Longenecker, *Galatians*, WBC 41 (Waco, TX: Word, 1990), 157.

117. Thomas R. Schreiner, *Galatians*, ZECNT (Grand Rapids: Zondervan, 2010), 258.

118. Troy W. Martin, "The Covenant of Circumcision (Genesis 17:9–14) and the Situational Antitheses of Galatians 3:28," *JBL* 122 (2003): 122.

119. Judith M. Gundry-Volf, "Christ and Gender: A Study of Difference and Equality in Gal 3,28," in *Jesus Christus als die Mitte der Schrift. Studien zur Hermeneutik des Evangeliums*, ed. C. Landmesser, H. J. Eckstein, and H. Lichtenberger (Berlin: Walter de Gruyter, 1997), 439.

Therefore, those who claim that Galatians 3:28 erases the sex binary or opens the door to multiple gender categories not only take it "far beyond its situational context,"[120] but misconstrue the apostle's meaning. Paul's words do not eliminate sex distinctions or proliferate gender options, nor do they indicate that he "expected a return to primal androgyny once God's elect received their heavenly bodies."[121] In fact, *the very statement that appears to relativize the significance of the sex binary underscores its abiding reality*. Straightforwardly, for male and female to be *united* (as opposed to *dissolved*) in Christ, the two sexes must remain *distinct*. Rather than announcing the eradication of sex difference, then, Galatians 3:28 encloses it "within a larger reality that constitutes a more basic identity, shared by all participants."[122] For this reason, sex "no longer serves as a metric with which to value the worth, esteem, or quality of a person."[123]

THE RESURRECTION OF THE BODY

We come now to the final section of this chapter and to a brief consideration of the Bible's hope, and, in particular, to what the promise of bodily resurrection reveals about the permanence and importance of embodied sex.

The backdrop to this discussion is, once again, the doubt that has been cast by queer theologians and trans-affirming authors over the present clarity and future certainty of the sex-and-gender binary and the sex-and-gender connection. For example, building on the thought of Gregory of Nyssa (in particular, his beliefs that sexual dimorphism was "a concession to the needs of reproduction" and that "eschatological transformation would mean the end of gender"), Linn Tonstad argues that "lived or reproductive heterosexuality belongs only to the order of fallen creation." The implication she draws from this "is that gender can't have the centrality for Christians that arguments for exclusive heterosexuality require it to have. If eschatological transformation takes human beings beyond gender, in some sense, then God isn't that concerned with enforcing normative

120. Martin, "Covenant of Circumcision," 124.

121. Knust, *Unprotected Texts*, 52.

122. Grant Macaskill, *Living in Union with Christ: Paul's Gospel and Christian Moral Identity* (Grand Rapids: Baker Academic, 2019), 56.

123. Do Vale, *Gender as Love*, 231.

gender standards on us."[124] Geoffrey Rees goes even further, seeing in the hope of resurrection the promise of a different ontological order, radically discontinuous with the present, in which identity is no longer determined by sex at all.[125]

Taking a different tack, Cornwall postulates that "it may be that clear sex-gender differentiation, rather than ambiguity, is what will be erased in the new humanity." Furthermore, she is convinced that the sexual domination of men over women, which she regards as an inevitable consequence of heteronormativity, "will not pass away until binaries are blurred and each referent is freed into a future truly different and truly transformed."[126] Present liberation, therefore, is dependent on the degree to which the sexual ambiguity of the future can be realized in history.

To assess such proposals, two passages will be considered: Matthew 22:23–33 (esp. v. 30) and 1 Corinthians 15:35–58 (esp. v. 53). The implications for trans theory will then be teased out. However, a brief comment on Jesus's resurrection is first necessary, for "if we want to know what God intends for bodily creatures, the resurrected body of the Son, and not our own sinful bodies, is the place we need to start."[127]

CHRIST THE FIRSTFRUITS

The apostle Paul is unequivocal that the Christian faith stands or falls with the bodily resurrection of Jesus Christ (1 Cor 15:14–19). Consequently, the claim that Christ "was raised on the third day in accordance with the Scriptures" was at the heart of his gospel and a matter of "first importance" (vv. 3–4). That he understood the resurrection to be a physical, space-time event is confirmed by his reference to Christ's postmortem burial (v. 4) and his numerous post-resurrection appearances (vv. 5–8). Moreover, as N. T. Wright has cogently argued, if Paul's notion of resurrection had been that of "a non-bodily survival of death," his entire argument would have been superfluous: "None of it, indeed,

124. Linn Marie Tonstad, *Queer Theology* (Eugene, OR: Cascade, 2018), 41.

125. Geoffrey Rees, *The Romance of Innocent Sexuality* (Eugene, OR: Cascade, 2011), 288.

126. Cornwall, *Sex and Uncertainty*, 70, 193.

127. Beth Felker Jones, *Marks of His Wounds: Gender Politics and Bodily Resurrection* (Oxford: Oxford University Press, 2007), 4.

would make sense: neither in outline nor in detail does 1 Corinthians 15 resemble an argument for the immortality of the soul."[128]

This helps clarify the meaning of Paul's statement in verse 45: "the last Adam became a life-giving spirit" (ὁ ἔσχατος Ἀδὰμ εἰς πνεῦμα ζῳοποιοῦν, *ho eschatos Adam eis pneuma zōopoioun*). The Old Testament background to this expression is Ezekiel 37. Here, as noted in chapter 8, the prophet's language deliberately echoes Genesis 2:7 (which Paul has just cited in the first half of the verse), as the Lord promises to resurrect his people by breathing into them "the spirit of life" (πνεῦμα ζωῆς, *pneuma zōēs*, LXX: Ezek 37:5). Paul's declaration, then, is not that Jesus is now a disembodied phantom—nor is this the meaning of "spiritual body" (σῶμα πνευματικόν, *sōma pneumatikon*) in verse 44, as we shall see shortly. It is, rather, that he "is the true resurrection of the dead, the one whose Spirit brings the rest of us to resurrection life."[129] Hence Paul calls him "the firstfruits of those who have fallen asleep" (v. 20).

That Jesus is not a ghost is also a point of emphasis in Luke 24:36–49. This is not to deny that there are indications of discontinuity between Christ's resurrection body and his temporal body.[130] Indeed, it is precisely Jesus's ability to suddenly appear among the disciples that made them wonder if they were seeing a spirit (v. 37). Nevertheless, Jesus quickly dispels this thought: "It is I myself. Touch me, and see. *For a spirit does not have flesh and bones* [ὅτι πνεῦμα σάρκα καὶ ὀστέα οὐκ, *hoti pneuma sarka kai ostea ouk*] as you see that I have" (v. 39). What is noteworthy is the expression, "it is I myself." This is language that not only communicates identity across time (pre- and post-resurrection) but connects this continuity to his body. As David Muthukumar writes:

> Jesus establishes his identity as 'I' and 'myself' by inviting his disciples to touch him and makes sense of his identity through his flesh and bones, demonstrating the essential embodiment of his personhood. In other words, Jesus's post-resurrection 'self' or egocentricity is extended here through his embodied continuity. … His sense

---

128. N. T. Wright, *The Resurrection of the Son of God* (Philadelphia: Fortress, 2003), 315.

129. Ciampa and Rosner, *Corinthians*, 820.

130. See Luke 24:31, 36 and 44 (compare John 20:19, 26; Acts 1:3; 10:40–41a).

> of diachronic unity ... is constructed around his bodily experiences of crucifixion and the resultant scars and wounds.[131]

This is the significance of the fact that Jesus "showed them his hands and his feet" (v. 40; compare John 20:27). Consequently, Article IV of the Thirty-Nine Articles of Religion ("*Of the Resurrection of Christ*") is right to declare that "Christ did truly rise again from death, and took again His body, with flesh, bones, and all things appertaining to the perfection of man's nature." The Scots Confession (1560) is likewise right to affirm that "the selfsame body which was born of the virgin, was crucified, dead, and buried, and which did rise again, did ascend into the heavens" (ch. 11).

Perhaps the most salient point, however, at least for our purposes, is that it is not only flesh and bone that has been raised from the dead and seated at the right hand of God, but it is "the man Christ Jesus" (1 Tim 2:5). For Jesus, as Todd Wilson rightly deduces, "is, and always will be, a crucified, circumcised Jewish male."[132]

MATTHEW 22:30

We turn now to Jesus's statement in Matthew 22:30 (compare Mark 12:25; Luke 20:35): "For in the resurrection they neither marry nor are given in marriage, but are like angels in heaven." As Mark Walton has helpfully catalogued, several of the early church fathers (including Clement of Alexandria and Athanasius) understood Jesus to mean that "the process of transformation that occurs concomitantly with the resurrection completely does away with all sex characteristics." As a consequence, "gender" not only becomes "irrelevant in the new creation; it becomes meaningless."[133] But is this what it will mean for us to be "like angels in heaven" (*ὡς ἄγγελοι ἐν τῷ οὐρανῷ, hōs angeloi en tō ouranō*)?

---

131. David S. Muthukumar, "Embodied and Socially Embedded 'Self': Understanding Jesus's Bodily Resurrection and Believers' Post Mortem Identity and Continuity," *Science and Christian Belief* 31 (2019): 126.

132. Wilson, *Mere Sexuality*, 36.

133. Mark David Walton, "What We Shall Be: A Look at Gender and the New Creation," *JBMW* 9 (2004): 18.

"Like angels in heaven"

The context of Jesus's statement holds the key to its meaning. It is a response to the Sadducees' question regarding the (presumably hypothetical) woman who had been married successively to seven brothers: "In the resurrection, therefore, of the seven, whose wife will she be?" (v. 28). Jesus's answer is clear: to none of them, for there will be no marriage in the resurrection. It is in *this respect* (not in *all respects*) that "those who are considered worthy to attain to that age and to the resurrection from the dead" (Luke 20:35) will be "like angels."[134] It makes no difference, then, whether angels are asexual or exclusively male beings. As Hagner writes: "The only point made here is that so far as marriage (and sex?) is concerned, human beings will be like angels, i.e., not marrying."[135]

Luke provides further confirmation of this interpretation. In his account, Jesus explains why marriage will not persist in the age to come: "*for they cannot die anymore* [οὐδὲ γὰρ ἀποθανεῖν ἔτι, *oude gar apothanein eti*], because they are *equal to angels* [ἰσάγγελοι, *isangeloi*] and are sons of God, being sons of the resurrection" (Luke 20:36). In other words, the reason marriage will end is because human life will not: death will be no more. While Jesus does not elaborate further on the connection between immortality and the cessation of marriage, the broader biblical witness would suggest that once God has brought

> the sad history of rebellion and sin to its ultimate end through the second, final death and the subsequent wedding between God and his people (Rev 20–21), the ultimate purpose of marriage will be reached. The divine covenant ideal it represents and the plan of redemption it symbolizes are then completely fulfilled and finished.[136]

Thus, the future for all of God's children (regardless of their marital status in this life) is participation in the marriage beyond marriage: that of Christ and the church.

---

134. Hagner, *Matthew 14–28*, 641. According to Jewish tradition, angels need neither food nor marriage (e.g., 1 En 15:6; 51:4; 104:4–6; Wis 5:5, 15–16; 2 Bar 51:10).

135. Hagner, *Matthew 14–28*, 641.

136. René Gehring, "'They Will Be Like Angels.' Paradise Without Marriage?," *JATS* 27 (2016): 83.

"They neither marry nor are given in marriage"

But will we be raised as males and females? Or was Gregory of Nyssa correct that "when all shall become one in Christ we shall be divested of the signs of this distinction together with the whole of the old man"?[137]

Careful attention to Jesus's words in Matthew 22:30 (compare Mark 12:25; Luke 20:35) yields a clear answer to this question. As Augustine rightly saw, the twin expressions "neither do they marry [οὔτε γαμοῦσιν, *oute gamousin*]" and "nor are they given in marriage [οὔτε γαμίζονται, *oute gamizontai*]" refer to males and females, respectively.[138] "The separate clauses for men and women reflect the asymmetry of the way that marriages were arranged, with the woman being given from her father's sphere to that of a husband."[139] Jesus, therefore, is doing more than stating that in the resurrection there will be no marriage. He is saying that in the resurrection males will not marry and females will not be given in marriage. In other words, he is not denying the continuing reality of embodied sex in the age to come; he is, in fact, affirming it.[140]

If further confirmation of post-mortem body-identity continuation is sought, the fact that Jesus insists that Abraham, Isaac, and Jacob remain themselves beyond the grave (v. 32a) indicates the persistence of their sex-determined gender even now in the intermediate state. Indeed, his entire point hinges on the force of the present tense of the verb "is" in Exodus 3:6 (LXX): "I *am* [εἰμι, *eimi*] the God of Abraham, and the God of Isaac, and the God of Jacob." From this Jesus draws the conclusion: "He is not God of the dead [νεκρῶν, *nekrōn*], but of the living [ζώντων, *zōntōn*]" (v. 32b). In sum, even as they await the resurrection of their bodies, Abraham, Isaac, and Jacob remain Abraham, Isaac, and Jacob.

Contrary to Gregory of Nyssa, then, Jesus is not saying that in the resurrection we shall all "be de-genitalized again, and so receive that angelic status that was our lot originally."[141] His point, rather, as Augustine rightly

---

137. Gregory of Nyssa, *Homilies on the Song of Songs,* Homily 7, cited in Verna E. F. Harrison, "Male and Female in Cappadocian Theology," *JTS* 41 (1990): 441.

138. Augustine, *The City of God*, 22.17 (*NPNF*[1] 2:496).

139. Nolland, *Matthew*, 904–5.

140. As Walton expresses: "Far from saying that there will be no distinctions of gender in the new creation, Jesus said in essence that those who are male in heaven will not take a wife, nor will those who are female be given in marriage" ("What We Shall Be," 19).

141. Coakley, "Eschatological Body," 68. This is Coakley's summary of Gregory's view.

discerned, is that he "who created both sexes will restore both."[142] Grenz's conclusion is therefore fitting: "Marriage and genital sexuality are limited to this penultimate age, of course. But sexuality is not. To leave sexuality behind is to undercut the significance of the resurrection."[143]

1 CORINTHIANS 15:53

We come finally to a consideration of Paul's teaching in 1 Corinthians 15:35–58, in particular verse 53: "For *this perishable body* [φθαρτὸν τοῦτο, *phtharton touto*] must put on the *imperishable* [ἀφθαρσίαν, *aphtharsian*], and *this mortal body* [θνητὸν τοῦτο, *thnēton touto*] must put on *immortality* [ἀθανασίαν, *athanasian*]." To properly elucidate the meaning and relevance of this statement, several features of Paul's larger argument first need to be appreciated.

"With what kind of body do they come?" (v. 35)

Paul begins this section by raising two related questions that were apparently being asked by his readers: "How are the dead raised? With what kind of body do they come?" (v. 35). The skeptical overtone of the opening "How" (πῶς, *pōs*), along with Paul's word of rebuke (v. 36a: "You foolish person!"), followed by his elucidation of the agriculturally obvious (v. 36b: "What you sow does not come to life unless it dies"), all suggest the questions are best viewed "not as a genuine enquiry but as a dismissive put down."[144]

Nonetheless, Paul provides an answer in three parts: first, verses 36–44 introduce the analogy of a seed growing into a plant to illustrate that "what you sow is not the body that is to be" (v. 37; compare v. 42); second, verses 45–49 draw a related contrast between "the first man" (Adam) and "the second man" (Christ) to make the point that "just as we have borne the image of the man of dust, we shall also bear the image of the man of heaven" (v. 49); and third, verses 50–58 highlight the necessity of bodily transformation to argue that if believers are to inherit God's kingdom, the "mortal and perishable body must give way to the immortal and

---

142. Augustine, *The City of God*, 22.17 (*NPNF*[1] 2:496).

143. Grenz, "The Social God," 88–89.

144. Wright, *Resurrection of the Son of God*, 342.

imperishable."[145] However, his short answer to the question, "With *what kind of body* are the dead raised?," is "a spiritual body" (v. 44).

"It is raised a spiritual body" (v. 44)

The meaning of "spiritual body" (σῶμα πνευματικός, *sōma pneumatikos*) has often been misunderstood.[146] In fact, Fernando Vidal has described the history of debates over the nature of the resurrection as "a two-thousand-year-old attempt at working out the oxymoron *spiritual body*."[147] Yet, when read in context, Paul's expression is not difficult to decipher. First, it is juxtaposed with the term "natural body" (σῶμα ψυχικός, *sōma psychikos*), which, as the preceding verses make plain, is essentially *earthly*—hence "perishable" (v. 42) and sown in "dishonor" and "weakness" (v. 43)—and so belongs to *the life of the present age*. By way of contrast, the "spiritual body" is essentially *heavenly*—hence "imperishable" (v. 42) and sown in "glory" and "power" (v. 43)—and so belongs to *the life of the coming age*. The "spiritual body," then, is an eschatological reality: the eternal body of the future.

Second, given that Paul's entire discussion of resurrection in verses 1–34 is inescapably *physical*, the "spiritual body" is clearly not "composed of 'spirit'; it is a *body* adapted to the eschatological existence that is under the ultimate domination of, and animated by, the Spirit."[148] Paul, then, is not contrasting a substantial body with an insubstantial one. Rather, in the face of our somatic frailty, he is holding forth the prospect of "the revivification and glorious transformation to immortality of the mortal body of flesh."[149] In this sense, the addition of "spiritual" (*pneumatikos*) to "body" (*sōma*) is "the most elegant way he can find of saying both that the new body is the result of the Spirit's work (answering the 'how does

---

145. Gardner, *1 Corinthians*, 721.

146. Dale Martin, for example, believes that as a *spiritual body*, "the raised body is stripped of flesh, blood, and soul" (Dale B. Martin, *The Corinthian Body* [New Haven: Yale University Press, 1995], 129).

147. Fernando Vidal, "Brains, Bodies, Selves and Science: Anthropologies of Identity and the Resurrection of the Body," *Critical Inquiry* 28 (2002): 941.

148. Fee, *Corinthians*, 869 (emphasis original).

149. James Ware, "Paul's Understanding of the Resurrection in 1 Corinthians 15:36–54," *JBL* 133 (2014): 835.

it come to be?') and that it is the appropriate vessel for the Spirit's life (answering 'what sort of thing is it?')."[150]

"This mortal body must put on immortality" (v. 53)

This brings us to verse 53. The "must" (δεῖ, *dei*) at the beginning of the verse in Greek emphasizes the *necessity* of the change that is scheduled for those in Christ (v. 22). The *reason* for this necessity has already been given: "flesh and blood cannot inherit the kingdom of God, nor does the perishable inherit the imperishable" (v. 50). As Troels Engberg-Pedersen explains, this statement does not mean that "flesh and blood will in some sense be 'shed' in such a way that it is only what remains that will be resurrected. No, the individual body of flesh and blood will be transformed as a whole so as to become through and through a pneumatic one"[151]—that is, characterized by the glory and power of the coming age and of "the man of heaven" himself (vv. 48–49).

Therefore, as necessary as is the change that Paul promises (v. 51), continuity between our present ("natural") body and our future ("spiritual") body is equally vital. And this is precisely what he asserts in verse 53, for when he declares "*this* perishable body must put on the imperishable, and *this* mortal body must put on immortality," "the subject of Paul's verbs of transformation is the present earthly body."[152] Christ's purpose is to renovate (not replace) our present bodies, that they might "be like his glorious body" (Phil 3:20–21).

The Westminster Confession of Faith, then, has rightly construed Paul's meaning: "the dead shall be raised up, *with the selfsame bodies, and*

150. Wright, *Resurrection of the Son of God*, 354 (emphasis original).

151. Troels Engberg-Pedersen, *Cosmology and Self in the Apostle Paul: The Material Spirit* (Oxford: Oxford University Press, 2010), 32.

152. Ware, "Paul's Understanding," 827. Engberg-Pedersen concurs: "Continuity," he writes, "is in fact the very point of the τοῦτο (*touto*) that Paul repeats four times in 15:53–54: that '*this* corruptible (some-thing)' and '*this* mortal (something)' " (meaning this individual body) "will put on incorruption and immortality. If 'this mortal and corruptible something,' which must consist of flesh and blood, is going to put on immortality and incorruption, then it must, as it were, *be* there for that operation to be successful" (Troels Engberg-Pedersen, "Complete and Incomplete Transformation in Paul: A Philosophical Reading of Paul on Body and Spirit," in *Metamorphoses: Resurrection, Body and Transformative Practices in Early Christianity*, Ekstasis 1, ed. Turid Karlsen Seim and Jorunn Økland, [Berlin: de Gruyter, 2009], 128 [emphasis original]).

none other (although with different qualities)."[153] What this means for our present study is that while radical bodily change is due for all who are "in Christ" (v. 22), Scripture gives us no reason to think (and every reason to doubt) that God intends to change our sex. The change will not be from men and women into something else. Rather, it will be from *mortal* and *perishable* men and women into *immortal* and *imperishable* men and women. It is in this way that we shall all come to "bear the image of the man of heaven" (v. 49).

IMPLICATIONS FOR TRANS THEORY

In view of Paul's teaching in 1 Corinthians 15 about the nature of the resurrection body, I conclude this chapter with a series of reflections on some of the more important questions raised by trans-affirming authors and disability theologians.

Ever since Nancy Eiesland's provocative claim that "the resurrected Jesus is revealed as the disabled God,"[154] disability theologians have been asking if "our resurrection bodies will still retain the injuries and defects of earthly life, whether they be an amputated leg, an intellectual disability, a hemiplegia, or a speech delay."[155] With intersex conditions particularly in mind, Cornwall similarly suggests that "bodies which have had different configurations during their time on earth provoke questions about which particular configuration, if any, will be reflected in the resurrection body." One of those questions is the following: "What body might we expect for someone shorn of an undersized penis and brought up as a girl, who has decided to make the best of a bad gender-assignment despite experiencing gender dysphoria?"[156]

In view of the complex somatic conditions with which some are afflicted, Robert Song argues that it is "ludicrously inappropriate to enquire what precise form the resurrection body might take." At the same time, Song expresses confidence that

153. XXXII.2 (emphasis added).

154. Nancy L. Eiesland, *The Disabled God: Toward a Liberatory Theology of Disability* (Nashville: Abingdon, 1994), 100.

155. Maja I. Whitaker, "Perfected Yet Still Disabled?: Continuity of Embodied Identity in Resurrection Life," *Stimulus* 26 (December 2019): https://hail.to/laidlaw-college/article/sRNklJP.

156. Cornwall, *Sex and Uncertainty*, 189.

> whatever the resurrection body is, it cannot be the end product of human manipulation: flesh and blood, however much human beings may intervene in them, cannot inherit the kingdom of God (1 Cor. 15:50). Rather, the New Testament emphasis is on the transformation of our bodies into bodies that will be fit for the life of the new heaven and the new earth, and that this transformation will be the work of God.[157]

This is certainly in keeping with Paul's thought in 1 Corinthians 15. For just as God gives to each kind of *seed* "a body as he has chosen" (v. 38), so shall it be with the resurrection of the dead (v. 42): he will give each *person* the body he has chosen. Moreover, given that the body that is sown "is not the body that is to be" (v. 37), perhaps there are some questions we need not try to answer.

But can any more be said? Paul's emphasis on the continuity between *the body that is* and *the body that will be* strongly suggests it can. As we have seen throughout both this and the previous chapter, the saving work of the Triune God is "to redeem, restore, renew and consummate his creation, in all its dimensions, including especially man in every aspect of his being."[158] Creation matters, therefore. Its form matters. Its structure matters. Its purpose matters. Its glorification matters. It is not just "the raw material out of which the world as we know it is composed," it is "the order and coherence *in* which it is composed."[159] This means that our bodies matter, as does their sex, for males and females differ all the way down to the cellular level. Consequently, *our sex is not only revelatory of the particular gift given to each of us but is fundamental to our personal identity*. "We are not androgynous persons who happen to have, as a matter of indifference, either a male or female body. ... Our bodies, therefore, give us our gender identity, which is inextricably linked to our bodily form as male or female."[160]

157. Robert Song, *Human Genetics: Fabricating the Future* (London: Darton, Longman & Todd, 2002), 73–74.

158. Matthew P. W. Roberts, "Thinking Like a Christian: The Prolegomena of Herman Bavinck," *ER* 1 (2009): 81.

159. O'Donovan, *Resurrection and Moral Order*, 31 (emphasis original).

160. Mason, "The Wounded It Heals," 139.

Cornwall appears to affirm this when she postulates that a person born with only one leg "might find in the resurrected body a leg present where there was none before." However, she then reverses herself, supporting David Hester's claim that because the Gospels contain no record of Jesus healing a eunuch, genital castration should not be seen as something in need of restoration.[161] Even more confusingly, she speculates that a "female-to-male transsexual who has invested much in a 'phantom' penis might well find a penis in his resurrected body."[162] Such an idea, however, not only inverts the sex and gender relationship, grounding embodiment in identity (rather than the other way around), but proclaims the eternal triumph of confused psychology over clear biology. This is not the change Paul anticipates or the victory he celebrates (vv. 51–57).

CONCLUDING REFLECTIONS

The Bible's expectation is that Christ will raise our bodies with their natal sex. As the realization of this hope will in no way shame or disappoint us (Rom 5:5), we may joyfully anticipate that any distress this sex has caused us in this life will be wondrously healed according to God's original design and eternal purpose. For rather than dispensing with either the sex-and-gender binary or the sex-and-gender connection, God's will is to "sanctify [us] wholly," so that our "*whole* spirit, soul, and body [may] be preserved, unblameably at the coming of our Lord Jesus Christ" (1 Thess 5:23 LSV). Therefore, "whether or not we 'have sex' and whether or not we have sexually distinct social roles in Heaven," our destiny is to be forever sexed.[163]

Furthermore, because sin will no longer corrupt or confuse us in the coming age, we may be confident not only that *fallen gendered stereotypes* will disappear but also that *true gendered archetypes* will remain—if not be fully revealed for the first time! Thus, with Fellipe do Vale, I affirm that one of the reasons we need gender to be restored in the resurrection is "because it is only then that the miseries of this world (including its

161. Cornwall, *Sex and Uncertainty*, 188, 137; compare J. David Hester, "Eunuchs and the Postgender Jesus: Matthew 19:12 and Transgressive Sexualities," *JSNT* 28 (2005): 38.

162. Cornwall, *Sex and Uncertainty*, 188–89.

163. Peter Kreeft, *Everything You Ever Wanted to Know About Heaven: But Never Dreamed of Asking!* (San Francisco: Ignatius Press, 1990), 120.

pernicious constructions of gender) will be seen for what they are, and gendered life lived as it was supposed to be."[164]

While much about our experience of gendered life in the world to come is yet to be disclosed, God's determination to raise these earthly bodies indicates that sex is not only the protological ground of gender but its eschatological ground as well. For those who presently endure the affliction of gender incongruence, this is vital to understand—not because such knowledge will bring an immediate end to their gender conflicts, but because it illuminates the path of true peace. For by ruling out what the experience of gender incongruence is not (ontological misalignment), it highlights what it likely is (epistemological misidentification). It thus signals the way in which personal integration is best sought—by exploring the reasons for the misidentification and by learning to align gender (in its various dimensions) with biological sex.

As stewards not only of the created world but of our own humanity, the task of all who have been redeemed by Jesus Christ and filled with his Spirit is to *grow with the grain of creation toward the goal of new creation*. The reason for this, as Matthew Mason rightly deduces, is because "*this* body, given to me by my Creator according to his original purpose, including its biological sex and the personal gender identity that entails, is the body that will rise on the last day—transformed, powerful, immortal, and glorious beyond my imagining."[165]

There are many things about our resurrection bodies that will remain a mystery until that which is mortal is swallowed up in life (2 Cor 5:4). At the same time, Scripture gives us every reason to believe (and no reason to doubt) that *the sex of the body God has given us in this world will determine the sex of the body he gives us in the world to come*. And as it is now, so it will be then: *the sex of the body both determines and reveals the gender of the person*.

---

164. Fellipe M. do Vale, "Cappadocian or Augustinian? Adjudicating Debates on Gender in the Resurrection," *IJST* 21, no. 2 (April 2019): 198.

165. Mason, "The Wounded It Heals," 143 (emphasis original).

CHAPTER 12

CONCLUSION

Man never exists as such, but always as the human male or the human female. ... He cannot wish to liberate himself from the differentiation and exist as mere man; for in everything that is commonly human he will always be in fact either the human male or the human female.[1]

—Karl Barth

Men and women's gender identities are rooted in the specificity of their distinct sexed bodies. ... A notion that cross gender identifications can make the differences inscribed in the body irrelevant is an illusion.[2]

—Miroslav Volf

The central claim of transgender theory (in both its soft and hard forms) is that the sexed body *does not* determine the gendered self and, as a consequence, *should not* (or, at least, *need not*) ground gender identity, guide gender roles, and govern gender expression.

To evaluate this claim, I have endeavored to do three things in this book. In part 1 (chs. 1–3), I described the main contours and challenges of the current "Transgender Moment," surveyed the most notable evangelical attempts to address transgender questions, and explained the nature of evangelical theological method and how it can be applied to transgender

1. Barth, *CD*, III/4, 117–18.

2. Volf, *Exclusion and Embrace*, 174–75.

theory. In part 2 (chs. 4–6), I attempted to unravel the recent changes that have taken place in conceptions of both sex and gender (and also the connection between them) and offered a philosophical analysis and appraisal of the coherence of trans theory. In part 3 (chs. 7–11), I provided a theological exposition of the key biblical texts that illuminate both sex and gender (as well as the relationship between them) and did so in dialogue with the trans-affirming interpretations of these texts. In this way, I have not only sought to supply an evangelical evaluation of trans theory but to fill an important gap in the evangelical literature.

~

The key conclusions arising from my theological exposition of Scripture may be summarized in seven points:

1. There are and remain only two human sexes—male and female. Intersex conditions do not constitute a third sex.
2. The two sexes are equal in dignity and value (both being made in the image of God) but different in form and function.
3. Because the biological (sex) undergirds the psychosocial-cultural (gender), sexed embodiment is foundational to personal identity.
4. Human beings are psychosomatic unities. Because sex is first and foremost a bodily property, the soul takes its sex from the body.
5. To the extent that the body's sex (or the male-female distinction) is denied, disguised, or diminished, gender will be inauthentic and unfaithful.
6. If a husband or wife transitions genders, the marriage and its witness will be formally (if not also substantially) undermined.
7. The divine purpose is to raise our bodies with their biological sex and the gender identity that corresponds to that sex.

In view of Scripture's consistent affirmation of both the sex-and-gender binary and the sex-and-gender connection, the claim of trans theory has been found to be without foundation and so its implication does not follow. The sexed body *does* determine the gendered self and so *should* ground gender identity, guide gender roles, and govern gender expression.

~

I embarked on my evaluation of trans theory cognizant of Susannah Cornwall's caution that "there is so little biblical material which could be interpreted as speaking specifically about transgender issues that it is dangerous to try to build a Christian theological-ethical response purely on the basis of it."[3] My exploration of the scriptural testimony, however, has shown this concern to be needless. While the Bible may only occasionally speak *about* transgender issues, it speaks *to* them in many and various ways and does so from its opening pages. As we have seen, Scripture "does not begin with the concrete commands in Exodus to Deuteronomy that make allowance for human willfulness. It begins with the vision in Genesis 1–2, and Jesus fulfills the Torah partly by reaffirming its vision, indicating its implications, and challenging his disciples to live by this vision."[4] Creation and Christ, then, are not in conflict. The latter comes to rescue and restore the former.

It is God's commitment to the liberation and transfiguration of the created order that explains why both the sex-and-gender binary and the sex-and-gender connection remain normative for his image bearers throughout all four acts of the biblical drama—creation, fall, redemption, and consummation. Furthermore, it is this anthropological and moral normativity that not only makes possible a coherent theo-ethical response to trans theory but also reveals the Christian's sexual vocation: to faithfully steward his or her sexed identity by *working with the grain of creation toward the goal of new creation.*

3. Cornwall, *Sex and Uncertainty*, 133.

4. See John E. Goldingay, Grant R. LeMarquand, George R. Sumner, and Daniel A. Westberg, "Same-Sex Marriage and Anglican Theology: A View of the Traditionalists," *ATR* 93 (2011): 19.

~

What I have not attempted to do in this book is provide advice and self-care strategies for sufferers. Nor have I sought to outline the contours (let alone develop the details) of a comprehensive pastoral response to those who are either wrestling personally with gender incongruence or seeking to support loved ones who do. Although some valuable work has been done in these domains, there is much work still to be done.[5] Moreover, the need is not just for deeper therapeutic insight and wiser ministry protocols, but for further theological exploration as well: of the biblical practice of lament and its relation to hope; of the importance of suffering and endurance in the life of faith; of the Christian calling to help the weak and bear one another's burdens; and of our duty to alleviate distress where possible, as well as the ethical limits surrounding that duty.[6]

At the larger level of Christian cultural engagement, there is also a need for further thought to be given to how evangelical Christians might better address (rather than reinforce) "the deep-seated fears and misunderstandings" of many of our contemporaries regarding "what the claims of Jesus mean for their gender and sexuality."[7] How can God's good pattern for human flourishing be communicated without it being perceived as a crushing burden? How might we affirm both the reality of the gender binary and the need for gender boundaries without creating overly rigid and needlessly restrictive gender norms?

---

5. Although lacking in evangelical convictional clarity, much therapeutic wisdom can be found in Mark A. Yarhouse and Julia Sadusky, *Emerging Gender Identities: Understanding the Diverse Experiences of Today's Youth* (Grand Rapids: Brazos, 2020); *Gender Identity and Faith: Clinical Postures, Tools and Cases Studies for Client-Centered Care* (Downers Grove, IL: IVP Academic, 2022); "Best Practices in Ministry to Youth Navigating Gender Identity and Faith," *Christian Education Journal* (2020): 1–12, https://doi.org/10.1177/0739891320941866. Brief but biblically founded advice to parents, church leaders, and those who experience gender dysphoria can be found in Samuel Ferguson's *Does God Care about Gender and Identity?*, 26–44. Finally, while not written from a Christian perspective, Sasha Ayad, Lisa Marchiano, and Stella O'Malley's *When Kids Say They're Trans: A Guide for Thoughtful Parents* (London: Swift, 2023) will prove to be of considerable help to many.

6. On the relevance of lament to the experience of gender dysphoria, Andrew Bunt's booklet *People Not Pronouns* provides a brief but valuable introduction (esp. ch. 4: "A Hope Response," 19–23). For an insightful discussion of the healing power of biblical eschatology for those who have experienced gender distress or gender-based violence in this world, see Vale, *Gender as Love*, 232–35.

7. Peter Sanlon, *Plastic People: How Queer Theory Is Changing Us* (London: The Latimer Trust, 2010), 38.

In Deryn Guest's view, this cannot be done—not by evangelicals, not via an evangelical reading of Scripture, and certainly not by affirming the view of sex and gender presented in this book. As she sees it, the way forward is to reject the idea of "a God-ordained, ordered, binaried world," to "undo creation," and to give "chaos a voice."[8] But whatever pain and disappointment may lie behind such a proposal, insisting that "gender must be eliminated for the injustices and sins embroiling it to be made right is," as Fellipe do Vale rightly discerns, "a Pyrrhic victory, a consolation achieved at too great a cost to be of value to the consoled."[9] The reason for this is that our hope lies not in the obliteration of sex-and-gender binary and the sex-and-gender connection, but in their purification from all that is fallen, fractured, and sinful, and their transformation into all that is true, good, and beautiful.

This is why, rather than attempting to "undo creation," the gospel of Jesus Christ points to another way—a way of redemption, restoration, and, finally, resurrection. Indeed, as "the image of the invisible God" in whom, through whom, and for whom "all things were created," Jesus himself is that way (John 14:6; Col 1:15–16). Accordingly, it is his acceptance that is the key to true self-acceptance, just as it is his indwelling that is the key to true transformation. Hence, we shall only become the men and women we were created to be by coming to Jesus, receiving his Spirit, sharing in his identity, and being conformed to his likeness (Matt 11:28; Rom 8:29).

As we have seen, the process of christification is, fundamentally, a matter of *character transformation*—for the "new self" in Christ is "created after the likeness of God in true righteousness and holiness" (Eph 4:24). Nevertheless, the process will ultimately issue in *bodily transformation* (Phil 3:21)—for "just as we have borne the image of the man of dust, we shall also bear the image of the man of heaven" (1 Cor 15:49). This should come as no surprise. The incarnation and resurrection of Jesus not only affirm the essential goodness of human embodiment but confirm that just as his sex is basic to his whole human existence, so our sex grounds our

---

8. Guest, "Troubling the Waters," 22.

9. Vale, *Gender as Love*, 234.

identities and will continue do so in the coming ages.[10] Thus, the body God gives will forever remain foundational to personal identity, and sex the eternal ground of gender.

10. Macleod, *Person of Christ*, 162; Daniel R. Heimbach, "The Unchangeable Difference: Eternally Fixed Sexual Identity for an Age of Plastic Sexuality," in *Biblical Foundations for Manhood and Womanhood*, ed. Wayne A. Grudem (Wheaton, IL: Crossway, 2002), 275–89.

BIBLIOGRAPHY

Achtemeier, Mark. *The Bible's Yes to Same-Sex Marriage: An Evangelical's Change of Heart*. Louisville: Westminster John Knox, 2014.

Adkins, Deanna. "Expert Declaration of Deanna Adkins, M.D." *U. S. District Court, Middle District of North Carolina*, Case 1:16-cv-00236-TDS-JEP (May 13, 2016). https://www.aclu.org/sites/default/files/field_document/AdkinsDecl.pdf.

Alcoff, Linda M. *Visible Identities: Race, Gender and the Self*. Oxford: Oxford University Press, 2006.

Aldous, J., and R. Hill. *International Bibliography of Research in Marriage and the Family*. Vol. 1: 1900–1964. Minneapolis: University of Minnesota Press, 1967.

Alexander, T. Desmond. "Genealogies, Seed and the Compositional Unity of Genesis." *TB* 44, no. 2 (1993): 255–70.

Allberry, Sam. *What God Has to Say about Our Bodies: How the Gospel Is Good News for Our Physical Selves*. Wheaton, IL: Crossway, 2021.

Allen, Prudence. *The Concept of Woman: The Aristotelian Revolution, 750 B.C.–A.D. 1250*. 2nd ed. Grand Rapids: Eerdmans, 1997.

Alter, Robert. *Genesis: Translation and Commentary*. New York: Norton, 1996.

Althaus-Reid, Marcella. *Indecent Theology: Theological Perversions in Sex, Gender and Politics*. London: Routledge, 2000.

Althaus-Reid, Marcella, and Lisa Isherwood, eds. *Trans/Formations*. London: SCM, 2009.

Altman, Meryl, and Keith Nightenhelser. "Book Review of *Making Sex: Body and Gender From the Greeks to Freud by Thomas Laqueur*." *Postmodern Culture* 2, no. 3 (1992). http://www.pomoculture.org/2013/09/26/book-review-of-making-sex.

American Psychiatric Association. *Diagnostic and Statistical Manual of Mental Disorders*, 5th ed (*DSM-5*). Washington, DC: American Psychiatric Publishing, 2013.

American Psychological Association "Answers to Your Questions About Transgender People, Gender Identity, and Gender Expression." *American Psychological Association* (2018). https://www.apa.org/topics/lgbtq/transgender-people-gender-identity-gender-expression.

Anderson, James N. "Transgenderism: A Christian Perspective." *Reformed Faith & Practice* 2, no. 2 (2017): 51–71.

Anderson, Matthew Lee. *Earthen Vessels: Why Our Bodies Matter to Our Faith.* Minneapolis: Bethany, 2011.

Anderson, Ray S. *On Being Human: Essays in Theological Anthropology*. Grand Rapids: Eerdmans, 1982.

Anderson, Ryan T. *When Harry Became Sally: Responding to the Transgender Moment*. New York: Encounter Books, 2018.

Andrews, Tom. "What Is Social Constructionism?" *The Grounded Theory Review* 11, no. 1 (2012): 39–46.

Anglican Church Diocese of Sydney. "Gender Identity: A Report from the Social Issues Committee" (November 21, 2017). https://www.sds.asn.au/sites/default/files/Gender%20Identity.Report2017.FINAL.v2.pdf?doc_id=NTU2MTI.

Aquinas, Thomas. *On Being and Essence*. Translated by A. Maurer. Toronto: Pontifical Institute of Medieval Studies, 1968.

———. *Summa Contra Gentiles*. 5 volumes. Translated by Anton C. Pegis, James F. Anderson, Vernon J. Bourke, and Charles J. O'Neil. Notre Dame: University of Notre Dame Press, 1975.

———. *Summa Theologiae: Latin Text and English Translation, Introductions, Notes, Appendices, and Glossaries*. Edited by T. Gilby and T. C. O'Brien. 60 vols. New York: McGraw Hill, 1963–1976.

Arndt, William F., Walter Bauer, and F. Wilbur Gingrich. *A Greek-English Lexicon of the New Testament and Other Early Christian Literature.* 3rd ed. Chicago: University of Chicago Press, 2001.

Arnold, Bill T. *Genesis*. NCBC. Cambridge: Cambridge University Press, 2009.

Ash, Christopher. *Marriage: Sex in the Service of God*. Leicester: Inter-Varsity Press, 2003.

Ashford, Bruce Riley, and Craig G. Bartholomew. *The Doctrine of Creation: A Constructive Kuyperian Approach*. Downers Grove, IL: InterVarsity Press, 2020.

Ashford, Bruce Riley, and David P. Nelson. "The Story of Mission: The Grand Biblical Narrative." Pages 6–16 in *Theology and Practice of Mission: God, the Church and the Nations*. Edited by Bruce Riley Ashford. Nashville: Broadman & Holman, 2011.

Atkinson, David. *The Message of Genesis 1–11*. Downers Grove, IL: InterVarsity Press, 1990.

Augustine. *The City of God*. Pages 1–511 in vol. 2 of *Nicene and Post-Nicene Fathers*. Series 1. Edited by Philip Schaff. 1887. Repr., Peabody, MA: Hendrickson, 1995.

———. *The Literal Meaning of Genesis: Books 1–6*. Translated and annotated by John Hammond Taylor. United States: Newman Press, 1982.

———. *On Genesis: Two Books on Genesis Against the Manichees and On the Literal Interpretation of Genesis: An Unfinished Book*. Volume 84 of The Fathers of the Church: A New Translation. Translated by Roland J. Teske. Washington, DC: The Catholic University of America Press, 1991.

Austin, John Langshaw. *How to Do Things with Words*. Cambridge: Harvard University Press, 1955.

Avrahami, Yael. "בוש in the Psalms: Shame or Disappointment?" *JSOT* 34 (2010): 295–313.

Ayad, Sasha, Lisa Marchiano, and Stella O'Malley. *When Kids Say They're Trans: A Guide for Thoughtful Parents*. London: Swift, 2023.

Bader-Saye, Scott. "The Transgender Body's Grace." *Journal of the Society of Christian Ethics* 39, no. 1 (2019): 75–92.

Barnes, Hannah. *Time to Think: The Inside Story of the Collapse of the Tavistock's Gender Service for Children*. London: Swift, 2023.

Barr, James. "The Image of God in the Book of Genesis: A Study of Terminology," *BJRL* 51 (1968): 11–26.

Barth, Karl. *Church Dogmatics*. Vol. II/1, *The Doctrine of the Word of God*. Edited by G. W. Bromiley and T. F. Torrance. Translated by T. H. L. Parker, W. B. Johnston, Harold Knight and J. L. M. Haire. Edinburgh: T&T Clark, 1957.

———. *Church Dogmatics*. Vol. III/1, *The Doctrine of Creation*. Edited by G. W. Bromiley and T. F. Torrance. Translated by Harold Knight, G. W. Bromiley, J. K. S. Reid and R. H. Fuller. Edinburgh: T&T Clark, 1958.

———. *Church Dogmatics*. Vol. III/2, *The Doctrine of Creation*. Edited by G. W. Bromiley and T. F. Torrance. Translated by Harold Knight, G. W. Bromiley, J. K. S. Reid and R. H. Fuller. Edinburgh: T&T Clark, 1960.

———. *Church Dogmatics*. Vol. III/4, *The Doctrine of Creation*. Edited by G. W. Bromiley and T. F. Torrance. Translated by A. T. Mackay, T. H. L. Parker, Harold Knight, H. A. Kennedy and J. Marks. Edinburgh: T&T Clark, 1961.

———. *The Humanity of God*. Translated by Thomas Wieser and John Newton Thomas. Richmond: John Knox, 1960.

Barton, Carlin A. *Roman Honor: The Fire in the Bones*. Berkeley: University of California Press, 2001.

Bauckham, Richard. *God and the Crisis of Freedom: Biblical and Contemporary Perspectives*. Louisville: Westminster John Knox, 2002.

Bavinck, Herman. *Reformed Dogmatics: God and Creation: Volume Two*. Edited by John Bolt. Translated by John Vriend. Grand Rapids: Baker, 2004.

———. *Reformed Ethics: The Duties of the Christian Life: Volume Two*. Edited by John Bolt. Grand Rapids: Baker, 2021.

Beardsley, Christina. "Taking Issue: The Transsexual Hiatus in *Some Issues in Human Sexuality*." Pages 69–79 in *This Is My Body: Hearing the Theology of Transgender Christians*. Edited by Christina Beardsley and Michelle O'Brien. London: Darton, Longman & Todd, 2016. Originally published in *Theology* 58, no. 845 (2005): 338–46.

———. *The Transsexual Person Is My Neighbour: Pastoral Guidelines for Christian Clergy, Pastors and Congregations (with an Appendix on Intersex by Michelle O'Brien)*. Brighton: Gender Trust, 2007. https://sibyls.co.uk/wp-content/uploads/2021/05/The-Transexual-Person-is-my-Neighbour-2007.pdf

Beardsley, Christina, and Michelle O'Brien, eds. *This Is My Body: Hearing the Theology of Transgender Christians*. London: Darton, Longman & Todd, 2016.

Beattie, Tina. "The Theological Study of Gender." Pages 33–52 in *The Oxford Handbook of Theology, Sexuality, and Gender*. Edited by Adrian Thatcher. Oxford: Oxford University Press, 2014.

Beauvoir, Simone de. *The Second Sex*. Translated by Constance Borde and Sheila Malovany-Chevallier. London: Vintage, 2011. First published in French as *Le Deuxième Sexe* in 1949.

Bedford, Elliott Louis, and Jason T. Eberl. "Is the Soul Sexed? Anthropology, Transgenderism, and Disorders of Sex Development." *Health Care Ethics USA* 24, no. 3 (2016): 18–33. https://www.chausa.org/docs/default-source/hceusa/is-the-soul-sexed-anthropology-transgenderism-and.pdf?sfvrsn=4.

Beet, Joseph Agar. *A Commentary on St. Paul's Epistle to the Galatians*. 4th ed. London: Hodder and Stoughton, 1893.

Behr, John. "The Rational Animal: A Rereading of Gregory of Nyssa's *De hominis opificio*." *JECS* 7 (1999): 219–47.

Bem, Sandra Lipsitz. "Gender Schema Theory: A Cognitive Account of Sex Typing." *Psychological Review* 88, no. 4 (1981): 354–64.

———. "The Measurement of Psychological Androgyny." *Journal of Consulting and Clinical Psychology* 42, no. 2 (1974): 155–62.

———. *The Lenses of Gender: Transforming the Debate on Sexual Inequality*. New Haven: Yale University Press, 1993.

Benhabib, Seyla. "Feminism and Postmodernism: An Uneasy Alliance." Pages 17–34 in Seyla Benhabib, Judith Butler, Drucilla Cornell and Nancy Fraser, *Feminist Contentions: A Philosophical Exchange*. London: Routledge, 1995.

———. "Subjectivity, Historiography, and Politics." Pages 107–25 in Seyla Benhabib, Judith Butler, Drucilla Cornell, and Nancy Fraser, *Feminist Contentions: A Philosophical Exchange*. London: Routledge, 1995.

Benjamin, Harry. *The Transsexual Phenomenon*. New York: The Julian Press, 1966.

Bensmaïa, Réda. "Poststructuralism." Pages 92–95 in *The Columbia History of Twentieth-Century French Thought*. Edited by Lawrence Kritzman. New York: Columbia University Press, 2006.

Bentley, Madison. "Sanity and Hazard in Childhood." *American Journal of Psychology* 58, no. 2 (1945): 212–46.

Berger, Peter L., and Thomas Luckmann. *The Social Construction of Reality: A Treatise in the Sociology of Knowledge*. New York: Anchor, 1966.

Bergeson, Samantha. "J. K. Rowling Doubles Down on Transphobia in International Women's Day Twitter Rant." *IndieWire* (Mar 8, 2022). https://www.indiewire.com/2022/03/jk-rowling-transphobia-international-womens-day-rant-1234705640.

Berkouwer, Gerrit C. *Man: The Image of God*. Translated by D. W. Jellema. Grand Rapids: Eerdmans, 1962.

Bernard, Jessie. *Women and the Public Interest: Policy and Protest in American Life*. Chicago: Aldine, 1971.

Bertens, Hans. *The Idea of the Postmodern: A History*. London: Routledge, 1995.

Bettcher, Talia Mae. "Feminist Perspectives on Trans Issues." *Stanford Encyclopedia of Philosophy* (January 8, 2014). https://plato.stanford.edu/archives/spr2014/entries/feminism-trans.

Betz, Hans Dieter. *Galatians: A Commentary on Paul's Letter to the Churches in Galatia*. Hermeneia. Minneapolis: Fortress, 1989.

Billington, James H. *Fire in the Minds of Men: Origins of the Revolutionary Faith*. New York: Basic Books, 1980.

Bird, Phyllis A. "'Male and Female He Created Them': Gen 1:27b in the Context of the Priestly Account of Creation." *HTR* 74, no. 2 (1981): 129–59.

———. "Bone of My Bone and Flesh of My Flesh." *Theology Today* 50, no. 4 (January 1994): 521–34.

Blackless, Melanie, Anthony Charuvastra, Amanda Derryck, Anne Fausto-Sterling, Karl Lauzanne, and Ellen Lee. "How Sexually Dimorphic Are We? Review and Synthesis." *American Journal of Human Biology* 12, no. 2 (2000): 151–66.

Blanchard, Ray. "Typology of Male-to-Female Transsexualism." *Archives of Sexual Behavior* 14, no. 3 (1985): 247–61.

Bleier, Ruth H. *Science and Gender: A Critique of Biology and Its Theories on Women*. New York: Pergamon, 1984.

Blevins, John. "Broadening the Family of God: Debating Same-Sex Marriage and Queer Family in America." *Theology & Sexuality* 12, no. 1 (2005): 63–80.

Blocher, Henri. "Women, Ministry and the Gospel: Hints for a New Paradigm?" Pages 239–49 in *Women, Ministry and the Gospel: Exploring New Paradigms*. Edited by Mark Husbands and Timothy Larson. Downers Grove, IL: InterVarsity Press, 2007.

———. *In the Beginning: The Opening Chapters of Genesis*. Translated by David G. Preston. Downers Grove, IL: InterVarsity Press, 1984.

———. *Original Sin: Illuminating the Riddle*. NSBT 5. Leicester: Apollos, 1997.

Block, Daniel I. *Deuteronomy: The NIV Application Commentary*. Grand Rapids: Zondervan, 2012.

Bloesch, Donald G. *A Theology of Word and Spirit: Authority & Method in Theology*. Downers Grove, IL: InterVarsity Press, 1992.

Bock, Darrell L. "Thinking Backwards about Adam and History." *TRINJ* N.S. 40, no. 2 (Fall 2019): 131–43.

———. *Luke 9:51–24:53*. BECNT. Grand Rapids: Baker, 1996.

———. *Proclamation from Prophecy and Pattern: Lucan Old Testament Christology*. JSNTSup 12. Sheffield: JSOT Press, 1987.

Boersma, Hans. "Putting on Clothes: Body, Sex, and Gender in Gregory of Nyssa." *CRUX* 54, no. 2 (Summer 2018): 27–34.

Bonhoeffer, Dietrich. *Creation and Fall: A Theological Exposition of Genesis 1–3*. Edited by John W. De Gruchy. Translated by Douglas S. Bax. Minneapolis: Fortress, 2004.

———. *Ethics*. Edited by Eberhard Bethge. New York: The Macmillan Company, 1962.

Bornstein, Kate. *Gender Outlaw: On Men, Women, and the Rest of Us*. New York: Routledge, 1994.

Boswell, Holly. "The Transgender Alternative." *Chrysalis Quarterly* 1, no. 22 (1991): 29–31.

Boucher, Geoff. "Judith Butler's Postmodern Existentialism: A Critical Analysis." *Philosophy Today* 48, no. 4 (Winter 2004): 355–69.

Boyarin, Daniel. "Paul and the Genealogy of Gender." *Representations* 41 (Winter, 1993):1–33.

Boylan, Jennifer Finney. "Throwing Our Voices: An Introduction." Pages xv–xviii in *'Trans Bodies, Trans Selves': A Resource for the Transgender Community*. Edited by Laura Erickson-Schroth. Oxford: Oxford University Press, 2014.

Branch, J. Alan. *50 Ethical Questions: Biblical Wisdom for Confusing Times*. Bellingham, WA: Lexham, 2022.

———. *Affirming God's Image: Addressing the Transgender Question with Science and Scripture*. Bellingham, WA: Lexham Press, 2018.

Brettler, Marc Zvi. "Happy Is the Man Who Fills His Quiver with Them (Ps. 127:5): Construction of Masculinities in the Psalms." Pages 198–220 in *Being a Man: Negotiating Ancient Constructs of Masculinity*. Edited by Ilona Zsolnay. London: Routledge, 2017.

Brock, Brian. *Disability: Living into the Diversity of Christ's Body*. Grand Rapids: Baker Academic, 2021.

Bromiley, Geoffrey W. *God and Marriage*. Grand Rapids: Eerdmans, 1980.

Brown, Harold O. J. "On Method and Means in Theology." Pages 147–70 in *Doing Theology in Today's World: Essays in Honor of Kenneth S. Kantzer*. Edited by J. D. Woodbridge and T. E. McComiskey. Grand Rapids: Zondervan, 1991.

Brownson, James V. *Bible, Gender, Sexuality: Reframing the Church's Debate on Same-Sex Relationships*. Grand Rapids: Eerdmans, 2013.

Brubaker, Rogers. *Trans: Gender and Race in an Age of Unsettled Identities*. Princeton: Princeton University Press, 2016.

Bruce, F. F. *The Epistle to the Hebrews*. Grand Rapids: Eerdmans, 1964.

Brunner, Emil. *Man in Revolt: A Christian Anthropology*. Translated by Olive Wyon. London: Lutterworth, 1939.

———. *The Divine-Human Encounter*. Translated by A. W. Loos. London: SCM, 1944.

Brunskell-Evans, Heather. "The Medico-Legal 'Making' of 'The Transgender Child.'" *Medical Law Review* 27, no. 4 (Autumn 2019): 640–57.

———. *Transgender: Body Politics*. North Geelong: Spinifex, 2020.

Budziszewksi, J. *On the Meaning of Sex*. Wilmington, DE: Intercollegiate Studies Institute, 2014.

Buhle, Mari Jo. *Feminism and Its Discontents: A Century of Struggle*. Cambridge: Harvard University Press, 1998.

Bullough, Vern L. "The Contributions of John Money: A Personal View." *The Journal of Sex Research* 40, no. 3 (August 2003): 230–36.

Bunt, Andrew. *People Not Pronouns: Reflections on Transgender Experience*. Cambridge: Grove Books, 2021.

Burk, Denny. "The Transgender Test." Pages 87–99 in *Beauty, Order, and Mystery: A Christian Vision of Human Sexuality*. Edited by Gerald Hiestand and Todd Wilson. Downers Grove, IL: InterVarsity Press, 2017.

———. *What Is the Meaning of Sex?* Wheaton, IL: Crossway, 2013.

Burr, Vivien. *Social Constructionism*. 3rd ed. London: Routledge, 2015.

Bury, Michael R. "Social Construction and the Development of Medical Sociology." *Sociology of Health and Illness* 8, no. 2 (1986): 137–69.

Busfield, Joan. *Men, Women and Madness: Understanding Gender and Mental Disorder*. London: Palgrave, 1996.

Butler, Christopher. *Postmodernism: A Very Short Introduction*. Oxford: Oxford University Press, 2002.

Butler, Judith. "Gender as Performance: An Interview with Judith Butler." *Radical Philosophy: A Journal of Socialist and Feminist Philosophy* 67 (Summer 1994): 32–39.

———. "Imitation and Gender Insubordination." Pages 307–20 in *Lesbian and Gay Studies Reader*. Edited by Henry Abelove, Michele Aina Barale, and David M. Halperin. New York: Routledge, 1993.

———. "Judith Butler on Her Philosophy and Current Events." *Interviews by Kian* (December 27, 2019). https://interviewsbykian.wordpress.com/2019/12/27/judith-butler-on-her-philosophy-and-current-events.

———. "Performative Acts and Gender Constitution: An Essay in Phenomenology and Feminist Theory." *Theatre Journal* 40, no. 4 (December 1988): 519–31.

———. "Sex and Gender in Simone de Beauvoir's *Second Sex*." *Yale French Studies 72: Simone de Beauvoir: Witness to a Century* (1986): 35–49.

———. *Antigone's Claim: Kinship Between Life and Death*. New York: Columbia University Press, 2000.

———. *Bodies that Matter: On the Discursive Limits of "Sex."* London: Routledge, 1993.

———. *Gender Trouble: Feminism and the Subversion of Identity*. New York: Routledge, 2007. First published 1990.

———. *Giving an Account of Oneself: A Critique of Ethical Violence*. New York: Fordham University Press, 2005.

———. *Senses of the Subject*. New York: Fordham University Press, 2015.

———. *The Psychic Life of Power: Theories in Subjection*. Stanford, CA: Stanford University Press, 1997.

———. *Undoing Gender*. New York & London: Routledge, 2004.

———. *Who's Afraid of Gender?* New York: Farrar, Straus and Giroux, 2024.

Byrne, Alex. "Is Sex Binary?" *ARC Digital* (November 2, 2018). https://medium.com/arc-digital/is-sex-binary-16bec97d161e.

———. "Is Sex Socially Constructed?" *ARC Digital* (December 1, 2018). https://medium.com/arc-digital/is-sex-socially-constructed-81cf3ef79f07.

Byrne, Patrick J., with John Whitehall and Lane Anderson. *Transgender: One Shade of Grey: The Legal Consequences for Man & Woman, Schools, Sports, Politics, Democracy*. Melbourne: Wilkinson, 2018.

Cadden, Joan. *Meanings of Sex Difference in the Middle Ages: Medicine, Science, and Culture*. Cambridge: Cambridge University Press, 1995.

Cahana, Jonathan. "Gnostically Queer: Gender Trouble in Gnosticism." *Biblical Theology Bulletin* 41, no. 1 (2011): 24–35.

Callahan, Gerald N. *Between XX and XY: Intersexuality and the Myth of Two Sexes*. Chicago: Chicago Review Press, 2009.

Calvin, John. *Genesis*. Translated and edited by John King. Edinburgh: Banner of Truth Trust, 1847.

———. *Institutes of the Christian Religion*. 2 vols. Edited by J. T. McNeill. Translated by L. F. Battles. Philadelphia: Westminster Press, 1960.

Cameron, Andrew J. *Joined-Up Life: A Christian Account of How Ethics Works*. Nottingham: Inter-Varsity Press, 2011.

Canceran, Delfo. "Image of God: A Theological Reconstruction of the Beginning." *The Asia Journal of Theology* 25, no. 1 (2011): 3–23.

Carden, Michael. "Genesis/Bereshit." Pages 21–60 in *The Queer Bible Commentary*. Edited by Deryn Guest, Bob Goss, Mona West, and Tom Bohache. London: SCM, 2006.

Carson, D. A. "Current Issues in Biblical Theology: A New Testament Perspective." *BBR* 5 (1995): 17–41.

———. "Matthew." Pages 3–599 in vol. 8 of *The Expositor's Bible Commentary*. Edited by Frank E. Gaebelein. Grand Rapids: Regency, 1984.

———. "Mystery and Fulfillment: Toward a More Comprehensive Paradigm of Paul's Understanding of the Old and New." Pages 393–436 in *The Paradoxes of Paul*. Vol. 2 of *Justification and Variegated Nomism*. Edited by D. A. Carson, Peter T. O'Brien, and Mark A. Seifrid. Grand Rapids: Baker Academic, 2004.

———. "Systematic Theology and Biblical Theology." Pages 89–104 in *New Dictionary of Biblical Theology*. Edited by T. D. Alexander and Brian S. Rosner. Leicester: Inter-Varsity Press, 2000.

———. "The Role of Exegesis in Systematic Theology" Pages 39–76 in *Doing Theology in Today's World: Essays in Honor of Kenneth S. Kantzer*. Edited by J. D. Woodbridge and T. E. McComiskey. Grand Rapids: Zondervan, 1991.

———. *The Gagging of God: Christianity Confronts Pluralism*. Grand Rapids: Zondervan, 1996.

Carter, Craig A. "The New Gender Gnostics." *Eikon* 2, no. 1 (Spring 2020): 28–39.

Cassuto, Umberto. *A Commentary on the Book of Genesis 1–11: Part 1: From Adam to Noah*. Translated by Israel Abrahams. Jerusalem: Magnes, 1961. Repr., Skokie, IL: Varda, 2005.

Chadwick, Henry, and J. E. L. Oulton, eds. *Alexandrian Christianity: Selected Translations of Clement and Origen*. London: SCM, 1954.

Chanter, Tina. *Gender: Key Concepts in Philosophy*. London: Continuum, 2006.

Childs, Brevard S. "The Etiological Tale Re-Examined." *VT* 24, no. 4 (1974): 387–97. https://doi.org/10.2307/1517173.

Chivers, Tom. "Of Course Biological Sex Exists." *UnHerd* (December 10, 2019). https://unherd.com/2019/12/yes-of-course-biological-sex-exists/?=refinnar.

Christensen, Duane L. *Deuteronomy 21:10–34:12*. WBC 6B. Waco, TX: Word, 2002.

Ciampa, Roy E., and Brian S. Rosner. *The First Letter to the Corinthians*. PNTC. Grand Rapids: Eerdmans, 2010.

Clark, David K. *To Know and Love God: Method for Theology*. Wheaton, IL: Crossway, 2003.

Clement of Alexandria. *The Instructor*. Pages 207–96 in vol. 2 of *Ante-Nicene Fathers: The Writings of the Fathers Down to A.D. 325*. Edited by Alexander Roberts & James Donaldson, 1885. 10 vols. Repr. Peabody, MA: Hendrickson, 1995.

———. *The Stromata, or Miscellanies*. Pages 299–568 in vol. 2 of *Ante-Nicene Fathers: The Writings of the Fathers Down to A.D. 325*. Edited by Alexander Roberts & James Donaldson, 1885. 10 vols. Repr. Peabody, MA: Hendrickson, 1995.

Clines, David J. A. "The Image of God in Man." *TB* 19 (1968): 53–103.

Clowney, Edmund P. "A Biblical Theology of Prayer." Pages 136–73 in *Teach Us to Pray: Prayer in the Bible and the World*. Edited by D. A. Carson. Exeter: Paternoster, 1990.

Coakley, Sarah. "The Eschatological Body: Gender, Transformation, and God." *Modern Theology* 16, no. 1 (January 2000): 61–73.

———. *God, Sexuality, and the Self: An Essay "On the Trinity."* Cambridge: Cambridge University Press, 2013.

Cole, Graham A. "Sola Scriptura: Some Historical and Contemporary Perspectives." *Churchman* 104, no. 1 (1990): 20–34.

Collins, C. John. "May We Say That Adam and Eve 'Fell'? A Study of a Term and Its Metaphoric Function." *Presbyterion* 46, no. 1 (2020): 53–74.

———. "What Happened to Adam and Eve? A Literary-Theological Approach to Genesis 3." *Presbyterion* 27, no. 1 (Spring 2001): 12–44.

———. *Genesis 1–4: A Linguistic, Literary and Theological Commentary.* Phillipsburg, NJ: P&R Publishing, 2006.

———. *Reading Genesis Well: Navigating History, Poetry, Science, and Truth in Genesis 1–11*. Grand Rapids: Zondervan, 2018.

Collins, Nate. *All But Invisible: Exploring Identity Questions at the Intersection of Faith, Gender & Sexuality*. Grand Rapids: Zondervan, 2017.

Collins, Raymond. *Christian Morality: Biblical Foundations*. Notre Dame: University of Notre Dame Press, 1986.

Comensoli, Peter A. *In God's Image: Recognizing the Profoundly Impaired as Persons*. Eugene, OR: Cascade, 2018.

Condren, Janson C. "Towards a Purge of the Battle of the Sexes and 'Return' for the Original Meaning of Genesis 3:16b." *JETS* 60, no. 2 (June 2017): 227–45.

Connell, Raewyn, and Rebecca Pearse. *Gender: In World Perspective*. Cambridge: Polity Press, 2015.

Conway, Colleen M. *Behold the Man: Jesus and Greco-Roman Masculinity*. Oxford: Oxford University Press, 2008.

———. "The Construction of Gender in the New Testament." Pages 222–38 in *The Oxford Handbook of Theology, Sexuality, and Gender*. Edited by Adrian Thatcher. Oxford: Oxford University Press, 2014.

Coole, Diana, and Samantha Frost. "Introducing the New Materialisms." Pages 1–43 in *New Materialisms: Ontology, Agency, and Politics*. Edited by Diana Coole and Samantha Frost. Durham, NC: Duke University Press, 2010.

Cooper, John W. "Dualism and the Biblical View of Human Beings (2)." *The Reformed Journal* (October 1982): 16–18.

———. "Reformed Apologetics and the Challenge of Post-Modern Relativism." *CTJ* 28 (1993): 108–20.

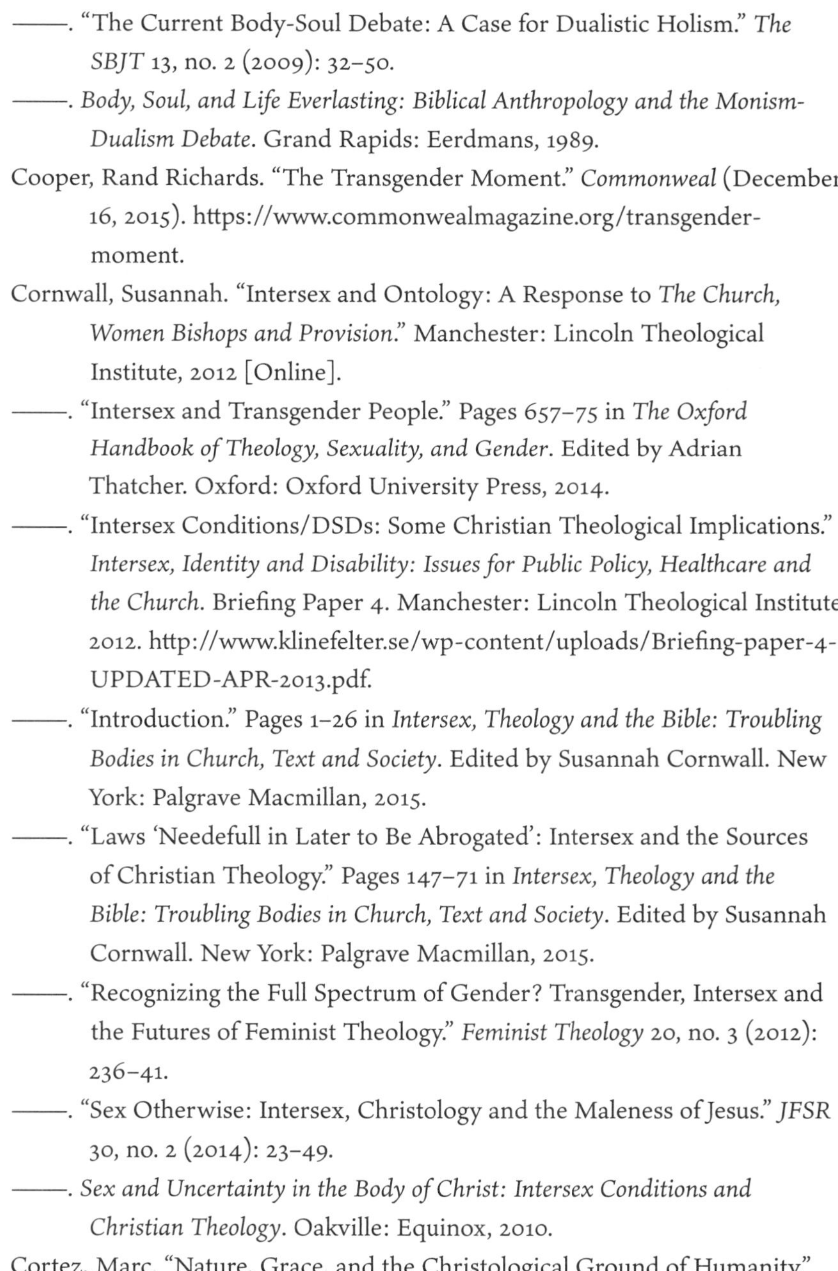

———. "The Current Body-Soul Debate: A Case for Dualistic Holism." *The SBJT* 13, no. 2 (2009): 32–50.

———. *Body, Soul, and Life Everlasting: Biblical Anthropology and the Monism-Dualism Debate*. Grand Rapids: Eerdmans, 1989.

Cooper, Rand Richards. "The Transgender Moment." *Commonweal* (December 16, 2015). https://www.commonwealmagazine.org/transgender-moment.

Cornwall, Susannah. "Intersex and Ontology: A Response to *The Church, Women Bishops and Provision*." Manchester: Lincoln Theological Institute, 2012 [Online].

———. "Intersex and Transgender People." Pages 657–75 in *The Oxford Handbook of Theology, Sexuality, and Gender*. Edited by Adrian Thatcher. Oxford: Oxford University Press, 2014.

———. "Intersex Conditions/DSDs: Some Christian Theological Implications." *Intersex, Identity and Disability: Issues for Public Policy, Healthcare and the Church*. Briefing Paper 4. Manchester: Lincoln Theological Institute, 2012. http://www.klinefelter.se/wp-content/uploads/Briefing-paper-4-UPDATED-APR-2013.pdf.

———. "Introduction." Pages 1–26 in *Intersex, Theology and the Bible: Troubling Bodies in Church, Text and Society*. Edited by Susannah Cornwall. New York: Palgrave Macmillan, 2015.

———. "Laws 'Needefull in Later to Be Abrogated': Intersex and the Sources of Christian Theology." Pages 147–71 in *Intersex, Theology and the Bible: Troubling Bodies in Church, Text and Society*. Edited by Susannah Cornwall. New York: Palgrave Macmillan, 2015.

———. "Recognizing the Full Spectrum of Gender? Transgender, Intersex and the Futures of Feminist Theology." *Feminist Theology* 20, no. 3 (2012): 236–41.

———. "Sex Otherwise: Intersex, Christology and the Maleness of Jesus." *JFSR* 30, no. 2 (2014): 23–49.

———. *Sex and Uncertainty in the Body of Christ: Intersex Conditions and Christian Theology*. Oakville: Equinox, 2010.

Cortez, Marc. "Nature, Grace, and the Christological Ground of Humanity." Pages 23–40 in *The Christian Doctrine of Humanity: Explorations in Constructive Dogmatics*. Edited by Oliver D. Crisp and Fred Sanders. Grand Rapids: Zondervan, 2018.

———. *ReSourcing Theological Anthropology: A Constructive Account of Humanity in the Light of Christ*. Grand Rapids: Zondervan, 2017.

———.*Theological Anthropology: A Guide for the Perplexed*. London: T&T Clark, 2010.

Cortez, Marina, Paula Gaudenzi, and Ivia Maksud. "Gender: Pathways and Dialogues between Feminist and Biomedical Studies from the 1950s to 1970s." *Physis: Revista de Saúde Coletiva* 29, no. 1 (2019): 1–20. https://www.scielo.br/j/physis/a/p4dXbydkK3jShSKdxxpgpCm/?format=pdf&lang=en.

Countryman, L. William. *Dirt, Greed, and Sex: Sexual Ethics in the New Testament and their Implications for Today*. Philadelphia: Fortress, 1988.

Cowdell, Scott. "Gender and Identity: Freeing the Bible from Modern Western Anxieties." *ABC Religion & Ethics* (14 September 2017). https://www.abc.net.au/religion/gender-and-identity-freeing-the-bible-from-modern-western-anxiet/10095390.

Cox, Jennifer Anne. *Intersex in Christ: Ambiguous Biology and the Gospel*. Eugene, OR: Cascade, 2018.

Craig, William Lane. *In Quest of the Historical Adam: A Biblical and Scientific Exploration*. Grand Rapids: Eerdmans, 2021.

Craigie, Peter C. *The Book of Deuteronomy*. NICOT. Grand Rapids: Eerdmans, 1976.

Crawford, David S. "Liberal Androgyny: 'Gay Marriage' and the Meaning of Sexuality in Our Time." *Communio* 33, no. 2 (Summer 2006): 239–65.

Cromby, John, and David J. Nightingale. "What's Wrong with Social Constructionism?" Pages 1–19 in *Social Constructionist Psychology: A Critical Analysis of Theory and Practice*. Edited by David J. Nightingale and John Cromby. Buckingham: Open University Press 1999.

Cross, F. L., and E. A. Livingstone, eds. *The Oxford Dictionary of the Christian Church*. 2nd ed. Oxford: Oxford University Press, 1997.

Curtis, Edward M. "Image of God (OT)." Pages 389–91 in vol. 3 of *The Anchor Bible Dictionary*. Edited by David Noel Freedman. New York: Doubleday, 1992.

Dabhoiwala, Faramerz. *The Origins of Sex: A History of the First Sexual Revolution*. London: Penguin, 2013.

Daly, Mary. *Beyond God the Father: Toward a Philosophy of Women's Liberation*. Boston: Beacon, 1973.

Daly, Todd T. W. "Gender Dysphoria and the Ethics of Transsexual (i.e., Gender Reassignment) Surgery." *Ethics & Medicine: An International Journal of Bioethics* 32, no. 1 (2016): 39–53.

Davidson, Richard J., and Bruce S. McEwen. "Social Influences on Neuroplasticity: Stress and Interventions to Promote Well-Being." *Nature Neuroscience* 15 (2012): 689–95.

Davidson, Richard M. "Cosmic Metanarrative for the Coming Millennium." *JATS* 11 (2000): 102–19.

———. "The Genesis Account of Origins." Pages 69–87 in *The Genesis Creation Account and its Reverberations in the Old Testament*. Edited by Gerald A. Klingbeil. Berrien Springs, MI: Andrews University Press, 2015.

———. "The Nature of the Human Being from the Beginning: Genesis 1–11." Pages 11–42 in *"What Are Human Beings that You Remember Them?": Proceedings of the Third International Bible Conference Nof Ginosar and Jerusalem June 11–21, 2012*. Edited by Clinton Wahlen. Silver Spring, MD: Review and Herald, 2015.

———. *Flame of Yahweh: Sexuality in the Old Testament*. Peabody, MA: Hendrickson, 2007.

Davie, Martin. "Transgender, Reality and Pastoral Care," *Reflections of an Anglican Theologian* (March 15, 2018). https://mbarrattdavie.wordpress.com/2018/03/16/transgender-reality-and-pastoral-care.

———. *Transgender Liturgies: Should the Church of England Develop Liturgical Materials to Mark Gender Transition?* London: The Latimer Trust, 2017.

———. *What Does the Bible Really Say? Addressing Revisionist Arguments on Sexuality and the Bible*. London: The Latimer Trust, 2020.

Davies, W. D., and Dale C. Allison. *A Critical and Exegetical Commentary on the Gospel According to Saint Matthew: Volume III: XIX–XXVIII*. ICC. Edinburgh: T&T Clark, 1997.

De Lauretis, Teresa. *Technologies of Gender: Essays on Theory, Film, and Fiction*. Bloomington: Indiana University Press, 1987.

Dean, Kathryn E. S., Jonathan Joseph, and Alan W. Norrie. "New Essays in Critical Realism." *New Formations* 56 (Autumn 2005): 7–26.

DeFranza, Megan K. "Good News for Gender Minorities." Pages 147–78 in *Understanding Transgender Identities: Four Views*. Edited by James K. Beilby and Paul Rhodes Eddy. Grand Rapids: Baker Academic, 2019.

———. "Response to Mark A. Yarhouse and Julia Sadusky." Pages 136–41 in *Understanding Transgender Identities: Four Views*. Edited by James K. Beilby and Paul Rhodes Eddy. Grand Rapids: Baker Academic, 2019.

———. *Sex Difference in Christian Theology: Male, Female, and Intersex in the Image of God*. Grand Rapids: Eerdmans, 2015.

Delphy, Christine. "Rethinking Sex and Gender." Pages 31–42 in *Sex in Question: French Materialist Feminism*. Edited by Diana Leonard and Lisa Adkins. London: Taylor & Francis, 1996.

DeRouchie, Jason S. "Confronting the Transgender Storm: New Covenant Reflections on Deuteronomy 22:5." *JBMW* 21, no. 1 (May 2016): 58–69.

Derrida, Jacques. "Le Facteur de la verite." *Poetique* 21 (1975): 96–147. Translated by Willis Domingo, et al., "The Purveyor of Truth." *Graphesis: Perspectives in Literature and Philosophy, Yale French Studies* 52 (1975): 31–113.

———. "Signature Event Context" ("Signature Evénement Contexte"). Pages 80–111 in *A Derrida Reader: Between the Blinds*. Edited by Peggy Kamuf. New York: Columbia University Press, 1999.

DeVun, Leah. "Heavenly Hermaphrodites: Sexual Difference at the Beginning and End of Time." *Postmedieval: A Journal of Medieval Cultural Studies* 9, no. 2 (2018): 132–46. https://doi.org/10.1057/s41280-018-0080-8.

———. *The Shape of Sex: Nonbinary Gender from Genesis to the Renaissance*. New York: Columbia University Press, 2021.

Dew, James K. Jr. *In Defense of Modified Thomistic Holism: A Proposal for Christian Anthropology*. PhD thesis, University of Birmingham, UK, 2019. https://etheses.bham.ac.uk//id/eprint/9396/1/Dew2019PhD.pdf

DeYoung, Kevin. *What Does the Bible Really Teach About Homosexuality?* Wheaton, IL: Crossway, 2015.

Diamond, Irene, and Lee Quinby, eds. *Feminism and Foucault: Reflections on Resistance*. Boston: Northeastern University Press, 1988.

Diamond, Milton. "Transsexualism as an Intersex Condition." Pages 43–54 in *Transsexuality in Theology and Neuroscience: Findings, Controversies, and Perspectives*. Edited by Gerhard Schreiber. Boston: de Gruyter, 2016.

Do Vale, Fellipe M. "Can a Male Savior Save Women?: The Metaphysics of Gender and Christ's Ability to Save." *Philosophia Christi* 21, no. 2 (2019): 309–24. https://doi.org/10.5840/pc201921230.

———. "Cappadocian or Augustinian? Adjudicating Debates on Gender in the Resurrection." *IJST* 21, no. 2 (April 2019): 182–98.

———. *Gender as Love: A Theological Account of Human Identity, Embodied Desire, and Our Social Worlds*. Grand Rapids: Baker Academic, 2023.

Dostoyevsky, Fyodor. *Notes from Underground*. Translated by Jessie Coulson. Melbourne: Penguin, 2010.

Dowd, Chris. "Five Things Cis Folk Don't Know About Trans Folk Because It Isn't on Trashy TV—My Right of Reply." Pages 101–7 in *This Is My Body: Hearing the Theology of Transgender Christians*. Edited by Christina Beardsley and Michelle O'Brien London. London: Darton, Longman & Todd, 2016.

Dragga, Sam. "Genesis 2–3: A Story of Liberation," *JSOT* 55 (1992): 3–13.

Dreger, Alice D. "Shifting the Paradigm of Intersex Treatment." *Intersex Society of North America* (2003). https://isna.org/pdf/compare.pdf.

Dresner, Samuel H. "Homosexuality and the Order of Creation." *Judaism* 40, no. 3 (1991): 309–21.

Driver, Samuel Rolles. *A Critical Commentary on Deuteronomy*. ICC. New York: Scribner's Sons, 1902.

Dryden, J. De Waal. *A Hermeneutic of Wisdom: Recovering the Formative Agency of Scripture*. Grand Rapids: Baker Academic, 2018.

Dumbrell, William J. *Covenant and Creation: An Old Testament Covenant Theology*. 2nd ed. Milton Keynes: Paternoster, 2013.

———. *The Faith of Israel: Its Expression in the Books of the Old Testament*. Leicester: Inter-Varsity Press, 1988.

Dunn, James D. G. *Romans 1–8*. WBC 38A. Dallas, TX: Word, 1988.

———. *The Epistle to the Galatians*. London: Black, 1993.

Dworkin, Andrea. *Woman Hating: A Radical Look at Sexuality*. New York: Plume Penguin Books, 1974.

Earl, Jessie. "Do You Need Gender Dysphoria to Be Trans?" *Advocate* (January 18, 2019). www.advocate.com/commentary/2019/1/18/do-you-need-gender-dysphoria-be-trans.

Eberstadt, Mary. "The Lure of Androgyny." *Commentary* (October 2019). https://www.commentary.org/articles/mary-eberstadt/the-lure-of-androgyny.

———. *Adam and Eve after the Pill: Paradoxes of the Sexual Revolution*. San Francisco: Ignatius Press, 2012.

Eddy, Paul Rhodes, and James K. Beilby. "Understanding Transgender Experiences and Identities: An Introduction." Pages 1–54 in *Understanding Transgender Identities: Four Views*. Edited by James K. Beilby and Paul Rhodes Eddy. Grand Rapids: Baker Academic, 2019.

Eichrodt, Walther. *Theology of the Old Testament*. Translated by J. A. Baker. Vol. 1. OTL. Philadelphia: Westminster, 1961.

Eiesland, Nancy L. *The Disabled God: Toward a Liberatory Theology of Disability*. Nashville: Abingdon, 1994.

Eilberg-Schwartz, Howard. "People of the Body: The Problem of the Body for the People of the Book." *Journal of the History of Sexuality* 2 (1991): 1–24.

Ekins, Richard, and Dave King. *The Transgender Phenomenon*. London: SAGE Publications, 2006.

Elder-Vass, Dave. *The Reality of Social Construction*. Cambridge: Cambridge University Press, 2012.

Eliot, Lise, Adnan Ahmed, Hiba Khan, and Julie Patel. "Dump the 'Dimorphism': Comprehensive Synthesis of Human Brain Studies Reveals Few Male-Female Differences beyond Size." *Neuroscience & Biobehavioral Reviews* (2021): 125:667–97. doi.org/10.1016/j.neubiorev.2021.02.026.

Elliot, Patricia. "Who Gets to Be a Woman?: Feminist Politics and the Question of Trans-Inclusion." *Atlantis* 29, no. 1 (Fall/Winter 2004): 13–20.

———. *Debates in Transgender, Queer, and Feminist Theory: Contested Sites*. Abingdon: Ashgate, 2010.

Eloit, Ilana, and Clare Hemmings. "Lesbian Ghosts Feminism: An Introduction." *Feminist Theory* 20, no. 4 (December 2019): 351–60.

Engberg-Pedersen, Troels. "Complete and Incomplete Transformation in Paul: A Philosophical Reading of Paul on Body and Spirit." Pages 123–46 in *Metamorphoses: Resurrection, Body and Transformative Practices in Early Christianity*, Ekstasis 1. Edited by Turid Karlsen Seim and Jorunn Økland (Berlin: de Gruyter, 2009).

———. *Cosmology and Self in the Apostle Paul: The Material Spirit*. Oxford: Oxford University Press, 2010.

Enke, Anne Finn. "Introduction." Pages 1–15 in *Transfeminist Perspectives in and Beyond Transgender and Gender Studies*. Edited by Anne Finn Enke. Philadephia: Temple University Press, 2012.

Erickson, Millard J. *Christian Theology*. 2nd ed. Grand Rapids: Baker, 1998.

Evangelical Alliance. *Transformed: A Brief Biblical and Pastoral Introduction to Understanding Transgender in a Changing Culture*. London: Evangelical Alliance, 2018.

———. *Transsexuality: A Report by the Evangelical Alliance Policy Commission*. London: Evangelical Alliance, 2000.

"The Evangelical Divide." Editorial, *The Economist* (October 14, 2017). https://www.economist.com/united-states/2017/10/14/the-evangelical-divide.

Evans, C. Stephen. *Preserving the Person: A Look at the Human Sciences*. Vancouver: Regent College Publishing, 1977.

Evans, Rachel Held. "The False Gospel of Gender Binaries." *RachelHeldEvans.com* (November 19, 2014). http://rachelheldevans.com/blog/gender-binaries.

Fairhurst, Gail T., and David Grant. "The Social Construction of Leadership: A Sailing Guide." *Management Communication Quarterly* 24, no. 2 (2010): 171–210.

Fausto-Sterling, Anne. "Gender/Sex, Sexual Orientation, and Identity Are in the Body: How Did They Get There?" *The Journal of Sex Research* (2019): 1–27.

———. "Nature." Pages 294–319 in *Critical Terms for the Study of Gender*. Edited by Catharine R. Stimpson and Gilbert Herdt. Chicago: Chicago University Press, 2014.

———. "The Bare Bones of Sex: Part 1—Sex and Gender." *Signs* 30, no. 2 (2005): 1491–527.

———. "The Five Sexes, Revisited." *The Sciences* 40, no. 4 (July/August 2000): 18–23.

———. "The Five Sexes: Why Male and Female are not Enough." *The Sciences* (March/April 1993): 20–25.

———. "The Problem with Sex/Gender and Nature/Nurture." Pages 123–32 in *Debating Biology: Sociological Reflections on Health, Medicine and Society*. Edited by S. J. Williams, L. Birke, and G. A. Bendelow. London & New York: Routledge, 2003.

———. "Why Sex Is Not Binary: The Complexity Is More Than Cultural. It's Biological, Too." *The New York Times* (October 25, 2018). https://www.nytimes.com/2018/10/25/opinion/sex-biology-binary.html.

———. *Sex/Gender: Biology in a Social World*. London: Routledge, 2012.

——. *Sexing the Body: Gender Politics and the Construction of Sexuality*. New York: Basic Books, 2000.

Favale, Abigail. *The Genesis of Gender: A Christian Theory*. San Francisco: Ignatius Press, 2022.

Fee, Gordon D. *The First Epistle to the Corinthians*. Rev. ed. NICNT. Grand Rapids: Eerdmans, 2014.

Feinberg, Leslie. *Transgender Warriors: Making History from Joan of Arc to Dennis Rodman*. Boston: Beacon, 1996.

Ferguson, Ann. "Androgyny as an Ideal for Human Development." Pages 45–69 in *Feminism and Philosophy*. Edited by Mary Vetterling-Braggin, Frederick A. Ellison and Jane English. Totowa, NJ: Littlefield, Adams, 1977.

Ferguson, Samuel D. *Does God Care about Gender and Identity?* Wheaton, IL: Crossway, 2023.

Fernando, Ajith. *Deuteronomy: Loving Obedience to a Loving God*. Wheaton, IL: Crossway, 2012.

Fine, Cordelia. *Testosterone Rex: Unmaking the Myths of our Gendered Minds*. New York: Norton, 2017.

Finney, Mark T. "Honour, Head-Coverings and Headship: 1 Corinthians 11.2–16 in Its Social Context." *JSNT* 33 (2010): 31–58.

Firestone, Shulamith. *The Dialectic of Sex: The Case for Feminist Revolution*. New York: Farrar, Straus and Giroux, 1970.

Fitzgibbons, Richard P., Philip M. Sutton, and Dale O'Leary. "The Psychopathology of 'Sex Reassignment' Surgery: Assessing Its Medical, Psychological, and Ethical Appropriateness." *The National Catholic Bioethics Quarterly* 9, no. 1 (2009): 97–125.

Flaherty, Colleen. "'TERF' War," *Inside Higher Ed* (August 19, 2018). https://www.insidehighered.com/news/2018/08/29/philosophers-object-journals-publication-terf-reference-some-feminists-it-really.

Foh, Susan T. "What Is the Woman's Desire?" *WTJ* 37 (1975): 376–83.

Fong, Edmund. "Gender Dysphoria and the Body-Soul Relationship." *Themelios* 47, no. 2 (August 2022): 348–65.

Fonrobert, Charlotte Elisheva. "Gender Identity in Halakhic Discourse." *Shalvi/Hyman Encyclopedia of Jewish Women* (December 31, 1999). https://jwa.org/encyclopedia/article/gender-identity-in-halakhic-discourse.

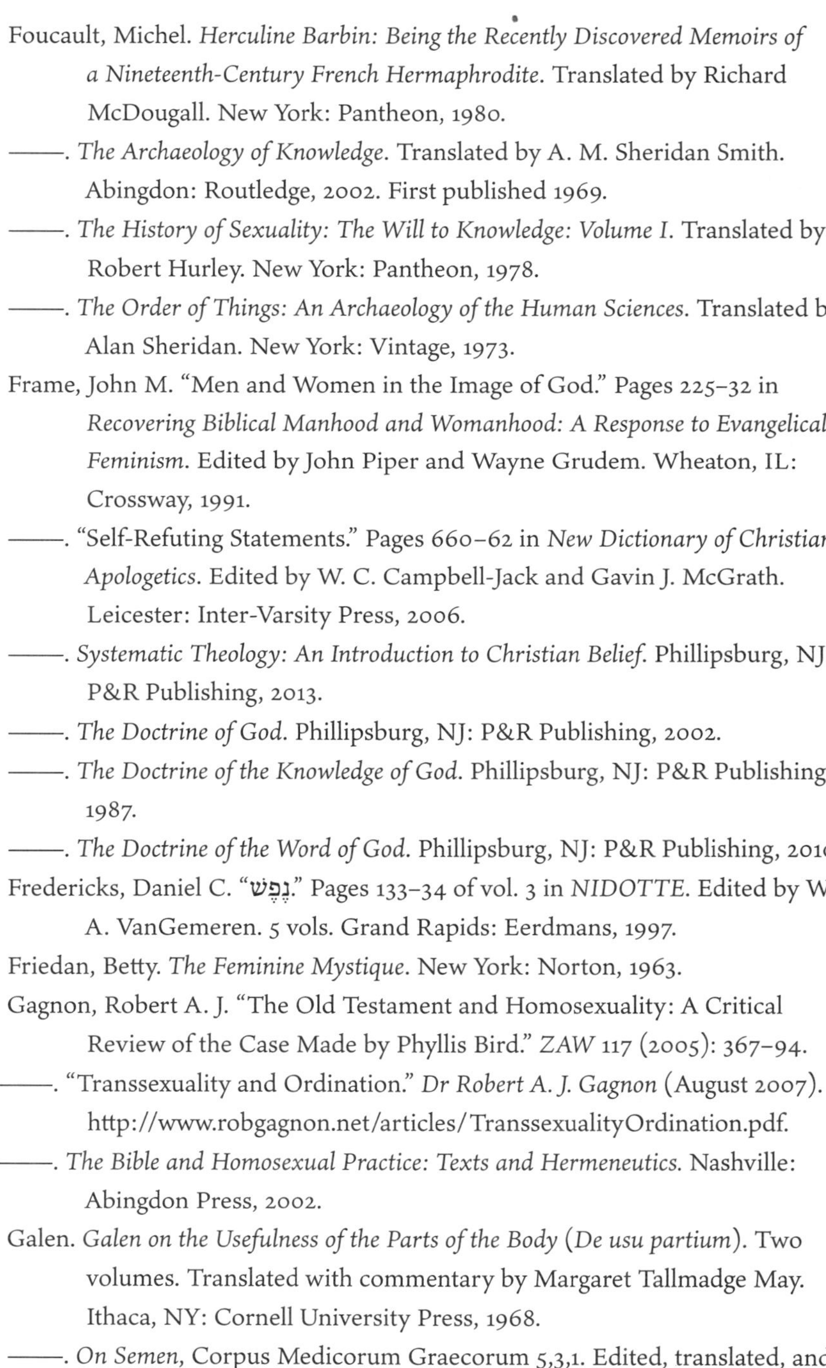

Foucault, Michel. *Herculine Barbin: Being the Recently Discovered Memoirs of a Nineteenth-Century French Hermaphrodite*. Translated by Richard McDougall. New York: Pantheon, 1980.

———. *The Archaeology of Knowledge*. Translated by A. M. Sheridan Smith. Abingdon: Routledge, 2002. First published 1969.

———. *The History of Sexuality: The Will to Knowledge: Volume I*. Translated by Robert Hurley. New York: Pantheon, 1978.

———. *The Order of Things: An Archaeology of the Human Sciences*. Translated by Alan Sheridan. New York: Vintage, 1973.

Frame, John M. "Men and Women in the Image of God." Pages 225–32 in *Recovering Biblical Manhood and Womanhood: A Response to Evangelical Feminism*. Edited by John Piper and Wayne Grudem. Wheaton, IL: Crossway, 1991.

———. "Self-Refuting Statements." Pages 660–62 in *New Dictionary of Christian Apologetics*. Edited by W. C. Campbell-Jack and Gavin J. McGrath. Leicester: Inter-Varsity Press, 2006.

———. *Systematic Theology: An Introduction to Christian Belief*. Phillipsburg, NJ: P&R Publishing, 2013.

———. *The Doctrine of God*. Phillipsburg, NJ: P&R Publishing, 2002.

———. *The Doctrine of the Knowledge of God*. Phillipsburg, NJ: P&R Publishing, 1987.

———. *The Doctrine of the Word of God*. Phillipsburg, NJ: P&R Publishing, 2010.

Fredericks, Daniel C. "נֶפֶשׁ." Pages 133–34 of vol. 3 in *NIDOTTE*. Edited by W. A. VanGemeren. 5 vols. Grand Rapids: Eerdmans, 1997.

Friedan, Betty. *The Feminine Mystique*. New York: Norton, 1963.

Gagnon, Robert A. J. "The Old Testament and Homosexuality: A Critical Review of the Case Made by Phyllis Bird." *ZAW* 117 (2005): 367–94.

———. "Transsexuality and Ordination." *Dr Robert A. J. Gagnon* (August 2007). http://www.robgagnon.net/articles/TranssexualityOrdination.pdf.

———. *The Bible and Homosexual Practice: Texts and Hermeneutics*. Nashville: Abingdon Press, 2002.

Galen. *Galen on the Usefulness of the Parts of the Body (De usu partium)*. Two volumes. Translated with commentary by Margaret Tallmadge May. Ithaca, NY: Cornell University Press, 1968.

———. *On Semen*, Corpus Medicorum Graecorum 5,3,1. Edited, translated, and commentary by Phillip de Lacy. Berlin: Akademie Verlag, 1992.

Gamble, Sarah. "Gender and Transgender Criticism." Pages 37–56 in *Criticism in the 21st Century*. Edited by Julian Wolfreys. 2nd ed. Edinburgh: Edinburgh University Press, 2015.

Gardner, Paul. *1 Corinthians*. ZECNT. Grand Rapids: Zondervan, 2018.

Garland, David E. *1 Corinthians*. BECNT. Grand Rapids: Baker, 2003.

Garrett, James Leo. *Systematic Theology: Biblical, Historical & Evangelical: Volume 1*. Grand Rapids: Eerdmans, 1990.

Gatens, Moira. *Imaginary Bodies: Ethics, Power, and Corporeality*. London: Routledge, 1996.

Gay, Craig M. "'Gender' and the Idea of the Social Construction of Reality." Pages 167–80 in *Christian Perspectives on Gender, Sexuality and* Community. Edited by Maxine Hancock. Vancouver: Regent College Publishing, 2003.

Gehring, René. "'They Will Be Like Angels.' Paradise Without Marriage?" *JATS* 27 (2016): 55–84.

George, Robert P. "Gnostic Liberalism." *First Things* (December 2016). https://www.firstthings.com/article/2016/12/gnostic-liberalism.

Gergen, Kenneth J. "The Social Constructionist Movement in Modern Psychology." *American Psychologist* 40, no. 3 (March 1985): 266–75.

Germon, Jennifer. *Gender: A Genealogy of an Idea*. New York: Palgrave MacMillan, 2009.

Gibbs, Jeffrey A. *Matthew 11:2–20:34*. Concordia Commentary. St. Louis: Concordia Publishing House, 2010.

Giddens, Anthony. *Modernity and Self-Identity: Self and Society in the Late Modern Age*. Oxford: Polity Press, 1991.

Giffney, Noreen. "Introduction: The 'q' Word." Pages 19–27 in *Ashgate Research Companion to Queer Theory*. Edited by Noreen Giffney and Michael O'Rourke. Burlington, VT: Ashgate, 2009.

Gilles, Donald. *Philosophy of Science in the Twentieth Century*. Oxford: Blackwell Publishers, 1993.

Gilson, Rachel. "Male and Female in Distinction and Glory: First Corinthians 11:2–16 and Contemporary Questions of Sex, Gender and Transgender Identities." *EQ* 93 (2022): 40–60.

Girgis, Sherif, Ryan T. Anderson, and Robert P. George. *What Is Marriage?: Man and Woman: A Defense*. New York: Encounter, 2012.

Gladwell, Malcolm. *The Tipping Point: How Little Things Can Make a Big Difference*. London: Abacus, 2000.

Gleason, Maud W. *Making Men: Sophists and Self-Presentation in Ancient Rome*. Princeton: Princeton University Press, 1995.

Goddard, Andrew. "James V. Brownson, *Bible, Gender, Sexuality*: A Critical Engagement." *The Kirby Laing Institute for Christian Ethics* (2014). https://kirbylaingcentre.co.uk/wp-content/uploads/2021/01/KLICEPaper-AGoddardreviewofBrownson-BibleGenderSexuality.pdf

Goldie, Terry. *The Man Who Invented Gender: Engaging the Ideas of John Money*. Vancouver: UBC Press, 2014.

Goldingay, John E., Grant R. LeMarquand, George R. Sumner, and Daniel A. Westberg. "Same-Sex Marriage and Anglican Theology: A View of the Traditionalists." *ATR* 93, no. 1 (Winter 2011): 1–50.

Goldschmidt, Richard B. "Intersexuality and the Endocrine Aspect of Sex." *Endocrinology* 1, no. 4 (1917): 433–56.

Goldsworthy, Graeme. "'Thus says the Lord!'—The Dogmatic Basis of Biblical Theology" Pages 25–40 in *God Who Is Rich in Mercy: Essays Presented to D. B. Knox*. Edited by P. T. O'Brien and D. G. Peterson. Sydney: Anzea Press; 1986.

Goss, Robert E. "Ephesians." Pages 630–38 in *The Queer Bible Commentary*. Edited by Deryn Guest, Bob Goss, Mona West, and Tom Bohache. London: SCM Press, 2006.

———. *Queering Christ: Beyond JESUS ACTED UP*. Cleveland: Pilgrim Press, 2002.

Goss, Robert E., and Mona West, eds. *Take Back the Word: A Queer Reading of the Bible*. Cleveland: The Pilgrim Press, 2000.

Gowing, Laura. "Women's Bodies and the Making of Sex in Seventeenth-Century England." *Signs* 37, no. 4 (2012): 813–22.

Grady, Constance. "The Waves of Feminism, and Why People Keep Fighting Over Them, Explained." *Vox* (July 20, 2018). https://www.vox.com/2018/3/20/16955588/feminism-waves-explained-first-second-third-fourth.

Graham, Elaine. *Making the Difference: Gender, Personhood and Theology*. London: Mowbray, 1995.

Green, Joel B. *Body, Soul and Human Life: The Nature of Humanity in the Bible*. Milton Keynes: Paternoster, 2008.

Greer, Germaine. *The Whole Woman*. London: Doubleday, 1999.

Gregory of Nyssa. *On the Making of Man*. Pages 387–427 in vol. 5 of *Nicene and Post-Nicene Fathers*, Series 2. Edited by Philip Schaff and Henry Wace, 1893. Repr., Peabody, MA: Hendrickson, 1995.

Grenz, Stanley J. "The Social God and the Relational Self: Toward a Theology of the *Imago Dei* in the Postmodern Context." Pages 70–92 in *Personal Identity in Theological Perspective*. Edited by Richard Lints, Michael S. Horton, and Mark R. Talbot. Grand Rapids: Eerdmans, 2006.

———. *A Primer on Postmodernism*. Grand Rapids: Eerdmans, 1996.

———. *The Social God and the Relational Self: A Trinitarian Theology of the* Imago Dei. Louisville: Westminster John Knox, 2001.

———. *Theology for the Community of God*. Grand Rapids: Eerdmans, 1994.

Griggs, Brandon. "America's Transgender Moment." *CNN* (June 1, 2015). https://edition.cnn.com/2015/04/23/living/transgender-moment-jenner-feat/index.html.

Grisanti, Michael A. "תָּעַב." Volume 4, pages 314–18 in *NIDOTTE*.

Gross, Sally. "Intersexuality and Scripture." *Theology & Sexuality* 11 (1999): 65–74.

Grosz, Elizabeth A. *Volatile Bodies: Towards a Corporeal Feminism*. Bloomington: Indiana University Press, 1994.

Gu, Jenny, and Ryota Kanai. "What Contributes to Individual Differences in Brain Structure?" *Frontiers in Human Neuroscience* 8, art. 262 (2014): 1–6. https://www.ncbi.nlm.nih.gov/pmc/articles/PMC4009419.

Guest, Deryn. "Deuteronomy." Pages 122–43 in *The Queer Bible Commentary*. Edited by Deryn Guest, Bob Goss, Mona West, and Tom Bohache. London: SCM Press, 2006.

———. "Troubling the Waters: תהום, Transgender, and Reading Genesis Backwards." Pages 21–44 in *Transgender, Intersex, and Biblical Interpretation*. Edited by Teresa J. Hornsby and Deryn Guest. Atlanta: SBL Press, 2016.

Guidero, Kirsten Lauren. "'No Longer Any Male and Female'? Galatians 3, Baptismal Identity, and the Question of an Evangelical Hermeneutic." *Priscilla Papers* 33, no. 3 (Summer 2019): 19–27.

Gundry, Robert H. *Sōma in Biblical Theology: With Emphasis on Pauline Anthropology*. Grand Rapids: Zondervan, 1987.

Gundry-Volf, Judith M. "Christ and Gender: A Study of Difference and Equality in Gal 3:28." Pages 439–78 in *Jesus Christus als die Mitte der Schrift. Studien zur Hermeneutik des Evangeliums*. Edited by C. Landmesser, H. J. Eckstein, and H. Lichtenberger. Berlin: Walter de Gruyter, 1997.

Gunton, Colin E. "Proteus and Procrustes: A Study in the Dialectic of Language in Disagreement with Sallie McFague." Pages 65–80 in *Speaking the Christian God: The Holy Trinity and the Challenge of Feminism*. Edited by Alvin F. Kimel, Jr. Grand Rapids: Eerdmans, 1992.

———. *A Brief Theology of Revelation*. Edinburgh: T&T Clark, 1995.

———. *The Triune Creator: A Historical and Systematic Study*. Grand Rapids: Eerdmans, 1998.

Habermas, Jürgen. *The Philosophical Discourse of Modernity*. Translated by Frederick Lawrence. Cambridge: Cambridge University Press, 1987.

Hacking, Ian. *The Social Construction of What?* Cambridge: Harvard University Press, 1999.

Hagner, Donald A. *Matthew 14–28*. WBC 33B. Waco, TX: Word, 1995.

Haig, David. "The Inexorable Rise of Gender and the Decline of Sex: Social Change in Academic Titles, 1945–2001." *Archives of Sexual Behavior* 33, no. 2 (April 2004): 87–96.

Hall, Gary Harlan. *Deuteronomy: The College Press NIV Commentary*. Joplin, MO: The College Press Publishing Co., Inc., 2000.

Halperin, David M. "Sex/Sexuality/Sexual Classification." Pages 449–86 in *Critical Terms for The Study of Gender*. Edited by C. R. Stimpson and G. Herdt. Chicago: University of Chicago Press, 2014.

———. *Saint Foucault: Towards a Gay Hagiography*. New York: Oxford University Press, 1995.

Hamilton, James M. Jr. "The Skull Crushing Seed of the Woman: Inner-Biblical Interpretation of Genesis 3:15." *SBJT* 10, no. 2 (Summer 2006): 30–54.

———. *Typology—Understanding the Bible's Promise-Shaped Patterns: How Old Testament Expectations Are Fulfilled in Christ*. Grand Rapids: Zondervan Academic, 2021.

Hamilton, Victor P. *The Book of Genesis Chapters 1–17*. NICOT. Grand Rapids: Eerdmans, 1990.

Hammond, George C. *It Has Not Yet Appeared What We Shall Be: A Reconsideration of the* Imago Dei *in Light of Those with Severe Cognitive Disabilities*. Phillipsburg, NJ: P&R Publishing, 2017.

Haraway, Donna Jeanne. "A Manifesto for Cyborgs: Science, Technology, and Socialist Feminism in the 1980s." *Socialist Review* 80 (1985): 65–108.

———. *Simians, Cyborgs, and Women: The Reinvention of Nature*. New York: Routledge, 1991.

Hare, John. "Hermaphrodites, Eunuchs, and Intersex People: The Witness of Medical Science in Biblical Times and Today." Pages 79–96 in *Intersex, Theology and the Bible: Troubling Bodies in Church, Text and Society*. Edited by Susannah Cornwall. New York: Palgrave Macmillan, 2015.

Harrison, Glynn. *A Better Story: God, Sex and Human Flourishing*. Leicester: Inter-Varsity Press, 2017.

Harrison, Verna E. F. "Male and Female in Cappadocian Theology." *Journal of Theological Studies* 41 (1990): 441–77.

Hart, Mark D. "Reconciliation of Body and Soul: Gregory of Nyssa's Deeper Theology of Marriage." *Theological Studies* 51 (1990): 450–78.

Hartke, Austen. *Transforming: The Bible and the Lives of Transgender Christians*. Louisville: Westminster John Knox, 2018.

Haslanger, Sally. *Resisting Reality: Social Construction and Social Critique*. Oxford: Oxford University Press, 2012.

Hausman, Bernice L. *Changing Sex: Transsexualism, Technology, and the Idea of Gender*. Durham, NC: Duke University Press, 1995.

Hays, Richard B. *First Corinthians*. Louisville: Westminster John Knox, 2011.

Heartfield, James. *The "Death of the Subject" Explained*. Sheffield: Sheffield Hallam University, 2006.

Heilbrun, Carolyn G. *Toward A Recognition of Androgyny*. New York: Knopf, 1973.

Heimbach, Daniel R. "The Unchangeable Difference: Eternally Fixed Sexual Identity for an Age of Plastic Sexuality." Pages 275–89 in *Biblical Foundations for Manhood and Womanhood*. Edited by Wayne A. Grudem. Wheaton, IL: Crossway, 2002.

Hekman, Susan J. "Constructing the Ballast: An Ontology for Feminism." Pages 85–119 in *Material Feminisms*. Edited by Stacy Alaimo and Susan J. Hekman. Bloomington: Indiana University Press, 2008.

Heldman, Breanne L. "Chaz Bono: Gender Is Between Your Ears, Not Legs." *ENews* (November 19, 2009). https://www.eonline.com/au/news/154524/chaz-bono-gender-is-between-your-ears-not-legs.

Hellerman, Joseph H. *The Ancient Church as Family*. Minneapolis: Fortress, 2001.

Herdt, Gilbert, "Preface." Pages 11–20 in *Third Sex, Third Gender: Beyond Sexual Dimorphism in Culture and History*. Edited by Gilbert Herdt. New York: Zone Books, 1993.

Herzer, Linda Tatro. *The Bible and the Transgender Experience: How Scripture Supports Gender Variance*. Cleveland: Pilgrim Press, 2016.

Hester, J. David. "Eunuchs and the Postgender Jesus: Matthew 19:12 and Transgressive Sexualities." *JSNT* 28, no. 1 (September 2005): 13–40.

Heyer, Walt. "Childhood Sexual Abuse, Gender Dysphoria, and Transition Regret: Billy's Story." *Public Discourse* (March 26, 2018). https://www.thepublicdiscourse.com/2018/03/21178.

Heyward, Carter. *Our Passion for Justice: Image of Power, Sexuality, and Liberation*. New York: Beacon, 1984.

Higton, Mike. "A Critique of 'Transformed' 4." *kaì* euthùs (February 28, 2019). https://mikehigton.org.uk/a-critique-of-transformed-4.

Hilary of Poitiers. *On the Trinity*. Pages 40–233 in vol. 9 of *Nicene and Post-Nicene Fathers*. Series 2. Edited by Philip Schaff and Henry Wace. Repr., Grand Rapids: Eerdmans, 1955.

Hilton, Emma, and Jenny Whyte. "Project Nettie: Scientists Supporting Biological Sex." *Project Nettie: Scientists Supporting Biological Sex*. https://projectnettie.wordpress.com.

Hodge, Charles. *Systematic Theology: Volume II*. Ontario: Devoted Publishing, 2016.

Hoehner, Harold W. *Ephesians: An Exegetical Commentary*. Grand Rapids: Baker, 2002.

Hoekema, Anthony A. *Created in God's Image*. Grand Rapids: Eerdmans, 1986.

Hogan, Pauline N. *"No Longer Male and Female": Interpreting Galatians 3.28 in Early Christianity*. LNTS 380. New York: T&T Clark, 2008.

Holder, Rodney. "The Ethics of Transsexualism, Part 1: The Transsexual Condition and the Biblical Background to an Ethical Response." *Crucible* 37, no. 2 (1998): 89–99.

———. "The Ethics of Transsexualism, Part 2: A Christian Response to the Issues Raised." *Crucible* 37, no. 3 (1998): 125–36.

Holmes, Brooke. "Let Go of Laqueur: Towards New Histories of the Sexed Body." *Eugesta: Journal on Gender Studies in Antiquity* 9 (2019): 136–75.

———. *Gender: Antiquity and Its Legacy*. Oxford: Oxford University Press, 2012.

Hornsby, Teresa J. "The Dance of Gender: David, Jesus, and Paul." *Neotestimentica* 48, no. 1 (2014): 75–91.

Hornsby, Teresa J., and Deryn Guest, eds. *Transgender, Intersex, and Biblical Interpretation*. Semeia Studies, No. 83. Atlanta: SBL Press, 2016.

Horton, David. *Changing Channels? A Christian Response to the Transvestite and Transsexual*. Nottingham: Grove Books, 1994.

Horton, Michael S. "Post Reformation Reformed Anthropology." Pages 45–69 in *Personal Identity in Theological Perspective*. Edited by Richard Lints, Michael S. Horton, and Mark R. Talbot. Grand Rapids: Eerdmans, 2006.

———. *The Christian Faith: A Systematic Theology for Pilgrims on the Way*. Grand Rapids: Zondervan, 2011.

House of Bishops. *Some Issues in Human Sexuality: A Guide to the Debate*. London: Church House Publishing, 2003.

Hull, Carrie L. "Letter to the Editor: How Sexually Dimorphic Are We? Review and Synthesis." *American Journal of Human Biology* 15 (2003): 112–15.

———. *The Ontology of Sex: A Critical Inquiry into the Deconstruction and Reconstruction of Categories*. London and New York: Routledge, 2006.

Instone-Brewer, David. *Divorce and Remarriage in the Bible: The Social and Literary Context*. Grand Rapids: Eerdmans, 2002.

Irenaeus. *Against Heresies*. Pages 309–567 in vol. 1 of *Ante-Nicene Fathers: The Writings of the Fathers Down to A.D. 325*. Edited by Alexander Roberts, James Donaldson, A. Cleveland Coxe, and Allan Menzies, 1884. 10 vols. Repr. Peabody, MA: Hendrickson, 1995.

Jagose, Annamarie Rustom. *Queer Theory: An Introduction*. Melbourne: Melbourne University Press, 1996.

James, Sharon. *Gender Ideology: What Do Christians Need to Know?* Fearn: Christian Focus Publications, 2019.

Jaulin, Annick. "La fabrique du sexe, Thomas Laqueur et Aristote." *Clio* 14 (2001): 195–205.

Jeeves, Malcolm A., and R. J. Berry. *Science, Life and Christian Belief: A Survey and Assessment*. Leicester: Apollos, 1998.

Jeffreys, Sheila. *Gender Hurts: A Feminist Analysis of the Politics of Transgenderism*. New York: Routledge, 2014.

Jenkins, Katharine. "Can a Woman Have a Penis? How to Understand Disagreements about Gender Recognition." *The Conversation* (August 28, 2018). https://theconversation.com/can-a-woman-have-a-penis-how-to-understand-disagreements-about-gender-recognition-101991.

Jensen, Peter F. "God and the Bible." Pages 477–96 in *The Enduring Authority of the Christian Scriptures*. Edited by D. A. Carson. Grand Rapids: Eerdmans, 2016.

Jewett, Paul K., with Marguerite Shuster. *Who We Are: Our Dignity as Human: A Neo-Evangelical Theology*. Grand Rapids: Eerdmans, 1996.

Jewett, Paul K. *Man as Male and Female: A Study in Sexual Relationships from a Theological Point of View*. Grand Rapids: Eerdmans, 1975.

John Paul II. *Man and Woman He Created Them: A Theology of the Body*. Translated by Michael Waldstein. Boston: Pauline Books & Media, 2006.

Johnson, Elizabeth. "Wisdom Was Made Flesh and Pitched Her Tent Among Us." Pages 95–117 in *Reconstructing the Christ Symbol: Essays in Feminist Christology*. Edited by Mary Anne Stevens. New York: Paulist Press, 1993.

Johnson, Eric L. "Playing Games and Living Metaphors: The Incarnation and the End of Gender." *JETS* 40, no. 2 (June 1997): 271–85.

Johnston, Jill. *Lesbian Nation: The Feminist Solution*. New York: Simon and Schuster, 1973.

Jones, Angela. "Rachel Dolezal Is Really Queer: Transracial Politics and Queer Futurity." *Social (In)Queery* (June, 17, 2015). https://socialinqueery.com/2015/06/17/rachel-dolezal-is-really-queer-transracial-politics-and-queer-futurity.

Jones, Beth Felker. *Marks of His Wounds: Gender Politics and Bodily Resurrection*. Oxford: Oxford University Press, 2007.

Joyce, Helen. *Trans: When Ideology Meets Reality*. London: Oneworld Publications, 2021.

Jung, Patricia Beattie, and Ralph F. Smith. *Heterosexism: An Ethical Challenge*. Albany: State University of New York Press, 1993.

Jung, Patricia Beattie. "Christianity and Human Sexual Polymorphism: Are They Compatible?" Pages 293–309 in *Ethics and Intersex*. Edited by Sharon E. Sytsma. Dordrecht: Springer, 2006.

Kacere, Laura. "Why the Feminist Movement Must Be Trans-Inclusive." *Everyday Feminism* (February 24, 2014). https://everydayfeminism.com/2014/02/trans-inclusive-feminist-movement.

Kearns, Madeleine. "Has Trans Orthodoxy Conquered the World?" *UnHerd* (January 6, 2020). https://unherd.com/2020/01/how-the-trans-orthodoxy-conquered-the-world.

Keller, Timothy. *Making Sense of God: An Invitation to the Skeptical*. New York: Viking, 2016.

Kelsey, David H. *Eccentric Existence: A Theological Anthropology*. 2 volumes. Philadelphia: Westminster, 2009.

Kennedy, John W. "The Transgender Moment." *Christianity Today* (February 12, 2008). http://www.christianitytoday.com/ct/2008/february/25.54.html.

Kessler, Suzanne J. *Lessons from the Intersexed*. New Brunswick: Rutgers University Press, 1998.

Khalidi, Muhammad Ali. "Three Kinds of Social Kinds." *Philosophy and Phenomenological Research* 90, no. 1 (January 2015): 96–112.

Kidd, Thomas S. *Who Is an Evangelical? The History of a Movement in Crisis*. New Haven: Yale University Press, 2019.

Kidner, Derek, *Genesis: An Introduction and Commentary*. TOTC. Leicester: Inter-Varsity Press, 1967.

———. *Psalms 1–72*. TOTC. Leicester: Inter-Varsity Press, 1973.

———. *Psalms 73–150*. TOTC. Leicester: Inter-Varsity Press, 1975.

Kierkegaard, Søren. *The Concept of Anxiety: A Simple Psychologically Orienting Deliberation on the Dogmatic Issue of Hereditary Sin*. Edited and translated by Reidar Thomte and Albert B. Anderson. Princeton: Princeton University Press.

Killermann, Sam. *A Guide to Gender: The Social Justice Advocate's Handbook*. 2nd ed. Austin, TX: Impetus Books, 2017.

Kilner, John F. *Dignity and Destiny: Humanity in the Image of God*. Grand Rapids: Eerdmans, 2015.

King, Helen. *The One-Sex Body on Trial: The Classical and Early Modern Evidence. The History of Medicine in Context*. Burlington, VT: Ashgate, 2013.

Kirby, Vicki, and Judith Butler. "Butler Live" (Interview). Pages 144–58 in *Judith Butler: Live Theory*. Edited by Vicki Kirby. London: Continuum, 2006.

Kirby, Vicki. "Natural Convers(at)ions: Or, What If Culture Was Really Nature All Along?" Pages 214–36 in *Material Feminisms*. Edited by Stacy Alaimo and Susan J. Hekman. Bloomington: Indiana University Press, 2008.

Klassen, Brad. "The Pauline Response to Today's Sexual and Gender Confusion." *MSJ* 28, no. 2 (Fall 2017): 145–66.

Kleinig, John W. *Wonderfully Made: A Protestant Theology of the Body*. Bellingham, WA: Lexham Press, 2021.

Kline, Meredith G. *Images of the Spirit*. Eugene, OR: Wipf & Stock, 1991.

——. *Kingdom Prologue: Genesis Foundations for a Covenantal Worldview.* Overland Park, KS: Two Age Press, 2002.

Klink III, Edward W., and Darian R. Lockett. *Understanding Biblical Theology: A Comparison of Theory and Practice.* Grand Rapids: Zondervan, 2012.

Knight, George W. III. "Husbands and Wives as Analogues of Christ and the Church: Ephesians 5:21–33 and Colossians 3:18–19." Pages 165–78 in *Recovering Biblical Manhood and Womanhood: A Response to Evangelical Feminism.* Edited by John Piper and Wayne Grudem. Wheaton, IL: Crossway, 1991.

Knust, Jennifer Wright. *Unprotected Texts: The Bible's Surprising Contradictions about Sex and Desire.* New York: HarperOne, 2011.

Kohli, Sonali. "Pop Culture's Transgender Moment: Why Online TV Is Leading the Way." *The Atlantic* (September 26, 2014). https://www.theatlantic.com/entertainment/archive/2014/09/why-online-streaming-wins-with-transgender-portrayals/380822.

Kolakowski, Victoria S. "Toward a Christian Ethical Response to Transsexual Persons." *Theology and Sexuality* 6 (1997): 10–31.

Köstenberger, Andreas J., with David W. Jones. *God, Marriage and Family: Rebuilding the Biblical Foundations.* 2nd ed. Wheaton, IL: Crossway, 2010.

Kotz, Liz, and Judith Butler. "The Body You Want: Liz Kotz Interviews Judith Butler." *Artforum International* 31, no. 3 (1992): 82–89. https://www.artforum.com/print/previews/199209/the-body-you-want-an-inteview-with-judith-butler-33505.

Koyama, Emi. "From 'Intersex' to 'DSD': Toward a Queer Disability Politics of Gender." *Intersex Initiative* (2006). http://www.intersexinitiative.org/articles/intersextodsd.html.

——. "The Transfeminist Manifesto" (2001). Pages 244–59 in *Catching a Wave: Reclaiming Feminism for the 21st Century.* Edited by Rory Cooke Dicker and Alison Piepmeier. Boston: Northeastern University Press, 2003.

Kreeft, Peter. *Everything You Ever Wanted to Know About Heaven: But Never Dreamed of Asking!* San Francisco: Ignatius Press, 1990.

Kreukels, B. P., and A. Guillamon. "Neuroimaging Studies in People with Gender Incongruence." *International Review of Psychiatry* 28, no. 1 (2016): 120–28.

Kuby, Gabrielle. *The Global Sexual Revolution: Destruction of Freedom in the Name of Freedom*. Translated by James Patrick Kirchner. Kettering: LifeSite, 2015. First published in German as *Die globale sexuelle Revolution: Zerstörung der Freiheit im Namen der Freiheit*. Fe-Medienverlags Gmbh, 2012.

Kuefler, Mathew. *The Manly Eunuch: Masculinity, Gender Ambiguity and Christian Ideology in Late Antiquity*. Chicago: University of Chicago Press, 2001.

Kuehne, Dale S. *Sex and the iWorld: Rethinking Relationship beyond an Age of Individualism*. Grand Rapids: Baker, 2009.

Ladin, Joy. "The Genesis of Gender." *Tikkun* 30, no. 3 (Summer 2015): 39–48.

Lafrance, Marc. "The Struggle for True Sex: *Herculine Barbin dite Alexina B* and the Work of Michel Foucault." *Canadian Review of Comparative Literature* 32, no. 2 (June 2005): 161–82.

Lakey, Michael. *Image and Glory of God: 1 Corinthians 11:2–16 as a Case Study in Bible, Gender and Hermeneutics*. LNTS 418. New York: T&T Clark, 2010.

Laqueur, Thomas W. "L'usage de la catégorie de genre. Réponse de Thomas Laqueur à Annick Jaulin." *Clio* 15 (2002): 209–11.

———. "Sex in the Flesh." *Isis* 94 (2003): 300–6.

———. "The Rise of Sex in the Eighteenth Century: Historical Context and Historiographical Implications." *Signs* 37, no. 4 (2012): 802–13.

———. *Making Sex: Body and Gender from the Greeks to Freud*. Cambridge: Harvard University Press, 1990.

Lawford-Smith, Holly. *Gender-Critical Feminism*. Oxford: Oxford University Press, 2022.

———. *Sex Matters: Essays in Gender-Critical Philosophy*. Oxford: Oxford University Press, 2023.

Lawrence, Anne A. "Shame and Narcissistic Rage in Autogynephilic Transsexualism." *Archives of Sexual Behavior* (2008): 457–61.

Lebacqz, Karen, "Difference or Defect? Intersexuality and the Politics of Difference." *Annual of the Society of Christian Ethics* 17 (1997): 213–29.

Leff, Arthur Allen. "Unspeakable Ethics, Unnatural Law." *1979 Duke Law Journal* 6 (December 1979): 1229–49.

Leicht, Reimund. "Planets in Ancient Hebrew Literature." Pages 15–38 in *Giving a Diamond: Essays in Honor of Joseph Yahalom on the Occasion of His Seventieth Birthday*. Edited by Wout van Bekkum and Naoya Katsumata. Leiden: Brill, 2011.

Liederbach, Mark D., and Evan Lenow. *Ethics as Worship: The Pursuit of Moral Discipleship*. Phillipsburg, NJ: P&R Publishing, 2021.

Lennon, Kathleen. "Judith Butler and the Sartrean Imaginary." *Sartre Studies International* 23 (2017): 22–37.

Lennon, Kathleen, and Rachel Alsop. *Gender Theory in Troubled Times*. Cambridge: Polity Press, 2020.

Lenski, R. C. H. *The Interpretation of St. Paul's Epistles to the Galatians, to the Ephesians, and to the Philippians*. Columbus, OH: Wartburg Press, 1946.

Letham, Robert. *Systematic Theology*. Wheaton, IL: Crossway, 2019.

Levering, Matthew. *Engaging the Doctrine of Creation: Cosmos, Creatures, and the Wise and Good Creator*. Grand Rapids: Baker, 2017.

Levine, Stephen. B., and E. Abbruzzese. "Current Concerns About Gender-Affirming Therapy in Adolescents." *Curr Sex Health Rep* 15 (2023): 113–23. https://doi.org/10.1007/s11930–023–00358-x.

Lincoln, Andrew T. *Ephesians*. WBC 42. Waco, TX: Word, 1990.

Lints, Richard. *Identity and Idolatry: The Image of God and Its Inversion*. NSBT 36. Downers Grove, IL: InterVarsity Press, 2015.

Lipka, Hilary. "The Prohibition of Cross-Dressing: What does Deuteronomy 22:5 Prohibit and Why?" *TheTorah.com – A Historical and Contextual Approach* (N.D.): 1–11. https://thetorah.com/the-prohibition-of-cross-dressing.

Lips, Hilary M. *Gender: The Basics*. 2nd ed. London and New York: Routledge, 2018.

Littman, Lisa. "Correction: Parent Reports of Adolescents and Young Adults Perceived to Show Signs of a Rapid Onset of Gender Dysphoria." *PLoS ONE* 14, no. 3 (March 19, 2019): 1–7. https://doi.org/10.1371/journal.pone.0214157.

———. "Individuals Treated for Gender Dysphoria with Medical and/or Surgical Transition Who Subsequently Detransitioned: A Survey of 100 Detransitioners." *Archives of Sexual Behavior* 50 (2021): 3353–69. https://doi.org/10.1007/s10508-021-02163-w.

———. "Parent Reports of Adolescents and Young Adults Perceived to Show Signs of a Rapid Onset of Gender Dysphoria." *PLoS ONE* 13, no. 8 (August 16, 2018): 1–41. https://doi.org/10.1371/journal.pone.0202330.

Loader, William. "Homosexuality and the Bible." Pages 17–48 in *Two Views on Homosexuality, the Bible, and the Church*. Edited by Preston Sprinkle. Grand Rapids: Zondervan, 2016.

———. *Sex, Then and Now: Sexualities and the Bible*. Eugene, OR: Cascade, 2022.

———. *The New Testament on Sexuality*. Grand Rapids: Eerdmans, 2012.

Longenecker, Richard N. *Galatians*. WBC 41. Waco, TX: Word, 1990.

Looby, Christopher. "The Man Who Thought Himself a Woman." *The Knickerbocker* 50, no. 6 (December 1857): 599–610.

Looy, Heather, and Hessell Bouma III. "The Nature of Gender: Gender Identity in Persons Who are Intersexed or Transgendered." *Journal of Psychology and Theology* 33, no. 3 (2005): 166–78.

Lorber, Judith. *The Variety of Feminisms and Their Contributions to Gender Equality*. Oldenburg: Bibliotheks- und Informationssystem, 1997.

Loughlin, Gerard. "Being Creature, Becoming Human: Contesting Oliver O'Donovan on Transgender, Identity and the Body." *ABC Religion & Ethics* (September 5, 2018). https://www.abc.net.au/religion/being-creature-becoming-human-contesting-oliver-odonovan-on-tran/10214276.

———. "Gender Ideology: For a 'Third Sex' Without Reserve." *Studies in Christian Ethics* 31, no. 4 (2018): 471–82.

Lowe, Mary Elise. "From the Same Spirit: Receiving the Theological Gifts of Transgender Christians." *Dialog: A Journal of Theology* 56 (2017): 28–37.

Luther, Martin. *Lectures on Genesis Chapters 1–5*. Volume 1 of *Luther's Works*. Edited by Jaroslav Pelikan. St. Louis: Concordia, 1958.

———. *The Estate of Marriage* (1522). Pages 11–49 in Volume 45 of *Luther's Works*. Edited by Jaroslav Pelikan. St. Louis: Concordia, 1955.

Lyotard, Jean-François. *The Postmodern Condition: A Report on Knowledge*. Translated by Geoff Bennington and Brian Massumi. Minneapolis: University of Minnesota Press, 1984.

Macaskill, Grant. *Living in Union with Christ: Paul's Gospel and Christian Moral Identity*. Grand Rapids: Baker Academic, 2019.

MacCulloch, Diarmaid. *The Reformation: A History*. New York: Penguin, 2004.

Macleod, Donald. "Original Sin in Reformed Theology." Pages 129–46 in *Adam, the Fall, and Original Sin: Theological, Biblical, and Scientific Perspectives*. Edited by Hans Madueme and Michael Reeves. Grand Rapids: Baker, 2014.

——. *The Person of Christ*. Downers Grove, IL: InterVarsity Press, 1998.

Magnuson, Ken. *Invitation to Christian Ethics: Moral Reasoning and Contemporary Issues*. Grand Rapids: Kregel, 2020.

Mann, Susan Archer, and Douglas J. Huffman. "The Decentering of Second Wave Feminism and the Rise of the Third Wave." *Science & Society* 69, no. 1 (2005): 56–91.

Manning, Gideon. "The History of 'Hylomorphism.'" *Journal of the History of Ideas* 74, no. 2 (2013): 173–87.

Marchiano, Lisa. "Trans Activism's Dangerous Myth of Parental Rejection." *Quillette* (July 20, 2018). https://quillette.com/2018/07/20/trans-activisms-dangerous-myth-of-parental-rejection.

Marcuse, Herbert. *Eros and Civilization: A Philosophical Inquiry into Freud*. Boston: Beacon, 1955.

Marshall, I. Howard. *The Gospel of Luke: A Commentary on the Greek Text*. Exeter: Paternoster, 1978.

Martin, Dale B. *Sex and the Single Savior: Gender and Sexuality in Biblical Interpretation*. Louisville: Westminster John Knox, 2006.

Martin, Dale B. *The Corinthian Body*. New Haven: Yale University Press, 1995.

Martin, Ralph P. "Approaches to New Testament Exegesis." Pages 220–51 in *New Testament Interpretation*. Edited by I. Howard Marshall. Exeter: Paternoster, 1979.

Martin, Troy W. "The Covenant of Circumcision (Genesis 17:9–14) and the Situational Antitheses of Galatians 3:28." *JBL* 122, no. 1 (2003): 111–25.

Maryniarczyk, Andrzej. "Is the Human Soul Sexed? In Search for the Truth on Human Sexuality." *Studia Gilsoniana* 9, no. 1 (January–March 2020): 87–142.

Mason, Matthew. "The Authority of the Body: Discovering Natural Manhood and Womanhood." *BET* 4, no. 2 (2017): 39–57.

——. "The Wounded It Heals: Gender Dysphoria and the Resurrection of the Body." Pages 135–47 in *Beauty, Order, and Mystery: A Christian Vision of Human Sexuality*. Edited by Gerald Hiestand and Todd Wilson. Downers Grove, IL: InterVarsity Press, 2017.

Mathews, Kenneth A. *Genesis 1–11:26*. NAC 1A. Nashville: Broadman & Holman, 1996.

Mavrode, George I. "Self-Referential Incoherence." *American Philosophical Quarterly* 22, no. 1 (1985): 65–72.

Mayer, Lawrence S., and Paul R. McHugh. "Sexuality and Gender: Findings from the Biological, Psychological, and Social Sciences." *The New Atlantis* 50 (Fall 2016): 10–143. http://www.thenewatlantis.com/publications/number-50-fall-2016.

McCarthy, Margaret H. "Gender Ideology and the Humanum." *Communio* 43 (Summer 2016): 274–98.

McConville, J. Gordon. *Deuteronomy*, AOTC. Downers Grove, IL: InterVarsity Press, 2002.

McCready, Douglas. *He Came Down from Heaven: The Preexistence of Christ and the Christian Faith*. Downers Grove, IL: IVP Academic, 2005.

McDonald, Nathan. "The *Imago Dei* and Election: Reading Genesis 1:26–28 and Old Testament Scholarship with Karl Barth." *IJST* 10, no. 3 (July 2008): 303–27.

McDowell, Catherine. "In the Image of God He Created Them: How Genesis 1:26–27 Defines the Divine-Human Relationship and Why It Matters." Pages 29–46 in *The Image of God in an Image Driven Age: Explorations in Theological Anthropology*. Edited by Beth Felker Jones and Jeffrey W. Barbeau. Downers Grove, IL: InterVarsity Press, 2016.

McFadyen, Alistair Iain. *The Call to Personhood: A Christian Theory of the Individual in Social Relationships*. Cambridge: Cambridge University Press, 1990.

McGowan, A. T. B. *The Person and Work of Christ: Understanding Jesus*. Milton Keynes: Paternoster, 2012.

McLaughlin, Eleanor. "Feminist Christologies: Re-Dressing the Tradition." Pages 118–49 in *Reconstructing the Christ Symbol: Essays in Feminist Christology*. Edited by Mary Anne Stevens. New York: Paulist Press, 1993.

McNay, Lois. *Foucault and Feminism: Power, Gender, and the Self*. Cambridge: Polity Press, 1992.

Mead, Margaret. *Male and Female: A Study of the Sexes in a Changing World*. New York: Morrow, 1949.

Meeks, Wayne A. "The Image of the Androgyne: Some Uses of a Symbol in Earliest Christianity." *History of Religions* 13 (1974): 165–208.

Meilaender, Gilbert. *Faith and Faithfulness: Basic Themes in Christian Ethics*. Notre Dame: University of Notre Dame Press, 1991.

Melcher, Sarah J. "A Tale of Two Eunuchs: Isaiah 56:1–8 and Acts 8:26–40." Pages 115–28 in *Disability Studies and Biblical Literature*. Edited by Candida R. Moss and Jeremy Schipper. New York: Palgrave MacMillan, 2011.

Merleau-Ponty, Maurice. *The Phenomenology of Perception*. Translated by Colin Smith. Boston: Routledge and Kegan Paul, 1962.

Merrick, James R. A., and Stephen M. Garrett, eds. *Five Views on Biblical Inerrancy*. Grand Rapids: Zondervan, 2013.

Merrill, Eugene H. *Deuteronomy*. NAC. Nashville: Broadman & Holman, 1994.

Merritt, Jonathan. "Defining 'Evangelical': Its Meaning Has Shifted throughout Christianity's Long History and Changes Depending on Who You Ask. Why?" *The Atlantic* (December 7, 2015). https://www.theatlantic.com/politics/archive/2015/12/evangelical-christian/418236.

Meyerowitz, Joanne. "A History of 'Gender.'" *American Historical Review* 113, no. 5 (December 2008): 1346–56.

Middleton, Richard J. *The Liberating Image: The* Imago Dei *in Genesis 1*. Grand Rapids: Brazos, 2005.

Migdon, Brooke. "Idaho Governor Signs Transgender Bathroom Bill." *The Hill* (March 24, 2023). https://thehill.com/homenews/state-watch/3916944-idaho-governor-signs-transgender-bathroom-bill.

Migliore, Daniel L. *Faith Seeking Understanding: An Introduction to Christian Theology*. Grand Rapids: Eerdmans, 2004.

Milbank, John. *Theology and Social Theory: Beyond Secular Reason*. 2nd ed. New York: Wiley-Blackwell, 2008.

Milgrom, Jacob. "Sex and Wisdom: What the Garden of Eden Story Is Saying." *BRev* 10, no. 6 (1994): 21, 52.

Mill, John Stuart. *The Subjection of Women*. New York: Appleton, 1869.

Millar, J. Gary. *Now Choose Life: Theology and Ethics in Deuteronomy*. NSBT 6. Leicester: Apollos, 1998.

Millett, Kate. *Sexual Politics*. New York: Doubleday, 1970.

Miscall, Peter D. "Jacques Derrida in the Garden of Eden." *USQR* 44 (1990): 1–9.

Mohammadi, Mohammad Reza, and Ali Khaleghi. "Transsexualism: A Different Viewpoint to Brain Changes." *Clinical Psychopharmacology Neuroscience* 16, no. 2 (2018): 136–43.

Mohler, R. Albert. Jr. "I Signed the Nashville Statement. It's an Expression of Love for Same-Sex Attracted People." *The Washington Post* (September 3, 2017). https://www.washingtonpost.com/news/acts-of-faith/wp/2017/09/03/i-signed-the-nashville-statement-its-an-expression-of-love-for-same-sex-attracted-people/.

———. *We Cannot Be Silent: Speaking Truth to a Culture Redefining Sex, Marriage, and the Very Meaning of Right and Wrong*. Nashville: Nelson, 2015.

Mollenkott, Virginia Ramey. "We Come Bearing Gifts: Seven Lessons Religious Congregations Can Learn from Transpeople." Pages 46–58 in *Trans/Formations*. Edited by Marcella Althaus-Reid and Lisa Isherwood. London: SCM, 2009.

———. *Omnigender: A Trans-Religious Approach*. Cleveland: Pilgrim Press, 2007.

Moltmann, Jürgen. "Liberate Yourselves by Accepting One Another." Pages 105–22 in *Human Disability and the Service of God: Reassessing Religious Practice*. Edited by Nancy L. Eisland and Don E. Saliers. Nashville: Abingdon, 1998.

———. *God in Creation: An Ecological Doctrine of Creation*. Translated by Margaret Kohl. London: SCM, 1985.

Money, John. "Hermaphroditism, Gender and Precocity in Hyperadrenocorticism: Psychologic Findings." *Bulletin of the Johns Hopkins Hospital* 96 (1955): 253–64.

———. "Linguistic Resources and Psychodynamic Theory." *British Journal of Medical Psychology* 28, no. 4 (1955): 264–66.

———."Psychosexual Differentiation." Pages 3–23 in *Sex Research, New Developments*. Edited by John Money. New York: Holt, Rinehart, and Winston, 1965.

———. "This Week's Citation Classic." *Current Contents* 11 (March 16, 1987): 12. http://garfield.library.upenn.edu/classics1987/A1987G240300001.pdf.

———. *Sin, Science and Sex Police: Essays on Sexology & Sexosophy*. Amherst, NY: Prometheus Books, 1998.

Money, John, J. G. Hampson, and J. L. Hampson. "An Examination of Some Basic Sexual Concepts: The Evidence of Human Hermaphroditism." *Bulletin of the Johns Hopkins Hospital* 97 (1955): 301–19.

Money, John, and Patricia Tucker. *Sexual Signatures: On Being a Man or a Woman*. Boston: Little, Brown, 1975.

Moo, Douglas J. *Galatians*. BECNT. Grand Rapids: Baker Academic, 2013.

——. *The Letter to the Romans*. NICNT. 2nd ed. Grand Rapids: Eerdmans, 2018.

Moore, Russell D. "Joan or John? An Ethical Dilemma." *SBJT* 13, no. 2 (2009): 52–56.

——. "The Transgender Revolution and the Rubble of Empty Promises." *TGC: U.S. Edition* (June 6, 2017). https://www.thegospelcoalition.org/article/transgender-revolution-and-rubble-of-empty-promises.

Moreland, J. P. "In Defense of Thomistic-like Dualism." Pages 102–122 in *The Blackwell Companion to Substance Dualism*. Edited by Jonathan J. Loose, Angus J. L. Menuge, and J. P. Moreland. Oxford: Oxford University Press, 2018.

Moreland, J. P., and Scott B. Rae. *Body & Soul: Human Nature & the Crisis in Ethics*. Downers Grove, IL: InterVarsity Press, 2000.

Morgan, Christopher W. "Sin in the Biblical Story." Pages 131–62 in *Fallen: A Theology of Sin*. Edited by Robert A. Peterson and Christopher W. Morgan. Wheaton, IL: Crossway, 2013.

Morris, Leon. *The Gospel According to Matthew*. PNTC. Grand Rapids: Eerdmans, 1992.

Moschella, Melissa. "Sexual Identity, Gender, and Human Fulfillment: Analyzing the 'Middle Way' Between Liberal and Traditionalist Approaches." *Christian Bioethics* 25, no. 2 (2019): 192–215.

Motschenbacher, Heiko. *Language, Gender and Sexual Identity: Poststructuralist Perspectives*. Philadelphia: John Benjamins Publishing Company, 2010.

Motyer, Alec. *The Prophecy of Isaiah*. Leicester: Inter-Varsity Press, 1993.

Moxnes, Halvor. *Putting Jesus in His Place: A Radical Vision of Household and Kingdom*. Louisville: Westminster John Knox, 2003.

Murray, Douglas. *The Madness of Crowds: Gender, Race and Identity*. London: Bloomsbury, 2019.

Muthukumar, David S. "Embodied and Socially Embedded 'Self': Understanding Jesus's Bodily Resurrection and Believers' Post Mortem Identity and Continuity." *Science and Christian Belief* 31, no. 2 (2019): 112–30.

Nagoshi, Julie L., and Stephan/ie Brzuzy. "Transgender Theory: Embodying Research and Practice." *Affilia: Journal of Women and Social Work* 25, no. 4 (2010): 431–43.

Nagoshi, Julie L., Craig T. Nagoshi and Stephan/ie Brzuzy. *Gender and Sexual Identity: Transcending Feminist and Queer Theory*. New York: Springer, 2014.

Namaste, Viviane K. "'Tragic Misreadings': Queer Theory's Erasure of Transgender Subjectivity." Pages 183–206 in *Queer Studies: A Lesbian, Gay, Bisexual, and Transgender Anthology*. Edited by Brett Beemyn and Mickey Eliason. New York: New York University Press, 1996.

———. "Undoing Theory: The 'Transgender Question' and the Epistemic Violence of Anglo-American Feminist Theory." *Hypatia: A Journal of Feminist Philosophy* 24, no. 3 (2009): 11–32.

———. *Invisible Lives: The Erasure of Transsexual and Transgendered People*. Chicago: The University of Chicago Press, 2000.

Neuer, Werner. *Man and Woman in Christian Perspective*. Translated by Gordon J. Wenham. Wheaton, IL: Crossway, 1991.

New, Caroline. "Feminism, Critical Realism, and the Linguistic Turn." Pages 57–74 in *Critical Realism: The Difference it Makes*. Edited by Justin Cruickshank. London: Routledge, 2003.

———. "Sex and Gender: A Critical Realist Approach." *New Formations* 56 (Autumn 2005): 54–70.

Nietzsche, Friedrich Wilhelm. *Beyond Good and Evil*. Translated by Walter Kaufmann. New York: Vintage, 1989.

———. *On the Genealogy of Morals*. Translated by Walter Kaufmann. New York: Vintage, 1969.

Nolland, John. *The Gospel of Matthew*. NIGTC. Grand Rapids: Eerdmans, 2005.

Nussbaum, Martha C. "The Professor of Parody: The Hip Defeatism of Judith Butler." *New Republic* 220 (February 22, 1999): 37–45.

O'Brien, Michelle. "Intersex, Medicine, Diversity, Identity and Spirituality." Pages 45–56 in *This Is My Body: Hearing the Theology of Transgender Christians*. Edited by Christina Beardsley and Michelle O'Brien. London: Darton, Longman & Todd, 2016.

O'Donovan, Oliver. "Transsexualism and Christian Marriage." *Journal of Religious Ethics* 11, no. 1 (1983): 135–62.

———. *Begotten or Made?* 2nd ed. Landrum, SC: Davenant Press, 2022.

———. *Crisis in the Church: The Gay Controversy and the Anglican Communion*. Eugene, OR: Cascade, 2008.

———. *Resurrection and Moral Order: An Outline for Evangelical Ethics*. 2nd ed. Leicester, UK: Apollos, 1994.

Oakley, Ann. *Sex, Gender, and Society*. New York: Harper Colophon, 1972.

Oliven, John F. *Sexual Hygiene and Pathology*. Philadelphia: J. B. Lippincott Company, 1965.

Olyan, Saul M. "Mary Douglas's Holiness/Wholeness Paradigm: Its Potential for Insight and its Limitations." *Journal of Hebrew Scriptures* 8 (2008): art. 10, pp. 1–9, https://doi.org/10.5508/jhs.2008.v8.a10.

Ortega, Rodrigo Pérez. "World Athletics Banned Transgender Women from Competing. Does Science Support the Rule?" *Science* (4 April, 2023). https://www.science.org/content/article/world-athletics-banned-transgender-women-competing-does-science-support-rule.

Ortlund, Gavin. "Image of Adam, Son of God: Genesis 5:3 and Luke 3:38 in Intercanonical Dialogue." *JETS* 57, no. 4 (2014): 673–88.

Ortlund, Raymond C. Jr. *God's Unfaithful Wife: A Biblical-Theology of Spiritual Adultery*. NSBT 2. Downers Grove, IL: InterVarsity Press, 2002.

Osborne, Grant R. *The Hermeneutical Spiral: A Comprehensive Introduction to Biblical Interpretation*. Downers Grove, IL: InterVarsity Press, 1991.

Oster, Richard. "When Men Wore Veils to Worship: The Historical Context of 1 Corinthians 11.4." *NTS* 34, no. 4 (1988): 481–505.

Osterhaven, M. Eugene. "Covenant Theology." Pages 301–3 in *Evangelical Dictionary of Theology*. Edited by Walter. A. Elwell. Grand Rapids: Baker, 2001.

Overall, Christine. "Sex/Gender Transitions and Life-Changing Aspirations." Pages 11–27 in *You've Changed: Sex Reassignment and Personal Identity*. Edited by Laurie Shrage. Oxford: Oxford University Press, 2009.

Pannenberg, Wolfhart. "Dogmatic Theses on the Doctrine of Revelation." Pages 123–58 in *Revelation as History*. Translated by David Granskou. New York: Macmillan, 1968.

Paris, Jenell Williams. *The End of Sexual Identity: Why Sex Is Too Important to Define Who We Are*. Downers Grove, IL: InterVarsity Press, 2011.

Park, Katharine, and Robert A. Nye. "Destiny Is Anatomy, Review of Laqueur's *Making Sex: Body and Gender from the Greeks to Freud*." *The New Republic* 18 (1991): 53–57.

Park, Katharine. "Cadden, Laqueur, and the 'One-Sex Body.'" *Medieval Feminist Forum* 46 no. 1 (2010): 96–100.

Parker, T. H. L. *The Doctrine of the Knowledge of God: A Study in the Theology of John Calvin*. Edinburgh: Oliver & Boyd, 1952.

Parler, Branson. "Hair Length and Human Sexuality: The Underlying Moral Logic of Paul's Appeal to Nature in 1 Corinthians 11:14." *CTJ* 51 (2016): 112–36.

Patterson, Dan. "A Brief History of Gender and Its Significance." *Essentials* (Spring 2016): 6–10.

Patterson, Daniel R. "The Law of Adam and Eve: Judith Butler Matters, and So Does the Fall and Jesus." Pages 292–309 in *1968: Culture and Counterculture*. Edited by Thomas V. Gourlay and Daniel Matthys. Eugene, OR: Pickwick, 2020.

———. *Reforming a Theology of Gender: Constructive Reflections on Judith Butler and Queer Theory*. Eugene, OR: Cascade, 2022.

Payne, Philip B. *Man and Woman, One in Christ: An Exegetical and Theological Study of Paul's Letters*. Grand Rapids: Zondervan, 2009.

Pearcey, Nancy R. *Love Thy Body: Answering Hard Questions about Life and Sexuality*. Grand Rapids: Baker, 2018.

Pelikan, Jaroslav. *Historical Theology: Continuity and Change*. Eugene, OR: Wipf & Stock, 2014.

Peppiatt, Lucy. *Women and Worship at Corinth: Paul's Rhetorical Arguments in 1 Corinthians*. Eugene, OR: Cascade, 2015.

Peter, J. F. "The Reformed View of the Scriptures," *EQ* 31, no. 4 (1959): 196–204.

Peterson, Brian Neil. "Does Genesis 2 Support Same-Sex Marriage? An Evangelical Response." *JETS* 60, no. 4 (December 2017): 681–96.

———. "Male and Female Sexual Exploitation in Light of the Book of Genesis." *JETS* 62, no. 4 (December 2019): 693–703.

———. "Postmodernism's Deconstruction of the Creation Mandates." *JETS* 62, no. 1 (December 2019): 125–40.

Peterson, Ryan S. *The* Imago Dei *as Human Identity: A Theological Interpretation*. JTI Supplement 14. Winona Lake, IN: Eisenbrauns, 2016.

Phillips, Elaine A. "Serpent Intertexts: Tantalizing Twists in the Tales," *BBR* 10 (2000): 233–45.

Phillips, Melanie. "How Feminists Have Weaponised Androgyny." *MelaniePhillips.com* (January 19, 2018). https://www.melaniephillips.com/feminists-weaponised-androgyny.

Philo. *On the Decalogue. On the Special Laws, Books 1–3*. Translated by F. H. Colson. LCL. Cambridge: Harvard University Press, 1937.

Pinker, Steven. "Why Nature & Nurture Won't Go Away." *Dædalus* (Fall 2002): 1–13.

Plantinga, Alvin. "Is Belief in God Properly Basic?" *Noûs* 15, no. 1 (1981): 41–51.

———. *Warranted Christian Belief*. New York: Oxford University Press, 2000.

Plato. *The Symposium*. Edited by M. C. Howatson and Frisbee C. C. Sheffield. Translated by M. C. Howatson. Cambridge: Cambridge University Press, 2008.

Posner, Richard A. *Sex and Reason*. Cambridge: Harvard University Press, 1994.

Poythress, Vern S. *Interpreting Eden: A Guide to Faithfully Reading and Understanding Genesis 1–3*. Wheaton, IL: Crossway, 2019.

Prosser, Jay. *Second Skins: The Body Narratives of Transsexuality*. New York: Columbia University Press, 1998.

Pujante, David. "The Discursive Construction of Reality in the Context of Rhetoric." Pages 42–65 in *Developing* New *Identities in Social Conflicts: Constructivist Perspectives*. Discourse Approaches to Politics, Society and Culture 71. Edited by Esperanza Morales-López and Alan Floyd. Amsterdam: John Benjamins Publishing Co, 2017.

Punt, Jeremy. "Power and Liminality, Sex and Gender, and Gal 3:28. A Postcolonial, Queer Reading of an Influential Text." *Neotestamentica* 44, no. 1 (2010): 140–66.

Putnam, Hilary. *Renewing Philosophy*. Cambridge: Harvard University Press, 1992.

Pydi, Aakash. "Jean Paul Sartre: The Concept of Bad Faith and Its Role in Ethical Analysis," *Aakash Pydi* (March 11, 2018). https://medium.com/@aakashpydi/jean-paul-sartre-the-concept-of-bad-faith-and-its-role-in-ethical-analysis-93f4553fa242.

Quarles, Charles L. *Matthew*. EGGNT. Nashville: Broadman & Holman, 2017.

Rabinow, Paul. "Introduction." Pages 3–29 in *The Foucault Reader: An Introduction to* Foucault's *Thought*. Edited by Paul Rabinow. London: Penguin, 1984.

Raun, Tobias. "Trans as Contested Intelligibility: Interrogating How to Conduct Trans Analysis with Respectful Curiosity." *lambda nordica* 1 (2014): 13–37.

Raymond, Janice G. *The Transsexual Empire: The Making of the She-Male*. New

York: Teachers College Press, 1994. First published 1979.
Reay, Lewis. "Towards a Transgender Theology: Que(e)rying the Eunuchs." Pages 148–67 in *Trans/Formations*. Edited by Marcella Althaus-Reid and Lisa Isherwood. London: SCM, 2009.
Rees, Geoffrey. *The Romance of Innocent Sexuality*. Eugene, OR: Cascade, 2011.
Reilly-Cooper, Rebecca. "Gender Is Not a Spectrum." *Aeon* (June 28, 2016). https://aeon.co/essays/the-idea-that-gender-is-a-spectrum-is-a-new-gender-prison.
———. "Why Self-Identification Shouldn't Be the Only Thing That Defines Our Gender." *The Conversation* (May 13, 2016). https://theconversation.com/why-self-identification-shouldnt-be-the-only-thing-that-defines-our-gender-57924.
Reis, Elizabeth. "Divergence or Disorder." *Perspectives in Biology and Medicine* 50, no. 4 (2007): 535–43.
Reisenberger, A. T. "The Creation of Adam as Hermaphrodite—and Its Implications for Feminist Theology." *Judaica* 42 (1993): 447–52.
Repo, Jemima. *The Biopolitics of Gender*. Oxford: Oxford University Press, 2016.
Reymond, Robert L. *A New Systematic Theology of the Christian Faith*. Nashville: Nelson, 1998.
Rich, Adrienne. "Compulsory Heterosexuality and Lesbian Existence." *Signs: Journal of Women in Culture and Society* 5 (1980): 631–60.
Ringe, Donald A. *From Proto-Indo-European to Proto-Germanic*. Oxford: Oxford University Press, 2006.
Roberts, Alastair. "The Music and the Meaning of Male and Female." Pages 26–43 in *True to Form: Primer 03 – Gender and Sexuality*. Edited by David Shaw. Market Harborough: The Fellowship of Independent Evangelical Churches, 2016.
———. "Podcast: Intersex." *Alastair's Adversaria* (August 25, 2015). https://alastairadversaria.com/2015/08/25/podcast-intersex.
Roberts, Christopher C. *Creation & Covenant: The Significance of Sexual Difference in the Moral Theology of Marriage*. New York: T&T Clark, 2007.
Roberts, Matthew P. W. "Thinking Like a Christian: The Prolegomena of Herman Bavinck." *ER* 1, no. 1 (2009): 70–91.
Roberts, Vaughan. *Transgender*. Epsom, UK: The Good Book Company, 2016.
Robinson, H. Wheeler. "Hebrew Psychology." Pages 353–82 in *The People and*

the Book. Edited by Arthur S. Peake. Oxford: Clarendon, 1925.

Rodwell, Craig. "The Tarnished Golden Rule." *Queen's Quarterly* 3, no. 1 (January/February 1971): 5, 38–39.

Rosenberg, Rosalind. *Beyond Separate Spheres: Intellectual Roots of Modern Feminism*. New Haven: Yale University Press, 1982.

Rosner, Brian. "Biblical Theology." Pages 3–11 in *New Dictionary of Biblical Theology*. Edited by T. D. Alexander and Brian S. Rosner. Leicester: Inter-Varsity Press, 2000.

———. *Known by God: A Biblical Theology of Personal Identity*. Biblical Theology for Life. Grand Rapids: Zondervan, 2017.

Rothenberg, Ronald M. "Relation of the Tripartite Division of the Law and the Public/Private Distinction: Examining the Streams of Thought Behind Them." *JETS* 61, no. 4 (2018): 805–23.

Rowbotham, Sheila. "Foreword." Pages ix–xix in Simone de Beauvoir, *The Second Sex*. Translated by Constance Borde and Sheila Malovany-Chevallier. London: Vintage, 2011.

Rubin, Gayle. "Of Catamites and Kings: Reflections on Butch, Gender, and Boundaries." Pages 466–82 in *The Persistent Desire: A Femme-Butch Reader*. Edited by Joan Nestle. Boston, Alyson, 1991.

———. "The Traffic in Women: Notes on the Political Economy of Sex." Pages 157–210 in *Toward an Anthropology of Women*. Edited by Rayna R. Reiter. New York: Monthly Review Press, 1975.

Rubin, Henry. "Phenomenology as Method in Trans Studies." *GLQ: A Journal of Lesbian and Gay Studies* 4, no. 2 (1998): 263–82.

Rudolph, Kurt. *Gnosis: The Nature and History of an Ancient Religion*. Edinburgh: T&T Clark, 1983.

Ruether, Rosemary Radford. "The Liberation of Christology from Patriarchy." *Religion and* Intellectual *Life* 2, no. 3 (1985): 116–28.

———. *To Change the World: Christology and Cultural Criticism*. New York: Crossroad, 1981.

Ryken, Leland. *How to Read the Bible as Literature ... and Get More Out of It*. Grand Rapids: Zondervan, 1984.

Sabia-Tanis, Justin. "Holy Creation, Wholly Creative." Pages 195–222 in *Understanding Transgender Identities: Four Views*. Edited by James K. Beilby and Paul Rhodes Eddy. Grand Rapids: Baker Academic, 2019.

Sailhamer, John H. *Genesis Unbounded: A Provocative New Look at the Creation*

Account. Sisters, OR: Multnomah Books, 1996.

Salamon, Gayle. *Assuming a Body: Transgender and Rhetorics of Materiality*. New York: Columbia University Press, 2010.

Salih, Sara. *Judith Butler*. Oxford: Routledge, 2003.

Sanders, Fred. *Jesus in Trinitarian Perspective: An Intermediate Christology*. Nashville: Broadman & Holman Academic, 2007.

Sanlon, Peter. *Plastic People: How Queer Theory Is Changing Us*. London: The Latimer Trust, 2010.

Sapp, Stephen. *Sexuality, the Bible, and Science*. Philadelphia: Fortress, 1977.

Saucy, Mark. "Personal Ethics of the New Covenant." *EQ* 86, no. 4 (October 2014): 343–57.

Sawicki, Jana. *Disciplining Foucault: Feminism, Power, and the Body*. New York: Routledge, 1991.

Sax, Leonard. "How Common Is Intersex? A Response to Anne Fausto-Sterling." *The Journal of Sex Research* 39, no. 3 (2002): 174–78.

Scarbrough, Kathy. "The Difference Between Sex and Gender and Why It Matters." Pages 26–37 in *Female Erasure: What You Need to Know About Gender Politics' War on Women, the Female Sex and Human Right*. Edited by Ruth Barrett. Pacific Palisades: Tidal Time Publishing, 2016.

Scherer, Michael. "Battle of the Bathroom," TIME (May 19, 2016). https://time.com/4341419/battle-of-the-bathroom.

Schiebinger, Londa. *The Mind Has No Sex? Women and the Origins of Modern Science*. Cambridge: Harvard University Press, 1989.

Schleiner, Winfried. "Early Modern Controversies about the One-Sex Model." *Renaissance Quarterly* 53, No. 1 (Spring 2000): 180–91.

Schreiner, Thomas R. "Head Coverings, Prophecies and the Trinity." Pages 124–39 in *Recovering Biblical Manhood and Womanhood: A Response to Evangelical Feminism*. Edited by John Piper and Wayne Grudem. Wheaton, IL: Crossways, 1991.

———. "Original Sin and Original Death: Romans 5:12–19." Pages 271–88 in *Adam, the Fall, and Original Sin: Theological, Biblical, and Scientific Perspectives*. Edited by Hans Madueme and Michael Reeves. Grand Rapids: Baker, 2014.

———. *Galatians*. ZECNT. Grand Rapids: Zondervan, 2010.

Schüle, Andreas. "Made in the 'Image of God': The Concepts of Divine Images in Gen 1–3." *ZAW* 117, no. 1 (2005): 1–20.

Schumacher, Lydia. "The 'Theo-Logic' of Augustine's Theory of Knowledge by

Divine Illumination." *Augustinian Studies* 41, no. 2 (2010): 375–99.

Schumacher, Michele M. *Metaphysics and Gender: The Normative Art of Nature and Its Human Imitations*. Steubenville, OH: Emmaus Academic, 2023.

Schüssler Fiorenza, Elisabeth. *In Memory of Her: A Feminist Theological Reconstruction of Christian Origins*. 2nd ed. New York: Crossroad, 1994.

Schwöbel, Christoph. "Human Being as Relational Being: Twelve Theses for a Christian Anthropology." Pages 141–70 in *Persons, Divine and Human*. Edited by Christoph Schwöbel and Colin E. Gunton. Edinburgh: T&T Clark, 1991.

Scotchmer, Paul F. "Lessons from Paradise on Work, Marriage, and Freedom: A Study of Genesis 2:4–3:24." *Evangelical Review of Theology* 28 (2004): 80–85.

Scott, Joan Wallach. "Deconstructing Equality-versus-Difference: Or, the Uses of Poststructuralist Theory for Feminism." *Feminist Studies* 14, no. 1 (Spring 1988): 32–50.

———. "Gender: Still a Useful Category of Historical Analysis?" *Diogenes* 225 (2010): 7–14.

Scruton, Roger. *Sexual Desire: A Philosophical Investigation*. London: Continuum, 2006.

Searle, John. *Speech Acts: An Essay in the Philosophy of Language*. Cambridge: Cambridge University Press, 1969.

Segal, Lynne. "After Judith Butler: Identities, Who Needs Them?" *Subjectivity* 25, no. 1 (December 2008): 381–94.

Serano, Julia. *Whipping Girl: A Transsexual Woman on Sexism and The Scapegoating of Femininity*. 2nd ed. Emeryville, CA: Seal Press, 2016.

Shaw, Jane. "Reformed and Enlightened Church." Pages 215–29 in *Queer Theology: Rethinking the Western Body*. Edited by Gerard Loughlin. Oxford: Blackwell, 2007.

Shibley, Mark A. "Contemporary Evangelicals: Born-Again and World Affirming." *The Annals of the American Academy of Political and Social Science* 558 (July 1998): 67–87.

Shrier, Abigail. *Irreversible Damage: The Transgender Craze Seducing Our Daughters*. Washington, DC: Regnery, 2020.

Simons, Margaret A. "*The Second Sex*: From Marxism to Radical Feminism." Pages 243–62 in *Feminist Interpretations of Simone* de *Beauvoir*. Edited by Margaret A. Simons. Pennsylvania: Pennsylvania University Press, 1995.

Singer, June. *Androgyny: Toward a New Theory of Sexuality*. New York: Anchor, 1976.

Sire, James W. *Naming the Elephant: Worldview as a Concept*. 2nd ed. Downers Grove, IL: InterVarsity Press, 2015.

Skalko, John. "Why There Are Only Two Sexes." *The Public Discourse* (June 5, 2017). http://www.thepublicdiscourse.com/2017/06/19389.

Skinner, John. *A Critical and Exegetical Commentary on Genesis*. ICC. Edinburgh: T&T Clark, 1910.

Sloane, Andrew. "'And He Shall Rule Over You': Evangelicals, Feminists, and Genesis 2–3." Pages 1–29 in *Tamar's Tears: Evangelical Engagements with Feminist Old Testament Hermeneutics*. Edited by Andrew Sloane. Eugene, OR: Wipf & Stock, 2012.

———. "'Male and Female He Created Them'? Theological Reflections on Gender, Biology and Identity." Pages 223–36 in *Marriage, Family and Relationships: Biblical, Doctrinal and Contemporary Perspectives*. Edited by Thomas A. Noble, Sarah K. Whittle, Philip S. Johnston. London: Apollos, 2017.

Smedes, Lewis B. *Sex for Christians*. Grand Rapids: Eerdmans, 1976.

Smith, Claire S. "Family Ties: Marriage, Sex, and Belonging in the New Testament." Pages 139–51 in *Marriage, Same-Sex Marriage and the Anglican Church of Australia: Essays from the Doctrine Commission*. Mulgrave: Broughton, 2019.

———. *Pauline Communities as "Scholastic Communities": A Study of the Vocabulary of "Teaching" in 1 Corinthians, 1 and 2 Timothy and Titus*. Tübingen: Mohr Siebeck, 2012.

———. *God's Good Design: What the Bible Really Says About Men and Women*. 2nd ed. Sydney: Matthias Media, 2019.

Smith, Dorothy E. *The Conceptual Practices of Power: A Feminist Sociology of Knowledge*. Boston: Northeastern University Press, 1990.

Smith, Gary V. *Isaiah 40–66*. NAC 15B. Nashville: Broadman & Holman, 2009.

Smith, J. Warren. "The Body of Paradise and the Body of the Resurrection: Gender and the Angelic Life in Gregory of Nyssa's *De hominis opificio*." *HTR* 92, no. 2 (2006): 207–28.

Smith, James K. A. *Who's Afraid of Postmodernism?: Taking Derrida, Lyotard, and Foucault to Church*. Grand Rapids: Baker, 2006.

Smith, Justin Erik Halldór. "The Anthropocentric Idealism of Judith Butler." *Justin Erik Halldór* Smith (January 6, 2018). https://www.jehsmith.com/1/2018/01/gender-trouble-as-anthropocentric-idealism.html.

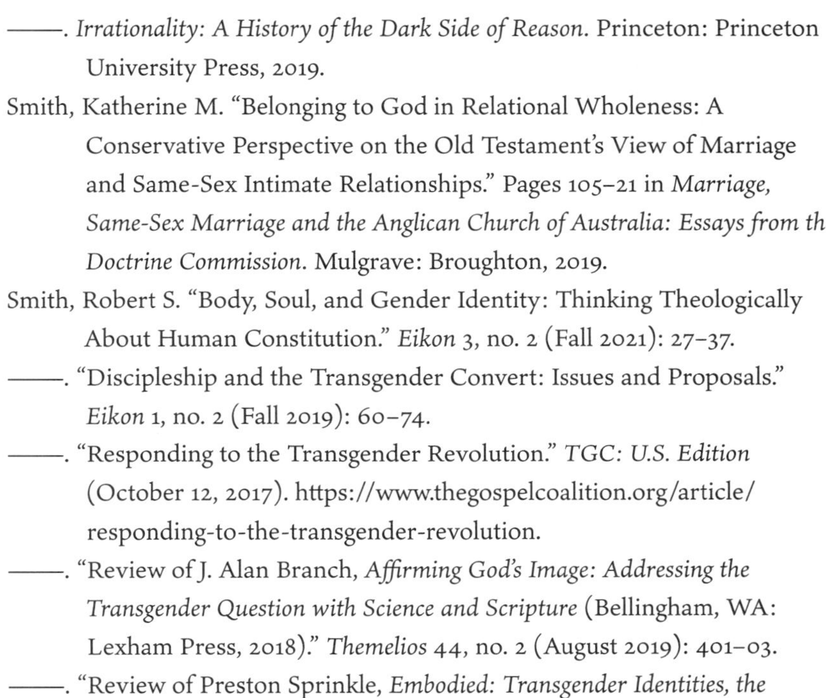

———. *Irrationality: A History of the Dark Side of Reason*. Princeton: Princeton University Press, 2019.

Smith, Katherine M. "Belonging to God in Relational Wholeness: A Conservative Perspective on the Old Testament's View of Marriage and Same-Sex Intimate Relationships." Pages 105–21 in *Marriage, Same-Sex Marriage and the Anglican Church of Australia: Essays from the Doctrine Commission*. Mulgrave: Broughton, 2019.

Smith, Robert S. "Body, Soul, and Gender Identity: Thinking Theologically About Human Constitution." *Eikon* 3, no. 2 (Fall 2021): 27–37.

———. "Discipleship and the Transgender Convert: Issues and Proposals." *Eikon* 1, no. 2 (Fall 2019): 60–74.

———. "Responding to the Transgender Revolution." *TGC: U.S. Edition* (October 12, 2017). https://www.thegospelcoalition.org/article/responding-to-the-transgender-revolution.

———. "Review of J. Alan Branch, *Affirming God's Image: Addressing the Transgender Question with Science and Scripture* (Bellingham, WA: Lexham Press, 2018)." *Themelios* 44, no. 2 (August 2019): 401–03.

———. "Review of Preston Sprinkle, *Embodied: Transgender Identities, the Church & What the Bible Has to Say*. Colorado Springs: David C Cook, 2021." *Themelios* 46, no. 1 (April 2021): 235–37.

———. "Review of Sharon James, *Gender Ideology: What Do Christians Need to Know?* Fearn: Christian Focus Publications, 2019." *Themelios* 46, no. 3 (December 2021): 714–16.

———. *How Should We Think about Gender and Identity?* Bellingham, WA: Lexham Press, 2022.

Smothers, Colin J. "On the Body and Its Meaning." *Eikon* 3, no. 1 (Spring 2021): 98–103.

Soble, Alan G. "The History of Sexual Anatomy and Self-Referential Philosophy of Science." *Metaphilosophy* 34, no. 3 (2003): 229–49.

Soh, Debra. *The End of Gender: Debunking the Myths about Sex and Identity in Our Society*. New York: Threshold Editions, 2020.

Sokal, Alan. *Beyond the Hoax: Science, Philosophy and Culture*. Oxford: Oxford University Press, 2008.

Solomon, Robert C. *Continental Philosophy since 1750: The Rise and Fall of the Self*. Oxford: Oxford University Press, 1988.

Song, Robert. *Human Genetics: Fabricating the Future*. London: Darton,

Longman & Todd, 2002.

Soughers, Tara. *Beyond a Binary God: A Theology for Trans* Allies*. New York: Church Publishing, 2018.

Spargo, Tamsin. *Foucault and Queer Theory*. Cambridge: Icon Books, 1999.

Spear, Susan A., and Jonathan Potter. "From Performances to Practices: Judith Butler, Discursive Psychology and the Management of Heterosexist talk." Pages 151–80 in *Talking Gender and Sexuality*. Edited by Paul McIlvenny. Philadelphia: John Benjamin Publishing Company, 2002.

Spelman, Elizabeth V. *Inessential Woman: Problems of Exclusion in Feminist Thought*. Boston: Beacon, 1988.

Sprinkle, Preston. "A Biblical Conversation About Transgender Identities." *The Center for Faith,* Sexuality *&* *Gender* (2018): 1–29. https://www.centerforfaith.com/resources/pastoral-papers/a-biblical-conversation-about-transgender-identities.

———."My Nashville Statement." *Preston Sprinkle* (September 3, 2017). https://www.prestonsprinkle.com/blog/2017/9/3/my-nashville-statement.

———. *Embodied: Transgender Identities, the Church & What the Bible Has to Say*. Colorado Springs: David C. Cook, 2021.

———. *People to Be Loved: Why Homosexuality Is Not Just an Issue*. Grand Rapids: Zondervan, 2015.

Steinmetz, Katy. "The Transgender Tipping Point." *TIME* (May 29, 2014). http://time.com/135480/transgender-tipping-point.

Stendahl, Krister. *The Bible and the Role of Women: A Case Study in Hermeneutics*. Translated by E. T. Sander. Philadelphia: Fortress, 1966.

Stewart, David Tabb. "Leviticus." Pages 77–104 in *The Queer Bible Commentary*. Edited by Deryn Guest, Bob Goss, Mona West, and Tom Bohache. London: SCM Press, 2006.

Stiegemeyer, Scott E. "How Do You Know Whether You Are a Man or a Woman?" *CTQ* 79 (2015): 19–48.

Stock, Kathleen. "Can You Change Your Gender?" *The Philosopher* 107, no. 3 (2019): 19–23.

———. "Changing the Concept of 'Woman' Will Cause Unintended Harms." *The Economist* (July 6, 2018). https://www.economist.com/open-future/2018/07/06/changing-the-concept-of-woman-will-cause-unintended-harms.

———. *Material Girls: Why Reality Matters for Feminism*. London: Fleet, 2021.

Stolberg, Michael. "A Woman Down to Her Bones: The Anatomy of Sexual Difference in the Sixteenth and Early Seventeenth Centuries." *Isis* 94, no. 2 (2003): 274–99.

Stoller, Robert J. "A Contribution to the Study of Gender Identity." *International Journal of Psycho-Analysis* 45 (1964): 220–26.

———. "Male Childhood Transsexualism." *Journal of the American Academy of Child and Adolescent Psychiatry* 7, no. 2 (April 1968): 193–201.

———. *Sex and Gender: The Development of Masculinity and Femininity*. New York: Science House, 1968.

Stone, Ken. "The Garden of Eden and the Heterosexual Contract." Pages 48–70 in *Bodily Citations: Religion and Judith Butler*. Edited by Ellen T. Armour and Susan M. St. Ville. New York: Columbia University Press, 2006.

Stone, Lawson G. "The Soul: Possession, Part, or Person?" Pages 47–61 in *What About the Soul? Neuroscience* and *Christian Anthropology*. Edited by Joel B. Green. Nashville: Abingdon, 2004.

Stone, Sandy. "The Empire Strikes Back: A Posttranssexual Manifesto." Pages 221–35 in *The* Transgender *Studies Reader*. Edited by Susan Stryker and Stephen Whittle. New York: Routledge, 2006.

Storkey, Elaine. *Created or Constructed?: The Great Gender Debate*. Carlisle: Paternoster, 2000.

Stott, John R. W. "Am I Supposed to Love Myself or Hate Myself?: The Cross Points the Way between Self-Love and Self-Denial." Pages 65–71 in *Christ the Cornerstone: Collected Essays of John Stott*. Bellingham, WA: Lexham Press, 2019. First published in *Christianity* Today 28, no. 7 (April 20, 1984): 26–28.

Strachan, Owen. "The Clarity of Complementarity: Gender Dysphoria in Biblical Perspective." *JBMW* (Fall 2016): 31–43.

———. "Transgender Identity in Theological and Moral Perspective." Pages 316–30 in *Scripture and the People of God: Essays in Honor of Wayne Grudem*. Edited by John DelHousaye, Jeff T. Purswell and John J. Hughes. Wheaton, IL: Crossway, 2018.

———. "Transition or Transformation? A Moral-Theological Exploration of Christianity and Gender Dysphoria." Pages 55–83 in *Understanding Transgender Identities: Four Views*. Edited by James K. Beilby and Paul Rhodes Eddy. Grand Rapids: Baker Academic, 2019.

———. *Reenchanting Humanity: A Theology of Mankind*. Fearn: Christian Focus

Publications, 2019.

Strachan, Owen, and Gavin Peacock. *What Does the Bible Teach About Transgenderism?* Fearn: Christian Focus Publications, 2020.

Strohschein, Jörg. "How sports are handling transgender women in competition." *DW* (October 1, 2023). https://www.dw.com/en/how-sports-are-handling-transgender-women-in-competition/a-66973847.

Stryker, Susan. *Transgender History: The Roots of Today's Revolution*. New York: Seal Press, 2017.

Sveinsdóttir, Ásta Kristjana. "The Metaphysics of Sex and Gender." Pages 47–66 in *Feminist Metaphysics: Explorations in the Ontology of Sex, Gender and Self*. Edited by Charlotte Witt. Dordrecht: Springer, 2011.

Swain, Scott. "More Thoughts on Theological Anthropology: Man as Male and Female." *Reformed Blogmatics* (May 14, 2020). https://www.scottrswain.com/2020/05/14/more-thoughts-on-theological-anthropology-man-as-male-and-female.

Swancutt, Diana, M. "'The Disease of Effemination': The Charge of Effeminacy and the Verdict of God (Romans 1:18–2:16)." Pages 193–234 in *New Testament Masculinities*. Edited by S. D. Moore and J. C. Anderson. Atlanta: Society of Biblical Literature, 2003.

Swinburne, Richard. *The Existence of God*. 2nd ed. Oxford: Clarendon, 2004.

Sykes, S. W. "Systematic Theology." Pages 560–62 in *A New Dictionary of Christian Theology*. Edited by Alan Richardson and John Bowden. London: SCM, 1983.

Sytsma, Sharon E. "Introduction." Pages xvii–xxv in *Ethics and Intersex*. Edited by Sharon E. Sytsma. Dordrecht: Springer, 2006.

Talley, David. "תְּשׁוּקָה." Volume 4, pages 341–42 in *NIDOTTE*.

Tanis, Justin. *Trans-Gender: Theology, Ministry, and Communities of Faith*. Eugene, OR: Wipf & Stock, 2018.

Tate, Marvin E. *Psalms 51–100*. WBC 20. Waco, TX: Word, 1990.

Taylor, Charles. *Sources of the Self: The Making of the Modern Identity*. Cambridge: Harvard University Press, 1989.

Taylor, Joan E. "'The Woman Ought to Have Control over Her Head because of the Angels' (1 Corinthians 11.10)." Pages 37–57 in *Gospel and Gender: A Trinitarian Engagement with Being Male and Female in Christ*. Edited by Douglas A. Campbell. London; New York: T&T Clark, 2003.

Terhune, Chad, Robin Respaut, and Michelle Conlin. "As More Transgender

Children Seek Medical Care, Families Confront Many Unknowns." *Reuters* (October 6, 2022). https://www.reuters.com/investigates/special-report/usa-transyouth-care.

Terrien, Samuel L. "Toward a Biblical Theology of Womanhood." Pages 17–27 in *Male and Female: Christian Approaches to Sexuality*. Edited by Ruth T. Barnhouse and Urban T. Holmes. New York: Seabury Press, 1976.

Tertullian. *A Treatise on the Soul*. Pages 181–235 in vol. 3 of *Ante-Nicene Fathers: The Writings of the Fathers Down to A.D. 325*. Edited by Alexander Roberts & James Donaldson, 1885. 10 vols. Repr. Peabody, MA: Hendrickson, 1995.

Thatcher, Adrian. "Some Issues with 'Some Issues in Human Sexuality.' " *Theology & Sexuality* 11, no. 3 (2005): 9–29.

———. *God, Sex, and Gender: An Introduction*. Oxford: Wiley-Blackwell, 2011.

———. *Redeeming Gender*. Oxford: Oxford University Press, 2016.

The Merriam-Webster.com Dictionary, s.v. "gender (n.)." https://www.merriam-webster.com/dictionary/gender.

Thielman, Frank S. "Ephesians." Pages 813–33 in *Commentary on the New Testament Use of the Old Testament*. Edited by G. K. Beale and D. A. Carson. Grand Rapids: Baker Academic, 2007.

Thiselton, Anthony C. *The First Epistle to the Corinthians*, NIGTC. Grand Rapids: Eerdmans, 2000.

Thompson, Mark D. "The Generous Gift of a Gracious Father: Toward a Theological Account of the Clarity of Scripture." Pages 615–43 in *The Enduring Authority of the Christian* Scriptures. Edited by D. A. Carson. Grand Rapids: Eerdmans, 2016.

Thornton, Stephen. "Popper, Basic Statements and the Quine-Duhem Thesis." *Yearbook of the Irish Philosophical Society* 9 (2007): 1–10.

Tiessen, Terrance. "A Female Soul in a Male Body?: A Theological Proposal." *Theological Thoughts* (June 20, 2015). https://www.thoughtstheological.com/a-female-soul-in-a-male-body-a-theological-proposal.

Tollefsen, Christopher O. "Sex Identity." *The Public Discourse* (July 13, 2015). http://www.thepublicdiscourse.com/2015/07/15306.

Tonstad, Linn Marie. *Queer Theology*. Eugene, OR: Cascade, 2018.

Torrance, Thomas F. *The Christian Doctrine of God, One Being Three Persons*. Edinburgh: T&T Clark, 1996.

Tosato, Angelo. "On Genesis 2:24," *CBQ* 52 (1990): 389–409.

Travers, Ann. *The Trans Generation: How Trans Kids (and Their Parents) Are Creating a Gender Revolution*. New York: New York University Press, 2018.

Trible, Phyllis. *God and the Rhetoric of Sexuality*. Philadelphia: Fortress, 1978.

Trueman, Carl R. "The Triumph of the Social Scientific Method." *First Things* (June 15, 2020). https://www.firstthings.com/web-exclusives/2020/06/the-triumph-of-the-social-scientific-method.

———. *Strange New World: How Thinkers and Activists Redefined Identity and Sparked the Sexual Revolution*. Wheaton, IL: Crossway, 2022.

———. *The Rise and Triumph of the Modern Self: Cultural Amnesia, Expressive Individualism, and the Road to Sexual Revolution*. Wheaton, IL: Crossway, 2020.

Tuohey, John F. "The Gender Distinctions of Primeval History and a Christian Sexual Ethic." *Heythrop Journal* 36, no. 2 (April 1995): 173–89.

Turner-Smith, Sarah G. "Naked but Not Ashamed: A Reading of Gen 2:25 in Textual and Cultural Context." *JTS* 69 (2018): 425–46.

Turner, William. *A Genealogy of Queer Theory*. Philadelphia: Temple University Press, 2000.

Tushima, Cephas T. A. "The Paradigmatic Role of Genesis 3 for Reading Biblical Narratives about Desire." *Unio Cum Christo* 5, no. 1 (April 2019): 87–102.

Vaid-Menon, Alok. *Beyond the Gender Binary*. New York: Penguin, 2020.

Van der Miesen, Anna I. R., Annelou. L. C. de Vries, Thomas D. Steensma, and Catharina A. Hartman. "Autistic Symptoms in Children and Adolescents with Gender Dysphoria." *Journal of Autism* and *Developmental Disorders* 48 (2018): 1537–48.

Van Til, Cornelius. "Introduction." Pages 3–68 in Benjamin B. Warfield, *The Inspiration and Authority of the Bible*. Phillipsburg, NJ: P&R Publishing, 1948.

Vanhoozer, Kevin J. "A Drama of Redemption Model: Always Performing?" Pages 151–99 in *Four Views on Moving Beyond the Bible to Theology*. Edited by Gary T. Meadors. Grand Rapids: Zondervan, 2009.

———. "Human Being, Individual and Social." Pages 158–88 in *The Cambridge Companion to Christian Doctrine*. Edited by C. E. Gunton. Cambridge: Cambridge University Press, 1997.

———. "Love's Wisdom: The Authority of Scripture's Form and Content for

Faith's Understanding and Theological Judgment." *Journal of Reformed Theology* 5 (2011): 247–75.

———. "May We Go Beyond What Is Written After All?" Pages 747–92 in *The Enduring Authority of the Christian Scriptures*. Edited by D. A. Carson. Grand Rapids: Eerdmans, 2016.

Vedeler, Harold Torger. "Reconstructing Meaning in Deuteronomy 22:5: Gender, Society, and Transvestitism in Israel and the Ancient Near East." *JBL* 127, no. 3 (2008): 459–76.

Vidal, Fernando. "Brains, Bodies, Selves and Science: Anthropologies of Identity and the Resurrection of the Body." *Critical Inquiry* 28, no. 4 (2002): 930–74.

Vigo, Julian. "Why Women Should Stand Up to the Trans Ideology." *Spiked* (November 29, 2017). http://www.spiked-online.com/newsite/article/why-women-should-stand-up-to-the-trans-ideology/20586#.WsGNWmZL2YU.

Volf, Miroslav. *Exclusion and Embrace: A Theological Exploration of Identity, Otherness, and Reconciliation*. Nashville: Abingdon, 1996.

Von Rad, Gerhard. *Genesis*. Translated by J. H. Marks & J. Bowden. London: SCM, 1972.

Vos, Geerhardus. *Biblical Theology: Old and New Testaments*. Grand Rapids: Eerdmans, 1948.

Walker, Andrew T. *God and the Transgender Debate: What Does the Bible Actually Say About Gender Identity?* Epsom, UK: The Good Book Company, 2022.

Waltke, Bruce K. *An Old Testament Theology: An Exegetical, Canonical, and Thematic Approach*. Grand Rapids: Zondervan, 2007.

Waltke, Bruce K., with Cathi J. Fredricks. *Genesis: A Commentary*. Grand Rapids: Zondervan, 2001.

Walton, John H. *Genesis: The NIV Application Commentary*. Grand Rapids: Zondervan, 2001.

———. *The Lost World of Genesis 1: Ancient Cosmology and the Origins Debate*. Downers Grove, IL: InterVarsity Press, 2009.

Walton, John H., with a contribution by N. T. Wright. *The Lost World of Adam and Eve: Genesis 2–3 and the Human Origins Debate*. Downers Grove, IL: InterVarsity Press, 2015.

Walton, Mark David. "What We Shall Be: A Look at Gender and the New

Creation." *JBMW* 9, no. 1 (Spring 2004): 17–28.

Ward, Graham. "The Erotics of Redemption—After Karl Barth." *Theology & Sexuality* 8 (March 1998): 52–72.

Wardlaw, Terrance Randall, Jr. *Created Male and Female*. Eugene, OR: Wipf & Stock, 2021.

Ware, Bruce. "Male and Female Complementarity and the Image of God." Pages 71–92 in *Biblical Foundations for Manhood and Womanhood*. Edited by Wayne A. Grudem. Wheaton, IL: Crossway, 2002.

Ware, James. "Paul's Understanding of the Resurrection in 1 Corinthians 15:36–54." *JBL* 133, no. 4 (Winter 2014): 809–35.

Warfield, Benjamin Breckinridge. "The Idea of Systematic Theology." Pages 49–87 in Benjamin Breckinridge Warfield, *Studies in Theology*. New York: Oxford University Press, 1932.

Warner, Megan. "'Therefore a Man Leaves His Father and His Mother and Clings to His Wife': Marriage and Intermarriage in Genesis 2:24." *JBL* 136, no. 2 (2017): 269–88. https://doi.org/10.15699/jbl.1362.2017.241017.

Warner, Michael. "From Queer to Eternity: An Army of Theorists Cannot Fail." *Village Voice Literary Supplement* (June 1992): 18–19.

Watkin, Christopher. *Biblical Critical Theory: How the Bible's Unfolding Story Makes Sense of Modern Life and Culture*. Grand Rapids: Zondervan, 2022.

———. *From Plato to Postmodernism: The Story of Western Culture Through Philosophy, Literature and Art*. London: Bristol Classical Press, 2011.

———. *Thinking Through Creation: Genesis 1 and 2 as Tools of Cultural Critique*. Phillipsburg, NJ: P&R Publishing, 2017.

Watts, Fraser. "Transsexualism and the Church." *Theology and Sexuality* 9, no. 1 (2002): 63–85.

Watts, John D. W. *Isaiah 34–66*. WBC 25. Waco, TX: Word, 1987.

Webster, John. "Introduction: Systematic Theology." Pages 1–15 in *The Oxford Handbook of Systematic Theology*. Edited by K. Tanner, J. Webster, and I. Torrance. Oxford: Oxford University Press, 2007.

Wedgeworth, Steven. "What Is Effeminacy?" *The Calvinist International* (July 15, 2018) [Online].

Weerakoon, Patricia, and Kamal Weerakoon. "The Biology of Sex and Gender." Pages 317–30 in *The Gender Conversation: Evangelical Perspectives on Gender, Scripture, and the Christian Life*. Edited by Edwina Murphy and David Starling. Eugene, OR: Wipf & Stock, 2016.

Weerakoon, Patricia, with Robert Smith and Kamal Weerakoon. *The Gender Revolution: A Biblical, Biological and Compassionate Response*. Sydney: Matthias Media, 2023.

Wenham, Gordon J. "The Old Testament Attitude to Homosexuality." *Expository Times* 102 (1990–91): 359–63.

Wenham, Gordon J. *Genesis 1–15*. WBC 1. Waco, TX: Word, 1987.

West, Candice, and Don H. Zimmerman. "Accounting for Doing Gender." *Gender and Society* 23, no. 1 (February 2009): 112–22.

———. "Doing Gender." *Gender & Society* 1, no. 2 (June 1987): 125–51.

West, Candice, and Sarah Fenstermaker. "Doing Difference." *Gender and Society* 9, no. 1 (February 1995): 8–37.

Westermann, Claus. *Creation*. Translated by John J. Scullion. London: SPCK, 1974.

———. *Genesis 1–11: A Commentary*. Translated by John J. Scullion. Minneapolis: Augsburg, 1984.

———. *Isaiah 40–66: A Commentary*. Philadelphia: Westminster, 1969.

Weston, Kath. "Do Clothes Make the Woman?: Gender, Performance Theory, and Lesbian Eroticism." *Genders* 17 (1993): 1–21.

Westfall, Cynthia Long. *Paul and Gender: Reclaiming the Apostle's Vision for Men and Women in Christ*. Grand Rapids: Baker, 2016.

Whitaker, Maja I. "Perfected Yet Still Disabled?: Continuity of Embodied Identity in Resurrection Life." *Stimulus* 26, no. 2 (December, 2019): 18–25. https://hail.to/laidlaw-college/article/sRNklJP.

White, David. *God, You, and Sex: A Profound Mystery*. Greensboro, NC: New Growth, 2019.

Whittle, Stephen. "Where Did We Go Wrong? Feminism and Trans Theory—Two Teams on the Same Side?" Pages 194–202 in *The Transgender Studies Reader*. Edited by Susan Stryker and Stephen Whittle. New York: Routledge, 2006.

Williams, Cristan and Judith Butler. "Judith Butler on Gender and the Trans Experience: 'One Should Be Free to Determine the Course of One's Gendered Life' " (interview). *Verso* (26 May, 2015). https://www.versobooks.com/blogs/2009-judith-butler-on-gender-and-the-trans-experience-one-should-be-free-to-determine-the-course-of-one-s-gendered-life.

Williams, Lesley-Anne Dyer. "Beautiful Bodies and Shameful Embodiment in

Plotinus's Enneads." Pages 69–86 in *Embodiment: A History*, Oxford Philosophical Concepts. Edited by Justin E. H. Smith. Oxford: Oxford University Press, 2017.

Williams, Michael D. "'For You Are with Me': Physical Anthropology and the Intermediate State." *Presbyterion* 45, no. 2 (Fall 2019): 17–34.

———. "Theology as Witness: Reading Scripture in a New Era of Evangelical Thought. Part II: Kevin Vanhoozer, The Drama of Doctrine." *Presbyterion* 37, no. 1 (Spring 2011): 16–30.

Wilson, Elizabeth A. *Psychosomatic: Feminism and the Neurological Body*. Durham, NC: Duke University Press, 2004.

Wilson, Todd A. *Mere Sexuality: Rediscovering the Christian Vision of Sexuality*. Grand Rapids: Zondervan, 2017.

Witherington, Ben, III. *The Acts of the Apostles: A Socio-Rhetorical Commentary*. Grand Rapids: Eerdmans, 1998.

Witt, Charlotte. "What is Gender Essentialism?" Pages 11–26 in *Feminist Metaphysics: Explorations in the Ontology of Sex, Gender and Self*. Edited by Charlotte Witt. Dordrecht: Springer, 2011.

Wittgenstein, Ludwig. *Philosophical Investigations*. 3rd ed. Translated by G. E. M. Anscombe. Oxford: Basil Blackwell, 1986.

Wittig, Monique. "One Is Not Born a Woman." *Feminist Issues* 1, no. 2 (1981): 47–54.

———. "The Category of Sex." Pages 1–8 in *The Straight Mind and Other Essays*. Boston, MA: Beacon, 1992.

———. "The Mark of Gender," *Feminist Issues* 5, no. 2 (Fall 1985): 3–12.

———. "The Straight Mind." Pages 21–32 in *The Straight Mind and Other Essays*. Boston, MA: Beacon, 1992.

Wolff, Hans Walter. *Anthropology of the Old Testament*. Translated by Margaret Kohl. Philadelphia: Fortress, 1974. Repr., Mifflintown, PA: Sigler Press, 1996.

Wolters, Albert M. *Creation Regained: Biblical Basics for a Reformational Worldview*. Grand Rapids: Eerdmans, 2005.

Wright, Christopher J. H. *Deuteronomy*. UBC. Grand Rapids: Baker, 1996.

———. *Walking in the Ways of the Lord: The Ethical Authority of the Old Testament*. Downers Grove, IL: InterVarsity Press, 1995.

Wright, N. T. *Creation, Power and Truth: The Gospel in a World of Cultural Confusion*. London: SPCK, 2013.

———. *The Resurrection of the Son of God*. Philadelphia: Fortress, 2003.

Wu, Daniel Y. *Honor, Shame, and Guilt: Social-Scientific Approaches to the Book of Ezekiel*. BBRS 14. Winona Lake, IN: Eisenbrauns, 2016.

Xie, J., S. Sreenivasan, G. Korniss, W. Zhang, C. Lim, and B. K. Szymanski. "Social consensus through the influence of committed minorities." *Phys. Rev. E* 84, 011130 (July 22, 2011). https://pdfs.semanticscholar.org/21ce/52e518edef55a4eb05edb19286132c5eb1a6.pdf.

Yang, Hongyi. *A Development, Not a Departure: The Lacunae in the Debate of the Doctrine of the Trinity and Gender Roles*. Phillipsburg, NJ: P&R Publishing, 2018.

Yarhouse, Mark A. *Understanding Gender Dysphoria: Navigating Transgender Issues in a Changing Culture*. Downers Grove, IL: InterVarsity Press, 2015.

Yarhouse, Mark A., and Julia Sadusky. "Best Practices in Ministry to Youth Navigating Gender Identity and Faith." *Christian Education Journal* (2020): 1–12, https://doi.org/10.1177/0739891320941866.

———. *Emerging Gender Identities: Understanding the Diverse Experiences of Today's Youth*. Grand Rapids: Brazos, 2020.

———. *Gender Identity and Faith: Clinical Postures, Tools and Cases Studies for Client-Centered Care*. Downers Grove, IL: IVP Academic, 2022.

Yudkin, Marcia. "Transsexualism and Women: A Critical Perspective." *Feminist Studies* 4, no. 3 (1978): 97–106.

Zimman, L. "The Discursive Construction of Sex: Remaking and Reclaiming the Gendered Body in Talk About Genitals Among Trans Men." Pages 13–34 in *Queer Excursions:* Retheorizing *Binaries in Language, Gender, and Sexuality*. Edited by L. Zimman, J. Davis, and J. Raclaw. New York: Oxford University Press, 2014.

Zizioulas, John D. "Human Capacity and Human Incapacity: A Theological Exploration of Personhood." *Scottish Journal of Theology* 28, no. 5 (1975): 401–48.

Zucker, Kenneth J. "The Myth of Persistence: Response to 'A Critical Commentary on Follow-up Studies and "Desistance" Theories about Transgender and Gender Non-conforming Children' by Temple Newhook et al. (2018)." *IJT* 19, no. 2 (2018): 231–45.

Zucker, Kenneth J., and Myra Kuksis. "Gender Dysphoria and Sexual Abuse: A Case Report." *Child Abuse & Neglect* 14, no. 2 (1990): 281–83.

SUBJECT AND AUTHOR INDEX

Y

SCRIPTURE INDEX

Old Testament

Exodus

Leviticus

Numbers

Deuteronomy

New Testament

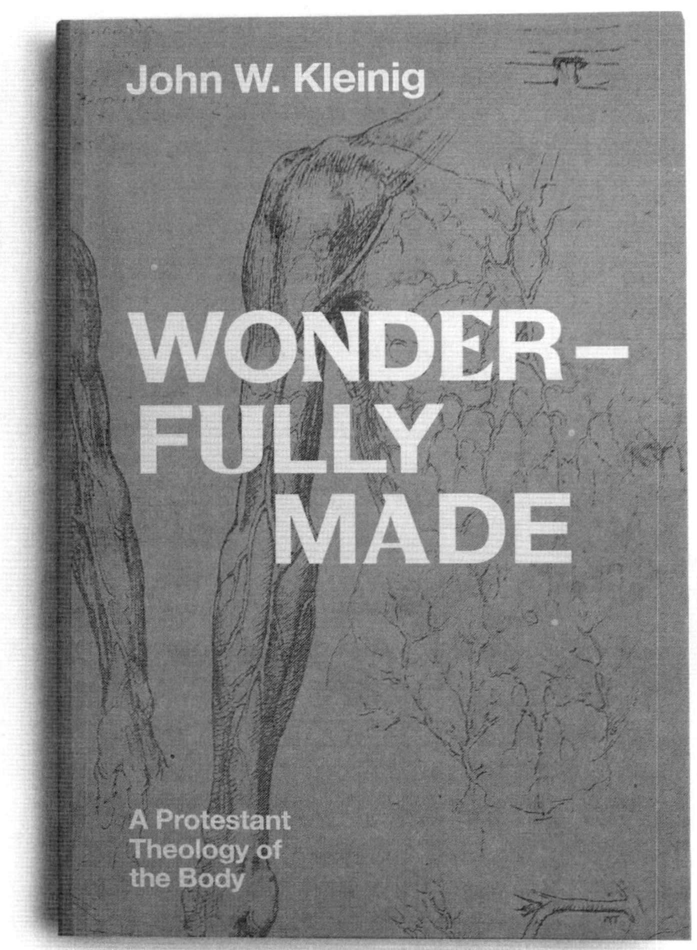

ALSO AVAILABLE FROM LEXHAM PRESS

Think deeply about God's word and the body

Visit lexhampress.com to learn more